Directory of the
AMERICAN THEATER
|1894–1971

Directory of the
AMERICAN THEATER
1894-1971

Indexed to the Complete Series of
BEST PLAYS *Theater Yearbooks*

TITLES, AUTHORS, AND COMPOSERS OF
BROADWAY, OFF-BROADWAY, AND OFF-OFF BROADWAY
SHOWS AND THEIR SOURCES

Compiled and Edited by
OTIS L. GUERNSEY JR.

DODD, MEAD & COMPANY • NEW YORK

To

HENRY HEWES

LOUIS KRONENBERGER

JOHN CHAPMAN

GARRISON P. SHERWOOD

AND ESPECIALLY

BURNS MANTLE

ISBN: 0–396–06428–0
Library of Congress Catalog Card Number: 71–180734

Printed in the United States of America
by The Haddon Craftsmen, Inc., Scranton, Penna.

Editor's Note

Glancing backward over my shoulder at the 77 years of theater streamed out behind me as I make the final 1970–71 entry in this Directory, I can't help remembering that I know more than half of it personally. I began going to the Broadway theater in the 1920s at matinees my parents thought suitable for children—the Marx Brothers in *Animal Crackers,* Ed Wynn in *Simple Simon, Hit the Deck* for some reason—and I began to cover the theater as a critic and editor in 1941 on the New York *Herald Tribune.*

I also remember one conversation with Burns Mantle and several with John Chapman at intermissions of Broadway openings concerning the clear, present and ever-increasing need for a cumulative index to the *Best Plays* series, to unlock its recorded memory for all time. If the idea had ever crossed my mind that *I* would be the one to compile it, I would have found some other line of work right there and then.

I'm happy that the future was hidden from me, because now that I've finished compiling this Directory of authors, composers and titles of Broadway, off-Broadway and off-off-Broadway shows and sources from the complete series of *Best Plays* yearbooks including the retrospective ones back to 1894, I'm beginning to forget the mind-boggling problems and to remember what a uniquely fascinating experience it proved to be. It was a constant discovery of new facts and stimulation of wild surmises, such as 1) Actors who play villains often try to write plays, but seldom actors who play heroes, or 2) William Shakespeare is by far the most-produced playwright in America, more than double anybody except Shaw and almost double him, Gilbert & Sullivan included—but in the season of 1933–34 for some strange reason probably having to do with the Depression, he wasn't produced at all, or 3) Eugene O'Neill's middle name is Gladstone, and Richard Rodgers' middle initial is C, etc., etc. The place where I thank the members of my editorial staff for helping me compile this Directory is going to be blank, because I prepared every entry myself, personally. I monopolized all the enjoyment of this labor of love for the theater, and I accept all the blame for any shortcomings.

This Directory's title and authorship data was gleaned directly from the cast-and-credits listing of each show in the series of *Best Plays* volumes, *not* from the individual volume indices which seldom list sources or borderline authorship credits. There were three overriding concerns in the preparation of the material:

accuracy, clarity and inclusion. Every care was taken to get each spelling and page reference right; each has been checked and double-checked. Ambiguities and contradictions were resolved by phoning the subjects whenever possible; the editor's own judgment had to make do for such matters as whether Aeschylus would prefer *The Libation-Pourers* or *The Libation-Bearers* for the title of his *Oresteia* centerpiece. Title spellings are based mostly on *The Oxford Companion to the Theater;* name spellings on Webster Two and *The Columbia Encyclopedia.* A paging change in the 1894–99 volume created numerous one-page errors in its own index; the 1894–99 page numbers given in this Directory are the correct ones.

Because the patterns of letter arrangement in names and titles differ, the two sections of the Directory are alphabetized differently. Names are listed in the absolute order of letters in the last name (for example, Lee comes before Le Gallienne), whereas the titles are alphabetized word by word (for example, *Do I Hear a Waltz?* comes before *Doctor's Dilemma, The*).

The entries have been kept as clear as possible of cross-reference clutter; they adhere to the guiding principle and convenience of one-stop shopping. The entries distinguish between the novel and the play, the play and the musical, the various adaptations of the same story. In the case of musicals, each page number of an entry which lists the song titles is clearly marked with a small "s".

As for inclusion, the policy has been: when in doubt, include it in (to paraphrase a famous malapropism). All borderline cases of authorship, both literary and musical (such as the billing "Revue assembled by" in the major credits, or "Dance music by" in small type among the arrangers and orchestrators), are listed in this Directory. Any useful or enlightening reference to titles or authors found in the *Best Plays* volumes outside this Directory's area of major concern —the "Plays Produced in New York" sections—have been included whenever I could find or come by them.

And so, quite a few months and 77 years of theater yearbooks after that first 1894 entry (*Dr. Syntax,* a musical with book by J. Cheever Goodwin and music by Woolson Morse), here are some 22,000 names of plays, playwrights, composers, lyricists and sources. If each entry averages at least three references—and I believe it does—that's at least 66,000 items of information. If they are as pure as that soap—99 and 44/100 per cent pure, isn't it?—there would nevertheless be .56 per cent of error, which would be 370 instances of inaccuracy, obfuscation or omission in this Directory. I don't believe there are 37, let alone 370, and I want to offer my sincerest thanks right here and now not only to those who have already helped me comb these pages for error but also to those of you who may in *future* come across an error of commission or omission while perusing this volume and will call it to my attention care of Dodd, Mead & Company (publishers of the *Best Plays* series), 79 Madison Ave., New York, N.Y. 10016, so that errata may be noted. Nothing short of perfection will suffice for a Directory of the American Theater, a volume intended not only as an index but also as a valuable entity in and of itself; an Alamanach de Gotha of a proud art form, a genealogy of the theater's ancestry; a permanent and complete record of the noble artists who created the American theater and of the delights they brought forth as the issue of their talents.

OTIS L. GUERNSEY JR.

Contents

Playwrights, Librettists, Composers, Lyricists and Other Authors of Shows and Sources, 1894–1971

Here are the names of all authors and composers of Broadway, off-Broadway, off-off-Broadway and other productions listed in the 52 *Best Plays* volumes dated 1919–20 to 1970–71, plus the three retrospective *Best Plays* volumes dated 1894–99, 1899–1909 and 1909–19. This Directory also includes the names mentioned in the *Best Plays* series as authors of literary and musical sources. This is a *complete* compilation of authorship data contained in the statistical "Plays Produced in New York" sections of all the volumes covering 77 years of American theater; plus the authorship data available in *Best Plays* articles during the years, for example, when the off-Broadway theater was covered in the form of a report rather than a listing; plus a few entries from other sections of the volumes which add to the general fund of information about authorship.

Names are alphabetized in order of the letters in the last name, then first name or initials (titles like Sir, Dr. or Mrs. are ignored in the alphabetizing). Each author's name appears in roman (regular) type, and opposite it is the abbreviated date of the *Best Plays* volume (in *italics*) and number of the page (again in roman) on which the name appears, as follows:

Goldsmith, (Dr.) Oliver   94–99, 167

The hyphenated number *94–99* in *italics* refers to the volume in which the author's name appears (in this case it is *The Best Plays of 1894–99*). The number 167 following the comma is the number of the 1894–99 volume's page on which the author's name appears. (Entries compiled from the 1970–71 *Best Plays* volume do not have page numbers, because the Directory went to press before that yearbook was paged.)

This Directory contains an entry for each time a name is mentioned as an author in the *Best Plays* listings, so that the author or composer of several shows or sources will have several volume entries, each separated by a semicolon. And an author produced more than once in a single theater season will have more than one page number after a volume number, as follows:

Bock, Jerry *55–56,* 339, 340, 341,
380; *57–58,* 311; *59–60,* 305; *60–61,*
301; *62–63,* 277, 289, 307, 331; *63–*
64, 372 (etc.)

Billing of authors' names sometimes varies through the decades, and the version used in our record is always the longest one (for example, George Bernard Shaw rather than Bernard Shaw or G.B. Shaw). Except in cases of obvious, glaring error, all variations in spelling are included and indicated by parentheses as in "Chekhov (Tchekhov), Anton" and all are cross-referenced. Closely similar names are listed separately unless the editor has found clear proof that they are the same person—and in such cases the telescoping is indicated by recording the name variations in parentheses.

A historical character has often provided the material for a play in some notable action or life, but this is not considered source authorship unless literary material like a letter or a speech was created and then used as the basis for all or part of a playscript. Thus, Queen Victoria has two references as an author, though not for *Victoria Regina* or other plays based on her life.

Composers of incidental music and music used in ballet programs are listed in this Directory, as are the authors of ballet stories and/or the sources for them, but choreographers, arrangers, orchestrators and other specialists are not included. The performer of a one-man show is presumed to be a co-author, at least as an adapter, unless other authorship credit is listed.

Accents and other punctuation marks of names are used when and as they appear in the *Best Plays* listings.

Playwrights, Librettists, Composers, Lyricists and Other Authors of Shows and Sources, 1894-1971

Aaron, Joyce *69–70,* 370
Aarons, Alfred E. *99–09,* 363, 367, 375, 473, 514; *09–19,* 426
Aarons, Franklin *37–38,* 463
Aart *70–71*
Abbott, George *24–25,* 558; *25–26,* 456, 546; *26–27,* 381; *27–28,* 406, 448; *28–29,* 365; *29–30,* 498; *32–33,* 388; *33–34,* 432; *34–35,* 400, 446; *35–36,* 499; *36–37,* 423; *38–39,* 429; *41–42,* 422; *42–43,* 435, 436; *48–49,* 388; *50–51,* 346, 363; *53–54,* 353; *54–55,* 366, 413; *56–57,* 373, 375; *59–60,* 305; *60–61,* 301, *61–62,* 260; *62–63,* 277, 331, 339; *64–65,* 336; *65–66,* 387, 407, 437; *66–67,* 422; *69–70,* 300
Abdullah, Achmed *20–21,* 438; *33–34,* 518
Abel, Lionel *59–60,* 41; *64–65,* 59
Abelard, Peter & Heloise *70–71*
Abrams, Leon *33–34,* 432
Accoe, Will *99–09,* 378
Achard, Marcel *32–33,* 381; *37–38,* 469; *49–50,* 359; *58–59,* 300; *61–62,* 263
Ackerly, J. R. *34–35,* 445
Ackerman, Michael *69–70,* 336
Ackland (Ackman), Rodney *33–34,* 464; *35–36,* 432; *45–46,* 457; *47–48,* 369; *56–57,* 331; *60–61,* 296

Actman, Irving *35–36,* 463
Actors (billed as authors or improvisers) *09–19,* 546; *35–36,* 503; *60–61,* 36, 37; *61–62,* 255, 318, 331; *62–63,* 283, 323, 330, 333, 335; *63–64,* 318, 319, 343, 345, 356, 363, 367; *64–65,* 297, 300, 303, 305, 320, 341, 346; *65–66,* 434; *68–69,* 426, 456, 457; *69–70,* 343, 345, 369, 370, 377; *70–71*
Adair, Laura *35–36,* 461
Adair, Tom *48–49,* 406
Adams, Mr. *09–19,* 406
Adams, F. *55–56,* 347
Adams, Frank R. *99–09,* 537, 541, 564, 576; *09–19,* 580; *24–25,* 497; *42–43,* 438
Adams, H. Austin *09–19,* 592; *19–20,* 400
Adams, Justin *99–09,* 413
Adams, Lee *55–56,* 338, 339, 391; *59–60,* 331; *61–62,* 292; *64–65,* 307; *65–66,* 405; *69–70,* 323
Adams, Roger *45–46,* 413; *46–47,* 407; *54–55,* 406; *56–57,* 344, 374; *64–65,* 308
Adams, Samuel Hopkins *27–28,* 401; *60–61,* 301
Adams, Stanley *33–34,* 421; *44–45,* 409
Adamson, Harold *30–31,* 455; *31–32,* 383; *41–42,* 422; *48–49,* 394; *63–64,* 343; *64–65,* 341

Addinsell, Richard *33–34,* 479; *46–47,* 439; *51–52,* 307; *55–56,* 352; *57–58,* 328; *62–63,* 316

Addison, John *56–57,* 338; *57–58,* 309, 318; *63–64,* 304

Addison, Thomas *99–09,* 578; *09–19,* 654

Ade, George *99–09,* 140, 386, 425, 436, 466, 468, 496, 497, 549, 559, 566, 577; *09–19,* 409, 500, 535, 605; *35–36,* 507

Adelson, Lenny *55–56,* 336

Aderer, Adolphe *26–27,* 434

Adkins, Robert F. *34–35,* 435

Adler, Hans *34–35,* 376; *35–36,* 456

Adler, Hyman *26–27,* 531; *28–29,* 448; *29–30,* 482; *35–36,* 501

Adler, Richard *53–54,* 326, 354; *54–55,* 413; *56–57,* 375; *61–62,* 264; *66–67,* 422

Adomian, Lan *41–42,* 460; *50–51,* 345

Aeschylus *50–51,* 331; *61–62,* 255; *68–69,* 398; *69–70,* 365

Afford, Max *44–45,* 427

Afinegenov, Alexander *43–44,* 443

Agee, James *60–61,* 308; *63–64,* 369; *68–69,* 454

Ager, Milton *19–20,* 439; *27–28,* 506; *29–30,* 382

Ahlert, Fred E. *40–41,* 384

Aicard, Jean *99–09,* 536, 562

Aidman, Charles *63–64,* 304

Aiken, Alfred *62–63,* 318

Aiken, Conrad *47–48,* 414, 417; *60–61,* 48

Aiken, G.L. *32–33,* 498

Ajayi, Afolabi *69–70,* 352

Akins, Zoe *09–19,* 561, 655; *19–20,* 363, 452; *21–22,* 408, 472; *22–23,* 492; *23–24,* 350, 403; *26–27,* 420, 497; *27–28,* 523; *28–29,* 493; *30–31,* 419; *34–35,* 436; *35–36,* 457; *40–41,* 425; *43–44,* 463

Akst, Harry *27–28,* 452; *34–35,* 424; *53–54,* 305, 306

Akutagawa, Ryunosuke *58–59,* 317

Albee, Edward *59–60,* 352; *60–61,* 47, 356; *61–62,* 305, 306, 323; *62–63,* 279, 313, 337; *63–64,* 312, 364; *64–65,* 322; *65–66,* 394, 416; *66–67,* 357, 395; *67–68,* 353, 401; *68–69,* 379, 425; *69–70,* 297; *70–71*

Albeniz, Isaac *46–47,* 486

Albert, Prince Consort (Wettin) *62–63,* 295

Albert, Allan *70–71*

Albert, Katherine *46–47,* 427

Albery, James *94–99,* 230

Albert, Jerry *37–38,* 469

Albini, Felix *09–19,* 427, 468

Albright, Hardie *37–38,* 435

Albyn, G.N. *32–33,* 426

Alcarez, Jose *70–71*

Alcott, Louisa May *09–19,* 480, 590; *31–32,* 444; *38–39,* 490; *44–45,* 379; *45–46,* 393; *63–64,* 358

Alderman, (Dr.) Van V. *39–40,* 468

Aldis, Mary *29–30,* 541

Aldrich, Azelle M. *09–19,* 606

Aldrich, Dorrough *09–19,* 647

Aldrich, Thomas Bailey *94–99,* 214; *99–09,* 475; *69–70,* 374

Aleichem, Sholom (Sholem) *31–32,* 396; *34–35,* 472; *36–37,* 497; *39–40,* 474; *45–46,* 460; *46–47,* 497; *48–49,* 430; *53–54,* 359; *64–65,* 302

Alevy, Maurice *61–62,* 329

Alexander, H. *29–30,* 548

Alexander, I.J. *38–39,* 484

Alexander, Irene *37–38,* 413

Alexander, Leon *37–38,* 419

Alexander, Larry *63–64,* 343; *65–66,* 424

Alexander, Melville *09–19,* 479

Alexander, Ronald *52–53,* 272; *54–55,* 393; *56–57,* 355; *63–64,* 317

Alford, Lamar *69–70,* 375

Alfred, William *65–66,* 425; *69–70,* 325

Alfriend, Edward M. *94–99,* 141, 194, 215

Alicoate, Jack *22–23,* 523; *25–26,*
 463
Allan, Gene *68–69,* 411
Allan, George *61–62,* 308
Allan, Ted *64–65,* 303
Allardice, James B. *48–49,* 415
Allegro, Alfred *38–39,* 486
Allen, Ben. G. *58–59,* 319
Allen, Donald M. *63–64,* 345
Allen, Frank *09–19,* 603; *21–22,*
 499
Allen, Fred *33–34,* 476
Allen, Grant *99–09,* 457
Allen, Inglis *99–09,* 519
Allen, Jay *67–68,* 358; *68–69,*
 400
Allen, John *60–61,* 42; *67–68,*
 401
Allen, Lester *25–26,* 420
Allen (Allan), Lewis *41–42,* 438;
 42–43, 433; *44–45,* 438
Allen, Ruth Collins *37–38,* 463
Allen, Steve *62–63,* 305
Allen, Woody *59–60,* 335, 336;
 62–63, 324; *66–67,* 369; *68–69,*
 406
Allensworth, Carl *41–42,* 393
Allerdice, W.H. *94–99,* 227
Allinson, Francesca *37–38,* 412
Alliot, Beatrice *40–41,* 418
Allison, Hughes *37–38,* 447
Allvine, Glendon *38–39,* 418
Alma, Richard *39–40,* 437
Almagor, Dan *67–68,* 372
Alphin, Charles *99–09.* 563
Alsberg, Arthur *67–68,* 378
Alsberg, Henry (Harry) G. *25–26,*
 517; *26–27,* 425
Alstone, Louis P. *62–63,* 294;
 64–65, 331
Alter, Louis *27–28,* 392; *30–31,* 468;
 33–34, 434
Alters, Gerald *64–65,* 358
Alton, Maxine *36–37,* 407
Alton, Robert *38–39,* 456
Alwaise, Francis *44–45,* 395
Amade, Louis *66–67,* 367; *68–69,*
 383

Aman (Amon), John *63–64,* 343;
 66–67, 35; *68–69,* 422
Ambient, Mark *94–99,* 223; *99–09,*
 346; *09–19,* 410
American humorists (unnamed
 authors) *65–66,* 432
Americans (unnamed composers)
 34–35, 459; *66–67,* 353
Ames, Winthrop *23–24,* 161; *27–28,*
 493; *30–31,* 448; *38–39,* 490
Amiel, Denys *21–22,* 468; *33–34,*
 449
Amira, John *69–70,* 375
Amram, David *58–59,* 298, 312,
 313, 321, 324, 333; *59–60,* 293,
 307, 314, 320, 325, 334; *60–61,*
 331; *61–62,* 324, 343; *62–63,* 319,
 354; *63–64,* 321, 325, 347, 387;
 64–65, 74, 76, 310; *65–66,* 95, 97;
 66–67, 106, 107, 385; *67–68,* 93,
 95
Amsterdam, Morey *48–49,* 379
Anania, Joan *60–61,* 42
Andersen, Hans Christian *99–09,*
 369; *09–19,* 540; *34–35,* 387;
 35–36, 479; *47–48,* 420
Anderson, Albert *94–99,* 158
Anderson, Arthur *99–09,* 546;
 09–19, 471, 474, 507
Anderson, Burnes *64–65,* 340
Anderson, Charles *68–69,* 433
Anderson, Doris *31–32,* 448
Anderson, Garland *25–26,* 473;
 28–29, 487
Anderson, Harold L. *41–42,*
 458
Anderson, Howard *41–42,* 461
Anderson, Hugh A. *28–29,* 490
Anderson, John *30–31,* 469; *31–32,*
 478
Anderson, John Murray *19–20,* 339,
 439; *20–21,* 374; *21–22,* 407;
 22–23, 452; *23–24,* 320; *24–25,*
 454; *53–54,* 328, 329
Anderson, Leroy *58–59,* 294
Anderson, Mary *09–19,* 455, 624
Anderson, Maxwell *23–24,* 339;
 24–25, 448; *25–26,* 436, 447, 459;

Anderson, Maxwell *(cont.)*
26–27, 468; 27–28, 538; 28–29,
402, 455; 30–31, 445; 31–32, 492;
32–33, 472; 33–34, 463; 34–35,
422; 35–36, 410; 36–37, 445, 452,
461; 37–38, 373; 38–39, 419;
39–40, 416; 40–41, 383; 41–42,
405; 42–43, 434; 43–44, 447;
45–46, 429; 46–47, 442; 48–49,
399, 426; 49–50, 358; 51–52, 289;
54–55, 381; 57–58, 320; 58–59, 55;
61–62, 332; 62–63, 339; 63–64,
342, 343; 65–66, 429; 66–67, 358;
67–68, 410; 69–70, 335

Anderson, Robert 45–46, 401;
49–50, 368; 53–54, 308; 54–55,
363; 59–60, 308; 66–67, 384;
67–68, 359, 413

Anderson, Sherwood 57–58, 316

Anderson, T. Diane 66–67, 423

Anderson, Walt 56–57, 58

Anderson, Will R. 09–19, 654

Andreas, Otto 39–40, 395

Andrews, Charlton 09–19, 611;
20–21, 364; 21–22, 421; 26–27,
463; 27–28, 545, 555; 28–29, 466;
44–45, 410

Andrews, D.H. 21–22, 490

Andrews, George H. 94–99, 185

Andreyev, Leon(id) 09–19, 547, 580;
21–22, 492; 22–23, 557; 27–28,
545; 28–29, 473; 30–31, 521;
45–46, 432; 67–68, 410

Anet, Claude 29–30, 413

Angelos, William 62–63, 337

Angoff, Charles 42–43, 487

Angus, Bernadine (Bernie) 37–38,
382, 397; 41–42, 421

Ankrum, Morris 27–28, 498

Anne, Jean 63–64, 345

Anonymous author (see also Others)
31–32, 512; 32–33, 447; 45–46,
400; 62–63, 295; 62–63, 322;
63–64, 314; 68–69, 433, 456, 457;
69–70, 375

Anouilh, Jean 37–38, 469; 38–39,
492; 45–46, 428; 49–50, 377;

50–51, 329; 51–52, 300; 52–53,
273; 53–54, 334; 54–55, 52, 56;
55–56, 362; 56–57, 349; 57–58, 52,
53, 301, 322; 59–60, 310, 357;
60–61, 44, 298; 63–64, 303, 369;
64–65, 301, 313, 355; 67–68, 409,
412; 68–69, 455; 69–70, 373

Ansky, S. 25–26, 517; 26–27, 440,
442; 46–47, 497; 47–48, 432;
63–64, 322

Anslee, Ancella 09–19, 616

Anspacher, Louis Kaufman 99–09,
514, 579; 09–19, 239, 557; 22–23,
469, 521; 25–26, 555; 30–31, 412

Anstey, F. (Thomas Anstey Guthrie)
99–09, 437; 09–19, 421; 28–29,
383; 43–44, 417; 46–47, 421

Antheil, Mr. 34–35, 459

Anthony, C. L. (Dodie Smith)
32–33, 425

Anthony, Charles 20–21, 419

Anthony, Earle C. 09–19, 464

Anthony, Joseph 34–35, 375

Anthony, Norman B. 32–33, 383;
43–44, 414

Anthony, Rock 58–59, 51; 59–60,
41

Anthony, Stuart 35–36, 484

Antoine, A. 29–30, 510

Antonia 69–70, 305

Apolinar, Danny 67–68, 398

Apollinaire, Guillaume 67–68,
411

Appell, Don 45–46, 439; 53–54,
339; 61–62, 259; 64–65, 302

Applebaum, Louis 57–58, 325;
62–63, 297

Appleman, Herbert 69–70, 356

Apstein, Theodore 55–56, 373;
59–60, 41

Aquino, Senor 27–28, 468

Aramburu, Silvo 42–43, 490

Arbuzov, Aleksei 67–68, 352

Archangelsky, Alexei 31–32, 414

Archer, Charles 99–09, 487; 22–23,
527; 24–25, 582

Archer, Daniel 49–50, 371

Archer, Harry *23–24,* 301, 414;
    24–25, 494; *25–26,* 454; *26–27,*
    429; *28–29,* 391; *29–30,* 377;
    35–36, 421
Archer, William *99–09,* 360, 459,
    487; *09–19,* 579; *20–21,* 422;
    22–23, 527; *25–26,* 538; *26–27,*
    458; *28–29,* 420
Archibald, H.A. *31–32,* 441
Archibald, Jean *20–21,* 375; *28–29,*
    496
Archibald, William *45–46,* 386;
    49–50, 371; *54–55,* 383; *58–59,* 52;
    59–60, 354; *61–62,* 320
Arden, Edwin *94–99,* 88
Arden, John *65–66,* 416, 431, 437;
    70–71
Arden, Willis *94–99,* 230
Ardrey, Robert *35–36,* 493; *37–38,*
    423, 426; *39–40,* 411; *45–46,* 428;
    54–55, 369; *61–62,* 314
Arene, Emmanuel *09–19,* 615
Arensky, Anton *25–26,* 515
Arent, Arthur *35–36,* 471; *36–37,*
    492; *37–38,* 395, 452; *38–39,* 470
Argento, Dominick *68–69,* 399
Argyll, Astrid *20–21,* 440
Ariosto, Lodovico *37–38,* 467;
    70–71
Aristophanes *25–26,* 514; *29–30,*
    548; *39–40,* 469; *46–47,* 428;
    59–60, 306, *60–61,* 332; *63–64,*
    344; *68–69,* 445, 456; *69–70,* 367,
    374
Arkell, T. Reginald *31–32,* 469;
    38–39, 491
Arlen, Harold *30–31,* 399, 480;
    32–33, 392, 395; *34–35,* 362;
    37–38, 397; *42–43,* 420; *44–45,*
    387; *45–46,* 436; *46–47,* 411;
    53–54, 306; *54–55,* 389; *57–58,*
    297; *59–60,* 309; *66–67,* 414;
    67–68, 399; *68–69,* 436
Arlen, Michael *25–26,* 445, 464
Arliss, George *99–09,* 432; *09–19,*
    607
Arluck, Elliot *60–61,* 41

Arm, Richard Allen *37–38,* 469
Armitage, Walter *45–46,* 458
Armont, Mons. *09–19,* 424, 438;
    21–22, 513, 535; *24–25,* 476
Armont, Paul *19–20,* 409
Armstrong, Anthony *33–34,* 443
Armstrong, Charlotte (Charl) *38–39,*
    468; *41–42,* 414
Armstrong, Eunice Burton *30–31,*
    525
Armstrong, Norman *42–43,* 449
Armstrong, Paul *99–09,* 458, 489,
    531, 555, 572, 581; *09–19,* 411,
    436, 467, 507, 530, 533; *21–22,*
    475; *24–25,* 513
Arne, Michael *94–99,* 200
Arne, Dr. Thomas Augustine *37–38,*
    412
Arnell, Richard *47–48,* 422
Arnheim, M. I. *35–36,* 476
Arno, Owen G. *63–64,* 314
Arno, Peter *29–30,* 382; *30–31,* 465;
    31–32, 379, 422
Arnold, Samuel *37–38,* 412
Arnold, Stanley *48–49,* 379
Aronson, Alvin *65–66,* 428
Arouet, François Marie (see Voltaire)
Arrabal, Fernando *59–60,* 46;
    61–62, 313, 323; *63–64,* 362;
    68–69, 450, 456
Arrieu, Claude *47–48,* 427
Arrighi, Mel *68–69,* 427; *70–71*
Artaud, Antonin *70–71*
Artemowsky, Simon *36–37,* 500
Arthur, Art *47–48,* 402
Arthur, Eric *39–40,* 469
Arthur, Frederick *09–19,* 528
Arthur, George K. *35–36,* 429
Arthur, Joseph *94–99,* 98, 116, 180,
    220, 253; *99–09,* 374
Arthur, Lee *94–99,* 188, 260; *09–19,*
    510, 634–5, 643
Arthur, Stewart *39–40,* 437
Arthur, T.S. *31–32,* 467
Arthurs, George *99–09,* 577
Artus, Mons. *94–99,* 259
Artzybashell *27–28,* 409

Arundell, Dennis *63–64*, 347–8
Arzoomanian, Ralph S. *65–66*, 431; *69–70*, 367
Asbury, Herbert *35–36*, 486
Asch (Ash), Shole(o)m *22–23*, 501; *38–39*, 493; *39–40*, 474
Ascham, Charles *63–64*, 314
Asche, Oscar *09–19*, 610; *20–21*, 390
Ascher, Leo *09–19*, 588
Ashbury, John *52–53*, 308
Ashford, Daisy *20–21*, 409
Ashley, Clayton *44–45*, 409
Ashmore, Basil *67–68*, 401
Ashton, Herbert Jr. *28–29*, 442, 495; *33–34*, 469
Ashton, Linda *65–66*, 417
Ashwood, Michael *38–39*, 486
Askew, Claude *99–09*, 524
Astori, Alda *56–57*, 333
Astray, (Pillar M.) *31–32*, 501
Atkinson, George *20–21*, 435
Atkinson, Oriana *60–61*, 320
Atlas, Helen Gillespie *69–70*, 314
Atlas, Leopold L. *33–34*, 481; *36–37*, 453
Atteridge, Harold *09–19*, 458, 467, 471, 485, 494, 503, 519, 524, 527, 534, 546, 547, 553, 562, 567, 571, 576, 585, 600, 610, 622, 631, 652; *19–20*, 381; *20–21*, 356, 416, 449; *21–22*, 397, 437, 523, 534; *22–23*, 457, 582; *23–24*, 358, 439; *24–25*, 432, 436, 446, 518, 551; *25–26*, 420, 427, 431, 527, 600; *26–27*, 422, 525; *27–28*, 391, 536; *28–29*, 469; *31–32*, 409; *34–35*, 432
Attmore, John *60–61*, 39
Atwell, Lester *64–65*, 336
Atwell, Roy *09–19*, 608
Atwood, A. *94–99*, 223
Auber, Daniel Francois Esprit *48–49*, 428
Aubrey, John *67–68*, 357
Auchincloss, Louis *67–68*, 408
Auden, W.H. *35–36*, 479; *36–37*, 448; *37–38*, 454; *38–39*, 487; *46–47*, 426; *47–48*, 425; *49–50*, 383; *58–59*, 52
Audiberti, Jacques *68–69*, 450
Audran, Edmond *94–99*, 212; *99–09*, 581
Audry, Paul *94–99*, 256
Auerbach, Arnold *45–46*, 438; *47–48*, 401; *50–51*, 334
Auerbach, S. Leonard *68–69*, 399
Augier, Emile *99–09*, 401; *22–23*, 488
Aulicino, Armand *60–61*, 352; *68–69*, 455
Aumont, Jean Pierre *48–49*, 411
Auracher, Harry *09–19*, 464; *19–20*, 414
Auric, Georges *56–57*, 353; 64–65, 315
Aurthur, Robert Alan *56–57*, 334; *61–62*, 264; *67–68*, 364
Austen, Jane *35–36*, 430; *58–59*, 331; *62–63*, 295
Austin, Frederick *20–21*, 416; *27–28*, 533
Austin, George *35–36*, 420
Austin, Mary *09–19*, 440, 591
Austin, Paul John *67–68*, 412
Austin, Sumner *42–43*, 487
Aveling, Claude *09–19*, 524
Aviva (see Hillel & Aviva)
Avshalomoff, Aaron *25–26*, 569; *55–56*, 353
Axe, Ronald *60–61*, 292; *62–63*, 324; *64–65*, 343
Axelrod, George *48–49*, 380; *52–53*, 270; *55–56*, 353; *59–60*, 311
Axelson, Mary Macdougal *31–32*, 496
Axlerod, David *62–63*, 324; *63–64*, 344; *64–65*, 343; *67–68*, 377, 378
Ayckbourn, Alan *70–71*
Ayer, Ethan *61–62*, 309; *64–65*, 353
Ayer, Nat D. *99–09*, 580
Aymé, Marcel *57–58*, 53; *59–60*, 295; *63–64*, 368; *64–65*, 315
Ayre, Robert *42–43*, 442

Aznavour, Charles *65–66,* 377;
  66–67, 367; *68–69,* 383; *69–70,*
  314

Baal, Frederic *70–71*
Babel, Isaac *65–66,* 435
Babgy, George *28–29,* 466
Bach, Johann Sebastian *37–38,* 412;
  38–39, 476; *42–43,* 485; *45–46,*
  452, 453; *47–48,* 344, 356, 414,
  416; *48–49,* 429; *54–55,* 386;
  62–63, 326; *66–67,* 404; *67–68,*
  391
Bacharach, Burt *68–69,* 395
Bacheller, Irving *99–09,* 398
Bachmann, (Dr.) Robert *45–46,* 459;
  50–51, 373
Bach(k)witz, Hans *25–26,* 537;
  30–31, 512
Backer, George *32–33,* 440
Backer, William *09–19,* 474
Bacon, Frank *09–19,* 634; *19–20,*
  372; *38–39,* 405
Bacon, Gaspar Jr. *36–37,* 499
Bacon, Glenn *39–40,* 400
Bacon, Robert *39–40,* 473
Baer, Abel *26–27,* 423, 510
Baer, Arthur ("Bugs") *20–21,* 415;
  21–22, 388; *25–26,* 420
Bafunno, Antonio *09–19,* 647
Bagley, Ben *55–56,* 391; *62–63,* 316;
  65–66, 428
Bagnold, Enid *51–52,* 307; *55–56,*
  358; *63–64,* 318
Bahr, Herman *09–19,* 427, 579, 589,
  621, 623; *24–25,* 505; *67–68,* 367
Bailey, Jeff *46–47,* 447
Bailey, Le Roy *36–37,* 481; *37–38,*
  464; *38–39,* 485
Bailey, Oliver D. *09–19,* 539, 571,
  607, 636, 640
Bailin, Harriet *66–67,* 416
Baird, Anthony *30–31,* 498
Baird, Bil *62–63,* 331; *64–65,* 328;
  66–67, 413; *67–68,* 395; *68–69,*
  436, 437; *69–70,* 351; *70–71*
Baird, Stewart *29–30,* 398

Bairnsfather, (Capt.) Bruce *09–19,*
  641; *26–27,* 423
Baker, Mr. *62–63,* 295
Baker, David *54–55,* 409; *57–58,*
  293; *60–61,* 292, 360; *65–66,* 391;
  68–69, 411
Baker, Dorothy & Howard *44–45,*
  407
Baker, Edith Ellis (see Edith Ellis)
Baker, Elizabeth *09–19,* 488
Baker, Elliott *69–70,* 300
Baker, H. *68–69,* 391
Baker, Herbert *43–44,* 470
Baker, Josephine *63–64,* 323
Baker, Josephine Turck *22–23,* 569
Baker, R. Melville *99–09,* 406, 462,
  549; *23–24,* 341; *24–25,* 514;
  33–34, 457
Baker, Robert *09–19,* 583
Balamos, John *61–62,* 267; *64–65,*
  361
Balch, David Arnold *26–27,* 469;
  34–35, 472
Balch, Jack *48–49,* 428
Balderston, John L. *27–28,* 422;
  29–30, 432; *30–31,* 515; *32–33,*
  437
Baldridge, Richard *56–57,* 360;
  66–67, 371
Baldwin, Faith *33–34,* 518
Baldwin, James *63–64,* 335; *64–65,*
  332
Baldwin, Winnie *29–30,* 409
Balf, Miriam *51–52,* 328
Balfe, Michael William *09–19,* 638;
  33–34, 423; *34–35,* 360
Balieff, M. Nikita *21–22,* 504;
  24–25, 526; *31–32,* 413; *43–44,*
  407
Ball, Jessica *32–33,* 484
Ballard, Clinton *70–71*
Ballard, Frederick *09–19,* 504, 556;
  26–27, 379; *27–28,* 560; *29–30,*
  423
Ballard, Lucinda *39–40,* 471
Balmer, E. *99–09,* 572
Balogh, Erno *32–33,* 494

Balzac (Honoré de Balzac) *99–09,* 558, 580; *09–19,* 653; *38–39,* 492

Balzer, George *45–46,* 405

Bamman, George *28–29,* 490

Bangs, John Kendrick *99–09,* 478, 519

Banks, Bobbie *69–70,* 373

Banks, John *29–30,* 512

Banks, Nathaniel *58–59,* 51

Ban(n)ister, Lemuel Jr. *39–40,* 473; *40–41,* 433

Bantock, Leedham *99–09,* 546; *09–19,* 404

Barab, Seymour *57–58,* 306

Baragwanath, John *37–38,* 416

Barasch, Norman *58–59,* 299; *60–61,* 311

Baratt, Louise Bascom *28–29,* 460

Barber, Samuel *46–47,* 487

Barbier, L. *45–46,* 390

Barbier, Pierre *37–38,* 469

Barbour, Edwin *94–99,* 125, 158

Barbour, Thomas *58–59,* 51

Barcus, James S. *09–19,* 525

Bard, Phil *48–49,* 427

Bardoly, Louis S. *38–39,* 420; *63–64,* 336

Barefield, Eddie *54–55,* 393

Barer, Marshall *56–57,* 314, 357; *58–59,* 335; *59–60,* 335; *65–66,* 403, 428; *66–67,* 422

Bargy, Jean *60–61,* 42

Barian, Joe *41–42,* 438

Barillet, Pierre *65–66,* 390; *68–69,* 400; *70–71*

Barkentin (Barkenstein), Marjorie *58–59,* 55

Barker, Albert Wineman *28–29,* 480; *31–32,* 388; *35–36,* 468; *44–45,* 432; *48–49,* 383

Barker, Edwin L. *28–29,* 480; *31–32,* 388; *35–36,* 468

Barker, Harley Granville & Helen (see Granville-Barker)

Barklie, Lance *61–62,* 313

Barlow, Anna Marie *61–62,* 327; *67–68,* 408; *69–70,* 372

Barlow, Howard *25–26,* 569; *26–27,* 503

Barlow, Samuel L.M. *09–19,* 520; *37–38,* 384

Barnard, Armand *09–19,* 419

Barnard, Charles *94–99,* 101, 152, 157

Barnes, Billy *59–60,* 289; *61–62,* 253

Barnes, Carman *30–31,* 459

Barnes, Charles *41–42,* 443

Barnes, Djuna *25–26,* 593

Barnes, Howard McKent *27–28,* 522

Barnes, Margaret Ayer *28–29,* 428; *29–30,* 415, 487; *37–38,* 400

Barnet, R.A. *94–99,* 103, 154, 182; *99–09,* 358, 388, 406, 409, 549

Barnett, Ella *26–27,* 508

Barnett, Jack *46–47,* 450

Barney, Betty *69–70,* 375

Baron, Henry *20–21,* 434; *21–22,* 515

Baron, Henry *24–25,* 594

Baron, Maurice *38–39,* 490

Barr, Michael *69–70,* 347

Barr, Richard *47–48,* 345

Barrangon, Eloise *36–37,* 404

Barras, Charles M. *94–99,* 95

Barratt, Augustus *99–09,* 549, 576; *09–19,* 476, 627, 643

Barrault, Jean-Louis *52–53,* 269; *63–64,* 326; *64–65,* 363; *69–70,* 329

Barre, Mons. (see Keroul & Barre)

Barre, Albert *94–99,* 211

Barre, Alfred *99–09,* 468

Barrett, Elizabeth (see Elizabeth Barrett Browning)

Barrett, Lillian *22–23,* 555

Barrett, Sheila *36–37,* 498

Barrett, William E. *69–70,* 321

Barrett, Wilson *94–99,* 105, 183, 217; *99–09,* 384

Barrie, (Sir) J(ames) M(atthew) *94–99,* 186, 209; *99–09,* 384, 399, 445, 450, 478, 500, 503, 575; *09–19,* 439, 464, 489, 504, 508, 509, 518, 557, 566, 568, 591, 596,

601, 629, 647; *20–21,* 414, 448;
24–25, 481, 522, 559; *25–26,* 583,
593; *26–27,* 501; *27–28,* 551;
28–29, 425, 501; *29–30,* 533;
30–31, 501; *31–32,* 406, 489;
37–38, 467; *40–41,* 431; *41–42,*
442; *46–47,* 436; *49–50,* 378;
50–51, 355; *52–53,* 289; *54–55,*
369, 384; *66–67,* 408, 409
Barriere, Theo. *94–99,* 167
Barrington, Lowell *35–36,* 462
Barron, Elwyn *99–09,* 456
Barron, P.J. *09–19,* 404
Barron, Robert M. *47–48,* 429
Barrows, John *51–52,* 318
Barry, Jeff *67–68,* 380; *70–71*
Barry, Julian *70–71*
Barry, Mae Howley *38–39,* 488
Barry, P.J. *70–71*
Barry, Peter *39–40,* 437; *40–41,*
389; *41–42,* 459
Barry, Philip *22–23,* 535; *24–25,*
507; *25–26,* 495; *26–27,* 404;
27–28, 444, 483, 489; *28–29,* 424;
29–30, 522; *30–31,* 479; *31–32,*
463; *33–34,* 486; *35–36,* 420;
36–37, 404; *38–39,* 436, 467;
39–40, 470; *40–41,* 414; *42–43,*
442; *44–45,* 420; *48–49,* 411;
50–51, 339; *60–61,* 45; *65–66,* 437
Barry, Richard *25–26,* 477
Barry, Tom *09–19,* 423; *24–25,* 493;
26–27, 391; *28–29,* 391
Barry, William E. *28–29,* 504;
31–32, 495
Barrymore, Maurice *94–99,* 183
Barsha, Tony *67–68,* 405; *70–71*
Barstow, Montague *09–19,* 428
Bart, Jean *26–27,* 425; *30–31,* 497;
32–33, 384
Bart, Lionel *62–63,* 292; *65–66,* 370;
69–70, 308
Bartfield, Carl *31–32,* 513
Bartholomae, Philip H. *09–19,* 435,
474, 504, 531, 567, 615, 620;
19–20, 339; *21–22,* 391, 402;
22–23, 541; *25–26,* 597

Bartley, Nalbro *09–19,* 635
Bartok, Bela *26–27,* 504; *51–52,*
330
Barton, Arthur *31–32,* 415; *32–33,*
488
Barton, John *62–63,* 295
Barton, John W. *99–09,* 423
Barton, Paul *32–33,* 438
Bartov, Hanoch *63–64,* 322
Barwinsky, Mr. *47–48,* 417
Barzini, Luigi *22–23,* 450
Barzman, Ben & Sol *40–41,* 403
Bascom, Ada Lee *94–99,* 155
Basinger, John *69–70,* 311
Bass, George Houston *68–69,* 433
Bass, Jules *68–69,* 428
Basshe, Em Jo (Emjo) *25–26,* 489;
26–27, 492; *27–28,* 461; *35–36,*
475
Bassman, George *40–41,* 403; *56–57,*
328
Baswitz, C. *99–09,* 516
Bataille, Henri *99–09,* 429; *09–19,*
427, 433, 611; *21–22,* 414; 22–23,
461, 489
Bataille-Henri, Mons. *64–65,* 332
Batchelor, W.H. *94–99,* 129, 259
Bates, Esther Willard *28–29,* 465
Batiste, John *67–68,* 403
Batson, George D. *38–39,* 484;
43–44, 446; *48–49,* 420; *52–53,*
300
Batterberry, Michael *61–62,* 308
Battista, Miriam (Mrs. Russell
Maloney) *48–49,* 375
Battle, John Tucker *26–27,* 470
Baty, Gaston *37–38,* 390
Bauer, Irv *70–71*
Baum, L. Frank *99–09,* 427; *68–69,*
436
Baum, Vicki *30–31,* 452; *33–34,*
450; *39–40,* 408; *43–44,* 439
Baumer, Marie *29–30,* 411, 508;
33–34, 511; *34–35,* 439; *36–37,*
406; *45–46,* 430
Bax, Clifford *09–19,* 487; *31–32,*
419; *50–51,* 328

Baxandall, Lee *67–68,* 396; *68–69,* 421

Baxt, George *55–56,* 391

Baxter, Alan *34–35,* 432

Baxter, James K. *62–63,* 321; *63–64,* 345

Baxter, Lora *31–32,* 462

Bayard, Mons. *94–99,* 115

Bayer, Carole *69–70,* 317

Bayer, Eleanor & Leo *58–59,* 316

Bayes, Nora *69–70,* 371

Bayesen, Algernon *99–09,* 485; *09–19,* 407

Bazelon, Irwin A. *52–53,* 307; *56–57,* 356

Beach, Albert A. *63–64,* 343; *65–66,* 383

Beach, Lewis *09–19,* 560; *22–23,* 525; *23–24,* 393; *28–29,* 459

Beach, Rex *99–09,* 535, 581; *09–19,* 409, 475; *24–25,* 513

Beach, Stewart *36–37,* 414

Beachner, Louis *51–52,* 333

Beahan, Charles *28–29,* 378, 480; *29–30,* 528; *33–34,* 433–4

Beals, Julia *66–67,* 423

Beamer, Nona *60–61,* 328

Bean, Orestes *09–19,* 476

Bean, Orson *53–54,* 329

Beane, Mr. *53–54,* 306

Beardsley, Bonnie *70–71*

Béart, Guy *64–65,* 315

Beatty, Bessie *32–33,* 429

Beauchamp, Guy *38–39,* 404

Beaumarchais (Pierre Augustin Caron) *42–43,* 444; *55–56,* 357; *63–64,* 326

Beaumont, Gerald *22–23,* 451; *24–25,* 539

Beban, George *09–19,* 453

Becaud, Gilbert *66–67,* 367; *68–69,* 382, 383

Becerra, M. Hernaiz *09–19,* 509

Bechhofer, C.E. *09–19,* 579

Beck, Sydney *63–64,* 314

Becker, George *62–63,* 300

Becker, Ivan *51–52,* 332

Becker, Will H. *09–19,* 472

Beckett, Samuel *55–56,* 385; *56–57,* 350; *57–58,* 53; *59–60,* 352; *60–61,* 47; *61–62,* 305, 323; *63–64,* 354, 362; *65–66,* 416, 420; *67–68,* 405; *68–69,* 379; *69–70,* 335, 363, 370, 376; *70–71*

Beckwith, Reginald *39–40,* 463

Becque, Henri *99–09,* 472; *50–51,* 312

Bedford, Ronnie *59–60,* 324; *60–61,* 289

Beer, Thomas *22–23,* 450

Beerbohm, Max *99–09,* 404; *68–69,* 427

Beeson, Nora *62–63,* 336

Beethoven (Ludwig van Beethoven) *44–45,* 439; *45–46,* 452; *46–47,* 491; *47–48,* 423; *54–55,* 386; *56–57,* 333; *62–63,* 296

Behan, Brendan *58–59,* 49; *60–61,* 295; *61–62,* 315; *66–67,* 422; *69–70,* 324

Behn, Susanne *27–28,* 520

Behrman, S(amuel) N(athaniel) *26–27,* 507, 509; *28–29,* 461; *29–30,* 465; *31–32,* 426; *32–33,* 434; *33–34,* 492; *34–35,* 427; *35–36,* 483; *37–38,* 384, 426; *38–39,* 470; *40–41,* 417; *42–43,* 446; *43–44,* 462; *45–46,* 416; *49–50,* 359; *51–52,* 308; *54–55,* 373; *58–59,* 309; *62–63,* 288; *63–64,* 321

Beich, Albert *58–59,* 300

Bein, Albert *32–33,* 487; *35–36,* 431; *39–40,* 456; *43–44,* 414

Bein, Mary *43–44,* 414

Beirne, Deborah *31–32,* 488

Beissier, Fernand *24–25,* 600

Beith, (Maj.) Ian Hay *25–26,* 596

Bela, Nicholas *48–49,* 426

Belafonte, Harry *53–54,* 328, 330

Belasco, David *94–99,* 84, 95, 96, 97, 149, 233, 250; *99–09,* 107, 359, 373, 395, 402, 448, 481, 500, 527, 547; *09–19,* 407, 454, 613; *19–20,*

387; *21–22,* 424, 470; *22–23,* 542;
23–24, 364; *26–27,* 384; *28–29,*
434, 451; *45–46,* 391; *57–58,* 56
Bell, A.R. *69–70,* 373
Bell, Charles J. *99–09,* 469, 497
Bell, Charles W. *09–19,* 501, 618;
22–23, 552; *23–24,* 414
Bell, Gail *66–67,* 423; *67–68,* 410
Bell, James *37–38,* 463
Bell, Mary Hayley *42–43,* 467;
47–48, 357
Bell, Thomas *43–44,* 433
Bellamy, Francis R. *26–27,* 397
Belledna, Alex *28–29,* 505
Bellak, George *49–50,* 384
Bellew, Kyrle (see also J.C.
Montesquison) *94–99,* 141
Belling, Edward *70–71*
Bellini, Vincenzo *42–43,* 484; *45–46,*
454
Bellman, Geoffrey *63–64,* 368
Bellow, Saul *64–65,* 305; *66–67,* 366
Bellson, Louis *57–58,* 320
Bellwood, Peter *69–70,* 315
Belmonte, Nene *33–34,* 447
Beloin, Edmund *52–53,* 257
Belot, Adolphe *94–99,* 126, 132,
143; *99–09,* 361
Belson, Hortense *52–53,* 306
Bemelmans, Ludwig *49–50,* 374
Benary, Barbara *69–70,* 375
Benatsky, Ralph *30–31,* 476; *36–37,*
413
Benavente, Jacinto (see Jacinto
Benevente)
Benchley, Nathaniel G. *37–38,* 469;
53–54, 311
Bendix, Max *09–19,* 536, 620
Benedict, Arden *94–99,* 138
Benedict, Stewart *70–71*
Benelli, Sem *09–19,* 432, 655; *19–20,*
353; *25–26,* 547
Benét, Stephen Vincent *24–25,* 441,
460; *38–39,* 474; *52–53,* 288, 308;
60–61, 45; *68–69,* 433, 455; *70–71*
Benét, William Rose *47–48,* 414,
417

Benevente (Benavente), Jacinto
09–19, 612, 655; *19–20,* 415;
25–26, 599; *26–27,* 411; *29–30,*
417; *31–32,* 500; *34–35,* 448;
36–37, 499; *53–54,* 322
Bengal, Ben *37–38,* 464, 465; *38–39,*
485, 487
Bennett, Alan *62–63,* 283
Bennett, Arnold *09–19,* 477, 495,
511; *19–20,* 429; *21–22,* 460, 541;
26–27, 445; *29–30,* 545; *67–68,*
360
Bennett, Dorothy Cheston *32–33,*
490; *34–35,* 439; *38–39,* 419
Bennett, Richard *09–19,* 543
Bennett, Robert Russell *33–34,* 434;
44–45, 399, 400; *46–47,* 433
Bennett, Tom *43–44,* 418; *44–45,*
383, 398
Bennison, Louis *25–26,* 558
Benny, Jack *62–63,* 299
Benrimo, J. Harry *09–19,* 483,
548, 587, 596; *26–27,* 499; *28–29,*
411
Benson, E.F. *99–09,* 417; *48–49,*
401
Benson, Sally *51–52,* 277; *55–56,*
348; *61–62,* 333
Bent, Gordon *41–42,* 461
Bentham, Josephine *42–43,* 427
Bentley, Eric (Russel) *44–45,* 443;
56–57, 345; *61–62,* 317, 318, 322;
62–63, 304, 314, 340; *63–64,* 359,
365; *64–65,* 359, 360; *65–66,* 379;
66–67, 371; *67–68,* 409; *69–70,*
378; *70–71*
Benton, Robert *65–66,* 405; *69–70,*
335
Benton, Sally *44–45,* 432
Beranger, Clara *19–20,* 454
Bercovici, Leonardo *35–36,* 422;
36–37, 439; *40–41,* 422
Bereny, Henri *09–19,* 459, 473
Berg, Gertrude *47–48,* 387; *62–63,*
299
Berg, Jimmy *39–40,* 395
Bergelson, David *44–45,* 444

Berger, Henning *09–19*, 603; *21–22*, 499; *34–35*, 453

Berger, Ted *66–67*, 415

Bergerat, Emile *99–09*, 352

Bergerse(o)n, Baldwin *37–38*, 429; *40–41*, 405; *42–43*, 471; *43–44*, 469; *45–46*, 386; *48–49*, 380; *59–60*, 354; *70–71*

Bergersen, Beau *41–42*, 438

Berghof, Herbert *47–48*, 341

Bergman, Alan & Marilyn *64–65*, 311

Bergman, Robert *41–42*, 461

Bergstrom, Hjalmar *09–19*, 619

Bergy, Jean *63–64*, 343

Beringer, Mrs. Oscar *94–99*, 169, 228

Berisso, Emilio *27–28*, 467

Berkeley, Lennox *55–56*, 350

Berkeley, Martin *36–37*, 406; *37–38*, 424

Berkeley, Reginald *20–21*, 402; *31–32*, 436

Berkey, Ralph *55–56*, 371

Berkman, Alexander *27–28*, 484

Berkman, John *68–69*, 411

Berkowitz, Sol *55–56*, 392; *62–63*, 284

Berlin, Irving *09–19*, 541, 567, 586, 619, 633, 643; *20–21*, 355; *21–22*, 426; *22–23*, 477; *23–24*, 320; *24–25*, 496; *25–26*, 511; *27–28*, 391; *31–32*, 379, 480; *32–33*, 457; *33–34*, 438; *39–40*, 465; *42–43*, 420, 421; *45–46*, 447; *49–50*, 354; *50–51*, 319; *53–54*, 306; *57–58*, 319; *62–63*, 280; *65–66*, 413; *66–67*, 356; *68–69*, 446

Berlioz, Louis Hector *46–47*, 489; *47–48*, 418

Berman, L.E. *99–09*, 567

Bermel, Albert *57–58*, 314; *63–64*, 369; *67–68*, 409; *68–69*, 457; *69–70*, 311

Bern, Mina *70–71*

Bernard, Anthony *45–46*, 421

Bernard, Ian *66–67*, 418

Bernard, Jean-Jacques *27–28*, 534; *28–29*, 388; *36–37*, 499; *37–38*, 469

Bernard, Sam *23–24*, 322

Bernard, Sam II *32–33*, 392

Bernard, Tristan *99–09*, 536, 548, 560; *09–19*, 514

Bernauer & Jacobson (see Rudolph Bernauer and Leopold Jacobson)

Bernauer, Rudolph *09–19*, 399; *21–22*, 476; *22–23*, 505; *27–28*, 416; *29–30*, 482; *31–32*, 394; *33–34*, 523; *42–43*, 419; *46–47*, 470

Berney, William *44–45*, 421; *49–50*, 369; *56–57*, 348; *57–58*, 56; *69–70*, 362

Bernhard, Emil *27–28*, 484

Bernhardt, Maurice *09–19*, 589 (and 605)

Bernhardt, Sarah *09–19*, 589 (and 605); *70–71*

Bernhauser, Mr. *22–23*, 479

Berns, Julie *43–44*, 490; *44–45*, 443; *48–49*, 395; *56–57*, 346

Bernstein, Elmer *54–55*, 369; *67–68*, 355

Bernstein, Henri *99–09*, 475, 544, 571; *09–19*, 403, 416, 453, 456, 477, 517, 614; *21–22*, 442; *24–25*, 547; *26–27*, 512; *30–31*, 517; *31–32*, 412, 500; *36–37*, 448, 500

Bernstein, Herman *09–19*, 446; *20–21*, 403; *22–23*, 557; *25–26*, 553, 573; *27–28*, 409, 545, 555; *28–29*, 366, 473, 503; *29–30*, 417

Bernstein, Leonard *43–44*, 486; *44–45*, 406–7; *46–47*, 489; *49–50*, 378; *52–53*, 290; *54–55*, 406; *55–56*, 363; *56–57*, 340; 57–58, 286, 323, 331; *58–59*, 315; *59–60*, 336; *62–63*, 297; *63–64*, 333; *64–65*, 363; *65–66*, 418, 419; *66–67*, 386; *68–69*, 373

Bernstein, Richard N. *60–61*, 42

Bernstein, Robert A. *55–56*, 335
Berr, Verneuil & Blum (see Georges Berr, Louis Verneuil and Mons. Blum)
Berr, Georges *99–09*, 428; *09–19*, 441, 455, 479, 643; *30–31*, 476
Berrigan, Daniel (S.J.) *70–71*
Berstl, Julius *30–31*, 504
Berte, Emile *28–29*, 486
Berte, Heinrich *09–19*, 464; *25–26*, 565; *30–31*, 500; *43–44*, 410
Berton, Eugene *39–40*, 468; *47–48*, 339
Berton, Pierre (1) *94–99*, 250; *99–09*, 373, 460, 472, 483, 501
Berton, Pierre (2) *64–65*, 358
Berton, Ralph *39–40*, 468
Bertram, Eugene *94–99*, 139
Besant, Walter *94–99*, 120
Besier, Rudolph *09–19*, 408, 409, 466, 623; *22–23*, 509; *23–24*, 320; *30–31*, 487; *34–35*, 456; *44–45*, 425
Besoyan, Rick *59–60*, 351; *63–64*, 304; *64–65*, 351; *69–70*, 373
Best, Charles *52–53*, 306
Betti, Henri *55–56*, 347; *64–65*, 294, 331
Betti, Ugo *52–53*, 258; *55–56*, 350; *59–60*, 46; *63–64*, 347; *64–65*, 355; *65–66*, 416; *68–69*, 458; *69–70*, 378
Bevan, Donald *50–51*, 368, 374
Beydts, Louis *55–56*, 357
Beye, Holly *61–62*, 329
Beyea, Basil *42–43*, 418
Beyerlein, Franz Adam *99–09*, 466; *24–25*, 576
Beyo, Mascha *63–64*, 366
Bhagat, Niranjan *63–64*, 368
Bhasa *63–64*, 368
Bhumibol (King of Thailand) *50–51*, 309
Bialik, Ch. N. *70–71*
Bialik, H.N. *63–64*, 322
Biancardo, Pascal *30–31*, 524; *46–47*, 493

Bibesco, Prince *30–31*, 400
Bibo, Irving *34–35*, 483
Bickford, Charles A. *27–28*, 560
Biddle, Cordelia Drexel *56–57*, 337
Biddle, Nicholas *94–99*, 137
Bideau, Jean *26–27*, 460
Bidwell, Martin *44–45*, 371
Bidwell, Patric *99–09*, 575
Bieber, Ethel *65–66*, 432
Biel, Nicholas *46–47*, 495
Bienbryer, Eddie *32–33*, 500
Biermann, Wolf *67–68*, 409
Bieville, Mons. *94–99*, 115
Bigbee, North *36–37*, 474
Bigelow, Joe *45–46*, 427
Bigelow, Otis *51–52*, 293; *64–65*, 347
Biggers, Earl Derr *09–19*, 166, 546, 624; *19–20*, 355, 395; *33–34*, 444; *34–35*, 481
Bilhaud, Paul *94–99*, 211; *99–09*, 347, 355, 361, 363, 460, 468, 502
Billetdoux, François *62–63*, 283
Bimonte, Dave *62–63*, 336
Bingham, Susan Hulsman *69–70*, 345
Birabeau, Andre *36–37*, 499; *38–39*, 408; *41–42*, 414
Birch-Pfeiffer, Charlotte *94–99*, 243
Bird, John *62–63*, 323
Bird, Dr. (Robert) Montgomery *94–99*, 226; *70–71*
Birimisa, George *68–69*, 455; *70–71*
Birinski, Leo *34–35*, 444; *44–45*, 374
Birmingham, George A. *09–19*, 513; *29–30*, 485
Birmingham, Michael *32–33*, 478
Birmingham, T.R. *94–99*, 197
Birney, F.O. *41–42*, 461
Birnkrant, Arthur *66–67*, 413
Birnkrant, Samuel *62–63*, 316
Biro, Lajos *21–22*, 502; *23–24*, 403
Bisch, Louis E. *24–25*, 552; *27–28*, 527
Bischoff, Edgar *60–61*, 291
Bishop, Gordon *62–63*, 334

Bishop, Stuart *58–59*, 53; *62–63*, 314
Bissell, Gene P. *66–67*, 404; *67–68*, 377
Bissell, Marian *57–58*, 327; *58–59*, 324; *65–66*, 436
Bissell, Richard *53–54*, 353; *56–57*, 375; *57–58*, 327; *58–59*, 324; *65–66*, 436
Bissell, Roger W. *41–42*, 461
Bissell, Tallman *38–39*, 491
Bisson, Alexandre *94–99*, 134, 176, 185, 243, 250; *99–09*, 391, 583; *09–19*, 413, 421, 432, 446, 616; *19–20*, 421; *27–28*, 387
Bixby, Carl *27–28*, 550
Bixby, Frank L. *94–99*, 85
Bizet, Georges *94–99*, 198; *09–19*, 638; *25–26*, 515; *43–44*, 432, 439, 472; *44–45*, 382, 443; *45–46*, 389, 394; *46–47*, 408; *47–48*, 343; *49–50*, 385; *55–56*, 393; *56–57*, 333
Bjorkman, Edwin *09–19*, 498, 619; *25–26*, 533
Bjornson, Bjornstjerne *99–09*, 403–4; *09–19*, 564
Black, Arnold *53–54*, 340; *61–62*, 308; *62–63*, 314; *67–68*, 409
Black, Frank *45–46*, 427
Black, Jack *32–33*, 429
Black, Jean Ferguson *33–34*, 453; *36–37*, 480; *44–45*, 441
Black, Kitty *51–52*, 300
Black, Leonard *40–41*, 431
Blackburn, Maurice *50–51*, 348
Blackmar, Beatrice *28–29*, 485
Blackmore, Peter *50–51*, 374
Blackwell, Donald *32–33*, 488; *33–34*, 424; *34–35*, 455
Blackwell, Earl *39–40*, 413
Blackwell, Vera *67–68*, 389; *69–70*, 348
Blaine, Marjorie *19–20*, 382
Blair, Richard *64–65*, 342
Blake, Eubie *20–21*, 450; *22–23*, 552; *24–25*, 442; *30–31*, 438;

32–33, 441; *37–38*, 447; *51–52*, 323
Blake, Gordon *99–09*, 474
Blake, Robert *29–30*, 175
Blake, William *37–38*, 468; *38–39*, 491; *62–63*, 322; *68–69*, 407
Blanchard, Benjamin F. *09–19*, 543
Blanchard, Dorothy *29–30*, 533
Blanchard, Edwin *94–99*, 158
Bland, Margaret *27–28*, 551
Blane, Ralph *41–42*, 400; *51–52*, 316; *62–63*, 330
Blaney, Charles E. *94–99*, 117, 192, 210, 221, 224–5, 248, 255
Blankfort, Dorothy *57–58*, 295
Blankfort, Henry *40–41*, 403
Blankfort, Michael *34–35*, 423; *35–36*, 477, 510; *36–37*, 497; *37–38*, 464; *57–58*, 295
Blasco, Senor *31–32*, 500
Blatt, Jerry *67–68*, 398
Blau, Eric *60–61*, 42; *67–68*, 399
Blau, Herbert *65–66*, 378
Blechman, Burt *62–63*, 303
Blethen, Joseph *99–09*, 541
Blitzer, Barry *56–57*, 316
Blitzstein, Marc *29–30*, 548; *37–38*, 388, 395, 411, 461; *38–39*, 424, 485; *39–40*, 468; *40–41*, 430; *42–43*, 433; *45–46*, 392; *46–47*, 437, 443; *47–48*, 343, 370; *48–49*, 429; *49–50*, 359; *50–51*, 338; *53–54*, 358; *55–56*, 369; *58–59*, 326; *59–60*, 48; *61–62*, 317; *63–64*, 343, 363; *64–65*, 347; *66–67*, 366, 408; *69–70*, 335
Bloch, Augustin *64–65*, 322
Bloch, Bertram *25–26*, 580; *29–30*, 492; *31–32*, 464; *34–35*, 404; *41–42*, 411
Bloch, Pedro *51–52*, 325
Block, Anita Rowe *63–64*, 316
Block, Arthur *38–39*, 485
Block, Hal *41–42*, 417
Block, Maxine *29–30*, 538
Blocki, Fritz *33–34*, 472; *36–37*, 476, 486

Blondeau, Henri *09–19,* 437

Blood Company, The *70–71*

Bloom, Philip *37–38,* 465

Bloom, Rube *38–39,* 459

Bloomstein, Henry *69–70,* 341

Blossom, Henry M. (Jr.) *99–09,* 423, 437, 455, 502, 504, 520, 548, 573; *09–19,* 435, 468, 469, 490, 502, 538, 560, 597, 624, 650; *91–20,* 448; *29–30,* 414; *33–34,* 530; *45–46,* 398

Blow, Sydney *09–19,* 513

Blue, Dan *61–62,* 323; *65–66,* 422

Blum, Mons. *30–31,* 476

Blum, Abraham *38–39,* 494; *39–40,* 474

Blum, David *44–45,* 441

Blum, Edwin Harvey *36–37,* 397; *37–38,* 430; *62–63,* 333

Blum, Ernest *94–99,* 218

Blumenthal, Oscar *94–99,* 121, 162, 217, 252; *99–09,* 365; *09–19,* 397; *36–37,* 413

Blun, Gustav *09–19,* 652

Blunden, Edmund *64–65,* 303

Boal, Augusto *69–70,* 339

Bobrick, Sam *69–70,* 316

Boccaccio, Giovanni *09–19,* 575; *60–61,* 42

Bock, Jerry *55–56,* 339, 340, 341, 380; *57–58,* 311; *59–60,* 305; *60–61,* 301; *62–63,* 277, 289, 307, 331; *63–64,* 372; *64–65,* 302; *65–66,* 374; *66–67,* 364; *68–69,* 455; *70–71*

Bodansky, Robert *09–19,* 395, 454, 468, 490, 562; *29–30,* 496

Boddington, E.F. *99–09,* 389, 423

Boden, William *09–19,* 476

Bodeen, DeWitt *47–48,* 375

Boehm, David *31–32,* 430

Bogart, Helen *94–99,* 188

Boggia, Signor *36–37,* 500

Bohnen, Roman *32–33,* 415

Boileau (Nicolas Boileau-Despréaux) *69–70,* 313

Boileau, Pierre *57–58,* 295

Boker, George H. *99–09,* 403

Bokwe, John Knox *63–64,* 330

Boland, Clay A. *37–38,* 468; *38–39,* 491; *39–40,* 472; *41–42,* 460

Bolcom, William *61–62,* 303, 325; *63–64,* 360; *66–67,* 416; *67–68,* 351; *68–69,* 393; *70–71*

Boleyn, Anne *62–63,* 295

Bolitho, Hector *39–40,* 459

Bolitho, William *30–31,* 465

Bologna, Joseph *68–69,* 377

Bolt, Robert *59–60,* 298; *61–62,* 272; *63–64,* 322

Bolton, Guy *09–19,* 522, 544, 552, 557, 561, 567, 583, 593, 595, 605, 606, 607, 613, 621, 638, 645; *19–20,* 338, 351, 390, 412; *20–21,* 369, 413; *21–22,* 391, 394, 526; *22–23,* 441, 518; *23–24,* 321, 340, 418; *24–25,* 457, 497; *25–26,* 525; *26–27,* 382, 420, 454, 475; *27–28,* 427, 486, 488; *28–29,* 451; *29–30,* 467, 497; *30–31,* 430, 502; *34–35,* 412; *39–40,* 466; *40–41,* 378; *41–42,* 413, 420; *43–44,* 448, 466; *46–47,* 470; *47–48,* 403; *54–55,* 388, 405; *56–57,* 334; *59–60,* 48; *61–62,* 330; *65–66,* 387; *67–68,* 400

Bolton, Muriel Roy *46–47,* 494

Bolton, Richard *46–47,* 494

Bond, Edward *70–71*

Bond, Julian *66–67,* 355

Bond, Raymond *36–37,* 458

Bone, Gene *68–69,* 439

Boni, John *66–67,* 404

Bonner, Eugene *30–31,* 496

Bonner, Geraldine *99–09,* 580; *09–19,* 443

Bontemps, Arna *45–46,* 436; *66–67,* 354, 355

Bonus, Ben *70–71*

Booraem, Hendrik *34–35,* 423

Boorde, Andrew *63–64,* 314

Boosey, William *99–09,* 485

Booth, Howard *19–20,* 424

Boyle, William *09–19,* 458–9, 494
Boynton-Devinney *68–69,* 449
Bracco, Roberto *99–09,* 539; *09–19,* 560
Bradbury, Ray *65–66,* 421
Braddell, Maurice *30–31,* 486; *34–35,* 448
Bradford, Joseph *94–99,* 129
Bradford, Perry *28–29,* 496
Bradford, Roark *34–35,* 457; *39–40,* 428; *50–51,* 358
Bradford, Roy *48–49,* 427
Bradley, Alice *09–19,* 475
Bradley, Mrs. (Lillian) Trimble *09–19,* 555, 634; *19–20,* 428; *24–25,* 453, 467
Bradshaw, Fanny *63–64,* 361
Bradshaw, George *33–34,* 452; *34–35,* 448
Brady, Jasper Ewing *21–22,* 402
Brady, Leo *42–43,* 434
Brady, William A. *94–99,* 87, 94
Brady, William S. *29–30,* 453
Bragdon, Helen *55–56,* 336
Bragg, Bernard *68–69,* 407; *69–70,* 311
Braggiotti, Mario *30–31,* 447
Braham, Dave *94–99,* 110, 175, 197, 245
Braham, George F. *94–99,* 197
Braham, John J. *94–99,* 259; *99–09,* 497
Brahms, Johannes *44–45,* 439; *45–46,* 452; *47–48,* 415
Brainin, Jerome *42–43,* 420
Bradley, Berton *09–19,* 624
Brammer, Julius *09–19,* 521, 578; *20–21,* 449; *22–23,* 467; *26–27,* 380, 517; *27–28,* 538
Bramson, (Mme.) Karen *23–24,* 404; *24–25,* 475
Brancati, John *69–70,* 352
Branch, William *54–55,* 57
Brand, Max *58–59,* 334
Brand, Millen *39–40,* 413
Brand, Oscar *66–67,* 376; *67–68,* 369; *68–69,* 428

Brand, Phoebe *61–62,* 331
Brandl, Johann *94–99,* 153
Brandon, Dorothy *23–24,* 405; *27–28,* 537
Brandon, James R. *67–68,* 411
Brandon, Jocelyn *09–19,* 528
Brandon, John G. *27–28,* 505; *32–33,* 417
Brandon, Johnny *63–64,* 361; *67–68,* 400; *69–70,* 359
Brandt, Eddie *29–30,* 467–8
Brandt, Mike *69–70,* 357
Brant, Henry *34–35,* 460; *39–40,* 471; *40–41,* 429; *41–42,* 457; *46–47,* 428
Brash, Arthur F. *29–30,* 380
Bratton, John W. *99–09,* 376, 460, 463, 492, 580
Bray, Vicar of *62–63,* 295
Bray, Barbara *70–71*
Brearley, William H. *99–09,* 392
Brecher, Irving *42–43,* 455
Brecht, Bertolt *32–33,* 483; *35–36,* 436; *38–39,* 486; *44–45,* 443; *47–48,* 393; *53–54,* 358; *56–57,* 345; *58–59,* 54; *60–61,* 355; *61–62,* 305, 317, 322, 331; *62–63,* 304, 314, 340; *63–64,* 312, 342, 344, 365, 369; *64–65,* 344, 359, 360; *65–66,* 379; *66–67,* 361, 366, 420; *67–68,* 345, 401; *68–69,* 398, 454, 456; *69–70,* 335, 366, 377, 378; *70–71*
Brecker, Richard L. *41–42,* 461
Bredschneider, Willy *09–19,* 517
Bredt, James *68–69,* 427
Breeden, Marshall *63–64,* 372
Breen, Bernice *28–29,* 500
Breen, Richard *39–40,* 473
Breen, Robert *39–40,* 468
Breese, Edmund *09–19,* 511
Breffort, Alexandre *60–61,* 296
Breil, Joseph Carl *99–09,* 581; *09–19,* 419, 650
Breiseth, Tillman *46–47,* 462
Breit, Harvey *58–59,* 308; *61–62,* 333; *67–68,* 366

Breitenbach, Robert *94–99,* 90, 178, 209, 238

Brel, Jacques *67–68,* 399

Brennan, Frederick Hazlett *34–35,* 442; *35–36,* 441; *41–42,* 394; *48–49,* 381

Brennan, J. Keirn *27–28,* 452; *28–29,* 463, 486, 506; *30–31,* 413

Brenner, S.M. *99–09,* 533

Brent, Romney *32–33,* 432; *35–36,* 456

Brentano, Felix *42–43,* 487; *43–44,* 479; *44–45,* 380

Brentano, Lowell *26–27,* 496; *27–28,* 517; *28–29,* 456; *29–30,* 461; *38–39,* 434

Bressler, Maxwell *34–35,* 483

Breton, Nicholas *63–64,* 314

Breton, Richard *63–64,* 314

Breton, Tomas *68–69,* 415

Bretton, Elise *70–71*

Breuer, Bessie *48–49,* 378

Breuer, Kurt *28–29,* 486

Breuer, Lee *70–71*

Brewer, George (Jr.) *34–35,* 404; *36–37,* 456

Briant, Roy *26–27,* 371

Brickman, Marshall *66–67,* 404

Bricusse, Leslie *62–63,* 278; *64–65,* 338; *65–66,* 372

Bridgers, Ann Preston *27–28,* 448

Bridgewater, Leslie *46–47,* 425, 481; *50–51,* 328; *59–60,* 291

Bridie, James *32–33,* 408; *34–35,* 389; *36–37,* 470, 493; *49–50,* 385; *50–51,* 314

Briel, Joseph Carl *32–33,* 502

Brieux, Eugene *99–09,* 472, 582; *09–19,* 408, 417, 497, 543; *19–20,* 430; *20–21,* 363; *21–22,* 511; *25–26,* 458; *36–37,* 484

Brighouse, Harold *09–19,* 526, 564, 612, 628; *66–67,* 374

Bright, Addison *99–09,* 365

Bright, John *41–42,* 420

Brightman, Melford & Furber *23–24,* 330

Brilant, Arthur M. *26–27,* 493

Brill, Leighton K. *30–31,* 468

Brill, Marty *63–64,* 334

Brine, John *63–64,* 350

Brink, Roscoe W. *23–24,* 433

Briquet, Jean *09–19,* 425, 505, 522, 554, 558

Brisebarre, Edouard *94–99,* 99, 235, 245

Bristol, W.D. *34–35,* 476

Britten, Benjamin *41–42,* 457; *46–47,* 426; *48–49,* 404; *50–51,* 333; *61–62,* 314; *62–63,* 334

Britton, Kenneth Phillips *29–30,* 389; *32–33,* 461

Broad, Jay *68–69,* 403

Broadhurst, George H. *94–99,* 172, 199, 205, 254; *99–09,* 347, 382, 428, 431, 460, 495, 512, 528, 535, 542, 559, 565, 568, 575; *09–19,* 396, 452, 456, 473, 510, 531, 533, 561, 580, 584(?), 605, 607, 633, 634; *19–20,* 339; *21–22,* 410, 475; *22–23,* 451; *24–25,* 453, 467

Broadhurst, Thomas William *99–09,* 543; *09–19,* 510, 656

Brod, Max *68–69,* 433

Broderick, Patricia *64–65,* 361

Broderson, Moishe *66–67,* 393; *67–68,* 339

Brody, Lee *39–40,* 394

Brody, Max *09–19,* 507, 568

Broekman, David *52–53,* 258

Brohn, William (Bill) *66–67,* 423; *69–70,* 372

Brokaw, Clare Boothe (see Clare Boothe)

Bromberg, Conrad *69–70,* 356, 372

Bromberger, Anne *36–37,* 493

Bromfield, Louis *27–28,* 418; *34–35,* 457, 461

Bronner, Edwin *45–46,* 400

Bronson-Howard, George (see also Bronson Howard) *09–19,* 395, 449, 485

Brontë, Anne *63–64,* 354

Browne, Maurice *28–29*, 432; *47–48*, 427; *48–49*, 427

Browne, Porter Emerson *99–09*, 580; *09–19*, 417, 488; *20–21*, 374

Browne, Raymond A. *99–09*, 403

Browne, Roscoe Lee *66–67*, 354, 355

Browne (Brown), Walter *99–09*, 397; *09–19*, 417, 440

Browne, William Maynadier *94–99*, 138

Brownell, Atherton *28–29*, 443

Brownell, John Charles *29–30*, 418; *33–34*, 513; *34–35*, 360, 464; *37–38*, 460

Browning, Elizabeth Barrett *64–65*, 361; *68–69*, 407

Browning, Robert *99–09*, 375, 378, 488, 525; *26–27*, 413; *28–29*, 421; *29–30*, 437; *64–65*, 361; *70–71*

Bruce, Lenney *70–71*

Bruce, Norman *43–44*, 415

Bruce, Renaud C. *64–65*, 362

Bruce, Richard *20–21*, 357

Bruckner, Ferdinand *38–39*, 430; *41–42*, 445, 458; *43–44*, 489

Bruguiere, Emil *99–09*, 473

Bruland, Ragnhilde *33–34*, 530

Brulin, Tone *70–71*

Brush, Albert *47–48*, 393

Brusie, Judson D. *99–09*, 555

Bryan, Alfred (Al.) *19–20*, 366; *20–21*, 425

Bryan, C.D. *63–64*, 345

Bryan, Vincent *99–09*, 427, 519, 526, 540, 568, 574

Bryant, Francis *99–09*, 381; *22–23*, 580

Bryant, George *31–32*, 445, 483

Bryant, Henry (see Henry Brant)

Bryce (Pryce), Richard *99–09*, 479; *23–24*, 430

Brymm, James *09–19*, 445

Brynner, Roc *70–71*

Bucci, Mark *50–51*, 373; *60–61*, 292; *61–62*, 284; *63–64*, 352

Buchanan, Robert *94–99*, 157, 182, 248

Buchanan, Thompson *99–09*, 578; *09–19*, 400, 418, 429, 450, 495, 536; *19–20*, 349; *22–23*, 532, 564; *24–25*, 507; *26–27*, 476; *30–31*, 446

Buchbinder, Bernhard *09–19*, 431

Buchman, Harold *44–45*, 391

Buchman, Sidney R. *30–31*, 438

Buchwald, Art *69–70*, 312

Buck, Charles Neville *09–19*, 537

Buck, Gene *09–19*, 502, 527, 553, 576, 601, 631; *19–20*, 361; *20–21*, 355; *21–22*, 388, 464, 555; *23–24*, 340; *24–25*, 429; *26–27*, 359; *27–28*, 457; *31–32*, 377

Buck, Pearl S. *32–33*, 401; *45–46*, 458; *58–59*, 332; *59–60*, 339

Buckminster, Harold C. *47–48*, 428

Buckner, Robert L. *30–31*, 458; *37–38*, 463; *38–39*, 444

Buckwald, N. *52–53*, 308

Buechner (Büchner), George *27–28*, 455, 471; *38–39*, 424; *65–66*, 378, 406; *67–68*, 412; *68–69*, 455; *70–71*

Bufano, Rocco *68–69*, 443

Buffery, Anthony *64–65*, 305

Bulgakov, Mikhail *34–35*, 453; *64–65*, 323

Bulger, Bozeman *25–26*, 420

Bulger, Harry *94–99*, 193, 254; *99–09*, 519

Bull, John *63–64*, 314

Buller, H.G. *31–32*, 482

Bul(l)finch, Thomas *60–61*, 332

Bulling, Erich *69–70*, 377

Bullins, Ed *67–68*, 391; *68–69*, 455; *69–70*, 338, 341, 371; *70–71*

Bullock, Michael *62–63*, 170

Bullock, Turner *34–35*, 466; *38–39*, 481

Bullock, Walter *49–50*, 371, 376

Bulwer-Lytton (see Lytton)

Bunim, Shmuel *68–69*, 385

Bunner, H.C. *94–99*, 171

Bunner, Rudolph *21–22*, 426

Bunuel, Rafael *70–71*

Bunyan, John *99–09*, 550

Burbage, Edward *41–42,* 459

Burg, Brad *70–71*

Burgess, Gelett *09–19,* 456

Burgess, Gilbert *94–99,* 148

Burgess, John *45–46,* 457

Burgie, Irving *63–64,* 348

Burk, Robert *32–33,* 392

Burke, Charles *94–99,* 130; *99–09,* 498

Burke, Edmund Laurence *09–19,* 595

Burke, Edwin *28–29,* 374

Burke, Johnny *45–46,* 422; *53–54,* 301; *60–61,* 339

Burke, Melville *27–28,* 522

Burke, Sonny *49–50,* 367

Burke, T. Patrick *60–61,* 39

Burkhardt, Addison *99–09,* 433, 525, 556, 564

Burman, Howard *44–45,* 422

Burnanad, Francis C. *94–99,* 121, 142, 149, 162, 217, 234; *99–09,* 458; *34–35,*364; *36–37,* 401; *43–44,* 456

Burnet(t), Dana *24–25,* 512; *27–28,* 406; *28–29,* 503; *29–30,* 488; *32–33,* 455

Burnett, (Mrs.) Frances Hodgson *94–99,* 111, 192, 213, 229; *99–09,* 426, 431, 444, 453, 576; *09–19,* 489, 591; *38–39,* 490

Burnett, Murray *43–44,* 476

Burney, Fanny *62–63,* 295

Burnham, Barbara *32–33,* 445

Burns, Arthur *62–63,* 331

Burns, Bernard K. *23–24,* 300

Burns, Robert *65–66,* 402

Burns, Walter *69–70,* 375

Burns, William J. *09–19,* 489

Burnside, R.H. *99–09,* 453, 517, 519, 540, 574; *09–19,* 398, 423, 457, 528, 535, 560, 580, 604, 610, 633; *19–20,* 346, 396; *20–21,* 365, 393; *21–22,* 534; *22–23,* 447; *23–24,* 348; *24–25,* 443; *28–29,* 395

Burr, Anne *68–69,* 434

Burr, Charles H. *41–42,* 461

Burrell, James L.A. *23–24,* 404; *26–27,* 513; *30–31,* 446; *31–32,* 449; *34–35,* 387

Burrell, Philippa *37–38,* 464

Burrell, Randal C. *25–26,* 534

Burrill, Mary *27–28,* 549

Burroughs, Edgar Rice *21–22,* 410

Burrows, Abe *50–51,* 329, 363; *51–52,* 315; *52–53,* 303; *54–55,* 400, 407; *57–58,* 327; *58–59,* 324, 331; *61–62,* 261, 300; *64–65,* 334; *65–66,* 390, 407, 436; *66–67,* 351, 396; *70–71*

Burrows, Joe *23–24,* 298

Burstein, Lonnie *67–68,* 398

Burston, Buddy *42–43,* 471

Burt, Benjamin Hapgood *99–09,* 463, 492, 517; *09–19,* 470, 552; *25–26,* 487

Burt, David *39–40,* 473

Burtis, Thom(p)son *28–29,* 478

Burton, G. Marion *24–25,* 544

Burton-Mercur, Paul *42–43,* 488

Burtson, Bud *55–56,* 338

Burwell, Basil *66–67,* 416

Bush, Alan *47–48,* 392

Bush, Beverly *45–46,* 457

Bush, Josef *68–69,* 452

Bush(Bus)-Fekete, Ladislaus *37–38,* 371; *39–40,* 403; *44–45,* 393, 414; *46–47,* 453; *51–52,* 287

Bushnell, Adelyn *33–34,* 527

Busnach, William *99–09,* 436

Buson, Mr. *62–63,* 322

Bussière, Tadema *25–26,* 564; *26–27,* 427

Butler, Frank *32–33,* 467

Butler, James E. *62–63,* 315

Butler, Rachel Barton *19–20,* 418

Buzzell, Eddie *28–29,* 463

Byram, Al *26–27,* 525

Byrd, William *63–64,* 314

Byrne, Charles Alfred *94–99,* 201, 225, 230

Byrne, Dolly *20–21,* 366

Byrne, Donn *26–27,* 441

Byrne, John *60–61,* 39

Byrne, John F. *94–99,* 101, 242

Byrnes, James *09–19,* 615
Byron, Henry J. *94–99,* 235; *99–09,*
536; *31–32,* 457
Byron, Lord (George Gordon)
24–25, 568

Cabanne, Martha (Mrs. Robert Lee
Kayser) *40–41,* 430
Cabell, James Branch *25–26,* 592
Cable, George W. *99–09,* 424
Cadou, André *55–56,* 357
Caesar, Arthur *23–24,* 354; *26–27,*
479
Caesar, Irving *21–22,* 503; *22–23,*
452; *23–24,* 320; *24–25,* 454, 512;
25–26, 446, 531; *26–27,* 359, 450,
534; *27–28,* 421, 547; *28–29,* 406,
451; *29–30,* 401, 491; *30–31,* 415,
507; *31–32,* 390; *32–33,* 428, 462;
33–34, 421; *36–37,* 413; *43–44,*
411; *70–71*
Cage, John *44–45,* 438; *46–47,* 488
Cahn, Sammy *47–48,* 358; *52–53,*
276; *55–56,* 391; *62–63,* 278, 279;
65–66, 384; *66–67,* 374; *69–70,*
321
Caillavet, Gaston A. *99–09,* 566;
09–19, 615; *20–21,* 419
Cain, Henri *09–19,* 589 (and 605)
Cain, James M. *35–36,* 488
Cain, Joe *70–71*
Caine, Hall *94–99,* 105, 125, 242;
99–09, 423, 494; *09–19,* 570
Calderisi, David *66–67,* 419
Calderón (Pedro Calderón de la
Barca) *45–46,* 458; *47–48,* 432;
53–54, 321, 322; *63–64,* 362;
64–65, 362; *67–68,* 401; *69–70,*
343
Calderon, George *22–23,* 573;
27–28, 521
Caldon, Walter *62–63,* 314; *68–69,*
457
Caldwell, Anne *99–09,* 512, 548;
09–19, 431, 456, 481, 521, 535,
571, 585, 610, 656, 657; *19–20,*
421; *20–21,* 375, 393, 397; *21–22,*

452; *22–23,* 495; *23–24,* 348, 427;
24–25, 443, 495; *25–26,* 483;
26–27, 400, 467; *27–28,* 457, 525;
28–29, 395
Caldwell, Ben *68–69,* 455; *69–70,*
338
Caldwell, Erskine *33–34,* 467;
36–37, 488; *37–38,* 419; *42–43,*
427; *43–44,* 409; *49–50,* 375
Caldwell, Joseph *61–62,* 305
Calhoun, Virginia *99–09,* 367
Callahan, Charles E. *94–99,* 84
Calmour, Alfred C. *99–09,* 353
Calthrop, Dion Clayton *09–19,* 508,
611
Calvi, Gerard *65–66,* 391
Cameron, George *99–09,* 570;
09–19, 395
Cameron, John *64–65,* 305
Cameron, Kenneth *68–69,* 430
Camoletti, Marc *64–65,* 323
Camp, Hamid Hamilton *70–71*
Camp, Shep *27–28,* 403
Camp, Wadsworth *22–23,* 477
Campanella, Philip *70–71*
Campanile, Festa *63–64,* 323
Campbell, Argyll *27–28,* 510
Campbell, Bartley *94–99,* 113, 165,
235; *99–09,* 482
Campbell, Charles J. *99–09,* 562;
09–19, 395
Campbell, C.E. *99–09,* 514
Campbell, Frank G. *94–99,* 228
Campbell, Gurney *70–71*
Campbell, Kane *25–26,* 429
Campbell, Lawton *27–28,* 441;
30–31, 430
Campbell, Maurice *09–19,* 413
Campbell, Roy *63–64,* 362
Campbell, Mrs. Patrick *59–60,* 329;
61–62, 326
Campbell, Mrs. Vere *09–19,* 526
Campion, Thomas *63–64,* 314
Campos, Roberto *64–65,* 349
Campton, David *62–63,* 338
Camus, Albert *59–60,* 319; *62–63,*
322

Canadian writers & composers
(unnamed authors) *69–70,* 354
Canfield, Mary Cass *41–42,* 402, 437
Cannan, Dennis *58–59,* 311; *64–65,*
355
Cannon, Alice *61–62,* 295
Cannon, Fanny *09–19,* 563
Cannon, Norman *28–29,* 489
Cantor, Arthur *68–69,* 436
Cantor, Eddie *27–28,* 391
Cantor, Eli *48–49,* 426
Cantwell, John *30–31,* 400
Capalbo, Carmen *69–70,* 366
Capek, Josef *22–23,* 480; *48–49,* 376
Capek, Karel *22–23,* 471, 480;
25–26, 534; *38–39,* 471; *42–43,*
450; *48–49,* 376; *57–58,* 304
Caplan, Arthur *35–36,* 406
Caples, Martha *33–34,* 507
Caplin, Elliott *70–71*
Capobianco, Tito *68–69,* 415
Capote, Truman *51–52,* 317; *52–53,*
306; *54–55,* 389; *66–67,* 395, 414;
67–68, 399
Capp, Al *56–57,* 335
Capus, Alfred *99–09,* 369, 385, 418;
35–36, 511
Carb, David *20–21,* 370; *23–24,* 353
Carco, Francis *22–23,* 502
Carelli, Cara *23–24,* 352
Carey, Henry *37–38,* 412
Carey, Henry D. *09–19,* 402
Carl, Joseph *09–19,* 539
Carle, Richard *99–09,* 363, 454, 462,
502, 522, 545, 562–3, 583; *09–19,*
440; *20–21,* 453
Carleton, Henry Guy *94–99,* 95,
143, 145, 148, 236, 256
Carlino, Lewis John *61–62,* 332;
63–64, 343, 351, 364; *67–68,* 373
Carlo & Sanders *22–23,* 552; *23–24,*
402; *24–25,* 437, 497; *25–26,* 510;
30–31, 399
Carlo, Monte *47–48,* 339
Carlson, Donna *69–70,* 378
.Carlson, John *69–70,* 377
Carlson, Richard *37–38,* 407

Carlton, Carl(e) *23–24,* 414; *26–27,*
456
Carlton, Henry Fisk *24–25,* 430;
26–27, 431
Carlton, Sidney *94–99,* 225
Carlton, Tom *09–19,* 561
Carlton, Will *68–69,* 380
Carmichael, Hoagy *39–40,* 466;
53–54, 306
Carmines, Al *63–64,* 346, 365;
66–67, 36, 418; *67–68,* 393, 411;
68–69, 425, 445, 456; *69–70,* 333,
375; *70–71*
Carmon, Eugene (see Eugene
Cormon)
Carney, Frank *55–56,* 366
Carole, Joseph *39–40,* 447
Caron, Pierre Augustine (see
Beaumarchais)
Carpenter, Edward Childs *99–09,*
575; *09–19,* 514, 569, 613, 614;
20–21, 397; *21–22,* 428; *23–24,*
313; *27–28,* 519; *31–32,* 466;
32–33, 415, 462; *34–35,* 390
Carpi, Fiorenzo *59–60,* 321
Carr, Alexander *31–32,* 375
Carr, J. Comyns *94–99,* 150; *99–09,*
353; *09–19,* 466
Carr, Leon *64–65,* 345
Carr, Dr. Osmond *94–99,* 147, 207
Carr, Philip *30–31,* 436
Carra, Lawrence *38–39,* 487
Carre, Fabrice *99–09,* 347, 363
Carré, Michel *94–99,* 185, 252;
99–09, 361; *09–19,* 581; *45–46,*
390
Carré, Michel (fils) *24–25,* 555
Carreño (see Sevilla & Carreño)
Carrette, Louis (see Felicien
Marceau)
Carril, Pepe *69–70,* 375
Carrington, Elaine Sterne *27–28,*
449
Carroll, Carroll *29–30,* 548
Carroll, Earl *09–19,* 532, 584, 594,
622; *20–21,* 368, 406; *21–22,* 516;
23–24, 294; *24–25,* 451; *28–29,*

Cavett, Frank *32–33,* 470
Caylor, Rose *29–30,* 524; *30–31,* 417
Caymmi, Dorival *42–43,* 420
Cazauran, A.R. *94–99,* 91, 143, 230, 236; *99–09,* 355, 486
Celestin, Jack *30–31,* 508
Cellier, Alfred *94–99,* 138
Centlivre, Susanna Freeman *94–99,* 198
Cervantes (Miguel de Cervantes Saavedra) *94–99,* 151; *99–09,* 470; *23–24,* 359; *36–37,* 497; *65–66,* 386
Cessna, Robert *66–67,* 423
Chabrier, Emmanuel *64–65,* 315
Chadwick, George Whitefield *09–19,* 440
Chagrin, Mme. Claude *65–66,* 382
Chaine, Pierre *09–19,* 509; *23–24,* 333; *26–27,* 447
Chakraband *50–51,* 309
Chamberlain, George Agnew *26–27,* 500
Chamberlain, Ida Hoyt *27–28,* 408
Chambers, C. Haddon *94–99,* 115, 120, 127, 234, 235; *99–09,* 347, 408, 453, 526, 544; *09–19,* 434, 450, 453, 509, 512, 572, 638; *26–27,* 512
Chambers, Ernest A. *60–61,* 317; *61–62,* 308; 64–65, 343
Chambers, H. Kellett *99–09,* 484, 488; *09–19,* 399, 460, 470
Chambers, Robert W. *94–99,* 197; *09–19,* 518
Champlin, Charles K. *31–32,* 469
Champlin, Stephen Gardner *09–19,* 658; *27–28,* 544
Chancel, Mons. *99–09,* 485
Chandler, F. *99–09,* 423
Chandler, Julia *23–24,* 392
Chandler, Richard *67–68,* 380
Chantler, Everett *26–27,* 520
Chapi, R. *68–69,* 416
Chapin, Anna Alice *09–19,* 425
Chapin, Anne Morrison *33–34,* 492

Chapin, Benjamin *99–09,* 511
Chapin, Frederic *99–09,* 540; *09–19,* 484
Chapin, Harold *09–19,* 538, 541, 615; *20–21,* 424
Chapin, Katherine Garrison *47–48,* 428
Chapler, Harold J. *69–70,* 352
Chaplin, Saul *58–59,* 315
Chapman, Christopher *67–68,* 359
Chapman, Henry Grafton *09–19,* 417
Chapman, John *70–71*
Chapman, Lonny *58–59,* 50; *60–61,* 38
Chapman, Robert H. *48–49,* 427; *50–51,* 349
Chapman, Virginia Hathaway *46–47,* 496
Chappell, Edna & Delos *32–33,* 414
Chappell, George S. *09–19,* 574
Chappelle, Frederick *21–22,* 503
Chapuis, Peret *45–46,* 460
Charash, Jack *25–26,* 575
Charell, Erik *39–40,* 417
Charig, Philip *26–27,* 363; *27–28,* 390, 421, 429; *28–29,* 451; *31–32,* 379, 398; *43–44,* 424, 466; *55–56,* 338
Charlap, Mark (Moose) *54–55,* 369; *58–59,* 314; *60–61,* 318; *64–65,* 325
Charles, Mr. *53–54,* 306
Charles I (King) *62–63,* 295
Charles II (King) *62–63,* 295
Charles, Theodore *28–29,* 421
Charlot, Andre *23–24,* 384
Charnin, Martin *62–63,* 306, 336; *64–65,* 358; *68–69,* 439; *70–71*
Charpentier, Marc Antoine *69–70,* 314
Chartres, Mme. Vivanti *94–99,* 251
Charvay, Robert *99–09,* 543
Chase, Ilka *31–32,* 499; *44–45,* 397
Chase, Marjorie *21–22,* 463
Chase, Mary (Coyle) *36–37,* 469; *44–45,* 394; *45–46,* 402; *51–52,*

Chase, Mary (Coyle) *(cont.)*
310; *52–53*, 260; *60–61*, 321;
69–70, 316

Chase, Mary Ellen *46–47*, 447

Chase, William P. *09–19*, 527

Chatrian, Erck(h)mann *94–99*, 150;
99–09, 353, 442; *40–41*, 432

Chatterton, Ruth *24–25*, 501

Chaucer, Geoffrey *68–69*, 404, 444

Chavez, Carlos *45–46*, 456; *47–48*,
417

Chayefsky, Paddy *55–56*, 374;
59–60, 302; *61–62*, 270; *63–64*,
324; *67–68*, 346

Chayes, Joel *66–67*, 393; *67–68*, 339

Cheese Club (revue authors) *23–24*,
442

Cheever, John *48–49*, 383

Cheffer, Ch. *70–71*

Chekhov (Tchekhov), Anton *09–19*,
547, 560–1, 579; *22–23*, 517;
23–24, 356; *26–27*, 414; *27–28*,
521; *28–29*, 396, 491, 507; *29–30*,
393, 402, 403, 501, 524; *30–31*,
417; *32–33*, 474; *34–35*, 453;
36–37, 497; *37–38*, 436; *38–39*,
488; *39–40*, 402, 446; *40–41*, 432;
42–43, 452, 489; *43–44*, 450, 490;
44–45, 380; *45–46*, 443, 450;
46–47, 485; *47–48*, 346; *49–50*,
376; *53–54*, 353; *54–55*, 56, 396;
55–56, 55; *56–57*, 55; *58–59*, 49,
333; *59–60*, 42, 50, 360; *60–61*, 45;
61–62, 323, 326; *62–63*, 319;
63–64, 332; *64–65*, 295, 323;
65–66, 410; *66–67*, 422; *67–68*,
353, 402, 413; *68–69*, 407; *69–70*,
297, 329; *70–71*

Chenery, Howard *28–29*, 437;
35–36, 486

Chernikhovsky, Saul *47–48*, 432

Chernis, Jay *52–53*, 300

Cherry, Paul *69–70*, 327

Chesnut, Mrs. *63–64*, 350

Chester, George Randolph *09–19*,
424, 529

Chester, Lillian *09–19*, 529

Chester, Robert F. *28–29*, 503

Chesterton, G.K. *09–19*, 595; *42–43*,
431

Chevalier, Albert *09–19*, 433

Chevalier, Maurice *29–30*, 517;
31–32, 475; *46–47*, 470; *47–48*,
388; *55–56*, 347; *62–63*, 294, 295;
64–65, 331, 332

Chiaramello, Giancarlo *67–68*, 380

Chiarelli, Luigi *24–25*, 450; *32–33*,
493

Child, Alan (Lawrence Langner)
33–34, 439, 441

Child, Nellise *35–36*, 444

Children, (unnamed authors) *69–70*,
369

Childress, Alice *68–69*, 440

Chilton, Charles *64–65*, 303; *67–68*,
365

Chilton, Eleanor Carroll *40–41*, 397

Chilvers, Thomas *94–99*, 248

Chine, Pierre *37–38*, 465

Chirikoff, Eugene *09–19*, 469

Chislanzoni, Antonio *43–44*, 473

Chivot, Henri *94–99*, 139

Chlumberg, Hans *29–30*, 489;
30–31, 505

Chodorov, Edward *31–32*, 415;
34–35, 473; *35–36*, 403; *40–41*,
376, 401; *43–44*, 400, 452; *44–45*,
430; *51–52*, 334; *53–54*, 331

Chodorov, Jerome *37–38*, 433;
40–41, 405; *41–42*, 415; *45–46*,
411; *47–48*, 427; *49–50*, 367;
52–53, 290; *53–54*, 343, 348;
55–56, 376; *57–58*, 323; *62–63*,
297; *64–65*, 319; *65–66*, 401;
66–67, 386, 389

Chodosh, Richard B. *62–63*, 316;
63–64, 349

Chopin, Frederic *28–29*, 370; *39–40*,
471; *45–46*, 396, 452, 453; *46–47*,
486; *47–48*, 423; *56–57*, 333

Chorpenning, Charlotte *35–36*, 479;
37–38, 467; *47–48*, 430; *48–49*,
426

Chorpenning, Ruth *29–30*, 548

Chotzinoff, Samuel *32–33*, 440
Christensen, Lew *38–39*, 476
Christie, Agatha *31–32*, 474; *44–45*,
 365; *46–47*, 420; *54–55*, 383;
 60–61, 44; *65–66*, 436
Christine, (Mr.) *94–99*, 236; *99–09*,
 526
Christine, Henri *62–63*, 295; *64–65*,
 331
Christopher, Don *67–68*, 397
Chueca & Valverde *68–69*, 416
Church, Harden *33–34*, 532
Churchill, Mr. *62–63*, 295
Churchill, M.L. *99–09*, 367
Churchill, Winston (novelist) *99–09*,
 370, 422, 505, 509
Chute, B.J. *59–60*, 327; *70–71*
Chute, M.G. *44–45*, 442
Chute, Marchette *44–45*, 442;
 63–64, 353
Ciannelli, Eduardo *26–27*, 487;
 32–33, 449
Cibber, Colley *50–51*, 328
Cicconi, T. *09–19*, 431
Cimarosa, Mr. *40–41*, 429
Clancy, James *67–68*, 411
Clapsadle, Robert *70–71*
Clarance, Rene *09–19*, 589 (and
 605)
Claretie, Jules *94–99*, 127
Clark, Alan *64–65*, 303
Clark, Alice *60–61*, 292
Clark, Barrett H.ᐟ *31–32*, 459
Clark, Bayard *39–40*, 473
Clark, Bobby *45–46*, 420; *50–51*,
 309
Clark, Calvin *24–25*, 513
Clark, Edward *09–19*, 576, 594, 606,
 609, 641; *19–20*, 342, 448; *20–21*,
 376; *21–22*, 506; *22–23*, 554;
 23–24, 414; *28–29*, 360
Clark, J.P. *69–70*, 353
Clark, Kenneth S. *99–09*, 524
Clark, Maurice *26–27*, *398; 29–30*,
 428
Clark, Norman *38–39*, 437
Clark, Ron *69–70*, 316

Clark, Sadie *99–09*, 538
Clarke, Mr. *53–54*, 305
Clarke, Cecil *36–37*, 398
Clarke, Creston *94–99*, 227
Clarke, Grant *24–25*, 479
Clarke, Harold A. *35–36*, 470
Clarke, Harry *20–21*, 439; *30–31*,
 400; *31–32*, 465, 487; *32–33*, 382
Clarke, Joseph I.C. *94–99*, 191, 194,
 228; *99–09*, 376, 520
Claudel, Paul *22–23*, 510; *56–57*,
 353; *61–62*, 303; *63–64*, 346;
 64–65, 357
Claypoole, Edward B. *99–09*, 559
Clayton, Don Allan *60–61*, 42
Cleary, Michael H. *30–31*, 453;
 31–32, 379, 520; *36–37*, 484
Clemens, Le Roy *09–19*, 635; *20–21*,
 428; *21–22*, 404; *24–25*, 579;
 25–26, 503; *29–30*, 432
Clement, Clay *94–99*, 199; *99–09*,
 523, 525
Clements, C.C. *39–40*, 470; *41–42*,
 459
Clements, Colin *40–41*, 394; *42–43*,
 466; *44–45*, 375; *47–48*, 376
Clements, John *23–24*, 409; *24–25*,
 462
Clements, Le Roy (see Clemens)
Clemons, Walter *47–48*, 428
Clifford, Charles L. *34–35*, 369
Clifford, Mrs. W.K. *99–09*, 505
Clift (Cliff), Denison *26–27*, 389;
 29–30, 407
Clift, Montgomery *53–54*, 353
Clifton, Burt *34–35*, 397
Clifton, Ethel *22–23*, 568
Clifton, John *66–67*, 406
Clifton, L. *99–09*, 384
Clork, Harry *33–34*, 526; *39–40*,
 399; *42–43*, 476
Closser, Myla Jo *32–33*, 479
Closson, Henry W. *37–38*, 463
Cluchey, Rick *70–71*
Clugston, Katharine *28–29*, 415
Coale, George B. *99–09*, 363
Coates, Eric *47–48*, 414

Cobb & Edwards *99–09*, 517, 526, 540
Cobb & Shields *99–09*, 514
Cobb, Elisabeth *47–48*, 377
Cobb, Humphrey *35–36*, 411
Cobb, Ira *46–47*, 418
Cobb, Irvin S. *99–09*, 554; *09–19*, 564, 584; *19–20*, 370
Coble, Tom *66–67*, 421
Coburn, Mary *47–48*, 425
Cochran, Dorcas *39–40*, 429
Cochran, Gifford *32–33*, 483
Cocteau, Jean *37–38*, 464; *46–47*, 410, 472; *53–54*, 359; *57–58*, 314; *60–61*, 354; *62–63*, 318, 322, 325; *66–67*, 423; *70–71*
Codina, (José) *31–32*, 501
Cody, Henry *39–40*, 468
Coffee, Lenore *38–39*, 463
Coggio, Roger *66–67*, 416
Coghill, Nevill *68–69*, 404
Coghlan, Charles *94–99*, 159, 170, 219, 257; *99–09*, 536; *28–29*, 422
Cohan, George M. *99–09*, 388, 432, 446, 472, 505, 509, 521, 552, 557, 562, 570; *09–19*, 166, 402, 424, 452, 468, 477, 532, 542, 557, 570, 600, 619, 647, 648, 652; *20–21*, 451; *21–22*, 520; *22–23*, 487; *23–24*, 375, 380; *25–26*, 461; *26–27*, 367; *27–28*, 402, 413, 513; *28–29*, 385; *29–30*, 384; *30–31*, 398; *31–32*, 384; *32–33*, 450; *34–35*, 481; *35–36*, 490; *36–37*, 463; *39–40*, 462; *61–62*, 326; *62–63*, 295; *63–64*, 359; *67–68*, 370
Cohan, Mary *67–68*, 370
Cohen, Coleman *63–64*, 343
Cohen, Frederic (A.) *41–42*, 430, 432, 456; *46–47*, 492
Cohen, Larry *69–70*, 362
Cohen, Leonard *68–69*, 407
Cohen, Michael *65–66*, 417; *66–67*, 404; *67–68*, 378
Cohen, Mortimer *37–38*, 469
Cohen, Octavius *94–99*, 244
Cohen, Octavus Roy *20–21*, 358

Cohen, Robert *09–19*, 630
Cohn, Al *63–64*, 365
Coit, Dorothy *37–38*, 468; *46–47*, 484
Colaizzi, Dominick *26–27*, 458
Colbron, Grace Isabel *99–09*, 539
Colby, Archie *34–35*, 483
Colby, Robert *61–62*, 327
Cole, Beatrice *46–47*, 447
Cole, Robert (Bob) *94–99*, 227; *99–09*, 378, 414, 427, 473, 478, 541, 583
Coleby, Wilfred T. *99–09*, 566
Coleman, Cy *51–52*, 311; *53–54*, 326; *60–61*, 313; *62–63*, 287, 324; *65–66*, 395
Coleman, John *32–33*, 496
Coleman, Lonnie *59–60*, 308; *66–67*, 391; *69–70*, 327
Coleman, Patricia *42–43*, 463
Coleman, Robert H. *40–41*, 433
Coleman, Val *61–62*, 322
Coleridge, Samuel Taylor *23–24*, 416
Coles, Stedman *38–39*, 485
Colette *51–52*, 295; *59–60*, 295, 331; *69–70*, 367; *70–71*
Coley, Thomas *48–49*, 420; *70–71*
Colicchio, Michael *57–58*, 290
Collier, Constance *28–29*, 490; *30–31*, 514
Collier, Edmund *94–99*, 86
Collier, Ronald *65–66*, 421
Collier, William (Willie) *94–99*, 98; *99–09*, 347, 530, 573; *09–19*, 431, 459, 484, 518; *19–20*, 433; *20–21*, 388; *23–24*, 322
Collinge, Patricia *38–39*, 408; *41–42*, 460
Collins, Anne *27–28*, 539
Collins, Arthur *99–09*, 398, 427, 446, 473, 499; *09–19*, 515
Collins, Frank J. *29–30*, 469
Collins, Sewell *09–19*, 422
Collins, Wilkie *99–09*, 496, *09–19*, 487

Collison, Wilson *09–19*, 649; *19–20*, 365; *20–21*, 366; *21–22*, 390, 443, 510; *27–28*, 485

Collodi, C. *38–39*, 479

Colt, Ethel Barrymore *36–37*, 467

Colton, John *21–22*, 490; *22–23*, 483; *24–25*, 443; *25–26*, 543; *27–28*, 507; *32–33*, 446, 488; *34–35*, 451; *44–45*, 397; *47–48*, 428

Colum, Padraic *09–19*, 598; *40–41*, 431; *66–67*, 416, 417

Coman, John J. *36–37*, 489

Combine, The *69–70*, 345

Comden, Betty (see also The Revuers) *44–45*, 406; *45–46*, 415; *51–52*, 278; *52–53*, 290; *54–55*, 369; *56–57*, 339; *57–58*, 323, 327; *58–59*, 54, 315, 324; *60–61*, 315; *61–62*, 276; *62–63*, 297; *63–64*, 339; *65–66*, 419, 436; *66–67*, 386, 391; *69–70*, 323

Committee, The *64–65*, 300

Comor, Henry *68–69*, 429

Comorthoon, James *60–61*, 39

Comstock, Howard Warren *29–30*, 530; *30–31*, 488

Conan Doyle (see Doyle)

Condon, Richard *52–53*, 302

Congreve, William *24–25*, 489, 564; *25–26*, 444; *30–31*, 530; *31–32*, 501; *39–40*, 466; *46–47*, 481; *54–55*, 56; *60–61*, 45; *65–66*, 423

Conheim, Martha Morton (see Martha Morton)

Conkle, Ellsworth Prouty *36–37*, 433; *37–38*, 457; *38–39*, 482; *39–40*, 444; *40–41*, 431; *47–48*, 397; *49–50*, 384

Conklin, Bill *62–63*, 315

Conlin, Richard *46–47*, 498

Connell, Louise Fox *29–30*, 442

Connell, Tom *31–32*, 513

Connell, Vivian *48–49*, 427

Connelly, D. Hubert *33–34*, 429

Connelly, Marc *09–19*, 582; *20–21*, 418; *21–22*, 393, 512; *22–23*, 485; *23–24*, 293, 346, 398; *24–25*, 447, 560; *25–26*, 551; *27–28*, 404; *29–30*, 502; *34–35*, 400, 457; *38–39*, 442; *41–42*, 438; *48–49*, 382, 425; *50–51*, 358; *69–70*, 303

Conners, Barry *23–24*, 297; *24–25*, 426, 529; *25–26*, 457, 522; *28–29*, 404; *30–31*, 532

Conor, Mr. *94–99*, 161

Conover, Grandin *66–67*, 420

Conquest, George *94–99*, 258

Conrad, Barnaby *63–64*, 303

Conrad, Con *23–24*, 320, 394; *24–25*, 512, 575; *25–26*, 597; *26–27*, 363

Conrad, Constance *62–63*, 312

Conrad, Eugene *24–25*, 440; *34–35*, 363, 482; *35–36*, 500; *40–41*, 395, *44–45*, 404

Conradt, Mark *65–66*, 424

Constanten, Tom *70–71*

Constantin, Jean *55–56*, 347; *64–65*, 316

Converse, Harry *29–30*, 377

Convy, Bert *70–71*

Conway, Shane *28–29*, 502

Cook, Charles Emerson *99–09*, 444, 533

Cook, George Cram *09–19*, 612; *21–22*, 425

Cook, Joan *67–68*, 358

Cook, Norman *41–42*, 461

Cook, Peter *62–63*, 283, 323; *63–64*, 350, 363

Cook, Phil *22–23*, 446; *23–24*, 435; *25–26*, 463

Cook, Roderick *68–69*, 378, 379

Cook, Whitfield *44–45*, 390

Cook, Will Marion *99–09*, 364, 429, 461, 509, 556; *53–54*, 306

Cooke, Charles L. *38–39*, 466

Cooke, Edmund Vance *94–99*, 236

Cooke, Emerson *94–99*, 229

Cooke, Marjorie Benton *38–39*, 488

Cool, Walter *65–66*, 437

Coolus, Romain *23–24*, 373

Cooney, Ray *70–71*

Cooper, Giles *62–63,* 303; *67–68,* 353

Cooper, Helen *63–64,* 315

Cooper, Hi *45–46,* 403

Cooper, Irving *63–64,* 315

Cooper, Lou *41–42,* 438; *42–43,* 433

Cooper, Norton *59–60,* 40

Cooper, Patricia *69–70,* 370

Coopersmith, Jerome *64–65,* 327; *66–67,* 364; *68–69,* 439

Coots, J. Fred *22–23,* 448; *24–25,* 474; *25–26,* 420, 424, 427, 527, 604; *27–28,* 428; *29–30,* 451

Copani, Peter *67–68,* 389

Copeau, Jacques *26–27,* 453

Copeland, Nick *32–33,* 499

Copland, Aaron *29–30,* 548; *36–37,* 448, 499; *38–39,* 477; *40–41,* 429; *41–42,* 457; *42–43,* 483, 484; *44–45,* 440; *45–46,* 453, 456

Copmann, Elizabeth *26–27,* 524

Coppe, Carlo *94–99,* 129

Coppee, Francois *94–99,* 93, 165, 194; *99–09,* 367

Coppel, Alec *42–43,* 426; *57–58,* 305, 315; *58–59,* 313

Coppel, Myra *58–59,* 313

Corbett, Edward *94–99,* 239

Corbett, Jim *61–62,* 284

Corbin, John *09–19,* 523

Cordoba, Daniel *49–50,* 354

Corelli, Marie *94–99,* 138, 248

Corey, George H. *40–41,* 432

Corey, Gertrude *61–62,* 326

Corey, Herb *60–61,* 42

Corey, Orlin *61–62,* 322

Corigliano, John *70–71*

Corio, Ann *64–65,* 329; *69–70,* 358

Corle, Edwin *41–42,* 436; *58–59,* 300

Corliss, E.W. *99–09,* 358, 406, 409

Cormack, Bartlett *27–28,* 456

Corman, Avery *70–71*

Cormon, Eugene *94–99,* 107, 149, 234, 235; *99–09,* 456, 536; *09–19,* 550; *25–26,* 579

Corneille, Pierre *58–59,* 295; *65–66,* 397

Cornell, Katharine *34–35,* 424

Cornish, Roger *68–69,* 446

Cort, Harry L. *09–19,* 647; *19–20,* 381; *20–21,* 391; *22–23,* 542; *23–24,* 358; *24–25,* 527

Cortelyou; Winthrop *27–28,* 388

Cortis, Ernest & Louise *26–27,* 528

Corvo, Baron (see Frederick William Rolfe)

Corwin, Norman *58–59,* 321; *60–61,* 294; *65–66,* 423; *67–68,* 410

Corwin, Walter *70–71*

Cosentino, Nicholas *35–36,* 401

Cosic, Ileana *68–69,* 425

Coslow, Sam *24–25,* 474

Cossa, Pietro *99–09,* 536

Costa, P. Mario *24–25,* 600

Costello, Charles S. *34–35,* 483

Costigan, James *60–61,* 309; *62–63,* 309; *63–64,* 335

Costikyan, Edward N. *46–47,* 498

Costillo, Mario *47–48,* 367

Cotton, Will *31–32,* 452

Cottrell, Harry D. *99–09,* 518

Couperin, François *54–55,* 386, 407

Cournos, John *39–40,* 446

Courteline, Georges *09–19,* 579, 589 (and 605); *21–22,* 468

Courtneidge, Robert *99–09,* 504, 542, 550

Courtney, C.C. *69–70,* 340; *70–71*

Courtney, Marguerite *63–64,* 308

Courtney, Ragan *70–71*

Courtney, Robert *22–23,* 573

Courtney, W.L. *99–09,* 501, 521; *23–24,* 343

Courtright, Eugenie *34–35,* 450

Coverly, Robert *94–99,* 140

Covington, Zella *09–19,* 555

Cowan, Sada *24–25,* 587

Coward, Noel *25–26,* 445, 460, 509; *26–27,* 431; *27–28,* 450, 463; *28–29,* 410; *29–30,* 382, 435; *30–31,* 483; *31–32,* 453, 494; *32–33,* 454; *33–34,* 524; *34–35,* 396, 440; *36–37,* 435; *38–39,* 451; *41–42,* 410; *43–44,* 410; *46–47,* 433; *47–48,* 384, 385; *48–49,* 385,

426; *51–52*, 334; *54–55*, 372;
55–56, 370; *57–58*, 301, 302, 314;
58–59, 325; *61–62*, 257; *63–64*,
315, 333; *64–65*, 362; *66–67*, 393;
67–68, 407, 408; *68–69*, 378, 457;
69–70, 307; *70–71*
Cowen, Ron *67–68*, 394; *69–70*, 350
Cowen, William Joyce *38–39*, 463
Cowl, Jane *09–19*, 594, 603, 639;
28–29, 421; *31–32*, 471
Cowles, Albert *26–27*, 510
Cowles, Virginia *46–47*, 453
Cowper, Mrs. Archie (see Eleanor
Merron)
Cox, Palmer *94–99*, 103
Cox, Ronny *70–71*
Cox, Wally *49–50*, 368
Coxe, Daniel *30–31*, 446
Coxe, Louis O. *48–49*, 427; *50–51*,
349
Coyle, J.J. *67–68*, 352
Crabtree, Paul *50–51*, 326; *61–62*,
320
Craig, Colin *40–41*, 432
Craig, David *54–55*, 409; *57–58*,
293
Craig, Gordon *41–42*, 457
Craigie, Mrs. (see John Oliver
Hobbs)
Crandall, Courtney *47–48*, 344
Crandall, Prudence *63–64*, 350
Crane, Elizabeth G. *09–19*, 499
Crane, Lor *70–71*
Crane, Stephen *70–71*
Cranko, John *56–57*, 338
Crankshaw, Edward *37–38*, 454
Cranton, Hal *52–53*, 259
Craven, Frank *09–19*, 522, 605;
19–20, 447; *20–21*, 398; *22–23*,
462, 484; *24–25*, 488; *26–27*, 488;
27–28, 428; *30–31*, 410; *31–32*,
522
Craven, Richard *62–63*, 317; *64–65*,
343
Craven, Tom *94–99*, 109
Crawford, Alice *31–32*, 455
Crawford, Clifton *99–09*, 406, 409,
446, 515; *09–19*, 476

Crawford, Dorothy *38–39*, 489
Crawford, F. Marion *94–99*, 193;
99–09, 383, 422; *09–19*, 400
Crawshay, Eliot *35–36*, 397
Creamer & Johnson *27–28*, 392
Creamer & Layton *19–20*, 444
Creamer, Henry *27–28*, 518; *28–29*,
449
Creatore, Luigi *68–69*, 387
Creighton, Anthony *58–59*, 301, 317
Creighton, Marion *09–19*, 571
Cressy, Will M. *99–09*, 560
Crichton, Kyle *34–35*, 478; *56–57*,
337
Criswell, Jeron *36–37*, 397
Crocitto, Frank *70–71*
Crocker, Bosworth *09–19*, 579
Crockett, Davy *47–48*, 398
Crockett, Otway *65–66*, 437
Croker, Mrs. B.M. *99–09*, 451
Cromwell, John *60–61*, 39; *63–64*,
346
Cronin, A.J. *40–41*, 377
Cronyn, George *09–19*, 612
Crooker, Earle *27–28*, 465; *28–29*,
456; *29–30*, 461; *31–32*, 497;
34–35, 432; *38–39*, 434
Crosby, Vivian *30–31*, 475; *31–32*,
481
Cross, Beverley *59–60*, 329; *64–65*,
323, 333
Cross, Joan *45–46*, 389
Crosswell (Croswell) Anne *59–60*,
359; *62–63*, 302; *64–65*, 358, 362;
67–68, 372
Crosswell, Rudolph *69–70*, 336
Crothers, Rachel *99–09*, 523, 550,
570; *09–19*, 414, 496, 514, 518,
586, 608, 628, 648, 654; *19–20*,
425; *20–21*, 433; *21–22*, 463;
22–23, 528; *23–24*, 420; *25–26*,
500; *27–28*, 476; *28–29*, 471;
30–31, 501; *31–32*, 423; *32–33*,
396, 451; *37–38*, 379; *39–40*, 397;
43–44, 435; *70–71*
Croue, Jean *26–27*, 453
Crouse, Russel *30–31*, 493; *33–34*,
433; *34–35*, 412; *36–37*, 424;

Crouse, Russel *(cont.)*
   37–38, 397; *39–40,* 410; *41–42,*
   460; *42–43,* 432; *45–46,* 407;
   48–49, 391; *50–51,* 319; *51–52,*
   283; *53–54,* 330; *55–56,* 368;
   56–57, 343; *58–59,* 318; *59–60,*
   303; *61–62,* 330; *62–63,* 280;
   66–67, 386; *67–68,* 346
Crow, Carl *63–64,* 343
Crowley, Mart *67–68,* 404
Croy, Homer *30–31,* 453
Crozier, Eric *45–46,* 389; *50–51,*
   333
Crozier, Jim *70–71*
Cruchaga, Luco *67–68,* 401
Crump, John *34–35,* 394; *36–37,*
   426
Crump, Owen *50–51,* 315
Cryer, Gretchen *67–68,* 386; *69–70,*
   356; *70–71*
Cucci, Frank *67–68,* 412; *69–70,*
   339
Cuitino, Senor *27–28,* 468
Culbertson, Ernest Howard *21–22,*
   387; *26–27,* 514
Cullen, Countee *45–46,* 436; *66–67,*
   354
Cullen, James *09–19,* 651
Cullinan, Ralph *24–25,* 537; *25–26,*
   554; *27–28,* 466; *28–29,* 366
Cumberland, Richard *94–99,* 245
Cumming, Dorothy *39–40,* 421
Cumming, Richard *69–70,* 330
Cummings, E.E. *27–28,* 541; *62–63,*
   322; *68–69,* 407
Cuney, Waring *66–67,* 354, 355
Cunningham, Leon *22–23,* 486;
   23–24, 377
Curchack, Fred *70–71*
Curci, Gennaro Mario *30–31,* 497
   32–33, 449
Curcio, Armando *61–62,* 317
Curley, Daniel *70–71*
Curran, Homer *44–45,* 369; *48–49,*
   381
Currimbhoy, Asif *67–68,* 402
Curti, Alfredo *09–19,* 444

Curti, Franz *94–99,* 224
Curtis, Jackie *69–70,* 375
Curtis, Margaret *43–44,* 475
Curtis, Norman *68–69,* 424
Curtis, Patricia Taylor *68–69,* 424
Curtis, Paul *67–68,* 410
Curtis, William C. *62–63,* 312
Curtright, Wesley *66–67,* 355
Curzon, Frank *09–19,* 438
Cushing, C.C.S. *09–19,* 519; *29–30,*
   484
Cushing, Catherine Chisholm *09–19,*
   447, 495, 519, 524, 582, 641;
   19–20, 444; *21–22,* 498; *24–25,*
   511; *25–26,* 461, 520
Cushing, Tom *21–22,* 422, 430;
   23–24, 364; *26–27,* 450; *27–28,*
   502; *69–70,* 319
Cushman, Dan *58–59,* 314
Cushman, Howard *35–36,* 471
Cuvillier, Charles *09–19,* 537, 581;
   20–21, 402
Czerny, Karl *47–48,* 415

Daab, Hyatt *28–29,* 365
Daavidson, Roy *30–31,* 510
Da Costa, Morton *59–60,* 309;
   68–69, 387
Dafora, Asadata *33–34,* 533; *34–35,*
   483; *45–46,* 456; *46–47,* 487
D'Aguzan, Jean (see D'Auguzan)
Dahdah, Robert *67–68,* 395
Dahl, Roald *54–55,* 411
Dale, Alan *09–19,* 620
Dale, Gretchen *09–19,* 455
Dalferes, Clayelle *70–71*
Dali, Salvador *44–45,* 439
Dallas, Mervyn *94–99,* 103
Dalrymple, Leona *25–26,* 521
D'Alton, Louis *40–41,* 413
Dalton, Test *28–29,* 511
Daly, Arnold *09–19,* 623
Daly, Augustin *94–99,* 85, 90, 107,
   111, 119, 128, 129, 134, 135, 143,
   157, 164, 208, 224; *99–09,* 536;
   25–26, 481; *28–29,* 488; *67–68,*
   410

Daly, William *21–22*, 514; *22–23*, 497

Dam, H.J.W. *94–99*, 102, 149; *99–09*, 433

Dale, Gretchen *09–19*, 455

Dalvin, Rae *50–51*, 374

Damrosch, Gretchen *29–30*, 548; *30–31*, 473; *31–32*, 444; *33–34*, 523; *42–43*, 487

Damrosch, Leopoldine *29–30*, 548

Damrosch, Walter *09–19*, 482, 621–2; *42–43*, 487; *46–47*, 423

Damroth, George *35–36*, 431

Dana, Bill *64–65*, 343

Dana, Frederick *94–99*, 205

Dance, George *94–99*, 164, 187; *99–09*, 394, 412

d'Ancourt, Grenet *09–19*, 538

Dane, Clemence *21–22*, 438; *22–23*, 515; *23–24*, 392; *26–27*, 480, 498; *33–34*, 479; *34–35*, 401; *35–36*, 459; *51–52*, 307

Dane, Essex *23–24*, 431

d'Angelo, Aristide *39–40*, 470

Danielou, Mons. *46–47*, 410

Daniels, Dan *68–69*, 456

Danner, Margaret *66–67*, 355

D'Annunzio, Gabriele *99–09*, 421; *23–24*, 366

Dante (Harry A. Jansen) *40–41*, 378

Dante, Ron *68–69*, 411

Danvers, Godfrey *68–69*, 446

Danzig, David *35–36*, 510

da Ponte, L. *47–48*, 347

Darby, Dermot *26–27*, 460

Dare, Danny *40–41*, 403

Dare, Frank *09–19*, 609, 612

Darewski, Herman *09–19*, 641; *19–20*, 420

Dargin, David *40–41*, 431

Darion, Joe *56–57*, 367; *65–66*, 386; *66–67*, 390; *68–69*, 385; *70–71*

Dark, Stanley *99–09*, 458, 519

D'Armond, Frank *34–35*, 363

Darnley, Herbert *99–09*, 466

Darnley, James H. *99–09*, 433

Darrell, Charles *94–99*, 175

Darrell, Rupert *32–33*, 461

d'Artois, Armand *94–99*, 182

Da Silva, Howard *65–66*, 383

Dassin, Jules *66–67*, 390

Daudet, Alphonse *94–99*, 126, 169, 198; *99–09*, 361, 472; *09–19*, 432; *59–60*, 42

Daugherty, Mick *69–70*, 376

D'Auguzan (D'Aguzan), Jean *09–19*, 497, 509

Davenport, Butler *09–19*, 428, 549, 552, 565, 587, 598, 617, 619, 622, 643, 646; *38–39*, 485; *40–41*, 432; *43–44*, 490

Davenport, Pembroke *40–41*, 405; *59–60*, 319

David, Frank *94–99*, 248

David, Hal *68–69*, 395

David, Lee *27–28*, 386–7; *29–30*, 379

David, Mack *43–44*, 414; *66–67*, 367; *68–69*, 383

David, Worton *20–21*, 402

Davidson, David Jr. *29–30*, 406

Davidson, Gustav *26–27*, 505

Davidson, N.R. *70–71*

Davies, Hubert Henry *99–09*, 430, 441, 447, 566; *09–19*, 449, 465, 537; *40–41*, 432

Davies, (Sir) John *63–64*, 314

Davies, Maria Thompson *09–19*, 648

Davies, Paul E. *59–60*, 47

Davies, Robertson *60–61*, 313

Davies, Valentine *31–32*, 382; *33–34*, 444; *37–38*, 370; *63–64*, 306

Daviot, Gordon (Agnes Mackintosh) *33–34*, 496; *36–37*, 417

Davis, Allan *23–24*, 428; *25–26*, 511

Davis, Bancroft G. Jr. *39–40*, 473; *40–41*, 433

Davis, Benny *27–28*, 452; *29–30*, 451; *43–44*, 484; *56–57*, 328

Davis, Blevins *44–45*, 399

Davis, Buster *66–67*, 413

Davis, Carl *63–64*, 350

Davis, Carl E. *39–40*, 472
Davis, Charles (1) *37–38*, 468
Davis, Charles (2) *69–70*, 372
Davis, Charles L. *94–99*, 110
Davis, Christopher *59–60*, 324
Davis, Donald *32–33*, 401; *35–36*, 462, 510
Davis, Dorrance *24–25*, 461; *26–27*, 386, 481; *29–30*, 495
Davis, Eddie *39–40*, 397; *40–41*, 378; *41–42*, 448; *43–44*, 466; *54–55*, 405
Davis, Eugene *27–28*, 405
Davis, Frank Marshall *66–67*, 354
Davis, Gwen *65–66*, 405
Davis, Hallie Flanagan *47–48*, 412
Davis, Herbert *43–44*, 490
Davis, Irving Kaye *23–24*, 440; *27–28*, 530; *29–30*, 459, 531; *34–35*, 404, 421; *44–45*, 373
Davis, J. *69–70*, 314
Davis, J. Frank *26–27*, 409
Davis, J.P. *69–70*, 329
Davis, Julia *62–63*, 317
Davis, Lee *28–29*, 506
Davis, Luther *44–45*, 423; (*51–52*, 325 omitted); *53–54*, 324; *63–64*, 367; *65–66*, 368
Davis, Mack *40–41*, 411
Davis, N. Newnham *99–09*, 519
Davis, Nathaniel *31–32*, 475
Davis, Ossie *52–53*, 308; *61–62*, 256; *68–69*, 455; 69–70, 318
Davis, Owen *99–09*, 551; *09–19*, 465, 498, 504, 535, 543, 570, 588, 607, 636; *19–20*, 337, 345; *20–21*, 360, 385; *21–22*, 400, 522, 538; *22–23*, 453, 480, 530; *23–24*, 304, 331; *24–25*, 444, 456; *25–26*, 482, 506, 545; *26–27*, 369; *26–27*, 386, 414; *27–28*, 405, 496; *28–29*, 416, 431, 463, 478; *30–31*, 404; *31–32*, 386; *32–33*, 401, 468; *33–34*, 468; *34–35*, 369, 385; *35–36*, 462; *37–38*, 367; *40–41*, 410; *43–44*, 408; *44–45*, 392; *47–48*, 425; *48–49*, 376

Davis, Paul *61–62*, 338
Davis, (Prof.) Philip H. *37–38*, 458
Davis, Richard Harding *94–99*, 140; *99–09*, 407, 431, 453, 457, 507, 541; *09–19*, 443, 507, 546; *19–20*, 447
Davis, Robert H. *09–19*, 427, 500, 570
Davis, Ruth Helen *09–19*, 577
Davis, Sheldon *43–44*, 403, 474
Davis, Sid *66–67*, 404
Davis, Stan *64–65*, 358
Davison, E. Mora *99–09*, 485
Davison, Lesley *62–63*, 317; *63–64*, 355, 372; *64–65*, 343, 359; *65–66*, 417, 422
Dawkins, Cecil *66–67*, 409
Dawn, Isabel *32–33*, 455
Dawson, David *37–38*, 469
Dawson, Gregory *65–66*, 424
Day, Clarence *39–40*, 410; *48–49*, 391; *67–68*, 346
Day, Edmund *99–09*, 485, 542; *09–19*, 399; *31–32*, 490
Day, Frederick Lansing *21–22*, 551
Day, George *94–99*, 183, 216
Day, Holman *09–19*, 522
Day, Lillian *32–33*, 471; *51–52*, 309
Day, Louis deV. Jr. *39–40*, 472; *41–42*, 460
Dayton, Helena *28–29*, 460
Dayton, Katharine *35–36*, 440; *37–38*, 428; *51–52*, 328
Dazey, Charles Turner *94–99*, 97, 165, 229; *99–09*, 478, 512; *09–19*, 456, 461
Dazey, Frank Mitchell *23–24*, 318; *26–27*, 395; *30–31*, 437
de Acosta, Mercedes *22–23*, 548; *27–28*, 423
Deal, Borden *66–67*, 376
Dean, Basil *26–27*, 438
Dean, Norman *66–67*, 404; *67–68*, 410
Dean, Philip *68–69*, 430
de Anda, Peter *70–71*

Deane, Hamilton *27–28*, 422; *30–31*, 515

Dearden, Harold *27–28*, 432

Deasy, Mary *63–64*, 347

de Azertis, Lorenzo *23–24*, 322

de Balzac, Honoré (see Balzac)

de Banfield, Raffaello *51–52*, 322

de Banville, Theodore *94–99*, 120

de Beaumarchais (see Beaumarchais)

Debesa, Fernando *67–68*, 401

Debussy, Claude *40–41*, 428; *45–46*, 453; *47–48*, 414, 417; *54–55*, 386

de Caillavet, (Armand) (Robert) *09–19*, 401, 424, 529, 589 (and 605); *21–22*, 434

de Casalis, Jeanne *36–37*, 414

de Cervantes (see Cervantes)

de Cordova, Rudolph *99–09*, 519

DeCosta, Leon *19–20*, 380; *24–25*, 604; *26–27*, 361

Decourcelle, Adrien *94–99*, 140

Decourcelle, Pierre *94–99*, 140, 141, 184; *99–09*, 375, 452

de Courville, Albert *21–22*, 503

de Croisset, Francis *99–09*, 446, 472, 522; *09–19*, 397, 493, 532, 541; *22–23*, 456

Decroux, Etienne *59–60*, 48

Dee, Sylvia *46–47*, 474

Deems, Mickey *60–61*, 292

Deevy, Teresa *37–38*, 374

de Falla, Mr. *34–35*, 460

de Filippo, Eduardo *56–57*, 328; *61–62*, 317

De Flers, Robert *99–09*, 566; *09–19*, 401, 424, 529, 589 (and 605), 615; *20–21*, 419; *21–22*, 434

de Forest, Marian *09–19*, 480, 569, 590; *31–32*, 444; *38–39*, 490; *44–45*, 379; *45–46*, 393

Defries, Amelia *26–27*, 504

de Gaw, Boyce *32–33*, 455

de Ghelderode, Michel (Michael) (see Ghelderode)

De Gorsse, Henri *09–19*, 453; *24–25*, 483

De Gresac, Fred *99–09*, 446, 472; *09–19*, 455, 461, 499, 506, 541, 617; *22–23*, 456; *29–30*, 400; *46–47*, 457

de Hartog, Jan *47–48*, 363, 394; *51–52*, 288; *54–55*, 391; *66–67*, 375

de Holthoir, Beatrice *09–19*, 612

DeJagers, Dorothy *30–31*, 414

De Karlo, Sergio *44–45*, 368

de Kay, John *09–19*, 432

Dekker, Thomas *37–38*, 409; *63–64*, 314; *66–67*, 415

d(D)e Koven, Reginald *94–99*, 101, 117, 135, 182, 218, 251, 258; *99–09*, 355, 360, 367, 379, 398, 405, 416, 436, 444, 497, 529, 550, 570, 580; *09–19*, 461, 471, 507, 511, 600, 638; *29–30*, 444; *31–32*, 471; *44–45*, 396

de Kruif, Paul *33–34*, 504, 505; *46–47*, 438

de la Barca, Pedro Calderon (see Calderon)

Delacour, Alfred *94–99*, 150, 159, 230, 247; *99–09*, 354, 521

Delafield, E.M. *34–35*, 475

Delamater, Eric *09–19*, 548

Deland, Margaret *09–19*, 400

Delaney, Shelagh *60–61*, 297; *62–63*, 334

de Lange, Eddie *39–40*, 417

de Lange, Louis *94–99*, 103, 180, 188, 248, 259; *99–09*, 380

de la Grange, Charles (see La Grange)

de Lano, Allen *26–27*, 472

Delanoe, Pierre *66–67*, 367; *68–69*, 383

de la Pasture, Mrs. Henry *09–19*, 642

Delard, Eugene *26–27*, 535

de la Roche, Mazo *37–38*, 434

Delavigne, Casimir *94–99*, 88, 150; *99–09*, 477, 536; *09–19*, 443, 545, 642

De Leon, Jack *30–31*, 508

Deleon, R. *69–70*, 314

DeLeon, Walter *22–23*, 576; *24–25*, 479; *25–26*, 570; *28–29*, 397, 406

Delerue, Georges *63–64*, 326, 363; *65–66*, 397; *66–67*, 416

De Letraz, Jean *09–19*, 589 (and 605); *62–63*, 311

Delf, Harry *09–19*, 638; *22–23*, 529; *25–26*, 427; *27–28*, 503; *29–30*, 471; *30–31*, 489; *33–34*, 451

Délibes, Léo *45–46*, 453

De Lima, C.A. *99–09*, 562

de Lisser, Alfred M. *94–99*, 133; *99–09*, 515

Delius, Frederick *42–43*, 484

Dell, Floyd *28–29*, 394; *31–32*, 384

Dell, Jeffrey *31–32*, 400; *32–33*, 425

Dello Joio (Della Goio), Norman *45–46*, 454; *46–47*, 491; *51–52*, 331; *55–56*, 350

de Madina, Francisco *64–65*, 342

Delmar, Viña *30–31*, 425; *45–46*, 404; *52–53*, 281

Deloney, Thomas *63–64*, 314

de Long, George *99–09*, 473

de Lorde, Andre *99–09*, 417; *09–19*, 509; *23–24*, 333; *26–27*, 447; *35–36*, 397

de Lozier, S. Bouvet *33–34*, 475

del Vecchio, Thomas *60–61*, 39

Demanoir, Mons. *94–99*, 252

de Marivaux, Pierre Carlet de Chamblain (see Marivaux)

de Marney, Terence *28–29*, 467

de Mattos, Alexander Teixeira *94–99*, 124; *09–19*, 644

de Maupassant, Guy *94–99*, 220; *29–30*, 421; *34–35*, 484; *48–49*, 427

de Meissner, Mme. S.R. *99–09*, 455, 486

de Menasce, Jacques *46–47*, 499

de Mille, Beatrice *99–09*, 374

de Mille, Cecil B. *99–09*, 521, 561; *09–19*, 512

De Mille, Henry C. *94–99*, 84, 96, 201

de Mille (DeMille), William C. *99–09*, 483, 521, 543, 552, 561; *09–19*, 451, 497, 512; *28–29*, 502

DeMilt, Aida Rodman *26–27*, 523

de Molina, Tirso *70–71*

de Montherlant, Henri *59–60*, 46; *65–66*, 397

Dempsey, Clifford *94–99*, 166

de Musset, Alfred *09–19*, 560; *37–38*, 469; *55–56*, 358; *58–59*, 295; *64–65*, 362

de Najac, Emile *94–99*, 126, 169, 196; *99–09*, 539; *09–19*, 499

de Navarro, Carlos *23–24*, 348

Denby, Edwin *36–37*, 448, 499; *41–42*, 458

Denes, Jules *44–45*, 442

Denger, Fred *67–68*, 401

Denham, Reginald *39–40*, 449, 454; *43–44*, 451; *44–45*, 403, 433; *52–53*, 280

Denker, Henry *55–56*, 371; *60–61*, 333; *61–62*, 296; *63–64*, 308; *67–68*, 347

Dennigan, Gib *70–71*

Dennee, Charles *99–09*, 359, 413

D'Ennery, Adolphe Philippe *94–99*, 102, 107, 149, 173, 234, 235; *99–09*, 456; *09–19*, 550; *25–26*, 579; *36–37*, 500

Denni, Lucien *26–27*, 391

Dennis, Nigel *58–59*, 51

Dennis, Patrick *56–57*, 329; *58–59*, 291; *62–63*, 287; *65–66*, 412

Denny, Ernest *99–09*, 455, 533; *22–23*, 566

De Noie, Vera *94–99*, 233

Denslow, W.W. *99–09*, 492

Dent, Wade *58–59*, 50

de Obaldia, Rene *61–62*, 326, 332; *68–69*, 389; *69–70*, 363

de Packh, Maurice *22–23*, 513

DePaul (de Paul), Gene *55–56*, 337; *56–57*, 335

de Paur, Leonard *37–38*, 456; *39–40*, 468

Dickens, Charles *(cont.)*
62–63, 292; 65–66, 370, 372;
70–71
Dickenson, Dan 46–47, 485
Dickey, Paul 09–19, 496, 515, 554,
561; 20–21, 409; 22–23, 439;
23–24, 424; 24–25, 569; 30–31,
402
Dickinson, Emily 66–67, 423
Dickinson, Thomas H. 29–30, 440
Dickson, Charles 99–09, 464, 563;
09–19, 415, 605
Dickson, W. Lee 24–25, 472
Diet, Edmond 09–19, 444
Dietz, Howard 24–25, 458; 26–27,
531; 28–29, 498; 30–31, 407, 432,
532; 32–33, 387; 34–35, 418;
35–36, 406; 36–37, 446; 37–38,
404; 39–40, 463; 43–44, 448;
44–45, 397; 47–48, 401; 56–57,
357; 61–62, 270–71; 63–64, 308
di Gioa, Giuseppe 46–47, 493
Dill, George 24–25, 440
Dillea, Herbert 99–09, 516
Dilley, J.J. 99–09, 384
Dimey, Bernard 64–65, 315, 316
Dimona, Joe 61–62, 325
Dinehart, Alan 34–35, 374; 39–40,
447
Dinelli, Mel 49–50, 368
Dinner, William 50–51, 327
Dinroe, Dorothy A. 67–68, 407;
69–70, 352; 70–71
Diop, Birago 69–70, 354
Di Prima, Diane 61–62, 311
di San Secundo, Rosso 26–27, 487;
27–28, 447
Dismond, Binga 66–67, 354
Ditrichstein, Leo 94–99, 127, 191,
206, 247; 99–09, 352, 368, 386,
390, 409, 434, 446, 450, 460, 462,
502, 537, 560; 09–19, 397, 427,
506, 516, 521, 564, 640; 32–33,
398
Divine, Charles 34–35, 372
Dix, Beulah Marie 99–09, 417, 530,
538; 09–19, 535, 558; 33–34, 502

Dix, Frank 09–19, 515
Dix, Sherman 09–19, 488
Dixon, John C. 94–99, 130; 99–09,
381
Dixon, MacIntyre 60–61, 354
Dixon, Roy 21–22, 467
Dixon, Thomas (Jr.) 99–09, 506,
19–20, 344; 20–21, 379
Dizenzo, Charles 68–69, 437; 69–70,
341
Dlugoszewski, Lucia 60–61, 348
do Barros, Theo 69–70, 339
Dodd, Lee Wilson 99–09, 579;
09–19, 450, 583, 596; 23–24, 317;
29–30, 393
Dodge, Mr. (see Pease, Nelson &
Dodge)
Dodson, Owen 66–67, 355
Doermann, Felix 99–09, 556; 09–19,
581, 588
Doherty, Brian 37–38, 391
Doherty, Felix 41–42, 458
Dolan, Robert Emmett 49–50, 361;
50–51, 350; 63–64, 325
Dolin, Anton 39–40, 471
Dolin, Gerald 35–36, 401
Don, Carl 39–40, 437
Donahue, Jack 29–30, 451; 30–31,
429
Donahue, Tom 44–45, 441
Donaldson, Walter 25–26, 531;
31–32, 377; 64–65, 331
Doniger, Paul E. 70–71
Donizetti, Gaetano 09–19, 638
Donleavy, J.P. 63–64, 352; 70–71
Donnay, Maurice 99–09, 472;
09–19, 463
Donnell, (Capt.) Cushing 28–29, 506
Donnelly, Dorothy 09–19, 595, 627,
641; 19–20, 403; 21–22, 427;
23–24, 313, 438; 24–25, 500;
25–26, 469, 529, 564; 27–28, 402,
424; 30–31, 485, 500; 38–39, 438;
42–43, 475; 43–44, 410; 61–62,
304, 332
Donnelly, H. Grattan 94–99, 87, 98,
104, 185, 193

Donnelly, Leo *27–28*, 428
Donoghue, Dennis *33–34*, 498;
  38–39, 487
Donohue, Jack (see Donahue)
Donovan, Gerry *63–64*, 343
Donovan, John *63–64*, 358
Dooley, John *60–61*, 41
Dorati, Antal *44–45*, 380
Doremus, Mrs. Charles A. *99–09*,
  477
Dorey, Milnor *22–23*, 571
Dorfman, Nat N. *29–30*, 500;
  31–32, 504; *33–34*, 466; *34–35*,
  373
Dorin, F. *69–70*, 314
Doris, Hubert *63–64*, 361
Dorland, Peter *99–09*, 419
Doro, Marie *99–09*, 516
Dorrian, Cecil *09–19*, 561
Dorst, Tankred *67–68*, 414; *70–71*
Dos Passos, John *25–26*, 566;
  59–60, 350
Dossert, Frank G. *09–19*, 416
D-Ossetynski, Leonides *61–62*, 314
Dostoevsky, Feodor *94–99*, 92;
  99–09, 470, 536; *22–23*, 517;
  23–24, 356; *26–27*, 402, 453;
  34–35, 443; *39–40*, 405; *47–48*,
  439; *59–60*, 49; *60–61*, 348; *69–70*,
  343; *70–71*
Doten, Jay *34–35*, 391
Doty, Charles W. *99–09*, 478,
  512
Dougherty, Richard *63–64*, 324
Douglas, Jane *61–62*, 313
Douglas, Jerry *69–70*, 345; *70–71*
Douglas, Malcolm *94–99*, 103
Douglas, W.A.S. *48–49*, 425
Dowell, Coleman *60–61*, 41
Dowland, John *63–64*, 314
Dowling, Eddie *22–23*, 448; *24–25*,
  561; *26–27*, 383; *27–28*, 420
Dowling, Edward Duryea *39–40*,
  394
Dowling, Mildred *94–99*, 223
Down, Oliphant *09–19*, 548
Downey, Robert *66–67*, 419

Downing, Todd *42–43*, 418
Doyle, (Sir) Arthur Conan *94–99*,
  151; *99–09*, 353, 354, 442, 525;
  09–19, 408, 430; *29–30*, 446;
  53–54, 314; *64–65*, 327
Doyle, William R. *28–29*, 497;
  30–31, 510
Dozer, David *63–64*, 352; *70–71*
Dragun, Oswaldo *70–71*
Drahos, Mary *63–64*, 368; *66–67*,
  423
Drake, Alfred *49–50*, 380; *52–53*,
  258; *63–64*, 323
Drake, Ervin *46–47*, 478; *63–64*,
  327; *68–69*, 386
Drake, William A. *25–26*, 575;
  27–28, 525; *30–31*, 452; *33–34*,
  490; *36–37*, 449
Draper, Ruth *32–33*, 419; *34–35*,
  430; *35–36*, 462; *36–37*, 498;
  38–39, 488; *40–41*, 433; *42–43*,
  488; *46–47*, 464; *47–48*, 371;
  53–54, 338; *54–55*, 386; *56–57*,
  347
Draper, Samuel *63–64*, 352
Draskic, Ljubomir *68–69*, 425
Drayton, Mary *55–56*, 377; *65–66*,
  389
Dreiser, Theodore *09–19*, 612;
  21–22, 473; *26–27*, 399; *30–31*,
  495; *35–36*, 494; *54–55*, 376
Drejac, Jean *64–65*, 315, 331
Dressler, Marie *09–19*, 497
Drexler, Rosalyn *63–64*, 365; *67–68*,
  406, 411
Dreyer, Dave *62–63*, 295
Drinkwater, John *19–20*, 399;
  20–21, 437; *23–24*, 357; *28–29*,
  489; *29–30*, 424; *30–31*, 449;
  42–43, 437, 487
Driscoll, Clara *99–09*, 508
Driver, Donald *67–68*, 398
Drix, Walter *39–40*, 395
Drouet, Robert *94–99*, 117, 235
Drum, J.C. *09–19*, 537
Drury, Allen *60–61*, 308
Drury, (Maj.) W.P. *09–19*, 397

Dryden, John *31–32*, 501; *69–70*, 373

Duane, Frank *59–60*, 40

Duay, Grant *66–67*, 36

Duberman, Martin B. *63–64*, 350; *64–65*, 359; *67–68*, 407; *69–70*, 354; *70–71*

Dubey, Matt *56–57*, 314, 343

Dubin, Al *27–28*, 428; *39–40*, 394, 463; *42–43*, 420

DuBois, W.E.B. *63–64*, 351

Du Bois, William *30–31*, 435; *32–33*, 398; *37–38*, 456; *38–39*, 440

Ducovny, Amram *67–68*, 351

Ducquois, Mons. *99–09*, 547

Duddy, Lyn *49–50*, 379

Dudley, Bide *09–19*, 614–5, 655; *19–20*, 371, 451; *22–23*, 434; *25–26*, 544; *26–27*, 460; *29–30*, 376

Dudley, Bronson *59–60*, 40

Duerrenmatt, Friedrich *57–58*, 56, 332; *59–60*, 46, 315, 326; *61–62*, 281; *64–65*, 306; *65–66*, 430; *67–68*, 410; *69–70*, 347

Duffet, Vincent *27–28*, 498; *37–38*, 413

Duffield, Pitts *21–22*, 434

Duffy, Bernard *34–35*, 410

Duffy, Gordon *59–60*, 293

Duffy, Jimmy *25–26*, 420; *29–30*, 377

Duffy, John *63–64*, 352; *66–67*, 414; *67–68*, 406; *68–69*, 443; *69–70*, 372; *70–71*

Dugan, Lawrence Joseph *39–40*, 423

Dugan, William Francis *24–25*, 447, 579; *26–27*, 462

Duggan, Thomas *20–21*, 358; *42–43*, 461

Duke, Robert *46–47*, 446

Duke, Vernon *29–30*, 548; *31–32*, 379; *32–33*, 433; *33–34*, 476; *36–37*, 405, 446; *37–38*, 369; *40–41*, 384, 388; *41–42*, 422, 427; *43–44*, 448; *44–45*, 397; *52–53*, 275; *53–54*, 306; *55–56*, 391; *57–58*, 301; *63–64*. 357, 371

Dukelsky, Vladimir (Vernon Duke) *34–35*, 460

Dukes, Ashley *21–22*, 548; *22–23*, 432; *25–26*, 483; *26–27*, 430; *27–28*, 494; *29–30*, 481; *50–51*, 312; *66–67*, 406

Dulud, Michel *36–37*, 499

Dumas, Alexandre *fils* *94–99*, 105, 124, 143, 146, 147, 148, 156, 163, 166, 169, 215, 219, 226, 234; *99–09*, 380, 459, 472, 536, 537, 557; *09–19*, 432, 446, 589 (and 605), 618; *28–29*, 422; *30–31*, 482; *32–33*, 414; *35–36*, 446; *37–38*, 470; *45–46*, 388; *47–48*, 418; *61–62*, 268; *62–63*, 303; *68–69*, 374

Dumas, Alexandre *pere* *94–99*, 141, 185, 195, 254, 255; *99–09*, 377, 452; *20–21*, 450; *27–28*, 526; *35–36*, 511

Du Maurier, Daphne *44–45*, 411

Du Maurier, George *94–99*, 121, 132, 235; *99–09*, 491; *09–19*, 549, 599; *21–22*, 481

Du Maurier, Gerald *99–09*, 393; *23–24*, 337

Du Maurier, (Maj.) Guy *99–09*, 579

Dumay, Henri *94–99*, 221; *99–09*, 485

Dumont, Frank *94–99*, 101, 123

Dunai, Ferenc *63–64*, 336

Dunbar, Barre *30–31*, 470

Dunbar, Paul Laurence *99–09*, 409, 429; *66–67*, 354; *68–69*, 433

Duncan, Raymond *46–47*, 499; *47–48*, 429

Duncan, Robert *59–60*, 40

Duncan, Ronald *46–47*, 472; *48–49*, 404; *59–60*, 357; *61–62*, 314

Duncan sisters *24–25*, 511

Duncan, William Cary *09–19*, 499, 600, 635, 652; *19–20*, 444; *20–21*, 426; *21–22*, 494; *22–23*, 446; *23–24*, 374; *24–25*, 497; *26–27*,

534; *27–28*, 421, 505; *28–29*, 386; *29–30*, 421

Dunham, Katherine *46–47*, 440

Dunlop, Geoffrey *38–39*, 424

Dunmore, James H. *38–39*, 487

Dunn, (Miss) B.F. *59–60*, 40

Dunn, Caesar *24–25*, 571; *27–28*, 392

Dunn, Edward Delaney *20–21*, 448, 449; *21–22*, 442; *22–23*, 576

Dunn, Geoffrey *37–38*, 412

Dunn, Isabel *55–56*, 377

Dunne, George H. (S.J.) *47–48*, 427

Dunning, Frances Fox *32–33*, 388

Dunning, Philip *09–19*, 630; *26–27*, 381; *27–28*, 555; *28–29*, 372; *29–30*, 401; *32–33*, 388; *34–35*, 374, 415; *35–36*, 409

Dunphy, Jack *59–60*, 49; *61–62*, 332

Dunsany, Lord *09–19*, 588, 590, 628, 649–50; *27–28*, 437; *29–30*, 537

Dupree, Frank *27–28*, 403

du Pury, Marianne *66–67*, 406, 408

Duran, Michel *34–35*, 425

Durant, Harry *26–27*, 371

Duras, Marguerite *60–61*, 44; *70–71*

Duru, Alfred *94–99*, 139

d(D)u Souchet, Henry A. *94–99*, 179, 200, 215, 235; *99–09*, 484, 583; *09–19*, 462

d'Usseau, Arnaud *42–43*, 472; *45–46*, 386; *50–51*, 318; *53–54*, 311

Duval, Georges *99–09*, 389, 499, 522, 532

Duvernois, Henri *25–26*, 542

Dvorak, Anton *41–42*, 456; *43–44*, 485; *44–45*, 437

Dyar, Ralph E. *19–20*, 341

Dyer, Charles *62–63*, 306; *67–68*, 358

Dyer, Doug *69–70*, 345; *70–71*

Dyer, William *59–60*, 336; *63–64*, 355, 358, 371; *65–66*, 424

Dylan, Bob *70–71*

Dymow, Ossip *09–19*, 597; *21–22*, 538; *38–38*, 470

Dyne, Michael *65–66*, 378

Dyrenforth, James *22–23*, 513

Dzeduszycka, Teresa *68–69*, 444

Dzerzhinsky, Ivan *44–45*, 445

Eagan, Louis *99–09*, 462

Eagan, Raymond B. *25–26*, 475

Eager, Edward *43–44*, 477; *49–50*, 380; *52–53*, 258; *62–63*, 329; *63–64*, 323, 348; *68–69*, 427

Earle, Edward *60–61*, 42

Earle, Fred *99–09*, 492

Earle, Georgia *09–19*, 563

Easdale, Brian *56–57*, 325, 326

Easton, Sidney *53–54*, 306

Eastwood, Oliver *24–25*, 526

Eastwood, Tom *57–58*, 288

Eaton, Billy *64–65*, 361

Eaton, Walter Prichard *23–24*, 353

Ebb, Fred *59–60*, 335, 336; *60–61*, 292; *62–63*, 336; *63–64*, 347; *64–65*, 336; *66–67*,, 370, 410; *67–68*, 359; *68–69*, 393; *70–71*

Ebenhack, Arthur *30–31*, 519; *32–33*, 477

Eberhart, Mignon G. *40–41*, 408

Ebin, Gala *62–63*, 336

Echegaray, José *99–09*, 355, 404, 572; *09–19*, 520; *31–32*, 500

Eckstein, Gustav *39–40*, 427

Eddy, Arthur J. *99–09*, 582

Eddy, David *63–64*, 356

Eddy, Jerome H. *94–99*, 172; *99–09*, 382

Edelman, Maurice *60–61*, 343

Edens, Roger *58–59*, 315

Edeson, Robert *09–19*, 626

Edgington (Eddington), May *22–23*, 509; *23–24*, 320

Edmonds, Walter D. *32–33*, 459; *34–35*, 400

Edson, Jesse *99–09*, 523

Edwards, Mr. (see Cobb & Edwards)

Edwards, Gus *99–09*, 376, 491, 514, 525, 540, 546, 562, 568; *09–19*, 420

Edwards, I.W. *99–09*, 572

Edwards, Joan *49–50*, 379

Edwards, Julian *94–99*, 125, 166, 182, 200, 245; *99–09*, 362, 378, 404, 424, 427, 468, 488, 514, 532, 533, 562; *09–19*, 395, 401, 417, 601

Edwards, Leo *09–19*, 420, 553; *42–43*, 456

Edwards, Maurice *63–64*, 366

Edwards, Ryan *65–66*, 434

Edwards, Sherman *60–61*, 328; *68–69*, 410

Edwardes, George *09–19*, 423

Edymar *21–22*, 465

Egan, Louis *94–99*, 232

Egan, Michael *34–35*, 466

Egan, Raymond B. *09–19*, 656

Egbert, Leslie Floyd *45–46*, 382

Egerton, George *99–09*, 570; *09–19*, 456, 477, 480, 529

Egri, Lajos N. *26–27*, 505; *37–38*, 464

Ehrlich, Ida Lublenski *33–34*, 521

Ehrmann, Herbert *41–42*, 441

Eichel, Leslie P. *25–26*, 528

Eichheim, Henry *25–26*, 569

Einhorn, Abe *66–67*, 376

Einstein, Albert *62–63*, 322

Eisenberg, Emanuel *37–38*, 395

Eisenberg, Lawrence B. *63–64*, 352

Eisenschiml, Otto *42–43*, 422

Eisinger, Jo *36–37*, 463; *41–42*, 447

Eisler, Hanns *35–36*, 436; *39–40*, 438, 455; *44–45*, 443; *47–48*, 393; *61–62*, 317; *63–64*, 365; *66–67*, 363

Eisner, Helen *63–64*, 349

Eldee, Lilian *99–09*, 499

Elder, Lonne III *68–69*, 440, 451

Eldridge, Paul *28–29*, 355

Elgas, Miriam *33–34*, 534

Elinson, Izzy *41–42*, 422

Eliot, Samuel A. Jr. *24–25*, 591

Eliot, T.S. *35–36*, 472; *37–38*, 425; *47–48*, 425, 429; *49–50*, 369; *50–51*, 373, 374; *51–52*, 333; *53–54*, 340; *58–59*, 297; *60–61*, 354; *62–63*, 322; *67–68*, 410; *68–69*, 383; *69–70*, 343

Eliscu, Edward *28–29*, 463; *31–32*, 465; *32–33*, 500; *36–37*, 459; *40–41*, 403; *61–62*, 320

Elizabeth I (Queen) *62–63*, 295; *63–64*, 314

Elizondo, J.F. *09–19*, 611

Ellington, Duke *44–45*, 431; *46–47*, 451; *54–55*, 365; *65–66*, 403

Elliott, Mr. *27–28*, 444

Elliott, (Capt.) Arthur *09–19*, 641

Elliott, Bob *70–71*

Elliott, Don *59–60*, 324; *60–61*, 289; *62–63*, 309

Elliott, Francis Perry *09–19*, 596

Elliott, James W. *21–22*, 423

Elliott, Robert *62–63*, 317; *63–64*, 355; *65–66*, 422

Elliott, Sumner Locke *51–52*, 287; *53–54*, 326

Elliott, William *09–19*, 571

Ellis, Edith (Edith Ellis Baker) *99–09*, 495, 574; *09–19*, 425, 439, 568; *19–20*, 442; *20–21*, 427; *24–25*, 546

Ellis, Edward *09–19*, 497

Ellis, Harold *99–09*, 524

Ellis, Lionel *94–99*, 225

Ellis, Melville *99–09*, 435, 510, 517, 530

Ellis, Sidney R. *94–99*, 158

Ellis, Vivian *25–26*, 526; *56–57*, 331

Ellis, Walter W. *09–19*, 578

Ellstein, Abe *37–38*, 470; *45–46*, 460; *46–47*, 497; *47–48*, 431; *48–49*, 429; *49–50*, 376

Elman, Irving *42–43*, 472; *51–52*, 317; *56–57*, 346

Elmer, Arthur *41–42*, 459

Elmslie, Kenward *55–56*, 391

Elser, Frank B. *30–31*, 424; *32–33*, 459; *34–35*, 400

Elsner, Edward *28–29,* 362
Eltinge, Julian *09–19,* 523
Elward, James *64–65,* 353
Elwell, Ambrose Jr. *37–38,* 437
Elwood, Walter *26–27,* 481
Ely, Lewis B. *24–25,* 449
Emanuel, James *66–67,* 354, 355
Emerson, Geraldine *34–35,* 414
Emerson, John *23–24,* 311; *25–26,* 433; *26–27,* 388; *31–32,* 426
Emery, Edward T. *32–33,* 499
Emery, Gilbert *20–21,* 434; *21–22,* 412; *23–24,* 324; *24–25,* 536; *25–26,* 582; *28–29,* 353; *31–32,* 503; *32–33,* 478
Eminory, Mons. *26–27,* 460
Emmanuel, Jack *45–46,* 422
Emmett, James K. *94–99,* 90
Engel, Alexander *99–09,* 573; *09–19,* 396; *26–27,* 449; *30–31,* 401
Engel, I. *26–27,* 440; *63–64,* 322
Engel, (A.) Lehman *34–35,* 395; *35–36,* 472; *37–38,* 448; *38–39,* 414, 463; *39–40,* 418, 456; *40–41,* 432; *41–42,* 412; *46–47,* 435, 494; *47–48,* 356, 395, 417; *48–49,* 400; *51–52,* 284; *53–54,* 307; *55–56,* 374; *59–60,* 324
Engelbracht, Mr. *64–65,* 303
England, Barry *70–71*
England, Elizabeth *35–36,* 510
Englander, Ludwig *94–99,* 86, 119, 135, 176, 177, 198, 202, 238, 255, 258; *99–09,* 346, 354, 364, 370, 372, 392, 397, 409, 414, 428, 443, 464, 474, 499, 524, 546, 573; *09–19,* 527; *26–27,* 459
Engvick, William *60–61,* 42; *62–63,* 317
Ensign, Herman Lee *94–99,* 215
Ensor, Clois *55–56,* 390
Enters, Angna *39–40,* 472; *42–43,* 485
Entrikin, Knowles *24–25,* 531; *26–27,* 417
Ephraim, Armand *26–27,* 434

Ephron, Henry *42–43,* 475; *61–62,* 274; *68–69,* 415
Ephron, Phoebe *42–43,* 475; *58–59,* 292; *61–62,* 274; *68–69,* 415
Epstein, Julius J. *36–37,* 416; *43–44,* 465; *68–69,* 408
Epstein, Philip G. *36–37,* 416; *43–44,* 465
Epstein, Mark *59–60,* 336
Erckmann-Chatrian (see Erckmann Chatrian)
Erdman, Jean *62–63,* 320; *66–67,* 420
Erens, Joseph *42–43,* 471; *43–44,* 414
Erlanger, Aline *27–28,* 389
Ernst, Jessie Hein *27–28,* 461; *34–35,* 376
Erskin, Chester *31–32,* 393, 394; *35–36,* 463; *38–39,* 411
Erskine, John *31–32,* 447
Erskine, Milton *63–64,* 345
Ervine, St. John *09–19,* 351, 459, 494; *19–20,* 431; *20–21,* 412; *23–24,* 315, 399; *29–30,* 470; *33–34,* 422; *40–41,* 384; *47–48,* 364
Esler, Lemist *28–29,* 400
Esmond, Henry V. *94–99,* 185, 225, 249; *99–09,* 358, 362, 401, 422, 484, 507, 553; *09–19,* 519, 521; *25–26,* 529
Essex, Francis *62–63,* 316
Essex, Harry J. *37–38,* 401
Esslin, Martin *64–65,* 359; *69–70,* 378
Estabrook, Howard *09–19,* 455
Estrin, Slava *65–66,* 426
Estry, Joseph L. *47–48,* 383
Ettlinger, Karl *09–19,* 579
Eunson, Dale *41–42,* 435; *43–44,* 465; *46–47,* 427
Euripides *19–20,* 439; *20–21,* 440; *37–38,* 458, 463; *40–41,* 431; *47–48,* 360; *48–49,* 421, 426; *50–51,* 374; *56–57,* 55; *61–62,* 326; *63–64,* 345, 354; *64–65,* 298;

Faulkner, Virginia *40–41*, 405; *46–47*, 458
Faulkner, William *58–59*, 319
Fauré, Gabriel *62–63*, 326
Fauset, Jessie *66–67*, 354
Faust, Walter Livingstone *42–43*, 464
Favina, Mr. *45–46*, 452
Favreau, Didi *69–70*, 363
Fay, F.G. *09–19*, 463
Fay, Frances C. *24–25*, 505
Fay, Frank *21–22*, 507; *32–33*, 499
Fay, Mary Helen *44–45*, 393, 414; *46–47*, 453; *51–52*, 287
Fazekas, Imre *29–30*, 519
Fearon, Ed *63–64*, 343; *65–66*, 424
Fechheimer, Richard *19–20*, 392
Federal Theater Project staff *35–36*, 471; *37–38*, 452
Fedorova, Nina *42–43*, 470
Fehr, Richard *36–37*, 497
Feibleman, Peter S. *62–63*, 291
Feiffer, Jules *63–64*, 369; *66–67*, 364, 391; *67–68*, 407, 409; *68–69*, 442; *69–70*, 335, 358
Feigl, Jane Mauldin *99–09*, 514
Feilbert, Edward Allen *43–44*, 463; *62–63*, 311
Fein, Lupin *37–38*, 468
Feiner, Benjamin Jr. *29–30*, 533
Feiner, Herman *29–30*, 523
Feirstein, Frederick *66–67*, 420
Feist, Gene *62–63*, 313; *69–70*, 377; *70–71*
Feld, Leo *09–19*, 453
Feld, Rose C. *44–45*, 405
Feldman, Gene *61–62*, 311
Felipe, Leon *66–67*, 107
Felix, (Dr.) Hugo *09–19*, 479, 571; *19–20*, 444; *20–21*, 375; *21–22*, 498; *23–24*, 359, 427
Fell, Marion *09–19*, 561
Fellini, Federico *65–66*, 395; *69–70*, 308
Fellow of the Royal Society of Literature (anon. author) *09–19*, 590
Fells, Richard *69–70*, 372

Felton, Dudley P. *41–42*, 461
Fendall, Percy *99–09*, 435
Fenn, Frederick *99–09*, 479; *09–19*, 531; *23–24*, 430
Fennelly, Parker W. *36–37*, 463; *41–42*, 396
Fenton, Frank *36–37*, 412
Fenton, Howard *68–69*, 439
Ferber, Edna *09–19*, 562; *24–25*, 459; *27–28*, 482, 483; *31–32*, 513; *32–33*, 407; *36–37*, 421; *41–42*, 406; *45–46*, 418; *48–49*, 378, 393; *50–51*, 341; *53–54*, 352; *59–60*, 309; *60–61*, 334; *66–67*, 352, 357
Ferguson, Barney *94–99*, 200
Ferlinghetti, Lawrence *63–64*, 369; *70–71*
Fernald, Chester Bailey *94–99*, 208; *99–09*, 348; *09–19*, 535, 590, 656; *21–22*, 482; *24–25*, 450
Ferrand, Jacques *44–45*, 444
Ferrat, Jean *64–65*, 315, 316
Ferrer, José *47–48*, 345; *57–58*, 315
Ferrere, Claude *24–35*, 483
Ferris, Mabel *09–19*, 637
Ferris, Walter *27–28*, 492; *28–29*, 461; *29–30*, 469; *30–31*, 492
Ferro, A.H. *99–09*, 421
Fertik, Fannie *69–70*, 333
Fessler, Walter *94–99*, 98
Fetter, Ted *36–37*, 446, 457; *37–38*, 369, 449; *46–47*, 429; *53–54*, 306; *63–64*, 357
Feuchtwanger, Lion *29–30*, 481; *52–53*, 308
Feuer, Cy *58–59*, 314
Feuillet, Octave *94–99*, 91, 120, 209, 236; *99–09*, 355, 486; *09–19*, 547
Fevrier, Henri *19–20*, 391
Feydeau, Georges *94–99*, 144, 211, 216; *99–09*, 346; *09–19*, 416, 473; *19–20*, 424; *52–53*, 271; *56–57*, 353, 366; *58–59*, 325; *60–61*, 326; *64–65*, 362; *65–66*, 397; *69–70*, 297, 377
Feyder, J. *53–54*, 301
Ficke, Arthur Davison *21–22*, 501
Field, Edward *68–69*, 407

Field, Jonathan *62–63,* 339
Field, Julian *94–99,* 192
Field, Martyn *94–99,* 256
Field, Rachel Lyman *22–23,* 574
Field, Salisbury *09–19,* 528, 546;
  19–20, 383; *22–23,* 556
Fielding, Henry *99–09,* 550
Fielding, Marjery *41–42,* 443
Fields, Dorothy *27–28,* 553; *28–29,*
  445; *29–30,* 500; *30–31,* 447;
  31–32, 379; *38–39,* 458; *41–42,*
  407; *42–43,* 423, 458; *43–44,* 451;
  44–45, 413; *45–46,* 447; *46–47,*
  413; *49–50,* 372; *50–51,* 363;
  53–54, 349; *57–58,* 319; *58–59,*
  319; *65–66,* 395, 413, 437; *66–67,*
  356, 414; *67–68,* 410
Fields, Frank Gaskin *60–61,* 352;
  68–69, 455
Fields, Herbert *25–26,* 448, 572;
  26–27, 447, 516; *27–28,* 445, 546;
  28–29, 445; *29–30,* 452; *30–31,*
  465, 488; *32–33,* 452; *39–40,* 420;
  40–41, 390; *41–42,* 407; *42–43,*
  423, 458; *43–44,* 428, 451; *44–45,*
  413; *45–46,* 447; *46–47,* 413;
  49–50, 372; *53–54,* 349; *57–58,*
  319; *58–59,* 319; *65–66,* 413;
  66–67, 356; *67–68,* 410
Fields, Joseph (A.) *37–38,* 433;
  40–41, 405; *41–42,* 415; *42–43,*
  457; *45–46,* 411; *47–48,* 351, 427;
  49–50, 363; *52–53,* 290; *53–54,*
  343, 348; *55–56,* 376; *56–57,* 354;
  57–58, 323; *58–59,* 306; *62–63,*
  297; *66–67,* 386, 389
Fields, Lew *09–19,* 658; *28–29,* 381;
  30–31, 447
Fields, W.C. *22–23,* 443
Figman, Max *99–09,* 541
Fillmore, John Eldon *32–33,* 447
Finch, John *46–47,* 460
Finch, Robert *52–53,* 275
Finck, Herman *09–19,* 563
Finckel, Edwin *55–56,* 367
Fine, Sylvia *38–39,* 486; *39–40,* 400
Fine, Vivian *38–39,* 483

Finkle, David *65–66,* 422, 424;
  66–67, 404; *67–68,* 372
Finklehoffe, Fred F. *36–37,* 441;
  42–43, 429
Finletter, Gretchen Damrosch (see
  Gretchen Damrosch)
Finn, Ben *70–71*
Finn, Caesar *47–48,* 429
Finn, Jonathan *36–37,* 473
Finsterwald, Maxine *28–29,* 501;
  29–30, 534
Firbank, Ronald *60–61,* 349
Fischer (see Yarno & Fischer)
Fischer, Charles *67–68,* 402
Fischer, Clifford C. *41–42,* 443, 448,
  454; *42–43,* 429
Fischer, William S. *70–71*
Fischoff, George *62–63,* 317; *63–64,*
  348, 349, 366; *65–66,* 390; *69–70,*
  317
Fish, Horace *21–22,* 456; *23–24,*
  429
Fishberg, Jacob *38–39,* 494
Fisher, Mr. *56–57,* 333
Fisher, Mark *64–65,* 331
Fisher, Parker *09–19,* 632
Fisher, Robert (Bob) *65–66,* 376;
  67–68, 378; *69–70,* 320
Fisher, Rudolph *35–36,* 470
Fisher, Steve *61–62,* 304
Fisher, William *69–70,* 427; *70–71*
Fiske, Harrison Grey *94–99,* 118,
  169, 196, 204; *99–09,* 411; *09–19,*
  469; *26–27,* 458
Fiske, (Mrs.) Minnie Maddern
  94–99, 169, 188; *99–09,* 487,
  513
Fitch, Clyde *94–99,* 91, 127, 146,
  167, 176, 191, 228, 247, 249;
  99–09, 1, 30, 355, 358, 361, 387,
  388, 399, 400, 401, 421, 424, 426,
  428, 438, 444, 449, 467, 471, 480,
  483, 486, 493, 502, 523, 528, 531,
  553, 557, 560, 573, 579, 581;
  09–19, 406, 526, 573; *19–20,* 382;
  25–26, 438; *27–28,* 403; *37–38,*
  454; *48–49,* 425; *69–70,* 371

Fitts, Dudley *59–60,* 306; *66–67,* 410; *70–71*

Fitzgerald, Edith *29–30,* 486

Fitzgerald, Edward *45–46,* 458

Fitzgerald, F. Scott *25–26,* 545; *28–29,* 492; *55–56,* 348; *61–62,* 324; *63–64,* 367

Fitzgerald, Robert *66–67,* 410; *70–71*

Flagg, Fanny *65–66,* 424

Flaiano, Ennio *65–66,* 395

Flamma, Ario *21–22,* 399

Flanagan, William *60–61,* 356; *63–64,* 312; *65–66,* 394; *68–69,* 380

Flanders, Michael *59–60,* 294; *66–67,* 379

Flanigan, Phyllis *36–37,* 467

Flaubert, Gustave *37–38,* 390

Flavin, Martin *23–24,* 303, 429; *24–25,* 595; *25–26,* 590; *26–27,* 370; *29–30,* 410, 436, 438; *35–36,* 419, 454; *36–37,* 447

Flaxman, John *68–69,* 387; *69–70,* 363

Flecker, James Elroy *24–25,* 455

Fleeson, Neville *19–20,* 448; *22–23,* 443

Fleg, Edmond *30–31,* 448

Fleischman, Maxine *68–69,* 449

Fleisler, Joseph R. *29–30,* 534

Fleming, Allan *35–36,* 449

Fleming, Carroll *99–09,* 489, 527; *09–19,* 442, 449, 474

Fleming, George *94–99,* 192, 196; *99–09,* 365, 444, 445; *09–19,* 509

Fleming, Leopoldo *69–70,* 372

Fletcher, Bramwell *62–63,* 322; *65–66,* 427, 436

Fletcher, Constance (see George Fleming)

Fletcher, Coyne *94–99,* 204–5

Fletcher, Percy E. *20–21,* 390

Flexner, Anne Crawford *99–09,* 396, 463; *09–19,* 411, 512, 632; *19–20,* 453; *36–37,* 443

Flexner, Hortense *09–19,* 588

Flick, Pat C. *40–41,* 382

Flicker, Theodore J. *58–59,* 336

Flint, Eva Kay *29–30,* 403; *30–31,* 408; *33–34,* 452

Florman, Irving *43–44,* 407

Flournoy, Richard F. *32–33,* 500; *33–34,* 528; *34–35,* 400

Flowers, Priscilla *25–26,* 591; *27–28,* 551

Floyd, Carlisle *62–63,* 316

Floyd, John *26–27,* 448; *33–34,* 497

Flynn, James D. *94–99,* 257–8

Fodor, Ladislaus *31–32,* 408; *33–34,* 421; *47–48,* 405

Fodor, Laszlo *24–25,* 528; *31–32,* 393, 464

Foerster, Wilhelm Meyer (see Wilhelm Meyer-Foerster)

Fogarty, Alexander *29–30,* 398; *35–36,* 507

Fogel, Al *69–70,* 298

Foldes, Irma *09–19,* 607

Foley, Charles *99–09,* 417

Fonson, Frantz *09–19,* 434, 522

Fomeen, Basil *29–30,* 548

Fontaine, Robert L. *49–50,* 370; *67–68,* 358

Foote,, Horton *40–41,* 431; *41–42,* 459; *42–43,* 488; *43–44,* 464; *47–48,* 397; *51–52,* 318; *53–54,* 315; *54–55,* 371

Foote, Jay *62–63,* 317; *63–64,* 358, 359

Foote, John Taintor *09–19,* 652; *34–35,* 370

Footner, Hulbert *09–19,* 591

Foran, Edward J. *30–31,* 499

Forbes, Elliott *38–39,* 491

Forbes, Esther *68–69,* 411

Forbes, James *99–09,* 518, 564; *09–19,* 421, 482, 543; *19–20,* 404; *22–23,* 448; *25–26,* 501; *28–29,* 454; *36–37,* 431

Forbes, Kathryn *44–45,* 389

Forbes-Phillips, Rev. *09–19,* 526

Ford, Corey *33–34,* 433

Ford, George *31–32,* 440

Ford, Harriet 99–09, 374, 402, 423;
  09–19, 402, 407, 489, 526, 540,
  581, 609; 19–20, 376; 21–22, 436;
  23–24, 364, 409
Ford, Harry Chapman 20–21, 384;
  24–25, 562; 30–31, 534
Ford, Hugh 22–23, 495
Ford, Joan 58–59, 294
Ford, John 58–59, 52; 70–71
Ford, Nancy 67–68, 386; 69–70,
  356; 70–71
Ford, Paul Leicester 99–09, 381
Ford, Ruth 58–59, 319
Ford, Walter 99–09, 376
Forest, Mons. 24–25, 483
Forester, C.S. 31–32, 400
Forman, Justus Miles 09–19, 551
Forman, Milos 64–65, 297
Fornes, Maria Irene 69–70, 333
Forrest, Belford 29–30, 541
Forrest, George 44–45, 370; 48–49,
  381; 53–54, 324; 61–62, 268;
  63–64, 367; 65–66, 368, 387
Forrest, Sam 23–24, 307; 24–25,
  449; 25–26, 504
Forsberg, Rolf 62–63, 318
Forsell, Lars 68–69, 458
Forshaw, Robert Pierpont 42–43,
  444
Forslund, R.V. 63–64, 361
Forsslung, Louise 09–19, 586
Forst, Rudolf 34–35, 411
Forster, E.M. 61–62, 283; 70–71
Forster, Margaret 69–70, 317
Forsythe, James 58–59, 51; 60–61,
  44; 67–68, 348; 70–71
Fort, Garrett 28–29, 378
Fortis, John 44–45, 365; 46–47, 414,
  482
Forza, Dario 27–28, 447
Foss, Lukas 45–46, 454; 70–71
Fosse, Bob 65–66, 395
Foster, Charles 35–36, 431
Foster, Claiborne 43–44, 468
Foster, Gladys S. 69–70, 351
Foster, Harry L. 26–27, 497
Foster, Maximilian 09–19, 584

Foster, Norman 31–32, 457
Foster, Paul 64–65, 354; 65–66, 433;
  66–67, 36; 67–68, 404
Foster, Ray 49–50, 355
Foster, Stephen 38–39, 475
Fothergill, Jessie 94–99, 228; 99–09,
  355
Fowler, A.N.C 99–09, 534
Fowler, Gene 32–33, 432; 69–70,
  302
Fox, John Jr. 09–19, 464
Fox, Paul Hervey 24–25, 597;
  29–30, 385; 30–31, 513; 31–32,
  506; 37–38, 417
Fox, Stuart 09–19, 583
Fraccaroli, Arnaldo 22–23, 450
Fracht, J. Albert 63–64, 356
Fragonard, Jean-Honoré 46–47, 491
Françaix, Jean 51–52, 330
France, Anatole 09–19, 441, 545;
  22–23, 573; 27–28, 510; 29–30,
  536; 31–32, 375; 46–47, 488;
  67–68, 411
Franciosa, Signor 63–64, 323
Francis, Alfred 09–19, 622
Francis, Arthur 20–21, 446
Francis, J.O. 09–19, 521; 25–26, 548
Francis, John 44–45, 441
Francis, William 67–68, 365
Francis, William T. 94–99, 248;
  99–09, 382, 416, 437, 463, 490,
  492, 567; 09–19, 465
Francisco, Hale 31–32, 506
Francke, Caroline 28–29, 401
Francisco, William 61–62, 308
Frangipane & Dante 67–68, 403
Frank, Anne 55–56, 350
Frank, Bruno 27–28, 525; 36–37,
  470, 475
Frank, Charles 62–63, 318
Frank, Gerald 67–68, 400
Frank, John (see The Revuers)
Frank, Larry 70–71
Frank, Leonhard 29–30, 412
Frank, Melvin 39–40, 463; 56–57,
  335
Frank, Pat 48–49, 423

Frank, Paul *09–19*, 548; *29–30*, 417

Frank, Yasha *38–39*, 479; *39–40*, 472

Franke, Caroline *43–44*, 463; *60–61*, 303

Franke, Wolfgang *65–66*, 429

Frankel, Doris *38–39*, 440; *49–40*, 360

Franken, Rose *31–32*, 508; *32–33*, 492; *40–41*, 417; *43–44*, 423, 444; *44–45*, 387; *47–48*, 389; *51–52*, 333

Frankin, Eva *39–40*, 394

Franklin, Benjamin *69–70*, 344

Franklin, Edgar *24–25*, 546

Franklin, Malvin M. *09–19*, 456, 502, 658

Franklin, Peg *19–20*, 354

Franklyn, Roy *61–62*, 327

Franks, Thetta Quay *31–32*, 490

Fraser, Robert *94–99*, 128

Fraser-Simson, Harold *09–19*, 637

Fraserwood, A.C. *94–99*, 238

Fratti, Mario *62–63*, 339; *70–71*

Fray, Jacques *30–31*, 447

Frazier, Cliff *67–68*, 410

Frechtman, Bernard *59–60*, 355; *60–61*, 361; *63–64*, 351

Fredericks, Claude *61–62*, 329

Freeborn, Cassius *99–09*, 515

Freed, Donald *69–70*, 327

Freed, Fred *55–56*, 347; *62–63*, 295; *64–65*, 331

Freedley, Vinton Jr. *38–39*, 491

Freedman, Betty 63–64, 352

Freedman, David *26–27*, 450; *29–30*, 448; *30–31*, 454; *33–34*, 476; *34–35*, 362; *36–37*, 405, 413, 446; *37–38*, 369

Freedman, Gerald *65–66*, 410

Freeman, Bud *59–60*, 317

Freeman, Charles K. *44–45*, 401

Freeman, Gary William (see Gary William Friedman)

Freeman, Helen *21–22*, 456

Freeman, Lea *31–32*, 438

Freeman, Louis *38–39*, 493

Freeman, Stan *64–65*, 319; *70–71*

Freiman, Louis *42–43*, 490; *48–49*, 430; *61–62*, 310; *64–65*, 344

Freitag, Dorothea *56–57*, 319; *57–58*, 284; *70–71*

Frelinghaus, Mark *39–40*, 473

French, (Field Marshal Sir) John *64–65*, 303

French officer (anon. author) *09–19*, 589 (and 605)

Freska, Friedrich *09–19*, 463

Freund, Mrs. F.E. Washburn (see Mrs. F.E. Washburn-Freund)

Freund, Julius *09–19*, 519

Freund, Philip *59–60*, 40

Freund, Dr. Washburn (see Dr. Washburn-Freund)

Friar, Kimon *63–64*, 352

Friberg, Carl *67–68*, 378

Fribourg, Arthur *27–28*, 548

Fridolin (Gratien Gélinas) *50–51*, 348

Friebus, Florida *32–33*, 434; *46–47*, 439

Fried, Emanuel *67–68*, 396; *69–70*, 345

Fried, Gerald *61–62*, 281

Friedberg, Billy (William) *51–52*, 278; *55–56*, 391

Friedland, Antol *09–19*, 456, 485

Friedlander, William B. *19–20*, 414; *20–21*, 387; *23–24*, 394; *24–25*, 575; *40–41*, 426; *42–43*, 438

Friedman, Mr. *56–57*, 333

Friedman, Alan (Foster) *64–65*, 342; *65–66*, 417, 424; *70–71*

Friedman(n) Armin *24–25*, 434; *29–30*, 429

Friedman, Bruce Jay *65–66*, 436; *67–68*, 388; *70–71*

Friedman, Charles *34–35*, 479; *37–38*, 395; *38–39*, 407, 470; *52–53*, 264

Friedman, Gary William *64–65*, 354, 357; *66–67*, 107; *69–70*, 368; *70–71*

Friedman, I.K. *09–19*, 526

Friedman, Isidor(e) *42–43*, 490;
 45–46, 460; *46–47*, 497; *48–49*,
 429
Friedman, Joel *66–67*, 423; *67–68*,
 408
Friedman, Leon 67–68, 351
Friel, Brian *65–66*, 398; *66–67*, 360;
 68–69, 375; *69–70*, 308
Frielinghaus, Henry *40–41*, 433
Frieman, Louis *47–48*, 431
Friend, Cliff *29–30*, 401
Frietas, Dick *61–62*, 329
Friml, Rudolph *09–19*, 487, 516,
 547, 566, 594, 613, 639, 641, 654;
 19–20, 371; *20–21*, 444; *21–22*,
 388; *22–23*, 554; *23–24*, 340;
 24–25, 445; *25–26*, 451; *26–27*,
 359, 408, 467; *27–28*, 480, 526;
 30–31, 413; *31–32*, 441; *34–35*,
 434; *43–44*, 402; *61–62*, 332
Frings, Ketti *42–43*, 442; *57–58*,
 303; *59–60*, 318; *66–67*, 374
Frisby, Terence *67–68*, 345
Frisch, Max *50–51*, 374; *62–63*, 296,
 325; *68–69*, 426; *69–70*, 347
Frith, Walter *99–09*, 380
Froeschel, George *31–32*, 454
Froissart, Jean *62–63*, 295
Frondaie, Pierre *19–20*, 391; *21–22*,
 509; *24–25*, 483
Frost, Jack *23–24*, 440
Frost, Robert *59–60*, 49; *62–63*,
 322; *65–66*, 422, 436
Frost, Thomas *94–99*, 153
Frost, Walter Archer *24–25*, 541
Fry, Alex *61–62*, 262
Fry, Christopher *49–50*, 378; *50–51*,
 324, 329; *51–52*, 286, 310; *54–55*,
 400; *55–56*, 349; *57–58*, 331;
 59–60, 334; *67–68*, 348; *70–71*
Fry, Horace B. *94–99*, 169; *99–09*,
 411, 459; *27–28*, 550
Frye, Emma Sheridan *94–99*, 165
Frye, Peter *46–47*, 496
Fuchs, Isidor *94–99*, 102
Fuchs, Peter Paul *56–57*, 333
Fuerst, Jim *61–62*, 286

Fugard, Athol *63–64*, 359; *68–69*,
 454; *69–70*, 340; *70–71*
Fulda, Ludwig *94–99*, 191, 201;
 99–09, 407; *42–43*, 446
Fulgora, Robert *94–99*, 215
Fulham, William H. *35–36*, 508
Fuller, Albert C. *29–30*, 390
Fuller, Charles H. Jr. *68–69*, 449
Fuller, Dean *56–57*, 314, 357;
 58–59, 335; *66–67*, 393, 422
Fuller, John G. *52–53*, 301; *57–58*,
 329
Fuller, Logan *94–99*, 140
Fuller, Lorenzo *47–48*, 395; *62–63*,
 312
Fuller, Raymond *24–25*, 584
Fulton, Maude *09–19*, 596; *22–23*,
 519
Funt, Julian *46–47*, 414; *53–54*, 351
Furber, Mr. (see Brightman, Melford
 & Furber)
Furher, Douglas *20–21*, 402
Furland, Maxime *65–66*, 435
Furniss, Grace Livingston *94–99*,
 244, 255; *99–09*, 364, 415, 425,
 497, 544
Furst, William W. *94–99*, 85, 139,
 140, 146, 220, 230, 242, 243, 256;
 99–09, 369, 374, 399, 417, 525,
 550, 572, 574; *09–19*, 510, 587
Furth, George *69–70*, 328
Furth, Seymour *99–09*, 540, 559,
 564; *24–25*, 564
Fyles, Franklin *94–99*, 95, 164, 212,
 218; *99–09*, 438
Fytrelle, Jacques *09–19*, 557

Gaard, David *69–70*, 343
Gabel, Martin *47–48*, 378
Gabel, Zac & Ruby *40–41*, 395
Gaberman, Phil *67–68*, 410
Gabler, Carl *63–64*, 371
Gabriel, M. *94–99*, 90
Gabrielson, Frank *34–35*, 360, 478;
 41–42, 395, 458
Gaburo, Kenneth *60–61*, 41
Gagel, Frederick *94–99*, 126, 259

Gagliano, Frank *63–64,* 371; *64–65,* 354; *66–67,* 409; *67–68,* 391; *68–69,* 448

Gaines, Frederick *69–70,* 361

Gaites, Joseph M. *94–99,* 254

Galantière, Lewis *33–34,* 449, 482; *45–46,* 428

Gale, David *67–68,* 411

Gale, Zona *09–19,* 612; *20–21,* 415; *23–24,* 391

Gallagher, Francis *36–37,* 420; *59–60,* 40

Gallaher, Donald *27–28,* 515

Gallarati-Scotti, Signor *23–24,* 366

Gallico, Paul *32–33,* 436

Gallon, Tom *99–09,* 432

Gallup, Sammy *53–54,* 327

Galperin, Mikail *25–26,* 514

Galpern, Lasar *34–35,* 387

Galsworthy, John *99–09,* 537; *09–19,* 404, 468, 573, 595, 597; *20–21,* 398; *21–22,* 503; *22–23,* 464; *23–24,* 329; *24–25,* 509, 593; *27–28,* 440, 493; *31–32,* 419

Galton, Ray *68–69,* 389

Galvin, W. Randolph *70–71*

Gandera, Felix *24–25,* 594; *26–27,* 504

Gandillot, Leon *94–99,* 237

Ganne, M. Louis *09–19,* 424

Gannon, Kim *51–52,* 277; *61–62,* 333

Gans, Sharon *69–70,* 370

Ganthony, Richard *99–09,* 397

Ganthony, Robert *94–99,* 237

Gantillon, Simon *27–28,* 514; *53–54,* 356

Gantt, Cora Dick *20–21,* 385

Ganzert, Albert *36–37,* 500

Garcia-Lorca (see Federico Garcia Lorca)

Gardel, Senor *27–28,* 468

Garden, Louis *42–43,* 444

Gardener, Helen H. *94–99,* 251

Gardenier, Edward *99–09,* 415, 435, 568

Gardiner, Becky *29–30,* 472

Gardner, Dorothy *47–48,* 365

Gardner, Edward F. *33–34,* 493

Gardner, Herb *61–62,* 296; *68–69,* 396

Gardner, John *55–56,* 371

Gardner, Lewis *63–64,* 369

Garey, James R. *94–99,* 191

Gari, Janet *69–70,* 361

Garinei, Pietro *63–64,* 323

Garisto, Louis A. *45–46,* 459

Garland, Patrick *67–68,* 357

Garlock, Tommy *60–61,* 292

Garnett, Constance *28–29,* 396; *29–30,* 393, 402; *32–33,* 474; *45–46,* 443; *62–63,* 338; *70–71*

Garnett, David *39–40,* 471

Garren, Joseph J. *24–25,* 434

Garrett, Charlie *44–45,* 395

Garrett, Oliver H.P. *38–39,* 423; *44–45,* 395

Garrick, David *94–99,* 224; *27–28,* 554; *54–55,* 52

Garrick, Thomas *94–99,* 86

Garringer, Nelson *63–64,* 371, 372; *65–66,* 422; *67–68,* 402

Garrison, Dan *38–39,* 488

Garson, Barbara *66–67,* 414

Garson, Henry *52–53,* 257

Garson, Toby *69–70,* 361

Garth, Caswell *34–35,* 377

Gartlan, George H. *99–09,* 530

Gartner, Mr. *56–57,* 333

Garvarentz, George *62–63,* 294; *64–65,* 331; *69–70,* 314

Garvey, Joseph *65–66,* 399

Garvey, Marcus *63–64,* 351

Gary, Romain *61–62,* 274

Gascoigne, Bamber *67–68,* 381

Gaskill, Clarence *25–26,* 420; *29–30,* 377

Gassman, Remi *47–48,* 421

Gassner, John *38–39,* 455

Gastineau, Mons. *99–09,* 436

Gaston, M. *99–09,* 540

Gaston, William *26–27,* 465

Gates, Eleanor *09–19,* 492, 517

Gattie, A.W. *94–99,* 148

Gatts, George M. *42–43*, 463

Gauba, Mr. *47–48*, 414

Gaumont, Irving *38–39*, 409

Gaunt, Percy *94–99*, 135

Gauthier, Guy *70–71*

Gautier, Mr. *56–57*, 333

Gautier, Judith *94–99*, 118; *09–19*, 480

Gavault, Paul *99–09*, 428, 443, 543, 578; *09–19*, 424, 479; *22–23*, 564

Gay French Author (anon. author) *09–19*, 589 (and 605)

Gay, John *20–21*, 416; *25–26*, 468; *27–28*, 533; *32–33*, 484; *34–35*, 483 *46–47*, 451; *56–57*, 360; *64–65*, 362; *66–67*, 366

Gaylor, Charles *94–99*, 127

Gaynor, Charles *48–49*, 400; *60–61*, 317; *69–70*, 373

Gaze, Heino *64–66*, 331

Gazzo, Michael V. *55–56*, 360; *58–59*, 308; *69–70*, 374

Gearon, John *34–35*, 461

Geary, Joyce *55–56*, 335, 336, 337

Gebest, Charles J. *09–19*, 457, 526

Gebirtig, Mordecai *66–67*, 367

Geddes, Ve(i)rgil *28–29*, 476; *36–37*, 492

Geer, Shippen *61–62*, 308

Geer, Will *65–66*, 436

Gehrecke, Frank *60–61*, 42; *63–64*, 343

Geiger, Milton *58–59*, 305

Geiss, Tony *61–62*, 285; *64–65*, 358; *65–66*, 422; *66–67*, 404; *67–68*, 378

Gelb, Phillip S. *63–64*, 350

Gelbart, Larry *60–61*, 318; *61–62*, 297

Gelber, Jack *59–60*, 350; *61–62*, 305, 315; *62–63*, 314; *64–65*, 360; *68–69*, 377

Gelber, Stanley Jay *67–68*, 397

Geld, Gary *69–70*, 318

Gélinas, Gratien (see Fridolin)

Geller, Bruce *56–57*, 371; *61–62*, 312; *66–67*, 422

Gellhorn, Martha *46–47*, 453

Gendron, Pierre *22–23*, 578; *26–27*, 381

Genee, Richard *53–54*, 355

Genet, Jean *58–59*, 51; *59–60*, 355; *60–61*, 361; *61–62*, 323; *63–64*, 351

Genovese, Gen *52–53*, 259

Gens, Oskar *43–44*, 488

Gensler, Lewis E. *22–23*, 473; *24–25*, 447; *25–26*, 438; *26–27*, 376; *28–29*, 392; *30–31*, 493; *32–33*, 383

Gentile, Robert *63–64*, 342

Genung, Charles Harvey *99–09*, 534

George III (King) *62–63*, 295

George, Charles *21–22*, 545; *37–38*, 399

George, David Lloyd *64–65*, 303

George, George S. *38–39*, 477

George, Grace *21–22*, 500; *22–23*, 476; *24–25*, 533; *32–33*, 381, 404; *36–37*, 431

Georgie, Leyla *32–33*, 494; *38–39*, 457

Gerald, John *41–42*, 461

Geraldy, Paul *21–22*, 500; *22–23*, 476; *24–25*, 533; *36–37*, 499

Gerard, Philippe *64–65*, 294

Gerard, Rosemonde *09–19*, 491

Gerbidon, Mons. *21–22*, 513, 535

Gerhard, Roberto *46–47*, 491

German, Edward *99–09*, 414, 435, 550

German soldiers (anon. authors) *65–66*, 383

Gernet, Nina *63–64*, 305

Gerould, Daniel C. *69–70*, 371, 372

Gerry, Alexander *29–30*, 525

Gershe, Leonard *49–50*, 367; *58–59*, 334; *69–70*, 301

Gershenson, M. *70–71*

Gershwin, Arthur *44–45*, 409

Gershwin, George *09–19*, 657; *19–20*, 407, 456; *20–21*, 388, 453; *21–22*, 388; *22–33*, 443, 497; *23–24*, 293, 390; *24–25*, 431, 497,

574; *25–26*, 525, 526; *26–27*, 363, 420; *27–28*, 457, 486, 488; *29–30*, 378, 479; *30–31*, 430; *31–32*, 451, 475; *32–33*, 452, 496; *33–34*, 445; *35–36*, 416; *37–38*, 369; *40–41*, 427; *41–42*, 433; *43–44*, 412, 438; *51–52*, 322; *52–53*, 293; *57–58*, 328, 329; *59–60*, 48; *60–61*, 338; *62–63*, 294; *63–64*, 336; *64–65*, 332; *68–69*, 447, 455; *70–71*

Gershwin, Ira *24–25*, 497, 574; *25–26*, 525; *26–27*, 363, 420; *27–28*, 457, 486, 488; *28–29*, 411; *29–30*, 378, 479, 548; *30–31*, 430; *31–32*, 379, 451; *32–33*, 452, 496; *33–34*, 445; *34–35*, 362; *35–36*, 416; *36–37*, 405; *37–38*, 369; *40–41*, 412; *41–42*, 392, 433; *42–43*, 465; *43–44*, 412, 438; *44–45*, 424; *46–47*, 434; *51–52*, 322; *52–53*, 293; *59–60*, 48; *60–61*, 338; *63–64*, 336, 342; *66–67*, 414; *68–69*, 447, 455; *69–70*, 335; *70–71*

Gerstad, John *49–50*, 384

Gerstenberg, Alice *09–19*, 548, 560; *22–23*, 574; *43–44*, 421

Gerstenberger, Emil *26–27*, 456

Gesner, Clark *63–64*, 355; *64–65*, 343; *65–66*, 422; *66–67*, 415; *67–68*, 376, 377

Gethers, Steven *61–62*, 263

Geto, Alfred D. *37–38*, 466; *39–40*, 446; *41–42*, 438; *42–43*, 478; *43–44*, 404

Geyer, Siegfried *09–19*, 548; *29–30*, 408; *38–39*, 406; *69–70*, 377

Ghelderode (Michel de Ghelderode) *60–61*, 44; *61–62*, 330; *63–64*, 352; *67–68*, 353, 402; *68–69*, 376

Ghersi, P.B. *09–19*, 463

Giacometti, Paolo *99–09*, 536; *36–37*, 500

Giacosa, Giuseppe *94–99*, 156, 220; *43–44*, 438; *44–45*, 378; *45–46*, 387, 388

Gibbons, Arthur *21–22*, 410

Gibbons, Orlando *62–63*, 295

Gibbs, Anthony *38–39*, 486

Gibbs, (Sir) Philip *64–65*, 303

Gibbs, Wolcott *50–51*, 317

Gibney, Sheridan *30–31*, 511; *44–45*, 419

Gibson, Charles Dana *99–09*, 484

Gibson, Preston *09–19*, 415, 434

Gibson, William *57–58*, 309; *59–60*, 297, 352; *64–65*, 307; *68–69*, 391

Gide, André *34–35*, 460; *52–53*, 269, 273; *53–54*, 339; *58–59*, 52; *63–64*, 351; *64–65*, 363

Gideon, Melville *27–28*, 500

Gielgud, John *46–47*, 481; *65–66*, 410

Giglio, Clement(e) *26–27*, 529; *35–36*, 511; *37–38*, 437, 470

Gignoux, Regis *27–28*, 501

Gilbert & Sullivan (see also W.S. Gilbert and Arthur Sullivan) *94–99*, 174; *99–09*, 413; *09–19*, 419, 445, 471, 472, 500, 501, 502, 525, 551, 639; *24–25*, 515, 569, 573; *25–26*, 581, 585; *26–27*, 436, 530; *27–28*, 406, 452, 458; *28–29*, 352; *30–31*, 522, 527, 531, 535; *31–32*, 377, 378, 379, 380, 381, 461; *32–33*, 485; *33–34*, 425, 426, 512, 514, 515, 516, 520; *34–35*, 364; *35–36*, 398, 496, 497, 498; *36–37*, 398; *37–38*, 460; *38–39*, 419, 446, 466, 472, 480; *39–40*, 469, 470; *40–41*, 381, 430; *41–42*, 430, 458; *43–44*, 455, 488; *44–45*, 434; *45–46*, 391, 457; *46–47*, 408, 494; *47–48*, 372, 423, 424; *49–50*, 356, 383; *50–51*, 345, 347, 350, 351, 353, 373, 374; *51–52*, 331, 332; *52–53*, 262; *55–56*, 344; *56–57*, 58; *59–60*, 48; *60–61*, 291; *61–62*, 304, 332; *62–63*, 286, 339; *63–64*, 328, 367; *64–65*, 313, 359; *65–66*, 419; *66–67*, 367, 399; *67–68*, 373, 388; *68–69*, 390; *70–71*

Gilbert, Anthony *46–47*, 441

Gilbert, Benjamin Thorne *09–19*, 577

Gilbert, Billy *52–53*, 259

Gilbert, Craig P. *47–48*, 344

Gilbert, Edwin *35–36*, 507; *36–37*, 405

Gilbert, Jean *09–19*, 462, 519, 552; *22–23*, 468; *26–27*, 406; *31–32*, 487

Gilbert, John *29–30*, 396

Gilbert, John D. *94–99*, 118

Gilbert, Robert *43–44*, 405

Gilbert, Stuart *46–47*, 497

Gilbert, (Sir) William S. (see also Gilbert & Sullivan) *94–99*, 147, 159, 199, 214; *09–19*, 410; *25–26*, 418; *46–47*, 484; *52–53*, 308

Gilbert, Willie *61–62*, 261; *62–63*, 306; *64–65*, 329; *65–66*, 407

Gilchrist, J.N. *32–33*, 486

Gilder, Jeannette L. *99–09*, 366

Giler, Berne *45–46*, 403

Gill, Brendan *57–58*, 320

Gill, Frank Jr. *44–45*, 366

Gill, William F. *94–99*, 110, 112, 128, 202, 217, 260

Gillespie, Ruth C. *61–62*, 329

Gillette, Don Carle *36–37*, 442

Gillette, William *94–99*, 107, 111, 178–9, 250; *99–09*, 354, 522; *09–19*, 428, 432, 562; *19–20*, 380; *21–22*, 466; *27–28*, 513; *29–30*, 446; *41–42*, 453, 63–64, 356

Gillpatrick, Wallace *99–09*, 440; *09–19*, 520

Gilmore, Barney *94–99*, 181

Gilmore, Edward *49–50*, 384

Gilmore, William J. *94–99*, 143

Gilner, Elias *48–49*, 429

Gilroy, Frank D. *61–62*, 318; *63–64*, 339; *66–67*, 385; *67–68*, 378

Gilroy, John *99–09*, 434

Gimbel, Norman *58–59*, 314; *60–61*, 318

Giminez, Senor *68–69*, 416

Gimpel, Rosemary *70–71*

Ginisty, Paul *94–99*, 92

Ginnes, Abram S. *58–59*, 293; *61–62*, 260

Ginsburg, Mirra *65–66*, 435

Ginsbury, Norman *41–42*, 402; *56–57*, 370; *59–60*, 313

Ginty, Elizabeth B. *38–39*, 405

Giordano, Umberto *46–47*, 412

Giorloff, Ruth *26–27*, 523; *32–33*, 436

Giovanni, Paul *67–68*, 413

Giovannini, Sandra *63–64*, 323

Girard, Harry *99–09*, 541

Giraud, Hubert *64–65*, 332

Giraudin, Mons. *94–99*, 150, 247; *99–09*, 354, 520

Giraudoux, Jean *30–31*, 436; *37–38*, 384; *48–49*, 403; *49–50*, 368; *50–51*, 308; *51–52*, 332; *53–54*, 342; *55–56*, 349; *56–57*, 353; *58–59*, 50; *59–60*, 334; *62–63*, 325; *64–65*, 348; *67–68*, 348, 350, 413; *68–69*, 405; *69–70*, 361

Giudici, Ann *62–63*, 334

Giunta, Aldo *68–69*, 453

Givens, Charles G. *46–47*, 424

Glaspell, Susan *09–19*, 579, 612, 628; *21–22*, 461, 540; *26–27*, 490; *27–28*, 550; *30–31*, 464; *32–33*, 486

Glass, Montague *09–19*, 503, 563, 585, 603, 634; *19–20*, 374; *21–22*, 542; *26–27*, 371; *32–33*, 406; *34–35*, 468

Glass, Philip *70–71*

Glasser, Stanley *65–66*, 402, 403

Glassman, Stephen *68–69*, 411

Glassner, Leonard *64–65*, 360

Glazer, Benjamin F. *09–19*, 579, 589, 623; *20–21*, 404; *21–22*, 440, 509; *22–23*, 498; *32–33*, 409; *39–40*, 408, 442, 448; *44–45*, 428; *54–55*, 359

Glazounov (Glazunoff), Alexander *42–43*, 484; *44–45*, 437; *45–46*, 454

Gleason, James *24–25*, 517, 558; *27–28*, 414, 506

Glenny, Peter *26–27,* 451; *27–28,*
    395
Glenville, Peter *56–57,* 366
Glick, Carl *31–32,* 437; *35–36,* 479
Glick, Harold *62–63,* 290
Glickman, Will *48–49,* 400, 422;
    49–50, 367; *54–55,* 394; *55–56,*
    380; *57–58,* 311; *63–64,* 368
Gliere, Reinhold *25–26,* 514, 515;
    45–46, 452, 453
Glinka, Mikhail Ivanovich *45–46,*
    452
Glitter, Jimmy *62–63,* 312
Glover, J.M. *99–09,* 398, 446,
    473
Glover, Leonard *94–99,* 132
Gluck (see von Gluck)
Gluckman, Leon *65–66,* 401
Godard, Mr. *34–35,* 459
Goddard, Charles W. *09–19,* 496,
    515, 554, 561; *20–21,* 409
Godfernaux, Andre *99–09,* 560
Godfrey, G.W. *94–99,* 115; *99–09,*
    458
Godfrey, John *09–19,* 614–5
Goethe (Johann Wolfgang von
    Goethe) *94–99,* 119, 150; *28–29,*
    389; *39–40,* 468; *45–46,* 390;
    48–49, 426; *49–50,* 383; *60–61,*
    322; *65–66,* 406; *69–70,* 347
Goetz, Mr. *22–23,* 443
Goetz, Augustus *44–45,* 416; *47–48,*
    353; *49–50,* 372; *53–54,* 339;
    56–57, 351; *63–64,* 351
Goetz, Curt *24–25,* 522; *44–45,* 419
Goetz, E. Ray *99–09,* 512, 540;
    09–19, 409, 419, 438, 453, 465,
    473, 486, 487, 502, 513, 553,
    575–6, 601; *23–24,* 293; *28–29,*
    390, 435; *30–31,* 465
Goetz, Ruth Goodman *44–45,* 416;
    47–48, 353; *49–50,* 372; *53–54,*
    339; *56–57,* 351; *63–64,* 351
Goetzl, Anselm *09–19,* 593, 652;
    19–20, 391; *20–21,* 426
Goff, Ivan *46–47,* 480
Goff, Madison *46–47,* 494

Gogol, Nikolai *22–23,* 563; *30–31,*
    469; *34–35,* 452, 453; *42–43,* 487;
    60–61, 291; *63–64,* 363; *64–65,*
    323; *65–66,* 423; *66–67,* 416
Gohei, Namiki *67–68,* 411
Goland, Arnold *67–68,* 365
Gold, Ernest *67–68,* 372
Gold, Michael *27–28,* 511; *29–30,*
    395; *35–36,* 477
Goldbaum, Peter *47–48,* 379
Goldberg, Dan *36–37,* 464; *37–38,*
    444
Goldberg, Eugene L. *47–48,* 428
Goldberg, Herman *62–63,* 315
Goldberg, Isaac *21–22,* 478
Goldberg, Rube *29–30,* 382
Golden, Alfred L. *36–37,* 412;
    43–44, 427; *46–47,* 477; *51–52,*
    309
Golden, Echard *94–99,* 160
Golden, Eleanor *25–26,* 594; *36–37,*
    404
Golden, Ernie *29–30,* 550
Golden, Harry *59–60,* 304
Golden, I.J. *30–31,* 515; *33–34,* 478
Golden, John *94–99,* 181; *28–29,*
    364; *31–32,* 383; *33–34,* 450
Golden, John L. *99–09,* 382, 548,
    582; *09–19,* 462, 560, 580, 585,
    604, 633
Golden, Ray *40–41,* 403; *42–43,*
    471; *49–50,* 367; *55–56,* 338
Golden, Richard *94–99,* 112
Goldenberg, William *60–61,* 299;
    63–64, 311, 333; *65–66,* 424;
    67–68, 347
Goldfaden, Abraham *46–47,* 497
Goldfein, Abraham L. *49–50,* 383
Golding, Samuel Ruskin (see also
    Kent Wiley) *21–22,* 538; *25–26,*
    516; *26–27,* 362, 452; *27–28,* 451,
    532; *30–31,* 402, 442; *37–38,* 371
Golding, William *69–70,* 372
Goldknopf, Abraham *09–19,* 487;
    24–25, 557
Goldman, Harold *29–30,* 548;
    35–36, 481

Goldman, James *61–62*, 258, 282; *65–66*, 400; *70–71*

Goldman, Richard Franko *63–64*, 359

Goldman, Robert *58–59*, 331

Goldman, William *61–62*, 258, 282

Goldoni, Carlo *94–99*, 166; *99–09*, 536; *23–24*, 356; *26–27*, 432; *27–28*, 455; *41–42*, 461; *49–50*, 380; *59–60*, 43, 321; *64–65*, 362; *67–68*, 379

Goldschmidt, Lena *35–36*, 494

Goldsmith, Bea *41–42*, 438

Goldsmith, Clifford *37–38*, 438

Goldsmith, Lee *59–60*, 336; *60–61*, 292

Goldsmith, Milton *09–19*, 645

Goldsmith, (Dr.) Oliver *94–99*, 167; *99–09*, 474, 489; *09–19*, 410, 484; *23–24*, 443; *27–28*, 554; *49–50*, 365; *60–61*, 304; *61–62*, 310; *70–71*

Goldstein, William *70–71*

Goldstone, Jean Stock *57–58*, 290

Goldsworthy, John *23–24*, 424

Gombrowicz, Witold *70–71*

Gomes, Alfredo Dias *70–71*

Gondinet, Mons. *99–09*, 583

Gondra, Arthur *44–45*, 368

Gonzalez, Gloria *70–71*

Gonzalez, Raoul *62–63*, 312

Goodall, William Richard *94–99*, 128

Goode, Herbert *31–32*, 379

Goode, Reginald *24–25*, 475; *25–26*, 507

Goodhart, William *65–66*, 374

Goodhue, Willis Maxwell *25–26*, 421, 527; *26–27*, 527; *30–31*, 521

Goodman, Alfred *19–20*, 388; *20–21*, 356, 453; *22–23*, 457, 468, 526, 576; *23–24*, 358; *24–25*, 551; *25–26*, 420, 427

Goodman, Arthur *30–31*, 525; *31–32*, 473; *35–36*, 473; *37–38*, 462; *47–48*, 405, 412; *63–64*, 356

Goodman, Benny *39–40*, 418

Goodman, David Z. *54–55*, 56

Goodman, Eckert *37–38*, 382

Goodman, Edward *09–19*, 509, 547, 579

Goodman, Jules Eckert *99–09*, 571; *09–19*, 423, 481, 543, 546, 556, 566, 580, 585, 603, 634; *19–20*, 374, 417; *21–22*, 505, 542; *23–24*, 319; *24–25*, 483; *26–27*, 371; *31–32*, 449; *37–38*, 382, 460

Goodman, Kenneth *09–19*, 579

Goodman, Kenneth Sawyer *23–24*, 433

Goodman, Lee *49–50*, 368

Goodman, Paul *51–52*, 334; *59–60*, 41; *65–66*, 430

Goodman, Randolph *47–48*, 395

Goodman, Ruth (see Ruth Goodman Goetz)

Goodrich, Arthur *09–19*, 617; *22–23*, 445; *25–26*, 496; *26–27*, 413; *28–29*, 421; *29–30*, 437, 468, 499; *32–33*, 422; *34–35*, 470

Goodrich, Frances *30–31*, 406; *31–32*, 409, 517; *42–43*, 447; *49–50*, 384; *55–56*, 350

Goodwin, J. Cheever *94–99*, 83, 87, 129, 135, 139, 170, 177, 178, 195, 225, 259; *99–09*, 370, 371, 398, 414–5, 427, 459

Goodwin, Joe *64–65*, 331

Gordin, Jacob *99–09*, 516; *23–24*, 436; *35–36*, 511; *67–68*, 345

Gordon & Revel (see Mack Gordon & Harry Revel)

Gordon, Alex *67–68*, 365

Gordon, Arthur *65–66*, 432

Gordon, Charles K. *31–32*, 454

Gordon, Dorothy *36–37*, 498

Gordon, Irving *42–43*, 420

Gordon, Kilbourn *19–20*, 419; *23–24*, 354; *25–26*, 578; *27–28*, 453

Gordon, Kurtz *37–38*, 463

Gordon, Leon *09–19*, 635; *20–21*, 428; *21–22*, 404; *23–24*, 347, 425;

24–25, 526; *25–26, 582; 33–34,*
439

Gordon, Mack *31–32,* 377, 487;
32–33, 382, 472

Gordon, Marie *61–62,* 285

Gordon, Marvin *68–69,* 422

Gordon, Richard H. Jr. *38–39,* 491

Gordon, Ruth *43–44,* 446; *46–47,*
445; *48–49,* 389; *65–66,* 372

Gordone, Charles *68–69,* 434, 457;
69–70, 310, 355

Gordon-Lennox, Cosmo (see Cosmo
Gordon Lennox)

Gore-Brown, R.F. *31–32,* 420

Gorelik, Mordecai *62–63,* 325

Gorky (Gorki), Maxim *99–09,* 560;
19–20, 404; *22–23,* 517; *23–24,*
356; *29–30,* 476; *34–35,* 472;
35–36, 436; *38–39,* 487; *42–43,*
490; *46–47,* 498; *47–48,* 395;
56–57, 55; *63–64,* 360; *69–70,*
373

Gorney, Jay *24–25,* 440; *25–26,* 420;
26–27, 531–2; *29–30,* 378; *30–31,*
399; *31–32,* 379; *32–33,* 395;
40–41, 403; *48–49,* 380; *49–50,*
357

Goss, (Rev.) Charles Frederic *99–09,*
506

Gosse, Edmund *94–99,* 227; *99–09,*
360

Gostony, Adam *32–33,* 379

Gotovac, Jacov *44–45,* 437

Gottesfeld, Chuno *38–39,* 494;
43–44, 411

Gottler, Archie *20–21,* 388

Gottlieb, Alex *39–40,* 447; *55–56,*
386; *61–62,* 304

Gottschalk, Ferdinand *99–09,* 522

Gottwald, Fritz *27–28,* 409

Gould, Bruce *28–29,* 485

Gould, E.H. *09–19,* 539

Gould, Frank *39–40,* 450; *46–47,*
474

Gould, Heywood *70–71*

Gould, Hull *28–29,* 446

Gould, Jack *37–38,* 469

Gould, Morton *45–46,* 415; *49–50,*
372; *58–59,* 315

Goulding, Edmund *24–25,* 432;
45–46, 384

Goulding, Ray *70–71*

Gounod, Charles *43–44,* 473; *45–46,*
390; *46–47,* 409; *47–48,* 420

Gow, James *42–43,* 472; *45–46,* 386;
50–51, 318

Gow, Ronald *33–34,* 483; *35–36,*
488

Gowers, Patrick *62–63,* 323

Go-Won-Go-Mohawk *94–99,* 225

Gowraud, Jackson *99–09,* 423

Goyen, William *63–64,* 369

Gozzi, Carlo *37–38,* 469

Grace, Michael *53–54,* 326

Grady, James *63–64,* 364

Grael, Barry Alan *54–55,* 56; *62–63,*
316; *63–64,* 349

Graeme, David *63–64,* 371

Graeve, Oscar *09–19,* 647

Graham, Benjamin *34–35,* 432

Graham, Carroll & Garrett *33–34,*
497

Graham, Hedley Gordon *38–39,* 483

Graham, (Capt.) Harry *09–19,* 568,
636–7; *22–23,* 468; *24–25,* 551;
26–27, 406; *46–47,* 418

Graham, Irvin *35–36,* 507; *37–38,*
429; *40–41,* 405, 411; *56–57,* 314

Graham, James *44–45,* 442

Graham, John McD. *37–38,* 469

Graham, Joseph H. *27–28,* 510

Graham, Ranald *70–71*

Graham, Ronny (*51–52,* 325
omitted); *56–57,* 314; *57–58,* 284;
61–62, 260, 284, 299; *62–63,* 324;
64–65, 358; *67–68,* 376, 377, 378

Graham-Lujan, James *70–71*

Grainger, Porter *24–25,* 601; *30–31,*
403

Granados, Enrique *39–40,* 471;
43–44, 485; *47–48,* 344

Grand, Murray (*51–52,* 325
omitted); *56–57,* 314; *61–62,* 308;
63–64, 371, 372; *67–68,* 377

Grandin, Elmer *94–99*, 87, 218
Grange, Mr. *99–09*, 536
Granichstaedten, Bruno *09–19*, 470
Granick, Harry *61–62*, 329
Grannis, Anita *52–53*, 306
Grant, Bert *09–19*, 576; *20–21*, 356
Grant, James Edward *41–42*, 441
Grant, Maxwell *56–57*, 357; *60–61*, 292
Grant, Micki *70–71*
Grant, Neil *30–31*, 466
Grant, Richard *99–09*, 461
Grant, Robert *99–09*, 386
Granville-Barker, Harley *99–09*, 367; *09–19*, 512, 595, 625; *20–21*, 414; *21–22*, 450; *25–26*, 596; *27–28*, 516; *28–29*, 436, 455; *29–30*, 409, 483; *30–31*, 480; *35–36*, 447, 448
Granville-Barker, Helen *25–26*, 596; *28–29*, 436, 455; *29–30*, 409, 483; *35–36*, 448
Grass, Günter *65–66*, 434; *66–67*, 411
Grattan, Harry *09–19*, 601
Grattan, Lawrence *26–27*, 512
Graves, Clotilde *99–09*, 394, 526
Graves, Rupert *36–37*, 460; *38–39*, 454
Gray, David *99–09*, 509; *24–25*, 435; *32–33*, 476
Gray, Nicholas Stuart *64–65*, 362
Gray, Roger *26–27*, 364; *31–32*, 514
Gray, Thomas J. *09–19*, 552, 558; *20–21*, 374
Gray, Timothy *63–64*, 333
Gray, Wallace *64–65*, 350
Grayhon, Joseph *61–62*, 305
Grayson, Helen *27–28*, 534
Gredy, Jean-Pierre *65–66*, 390; *68–69*, 400; *70–71*
Greeley, Dana Watterson *27–28*, 443
Greely, Augusta *29–30*, 525
Green, Adolph (see also The Revuers) *44–45*, 406; *45–46*, 415; *51–52*, 278; *52–53*, 290; *54–55*, 369; *56–57*, 339; *57–58*, 323, 327; *58–59*, 54, 315, 324; *60–61*, 315; *61–62*, 276; *62–63*, 297; *63–64*, 339; *65–66*, 419, 436; *66–67*, 387, 391; *69–70*, 323
Green, Anna Katherine *43–44*, 489
Green, Bernard *57–58*, 322
Green, Bud *33–34*, 421
Green, Carolyn *55–56*, 363
Green, Eddie *31–32*, 502
Green, Ellen *61–62*, 317
Green, Eric Mawby *43–44*, 463
Green, Gerald *64–65*, 311
Green, Howard J. *40–41*, 392
Green, Isaac Jr. *47–48*, 339
Green, Janet *53–54*, 313
Green, John(ny) W. *31–32*, 422; *33–34*, 430; *42–43*, 436
Green, Kenneth *60–61*, 39
Green, Mawby *62–63*, 311
Green, Paul *24–25*, 586; *26–27*, 453, 514, 524; *27–28*, 398; *28–29*, 503; *31–32*, 398; *34–35*, 384; *35–36*, 510; *36–37*, 432, 496; *37–38*, 459; *40–41*, 421, 431; *42–43*, 439; *49–50*, 385; *50–51*, 344; *54–55*, 53; *63–64*, 342; *69–70*, 335; *70–71*
Green, Phil *53–54*, 329; *56–57*, 316; *60–61*, 292
Green, Schuyler *09–19*, 567
Green, Sylvan *35–36*, 429
Greenbank, Harry *94–99*, 94, 158, 176, 201, 226, 233; *99–09*, 357, 373; *09–19*, 498; *31–32*, 403
Greenbank, Percy *99–09*, 395, 403, 417, 471, 499, 519–520, 522, 524, 538; *09–19*, 404, 455
Greenbaum, Fritz (see Fritz Grunbaum)
Greenburg, Dan *66–67*, 423; *67–68*, 357; *68–69*, 453; *69–70*, 335
Greenburg, Edwin *61–62*, 326
Greendale, Alexander *37–38*, 465; *41–42*, 415
Greene, Alan *62–63*, 312
Greene, Bertram *62–63*, 337
Greene, Brad *37–38*, 413

Greene, Clay M. *94–99*, 85, 97, 132, 174, 181, 233, 255; *99–09*, 363, 420, 430, 433, 469

Greene, G.A. *94–99*, 156

Greene, Graham *54–55*, 374; *56–57*, 352; *58–59*, 311; *61–62*, 268; *62–63*, 320, 339; *67–68*, 406

Greene, H.C. *28–29*, 391

Greene, Patterson *41–42*, 425

Greene, Robert *63–64*, 314

Greene, Will *62–63*, 300

Greenfeld, Josh *61–62*, 311

Greensfelder, Elmer *33–34*, 493; *37–38*, 462

Greenwood, Walter *35–36*, 488

Greer, Edward *69–70*, 314

Greer, Jesse *27–28*, 387, 460; *33–34*, 421

Gregg, Jess *64–65*, 346

Gregg, Norma *27–28*, 392

Gregory, Lady *99–09*, 555; *09–19*, 458, 459, 494, 591; *28–29*, 483; *32–33*, 407; *36–37*, 497; *37–38*, 463

Gregory, Frank J. *09–19*, 631; *34–35*, 437

Gregg, Bud *49–50*, 368

Greggory (Gregory), David *37–38*, 385; *38–39*, 470, 486; *39–30*, 394, 437; *40–41*, 389; *41–42*, 459

Grene, David *63–64*, 368

Grenfell, Joyce *55–56*, 352; *57–58*, 328

Grenzeback, Joe *48–49*, 427

Gresac, Fred (see Fred De Gresac)

Gressieker, Hermann *58–59*, 51; *62–63*, 332, 339

Greth, Roma *70–71*

Grever, Marie *41–42*, 403

Greville, Charles Cavendish Fulke *62–63*, 295

Grew, William A. *24–25*, 505; *25–26*, 420, 487; *26–27*, 368; *27–28*, 389; *28–29*, 468, 511; *29–30*, 381; *30–31*, 489

Grey, Clifford *20–21*, 413; *21–22*, 526; *22–23*, 522; *23–24*, 413; *24–25*, 432, 474; *25–26*, 420, 424, 427, 433, 502, 527, 600, 604; *26–27*, 406, 516–7; *27–28*, 500, 501, 505, 526; *28–29*, 386, 392; *30–31*, 455; *47–48*, 403

Grey, Frank H. *22–23*, 434; *25–26*, 544; *27–28*, 465

Gribble, George Dunning *25–26*, 561

Gribble, Harry Wagstaff(e) *20–21*, 395, *21–22*, 392; *23–24*, 358; *24–25*, 474; *25–26*, 420, 428; *27–28*, 398, 534; *28–29*, 408; *29–30*, 512; *30–31*, 476, 527; *31–32*, 391, 481; *33–34*, 506; *43–44*, 489; *51–52*, 333

Grieg, Edvard *22–23*, 527; *44–45*, 369

Griffes, Charles T. *26–27*, 504

Griffith, Hubert *36–37*, 475

Griffiths, Fred *41–42*, 460

Griggs, Johnny *69–70*, 372

Grimm, Jakob & Wilhelm *94–99*, 146; *99–09*, 499; *09–19*, 483; *38–39*, 490; *70–71*

Griscom, Lloyd *27–28*, 390

Grismaijer, Michael *30–31*, 441

Grismer, Joseph R. *94–99*, 209, 223, 233, 252, 259; *99–09*, 448

Grissmer, John *70–71*

Griswold, Grace *23–24*, 412

Grodin, Charles *65–66*, 432

Grogan, Walter E. *99–09*, 508

Gronemann, Sammy *67–68*, 372

Groob, Michael *70–71*

Gropper, Milton Herbert *23–24*, 384, 401; *24–25*, 510; *26–27*, 401; *27–28*, 494; *28–29*, 375; *29–30*, 463; *31–32*, 510; *33–34*, 494; *44–45*, 368

Grosbard, Ulu *66–67*, 359

Grosman, Bernard *19–20*, 388

Gross, Ben S. *26–27*, 461

Gross, Charles *60–61*, 312; *62–63*, 326; *69–70*, 330

Gross, Laurence *31–32*, 466; *32–33*, 415

Gross, Milt *40–41,* 403
Gross, Ronald *67–68,* 410
Gross, Stephen *34–35,* 477; *35–36,*
  442
Grossman, Lawrence (Larry) *62–63,*
  316; *65–66,* 383; *69–70,* 320
Grossman, Samuel S. *20–21,* 405
Grossman, Shirley *63–64,* 346
Grossmith, George Jr. *99–09,* 522,
  567, 577; *09–19,* 399, 460
Grossmith, Weedon *99–09,* 418
Grotowski, Jerzy *69–70,* 343
Grove, F.C. *94–99,* 109, 136; *19–20,*
  452
Grudeff, Marian *64–65,* 327
Gruen, John *67–68,* 412; *68–69,* 456
Gruenberg, Louis *19–20,* 357;
  31–32, 447; *34–35,* 460
Grunbaum, Fritz *09–19,* 399, 519;
  29–30, 484
Grundy, Sydney *94–99,* 103, 114,
  120, 159, 188, 215, 255; *99–09,*
  359, 385, 397, 403, 450, 557;
  09–19, 629; *37–38,* 465
Grunwald (Gruenwald), Alfred
  09–19, 521, 579; *20–21,* 449;
  22–23, 467; *26–27,* 380, 517;
  27–28, 538; *30–31,* 401; *45–46,*
  381
Gryparis, J. *52–53,* 269; *61–62,* 255;
  64–65, 298
Guare, John *67–68,* 405; *68–69,*
  412; *70–71*
Guarnieri, Gianfrancesco *69–70,* 339
Guenther, Felix *46–47,* 418
Guerdon, David *62–63,* 326
Guerney, Bernard Guilbert *39–40,*
  402
Guernon, Charles *09–19,* 604
Guevara, Sr. *53–54,* 322
Guiche, Gustav *09–19,* 463
Guilbert, Warburton *33–34,* 507
Guiles, Fred Laurence *59–60,* 40
Guillema(u)nd, Marcel *09–19,* 441,
  455, 479
Guimera, Angel *99–09,* 440; *09–19,*
  520; *36–37,* 499, 500

Guirand, Edmond *99–09,* 543
Guiterman, Arthur *33–34,* 442;
  41–42, 428
Guitreau, Christian *64–65,* 316
Guitry, Sacha *09–19,* 640; *20–21,*
  414; *21–22,* 451; *22–23,* 540, 542;
  26–27, 430, 446; *38–39,* 450;
  48–49, 404
Gulesian, Mr. & Mrs. M.H. *25–26,*
  475
Gullans, Charles *65–66,* 383
Gumble, Albert *21–22,* 552
Gunn, Bill *60–61,* 39
Gunter, Archibald Clavering
  94–99, 91, 181, 234, 254; *99–09,*
  355
Gunther, John *47–48,* 401
Gurney, A.R. Jr. *68–69,* 432; *69–70,*
  334; *70–71*
Gurney, Louise L. *94–99,* 105
Guss, Jack Raphael *64–65,* 361
Guthrie, Judith *45–46,* 432
Guthrie, Thomas Anstey (see F.
  Anstey)
Guthrie, Tyrone *55–56,* 366, 370;
  57–58, 304; *60–61,* 291; *61–62,*
  304
Guthrie, William *59–60,* 40
Gutman, Arthur *21–22,* 467
Gutzkow, Karl *39–40,* 475
Gyarmathy, Michel *64–65,* 295
Gynt, Kaj *27–28,* 388
Gyp *99–09,* 483

Haack, Bruce *60–61,* 322; *62–63,*
  312
Haag, Jackson D. *09–19,* 482
Haase, John *62–63,* 283
Habe, Hans *63–64,* 349
Hacgfeld (Hachfeld), Eckar(d)t
  61–62, 308; *65–66,* 429
Hackady, Hal *55–56,* 335; *67–68,*
  378; *69–70,* 320
Hackett, Albert *30–31,* 406; *31–32,*
  409, 517; *42–43,* 447; *49–50,* 384;
  55–56, 350
Hackett, Buddy *67–68,* 341

Hackett, Walter *99–09,* 567; *09–19,* 400, 438, 520, 530, 609, 648; *21–22,* 487; *29–30,* 440; *34–35,* 390

Hacks, Peter *69–70,* 348

Hadjidakis, Manos *66–67,* 390

Hadler, Walter *70–71*

Hadley, Arthur *63–64,* 371

Hadley, Henry K. *99–09,* 423, 428; *09–19,* 638

Hadley, Roberta *39–40,* 473

Haffner, C. *53–54,* 355

Hagan, James *28–29,* 356; *32–33,* 463; *35–36,* 457; *38–39,* 494

Hagedorn, Hermann *09–19,* 414

Haggart, John *33–34,* 484

Haggin, Ben Ali *26–27,* 359

Hagler, Stan *55–56,* 336

Hague, Albert *49–50,* 368; *54–55,* 363, 394; *58–59,* 319; *59–60,* 300; *62–63,* 283; *63–64,* 334, 335, 368; *67–68,* 410; *68–69,* 400

Hahn, Reynaldo *26–27,* 430, 446

Haig (Field Marshal Earl) *64–65,* 303

Haight, George *32–33,* 443; *35–36,* 417; *40–41,* 376; *43–44,* 425; *55–56,* 386

Hailey, Oliver *62–63,* 327; *65–66,* 400; *69–70,* 347; *70–71*

Hailparn, Dorothy *37–38,* 460

Haimsohn, George *63–64,* 372; *66–67,* 35; *68–69,* 422, 441; *70–71*

Haines, Genevieve Greville *99–09,* 410, 480

Haines, H.E. *99–09,* 492, 504

Haines, Will E. *69–70,* 365

Haines, William Wister *47–48,* 354

Hair, Roy Newton *99–09,* 432

Hairston, William *63–64,* 349

Haislip, Bill *68–69,* 452

Haislip, Harvey *51–52,* 315

Hajos, Karl *24–25,* 542; *28–29,* 370

Halasz, Laszlo *42–43,* 444

Halbe, Max *09–19,* 446; *20–21,* 399

Haldane, Harry M. *59–60,* 293

Hale, Eugen *09–19,* 578

Hale, Lionel *33–34,* 526

Hale, Ruth *30–31,* 496

Halevi, Asaf *66–67,* 393; *67–68,* 339

Halévy, Ludovic *94–99,* 134, 211, 229; *99–09,* 472; *43–44,* 432; *44–45,* 382; *45–46,* 389, 394; *55–56,* 393; *63–64,* 326

Hall (see Tremayne and Hall)

Hall, Arthur D. *94–99,* 171, 217, 233

Hall, Donald *65–66,* 422

Hall, Holworthy *25–26,* 591; *27–28,* 549

Hall, Howard *99–09,* 393

Hall, John *68–69,* 394, 451

Hall, John T. *99–09,* 574

Hall, Joseph *62–63,* 295

Hall, Lyle Weaver *28–29,* 510

Hall, Norman *50–51,* 373

Hall, Owen *94–99,* 94, 158, 176; *99–09,* 357, 379, 420, 442, 451, 490, 516; *09–19,* 498, 524; *19–20,* 443; *31–32,* 403

Hall, Willis *61–62,* 327; *63–64,* 359; *64–65,* 356; *66–67,* 358

Haller, Herman *22–23,* 526

Halley, Anne *68–69,* 407

Halliday, Johnny *64–65,* 316

Halliwell, David *66–67,* 375, 419

Halm, Frederick *99–09,* 461

Halman, Doris F. *22–23,* 574

Halsey, Forrest *09–19,* 425; *19–20,* 428, 454

Halvey, Ludovic *09–19,* 469

Halward, Cyril *99–09,* 485

Hamill, Stuart *26–27,* 362

Hamilton, C. *25–26,* 588

Hamilton, Cecily *99–09,* 567; *09–19,* 461

Hamilton, Clayton *09–19,* 539

Hamilton, Cosmo *99–09,* 490, 492, 528, 548; *09–19,* 401, 481, 581, 615; *19–20,* 350, 357; *21–22,* 411, 479; *23–24,* 383; *24–25,* 492; *27–28,* 396, 473; *38–39,* 486

Hamilton, Edith *37–38,* 463; *63–64,* 354; *65–66,* 420

Hamilton, Hale *20–21*, 421
Hamilton, Harry *31–32*, 457
Hamilton, Henry *94–99*, 139, 156, 216, 253, 254; *99–09*, 463, 482, 499, 503, 532, 557; *09–19*, 397, 486, 558
Hamilton, John *46–47*, 494
Hamilton, Morris *26–27*, 368; *28–29*, 355
Hamilton, Nancy *33–34*, 507; *38–39*, 456; *39–40*, 436; *42–43*, 434; *45–46*, 431
Hamilton, Patrick *29–30*, 399; *41–42*, 419; *43–44*, 449; *47–48*, 346
Hamilton, Wallace *63–64*, 353
Hamlin, Mary *09–19*, 607
Hamlisch, Marvin *64–65*, 342, 343; *69–70*, 321
Hammer, Alvin (see The Revuers)
Hammerschlag, Peter *39–40*, 394
Hammerstein, Arthur II (see Oscar Hammerstein II)
Hammerstein, Oscar *94–99*, 178, 198, 230; *99–09*, 434
Hammerstein, Oscar II *19–20*, 411; *20–21*, 367, 406; *22–23*, 441, 473, 529; *23–24*, 374, 384, 401; *24–25*, 445; *25–26*, 452, 526; *26–27*, 408, 435, 467; *27–28*, 462, 482; *28–29*, 368, 376, 423; *29–30*, 386; *30–31*, 493; *31–32*, 387, 417, 513; *32–33*, 416; *35–36*, 446; *39–40*, 412; *41–42*, 418; *42–43*, 424, 471; *43–44*, 432, 442; *44–45*, 428; *45–46*, 393, 394, 418; *46–47*, 433; *47–48*, 359; *48–49*, 378, 409, 419; *50–51*, 360, 372; *51–52*, 285; *52–53*, 304; *53–54*, 299, 352; *54–55*, 359, 412; *55–56*, 364, 384, 393; *56–57*, 369; *57–58*, 285, 325; *58–59*, 306; *59–60*, 303, 340; *60–61*, 334, 337; *62–63*, 298, 308; *63–64*, 302; *64–65*, 296; *65–66*, 366, 368, 392; *66–67*, 352, 378, 386; *67–68*, 339, 379; *69–70*, 295, 374

Hammond, Edward *24–25*, 501
Hammond, Natalie Hays *32–33*, 458
Hampton, Christopher *66–67*, 410; *70–71*
Hampton, Max *59–60*, 293
Hamsun, Knut *23–24*, 356; *27–28*, 469
Hanaford, Edwin *09–19*, 445
Handel, Georg Friedrich *41–42*, 457; *54–55*, 386, 407
Handleman, Stanley *64–65*, 358
Handy, W.C. *53–54*, 306; *66–67*, 354
Haney, Ray *62–63*, 318
Hanighen, Mr. *64–65*, 303
Hanighen, Bernard *45–46*, 426; *46–47*, 470; *58–59*, 329
Hanjoro, Mr. *60–61*, 45
Hankin, Clifford W. *47–48*, 428
Hankin, St. John *99–09*, 516
Hanley, James *64–65*, 353; *68–69*, 437
Hanley, James F. (Jimmy) *09–19*, 571; *20–21*, 391; *21–22*, 503; *24–25*, 518; *25–26*, 431; *26–27*, 259, 383; *27–28*, 420; *29–30*, 377; *34–35*, 432
Hanley, William *62–63*, 315; *64–65*, 318; *65–66*, 370; *69–70*, 368; *70–71*
Hanlon, George *94–99*, 118
Hanlon, W.M. *94–99*, 88, 118
Hannah, Link *38–39*, 419
Hannan, Charles *99–09*, 422
Hannay, Canon (see George A. Birmingham)
Hansberry, Lorraine *58–59*, 328; *64–65*, 307; *68–69*, 442, 456; *70–71*
Hansen, Waldemar *61–62*, 267
Hapgood, Elizabeth Reynolds *39–40*, 405; *62–63*, 331
Harbach (Hauerbach), Otto A. *99–09*, 563; *09–19*, 415, 423, 443, 447, 450, 487, 516, 523, 538, 566, 577, 578, 594, 613, 618, 649, 654; *19–20*, 371, 413; *20–21*, 367, 396,

406, 444; *21–22*, 432, 494; *22–23*,
446, 529, 547; *23–24*, 381; *24–25*,
445, 512; *25–26*, 446, 452, 526,
597; *26–27*, 400, 408, 435, 467,
495; *27–28*, 462; *28–29*, 368;
30–31, 415; *31–32*, 411, 441;
33–34, 458; *36–37*, 425; *45–46*,
393; *70–71*
Harben, Will N. *09–19*, 499
Harburg, E.Y. *29–30*, 378, 548;
30–31, 399, 447; *31–32*, 379;
32–33, 383, 395, 433; *33–34*, 476;
34–35, 362; *37–38*, 397; *40–41*,
378; *44–45*, 387, 431; *46–47*, 411,
455; *50–51*, 370; *53–54*, 306;
54–55, 414; *57–58*, 297; *59–60*,
338; *60–61*, 332; *63–64*, 368;
66–67, 386, 414; *67–68*, 360;
68–69, 436
Harcourt, Cyril *09–19*, 536, 575,
583, 625, 646
Hardinge, H.C.M. *19–20*, 406
Hardt-Warden, Bruno *29–30*, 523
Hardy, Thomas *94–99*, 170, 196;
99–09, 409
Hare, David *70–71*
Hare, Montgomery *66–67*, 400
Hare, Walter B. *35–36*, 510
Hargis, Frances *27–28*, 551
Hargrave, Roy *29–30*, 389; *30–31*,
411; *35–36*, 461
Harker, L. Allen *30–31*, 428
Harkins, James W. Jr. *94–99*, 100,
103, 155–6, 158
Harlan, Otis *94–99*, 161
Harling, W. Franke *09–19*, 625;
26–27, 392
Harman, Carter *46–47*, 488
Harned, Mary *99–09*, 470
Harnick, Sheldon (*51–52*, 325
omitted); *53–54*, 328; *55–56*, 391;
57–58, 311, 320; *59–60*, 305;
60–61, 292, 301, 360; *62–63*, 277,
289, 307, 331; *63–64*, 372; *64–65*,
302, 358; *66–67*, 364; *68–69*, 455;
70–71
Harnley, Leslie *67–68*, 400

Harper, H.H. & Marguerite *40–41*,
397
Harper, Jimmy *69–70*, 365
Harper, Wally *68–69*, 412; *70–71*
Harr, George *40–41*, 432
Harrigan, Edward *94–99*, 110, 123,
175, 197, 214; *99–09*, 437
Harrill, John *67–68*, 411
Harris, Augustus *94–99*, 98, 113,
139, 156, 164
Harris, Bob *63–64*, 363
Harris, Charles K. *99–09*, 492
Harris, Clifford *09–19*, 637
Harris, Cora *09–19*, 624
Harris, Edward Peyton *42–43*, 488
Harris, Edward W. *29–30*, 531
Harris, Elmer Blaney *99–09*, 569,
580; *09–19*, 450, 482, 532, 584,
594; *27–28*, 523; *28–29*, 505;
29–30, 454; *30–31*, 400, 518, 529;
31–32, 429; *32–33*, 473; *39–40*,
430; *40–41*, 379
Harris, Frank *09–19*, 415
Harris, Hamilton *94–99*, 236
Harris, Herbert *65–66*, 428
Harris, Howard *48–49*, 379
Harris, Jeff Steve *61–62*, 310; *63–64*,
372; *64–65*, 359
Harris, John *41–42*, 446
Harris, Mark *61–62*, 279
Harris, Mildred *35–36*, 481
Harris, Richard W. *64–65*, 352
Harris, Ted *60–61*, 41; *69–70*, 339
Harris, William Jr. *09–19*, 416
Harrison & Sloane *99–09*, 540
Harrison, Anthony *67–68*, 409
Harrison, Mrs. Burton *99–09*, 400
Harrison, Duncan Bradley *94–99*,
251
Harrison, George *70–71*
Harrison, Louis *94–99*, 153, 230,
245, 258; *99–09*, 347, 360, 372
Harrity, Richard *47–48*, 396, 404
Harrity, Rory *62–63*, 317; *64–65*,
343
Harron, Donald *57–58*, 326
Hart, Anita *30–31*, 486

Hart, Bruce *62–63*, 324
Hart, Daniel *99–09*, 368
Hart, Frances Noyes *30–31*, 519
Hart, Howard *61–62*, 303, 332
Hart, Joseph *99–09*, 406, 462, 515, 537
Hart, (Capt.) Liddell *64–65*, 303
Hart, Lorenz (M.) *20–21*, 359; *24–25*, 602; *25–26*, 448, 572, 598; *26–27*, 447, 450; *27–28*, 445, 486, 546; *28–29*, 381, 478; *29–30*, 439, 497; *30–31*, 488, 502; *35–36*, 435, 499; *36–37*, 446, 479; *37–38*, 369, 385, 445; *38–39*, 429; *39–40*, 404, 453; *40–41*, 375, 404; *41–42*, 391, 455; *43–44*, 428; *51–52*, 301; *54–55*, 366; *60–61*, 343; *62–63*, 295, 311, 332; *64–65*, 331, 362; *66–67*, 410; *67–68*, 409
Hart, Moss *29–30*, 520; *30–31*, 418; *31–32*, 480; *32–33*, 457; *33–34*, 438; *34–35*, 377, 380; *35–36*, 400, 418; *36–37*, 440, 446; *37–38*, 369, 385; *38–39*, 412, 452; *39–40*, 396, 397, 402; *40–41*, 387, 412; *41–42*, 392; *42–43*, 465; *43–44*, 429; *44–45*, 381, 402; *46–47*, 444; *47–48*, 401; *48–49*, 397; *52–53*, 268; *53–54*, 359; *63–64*, 357; *65–66*, 387; *66–67*, 371, 385
Hart, Stan *65–66*, 428
Hart, Walter *37–38*, 442; *38–39*, 444
Harte, Bret *94–99*, 177; *99–09*, 531
Hartford, Huntington *57–58*, 331
Hartig, Herbert *61–62*, 286; *62–63*, 316, 324; *64–65*, 358
Hartman, Don *41–42*, 428
Hartman, Grace & Paul *47–48*, 368
Hartnett, John *70–71*
Hartog, Cecile *99–09*, 449
Harvey, Ellison *31–32*, 375
Harvey, Frank *94–99*, 118, 132, 133, 135, 144, 150, 177, 187, 204, 205; *30–31*, 443; *31–32*, 463
Harvey, James Clarence *99–09*, 546, 560; *09–19*, 453

Harvey, Morris *23–24*, 328
Harvey, Roslyn *41–42*, 438; *42–43*, 433
Harvey, Roy *68–69*, 435
Harwell, George *60–61*, 42
Harwood, H.M. *09–19*, 509, 577, 618; *21–22*, 545, 554; *25–26*, 450; *30–31*, 444, 463; *31–32*, 420; *34–35*, 368; *36–37*, 448; *53–54*, 304
Hasek, Y(J)aroslav *37–38*, 470; *62–63*, 331
Hasenclever, Walter *24–25*, 530; *33–34*, 440; *60–61*, 44
Haskins, James Jr. *94–99*, 243
Hastings, Basil Macdonald *09–19*, 481, 538, 564; *22–23*, 551
Hastings, Charlotte *50–51*, 353
Hastings, Hal *49–50*, 379
Hastings, Hugh *52–53*, 255
Hastings, Milo *35–36*, 477
Hastings, Patrick *26–27*, 382
Hastings, Sue *32–33*, 439
Hatch, Cutler *31–32*, 431
Hatch, Eric *42–43*, 440
Hatch, Frank *09–19*, 572
Hatch, James *61–62*, 322
Hathway, Donald Lamotte *32–33*, 447
Hatton, Frederic & Fanny *09–19*, 490, 564, 582, 608, 621, 625, 638; *20–21*, 369; *21–22*, 458; *26–27*, 393, 533; *27–28*, 426; *29–30*, 510; *30–31*, 401, 439; *32–33*, 390, 398
Hatton, Joseph *94–99*, 91, 240; *99–09*, 486
Hatvany, (Baroness) Lili *28–29*, 493; *30–31*, 456; *40–41*, 409
Hauerbach, Otto A. (see Otto A. Harbach)
Hauff, Hugo *39–40*, 394
Haufrecht, Mr. *47–48*, 417
Hauger, George *67–68*, 353, 402; *68–69*, 376
Hauptmann, Gerhart *99–09*, 365, 470; *09–19*, 417, 566; *22–23*, 463;

23–24, 400; *36–37*, 500; *61–62*, 325; *65–66*, 406

Hauser, Franklin *34–35*, 431

Havel, Vaclav *67–68*, 389; *69–70*, 348

Havez, Jean C. *09–19*, 474

Havoc, June *63–64*, 317

Hawhe, Andrew *42–43*, 486

Hawkes, J. Kerby *33–34*, 490

Hawkes, John *68–69*, 455

Hawkins, Maxwell *35–36*, 423

Haworth, William *94–99*, 86, 100, 122, 233

Hawthorne, Irene *56–57*, 319

Hawthorne, Nathaniel *94–99*, 91; *99–09*, 486; *09–19*, 410; *63–64*, 369; *64–65*, 346

Hawthorne, Ruth *24–25*, 516; *29–30*, 442

Hay, Ian *09–19*, 625; *20–21*, 372; *29–30*, 419; *37–38*, 418

Hay, (Hon.) John *99–09*, 425

Hay, Mary (see Bruce Spaulding)

Hayden, John *34–35*, 392

Hayden, Robert *66–67*, 354, 355; *68–69*, 433

Haydn, Joseph *25–26*, 569

Hayes, Alfred *37–38*, 419; *38–39*, 485; *39–40*, 468; *40–41*, 389, 430; *41–42*, 438; *53–54*, 340, 358

Hayes, Donald *66–67*, 355

Hayes, Hubert *34–35*, 370

Hayes, Joseph *48–49*, 408; *54–54*, 397; *62–63*, 284

Hays, H.R. *39–40*, 455; *61–62*, 317

Hays, Hoffman *35–36*, 479

Hayward, Grace *27–28*, 522

Hayward, (Sir) John *63–64*, 314

Hayward, Thomas *09–19*, 524

Hazard, Lawrence *34–35*, 400

Hazel, Rupert *21–22*, 503

Hazelwood, Colin H. *36–37*, 496

Hazelton, George C. *99–09*, 375, 415; *09–19*, 483, 587; *19–20*, 391, 405; *28–29*, 411

Hazzard, John E. (Jack) *09–19*, 578, 585; *28–29*, 444; *31–32*, 379

Head, Cloyd *25–26*, 478

Heagney, William *31–32*, 513

Healey, Joseph F. *94–99*, 197

Healey, Robert C. *49–50*, 383

Healon & Helf *99–09*, 446

Heartz, H. L. *99–09*, 406, 409, 454, 545, 583

Heath, E.P. *09–19*, 520; *29–30*, 484

Heath, Fenno *60–61*, 45

Heathfield, Mary *35–36*, 440

Heaton, Harold *99–09*, 517

Hebbel, Friederich *47–48*, 432

Hebert, Fred *60–61*, 42

Hecht, Ben *09–19*, 579; *22–23*, 513; *24–25*, 528; *28–29*, 358; *32–33*, 432, 444; *35–36*, 435; *36–37*, 498–9; *37–38*, 378; *39–40*, 403; *41–42*, 436, 460; *44–45*, 403; *45–46*, 446; *46–47*, 416, 417; *47–48*, 431; *50–51*, 337; *52–53*, 286; *57–58*, 56; *68–69*, 414; *69–70*, 301

Hecht, Harold *38–39*, 481

Hecht, Marie Armstrong *27–28*, 395; *29–30*, 523

Heckman, Don *66–67*, 420

Hedman, Martha *25–26*, 576; *35–36*, 435

Heefner, David Kerry *68–69*, 458; *69–70*, 378

Heege, Gus *94–99*, 96, 106, 135

Heelan, Will *99–09*, 559

Hefer, Hayim *68–69*, 385

Heggen, Thomas *47–48*, 383; *56–57*, 343; *62–63*, 339

Heghinian, (Lieut.) Edward N. *44–45*, 395

Heide, Robert *61–62*, 304

Heijermans, Hermann *99–09*, 348, 506, 532; *25–26*, 507; *27–28*, 433, 550

Heijermans-Houwink, Caroline *25–26*, 507; *27–28*, 433

Heilbron, Adelaide *34–35*, 474

Heim, Alyn *63–64*, 355

Heimann, Philip *34–35*, 372

Hein, Silvio *99–09*, 499, 517, 540, 571; *09–19*, 414, 419, 427, 504, 531, 536, 609, 617, 620, 633; *19–20*, 434, 447; *21–22*, 534

Helburn, Theresa *09–19*, 612, 637; *37–38*, 448; *41–42*, 414

Helf (see Healon & Helf)

Heller, Barbara *60–61*, 292

Heller, Joseph *68–69*, 385

Hellerman, Fred *62–63*, 291; *67–68*, 377

Hellinger, Mark *22–23*, 572; *31–32*, 377, 491

Hellman, Lillian *34–35*, 412; *36–37*, 441; *38–39*, 460; *40–41*, 422; *43–44*, 467; *46–47*, 443; *49–50*, 358, 359; *50–51*, 355; *52–53*, 279, 306; *55–56*, 362; *56–57*, 340; *59–60*, 322; *60–61*, 45; *62–63*, 303; *63–64*, 363–4; *65–66*, 419; *67–68*, 348

Heloise (see Peter Abelard)

Hemingway, Ernest *30–31*, 416; *39–40*, 442

Hemmerde, Edward G. *09–19*, 463

Henderson, Al *44–45*, 368

Henderson, Charles *49–50*, 355

Henderson, Isaac *99–09*, 415

Henderson, Luther *70–71*

Henderson, Ray *25–26*, 419, 604; *27–28*, 399, 412; *28–29*, 353, 395; *29–30*, 503; *31–32*, 390, 491; *32–33*, 472; *34–35*, 405; *35–36*, 453; *42–43*, 471

Henderson, W.J. *94–99*, 171

Hendl, Walter *44–45*, 421

Hendra, Tony *64–65*, 305

Hendricks, Adeline *21–22*, 539

Hendrie, Ernest *99–09*, 356

Hendryx, Shirl *69–70*, 357

Heneker, David *60–61*, 296; *64–65*, 333

Henie, Sonja *40–41*, 384; *42–43*, 421, 489; *46–47*, 482

Heniger, Jacob *09–19*, 591

Henkle, Carl *28–29*, 508; *32–33*, 381

Hennefeld, Edmund B. *46–47*, 495; *47–48*, 427

Hennequin, Maurice *94–99*, 153, 207, 211, 216, 230; *99–09*, 347, 355, 361, 389, 460, 502, 555, 576; *09–19*, 507; *23–24*, 373; *25–26*, 433; *26–27*, 443; *27–28*, 505; *28–29*, 386

Henning, Ervin *65–66*, 416

Henning, Magnus *36–37*, 448

Hennique, Leon *94–99*, 169

Henry VI (King) *62–63*, 295

Henry VIII (King) *62–63*, 295

Henry, Alice *38–39*, 488

Henry, Arthur *23–24*, 361

Henry, Creagh *94–99*, 248

Henry, Grace *26–27*, 368; *28–29*, 355

Henry, O. *09–19*, 411, 646; *21–22*, 475; *45–46*, 454

Henry, S.R. *20–21*, 376

Henshaw, T.W. *94–99*, 122

Henschke, Alfred (see Klabund)

Hentel, Nathan *37–38*, 469

Hentzner, Paul *63–64*, 314

Hepburn, Richard *60–61*, 39

Hepenstall, W.D. *09–19*, 656; *27–28*, 466

Herbert, F. Hugh *40–41*, 393; *42–43*, 467; *43–44*, 483; *47–48*, 364; *50–51*, 356; *53–54*, 313; *56–57*, 328

Herbert, Henry *31–32*, 520; *36–37*, 484

Herbert, John *66–67*, 414; *69–70*, 344

Herbert, Joseph W. *94–99*, 137, 179, 180, 226, 237; *99–09*, 420, 423, 447, 512, 517, 538, 540, 556, 580; *09–19*, 427, 454, 494, 562; *20–21*, 377; *22–23*, 434

Herbert, Victor *94–99*, 104, 152, 177, 198, 213, 239; *99–09*, 349, 352, 358, 367, 440, 445, 475, 493, 499, 504, 517, 520, 529, 534, 537, 566, 571, 573; *09–19*, 400, 405, 430, 450, 454, 455, 481, 502, 506,

514, 538, 540, 560, 586, 597, 601, 613, 614, 638, 650; *19–20*, 407, 422; *20–21*, 355, 357, 413; *21–22*, 388, 555; *22–23*, 456; *23–24*, 340; *24–25*, 429, 436; *29–30*, 400, 414, 425, 434, 466, 505; *30–31*, 467; *31–32*, 433; *33–34*, 530; *45–46*, 398; *46–47*, 419

Herczeg, Geza *30–31*, 507; *45–46*, 381

Herczegh, Ferencz *09–19*, 439; *21–22*, 411; *22–23*, 521

Herendeen, Frederick *09–19*, 577; *30–31*, 399; *32–33*, 377; *33–34*, 489; *35–36*, 429; *36–37*, 482; *40–41*, 415

Herford, Beatrice *36–37*, 498

Herford, Oliver *99–09*, 565; *09–19*, 396, 398, 424

Hériat, Philippe *65–66*, 372

Heriot, Wilton *99–09*, 346

Herlihy, James Leo *57–58*, 321; *68–69*, 448

Herman, Alexander C. *25–26*, 528

Herman, Henry *94–99*, 105, 234

Herman, Jerry *54–55*, 56; *59–60*, 335; *61–62*, 259, 317; *63–64*, 319; *64–65*, 331; *65–66*, 412; *68–69*, 405

Herman, William *61–62*, 237

Hermant, Abel *24–25*, 553

Hernández, Antonio Acevedo *67–68*, 401

Herndon, Agnes *94–99*, 129

Herndon, Venable *66–67*, 400; *70–71*

Herne, James A. *94–99*, 154, 251, 252; *99–09*, 372

Herne, Julie *99–09*, 484

Hernton, Calvin *68–69*, 433

Herold, Don *40–41*, 411

Heron, Matilda *94–99*, 234

Herrick, Howard *21–22*, 553

Herrick, Landon *29–30*, 548

Herrick, Robert *25 26*, 520

Herrmann, Harry *49–50*, 379

Herrod, Bro *69–70*, 365

Hersey, John *44–45*, 402; *60–61*, 300; *64–65*, 350

Hershey, Burnet *38–39*, 473

Herston, Jester *54–55*, 404

Hertz, Henrik *99–09*, 520

Herve, Florimond *94–99*, 205

Herve, Paul *09–19*, 425, 505, 522, 554, 558

Hervey, Harry *28–29*, 428

Hervey, (Lord) John *62–63*, 295

Hervieu, Paul *99–09*, 501, 557; *09–19*, 407

Herzer, Ludwig *22–23*, 539

Herzig, S.M. *42–43*, 430

Herzig, Sig *30–31*, 447; *31–32*, 379; *44–45*, 387; *46–47*, 411; *63–64*, 343; *64–65*, 341; *65–66*, 417; *66–67*, 401

Herzog, Arthur *25–26*, 589

Hess, George Elliott *36–37*, 499; *37–38*, 468; *38–39*, 491

Hess, John D. *52–53*, 279

Hester, Hal *67–68*, 398

Heuberger, Richard *09–19*, 465–6

Hewett, Christopher *59–60*, 336

Hewlett, Maurice *99–09*, 394; *09–19*, 625

Heyer, Georgette *37–38*, 398

Heyer, Grace *19–20*, 347

Heyman, Edward *33–34*, 430, 438, 532; *50–51*, 317

Heyn, Ernest V. *38–39*, 473

Heyse, Paul *99–09*, 422

Heyward, Donald (see Donald Heywood)

Heyward, Dorothy *23–24*, 414; *27–28*, 425; *29–30*, 391, 520; *30–31*, 414; *35–36*, 416; *38–39*, 443; *39–40*, 447; *41–42*, 433; *43–44*, 412, 438, 445; *48–49*, 392, 425; *52–53*, 293; *60–61*, 338; *63–64*, 336

Heyward, Du Bose *27–28*, 425; *29–30*, 391; *30–31*, 520; *35–36*, 416; *38–39*, 443; *39–40*, 447; *41–42*, 433; *43–44*, 412, 438;

Heyward, Du Bose *(cont.)*
52–53, 293; 60–61, 338; 63–64, 336

Heywood (Heyward), Donald 27–28, 388, 530; 30–31, 403; 31–32, 502; 32–33, 394; 34–35, 414; 36–37, 443; 37–38, 373

Hichens, Robert 99–09, 466; 09–19, 436, 455, 484, 624; 21–22, 500

Hickerson, (G.) Harold 28–29, 402; 61–62, 332

Hickman, Howard 21–22, 455

Hicks, Eddie 67–68, 405

Hicks, Seymour 94–99, 233, 240; 99–09, 452, 492, 499; 27–28, 431

Hickson, Leslie 24–25, 472

Higashi, Yutaka 70–71

Higbee, Dolly 94–99, 206

Higgins, David K. 94–99, 184, 195, 213, 230, 258; 99–09, 395; 26–27, 501

Higginson, Thomas Wentworth 63–64, 350

Higley, Philo 35–36, 409

Hiken, Nat 48–49, 407; 51–52, 278; 55–56, 391

Hildesheimer, Wolfgang 70–71

Hildreth, Carleton 28–29, 428

Hill, Abram 38–39, 487; 43–44, 489; 45–46, 415, 435

Hill, Alexander 32–33, 482

Hill, Billy 33–34, 476

Hill, Brownlow 99–09, 476

Hill, Errol 69–70, 336

Hill, Francis 20–21, 377

Hill, Graham 99–09, 577

Hill, J. Leubrie 09–19, 448, 553

Hill, Lucienne 56–57, 349; 57–58, 53, 322; 59–60, 310, 331; 60–61, 298; 63–64, 369; 64–65, 301, 313; 67–68, 409; 69–70, 373

Hill, M. Wood 37–38, 468

Hill, R.L. 35–36, 501

Hill, Tom 49–50, 383; 52–53, 306; 54–55, 53

Hillel & Aviva 50–51, 345

Hiller, J. Sebastian 99–09, 507

Hilliam, B.C. 19–20, 379, 392; 20–21, 447

Hilliard, Bob 47–48, 368; 50–51, 309; 52–53, 286; 64–65, 358

Hilliard, Frank 38–39, 484

Hilliard, Robert 94–99, 140

Hilton, James 36–37, 457; 56–57, 313

Hind, C. Lewis 09–19, 640

Hindemith, Paul 34–35, 460; 41–42, 456; 42–43, 487; 44–45, 440; 45–46, 456; 47–48, 417; 62–63, 328

Hines, Arline Van Ness 09–19, 630

Hines, Carl Wendell 68–69, 433

Hinkley, Eleanor Holmes 32–33, 420

Hinkley, Laura 09–19, 637

Hinsdale, Harriett 45–46, 446

Hinton, Jane 31–32, 412, 439; 32–33, 424; 44–45, 388; 46–47, 421

Hippius, Zinaida 21–22, 532

Hirsch, Louis A. 99–09, 556; 09–19, 425, 567, 553, 576, 616, 618, 626, 631, 645; 19–20, 355; 20–21, 396; 21–22, 432, 555; 22–23, 452; 23–24, 320; 24–25, 512

Hirsch, M. Henry 23–24, 333

Hirschmann, Henri 09–19, 467

Hirshbein, Peretz 21–22, 478

Hirshfeld, Ludwig 39–40, 446

Hirshhorn, Naomi Caryl 63–64, 304

Hirson, Roger O. 63–64, 351; 66–67, 374; 68–69, 449

Hitchcock, Jack 64–65, 353

Hitchcock, M.W. 99–09, 372

Hitchcock, R. 99–09, 372

Hivnor, Robert 63–64, 369

Hoag, Jackson D. 99–09, 484

Hoare, Douglas 09–19, 513

Hoare, J.E. 32–33, 437

Hobart, Doty 33–34, 455, 528; 36–37, 430

Hobart, George V. 94–99, 199; 99–09, 360, 372, 375, 376, 382, 392, 397, 405, 407, 409, 414, 433,

434, 435, 436, 446, 464, 472, 489,
493, 494, 499, 507, 525, 537, 554,
568, 571, 582; *09–19*, 405, 414,
420, 423, 425, 446, 450, 462, 480,
502, 527, 536, 562, 570, 576, 601,
614, 620, 651, 654; *19–20*, 366,
379, 437, 457; *20–21*, 392; *21–22*,
396, 533; *22–23*, 452
Hobble, John L. *09–19*, 635
Hobbs, Bertram *34–35*, 446
Hobbs, John Oliver (Mrs. Craigie)
94–99, 151; *99–09*, 361, 429
Hochhauser, Jeff *70–71*
Hochhuth, Rolf *63–64*, 327; *67–68*,
376
Hochman, Sandra *65–66*, 434
Hochwa(e)lder, Fritz *46–47*, 498;
53–54, 307
Hock, Robert D. *60–61*, 353
Hodgdon, Ray *27–28*, 560
Hodge, Merton *33–34*, 491
Hodge, William *20–21*, 383; *21–22*,
429; *23–24*, 334; *26–27*, 387;
28–29, 389; *29–30*, 516
Hodges, Horace *09–19*, 515, 591;
40–41, 432
Hodges, James *68–69*, 438
Hodges, John King *32–33*, 408
Hodges, Mitchell *39–40*, 394, 468
Hodson, J.L. *66–67*, 416
Hoerl, Arthur *31–32*, 494
Hoerr, Janice *39–40*, 473
Hoey, Dennis *46–47*, 441
Hoey, George *94–99*, 102, 108, 128,
171
Hoff, Frank *64–65*, 362
Hoffe, Monckton *09–19*, 425, 524,
611; *22–23*, 472, 511; *25–26*, 466;
29–30, 404
Hoffenstein, Samuel *32–33*, 431
Hoffert, Paul *68–69*, 444
Hoffman, Aaron *99–09*, 543, 568,
580; *09–19*, 412, 474, 631, 640;
20–21, 381; *21–22*, 406; *22–23*,
521; *23–24*, 299; *24–25*, 433;
30–31, 450; *43–44*, 415
Hoffman, Armin *60–61*, 294

Hoffman, Bill *55–56*, 383
Hoffman, Charles B. *94–99*, 90
Hoffman, Gertrude *99–09*, 519
Hoffman, Guy *68–69*, 428
Hoffman, Louis *41–42*, 428
Hoffman(n), Max *99–09*, 435, 464,
494, 526, 543; *09–19*, 412, 485
Hoffman, William *65–66*, 432
Hoffstein, David *39–40*, 475
Hofmann, Gert *66–67*, 422; *67–68*,
408
Hogan, Ernest *99–09*, 381
Hogan, James *42–43*, 461
Hoiby, Lee *56–57*, 362; *60–61*, 304,
360; *62–63*, 320; *63–64*, 338;
64–65, 310; *65–66*, 399
Holbrook, Walter *36–37*, 474
Holcroft, T. *94–99*, 112
Holden, Harold *46–47*, 497
Holden, Richard *39–40*, 437
Holden, Steve *68–69*, 422
Holdridge, Lee *63–64*, 343; *65–66*,
424; *66–67*, 377
Holiner, Mann *26–27*, 422; *28–29*,
463; *33–34*, 466; *53–54*, 305, 306
Hollaender, Victor *94–99*, 209;
09–19, 463, 479, 552
Holliday, Judy (see The Revuers)
Hollins, M.H. *09–19*, 448
Holinshed, Raphael *62–63*, 295
Hollister, Len D. *25–26*, 421; *28–29*,
457
Holloway, John *66–67*, 354
Holloway, Stanley *60–61*, 299
Holloway, Sterling *29–30*, 548
Holm, Jan *63–64*, 370
Holm, John Cecil *34–35*, 446;
41–42, 400, 422; *42–43*, 435;
45–46, 412; *46–47*, 457; *50–51*,
366; *54–55*, 397; *61–62*, 260;
62–63, 330; *69–70*, 300
Holman, Libby *54–55*, 365
Holman, M. Carl *66–67*, 355
Holmes, Jack *59–60*, 335, 336;
61–62, 284; *62–63*, 315, 317
Holmes, (Dr.) John Haynes *35–36*,
408

Honickman, Lynne 70–71

Holofcener, Lawrence (Larry)
55–56, 339, 340, 341, 380; 67–68,
358; 69–70, 368

Holst, Edouard 94–99, 215

Holt, Bernard 99–09, 454

Holt, Henry 29–30, 443; 41–42, 404

Holt, Sandy 69–70, 343

Holt, Will 61–62, 316; 63–64, 342,
343; 64–65, 344; 65–66, 419, 434;
66–67, 421; 68–69, 411; 69–70,
335, 368; 70–71

Holton, Robert 61–62, 308

Holtz, Hugo 99–09, 561

Holy Modal Rounders, The 79–70,
305

Homans, Robert E. 09–19, 572

Home, William Douglas 49–50, 356;
56–57, 322

Homer 37–38, 458; 69–70, 343;
70–71

Honegger, Arthur 26–27, 434;
39–40, 471; 47–48, 423; 52–53,
271; 63–64, 346

Honig, Edwin 64–65, 362

Honigman, Saul 70–71

Honrath, Donald 33–34, 507

Hood, (Capt.) Basil 94–99, 161, 209;
99–09, 369, 402, 414, 435; 09–19,
476

Hook, Basil 09–19, 496

Hook, Nina Warner 59–60, 336

Hooker, Brian 20–21, 444; 21–22,
498; 22–23, 497; 23–24, 345, 395;
25–26, 418, 451, 556, 602; 26–27,
430; 27–28, 480; 28–29, 439;
31–32, 471; 32–33, 440; 34–35,
431; 35–36, 504; 43–44, 402;
46–47, 422; 53–54, 318

Hope, Anthony 94–99, 141, 237,
249, 258; 99–09, 436, 568; 09–19,
437, 547; 25–26, 485

Hope, Edward 33–34, 459

Hopkins, Anthony 45–46, 444;
57–58, 291

Hopkins, Arthur 09–19, 466; 27–28,
396; 32–33, 464; 46–47, 448

Hopkins, Charles 37–38, 455

Hopwood, Aubrey 94–99, 233

Hopwood, Avery 99–09, 519, 578;
09–19, 404, 427, 430, 492, 564,
565, 587, 634; 19–20, 360, 365;
20–21, 364, 366, 371; 21–22, 390,
443; 22–23, 452; 23–24, 310, 373;
24–25, 435, 499; 25–26, 493;
27–28, 416; 32–33, 476; 36–37,
486; 44–45, 410; 52–53, 281

Horan, Charles 24–25, 558

Horan, Edward A. 33–34, 489

Hord, Parker A. 09–19, 542

Horgan, Paul 42–43, 422

Horine, Charles 65–66, 390

Horkheimer, H.M. 09–19, 457

Hornblow, Arthur 99–09, 485

Hornblow, Arthur Jr. 21–22, 511;
22–23, 540; 26–27, 390; 30–31,
463

Horne, Marie 09–19, 404

Horner, Charles 51–52, 320

Horner, Chuck 69–70, 361

Horner, Frederick 94–99, 132

Horner, Harry 37–38, 441

Hornez, André 55–56, 347

Hornimann, Ray (Roy) 09–19, 403;
28–29, 363

Hornsby, Joe 58–59, 319

Hornthal, Larry 27–28, 549

Hornung, E.W. 99–09, 442; 09–19,
429

Horovitz, Israel 67–68, 398, 407,
412; 68–69, 394, 451; 70–71

Horowitz, Herschel 63–64, 345

Horst, Julius 99–09, 573; 09–19, 396

Horst, Louis 34–35, 451

Horton, Asadata Dafora (see
Asadata Dafora)

Horton, George Moses 66–67, 354

Horton, Kate 25–26, 449; 26–27,
455

Horwin, Jerry 39–40, 434

Horwitt, Arnold B. 41–42, 459;
45–46, 405, 438; 47–48, 377, 401;
54–55, 394; 59–60, 300; 63–64,
368

Horwitz, Charles *99–09*, 415
Hoschna, K(C)arl *99–09*, 563; *09–19*, 415, 423, 440, 443, 447, 470
Hosmer, Lucius *94–99*, 229; *99–09*, 533
Hotchkis, John *51–52*, 300
Hotchner, A.E. *63–64*, 338
Hough, M. *55–56*, 347
Hough, William M. *99–09*, 537, 541, 564, 576; *09–19, 406, 552; 20–21*, 387; *42–43*, 438
Houghton, Mr. *65–66*, 423
Houghton, Stanley *09–19*, 487, 497, 508, 509, 535; *21–22*, 546; *28–29*, 501
House, Henry Arthur *25–26*, 576; *35–36*, 435
House, Roy Temple *09–19*, 547, 579
Houseman, John *33–34*, 449, 482
Housman, A.E. *67–68*, 277
Housman, Laurence *09–19*, 512; *35–36*, 453; *36–37*, 402; *38–39*, 410
Houston, Noel *39–40*, 444, 446; *43–44*, 480
Houston, Norman *23–24*, 307
Housum, Robert *09–19*, 528, 616; *22–23*, 478
Houwink, Caroline Heijermans (see Caroline Heijermans-Houwink)
Hovhaness, Alan *54–55*, 388
Howard, Bart *53–54*, 326; *62–63*, 317
Howard, Bronson (see also George Bronson-Howard) *94–99*, 86, 230, 234; *99–09*, 350; *09–19*, 516–7
Howard, Eleanor Harris *65–66*, 383
Howard, Garland *29–30*, 549
Howard, Joseph E. *99–09*, 514, 537, 541, 561, 564, 576; *09–19*, 406; *42–43*, 438; *55–56*, 347
Howard, Leslie *27–28*, 418; *29–30*, 489; *35–36*, 503
Howard, Louise *37–38*, 461
Howard, Peter *58–59*, 332; *68–69*, 386

Howard, Philip *36–37*, 457
Howard, Richard *61–62*, 313
Howard, Shafter *99–09*, 511
Howard, Sidney *21–22*, 409; *23–24*, 322; *24–25*, 463, 492; *25–26*, 480, 492; *26–27, 433, 444; 27–28*, 501; *28–29*, 398; *29–30*, 464; *30–31*, 453; *32–33*, 413, 465; *33–34*, 501, 504; *34–35*, 361, 425; *35–36*, 411; *37–38*, 394, 468; *39–40*, 401; *45–46*, 426; *46–47*, 438; *48–49*, 413; *53–54*, 323; *55–56*, 387; *58–59*, 54, 329; *64–65*, 362; *65–66*, 407
Howard, Tom *24–25*, 479
Howard, Walter *99–09*, 460; *09–19*, 530, 619
Howard, Willie *36–37*, 476
Howe, Frank Jr. *09–19*, 649
Howe, Helen *34–35*, 484; *36–37*, 498; *37–38*, 466; *39–40*, 472
Howe, Tina *69–70*, 364
Howell, Lois *31–32*, 402; *32–33*, 393
Howells, William Dean *94–99*, 134; *19–20*, 390
Howson, Frank A. *94–99*, 142, 176, 206, 246, 252; *99–09*, 403, 557
Hoyt, Charles Bamfield *25–26*, 530
Hoyt, Charles H. *94–99*, 89, 96, 98, 157, 161, 178, 190, 194, 199, 208, 236; *09–19*, 470, 585
Hsiung, S.I. *35–36*, 464
Hubbell, Raymond *99–09*, 433, 482, 508, 517, 526, 552, 583; *09–19*, 409, 429, 446, 457, 469, 470, 481, 502, 527, 548, 560, 580, 601, 604, 629, 630, 653; *19–20*, 346, 396; *20–21*, 365; *21–22*, 396; *22–23*, 447; *24–25*, 429; *26–27*, 467; *27–28*, 525; *28–29*, 395
Hubert, Philip G. *94–99*, 157
Huddleston, Floyd *51–52*, 323
Hudson, Holland *09–19*, 547
Hughes, Babette *38–39*, 488
Hughes, Catherine *59–60*, 40
Hughes, Dickson *59–60*, 335
Hughes, Eric *63–64*, 370

Hughes, Hatcher *20–21*, 420; *23–24*, 382; *24–25*, 567; *29–30*, 489; *34–35*, 416
Hughes, Henry H. Jr. *38–39*, 491; *39–40*, 472
Hughes, Langston *35–36*, 424; *37–38*, 464; *44–45*, 438; *46–47*, 454; *49–50*, 384; *50–51*, 323; *52–53*, 306; *56–57*, 58; *57–58*, 283; *59–60*, 49; *61–62*, 315; *63–64*, 312, 356; *64–65*, 360, 361; *65–66*, 371, 436; *66–67*, 354, 355, 423; *68–69*, 433, 454
Hughes, Richard *29–30*, 533; *37–38*, 464; *43–44*, 427; *48–49*, 391
Hughes, Robette *32–33*, 436
Hughes, Rupert *94–99*, 140; *99–09*, 420, 423, 510, 565; *09–19*, 399, 431, 439, 485, 624; *19–20*, 427
Hugo, Victor *99–09*, 406, 529; *20–21*, 442; *57–58*, 56; *58–59*, 295
Hull, Henry *22–23*, 437
Hull, Stacey *49–50*, 385
Hummel, George F. *33–34*, 448
Humperdinck, Englebert *94–99*, 146; *99–09*, 421; *47–48*, 425
Humphrey, Harry E. *27–28*, 544
Humphreys, Joseph *94–99*, 251
Humphries, Rolfe *38–39*, 483
Hunt, Estelle *29–30*, 467
Hunt, F.V. *67–68*, 414; *70–71*
Hunt, Hugh *37–38*, 376
Hunt, J. Ray *47–48*, 421
Hunter, Eddie *22–23*, 558; *26–27*, 360
Hunter, Evan *64–65*, 336
Hunter, Ian McLellan *63–64*, 325
Hunter, Kenneth *36–37*, 498
Hunter, N.C. *55–56*, 343
Hunter, Ruth *49–50*, 383
Huntley, Jobe *63–64*, 312; *64–65*, 361
Hupfeld, Herman *25–26*, 604; *27–28*, 392; *32–33*, 395; *33–34*, 430; *49–50*, 368; *56–57*, 359
Hurgon, Austen *99–09*, 554

Hurlbut, Gladys *33–34*, 485; *39–40*, 414, 453; *40–41*, 375; *42–43*, 445
Hurlbut, William J. *99–09*, 569, 582; *09–19*, 427, 442, 501, 509, 515, 608, 610; *19–20*, 423; *21–22*, 433; *22–23*, 463, 533; *23–24*, 351; *25–26*, 517, 577; *27–28*, 422, 477; *29–30*, 444
Hurley, Edward *30–31*, 403
Hurst, Fannie *09–19*, 609; *21–22*, 405; *22–23*, 537; *27–28*, 478
Hurst, Hawthorne *31–32*, 518
Hussey, James *21–22*, 397
Husson, Albert *52–53*, 295; *55–56*, 359
Huston, John *41–42*, 424; *52–53*, 307
Huston, Philip *43–44*, 489
Hutchinson, A.S.M. *22–23*, 551
Hutchinson, Ernest *21–22*, 447
Hutchinson, Harold *27–28*, 432
Hutton, Michael Clayton *47–48*, 376
Hutty, Leigh *26–27*, 516
Huxley, Aldous *50–51*, 318; *57–58*, 305; *65–66*, 385
Hyde, Herbert E. *09–19*, 649
Hydes, Watty *94–99*, 188
Hyland, Lily *23–24*, 439; *24–25*, 565; *25–26*, 418, 605; *27–28*, 558
Hyman, Mac *55–56*, 355
Hyman, Richard *46–47*, 498
Hyman, Sarah Ellis *26–27*, 521
Hymer, John B. *09–19*, 648; *24–25*, 579; *25–26*, 503; *26–27*, 485; *28–29*, 381; *29–30*, 388; *31–32*, 495; *34–35*, 436

Ibanez, Blasco *21–22*, 422
Ibn-Zahav, Ari *47–48*, 431
Ibsen, Henrik *94–99*, 121, 126, 136, 169, 216, 227; *99–09*, 360, 404, 410, 411, 430, 438, 456, 459, 487, 560; *09–19*, 415, 416, 418, 457, 468, 549, 551, 579, 625, 627, 629, 651; *21–22*, 516; *22–23*, 527; *23–24*, 356, 366, 437; *24–25*, 549,

582; *25–26*, 490, 538, 541, 545, 570; *26–27*, 418, 423, 458; *27–28*, 419, 532; *28–29*, 410, 420, 464, 481; *29–30*, 393, 403, 543; *31–32*, 410; *32–33*, 498; *33–34*, 522; *34–35*, 403, 483; *35–36*, 445, 450, 512; *36–37*, 432, 465, 499; *37–38*, 406, 439; *40–41*, 432; *41–42*, 437; *43–44*, 488; *45–46*, 459, 460; *46–47*, 437, 498; *47–48*, 386; *50–51*, 312, 339, 344, 373, 374; *51–52*, 301, 332; *54–55*, 401; *55–56*, 55; *56–57*, 55; *57–58*, 56; *59–60*, 313; *60–61*, 353; *61–62*, 306, 328; *62–63*, 325; *63–64*, 361; *65–66*, 423, 433; *66–67*, 371; *67–68*, 410; *69–70*, 337, 355; *70–71*

Ide, Leonard *28–29*, 408; *32–33*, 397; *38–39*, 428

Igo, Harold *39–40*, 422

Ileo, J. *68–69*, 416

Illica, L. *43–44*, 438; *44–45*, 378; *45–46*, 388

Imbrie, McCrea *68–69*, 449

Improvisers (other than actors; see also Actors) *60–61*, 37

Indig, Otto *34–35*, 371

Ingalls, Phil *49–50*, 379

Inge, Benson *31–32*, 519

Inge, William *49–50*, 373; *52–53*, 290, 306; *54–55*, 402; *57–58*, 305; *59–60*, 49, 307; *62–63*, 296; *65–66*, 400, 436

Ingerlid, Joseph Jay *32–33*, 380

Ingham, Hannah May *94–99*, 234

Ingraham, Mr. *99–09*, 540

Ingrassio, Anthony J. *70–71*

Inlender, Avraham *62–63*, 294

Ionesco, Eugene *57–58*, 308; *58–59*, 51; *59–60*, 46, 49, 356; *60–61*, 47, 316; *61–62*, 254, 323; *63–64*, 326, 345, 366; *67–68*, 353, 402; *69–70*, 363

Irving, H.B. *99–09*, 521

Irving, Henry *94–99*, 150; *99–09*, 520

Irving, Laurence *94–99*, 150, 151; *99–09*, 353, 394, 442, 470, 582; *09–19*, 408, 417; *26–27*, 402

Irving, Robert *49–50*, 371

Irving, Washington *94–99*, 130; *99–09*, 497; *46–47*, 494; *47–48*, 341; *66–67*, 404

Irwin, Rea *40–41*, 427

Irwin, Wallace *99–09*, 541, 554, 567; *09–19*, 482, 568

Irwin, Will(iam) *28–29*, 499; *29–30*, 548; *34–35*, 429, 482; *38–39*, 407; *40–41*, 405; *42–43*, 420, 434; *45–46*, 426; *50–51*, 343; *57–58*, 320; *58–59*, 329

Isaacs, Bryna Rachel *29–30*, 533

Isham, Frederick S. *09–19*, 582; *20–21*, 388; *22–23*, 547; *27–28*, 421, 544; *32–33*, 411

Isherwood, Christopher *38–39*, 487; *47–48*, 425; *49–50*, 383; *51–52*, 295; *66–67*, 370

Israel, William *09–19*, 630

Ito, Teiji *60–61*, 356; *61–62*, 305; *62–63*, 320; *63–64*, 313; *65–66*, 435; *66–67*, 420; *67–68*, 382, 402

Itow, Michi *21–22*, 556

Ivan, Rosalind *09–19*, 597; *26–27*, 453

Ives, Alice E. *94–99*, 90, 172; *99–09*, 382; *09–19*, 496

Ivor-Szinney, Stephen *09–19*, 652

Izumo, Takeda *09–19*, 579

Jacks, Leopold *29–30*, 482

Jackson, Alfred G. *25–26*, 568; *26–27*, 459; *34–35*, 483

Jackson, Arthur J. *09–19*, 657; *19–20*, 456; *20–21*, 388; *21–22*, 388, 514

Jackson, C. *61–62*, 322

Jackson, Delmar *59–60*, 315

Jackson, Frederick *09–19*, 552, 614, 650, 657; *19–20*, 440; *20–21*, 446; *21–22*, 514; *22–23*, 578; *33–34*, 515; *34–35*, 454; *43–44*, 482; *54–55*, 360

Jackson, Horace *37–38*, 414
Jackson, Howard *32–33*, 499
Jackson, Joseph *31–32*, 448
Jackson, Josephine *67–68*, 407
Jackson, N. Hart *94–99*, 107, 235;
    99–09, 456; *25–26*, 579
Jackson, Peter *41–42*, 460
Jackson, R. *99–09*, 397
Jackson, Roe Lee *24–25*, 587
Jackson, Shirley *60–61*, 48; *66–67*,
    365
Jacob, Bill & Patti *69–70*, 302
Jacobi, Georgio *94–99*, 129
Jacobi, Victor *09–19*, 507, 568, 606;
    19–20, 367; *20–21*, 401; *21–22*,
    435
Jac(k)obowski, Edward *94–99*, 87,
    102, 202; *99–09*, 441, 446; *20–21*,
    418
Jacobs, Arthur *37–38*, 469
Jacobs, Jacob *38–39*, 493, 494;
    45–46, 460; *46–47*, 497; *47–48*,
    432; *61–62*, 310; *64–65*, 344;
    65–66, 423; *70–71*
Jacobs, W.W. *99–09*, 494, 539;
    09–19, 514, 515; *22–23*, 575;
    28–29, 502
Jacobson, Dan *65–66*, 383
Jacobson, Hy *51–52*, 281
Jacobson, Kenneth *69–70*, 360
Jacobson, Leopold *99–09*, 556;
    09–19, 399; *21–22*, 476; *31–32*,
    394; *33–34*, 523; *42–43*, 419;
    46–47, 470
Jacobus, J. *24–25*, 459
Jacoby, Coleman *56–57*, 357
Jacoby, Elliott *37–38*, 400
Jacoby, Wilhelm *94–99*, 128; *09–19*,
    421
Jacquet, H. Maurice *29–30*, 453;
    30–31, 448
Jaffe, Chris *50–51*, 373
Jaffe, M. *37–38*, 468
Jaffe, Moe *28–29*, 506; *29–30*, 379
Jagendorf, Mauritz *35–36*, 510;
    37–38, 467
Jaime, Mons. *99–09*, 522
Jamaique, Yves *63–64*, 329

Jamerson, Pauline *43–44*, 443;
    48–49, 402
James I (King) *62–63*, 295
James, Benedict *09–19*, 645
James, Bob *67–68*, 354; *68–69*, 376,
    384
James, Daniel Lewis *42–43*, 448;
    44–45, 387; *46–47*, 411
James, Edgar *09–19*, 474
James, Harry *94–99*, 192, 221
James, Henry (1) *99–09*, 579; *47–48*,
    166, 353, 423; *49–50*, 371; *54–55*,
    383; *56–57*, 334, 353; *58–59*, 52;
    61–62, 288, 309; *62–63*, 337;
    68–69, 454
James, Henry (2; composer) *09–19*,
    532
James, Lilith *44–45*, 387; *46–47*,
    411
James, Paul *29–30*, 548; *30–31*, 417
James, Philip *36–37*, 472
James, Ted *65–66*, 422
Jameson, Storm *56–57*, 351
Jamison, William *41–42*, 461
Janacek, Leos *63–64*, 364
Jane, John *63–64*, 314
Janis, Elsie *19–20*, 392; *21–22*, 495;
    24–25, 534; *38–39*, 489
Janney, Russell *34–35*, 431; *43–44*,
    402
Janney, Sam *26–27*, 365, 532;
    31–32, 476
Jannings, Orin *46–47*, 422
Jansen, Harry A. (see Dante)
Jansen, Neil *62–63*, 283
Janssen, Werner *21–22*, 441, 533;
    22–23, 522; *26–27*, 364; *28–29*,
    463
Jara, Victor *67–68*, 401
Jarno, Georg *09–19*, 431
Jarre, Maurice *58–59*, 295
Jarrell, Randall *64–65*, 296; *68–69*,
    407
Jarrett, Arthur L. *40–41*, 420
Jarrett, Dan *29–30*, 449; *32–33*, 406
Jarry, Alfred *52–53*, 308; *68–69*,
    325, 457; *69–70*, 375
Jaspar, Bobby *60–61*, 289

Javits, Joan *60–61,* 42; *62–63,* 302; *65–66,* 423

Jay, Harriet *94–99,* 248

Jay, Leticia *69–70,* 338

Jay, William *41–42,* 420

Jeans, Ronald *25–26,* 526; *29–30,* 382, 548; *31–32,* 408; *41–42,* 398

Jeffers, Robinson *47–48,* 356, 360; *48–49,* 421; *50–51,* 331; *54–55,* 52; *65–66,* 427; *68–69,* 454

Jefferson, Joseph *94–99,* 258; *47–48,* 341

Jefferson, Thomas *63–64,* 350

Jefferson, William *99–09,* 378

Jeffreys, Alan *56–57,* 357; *60–61,* 292

Jeffries, Jay *67–68,* 402

Jellicoe, Ann *63–64,* 366

Jenbach, Bela *09–19,* 537, 554

Jenkins, Bunker *61–62,* 330

Jenkins, Gordon *48–49,* 406; *62–63,* 278

Jenks, George E. *94–99,* 83

Jennings, John *62–63,* 322

Jennings, Talbot *31–32,* 414

Jerome, Ben M. *99–09,* 462, 463, 564, 575; *09–19,* 425; *27–28,* 421

Jerome, Edwin *94–99,* 239

Jerome, Helen *35–36,* 430; *41–42,* 453; *58–59,* 331

Jerome, Jerome K. *94–99,* 96, 256; *99–09,* 347, 526, 577; *09–19, 401, 509, 541, 626; 24–25,* 596; *47–48,* 427

Jerome, William *99–09,* 427, 432, 436, 446, 457, 490, 491, 493, 498, 499, 524, 540, 541, 544; *09–19,* 397, 421

Jesse, F. Tennyson *09–19,* 509, 618; *21–22,* 545; *24–25,* 506; *25–26,* 450; *53–54,* 304

Jessel, George *28–29,* 379; *41–42,* 408

Jessel, Raymond *64–65,* 327

Jessop, George H. *94–99,* 97, 110, 119, 147, 153, 191, 235; *99–09,* 451

Jires, Jaromil *64–65,* 297

Joans, Ted *66–67,* 354

Job, Thomas *37–38,* 396; *41–42,* 452; *45–46,* 397; *46–47,* 447

Joffre, (Marshal) *64–65,* 303

Johannsen, Sigurd *28–29,* 370

John, Errol *61–62,* 319; *70–71*

John, Graham *25–26,* 526; *29–30,* 396, 491

John, Miriam *59–60,* 357; *69–70,* 373

Johns, Florence *33–34,* 488

Johns, Kenneth *34–35,* 360

Johns, Pierce *34–35,* 423

Johnson (see Cole & Johnson; Creamer & Johnson)

Johnson, (Pres.) Andrew *63–64,* 350

Johnson, Billy *94–99,* 227; *99–09,* 446

Johnson, Chic *38–39,* 407; *41–42,* 417; *44–45,* 404; *50–51,* 317

Johnson, F.G. *38–39,* 488

Johnson, Fenton *66–67,* 354; *68–69,* 433

Johnson, Freddie *24–25,* 601

Johnson, Greer *54–55,* 379; *60–61,* 39

Johnson, Hall *32–33,* 469; *43–44,* 406

Johnson, Haven *37–38,* 397

Johnson, Howard *23–24,* 414; *26–27,* 456

Johnson, Hunter *43–44,* 487; *45–46,* 456; *47–48,* 416

Johnson, J.C. *29–30,* 549

Johnson, Jack *63–64,* 343

Johnson, James *23–24,* 344

Johnson, James P. *38–39,* 486

Johnson, James W. *99–09,* 378, 473, 478, 541

Johnson, James Weldon *63–64,* 354; *66–67,* 354; *68–69,* 413

Johnson, Jimmy *27–28,* 518; *28–29,* 496; *31–32,* 451

Johnson, Julian *09–19,* 509

Johnson, Larry (Laurence) E. *25–26,* 444; *26–27,* 484; *27–28,* 424; *28–29,* 445; *29–30,* 381; *32–33,* 497

Johnson, Nora *67–68*, 347
Johnson, Nunnally *31–32*, 379; *43–44*, 433; *46–47*, 434; *67–68*, 347, 360
Johnson, Owen *99–09*, 553; *09–19*, 463, 536
Johnson, Page *61–62*, 332; *63–64*, 370
Johnson, Philander *20–21*, 392
Johnson, Philip *29–30*, 533; *35–36*, 487; *41–42*, 459
Johnson, Richard *63–64*, 314
Johnson, (A.) (J.) Rosamond *99–09*, 378, 414, 473, 478, 541, 583; *09–19*, 403, 448
Johnson, (Dr.) Samuel *99–09*, 387
Johnston, Agnes Christine *30–31*, 437
Johnston, Arthur *24–25*, 479
Johnston, Ben *70–71*
Johnston, Denis *31–32*, 485; *47–48*, 382; *60–61*, 357
Johnston, Howard *21–22*, 391
Johnston, Mary *99–09*, 389, 423, 578
Johnston, Robert *94–99*, 102
Johnstone, Alexander *09–19*, 460, 489, 525, 635
Johnstone, Lorimer *94–99*, 207
Johnstone, Tom (Thomas A.) *19–20*, 414; *21–22*, 491; *22–23*, 446; *23–24*, 435, 437; *25–26*, 463; *40–41*, 426
Johnstone, Will B. *09–19*, 469, 489, 525, 654; *21–22*, 491; *23–24*, 437
Jolliver, Simone *38–39*, 492
Jolson, Al *09–19*, 622; *62–63*, 295
Jonah, Dolly *61–62*, 316; *64–65*, 358
Jones, Nita *61–62*, 328
Jones, Agnes Hamilton *26–27*, 403
Jones, Archer *09–19*, 405
Jones, Arthur *35–36*, 430; *36–37*, 497; *52–53*, 259
Jones, E. Boyd *19–20*, 443
Jones, Earl C. *99–09*, 509
Jones, Edward *94–99*, 216

Jones, Elinor *69–70*, 367; *70–71*
Jones, Ellis O. *30–31*, 447
Jones, Frank *61–62*, 318; *63–64*, 369; *66–67*, 420
Jones, G. Edward *09–19*, 530
Jones, Henry (1) *29–30*, 512
Jones, Henry (2) *46–47*, 485
Jones, Henry (Arthur) (3) *94–99*, 90, 105, 109, 113, 121, 162, 186, 187, 217, 234, 240; *99–09*, 356, 383, 384, 447, 468, 481, 518, 546; *09–19*, 434, 465, 535, 538, 542, 559, 567; *27–28*, 503; *31–32*, 501; *40–41*, 432
Jones, LeRoi *61–62*, 311; *63–64*, 362, 364, 370; *64–65*, 350; *66–67*, 354, 355; *68–69*, 433, 455; *69–70*, 338, 354, 372
Jones, Leslie Julian *53–54*, 328
Jones, Robert Edmond *32–33*, 414; *36–37*, 449
Jones, Sidney *94–99*, 94, 105, 158, 176; *99–09*, 357, 373, 451; *09–19*, 409, 498, 529; *31–32*, 403
Jones, Stephen *23–24*, 313; *24–25*, 432; *25–26*, 438; *26–27*, 534
Jones, Terry *64–65*, 305
Jones, Tom *59–60*, 358; *63–64*, 311; *65–66*, 422; *66–67*, 375; *68–69*, 402; *69–70*, 367; *70–71*
Jones, Trevor *35–36*, 430
Jones, Walter *70–71*
Jonson, Ben *27–28*, 535; *29–30*, 509; *38–39*, 492; *46–47*, 467; *47–48*, 345, 348; *56–57*, 55, 353; *57–58*, 56; *63–64*, 325; *64–65*, 342; *66–67*, 361; *67–68*, 94
Joplin, Scott *68–69*, 446
Jordan, Carian *09–19*, 443, 516
Jordan, Hal *69–70*, 345
Jordan, Joe *28–29*, 449; *30–31*, 427
Jordan, Kate *99–09*, 562; *09–19*, 406, 543; *22–23*, 504
Jordan, Elizabeth *09–19*, 499
Joseph, Allen *68–69*, 457
Joseph, Edmund *39–40*, 447
Joseph, Irving *64–65*, 313

Joseph, Robert L. *49–50*, 360; *60–61*, 302; *61–62*, 292

Joseph, Stephen M. *69–70*, 368; *70–71*

Josephson, Gilbert *39–40*, 472

Joudry, Patricia *54–55*, 56; *59–60*, 328

Joullot, Eugene *23–24*, 333

Joyce, James *24–25*, 545; *46–47*, 485; *56–57*, 55; *58–59*, 55; *61–62*, 331; *62–63*, 320, 322; *63–64*, 368; *66–67*, 420; *67–68*, 386; *68–69*, 458

Jubin, George *94–99*, 256

Judge, James P. *25–26*, 560

Judson, Lester *55–56*, 335

Jules, Charles *19–20*, 342

Julian-Jones, Leslie *56–57*, 315

Junger, Esther *47–48*, 357

Jupp, Kenneth *61–62*, 312

Jurist, Irma *49–50*, 364, 367; *50–51*, 352; *61–62*, 331; *67–68*, 409

Justin, Mark *61–62*, 330

Jutte, William B. *32–33*, 455

Kadelburg, Gustav(e) *94–99*, 119, 121, 162, 217, 252; *99–09*, 365; *09–19*, 397, 415; *36–37*, 413

Kadison, Luba *61–62*, 323

Kadison, Philip *39–40*, 473; *40–41*, 433

Kadison, Pola *37–38*, 470

Kafka, Franz *49–50*, 385; *52–53*, 269; *61–62*, 330; *64–65*, 363; *68–69*, 433

Kaghan, Leonora *35–36*, 407

Kaghan, Theodore *37–38*, 464

Kahál, Irving *37–38*, 413; *40–41*, 382; *64–65*, 331

Kahane, Eric *68–69*, 453

Kahn, Alex *41–42*, 457

Kahn, Ali Akbar *67–68*, 402

Kahn, Gus *25–26*, 475, 597; *29–30*, 378

Kahn, Herman *64–65*, 303

Kahn, Roger Wolfe *27–28*, 547; *28–29*, 406

Kaiser, Georg *21–22*, 548; *22–23*, 423; *28–29*, 366; *43–44*, 488; *47–48*, 425; *63–64*, 342

Kalbfuss, F. *31–32*, 465

Kalcheim, Lee *63–64*, 370, 371; *66–67*, 402

Kalfin, Robert *62–63*, 331

Kalich, Jacob *42–43*, 435

Kalidasa *09–19*, 656

Kallen, Lucille *49–50*, 379; *57–58*, 312

Kallesser, Michael *25–26*, 600; *26–27*, 473; *27–28*, 520; *28–29*, 357, 495; *41–42*, 395; *67–68*, 408

Kalman, Emmerich (Emerich) *09–19*, 395, 520, 583, 589, 607; *22–23*, 467; *26–27*, 380, 517; *27–28*, 462, 538; *29–30*, 484; *45–46*, 380

Kalmanov, H. *70–71*

Kalmanovich, Harry *39–40*, 474; *61–62*, 312; *65–66*, 423

Kalmar, Bert *23–24*, 293; *24–25*, 433; *25–26*, 475; *26–27*, 382, 429, 495; *27–28*, 427, 486; *28–29*, 368, 402; *29–30*, 467; *41–42*, 408

Kalworth, Lincoln *29–30*, 521

Kaminska, Ida *67–68*, 345

Kaminski, Mark *69–70*, 376; *70–71*

Kamlot, Robert *66–67*, 422

Kamp, Irene *65–66*, 396

Kampf, Leopold *09–19*, 401

Kanaley, John *28–29*, 500

Kandel, Aben *30–31*, 507; *31–32*, 425

Kandel, Judith *35–36*, 428

Kander, John *60–61*, 297; *61–62*, 282; *62–63*, 289; *64–65*, 336; *66–67*, 370; *67–68*, 358; *68–69*, 393; *70–71*

Kane, Whitford *09–19*, 656

Kanfer, Stefan *61–62*, 305

Kanin, Fay *48–49*, 395; *53–54*, 335; *58–59*, 317; *61–62*, 270

Kanin, Garson *45–46*, 425; *48–49*, 406; *49–50*, 364; *50–51*, 313;

Kanin, Garson *(cont.)*
 59–60, 325; *60–61,* 315; *61–62,*
 289; *62–63,* 279
Kanin, Michael *53–54,* 335; *58–59,*
 317; *61–62,* 270
Kanka, Allena *09–19,* 557
Kanter, Phil *34–35,* 482
Kantor, Lenard *53–54,* 332
Kao-Tong-Kia *45–46,* 345
Kaper, Bronislaw *45–46,* 396
Kaplan, Elliot *63–64,* 351
Kaplan, Isabel De Witte *99–09,* 519
Kaplan, Samuel *09–19,* 612
Kaplan, Sol *54–55,* 398, 415; *56–57,*
 347; *59–60,* 329, 356; *60–61,* 306,
 321; *61–62,* 320
Karlin, George *47–48,* 426
Karlweiss, H. *99–09,* 352
Karp, David *66–67,* 423
Karr, Harold *56–57,* 314, 343
Kaser, A.L. *38–39,* 488
Kaslik, Vaclav *64–65,* 297
Kason, James *63–64,* 343
Kass, Jerome A. *61–62,* 317; *65–66,*
 431; *67–68,* 402
Kastner, Rose & Martin *69–70,* 377
Kasznar, Kurt S. *42–43,* 477; *43–44,*
 404
Katayev, Valentine *35–36,* 414, 510
Katscher, Robert *30–31,* 507; *38–39,*
 406
Katz, Leon *70–71*
Katzin, Olga *29–30,* 460
Katzin, Winifred *23–24,* 355; *25–26,*
 160; *26–27,* 396
Kauffman, Reginald Wright *09–19,*
 520
Kauffman, Stanley *37–38,* 468
Kaufman, Alvin *32–33,* 392
Kaufman, Beatrice *34–35,* 383
Kaufman, Bill *64–65,* 342; *65–66,*
 424; *66–67,* 404
Kaufman, Bob *68–69,* 433
Kaufman, Esther *60–61,* 39
Kaufman, George S. *09–19,* 636;
 21–22, 393, 512; *22–23,* 485;
 23–24, 293, 346, 398; *24–25,* 447,

459, 560; *25–26,* 453, 511; *26–27,*
 394; *27–28,* 483; *28–29,* 402;
 29–30, 416, 421, 479; *30–31,* 418,
 532; *31–32,* 451; *32–33,* 407, 495,
 496; *33–34,* 445, 462; *34–35,* 380;
 35–36, 440; *36–37,* 421, 440;
 37–38, 385; *38–39,* 412, 452;
 39–40, 396, 397, 402; *40–41,* 387;
 41–42, 406; *44–45,* 381, 399, 402,
 434; *46–47,* 434; *48–49,* 393, 425;
 50–51, 341, 351; *51–52,* 305, 322,
 328; *53–54,* 316; *54–55,* 400;
 63–64, 357; *65–66,* 387; *66–67,*
 357, 371, 385, 403; *68–69,* 447,
 455; *69–70,* 303
Kaufman, Mildred *32–33,* 392
Kaufman, Nico *46–47,* 487
Kaufman, S. Jay *23–24,* 439; *39–40,*
 394, 463
Kavanau, Alexander *34–35,* 483
Kay, Arthur *46–47,* 419
Kayden, Mildred *68–69,* 448; *69–70,*
 336
Kaye, B. *69–70,* 314
Kaye, B(enjamin) M. *26–27,* 372;
 29–30, 514, 548; *33–34,* 444;
 35–36, 426
Kaye, Buddy *48–49,* 379
Kaye, Danny *62–63,* 304
Kaye, Jim *55–56,* 336
Kaye, William *63–64,* 354
Kayser, Mrs. Robert Lee (see
 Martha Cabanne)
Kaz, Fred *69–70,* 343; *70–71*
Kazan, Molly *57–58,* 290; *60–61,* 38
Kazantzakis, Nikos *63–64,* 352;
 68–69, 393
Kazunoff (Kazounoff), Berenice
 38–39, 486; *39–40,* 437, 468
Keable, Robert *24–25,* 483
Kean, Gordon *21–22,* 528; *27–28,*
 442
Keane, John B. *61–62,* 312
Kearney, Patrick *25–26,* 472; *26–27,*
 399; *28–29,* 356; *30–31,* 495, 527,
 533; *31–32,* 391
Keats, John *62–63,* 322

Keays, Ethelyn Emery *09–19*, 490;
  22–23, 571
Keefe, Willard *27–28*, 476; *30–31*,
  499
Keeler, Eloise *33–34*, 506
Keeling, Henry *94–99*, 165
Keen, Herbert *94–99*, 183
Keith (see Kemble & Keith)
Keith, Nora *99–09*, 486
Keith, Robert *26–27*, 508; *32–33*,
  420
Kellam, Ian *66–67*, 365
Keller, Alvin *50–51*, 374
Kelley, Edgar Stillman *94–99*,
  208–9; *99–09*, 357
Kelly, Mr. *94–99*, 161
Kelly, Anthony Paul *09–19*, 632;
  19–20, 397
Kelly, George *22–23*, 444; *23–24*,
  396; *25–26*, 470; *26–27*, 410;
  27–28, 392, 475; *29–30*, 422;
  30–31, 478; *32–33*, 436; *36–37*,
  408; *44–45*, 423; *45–46*, 459;
  46–47, 442, 464; *49–50*, 381, 385;
  67–68, 353; *68–69*, 376
Kelly, Joe *94–99*, 224
Kelly, John Walter *39–40*, 459
Kelly, Tim *62–63*, 328
Kelm, William & Karlton *47–48*,
  427
Kelsey, Carlton *24–25*, 551
Kemble & Keith *99–09*, 540
Kemp, Harry *22–23*, 570
Kempner, David *09–19*, 456
Kempner, Nicholas *29–30*, 396
Kennard, Mrs. Arthur *99–09*, 538
Kennedy, Adrienne *63–64*, 356;
  65–66, 436; *68–69*, 434; *69–70*,
  375; *70–71*
Kennedy, Alfred C. *23–24*, 314
Kennedy, Aubrey *20–21*, 355;
  27–28, 442
Kennedy, Charles O'Brien *19–20*,
  370; *30–31*, 524
Kennedy, Charles Rann *99–09*, 561,
  574; *09–19*, 469, 627, 628; *20–21*,
  446; *22–23*, 531; *23–24*, 425;
24–25, 567; *24–26*, 595; *41–42*,
  416
Kennedy, Harold J. *44–45*, 411
Kennedy, Margaret *26–27*, 438;
  34–35, 442
Kennedy, Mary *24–25*, 516
Kennedy, Matt *26–27*, 364
Kennell, Ruth *32–33*, 494
Kennelly, Norman *66–67*, 399
Kenney, Charles Lamb *94–99*,
  110
Kenny, Charles *32–33*, 392
Kent, Charlotte *38–39*, 481
Kent, Walter *42–43*, 433; *51–52*,
  277; *61–62*, 333
Kenward, Allan R. *42–43*, 454
Kenyon, Charles A. *99–09*, 539,
  547; *09–19*, 460, 558, 609; *29–30*,
  450
Kenzel, Francis L. *09–19*, 539
Keohler, Ted *30–31*, 399
Kerby, Paul *42–43*, 441
Kerker, Gustave A. *94–99*, 99, 138,
  164, 173, 189, 202, 210, 219, 232,
  258; *99–09*, 385, 425, 434, 446,
  474, 512, 517, 518, 534, 540, 542;
  09–19, 471; *20–21*, 453; *21–22*,
  534; *48–49*, 426
Kerley, Jane *24–25*, 584
Kerman, Sheppard *59–60*, 315;
  63–64, 349
Kern, Jerome D. *99–09*, 466, 492,
  524, 540, 567; *09–19*, 409, 442,
  473, 484, 513, 529, 544, 552, 556,
  561, 567, 576, 593, 595, 605, 621,
  624, 630, 635, 656; *19–20*, 421;
  20–21, 397, 413; *21–22*, 452;
  22–23, 495; *23–24*, 348, 418;
  24–25, 443, 458; *25–26*, 452, 483;
  26–27, 400, 495; *27–28*, 482;
  29–30, 386; *31–32*, 411, 513;
  32–33, 416; *33–34*, 458; *38–39*,
  444; *39–40*, 412; *45–46*, 418;
  47–48, 403; *48–49*, 378; *51–52*,
  285; *53–54*, 306, 352; *59–60*, 48;
  60–61, 334; *66–67*, 352; *69–70*,
  371

Kernell, William B. *19–20*, 392;
25–26, 529
Kerner, Ben *64–65*, 352
Keroul & Barre *09–19*, 501, 513,
648
Kerr, C. Herbert *99–09*, 427
Kerr, C.V. *09–19*, 528
Kerr, Geoffrey *30–31*, 434
Kerr, Jean *45–46*, 434; *48–49*, 401;
49–50, 357; *53–54*, 326, 348;
58–59, 294; *60–61*, 329; *64–65*,
318
Kerr, Sophie *33–34*, 473
Kerr, Walter *42–43*, 434; *44–45*,
406; *45–46*, 434; *49–50*, 357;
58–59, 294
Kerrigan, Jeff *46–47*, 493
Kesey, Ken *63–64*, 313; *70–71*
Kesler, Lew *55–56*, 335, 336
Kesselring, Joseph O. *35–36*, 427;
36–37, 472; *40–41*, 410; *41–42*,
459; *50–51*, 342
Kessler, Lyle *66–67*, 422; *68–69*,
409
Kessler, Robert (Bob) *61–62*, 310;
62–63, 336; *64–65*, 358
Kester, Paul *99–09*, 383, 386, 424,
448, 470; *09–19*, 551; *20–21*, 378;
22–23, 576; *26–27*, 535; *28–29*,
447; *31–32*, 449; *47–48*, 430
Kettering, Ralph Thomas *24–25*,
434; *27–28*, 509
Keveson, Peter *69–70*, 366
Keyserling, Baron *09–19*, 598
Kidder, Edward E. *94–99*, 220;
99–09, 407, 492
Kiefert, Carl *94–99*, 219
Kiernan, Chris *47–48*, 428
Kilbourn, Fannie *23–24*, 313
Kildare, Owen *99–09*, 567
Kilgallen, Dorothy *43–44*, 477
Killens, John O. *64–65*, 362
Kilty, Jerome *59–60*, 329; *61–62*,
326; *68–69*, 431
Kimmel, Stanley *32–33*, 466
Kimmins, Anthony *33–34*, 531
King of Thailand (see Bhumibol)
King, Alexander *42–43*, 488

King, Clement *94–99*, 205
King, Edith *46–47*, 484
King, Emmett C. *94–99*, 236
King, Fitzmaurice *99–09*, 422
King, Harrison *31–32*, 501
King, Rufus *33–34*, 430, 529; *35–36*,
460
King, Thomas J. *47–48*, 428
King, Woodie Jr. *66–67*, 423
King-Hall, Stephen *29–30*, 419
King-Reeves, Hattie *46–47*, 495
Kingman, Tracy *38–39*, 485
Kingsbury (Kinsbury), Howard
Thayer *94–99*, 240; *99–09*, 355
Kingsley, Gershon *61–62*, 329
Kingsley, Herbert *42–43*, 446;
46–47, 494
Kingsley, Sidney (S.) *33–34*, 435;
35–36, 426; *36–37*, 422; *39–40*,
413; *42–43*, 460; *43–44*, 436;
48–49, 416; *50–51*, 341; *54–55*,
382; *62–63*, 282, 339
Kinkead, Cleves *09–19*, 555; *21–22*,
518
Kinnard, Jack *44–45*, 441
Kinoy, Ernest *46–47*, 498; *61–62*,
279; *64–65*, 316; *67–68*, 362
Kinsey, Tony *62–63*, 323
Kipling, Rudyard *99–09*, 385, 444;
09–19, 509
Kipnis, Claude *66–67*, 402
Kipphardt, Heinar *68–69*, 391;
69–70, 296
Kirby, Maurice Browne *09–19*, 395
Kirby, Nan *43–44*, 488
Kirchback, Wolfgang *94–99*, 224
Kirchon, V. *29–30*, 462
Kirkland, Alexander *44–45*, 426
Kirkland, Jack *33–34*, 467; *36–37*,
488; *37–38*, 416; *38–39*, 457;
42–43, 427; *43–44*, 409, 447;
48–49, 423; *49–50*, 375; *60–61*,
341
Kirkland, John M. *30–31*, 420
Kirkley, Donald *44–45*, 422
Kirkpatrick, John *25–26*, 435;
29–30, 402, 455, 542
Kirkup, James *64–65*, 306

Kirkwood, James *65–66*, 394
Kirkwood, Jimmy *49–50*, 368
Kirle, Bruce *67–68*, 409
Kishon, Ephraim *66–67*, 393; *67–68*, 339; *69–70*, 356
Kistemaecker (Kistenmaeckers), Henry *09–19*, 492, 634; *26–27*, 535
Kitchell, Iva *56–57*, 333
Kittredge, Helen Gholson *40–41*, 431
Kitts, W.P. *94–99*, 258
Klabund (Alfred Henschke) *40–41*, 432
Klages, Raymond *22–23*, 448
Klauber, Marcel *40–41*, 420
Kleban, Edward *70–71*
Klein, A.M. *51–52*, 325
Klein, Charles *94–99*, 118, 153, 154, 172, 184, 191, 200, 237; *99–09*, 382, 396, 405, 427, 444, 467, 501, 525, 547, 577; *09–19*, 407, 428, 449, 475, 510, 533, 556, 577, 584, 643; *21–22*, 533; *34–35*, 468; *48–49*, 425
Klein, Manuel *99–09*, 427, 445, 489, 503, 519, 527, 528, 548, 551, 574; *09–19*, 398, 423, 442, 449, 458, 474, 505, 515, 530
Klein, Maxine *70–71*
Klein, Paul *59–60*, 335, 336; *60–61*, 292; *63–64*, 347
Klein, Robert *67–68*, 376
Kleiner, Harry *45–46*, 406
Kleinman, Sy *55–56*, 339, 340
Kleinsinger, George *38–39*, 485; *39–40*, 468; *40–41*, 430; *41–42*, 438; *56–57*, 367; *70–71*
Klima, Ivan *70–71*
Kline, A.A. *24–25*, 532
Kline, Norman *67–68*, 377; *69–70*, 340
Kling, Saxon *28–29*, 405, 446; *32–33*, 474
Knepler, Paul *32–33*, 427; *37–38*, 405
Knight, Gwenn *37–38*, 412
Knight, Michael *69–70*, 357

Knight, Percival *09–19*, 616, 625, 641; *22–23*, 465
Knight, Raymond *38–39*, 424
Knoblock (Knoblauch), Edward *99–09*, 524; *09–19*, 404, 436, 461, 475, 477, 534, 544, 581, 644; *20–21*, 382; *23–24*, 316; *24–25*, 483; *27–28*, 414, 440; *29–30*, 545; *31–32*, 400; *32–33*, 456; *34–35*, 476; *53–54*, 324; *63–64*, 367; *65–66*, 368
Knott, Frederick *52–53*, 266; *61–62*, 267; *65–66*, 396
Knowles, James Sheridan *94–99*, 105, 145, 167; *99–09*, 412, 545
Knox, Alexander *49–50*, 362
Knox, Florence Clay *24–25*, 583
Kober, Arthur *36–37*, 467; *52–53*, 253; *59–60*, 313
Koblitz, Albert *23–24*, 343
Koch, Howard *33–34*, 450; *41–42*, 424
Koch, Kenneth *61–62*, 325
Kochno, Boris *34–35*, 460
Kock, Howard E. *29–30*, 386
Koehler, Ted *32–33*, 392; *34–35*, 405; *66–67*, 414
Koenig, Laird *68–69*, 409
Koestler, Arthur *50–51*, 341
Kohan, Alan *62–63*, 337
Kohn, Rose Simon *43–44*, 434
Kohner, Frederick *46–47*, 420
Kolitz, Zvi *67–68*, 372
Kollo, Walter *09–19*, 517; *20–21*, 448; *29–30*, 523
Komisarjevsky, Theodore *39–40*, 464
Komparu, Zenou *64–65*, 362
Kon, Henoch *64–65*, 347; *66–67*, 393; *67–68*, 339
Konecky, Jennifer *64–65*, 358
Konta, Alexander *99–09*, 564
Kookoolis, Joseph Martinez *70–71*
Kootz, Samuel M. *45–46*, 414
Kopit, Arthur L. *61–62*, 324; *63–64*, 303; *64–65*, 356; *69–70*, 299
Koppel, Holger *27–28*, 459
Kops, Bernard *58–59*, 51

Kore(n)to, Paul *64–65*, 342; *65–66*, 424; *66–67*, 404

Korey, Lois Balk *64–65*, 358

Korman, Jess J. *61–62*, 305

Kornblum, I.B. *20–21*, 428

Kornfeld, Robert *66–67*, 410

Korngold, Erich Wolfgang *43–44*, 470

Kortner, Fritz *39–40*, 439

Kosma, Mons. *52–53*, 268

Kostic, Vojislav *68–69*, 426

Kottow, Hans *32–33*, 390

Koutoukas, H.M. *67–68*, 403

Koven, Stanley *63–64*, 365

Kozlenko, William *39–40*, 444, 446

Kraatz, Curt *99–09*, 351, 390, 510, 569

Krafft, Paul *29–30*, 419

Kraft, H. *37–38*, 464

Kraft, H.S. *31–32*, 491; *40–41*, 401; *41–42*, 434; *43–44*, 460

Kraft, Helen *09–19*, 482

Kraft, Hy *51–52*, 290; *63–64*, 334

Kralj, Lado *70–71*

Kraly, Hans *40–41*, 393

Kramm, Joseph *51–52*, 305; *53–54*, 322; *61–62*, 280; *63–64*, 367

Krasna, Norman *31–32*, 429; *34–35*, 378; *41–42*, 409; *44–45*, 404; *46–47*, 459; *48–49*, 384; *53–54*, 316; *57–58*, 322; *61–62*, 272; *66–67*, 382

Kraus, John *69–70*, 377

Krause, Werner *61–62*, 308

Kreiner, Marty *63–64*, 343

Kreisler, Fritz *19–20*, 367; *44–45*, 400

Kreitzberg, Yasha *47–48*, 432

Kremer, Theodore *94–99*, 183; *99–09*, 398; *09–19*, 441; *23–24*, 441

Kremm, L. *99–09*, 392

Kresley, Ed *65–66*, 424; *66–67*, 404

Kretzmer, H. *69–70*, 314

Kreuder, Peter *36–37*, 448

Kreutz, Arthur *46–47*, 460

Kreymborg, Alfred *24–25*, 586; *26–27*, 522; *35–36*, 479; *47–48*, 430

Krimsky, Jerrold *32–33*, 483

Krimsky, John (see John Van Ostend Van Antwerp)

Krob, Lillian Wood *39–40*, 440

Kroll, Bernice *50–51*, 352

Kronenberger, Louis *53–54*, 334; *62–63*, 326

Kruger, Jess *39–40*, 447

Krummer (Kummer), Frederic Arnold *09–19*, 411, 480, 496; *19–20*, 385, 422, 445

Kruse, Werner *36–37*, 448; *65–66*, 429

Kubly, Herbert *44–45*, 386

Kuhn, Victoria *46–47*, 431

Kulkin, Philip *24–25*, 432

Kuller, Sid *40–41*, 403; *42–43*, 471; *49–50*, 367

Kummer, Clare *99–09*, 442, 490; *09–19*, 281, 465, 593, 609, 642; *20–21*, 408, 431, 432; *21–22*, 477; *22–23*, 458; *23–24*, 363; *24–25*, 480, 485; *25–26*, 585; *29–30*, 535; *33–34*, 436, 446, 495; *37–38*, 405, 433; *44–45*, 408; *64–65*, 351

Kummer, Frederic Arnold (see Frederic Arnold Krummer)

Kunneke, Edward *22–23*, 526; *24–25*, 524; *25–26*, 502

Kuntz, John B. *68–69*, 422; *70–71*

Kunz-Schmidt, Katherine *38–39*, 492

Kupferberg, Tuli *69–70*, 305

Kupferman, Meyer *65–66*, 431

Kurnitz, Harry *54–55*, 365; *58–59*, 298; *61–62*, 263; *63–64*, 315

Kurtz, Maurice *41–42*, 458

Kusell, Daniel *22–23*, 443; *26–27*, 459; *28–29*, 375; *32–33*, 480

Kushner, William *70–71*

Kvapil, Jaroslav *09–19*, 445

Kvares, Donald *67–68*, 408, 412; *68–69*, 456; *70–71*

Kwan, Kiruchi *28–29*, 500

Kydoniatis, Konstantinos *61–62,*
   255; *64–65,* 298; *68–69,* 434
Kyle, Billy *49–50,* 367
Kyne, Peter B. *09–19,* 649

LaBar, Tom *70–71*
Labiche, Eugene Marie *94–99,* 159;
   99–09, 480; *26–27,* 403; *37–38,*
   469
Lacey, Bill *62–63,* 324
Lacey, Franklin *57–58,* 306; *65–66,*
   366
Lachaume, Aimee *99–09,* 391
Lackaye, Wilton *99–09,* 529; *25–26,*
   428; *33–34,* 488
Lackey, R.B. *31–32,* 503
Lacy, Ernest *94–99,* 251; *99–09,* 439
Ladd, Hank *47–48,* 368
Lady of Quality, A *28–29,* 461
Lafiaji, Mr. *69–70,* 353
La Gattuta, Joseph *38–39,* 485
La Grange (Charles de la Grange)
   69–70, 313
Lahr, John *69–70,* 305
Lai, Francis *64–65,* 315
Laird, Marvin *65–66,* 410
Laise, Wenner *38–39,* 487
Lait, Jack *09–19,* 522, 636; *22–23,*
   433; *34–35,* 477
Lakatos, Laszlo *24–25,* 577; *26–27,*
   422
Lalic, Ivan *68–69,* 426
Laloy, Louis *09–19,* 469
Lamb, A.J. *24–25,* 589
Lamb, Arthur *99–09,* 438
Lamb, Myrna *69–70,* 345
Lambert, Edward J. *35–36,* 401
Lambert, John *61–62,* 288
Lamkin, Speed *58–59,* 302
La Montaine, John *62–63,* 321
Lamoureux, Robert *55–56,* 347
Lampell, Millard *60–61,* 300
Lampl, Carl *48–49,* 379
Lamson, Peggy *46–47,* 432
La Mure, Pierre *67–68,* 387
Lancaster, A.E. *94–99,* 100, 124–5,
   223, 229; *99–09,* 394

Lancourt, Saul *42–43,* 488
Land, Andrew *46–47,* 499
Landeck, Benjamin *94–99,* 162, 171,
   246; *99–09,* 366
Landesman, Fran *58–59,* 336
Landesman, Jay *58–59,* 336
Landis, Frederick *09–19,* 623
Landman, Isaac *09–19,* 450
Landman, Michael L. *09–19,* 568
Landon, Allan *69–70,* 372
Landon, Margaret *50–51,* 360;
   55–56, 384; *59–60,* 340; *63–64,*
   302; *64–65,* 296; *67–68,* 379
Landowski, Marcel *65–66,* 397
Landsbergis, Algirdas *60–61,* 39
Lane, Burton *31–32,* 383; *40–41,*
   378; *44–45,* 404; *46–47,* 455;
   54–55, 414; *59–60,* 338; *65–66,*
   377; *66–67,* 386
Lane, Eleanor Macartney *99–09,*
   486
Lane, Robert M. *70–71*
Langbridge, Frederick *99–09,* 421
Lang, Andrew *37–38,* 448
Lang, Jerry *34–35,* 483
Lang, Matheson *19–20,* 406, 409
Lang, Philip J. *63–64,* 372
Langdon, Dory *66–67,* 414
Langdon, Gwynn *35–36,* 429
Lange, Sven *20–21,* 405
Langer, Frantisek *27–28,* 455;
   28–29, 493
Langley, A.N. *41–42,* 410
Langley, Noel *39–40,* 416; *48–49,*
   385; *49–50,* 384
Langner, Lawrence *09–19,* 560, 579,
   607; *21–22,* 414; *22–23,* 575;
   26–27, 367; *27–28,* 508; *32–33,*
   436; *33–34,* 439, 441, 442; *34–35,*
   447; *40–41,* 390; *49–50,* 372
Langner, (Mrs.) Lawrence (see
   Isabelle Louden)
Langner, Ruth *25–26,* 535; *27–28,*
   535; *29–30,* 412; *30–31,* 440;
   34–35, 371
Langtry, (Mrs.) Lillie *99–09,* 425
Languirand, Jacques *63–64,* 369

Lania, Leo *30–31*, 440

Lankester, E.G. *94–99*, 236

Lanner, Joseph *41–42*, 431

Lannin, Paul *20–21*, 446; *21–22*, 514; *27–28*, 392

Lannon, J. David *37–38*, 469; *38–39*, 491

Lanteau, William *60–61*, 292

Lanusse, Armand *66–67*, 354

La Prade, Malcolm L. *23–24*, 422; *63–64*, 355

Lardner, Ring *21–22*, 555; *27–28*, 472; *28–29*, 377; *29–30*, 416; *30–31*, 455; *32–33*, 495; *69–70*, 371

Lardner, Ring Jr. *63–64*, 325

Larimer, Robert *61–62*, 328

Larkin, John Jr. *31–32*, 456

Larkin, Margaret *25–26*, 594; *31–32*, 490

Larned, William Trowbridge *99–09*, 564

Larnen, Brendan (O.P.) *52–53*, 308; *61–62*, 321; *64–65*, 363

Larric, J.B. *09–19*, 535

Larric, Jack *30–31*, 450

Larrie, Jack *09–19*, 652; *24–25*, 438

L'Arronge, A. *94–99*, 125, 247

Larsen, Carl *63–64*, 352

Larson, Brent *69–70*, 369

Larson, Jack *67–68*, 406

Lascal, Milton *43–44*, 424

Lash, Isidore *38–39*, 493; *47–48*, 432

La Shelle, Kirke *99–09*, 358, 362, 420, 451

Lashin, Orrie *35–36*, 477

Laska, Edward *23–24*, 305

Lasker, Harvey *62–63*, 318

Lasswell, Mary *43–44*, 447

Laszlo, Miklos *62–63*, 307

Latham, Claude & Howard *37–38*, 461

Latham, Jean Lee *35–36*, 479

Lathom, Lord *26–27*, 390

Latouche (LaTouche), John *36–37*, 448; *38–39*, 470, 481, 486; *39–40*, 394, 468; *40–41*, 388; *41–42*, 422, 427; *42–43*, 433; *44–45*, 399; *45–46*, 396; *46–47*, 451; *47–48*, 397; *53–54*, 306, 346; *55–56*, 360, 361, 391; *56–57*, 340; *60–61*, 45; *61–62*, 323; *63–64*, 357

Lauf, Herr *99–09*, 390

Laufs, Carl *94–99*, 128; *41–42*, 453

Laughton, Charles *47–48*, 393; *52–53*, 288; *61–62*, 318; *66–67*, 361

Laun, Louis *48–49*, 380

Laure, Katharine *44–45*, 394

Lauren, S.K. *29–30*, 498; *32–33*, 401

Laurence, Mark *39–40*, 473

Laurence, William L. *29–30*, 476; *30–31*, 521

Laurents, Arthur *45–46*, 418; *46–47*, 495; *49–50*, 374; *52–53*, 260; *56–57*, 349; *57–58*, 286; *58–59*, 52, 337; *59–60*, 336; *60–61*, 303; *63–64*, 330, 333; *64–65*, 330; *66–67*, 391, 423; *68–69*, 373

Lavedan, Henri *94–99*, 243; *99–09*, 509; *09–19*, 437, 628, 650

LaVer (Laver), James *39–40*, 394; *40–41*, 432

La Verne, Lucille *09–19*, 499

Lavery, Emmet *34–35*, 382; *45–46*, 423; *47–48*, 367

Lavrenoff, B. *34–35*, 453

Law, Arthur *94–99*, 94; *99–09*, 418

Lawes, (Warden) Lewis E. *36–37*, 473

Lawler, Ray *57–58*, 310; *67–68*, 396

Lawless, Sue *66–67*, 423; *68–69*, 422

Lawlor, James Reed *50–51*, 352; *67–68*, 402

Lawlor, Nora *35–36*, 405

Lawrence, Basil *09–19*, 547

Lawrence, Bert *40–41*, 403

Lawrence, D.H. *45–46*, 385; *62–63*, 322

Lawrence, Eddie *64–65*, 325

Lawrence, Francis C. *38–39*, 491

Lawrence, Jack *51–52*, 276; *56–57*, 357; *63–64*, 319

Lawrence, Jerome *47–48*, 379; *54–55*, 409; *56–57*, 313, 329; *58–59*, 291; *59–60*, 292, 304; *60–61*, 342; *64–65*, 326; *65–66*, 412; *68–69*, 405

Lawrence, John *37–38*, 381

Lawrence, Lester *42–43*, 471

Lawrence, Mark *38–39*, 491; *41–42*, 461; *64–65*, 314; *66–67*, 358

Lawrence, Reginald *32–33*, 401; *35–36*, 408; *43–44*, 443; *50–51*, 336; *58–59*, 321; *62–63*, 339

Lawrence, Stephen (Steven) *62–63*, 316; *65–66*, 424; *66–67*, 404

Lawrence, Vincent *20–21*, 436; *23–24*, 295; *24–25*, 523; *25–26*, 422; *26–27*, 373; *27–28*, 465, 495, 554; *28–29*, 411; *29–30*, 411; *31–32*, 399; *44–45*, 415

Lawrence, Warren F. *27–28*, 508; *28–29*, 477

Laws, Maury *68–69*, 428

Lawson, Charles *63–64*, 350

Lawson, John Howard *22–23*, 538; *24–25*, 521; *25–26*, 562; *26–27*, 490; *27–28*, 491; *32–33*, 391; *33–34*, 508, 509; *36–37*, 466; *37–38*, 450

Lawton, Martin *24–25*, 426

Layton, Mr. (see Creamer & Layton)

Layton, Joe *70–71*

Layton, William *67–68*, 342

Lazarus, Andrew J. *46–47*, 498

Lazarus, Milton *35–36*, 439, 460; *40–41*, 400; *42–43*, 450; *44–45*, 369; 297

Lazarus, Sidney *24–25*, 479

Lea, Fanny Heaslip *29–30*, 420

Leach, Arthur C. *34–35*, 483

Leach, Wilford *70–71*

Lean, Cecil *19–20*, 434

Learsi, Rufus *25–26*, 590

Leary, Helen & Nolan *32–33*, 392

Leasor, James *70–71*

Leavitt, Douglas *20–21*, 439

Le Baron (LeBaron), William *09–19*, 422, 448, 525, 602, 614, 647, 656; *19–20*, 367; *20–21*, 401; *21–22*, 397, 398, 435; *22–23*, 467; *23–24*, 394; *25–26*, 426

Leblanc, Maurice *09–19*, 397

Lebowsky, Stanley *63–64*, 355; *64–65*, 343; *65–66*, 422; *69–70*, 315

Le Brandt, Joseph *94–99*, 238

Leclercq, Henri *94–99*, 250

Lecocq, (Alexander) Charles *94–99*, 171; *99–09*, 479; *31–32*, 414; *43–44*, 485

Lecuona, Mr. *54–55*, 386

Lederer, Charles *53–54*, 324; *63–64*, 367; *65–66*, 368

Ledru, J. *64–65*, 295

Lee, Albert *09–19*, 513

Lee, Bert *09–19*, 615; *32–33*, 411

Lee, C.Y. *58–59*, 306

Lee, Charles *26–27*, 524

Lee, Dai-Keong *53–54*, 310; *56–57*, 333

Lee, Gypsy Rose *43–44*, 419; *58–59*, 337; *60–61*, 48

Lee, Harry *25–26*, 423

Lee, James *56–57*, 58

Lee, Jessica *37–38*, 431

Lee, Kenneth *94–99*, 180

Lee, Leonard *55–56*, 359

Lee, Lester *27–28*, 460; *29–30*, 377; *42–43*, 420, 429, 471; *48–49*, 408

Lee, Maryat *50–51*, 375

Lee, Robert E. *47–48*, 379; *54–55*, 409; *56–57*, 313, 329; *58–59*, 291; *59–60*, 292, 304; *60–61*, 342; *64–65*, 326; *65–66*, 412; *68–69*, 405

Lee, Theophane *54–55*, 53

Leech, Margaret *34–35*, 383

Leeds, Nancy *65–66*, 424

Lees, G. *69–70*, 314

LeFanu, S. *70–71*

Lefebre, Hans *39–40*, 437

Leffingwell, Miron J. *94–99*, 238

Leonard, Michael *62–63*, 318;
  65–66, 390; *67–68*, 357
Leoncavallo, Ruggiero *99–09*, 557;
  43–44, 441; *44–45*, 378; *45–46*,
  388; *46–47*, 409; *47–48*, 343
Leongrande, Ernest *63–64*, 352
Leonidoff, Leon *38–39*, 491
Leontovich, Eugenie *42–43*, 459
Lepere, William H. *94–99*, 106
Lerner, Alan Jay *37–38*, 469; *38–39*,
  491; *43–44*, 426; *45–46*, 409;
  46–47, 471; *48–49*, 386; *49–50*,
  379; *51–52*, 292; *55–56*, 378;
  56–57, 363; *60–61*, 310; *61–62*,
  301, 333; *62–63*, 294, 295, 296;
  63–64, 338; *64–65*, 321, 331;
  65–66, 377; *67–68*, 356; *68–69*,
  373; *69–70*, 309, 335
Lerner, Sam *43–44*, 411; *47–48*,
  402
Leroux, Gaston *09–19*, 407
Le Roux, Hugh *94–99*, 92
Leroy, Nat *24–25*, 564
Lesan, David *34–35*, 478; *38–39*,
  481
Leslie, Aleen *43–44*, 420
Leslie, Lew *24–25*, 479; *29–30*, 500;
  30–31, 523; *33–34*, 466; *38–39*,
  459
Lessing, Doris *64–65*, 352
Lessing, (von) Gotthold Ephraim
  41–42, 445; *61–62*, 325, 327;
  66–67, 412; *68–69*, 433
Lessner, George *48–49*, 375
Lester, Edwin *64–65*, 297
Lester, Elliott *25–26*, 429; *31–32*,
  407
Lestocq, William *94–99*, 103, 124
L'Estrange, David *24–25*, 538
Leterrier, Mons. *94–99*, 177, 225
Letraz, Jean *36–37*, 499
Levant, Oscar *29–30*, 491; *38–39*,
  452; *39–40*, 396
Leveen, Raymond *41–42*, 403
Leveillee, Claude *64–65*, 343
Level, Maurice *09–19*, 509
Levenson, Leonard L. *45–46*, 381

Levey, Harold (A.) *20–21*, 411;
  22–23, 507; *23–24*, 325; *24–25*,
  495; *25–26*, 522, 570; *27–28*, 484
Levi, Maurice *94–99*, 193; *99–09*,
  371, 393, 415, 471, 506, 556, 563,
  584; *09–19*, 446
Levi, Stephen *67–68*, 344
Levik, H. *47–48*, 432
Levin, Donald *63–64*, 366
Levin, Ira *55–56*, 355; *57–58*, 317;
  60–61, 313; *61–62*, 290; *65–66*,
  375; *67–68*, 341
Levin, Jack *41–42*, 405
Levin, Meyer *57–58*, 296
Levin, Sylvan *54–55*, 399
Levine, Isaac Don *26–27*, 425
Levine, Milton *43–44*, 489
Levine, William (Bill) *62–63*, 316,
  317, 324; *63–64*, 355; *64–65*, 342,
  343
Levins, Peter *40–41*, 431
Levinson, Ben *39–40*, 470; *40–41*,
  430, 431
Levinson, Leonard Louis *44–45*,
  399
Levinson, Richard *60–61*, 292
Levister, Alonzo *67–68*, 376; *68–69*,
  442
Levitt, Saul *59–60*, 312; *70–71*
Levy, Benn W. *26–27*, 438; *28–29*,
  412; *29–30*, 493; *30–31*, 403, 423,
  457; *31–32*, 446, 458; *32–33*, 489;
  36–37, 475; *37–38*, 390, 417;
  38–39, 487; *47–48*, 371; *49–50*,
  362; *50–51*, 357; *59–60*, 321;
  60–61, 306
Levy, Charles *38–39*, 472, 480
Levy, Eric *69–70*, 357
Levy, Jacques *69–70*, 335
Levy, Jonathan *70–71*
Levy, Jose G. *09–19*, 507
Levy, Leo A. *32–33*, 491
Levy, Martin David *67–68*, 394
Levy, Melvin *34–35*, 417; *36–37*,
  452
Levy, Newman *29–30*, 548; *34–35*,
  362

Levy, Parke *37–38*, 413; *39–40*, 463, 466; *41–42*, 426
Lewin, John *68–69*, 398; *69–70*, 319, 365; *70–71*
Lewine, Richard *34–35*, 429; *36–37*, 457; *37–38*, 449; *40–41*, 389; *46–47*, 429; *47–48*, 377; *59–60*, 300
Lewis, Mr. *53–54*, 306
Lewis, Allen Jack *68–69*, 446
Lewis, Andy & Dave *66–67*, 408
Lewis, Catherine *94–99*, 100
Lewis, Cecil *27–28*, 520; *28–29*, 404; *31–32*, 416; *32–33*, 390
Lewis, David *64–65*, 305
Lewis, Harry *09–19*, 578
Lewis, John *62–63*, 296
Lewis, Leopold *94–99*, 150; *99–09*, 353, 442; *25–26*, 584
Lewis, Lillian *94–99*, 183, 202
Lewis, Lloyd *34–35*, 403
Lewis, Milton *46–47*, 414
Lewis, Morgan *33–34*, 507; *38–39*, 456; *39–40*, 436; *45–46*, 431
Lewis, Mort *39–40*, 463
Lewis, Peter *63–64*, 350
Lewis, Philip *40–41*, 397; *59–60*, 40
Lewis, Richard *68–69*, 407
Lewis, Sam M. *26–27*, 510
Lewis, Seaman *27–28*, 391; *28–29*, 354
Lewis, Sinclair *09–19*, 651; *21–22*, 436; *28–29*, 356; *33–34*, 501; *34–35*, 361, 403; *36–37*, 490; *69–70*, 315
Lewis, Ted *27–28*, 452
Lewisohn, Irene *25–26*, 569; *26–27*, 504
Lewisohn, Ludwig *36–37*, 449
Leyssac, Paul *27–28*, 532
Liadoro, Mr. *47–48*, 417
Liberata, Franco *99–09*, 536
Libertini, Richard *60–61*, 354
Libott, Robert Yale *56–57*, 322
Licht, David *46–47*, 497; *47–48*, 432; *65–66*, 426
Lichtman, Nat *38–39*, 486
Lieberman, Herbert *64–65*, 356

Lieberman, Leo *61–62*, 278
Liebermann, Rolf *61–62*, 308–9
Lieberson, Martin R. *50–51*, 354
Lieberson, William H. *50–51*, 354
Liebler, Theodore A. Jr. *09–19*, 621
Liebling, Howard *64–65*, 342, 343; *65–66*, 422
Liebling, Leonard *09–19*, 431, 458, 496
Liebman, Max *38–39*, 461; *39–40*, 400; *40–41*, 411
Liebovits, David *20–21*, 422
Lief, Max & Nathaniel *27–28*, 536; *28–29*, 373, 469; *31–32*, 379, 520
Lieferant, Henry & Sylvia *32–33*, 490
Liepolt, Werner *68–69*, 430
Liev, Siskind *35–36*, 510
Lifson, David S. *43–44*, 488; *61–62*, 327
Lightfoot, Gordon *69–70*, 354
Lightner, Frances *24–25*, 556
Liljencrantz, Torvald *31–32*, 397
Liljenquist, Don C. *68–69*, 378
Lillard, Robert *29–30*, 433
Lilley, Edward Clarke *30–31*, 400; *38–39*, 456
Lillian, Isador(e) *44–45*, 443; *45–46*, 460; *46–47*, 497
Lillie, Beatrice *56–57*, 358
Lillo, George *28–29*, 384
Lincke, Paul *99–09*, 556
Lincoln, Florence *09–19*, 613
Lincoln, Joseph C. *19–20*, 426
Lind, Jacov *67–68*, 389
Lindau, K(C)arl *99–09*, 392; *09–19*, 398, 459, 480; *44–45*, 444
Linder, Jack *48–49*, 410
Linder, Mark *27–28*, 536; *28–29*, 415; *29–30*, 529; *30–31*, 528; *32–33*, 389; *35–36*, 500
Lindsay, Howard *26–27*, 457; *29–30*, 442; *30–31*, 459; *33–34*, 425, 459; *34–35*, 412; *35–36*, 403; *36–37*, 424; *37–38*, 397; *39–40*, 410; *41–42*, 460; *42–43*, 432; *45–46*, 407; *48–49*, 391; *50–51*, 319; *51–52*, 283; *53–54*, 330; *55–56*,

368; *56–57*, 343; *58–59*, 318;
59–60, 303; *61–62*, 330; *62–63*,
280; *66–67*, 386; *67–68*, 346
Lindsey, William *09–19*, 592
Lineberger, James *70–71*
Lingeman, Richard *63–64*, 346
Lingham, M.V. *94–99*, 173
Link, Peter *69–70*, 340; *70–71*
Link, Ron *69–70*, 374
Link, William *60–61*, 292
Linne, Hans S. *09–19*, 472
Linsenmann, George W. *62–63*, 335;
64–65, 343
Lion, Leon M. *99–09*, 432; *25–26*,
466
Liorat, Mons. *94–99*, 195
Lipkind, Goodman *37–38*, 461
Lipman, Clara *99–09*, 505; *09–19*,
464, 515; *21–22*, 461
Lippa, Louis *59–60*, 41
Lippman, Morton *41–42*, 461
Lippman, Sidney *46–47*, 474
Lipscomb, David *64–65*, 305
Lipscott, Allen (Alan) *37–38*, 413;
39–40, 463, 466; *41–42*, 426
Lipshitz, Arthur *09–19*, 421
Lipschultz, Bess *09–19*, 631
Lipskeroff, Constantin *25–26*, 515
Lipton, James *59–60*, 47; *62–63*,
284; *66–67*, 385
Liska, Zdenek *64–65*, 297
Lister, Walter B. *26–27*, 503
Liszt, Franz *34–35*, 459; *41–42*, 456;
47–48, 418
Littell, Philip *09–19*, 405, 417, 506
Little, Homer *32–33*, 479
Littlefield, James *44–45*, 365; *46–47*,
414, 482
Littlewood, Joan (Theater Workshop)
64–65, 303
Litvak, Barry *70–71*
Living Theater Company *68–69*, 456
Livings, Henry *66–67*, 403
Livingston, Arthur *26–27*, 421
Livingston, James *46–47*, 433
Livingston, Jay *57–58*, 315; *61–62*,
260
Livingston, Jerry *43–44*, 414

Livingston, Robert H. *70–71*
Livingstone, Ruth *21–22*, 468
Livshitz, Moshe *48–49*, 429
Livy (Titus Livius) *48–49*, 405
Llewellyn, Richard *65–66*, 410
Lloyd, David D. *94–99*, 111, 186,
235, 236
Lloyd, Henry *32–33*, 392
Lloyd, Norman *46–47*, 487
Lobo, Edu *69–60*, 339
Lochbiler, Don *32–33*, 488
Locke, Edward J. *99–09*, 581;
09–19, 419, 479, 503, 549, 550,
650; *19–20*, 359; *22–23*, 438, 516;
25–26, 599; *27–28*, 437, 498;
32–33, 502
Locke, Edwin A. *94–99*, 84
Locke, Sam(uel) D. *39–40*, 400;
40–41, 389; *41–42*, 438, 459;
42–43, 433; *46–47*, 415; *55–56*,
360; *57–58*, 299
Locke, William J. *99–09*, 551;
09–19, 405; *22–23*, 566
Locke-Elliott, Sumner (see Sumner
Locke Elliott)
Lockhart, Gene *25–26*, 555
Lockname, Clement *94–99*, 188
Lockridge, Frances & Richard
40–41, 410
Lockwood, Lee *68–69*, 377
Lodge, Mark *52–53*, 308
Loeb, John Jacob *33–34*, 430;
55–56, 347; *61–62*, 303–4; *62–63*,
313; *65–66*, 417; *66–67*, 401
Loeb, Lee *44–45*, 372; *70–71*
Loesser, Frank *35–36*, 463; *48–49*,
388; *50–51*, 329, 346; *54–55*, 407;
55–56, 387; *58–59*, 322; *59–60*,
327; *61–62*, 261; *64–65*, 334;
65–66, 407, 408; *66–67*, 351;
70–71
Loewe, Frederick *38–39*, 434; *43–44*,
426; *45–46*, 409; *46–47*, 471;
49–50, 379; *51–52*, 292; *55–56*,
378; *56–57*, 363; *60–61*, 311;
61–62, 301, 333; *62–63*, 294, 295,
296; *63–64*, 338; *64–65*, 321, 331;
67–68, 356; *68–69*, 373

Loftus, Cecilia *37–38*, 466; *38–39*, 488

Loftus, Cissie *99–09*, 378

Logan, Danny *63–64*, 363

Logan, Joshua *39–40*, 453; *40–41*, 375; *47–48*, 383; *48–49*, 419; *49–50*, 376; *52–53*, 253; *54–55*, 373, 396, 412; *56–57*, 343, 369; *60–61*, 337; *62–63*, 339; *65–66*, 366; *67–68*, 339

Logan, Stanley *26–27*, 447

Logue, Christopher *62–63*, 323

Lohmann, Helen *26–27*, 432

Lollos, John *67–68*, 397

Lomax, Alan *66–67*, 355

Lombardo, Carmen *55–56*, 347; *61–62*, 303; *62–63*, 313; *65–66*, 417; *66–67*, 401

London, Marc *64–65*, 358

Lonergan, Lester *27–28*, 545; *28–29*, 457

Long, Dillard *32–33*, 447

Long, John Luther *99–09*, 107, 359, 481, 513, 576; *45–46*, 391

Long, Kenn *70–71*

Long, Sumner Authur *62–63*, 289; *69–70*, 306

Longfellow, Henry Wadsworth *09–19*, 510; *47–48*, 429

Longstreet, Stephen *47–48*, 358, 359

Lonsdale, Frederick *09–19*, 409, 438, 492, 583, 636; *22–23*, 468, 577; *23–24*, 349; *24–25*, 466, 576; *25–26*, 491; *26–27*, 404, 406; *28–29*, 369; *30–31*, 434; *37–38*, 424; *39–40*, 419; *43–44*, 418; *50–51*, 322

Loomis, Clarence *38–39*, 475

Loos, Anita *23–24*, 311; *25–26*, 433; *26–27*, 388; *31–32*, 426; *46–47*, 433; *49–50*, 363; *51–52*, 295; *59–60*, 295; *64–65*, 343

Lopez, Francis *55–56*, 347

Lopez, Sabatino *09–19*, 656; *21–22*, 485

Lorca, Federico Garcia *34–35*, 449; *42–43*, 484; *44–45*, 442; *46–47*, 486, 487; *48–49*, 426, 427; *49–50*, 383; *50–51*, 340; *56–57*, 320; *57–58*, 53; *61–62*, 330; *64–65*, 341; *66–67*, 361; *69–70*, 374; *70–71*

Lord, Mindret *35–36*, 507

Lord, William *37–38*, 461

Loredo, Armando *38–39*, 480

Lorentz, Kay & Lore *61–62*, 308; *65–66*, 429

Lorenz, Herbert Richard *23–24*, 434

Lorimer, Wright *99–09*, 458

Lorin, Will *41–42*, 459; *60–61*, 311

Loring, Eugene *38–39*, 477

Lorraine, William *99–09*, 436, 502

Lothar & Sebesi *31–32*, 478

Lothar, Mark *60–61*, 323; *65–66*, 407

Lothar, Rudolph *24–25*, 437; *27–28*, 409, 555; *30–31*, 512; *34–35*, 376

Loti, Pierre *09–19*, 480

Louden, Isabelle (Mrs. Lawrence Langner) *33–34*, 439

Louden, Thomas *20–21*, 417; *22–23*, 545

Louiguy, Mons. *55–56*, 347; *62–63*, 295; *64–65*, 331

Loux, Constance *67–68*, 387

Louys, Pierre *19–20*, 391

Love, Charles *69–70*, 334

Love, Edmund G. *61–62*, 276

Lovelace, John B. Jr. *47–48*, 428

Lovell, Kirk *70–71*

Lovell, (Mrs.) Maria *94–99*, 214; *99–09*, 461

Lovell, Roderick *60–61*, 46

Lovett, Robert *45–46*, 459

Lowe, Allen *99–09*, 413, 462, 531

Lowe, Florence *60–61*, 303

Lowell, Robert *63–64*, 369; *64–65*, 346, 362; *67–68*, 391, 409

Lowenthal, Jean *53–54*, 332

Lowery, Robert J. *69–70*, 357

Lowndes, Mrs. Belloc *09–19*, 592

Lubin, Harry *31–32*, 389

Lublenski, Ida *23–24*, 416
Lucas, W.J. *94–99*, 223
Luce, Alethea *23–24*, 392; *28–29*, 397
Luce, Ted *47–48*, 368; *49–50*, 379
Ludendorff, (Gen.) Erich *64–65*, 303
Luders, Gustav *99–09*, 383, 410, 430, 447, 468, 474, 503, 537, 570, 577; *09–19*, 409, 485, 492; *29–30*, 478
Ludl(e)am, Charles *66–67*, 35; *67–68*, 413; *70–71*
Luening, Otto *47–48*, 429; *55–56*, 369
Lujan, James Graham *50–51*, 341
Luke, Peter *68–69*, 401
Lully (Lulli), Jean-Baptiste *45–46*, 420; *55–56*, 357; *57–58*, 330; *69–70*, 314
Lumet, Baruch *54–55*, 415
Lumley, Ralph *94–99*, 172
Lumpkin, Grace *35–36*, 431
Lund, John *42–43*, 453
Luneau, Sylvie *66–67*, 416
Lunt, Carroll *25–26*, 569
Luria, Lajos *26–27*, 513
Lusk, Milton *99–09*, 522; *09–19*, 528; *34–35*, 395; *37–38*, 382
Luster, Betty *54–55*, 399
Luther, Frank *43–44*, 424
Lutz, H.B. *59–60*, 40
Lutz, Myer *94–99*, 259
Lyles, A.L. *23–24*, 344
Lyles, Aubrey *27–28*, 518
Lyman, George D. *39–40*, 471
Lyman, John *32–33*, 415
Lynch, Frances *28–29*, 357
Lynde, Paul *56–57*, 314; *61–62*, 284; *64–65*, 358
Lyndon, Barre *36–37*, 468
Lynn, John Jr. *47–48*, 424
Lynne, James Broom *65–66*, 421
Lyons, Eugene *35–36*, 414
Lytton, (Sir) Edward Bulwer *94–99*, 88, 145, 167, 206; *99–09*, 410, 470, 476, 477; *09–19*, 545, 599, 642; *29–30*, 468

Maas, Willard *60–61*, 348
Mabley, Edward *46–47*, 452; *51–52*, 286
Macaire, Robert *94–99*, 202
MacArthur, Charles *25–26*, 549; *27–28*, 501; *28–29*, 358; *32–33*, 444; *35–36*, 435; *39–40*, 403; *41–42*, 426, 460; *45–46*, 446; *46–47*, 416; *50–51*, 337; *68–69*, 414; *69–70*, 301
MacArthur, James *99–09*, 396, 535, 550
Macaulay, Pauline *66–67*, 380
MacColl, Ewan *65–66*, 402
MacConnell, Harry T. *99–09*, 364, 372, 376
MacCulloch, Campbell *09–19*, 509
MacDermot, Galt *67–68*, 374, 389, 390; *69–70*, 337
MacDonagh (McDonagh), Donagh *49–50*, 366; *60–61*, 46
Macdonald, Ann *25–26*, 569
MacDonald, Ann Sprague *23–24*, 324
MacDonald, Anne *30–31*, 446
MacD(d)onald, Ballard *20–21*, 435; *21–22*, 503; *23–24*, 293, 330; *25–26*, 531; *26–27*, 499; *27–28*, 386, 460; *30–31*, 403; *33–34*, 476; *34–35*, 432
MacDonald, Hugh *64–65*, 305, 346
Macdonald, Murray *33–34*, 470
MacDonald, Robert David *64–65*, 348; *66–67*, 371; *67–68*, 376
MacDonald, Ronald *99–09*, 418
Mac(d)Donough, Glen *94–99*, 85, 102, 134, 177, 239, 244; *99–09*, 353, 358, 378, 386, 397, 421, 440, 471, 475, 499, 566, 583; *09–19*, 400, 409, 420, 438, 453, 476, 490, 519, 548, 601, 629, 630, 653; *20–21*, 397; *22–23*, 559; *29–30*, 466, 496; *30–31*, 467
MacDougall, Roger *51–52*, 293; *53–54*, 321; *56–57*, 364
MacEntee, George *36–37*, 494
Macero, Teo *65–66*, 427

MacGill, Patrick *30–31,* 401
MacGowran, Jack *70–71*
MacGrath, Harold *99–09,* 497;
 21–22, 553, 554
MacGrath, Leueen *50–51,* 351;
 51–52, 305; *54–55,* 400
MacGregor, Edgar *25–26,* 553
MacGunigle, Robert *32–33,* 433
Machiavelli, Niccolo (*45–46,* 450
 omitted); *67–68,* 410
Machiz, Herbert *69–70,* 350
MacHugh, Augustin *09–19,* 465,
 522, 555; *20–21,* 395, 439
MacInnis, M. Donald *47–48,* 428
Mack, Adrian *38–39,* 432
Mack, Cecil *23–24,* 344; *37–38,* 447
Mack, Willard *09–19,* 534, 540, 577,
 609, 616, 640, 642; *19–20,* 382,
 424; *20–21,* 424, 429; *21–22,* 388;
 24–25, 450, 539; *25–26,* 432, 437;
 26–27, 384, 407, 428, 441, 469;
 27–28, 435, 490, 510, 533; *28–29,*
 359, 397
Mackall, Lawton *26–27,* 397
Mackay, Charles *21–22,* 444
Mackay, Robert Mears *09–19,* 643
Mackay, W. Gayer *99–09,* 551;
 20–21, 372
MacKaye, Percy *99–09,* 470, 549,
 569; *09–19,* 417, 425, 437, 518,
 560, 575; *19–20,* 432; *23–24,* 336,
 377; *53–54,* 356
Mackaye, Steele *94–99,* 84, 218,
 237, 244
Macken, Walter *54–55,* 362
MacKenzie, Margaret *20–21,* 409
Mackey, William Wellington *69–70,*
 359; *70–71*
Mackie, James B. *94–99,* 112, 133
Mackintosh, Agnes (see Gordon
 Daviot)
MacLane, Barton *32–33,* 399
MacLaren, Donald *99–09,* 510
MacLaren, Ian *99–09,* 396
MacLeish, Archibald *33–34,* 519;
 34–35, 460, 462; *40–41,* 428;
 52–53, 306; *58–59,* 312; *59–60,* 49;
 61–62, 333; *62–63,* 322; *70–71*

MacLiammoir, Micheal *47–48,* 382;
 60–61, 330; *67–68,* 394
Macloon, Louis *33–34,* 454
MacLow, Jackson *60–61,* 347
MacNamara, Brinsley *34–35,* 408
Macomber, Ken *31–32,* 517
MacOwen (Macowan), Norman
 21–22, 418; *29–30,* 494; *38–39,*
 431
MacPherson, J & L. du Rocher
 09–19, 533, 572, 578
Macpherson, Susan *51–52,* 332
Macrae, Arthur *47–48,* 356; *53–54,*
 326
Madden, Edward *99–09,* 492, 543,
 564, 575; *09–19,* 401, 425, 442;
 20–21, 356
Madden, Harry *34–35,* 374; *38–39,*
 457
Maddow, Ben *63–64,* 367
Madison, Marie *94–99,* 157
Madeira, Louis C. IV *36–37,* 499;
 37–38, 468
Madison, Martha *29–30,* 403; *30–31,*
 408; *34–35,* 415
Maeterlinck, Maurice *99–09,* 404,
 498, 560; *09–19,* 415, 426, 431,
 446, 451, 547, 560, 579, 644, 653;
 23–24, 367, 376; *66–67,* 36
Magdalany, Philip *69–70,* 312
Magidson, Herb *50–51,* 309
Magnier, Claude *65–66,* 401
Magnus, Julian *94–99,* 100
Magoon, Eaton Jr. *60–61,* 327
Maguire, Sylvester *99–09,* 543
Mahler, Gustav *46–47, 491; 47–48,*
 419
Mahoney, Bill *66–67,* 402
Maibaum, Richard *31–32,* 505;
 33–34, 460; *35–36,* 417; *39–40,*
 399
Mailer, Norman *66–67,* 412
Maissel, Alexander *44–45,* 441
Major, Austin *33–34,* 503
Major, Charles *99–09,* 386, 448, 464
Malament, Sarah *44–45,* 438
Malamuth, Charles *35–36,* 414, 511
Malats, Mr. *45–46,* 452

Malcolm *69–70*, 367

Malcolm, Charles Horace *24–25*, 597

Malcolm-Smith, George *45–46*, 405

Maldener, Fritz *65–66*, 429

Malet, Lucas *99–09*, 539–40

Malina, Judith *68–69*, 456

Maljean, Jean Raymond *67–68*, 412

Mallarmé, Stéphane *44–45*, 440

Malleson, Miles *09–19*, 612; *27–28*, 447; *38–39*, 471; *66–67*, 392

Mallory, Jay *35–36*, 491

Mallory, Louise *99–09*, 498

Malloy, Thomas *30–31*, 524

Maloney, Russell *48–49*, 375

Maloney, Mrs. Russell (see Miriam Battista)

Malory, (Sir) Thomas *62–63*, 296

Malot, Hector *38–39*, 490

Maltby, H.F. *21–22*, 549; *25–26*, 552; *29–30*, 517; *35–36*, 397

Maltby, Richard Jr. *61–62*, 308; *62–63*, 324; *67–68*, 378

Maltin, Bernard *29–30*, 377

Maltz (Malz), Albert *31–32*, 507; *33–34*, 465; *34–35*, 463; *35–36*, 510; *37–38*, 465; *38–39*, 485, 486, 487; *62–63*, 293

Malyon, E.G. *99–09*, 490

Malzkuhn, Eric *68–69*, 407; *69–70*, 311

Mamorsky, Morris *67–68*, 385

Mamoulian, Rouben *44–45*, 397; *49–50*, 372

Manchester, George *94–99*, 160

Manchester, Joe *64–65*, 345

Mandel & Schizzano *70–71*

Mandel, Alice *23–24*, 407

Mandel, Frank *09–19*, 482, 489, 529, 538, 563, 598; *19–20*, 338, 394, 434; *20–21*, 367, 396, 406; *21–22*, 432; *22–23*, 473; *23–24*, 340, 390, 407; *25–26*, 438, 446; *26–27*, 435; *28–29*, 376; *31–32*, 417; *33–34*, 530; *35–36*, 446; *42–43*, 424; *43–44*, 442; *45–46*, 393; *70–71*

Mandel, Loring *60–61*, 308

Mandley, Percy G. *33–34*, 452

Manet, Eduardo *70–71*

Manger, Itzik *64–65*, 347; *66–67*, 367; *68–69*, 385

Manges, Herbert (see Herbert Menges)

Manhattan Project *70–71*

Manheim, Ralph *66–67*, 416; *68–69*, 444; *69–70*, 348; *70–71*

Manheimer, Wallace A. *27–28*, 398; *29–30*, 539; *31–32*, 509

Manhoff, Bill *64–65*, 314

Manilow, Barry *68–69*, 422; *69–70*, 365

Manings, Allan *55–56*, 391

Mankiewicz, Herman J. *23–24*, 439; *26–27*, 394; *27–28*, 404

Mankiewicz, Tom *69–70*, 317

Mankowitz, Wolf *65–66*, 372

Manley, Charles *94–99*, 243

Manley, F.G. *37–38*, 463

Manley, William Ford *22–23*, 572; *24–25*, 430; *31–32*, 481

Mann, Charlton *21–22*, 418

Mann, Erica *36–37*, 448

Mann, Klaus *36–37*, 448

Mann, Louis *09–19*, 421

Mann, Stanley *56–57*, 364; *65–66*, 429

Mann, Thomas *40–41*, 422

Manners, J. Hartley *99–09*, 425, 496, 538, 552, 573, 581, 582; *09–19*, 401, 409, 487, 488, 523, 588, 597, 613, 619, 625, 630; *19–20*, 393; *20–21*, 426; *21–22*, 497; *23–24*, 427; *32–33*, 431

Mannes, Marya *30–31*, 405; *49–50*, 368

Mannheimer, Albert *46–47*, 420

Manning, Samuel L. *38–39*, 486; *47–48*, 367

Manoff, Arnold *49–50*, 373

Manoussi, Jean *19–20*, 409; *26–27*, 460

Mansfield, John *26–27*, 429

Mansfield, Richard (see also Merridan Phelps) *94–99*, 91, 229; *09–19*, 574

Manzori, Alessandro *38–39*, 492
Mao Tse-Tung *67–68*, 411; *68–69*, 380
Mapes, Victor *99–09*, 394, 445 *09–19*, 516, 554, 602, 643; *19–20*, 433
Marais, Josef *56–57*, 323
Marasco, Robert *69–70*, 316
Marble, Scott *94–99*, 89, 93, 115, 116, 157, 174, 182, 214, 242, 244, 247, 250
Marburg, Guido *99–09*, 440; *09–19*, 520
Marburgh, Bertram *09–19*, 524; *38–39*, 488
Marceau, Felicien (Louis Carrette) *59–60*, 325; *61–62*, 281
Marceau, Marcel *55–56*, 341, 373; *57–58*, 309; *60–61*, 290, 291; *62–63*, 292; *65–66*, 386; *69–70*, 325
Marcel, Gabriel *50–51*, 374
March, Charles *34–35*, 473
March, William *54–55*, 381
Marchand, Leopold *31–32*, 499
Marchant, William *51–52*, 320; *55–56*, 355
Marchette, Gerard *60–61*, 39
Marcin, Max *09–19*, 556, 577, 604, 608, 649; *21–22*, 394; *24–25*, 486, 501; *27–28*, 469; *28–29*, 372, 375; *29–30*, 452; *37–38*, 427
Marco, Mr. (see Fanchon & Marco)
Marco, Sano *62–63*, 312
Marcus, D. Frank *29–30*, 377, 433; *32–33*, 491
Marcus, Frank *66–67*, 360
Marcus, M.C. *09–19*, 579
Marcy, Everett *35–36*, 507; *37–38*, 429; *40–41*, 405
Marcy, Jor (Nathan Sherman) *38–39*, 464
Mareuil, Jacques *62–63*, 295
Mariani, Federico *99–09*, 583
Marion, George Jr. *39–40*, 404; *42–43*, 436; *43–44*, 400, 469; *45–46*, 380; *46–47*, 450

Marischka, Ernst *34–35*, 377
(de) Marivaux, (Pierre Carlet de Chamblain) *52–53*, 267; *55–56*, 357, 358; *58–59*, 295; *62–63*, 340; *70–71*
Markham, Gervase *63–64*, 314
Markowski, Andrzej *64–65*, 322
Marks, Duke *62–63*, 315
Marks, Gerald *43–44*, 411; *47–48*, 402
Marks, Maurice *26–27*, 523; *27–28*, 506; *34–35*, 363
Marks, Walter *64–65*, 316, 322; *65–66*, 422; *67–68*, 362
Marlin, Max *53–54*, 323; *54–55*, 385, 393, 396, 402; *66–67*, 359
Marlow, Brian *25–26*, 454; *27–28*, 409, 555; *30–31*, 425, 504; *35–36*, 425
Marlowe, Charles *94–99*, 157; *99–09*, 542
Marlowe, Christopher *09–19*, 410; *36–37*, 491; *47–48*, 429; *55–56*, 370; *57–58*, 56; *63–64*, 314; *64–65*, 343
Marnick, Burt *53–54*, 359
Marquand, John P. *44–45*, 399; *51–52*, 298
Marques, Rene *66–67*, 36, 408
Marquina, Eduardo *26–27*, 519; *31–32*, 500
Marquis, Don *22–23*, 441; *27–28*, 464; *29–30*, 480; *32–33*, 418; *56–57*, 367; *62–63*, 322
Marquiss, Walter *29–30*, 456
Marre, Albert *69–70*, 325
Marriott, Crittenden *31–32*, 462
Marrow, Macklin *39–40*, 466; *41–42*, 428
Marryat, Florence *94–99*, 234
Mars, Anthony *94–99*, *134*, *197*; *99–09*, 576; *09–19*, 428, 657
Marsden, Fred *94–99*, 99, 100, 166
Marsh, Buddy *39–40*, 446
Marshall, Armina *34–35*, 447; *40–41*, 390; *49–50*, 372
Marshall, Bruce *37–38*, 391

Marshall, Frederick *56–57*, 327; *58–59*, 311

Marshall, Harry B. *99–09*, 461

Marshall, Jack *70–71*

Marshall, Rachael *09–19*, 539

Marshall, (Capt.) Robert *94–99*, 260; *99–09*, 369, 389, 394, 416, 419, 426, 464; *09–19*, 513, 557; *28–29*, 430

Marston, Lawrence *94–99*, 183, 202, 211; *99–09*, 400

Martens, G.M. *47–48*, 427

Martialis (Martial), Marcus Valerius *62–63*, 322

Martin, Allan Langdon *19–20*, 408

Martin, Christopher *69–70*, 373; *70–71*

Martin, David *57–58*, 283

Martin, Dolphe *34–35*, 384; *67–68*, 401

Martin, Ernest H. *58–59*, 314

Martin, Gabriel *94–99*, 256

Martin, Helen R. *09–19*, 569, 649; *37–38*, 465

Martin, Herbert *65–66*, 390; *67–68*, 357

Martin, Hugh *41–42*, 400; *47–48*, 379; *50–51*, 363; *62–63*, 330; *63–64*, 333

Martin, Nancy *69–70*, 376; *70–71*

Martin, Norman L. *55–56*, 340; *59–60*, 335; *62–63*, 336; *67–68*, 402; *70–71*

Martin, Paul *67–68*, 347

Martin, Peter *34–35*, 479; *36–37*, 498

Martin, Robert Dale *61–62*, 329

Martin, Ruth & Thomas *53–54*, 355

Martin, Townsend *28–29*, 426

Martindale, Max *09–19*, 592

Martinez Sierra, Gregorio and Maria (see Sierra)

Martini, Faurto *23–24*, 364

Martins, Frank *30–31*, 398

Martos, Wimperis & Wylie *30–31*, 429

Martos, Franz *09–19*, 507, 538, 568

Martyn, Edward *99–09*, 367

Marum, Eleanor *24–25*, 584

Marvell, Andrew *62–63*, 322

Marvin, Jessie Lou *38–39*, 485

Marvin, Mel *66–67*, 415

Marx, Arthur *65–66*, 376; *69–70*, 320

Marx, Groucho *48–49*, 384

Mary I (Queen) *62–63*, 295

Mascagni, Pietro *99–09*, 423; *43–44*, 441; *44–45*, 377; *45–46*, 387; *46–47*, 409; *47–48*, 343

Masefield, John *09–19*, 492; *19–20*, 369, 427

Mason, A.E.W. *99–09*, 396; *09–19*, 452, 460

Mason, Carl *21–22*, 528

Mason, Charles A. *94–99*, 224

Mason, Jackie *69–70*, 294

Mason, Mark *66–67*, 423

Mason, Richard *58–59*, 296

Massenet, Jules *47–48*, 343

Massey, Edward *09–19*, 579; *27–28*, 543

Massey, Valgene *58–59*, 50

Massinger, Philip *49–50*, 384

Massingham, Dorothy *33–34*, 470

Mast, Jane *25–26*, 587

Masteroff, Joseph (Joe) *59–60*, 298; *62–63*, 307; *66–67*, 370; *68–69*, 455; *70–71*

Masters, Edgar Lee *27–28*, 559; *63–64*, 304

Matamoros, Ricardo *70–71*

Matarrese, Tony *63–64*, 346

Mat(t)hews, Frances Aymar *94–99*, 222; *99–09*, 431, 432

Mathews, Vera *45–46*, 384

Mathieu, William *61–62*, 255, 318, 331

Matthias, Rita *41–42*, 458

Mathewson, Christy *09–19*, 511

Mathieu, William *65–66*, 434

Matlowsky, Samuel *55–56*, 383

Matson, Norman *32–33*, 486

Matson, Ralph *43–44*, 490

Matsuda, Wackichi *65–66*, 403

Mattheus, H.V. *09–19*, 545, 642
Matthews, A. Kenward *25–26*, 441
Matthews, Adelaide *19–20*, 348;
    20–21, 364, 445; *21–22*, 389;
    25–26, 540; *27–28*, 439
Matthews, Brander *94–99*, 169, 235;
    99–09, 350; *09–19*, 442
Matthews, J. Sherrie *94–99*, 193,
    254
Matthews, John F. *49–50*, 385
Matthews, W.C. *41–42*, 461
Matthias, Rita *24–25*, 530
Matz, Peter *62–63*, 332
Maugham, W. Somerset *99–09*, 568,
    572; *09–19*, 400, 406, 412, 423,
    472, 517, 582, 596; *19–20*, 368,
    388; *21–22*, 416; *22–23*, 459, 483;
    23–24, 353; *26–27*, 433; *27–28*,
    411, 512; *28–29*, 418; *31–32*, 395;
    32–33, 482, 493; *34–35*, 451;
    37–38, 440; *41–42*, 413; *43–44*,
    469; *44–45*, 397; *46–47*, 485;
    47–48, 428; *51–52*, 296, 308;
    52–53, 257; *69–70*, 374
Maurette, Marcelle *38–39*, 421;
    54–55, 388; *65–66*, 387
Maurey, Max *94–99*, 256; *09–19*,
    509, 589 (and 605)
Mauriac, François *59–60*, 46
Maurice, Albert *94–99*, 160
Maury, Richard *56–57*, 314; *61–62*,
    284
Mawson, Harry P. *99–09*, 365
Mawson, Jean *94–99*, 238
Max, Jerome *65–66*, 422
Maxwell, H.R. *99–09*, 353, 422,
    477; *09–19*, 443
Maxwell, Sanders *37–38*, 468;
    38–39, 491
Maxwell, William B. *09–19*, 568;
    25–26, 592
May, Elaine *60–61*, 299; *61–62*, 325;
    68–69, 445
Mayer, Edwin Justus *24–25*, 473;
    29–30, 475; *44–45*, 424; *57–58*, 52;
    65–66, 436
Mayer, Jerome *39–40*, 443

Mayer, Paul Avila *62–63*, 328;
    66–67, 407; *70–71*
Mayfield, Julian *52–53*, 308; *60–61*,
    39
Maynard, Cora *99–09*, 523; *09–19*,
    412
Mayne, Rutherford *09–19*, 490
Mayo, Earl W. *99–09*, 522
Mayo, Frank *94–99*, 131
Mayo, Margaret *99–09*, 501, 539,
    553; *09–19*, 402, 422, 470, 499,
    528, 577, 630; *20–21*, 355; *26–27*,
    534
Mayo, Vivian *37–38*, 463
Mazza, Richard *64–65*, 362
Mbiti, J. *69–70*, 353
McAfee, Don *65–66*, 424
McAvity, Helen *65–66*, 383
McAvoy, Dan *99–09*, 427
McBride, Robert *41–42*, 457; *43–44*,
    487
McCardell, Roy L. *99–09*, 582
McCarthy, Daniel *94–99*, 168, 255
McCall, G.H. *33–34*, 475
McCann, John Ernest *94–99*, 97
McCarthy, Joseph (J.) *09–19*, 624;
    19–20, 386; *20–21*, 355, 453;
    22–23, 484, 513; *23–24*, 381;
    24–25, 429; *28–29*, 375; *62–63*,
    295
McCarthy, Joseph Jr. *53–54*, 326
McCarthy, Justin Huntley *94–99*,
    118, 216; *99–09*, 66, 440, 470, 471;
    09–19, 508, 514, 574; *25–26*, 451;
    34–35, 431; *43–44*, 402; *61–62*,
    332
McCarthy, Kevin *53–54*, 353
McCarthy, Mary *38–39*, 465
McCarty, Ernest *69–70*, 358
McCarty, Lawrence *09–19*, 481
McCay, Winsor *99–09*, 571
McClain, Billy *94–99*, 188
McCleery, William *44–45*, 415;
    46–47, 469
McClellan, Jack *25–26*, 576; *26–27*,
    510
McClellan, Walter *26–27*, 524

McCloskey, J.J. *94–99*, 194
McClung, Robert Marshall *38–39*, 491
McClure, Michael *61–62*, 311; *67–68*, 389
McColl, James *42–43*, 421
McComb, Malcolm *29–30*, 548
McConnor, Vincent *45–46*, 419
McCord, Joe *70–71*
McCormack, Herbert P. *33–34*, 426
McCormick, Elizabeth *39–40*, 446
McCormick, Langdon *19–20*, 361; *24–25*, 487
McCormick, Pat *64–65*, 358
McCrae, Arthur *62–63*, 316
McCree, Junie *09–19*, 439, 472
McCreery (McReary), Bud *55–56*, 391; *60–61*, 294; *62–63*, 316, 317, 336; *63–64*, 355; *64–65*, 356; *65–66*, 428
McCue, Frank *42–43*, 420
McCullers, Carson *49–50*, 366; *57–58*, 297; *62–63*, 339; *63–64*, 312
McCutcheon, George Barr *99–09*, 530; *20–21*, 406
McCutcheon, John T. *99–09*, 471
McDaniels, Gene *69–70*, 342
McDermott, John *31–32*, 467
McDonagh, Donagh (see Donagh MacDonagh)
McDonald, Joe *70–71*
McDonald, Julian L. *31–32*, 472
McDonald, Laetitia *26–27*, 464
McDowell, David *68–69*, 454
McDowell, John Herbert *63–64*, 346; *66–67*, 363; *67–68*, 412; *70–71*
McEnroe, Robert E. *48–49*, 397; *60–61*, 339
McEvoy, J.P. *23–24*, 369; *26–27*, 363, 405; *27–28*, 390; *28–29*, 406; *29–30*, 378; *32–33*, 395; *38–39*, 458
McFadden, Elizabeth *33–34*, 433; *44–45*, 417
McGee, James *47–48*, 412

McGee, John *35–36*, 467
McGinley, Phyllis *48–49*, 380
McGlynn, (Rev.) Thomas *43–44*, 458
McGovern, John *99–09*, 523
McGowan, John (Jack) *25–26*, 557; *27–28*, 390, 479; *28–29*, 395; *29–30*, 382, 399, 439, 503; *30–31*, 430; *31–32*, 392, 516; *32–33*, 392; *34–35*, 405
McGowan, Mary *39–40*, 470
McGrane, Paul *37–38*, 429; *42–43*, 421; *46–47*, 482
McGrath, Frank *32–33*, 412
McGrath, Harold *09–19*, 553
McGrath, Russell *68–69*, 434
McGuire, Ken *69–70*, 319
McGuire, William Anthony *09–19*, 412, 654; *19–20*, 414; *21–22*, 402; *22–23*, 455; *23–24*, 381; *25–26*, 497; *26–27*, 373; *27–28*, 488, 526; *28–29*, 431; *29–30*, 378, 491; *30–31*, 455
McHugh, Jimmy (James) *27–28*, 553; *29–30*, 500; *30–31*, 447; *31–32*, 379; *39–40*, 394, 463; *48–49*, 394
McIntyre, Dennis *70–71*
McIntyre, John T. *09–19*, 478; *19–20*, 375; *20–21*, 377
McIver, Ray *68–69*, 440
McKay, Claude 66–67, 354
McKean, Thomas *09–19*, 457; *23–24*, 412
McKellar, John *63–64*, 343
McKenna, William *09–19*, 572
McKennan, Arnett *36–37*, 499
McKenney, Ruth *40–41*, 405; *52–53*, 290; *56–57*, 320; *57–58*, 323; *62–63*, 297; *66–67*, 389
McKenzie, Neil *58–59*, 50
McKnight, Tom *36–37*, 430; *39–40*, 394
McLaughlin, Mignon *48–49*, 422
McLaughlin, Robert *09–19*, 563, 644; *26–27*, 415; *48–49*, 422

McLaurin, Kate L. *20–21*, 407; *21–22*, 448; *22–23*, 435; *25–26*, 425, 462

McLellan, C.M.S. (Hugh Morton) *99–09*, 169, 547; *09–19*, 435, 437, 441, 479, 509, 514, 563; *23–24*, 421

McLeod, Jane *41–42*, 460

McLiam, John *56–57*, 360

McMahon, Frank *69–70*, 324

McManus, George *99–09*, 580; *24–25*, 564

McMasters, William H. *24–25*, 535

McNab, Duncan *22–23*, 539

McNally, John J. *94–99*, 112, 118, 144, 153, 181, 189, 205; *99–09*, 350, 371, 380, 393, 398, 401, 414, 427, 435, 446, 461, 464, 473, 478, 491, 494, 498, 544, 567; *09–19*, 397

McNally, Terrence *62–63*, 303; *64–65*, 334; *67–68*, 407; *68–69*, 394, 436, 445, 454

McNally, William J. *24–25*, 536; *25–26*, 419; *36–37*, 438

McNamara, Edward J. *31–32*, 379

McNaughton, Charles *23–24*, 424

McNeal, Claudia *70–71*

McNutt, Patterson *24–25*, 440

McOwen, Bernard J. *23–24*, 424; *27–28*, 417, 544; *29–30*, 509; *31–32*, 376; *33–34*, 464; *34–35*, 435

McReary, Bud (see Bud McCreery)

McWhinney, Michael *61–62*, 286; *62–63*, 316, 329; *63–64*, 358, 359, 371, 372; *64–65*, 342, 259; *65–66*, 417, 424; *66–67*, 404; *67–68*, 377

Mead(e), George *42–43*, 444; *44–45*, 379; *45–46*, 390; *63–64*, 321

Mead, Phyllis *46–47*, 498

Mead, Shepherd *61–62*, 261

Meader, Clarence L. *09,–19*, 580

Meaney, Lottie M. *09–19*, 571, 640

Mears, John Henry *19–20*, 407; *20–21*, 453

Mears, Stannard *09–19*, 620

Mearson, Lyon *27–28*, 458; *32–33*, 471

Medcraft, Russell *25–26*, 436; *26–27*, 397; *32–33*, 423; *41–42*, 408

Mednick, Murray *66–67*, 36; *67–68*, 405, 413; *68–69*, 457; *69–70*, 378

Mee, Charles L. Jr. *67–68*, 412

Meehan, John *09–19*, 598; *22–23*, 541; *24–25*, 447, 507; *27–28*, 475 *28–29*, 426

Meehan, John Jr. *42–43*, 441; *43–44*, 470

Mehul, Etienne *46–47*, 498

Megrue, Roi Cooper *09–19*, 464, 509, 529, 530, 555, 563, 576, 584, 634, 638; *21–22*, 392

Meighan, Thad W. *94–99*, 108

Meilhac, Henri *94–99*, 126, 134, 211, 229, 257, 260; *99–09*, 472; *09–19*, 469; *43–44*, 432; *44–45*, 382; *45–46*, 389, 394; *55–56*, 393; *63–64*, 326

Meinhard, Herr *22–23*, 505

Meiser, Edith *39–40*, 460

Melcher, Rose *48–49*, 426

Meldon, H. Percy *94–99*, 258

Melfi, Leonard *65–66*, 432; *67–68*, 406; *68–69*, 394; *69–70*, 335; *70–71*

Melford, Mr. (see Brightman, Melford & Furber)

Melford, Austin *27–28*, 500

Meller, Raquel *26–27*, 412

Meltzer, Charles Henry *94–99*, 92, 141, 198, 229; *99–09*, 352, 360, 365, 470; *09–19*, 628

Meltzer, Newton *37–38*, 469

Melville, Al(l)an *53–54*, 329; *54–55*, 360; *59–60*, 336

Melville, Herman *48–49*, 427; *50–51*, 349; *60–61*, 38; *62–63*, 290, 322; *63–64*, 369; *64–65*, 346; *68–69*, 411; *69–70*, 336, 373; *70–71*

Melville, June (*51–52*, 325 omitted)

Menasci, G. *43–44*, 441; *44–45*, 377; *45–46*, 387

Mencher, Murray *34–35*, 482

Mendelssohn, Jakob Ludwig Felix *42–43*, 485; *45–46*, 452; *47–48*, 423; *51–52*, 330; *54–55*, 361; *67–68*, 387; *70–71*

Mendes, Catulle *99–09*, 485

Mendez-Ballester, Manuel *60–61*, 39

Mendoza, Dorothy *63–64*, 343

Menges (Mengies, Manges), Herbert *36–37*, 460; *37–38*, 368; *39–40*, 451; *50–51*, 344; *51–52*, 299, 300, 310

Menken, Marie *60–61*, 348

Menkiti, Ifeanyi *69–70*, 353

Menotti, Gian Carlo *44–45*, 439; *45–46*, 459; *46–47*, 477, 487, 488; *47–48*, 347; *48–49*, 399; *49–50*, 375; *50–51*, 311; *54–55*, 387; *58–59*, 302; *63–64*, 321; *65–66*, 371; *66–67*, 361

Menten, Dale F. *69–70*, 361

Mention, Michel *64–65*, 315

Meranus, Norman *52–53*, 307

Meranze, David S. *70–71*

Mercer, John(ny) *29–30*, 548; *38–39*, 459; *39–40*, 466; *42–43*, 420; *45–46*, 436; *49–50*, 361; *51–52*, 290; *56–57*, 335; *59–60*, 309; *62–63*, 295; *63–64*, 325; *64–65*, 331; *66–67*, 414

Mercer, Will *99–09*, 461

Merchant, Abby *22–23*, 474; *23–24*, 397; *40–41*, 423

Mercier, Mary *67–68*, 343; *70–71*

Mere, M. Charles *23–24*, 333

Mereshkovsky, Dmitry *09–19*, 469

Mergendahl, Charles *41–42*, 459

Merimée, Prosper *94–99*, 156; *99–09*, 503, 557; *38–39*, 492; *43–44*, 432; *44–45*, 382; *45–46*, 394; *55–56*, 393

Merington, Marguerite *94–99*, 131, 169, 228

Meritt, Paul *94–99*, 113

Merivale, Bernard *27–28*, 517

Merivale, Herman C. *94–99*, 109, 114, 136, 186; *99–09*, 384; *19–20*, 452

Meriwether, Susan *28–29*, 470

Meriwether, William *65–66*, 416

Merle, Martin V. *99–09*, 528

Merley, Heinz *28–29*, 486

Merli, Madeline *99–09*, 393

Merlin, F(rank) S. *24–25*, 580; *25–26*, 454; *26–27*, 525; *27–28*, 453; *30–31*, 490; *35–36*, 425; *58–59*, 50; *62–63*, 324

Merling, Howard *27–28*, 527

Merlyn, Iva *99–09*, 562

Merola, Gaetano *09–19*, 562

Merrick, Leonard *09–19*, 433

Merrill, Blanche *25–26*, 420

Merrill, Bob (Robert) *56–57*, 373; *59–60*, 299; *60–61*, 336; *62–63*, 339; *63–64*, 329; *66–67*, 395; *67–68*, 347; *68–69*, 397

Merrill, Fenimore *09–19*, 612

Merrill, James *54–55*, 56

Merron, Eleanor *99–09*, 348

Merton, Thomas *70–71*

Merwin, Samuel *32–33*, 408

Merwin, W.S. *62–63*, 340; *66–67*, 361; *70–71*

Messager, Andre *99–09*, 499, 532; *19–20*, 398

Meszel, Max *70–71*

Metcalf, Henriette *30–31*, 482; *35–36*, 446

Metcalfe, Felicia *33–34*, 428

Metzl, Lothar *39–40*, 394, 437

Meyer, Adolph E. *28–29*, 366

Meyer, Annie Nathan *21–22*, 543; *31–32*, 499

Meyer, George W. *24–25*, 479

Meyer, Dede (Deed) *58–59*, 53; *61–62*, 313

Meyer, Don *55–56*, 392

Meyer, Hans Bruno *36–37*, 490; *37–38*, 457; *38–39*, 478

Meyer, John *62–63*, 324; *64–65*, 342; *65–66*, 424; *66–67*, 404

Meyer, Joseph (Joe) *24–25*, 518; *25–26*, 431, 531; *27–28*, 429, 547; *28–29*, 463; *29–30*, 520; *51–52*, 323

Meyer, Josephine A. *09–19*, 560

Meyer, Michael *60–61*, 353; *69–70*, 337; *70–71*

Meyerbeer, Giacomo *46–47*, 489

Meyer-Foerster, Wilhelm *99–09*, 424, 439; *09–19*, 433

Meyers, Johnny *62–63*, 312

Meyers, Richard (see Richard Myers)

Meyers, William *68–69*, 453

Meyers, Z. *20–21*, 428

Mey(e)rowitz, Jan *49–50*, 384; *50–51*, 323

Mgrdichian, George *70–71*

Mica, Luigia *45–46*, 387; *46–47*, 412

Michael, Margaret *19–20*, 380

Michaelis, Karen *20–21*, 427

Michaelis, Sophus *09–19*, 415

Michaels, Sidney *62–63*, 283; *63–64*, 320; *64–65*, 308; *70–71*

Michajilov, Boris *64–65*, 297

Michalek, Stanislaw *64–65*, 322

Michel, Scott *50–51*, 362; *56–57*, 321

Michel, Werner *39–40*, 394, 395, 437

Michelson, Lottie *52–53*, 308

Michelson, Miriam *99–09*, 534

Michener, James A. *48–49*, 419; *54–55*, 412; *56–57*, 369; *60–61*, 337; *65–66*, 366; *67–68*, 339

Middlemas(s), Robert *25–26*, 591; *27–28*, 549; *32–33*, 389

Middleton, Edgar C. *28–29*, 437

Middleton, George (C.) *99–09*, 424, 554; *09–19*, 557, 606; *19–20*, 351, 412; *20–21*, 369; *23–24*, 371, 387; *25–26*, 458; *27–28*, 394; *28–29*, 360, 451; *38–39*, 412

Middleton, Horace *41–42*, 416

Middleton, Thomas *64–65*, 309

Miele, Elizabeth *29–30*, 470; *31–32*, 396; *54–55*, 380

Mignone, Francisco *46–47*, 488

Miguel, Muriel *69–70*, 370

Mihanovich, Sergio *68–69*, 432

Milan, Judith *64–65*, 358

Milbert, Seymour *40–41*, 432

Miles, Carleton *32–33*, 488; *34–35*, 433

Miles, Cherrilyn *69–70*, 377

Miles, Dorothy *69–70*, 311

Miles, Hank *65–66*, 390

Miles, Henry *51–52*, 320

Miles, William *32–33*, 488; *33–34*, 424

Milhaud, Darius *39–40*, 471; *44–45*, 381; *46–47*, 490; *56–57*, 353; *64–65*, 315

Milholland, (Charles) Bruce *32–33*, 444; *50–51*, 337

Millar, Robins *29–30*, 438

Millar, Ronald *62–63*, 277; *70–71*

Millaud, Albert *94–99*, 153

Millay, Edna St. Vincent *23–24*, 332; *24–25*, 583; *36–37*, 499; *59–60*, 316; *62–63*, 324; *63–64*, 357; *64–65*, 313

Millen, James Knox *31–32*, 460; *37–38*, 393

Miller, Albert G. *33–34*, 430

Miller, Alice Duer *09–19*, 585; *20–21*, 362; *24–25*, 495; *25–26*, 424; *27–28*, 430; *33–34*, 458

Miller, Allen C. *30–31*, 488

Miller, Arthur *44–45*, 400; *46–47*, 458; *48–49*, 412; *50–51*, 339; *52–53*, 282, 306; *55–56*, 347; *56–57*, 58; *57–58*, 52; *58–59*, 52; *61–62*, 310; *63–64*, 321, 332; *64–65*, 309, 353, 362; *67–68*, 363, 401, 410; *68–69*, 455; *69–70*, 376; *70–71*

Miller, Ashley *29–30*, 482

Miller, Bob *62–63*, 315

Miller, Carol *67–68*, 411

Miller, Everett *29–30*, 548

Miller, Flournoy E. *23–24*, 344; *27–28*, 518; *30–31*, 438; *32–33*, 441; *51–52*, 323

Miller, Frank *52–53*, 308

Miller, Freda *47–48*, 416, 417

Miller, Gilbert *40–41,* 398

Miller, Henry *99–09,* 496

Miller, Irvin C. *22–23,* 494

Miller, J. *68–69,* 391

Miller, Jason *69–70,* 361, 374

Miller, Joaquin *94–99,* 202

Miller, Jonathan *62–63,* 282

Miller, Katherine Browning *09–19,* 557

Miller, Louis *39–40,* 474

Miller, Patsy Ruth *47–48,* 355

Miller, Robert *66–67,* 35

Miller, Robin *68–69,* 441; *70–71*

Miller, Sigmund *51–52,* 314; *58–59,* 330

Miller, Stanley *37–38,* 469

Miller, Warren *59–60,* 320

Millhauser, Bertram *33–34,* 502

Milliken, J.F. *94–99,* 207

Millinder, Lucky *44–45,* 438

Millman, David *42–43,* 488

Millocker, K(C)arl *09–19,* 498; *32–33,* 427; *42–43,* 486

Mills & Scott *99–09,* 540

Mills, Billy *31–32,* 517

Mills, Carley *55–56,* 336

Mills, Charles *44–45,* 440; *62–63,* 334

Mills, Clifford *09–19,* 586; *19–20,* 373

Mills, Hugh *55–56,* 381

Milne, (Alan Alexander) A.A. *09–19,* 629; *20–21,* 430; *21–22,* 462, 480, 527; *22–23,* 488, 491; *23–24,* 428; *24–25,* 546; *26–27,* 511; *27–28,* 434; *28–29,* 429, 474; *29–30,* 462; *30–31,* 499; *31–32,* 484, 504; *39–40,* 470; *40–41,* 430; *67–68,* 395; *68–69,* 437; *70–71*

Milton, Ernest *45–46,* 400

Milner, Roger *66–67,* 365

Milner, Ronald *66–67,* 403; *68–69,* · 455, 457; *69–70,* 338

Milton, David Scott *69–70,* 341

Milton, Robert *20–21,* 362; *25–26,* 424

Milward, Jo *30–31,* 469; *33–34,* 490

Mims, Stuart *39–40,* 464

Miner, Worthington *38–39,* 455

Minkoff, Fran *67–68,* 377

Minkus, Leon *47–48,* 419

Minnelli, Vincente *36–37,* 446; *37–38,* 369; *49–50,* 368

Minoff, Lee *66–67,* 381

Minor, A.J. *32–33,* 478

Mins, Leonard *46–47,* 452

Minturn, Harry *38–39,* 472, 480

Minucci, Uhpio *56–57,* 359

Miramova, Elena *42–43,* 459

Mirande, T. *27–28,* 431

Mirande, Yves *09–19,* 506; *23–24,* 363; *24–25,* 501; *28–29,* 475

Mirbeau, Octave *99–09,* 466; *23–24,* 406

Mireille, Mons. *64–65,* 331

Mishima, Yukio *60–61,* 44, 47

Mishkin, William *44–45,* 441

Misrock, Henry R. *36–37,* 409; *46–47,* 444

Mitchell, Adrian *65–66,* 393; *66–67,* 379; *67–68,* 409; *69–70,* 359

Mitchell, Basil *36–37,* 439

Mitchell, Dodson L. *20–21,* 410; *31–32,* 439

Mitchell, Fanny Todd *28–29,* 430, 463, 486; *29–30,* 431

Mitchell, Georges *99–09,* 471, 480; *09–19,* 424

Mitchell, Joseph *35–36,* 437; *64–65,* 316

Mitchell, Langdon *94–99,* 136; *99–09,* 348, 516, 526; *09–19,* 441, 559, 586; *23–24,* 436; *28–29,* 509; *32–33,* 480

Mitchell, Leontrovitch *28–29,* 458

Mitchell, Loften *56–57,* 58; *63–64,* 348

Mitchell, Norma *25–26,* 436; *26–27,* 397; *32–33,* 423; *34–35,* 420; *41–42,* 408, 446

Mitchell, Ruth C. *09–19,* 531

Mitchell, Sydney *22–23,* 473

Mitchell, Thomas *25–26,* 580; *28–29,* 394; *31–32,* 384; *35–36,* 406

Mitford, Nancy *53–54,* 309

Mitropoulis, Dimitri *52–53,* 269
Mitropoulos, Dimitrios *68–69,* 434
Mittelholzer, Edgar *52–53,* 268
Miyoshi, Shoraku *65–66,* 403
Mizner, Wilson *09–19,* 395, 436, 467
Moeller, Philip *09–19,* 547, 560, 579, 612, 615, 653; *19–20,* 434; *28–29,* 446, 493
Moffatt, Graham *09–19,* 453, 478; *20–21,* 387
Moffett, Cleveland *99–09,* 574
Moffitt, John C. *36–37,* 490
Mohapeloa, J.P. *63–64,* 330
Mohr, Max *27–28,* 520
Molette, Carlton & Barbara *70–71*
Molière (Jean-Baptiste Poquelin) *99–09,* 486; *09–19,* 457, 579, 597; *23–24,* 416; *24–25,* 483; *28–29,* 383; *29–30,* 393, 403; *33–34,* 442; *35–36,* 475; *37–38,* 469; *38–39,* 492; *43–44,* 489; *44–45,* 437; *45–46,* 420; *49–50,* 383, 384; *50–51,* 359, 373; *52–52,* 270; *55–56,* 59, 356; *56–57,* 55, 353; *57–58,* 330; *58–59,* 295; *59–60,* 50; *60–61,* 325; *61–62,* 313; *63–64,* 327, 359, 360; *64–65,* 309; *65–66,* 397; *66–67,* 36, 392, 412, 419; *67–68,* 405; *68–69,* 374, 383, 391; *69–70,* 311, 313, 360; *70–71*
Molinaro, Ursula *63–64,* 371
Molineux, Roland Burnham *09–19,* 514
Moll, Elick *62–63,* 280
Moll, William *29–30,* 520
Molloy, (Rev.) Edward A. *63–64,* 368; *64–65,* 363; *65–66,* 437; *67–68,* 408; *69–70,* 372
Molloy, Michael J. *50–51,* 354
Molnar, Ferenc (Franz) *99–09,* 564, 565; *09–19,* 506, 533; *20–21,* 443; *21–22,* 435; *22–23,* 498; *23–24,* 332, 341; *24–25,* 470, 514; *25–26,* 465, 476; *26–27,* 419; *27–28,* 537; *28–29,* 398, 434; *29–30,* 537; *30–31,* 422, 423; *31–32,* 439; *32–33,* 409, 424; *37–38,* 467; *39–40,* 448; *40–41,* 398; *44–45,* 428; *46–47,* 476, 485; *47–48,* 400; *48–49,* 409; *50–51,* 362; *54–55,* 359; *60–61,* 44; *65–66,* 368; *66–67,* 378
Molnar, Robert *66–67,* 423
Monaco, James V. (Jimmy) *27–28,* 460; *62–63,* 295
Monaster, Nate *64–65,* 311
Monckton, Lionel *94–99,* 149, 176, 201, 233, 242; *99–09,* 357, 395, 403, 417, 471, 522, 538, 567, 576; *09–19,* 410, 422, 455, 524, 651
Monk, Julius *62–63,* 317; *63–64,* 355; *64–65,* 343; *65–66,* 422
Monks, John Jr. *36–37,* 441
Monnot, Marguerite *60–61,* 296; *62–63,* 295; *64–65,* 332
Montague, John *99–09,* 584; *31–32,* 521
Montanaro, Tony *62–63,* 312
Montayne, C.S. *22–23,* 434
Montesquison, J.C. *94–99,* 124
Montgomery, Bruce *63–64,* 359
Montgomery, James *09–19,* 433, 459, 473, 482, 582, 618, 624; *19–20,* 386; *22–23,* 513; *25–26,* 483; *27–28,* 421; *32–33,* 411
Montgomery, Robert *70–71*
Montgomery, Victoria *24–25,* 490
Moock, Senor *27–28,* 468
Moody, William Vaughn *99–09,* 242; *09–19,* 411, 594; *69–70,* 371
Mooney, Martin *28–29,* 478; *30–31,* 436; *33–34,* 420
Mooney, William *65–66,* 432
Moorat, Joseph *09–19,* 512
Moore, Carlyle *09–19,* 490, 637; *22–23,* 497
Moore, Carman *69–70,* 374
Moore, Carroll *58–59,* 299; *60–61,* 311
Moore, Douglas *38–39,* 474; *50–51,* 375; *61–62,* 309
Moore, Dudley *62–63,* 283; *65–66,* 432

Moore, Frances *94–99,* 160
Moore, Frankfort W. *94–99,* 186
Moore, Irene *70–71*
Moore, Joseph *37–38,* 465; *38–39,* 487
Moore, Mavor *61–62,* 285
Moore, McElbert *23–24,* 435; *25–26,* 527, 544; *27–28,* 465; *28–29,* 456
Moore, Percival T. *99–09,* 538
Moore, Sam *49–50,* 361
Moore, Sonia *70–71*
Moran, Alan *48–49,* 377, 424
Morand, Eugene *94–99,* 163; *99–09,* 380
Morando, Estelle *33–34,* 421
Morath, Max *68–69,* 446
More, Julian *60–61,* 296
Moreau, Emile *94–99,* 117, 126, 150, 247; *99–09,* 353, 354, 442, 520; *09–19,* 432, 589 (and 605); *20–21,* 440
Moreau, Jean-Baptiste *65–66,* 430
Morehouse, Ward *28–29,* 362; *36–37,* 477
Moreland, Donald *65–66,* 435
Morell, Peter *36–37,* 496
Morgan, Mr. *09–19,* 548
Morgan, Agnes *09–19,* 493; *23–24,* 439; *24–25,* 565; *25–26,* 418, 605; *26–27,* 529; *27–28,* 558; *28–29,* 499; *37–38,* 448
Morgan, Al *57–58,* 315; *65–66,* 374
Morgan, Cary *21–22,* 407
Morgan, Charles *38–39,* 467; *53–54,* 342; *56–57,* 58
Morgan, Diana *53–54,* 336
Morgan, Dixon *37–38,* 468
Morgan, Mrs. Edward Nash *99–09,* 451
Morgan, Henry *49–50,* 367
Morgenstern, Joseph *64–65,* 354
Morgenstern, Sam *47–48,* 430
Morin, Terry *62–63,* 312
Moritz, Al *44–45,* 395, 431
Moritz, Henry K. *38–39,* 486

Morley, Christopher *19–20,* 395; *22–23,* 572; *33–34,* 453; *44–45,* 441
Morley, Robert *39–40,* 469; *48–49,* 385
Morley, Thomas *63–64,* 314
Morlock, Martin *65–66,* 429
Morosco, Oliver *99–09,* 518; *09–19,* 532, 584, 594; *21–22,* 441, 533
Moroso, John *25–26,* 437
Moross, Jerome *34–35,* 478; *35–36,* 437, 510; *44–45,* 437; *45–46,* 420, 454; *47–48,* 397; *53–54,* 347; *60–61,* 45; *61–62,* 323; *63–64,* 348
Morrell, H.H. *99–09,* 490
Morrill, Katherine *59–60,* 314
Morris, Aldyth *55–56,* 353; *59–60,* 356
Morris, E.B. *43–44,* 454
Morris, Edmund *55–56,* 351; *65–66,* 426
Morris, Gordon *24–25,* 518
Morris, Gouverneur *09–19,* 543
Morris, Grant *09–19,* 642
Morris, I.N. *94–99,* 170; *99–09,* 425, 475, 530
Morris, John *54–55,* 410; *56–57,* 340; *63–64,* 387; *64–65,* 74, 356; *65–66,* 95, 410; *66–67,* 106; *67–68,* 93, 94, 390, 391; *68–69,* 391, 422, 424, 435; *69–70,* 337
Morris, Lee *55–56,* 340
Morris, Lloyd *42–43,* 439
Morris, Ramsay *94–99,* 217; *99–09,* 346, 381, 418, 438
Morris, Richard *60–61,* 304
Morrison, Anne *23–24,* 372; *24–25,* 440; *28–29,* 491
Morrison, Lee *09–19,* 557
Morrison, Mary *09–19,* 566
Morrissey, Will(iam) *20–21,* 356; *23–24,* 298; *26–27,* 483; *29–30,* 377; *30–31,* 403; *34–35,* 363; *42–43,* 438
Morrisson, B. *69–70,* 314
Morse, Ben *51–52,* 333
Morse, Leon *46–47,* 493

Morse, Michael 67–68, 398
Morse, N. Brewster 25–26, 603
Morse, Paul 70–71
Morse, Theodore F. 99–09, 403, 427, 492
Morse, Woolson 94–99, 83, 170, 177; 99–09, 459
Mortimer, John 61–62, 314
Mortimer, Lillian 33–34, 534
Mortman, Mike 69–70, 294
Morton, David 60–61, 292
Morton, Edward 99–09, 373
Morton, Frederic 70–71
Morton, Howard E. 21–22, 466
Morton, Hugh (see also C.M.S. McLellan) 94–99, 173, 189, 202, 210, 219, 232; 99–09, 385, 454; 20–21, 453; 48–49, 426
Morton, Jelly Roll 68–69, 446
Morton, John Maddison 94–99, 131, 146, 207; 34–35, 364; 36–37, 401, 496
Morton, Martha 94–99, 111, 125, 186, 208, 235; 99–09, 406, 408, 454, 544; 09–19, 401, 459, 463, 553
Morton, Michael 94–99, 215; 99–09, 352, 370, 429, 492, 543, 578; 09–19, 396, 433, 453, 479, 520, 530, 544, 599, 611, 644; 20–21, 423; 22–23, 546; 31–32, 474
Morum, William 50–51, 327
Mosel, Tad 51–52, 334; 60–61, 308; 61–62, 317
Mosenthal, Solomon 94–99, 208, 218
Moses, Gilbert 69–70, 355, 371, 372
Moszkowski 46–47, 490
Moss, Al 40–41, 389; 41–42, 459
Moss, Arnold 57–58, 326
Moss, Kurt 63–64, 345
Mossolow, Mr. 34–35, 460
Motter, Vail 43–44, 490
Motzan, Otto 09–19, 576, 585, 600
Mouesy-Eon, Mons. 27–28, 431
Mouillot, Frederick 99–09, 513
Moulin, Jean-Pierre 62–63, 295
Moulton, Powers 50–51, 374

Mountford, Eva 94–99, 218
Mountoy, Henry 09–19, 486
Moussorgsky (Mussorgsky), Modest 42–43, 485, 487; 43–44, 485; 44–45, 437, 439; 46–47, 489
Mowatt, Anna Cora 23–24, 395
Mowbray, Alan 29–30, 382
Mowell, Shelley 50–51, 352
Moyes, Patricia 57–58, 301
Mozart, Wolfgang Amadeus 37–38, 412; 44–45, 437; 45–46, 452, 454; 47–48, 343, 347, 415, 423, 425; 54–55, 386; 56–57, 320; 66–67, 379; 68–69, 436
Mrozek, Slawomir 61–62, 314, 329; 67–68, 413; 68–69, 444
Mrwebe, Gwigwi 65–66, 403
Mueller, Don A. 61–62, 327
Mueller, Hans 99–09, 556; 24–25, 530; 36–37, 413
Muhsam, Erich 36–37, 448
Muir, Jessie 99–09, 404
Mulcahy, Lance 63–64, 343; 69–70, 327
Mullally, Don 24–25, 452, 491; 25–26, 488; 28–29, 354; 31–32, 401, 441
Müller, Adolf 67–68, 367
Muller, Romeo 68–69, 428
Mulligan, Andy 63–64, 344
Mulligan, Lawrence 09–19, 405
Mumford, Ethel Watts 94–99, 230; 09–19, 542, 623
Munch-Bellinghausen 94–99, 214
Mundy, James 55–56, 360
Mundy, John 49–50, 380
Munford, (Col.) Robert 69–70, 371; 70–71
Munn, Margaret Crosby 32–33, 405
Munro, C.K. 25–26, 586, 587
Munro, H.H. (see Saki)
Murchison, Kenneth M. 09–19, 574
Murdoch, Iris 64–65, 309
Murfin, Jane 09–19, 594, 603, 639; 29–30, 424
Murger, Henri 94–99, 167; 45–46, 388
Murphey, Ralph 23–24, 441

Murphy, Cón T. *94–99,* 99, 109, 122

Murphy, Elliott *46–47,* 494

Murphy, Owen *21–22,* 397, 552; *24–25,* 440; *25–26,* 420, 522, 570; *27–28,* 506; *30–31,* 493; *33–34,* 434

Murphy, Ralph (Rolph) *24–25,* 557; *26–27,* 408; *27–28,* 515; *29–30,* 432; *31–32,* 462

Murphy, Thomas *69–70,* 341

Murray, Alfred *99–09,* 395

Murray, Douglas *09–19,* 641; *26–27,* 359

Murray, George *23–24,* 402

Murray, Gerard M. *43–44,* 479

Murray, (Sir) Gilbert *19–20,* 439; *23–24,* 343; *40–41,* 431; *61–62,* 326

Murray, J.P. *31–32,* 377

Murray, John *36–37,* 485; *52–53,* 297; *62–63,* 339; *69–70,* 367

Murray, T.C. *09–19,* 458, 494; *26–27,* 412; *32–33,* 407; *34–35,* 411

Murray, Ted *43–44,* 484

Murray, Warren *40–41,* 431

Murray, William *66–67,* 418; *68–69,* 451

Murray, William B. *31–32,* 499

Murril, Herbert *36–37,* 448

Muscari, Julius *38–39,* 485

Muse, Mr. *53–54,* 305

Musset, Alfred (see Alfred de Musset)

Musson, Bennett *26–27,* 501; *38–39,* 488

Mussorgsky, Modest (see Moussorgsky)

Myerberg, Michael *47–48,* 356; *57–58,* 296

Myers, Henry *21–22,* 525; *25–26,* 500; *26–27,* 362, 492; *28–29,* 368; *29–30,* 548; *32–33,* 393; *35–36,* 486; *37–38,* 393; *40–41,* 403; *46–47,* 419; *60–61,* 332

Myers, Johnny *64–65,* 358

Myers, Peter *62–63,* 316

Myers, Richard *27–28,* 390; *31–32,* 422; *32–33,* 395; *33–34,* 430, 438, 508; *56–57,* 357

Myers, Stanley *62–63,* 316, 323

Mysell, Bella *61–62,* 312

Mysels, George *61–62,* 329

Nabo(a)koff, Nicolas *33–34,* 519; *34–35,* 460; *40–41,* 428; *44–45,* 439; *45–46,* 452

Nabokov, Vladimir *68–69,* 434

Nagle, Urban (O.P.) *41–42,* 459; *46–47,* 432; *47–48,* 427; *48–49,* 426; *49–50,* 385

Nagler, A.N. *44–45,* 399

Namboku, Tsurya *68–69,* 406

Namiki, Senryu *65–66,* 403

Nancey (Nacey), Mons. *09–19,* 424, 438

Naoya, Shiga *60–61,* 45

Narayan, R.K. *67–68,* 366

Narcejac, Thomas *57–58,* 295

Nash, N. Richard *46–47,* 407; *48–49,* 396; *52–53,* 274; *54–55,* 371; *56–57,* 336; *58–59,* 292; *60–61,* 313; *63–64,* 311; *67–68,* 358

Nash, Ogden *43–44,* 417; *52–53,* 275; *55–56,* 391; *63–64,* 342, 371; *69–70,* 335

Nassau, Paul *56–57,* 314; *59–60,* 293; *66–67,* 376; *67–68,* 369, 376

Natanson, Jacques *28–29,* 435; *33–34,* 457

Nathan, Adele Gutman *38–39,* 418

Nathan, Alfred *27–28,* 389

Nathan, George Jean *09–19,* 509

Nathan, Paul *56–57,* 323

Naughton, Bill *64–65,* 320, 328; *67–68,* 341

Navarre, Jay *55–56,* 340

Naya, Ramon *41–42,* 459; *44–45,* 441

Naylor, Charles *66–67,* 417

Nazimova, Alla *99–09,* 360; *36–37,* 432

Neal, M. *99–09,* 510

Nedbal, Oskar *09–19,* 547

Neely, W. Hamlin Jr. *47–48,* 428

Neff, John *42–43,* 438

Neff, Morty *61–62,* 329

Negin, Louis *69–70,* 354

Neidlinger, W.H. *99–09,* 380

Neison, Francis *94–99,* 104; *09–19,* 463

Neilson, Keith *69–70,* 378

Neiman, Irving Gaynor *42–43,* 477; *43–44,* 404

Nellhaus, Gerhard *60–61,* 355; *61–62,* 305; *62–63,* 314

Nelson, Mr. (see Pease, Nelson & Dodge)

Nelson, Jack T. *29–30,* 390

Nelson, John L. *09–19,* 655

Nelson, Mervyn *48–49,* 418

Nelson, Portia *55–56,* 335

Nelson, Ralph *42–43,* 478; *43–44,* 404; *45–46,* 379

Nemerov, Howard *58–59,* 318

Nemiroff, Mr. *47–48,* 417

Nemiroff, Robert *65–66,* 382; *68–69,* 442; *70–71*

Nemirovitch-Dantchenko, Vladimir *25–26,* 514

Nepoly, Lucien *09–19,* 531

Nepoty, Mons. (see Farrere & Nepoty)

Ner(t)z, Louis *24–25,* 434; *29–30,* 429

Neruda, Pablo *67–68,* 401

Nesbit, Wilbur *09–19,* 447

Nestroy, Johann *38–39,* 441; *67–68,* 367

Nethersole, Olga *99–09,* 557

Neu, M. *66–67,* 393; *67–68,* 339

Neubach, Ernst *31–32,* 487

Neuman, Al *94–99,* 171

Neumann, Alfred *27–28,* 494; *41–42,* 458; *64–65,* 348; *66–67,* 371

Neuville, Mme. *94–99,* 122

Neveux, Georges *56–57,* 353

Neville, Henry *94–99,* 93

Nevill, Hugh *63–64,* 355

Nevin, Arthur *99–09,* 364

Nevin, Hardwick *28–29,* 480; *33–34,* 485

Nevius, J.A. *41–42,* 461

Newberry, Cammann *36–37,* 499

Newburg(e), David *69–70,* 314; *70–71*

Newing, DeWitt *24–25,* 593

Newley, Anthony *62–63,* 278; *64–65,* 338

Newman, Charles *99–09,* 483; *34–35,* 482

Newman, David *65–66,* 405; *69–70,* 335

Newman, Greatrix *27–28,* 500

Newman, Howard *40–41,* 418

Newmarch, Rosa *45–46,* 389

Newmeyer, Sarah *38–39,* 475

Ney, Richard *57–58,* 320

Niccodemi, Dario *99–09,* 472; *09–19,* 530, 544, 644; *23–24,* 370; *25–26,* 465, 524; *31–32,* 501

Nichols, Alberta *26–27,* 422; *33–34,* 466; *53–54,* 305, 306

Nichols, Anne *20–21,* 445; *21–22,* 441, 550; *35–36,* 505; *36–37,* 483; *54–55,* 375

Nichols, Beverly *32–33,* 456

Nichols, C.T. *94–99,* 251

Nichols, Dudley *35–36,* 484

Nichol(l)s, Harry *94–99,* 103, 233; *99–09,* 403

Nichols, Mike *60–61,* 299

Nichols, Peter *67–68,* 361; *69–70,* 317

Nichols, Robert *28–29,* 432; *47–48,* 427; *48–49,* 427

Nicholson, Kenyon *26–27,* 462, 509, 522; *28–29,* 364, 494; *30–31,* 404, 425, 447; *33–34,* 437; *34–35,* 477; *36–37,* 419; *37–38,* 416; *40–41,* 406; *45–46,* 425; *51–52,* 282

Nicholson, Leta Vance *19–20,* 437

Nicholson, Meredith *99–09,* 554

Nicol, Eric *67–68,* 342

Nicolaeff, Ariadne *65–66,* 410; *67–68,* 352

Niessner, Tony *64–65,* 299

Nilioff, G. *45–46*, 460; *46–47*, 497
Nilson, Einar *27–28*, 466
Nin, Joaquin *56–57*, 320
Nirdlinger, Charles Frederick *99–09*,
    352, 426, 547, 572; *09–19*, 460
Nivoix, Paul *25–26*, 515
Niwa, Tamako *67–68*, 411
Nizer, Louis *63–64*, 308
Noah, Robert *63–64*, 308
Noble, Sheldon *37–38*, 408
Noble, William *57–58*, 321
Nobles, Milton *94–99*, 84, 247
Noe, Yvan *36–37*, 499; *37–38*, 444
Noel, Joseph *09–19*, 472; *19–20*, 362
Noel, Maurice *69–70*, 373
Noel-Baker, Philip *64–65*, 303
Nolan, Peter *29–30*, 548
Noll, Joseph *09–19*, 606
Nolte, Charles *64–65*, 358
Noonan, John Ford *68–69*, 437;
    70–71
Norcross, Richard *41–42*, 395
Nord, Paul *42–43*, 489; *63–64*, 344
Norden, A.M. *99–09*, 452, 468
Nordoff, Paul *34–35*, 424; *43–44*,
    487; *45–46*, 456; *47–48*, 365
Nordstrom, Frances *19–20*, 416;
    21–22, 536
Norman, Mrs. George *20–21*, 409
Norman, Monty *60–61*, 296
Norman, Pierre *64–65*, 331
Norris, E.E. Jr. *47–48*, 428
Norris, Frank *99–09*, 454
North, Alex *35–36*, 437; *38–39*, 482;
    40–41, 389; *41–42*, 438; *46–47*,
    461, 463; *48–49*, 412, *49–50*, 371;
    53–54, 326, 337
North, Caroline *39–40*, 413
North, Carrington *24–25*, 434
North, Clyde *26–27*, 467; *27–28*,
    525; *29–30*, 390; *31–32*, 439;
    36–37, 444
North, E. *30–31*, 447
North, Joseph *35–36*, 510
North, Oliver *94–99*, 220
Northrup, Theodore H. *99–09*, 381
Norton, Frederick *09–19*, 610

Norworth, Jack *99–09*, 517; *54–55*,
    404
Noto, Lore *65–66*, 390
Nourse, Joan & Philip *66–67*, 423
Novelli, Ermete *99–09*, 536
Novello, Ivor *30–31*, 412, 472;
    33–34, 427; *35–36*, 480
Novion, Senor *27–28*, 468
Nowak, Lionel *41–42*, 457; *47–48*,
    417
Nudelman, M. *66–67*, 367, 393;
    67–68, 339
Nugent, Elliott *21–22*, 547; *23–24*,
    362; *24–25*, 478, 581; *25–26*, 455,
    563; *26–27*, 527; *27–28*, 449, 541;
    28–29, 382; *31–32*, 434; *39–40*,
    427; *44–45*, 427; *51–52*, 321
Nugent, J.C. *21–22*, 547; *23–24*,
    362; *24–25*, 478, 581; *25–26*, 455,
    563; *26–27*, 527; *27–28*, 449, 541;
    28–29, 382; *31–32*, 434; *34–35*,
    379; *43–44*, 481
Nurnberg, Maxwell *35–36*, 470
Nurock, Kirk *70–71*
Nus, Eugene *94–99*, 99, 143, 235,
    245
Nutter, Eileen *32–33*, 482
Nxumalo, Gideon *63–64*, 330
Nyburg, Sidney *39–40*, 468
Nye, Bill *94–99*, 158
Nyitray, Emil *09–19*, 467, 531;
    19–20, 394; *21–22*, 521; *23–24*,
    326; *24–25*, 575

Oakland, Ben *31–32*, 377; *33–34*,
    434
Oates, Joyce Carol *64–65*, 355;
    70–71
Obayashi, Kazu *65–66*, 403
Ober, Ruth Boyd *09–19*, 611
Obey, André *21–22*, 468; *32–33*,
    438; *34–35*, 451; *46–47*, 493;
    47–48, 427; *49–50*, 384; *54–55*, 58
Oboler, Arch *56–57*, 342; *62–63*,
    337
Obratsov, Sergei *63–64*, 305
O'Brien, Fitz James *94–99*, 104

O'Brien, Jack 67–68, 354; 68–69, 376

O'Brien, Joan 61–62, 325

O'Brien, Justin 59–60, 319; 65–66, 378

O'Brien, Kate 49–50, 361

O'Brien, Liam 53–54, 334

O'Brien, Seumas 37–38, 463

O'Casey, Sean 25–26, 567; 27–28, 459, 469; 29–30, 429; 32–33, 407; 34–35, 395, 406, 411; 35–36, 511; 37–38, 375, 377; 39–40, 430; 46–47, 438; 49–50, 383; 51–52, 332; 52–53, 308; 55–56, 367; 56–57, 55, 319; 57–58, 288; 58–59, 52, 305, 326, 333; 59–60, 49, 311; 60–61, 312, 351; 61–62, 314; 62–63, 338; 64–65, 347, 350; 68–69, 383; 70–71

Ochs, Phil 68–69, 453

O'Connell, Richard L. 44–45, 442; 50–51, 340; 70–71

O'Connor, Edwin 64–65, 311

O'Connor, Flannery 66–67, 409

O'Connor, Frank 37–38, 376; 58–59, 50

O'Connor, Giles 64–65, 358

O'Connor, Larry 34–35, 419

O'Connor, Shamus 65–66, 422

O'Connor, Vincent 42–43, 486

Oddie, Bill 64–65, 305, 346

O'Dea, James 99–09, 381, 512, 540, 548; 09–19, 456, 481, 535

O'Dea, John B. 42–43, 477; 43–44, 404

Oden, G.C. 66–67, 354

Odets, Clifford 34–35, 454, 464, 465, 483; 35–36, 402, 448; 37–38, 386; 38–39, 430, 463, 482, 484; 39–40, 438; 41–42, 423; 42–43, 455; 48–49, 413; 50–51, 325, 361; 51–52, 312; 54–55, 387; 64–65, 307; 66–67, 358; 67–68, 403, 409, 413; 69–70, 370; 70–71

O'Donnell, E.P. 42–43, 447

O'Donnell, Jack 29–30, 475

O'Donnell, Judson 41–42, 447

Oesterreicher, Rudolph 27–28, 416

Offenbach, Jacques 94–99, 110, 134, 250; 99–09, 461; 09–19, 638; 24–25, 524; 31–32, 414; 41–42, 456; 42–43, 487; 43–44, 470; 44–45, 380; 45–46, 454; 60–61, 332; 63–64, 326; 64–65, 297

Offner, Mortimer 40–41, 403

O'Flaherty, Liam 30–31, 424; 35–36, 463

Ogilvie, Stuart 94–99, 225

O'Hara, Constance M. 36–37, 497; 39–40, 470

O'Hara, Frank 63–64, 364

O'Hara, Geoffrey 29–30, 535

O'Hara, John 40–41, 404; 41–42, 391; 51–52, 301; 60–61, 343; 62–63, 311

O'Hara, Michael 46–47, 431

O'Hea, Murphy 94–99, 128

O'Higgins, Harvey J. 09–19, 489, 526, 540, 581; 19–20, 376; 21–22, 436; 23–24, 409

O'Higgins, Myron 66–67, 355

Ohnet, Georges 94–99, 114, 212, 234

O'Horgan, Tom 62–63, 330; 63–64, 345, 363; 65–66, 433; 68–69, 425; 70–71

Okala-Abuta, Etuka C. 46–47, 487

O'Keefe, Walter 28–29, 391

Okonkowsky, Georg 09–19, 462, 519

O'Kun, Lan 63–64, 372

O-lan (Mrs. Sam Shepard) 70–71

Oland, Edith 09–19, 497

Oland, Warner 09–19, 497

Olcott, Rita 19–20, 347

Oliver, Barrie 35–36, 429

Oliver, George W. 25–26, 550

Oliver, Roland 09–19, 535, 605; 24–25, 550; 26–27, 446; 27–28, 393, 540; 28–29, 413

Oliver, Tom 63–64, 371

Olivier, Laurence 39–40, 461

Olivier, Stuart 23–24, 426; 25–26, 580

Olney, Dorothy *64–65,* 361
Olsen, Harry B. *09–19,* 605
Olsen, Ole *38–39,* 407; *41–42,* 417;
44–45, 404; *50–51,* 317
Olshanetsky, Alexander *36–37,* 500;
38–39, 493, 494; *39–40,* 474;
43–44, 490; *44–45,* 443
O'Malley, Tom *61–62,* 313
OM Theater Workshop *68–69,* 457
O'Neal, Charles *51–52,* 315
O'Neil, George *32–33,* 465; *34–35,*
426
O'Neil, Rose Meller *09–19,* 410
O'Neill, Eugene (Gladstone) *09–19,*
612, 628; *19–20,* 420; *20–21,* 399,
417, 452; *21–22,* 454, 459, 519,
524; *23–24,* 409; *24–25,* 480, 485,
540, 587; *25–26,* 512, 535, 556;
26–27, 424, 435; *27–28,* 487, 500,
550, 551; *28–29,* 452, 467, 477,
502; *29–30,* 504; *31–32,* 417, 501,
511; *33–34,* 438, 478; *37–38,* 451,
453; *38–39,* 489; *41–42,* 401;
44–45, 441; *46–47,* 424; *47–48,*
348, 428; *51–52,* 304, 306, 333;
55–56, 55; *56–57,* 332, 372, 373;
58–59, 293; *59–60,* 49, 292, 299;
61–62, 298, 309; *62–63,* 300, 323,
339; *63–64,* 321; *64–65,* 321;
66–67, 392; *67–68,* 351, 401;
68–69, 424; *70–71*
O'Neill, Frank *54–55,* 380
O'Neill, Norman *09–19,* 640
Ongley, Byron *99–09,* 530, 560;
09–19, 467, 531
Onstott, Kyle *60–61,* 341
Open Theater Ensemble, The *68–69,*
457; *69–70,* 369, *70–71*
Open Window, The *68–69,* 449;
69–70, 335
Ophir, Shai K. *59–60,* 48
Oppenheim, James *24–25,* 588
Oppenheimer, George S. *27–28,* 389,
390; *32–33,* 383; *33–34,* 507;
49–50, 368; *59–60,* 313; *67–68,*
409
Orbier, Stanley *99–09,* 472

Orczy, Baroness *09–19,* 428; *63–64,*
354
Ord, Robert *99–09,* 551; *20–21,*
372
Ordonneau, Maurice *94–99,* 107,
195, 212, 242; *99–09,* 443
O'Reilly, Art *69–70,* 376
O'Reilly, Jeannine *70–71*
O'Reilly, Nan *32–33,* 461
Organic Theater Company *70–71*
O'Riada, Sean *70–71*
Oriovitz, Gil *52–53,* 307
Orkow, B. Harrison *24–25,* 508;
27–28, 524; *44–45,* 428
Orlob, Harold *09–19,* 448, 476, 525,
558, 647; *19–20,* 374, 381; *23–24,*
337; *26–27,* 534; *43–44,* 416
Orme, Michael *24–25,* 475
Ormiston, George *67–68,* 377
Ormont, Dave *55–56,* 339
Ornadel, Cyril *65–66,* 372
Ornitz, Samuel *34–35,* 398; *35–36,*
510
Orr, Mary *43–44,* 451; *44–45,* 403,
433; *52–53,* 280; *69–70,* 323
Ortman, Will *25–26,* 475
Orton, Joe *65–66,* 376; *67–68,* 367;
69–70, 344, 367
O'Ryan, Anna Wynne *19–20,* 439;
21–22, 529
Osborn, Lincoln *22–23,* 553
Osborn, Paul *28–29,* 413; *29–30,*
443; *30–31,* 457; *33–34,* 476;
37–38, 421; *39–40,* 418; *43–44,*
427; *44–45,* 402; *51–52,* 298;
52–53, 286; *55–56,* 58; *58–59,*
296
Osborne, Hubert *09–19,* 627, 630;
22–23, 435, 534; *24–25,* 427
Osborne, John *57–58,* 288, 317;
58–59, 301, 317; *60–61,* 45; *63–64,*
304; *65–66,* 389; *69–70,* 299
Osbo(u)rne, Lloyd *99–09,* 510;
09–19, 595; *29–30,* 546
Osgood, Lawrence *63–64,* 370;
64–65, 354; *70–71*
O'Shaughnessy, John *35–36,* 503

Osmun, Leighton Graves *09–19*, 652; *22–23*, 437, 562; *23–24*, 318; *30–31*, 497

Ossetynski (see D-Ossetinsky)

Osterman, Jack *27–28*, 452

Ostrov, Dmitri *35–36*, 414

Ostrovsky, Alexander N. *99–09*, 363, 560; *23–24*, 356; *34–35*, 453; *56–57*, 331; *61–62*, 325; *63–64*, 364

Ostrow, Dmitri *30–31*, 484

Others (unnamed authors) *09–19*, 633; *30–31*, 432; *32–33*, 428; *35–36*, 471, 479; *37–38*, 369, 469; *38–39*, 459, 487; *46–47*, 490; *47–48*, 414; *49–50*, 367; *51–52*, 333; *68–69*, 446; *70–71*

Otvos, A. *23–24*, 414

Otrabanda Company of Curacao *70–71*

Otvos, Dorian *29–30*, 548; *44–45*, 419

Otway, Howard *66–67*, 405

Ouelette, Gratie(a)n *63–64*, 343, 372

Ouida *99–09*, 387

Oursler, Fulton *26–27*, 386, 496; *27–28*, 442, 517; *28–29*, 465; *41–42*, 450

Ouspensky, A. *29–30*, 462

Outcault, R.F. *99–09*, 483

Overbury, (Sir) Thomas *63–64*, 314

Overstreet, Bonaro W. *43–44*, 490

Overton, Hal *50–51*, 309

Ovid *70–71*

Owen, Harold *09–19*, 534, 588

Owen, Harrison *27–28*, 548

Owens, Rochelle *66–67*, 36; *68–69*, 425, 439; *70–71*

Pachecho, Mrs. Romualdo *94–99*, 109; *99–09*, 563

Packard, Frank L. *09–19*, 532

Packard, William *61–62*, 332; *64–65*, 362; *65–66*, 430, 438

Padnos, Don *70–71*

Padrian, Thomas H.F. *42–43*, 486

Padula, Edward *66–67*, 376

Paganini, Nicolo *39–40*, 471; *40–41*, 427–8; *44–45*, 439

Pagano, Ernest *54–55*, 53

Pagat, Henry *94–99*, 182

Page, Austin *09–19*, 645

Page, Curtis Hidden *09–19*, 457

Page, Mann *22–23*, 439; *24–25*, 569; *25–26*, 557, 568; *29–30*, 518

Page, N. Clifford *94–99*, 209

Page, William A. *22–23*, 493

Paget, Daniel *63–64*, 369

Pagni, Mr. *45–46*, 452

Pagnol, Marcel *25–26*, 515; *29–30*, 493; *30–31*, 403, 453, 491; *47–48*, 371; *54–55*, 373

Pailleron, Edmond *94–99*, 224

Paine, Albert B. *94–99*, 211

Pakulski, Jerzy *64–65*, 322

Palacios (see Perrin & Palacious)

Palestrant, Judith *60–61*, 39

Paley, Paul K. *43–44*, 459

Pallings, W. *94–99*, 201

Palma, Anthony *49–50*, 384

Palmer, David *64–65*, 305, 346

Palmer, Rose A. *26–27*, 413; *28–29*, 421; *29–30*, 437

Palmer, Winthrop B. *41–42*, 457; *44–45*, 439; *59–60*, 47; *63–64*, 366

Panama, Norman *39–40*, 463; *56–57*, 335

Panara, Robert F. *68–69*, 406, 407; *69–70*, 311

Pandel, Ted *62–63*, 312

Panetta, George *57–58*, 56; *59–60*, 330; *61–62*, 328, 329; *64–65*, 342; *67–68*, 371

Panich, David *62–63*, 336; *64–65*, 358

Panzer, Mart(y) *68–69*, 422; *69–70*, 365

Papaconstantieou, Alkis *63–64*, 344

Papps, Frank *62–63*, 334

Paradis, Marjorie Bartholomew *29–30*, 539

Paramore, Edward E. (Jr.) *26–27*, 483; *28–29*, 365; *46–47*, 424

Parent, Gayle (Gail) *65–66,* 417,
424; *67–68,* 378
Parenteau, Zoel *09–19,* 582, 624
Paris, Ronnie *68–69,* 442
Parish, James *37–38,* 464; *46–47,*
475
Park, Andy *67–68,* 361
Park, Samuel John *29–30,* 395;
35–36, 483; *38–39,* 486
Parker, Austin *29–30,* 427
Parker, Don *70–71*
Parker, Dorothy *24–25,* 496; *31–32,*
379; *33–34,* 493; *52–53,* 306;
53–54, 311; *56–57,* 340; *66–67,*
423
Parker, George D. *09–19,* 589, 657
Parker, (Sir) Gilbert *94–99,* 121;
99–09, 549, 570
Parker, Harry Doel *94–99,* 240
Parker, Helen Pitts *38–39,* 488
Parker, Horatio *99–09,* 520
Parker, Ken *51–52,* 332; *52–53,*
309; *53–54,* 358
Parker, Lottie Blair *94–99,* 223;
99–09, 399, 448, 506
Parker, Louis Napoleon *94–99,* 92,
175, 196, 206, 249; *99–09,* 365,
376, 384, 403, 407, 468, 480, 494,
509, 539; *09–19,* 79, 434, 437, 459,
471, 486, 491, 509, 514, 536, 543,
598; *21–22,* 498; *22–23,* 505, 575;
26–27, 522; *27–28,* 478; *35–36,*
511; *53–54,* 322
Parker, Rod *70–71*
Parker, Ross *58–59,* 303
Parkington, Mary *28–29,* 501;
29–30, 535
Parkinson, John *69–70,* 378
Parks, Don(ald) *59–60,* 336; *63–64,*
355, 358, 371; *65–66,* 424
Parrish, Claire *46–47,* 415
Parrish, Mitchell *39–40,* 429
Parry, Edward A. *99–09,* 513
Parry, John C. *41–42,* 460
Parry, Maxwell *09–19,* 649
Parsons, J. Palmer *25–26,* 489
Parsons, Kate *29–30,* 387

Partridge, Bellamy *45–46,* 424
Pascal, Ernest *21–22,* 537; *28–29,*
448; *29–30,* 455; *37–38,* 430;
43–44, 453
Pascal, Gabriel *68–69,* 373
Pascal, John & Fran *67–68,* 370
Pascal, Milton *43–44,* 466; *48–49,*
407; *55–56,* 339
Paso, Alfonso *67–68,* 342
Pasos, Antonio *42–43,* 490
Passman, Ray *62–63,* 312
Patchem, Kenneth *67–68,* 414
Paton, Alan *49–50,* 358; *56–57,* 322;
63–64, 330
Patrick, John *35–36,* 455; *42–43,*
451; *44–45,* 408; *46–47,* 459;
50–51, 321; *51–52,* 297; *53–54,*
310; *56–57,* 58, 332, 359; *61–62,*
260, 332; *69–70,* 310; *70–71*
Patrick, Pat *67–68,* 393
Patrick, Robert *67–68,* 407; *69–70,*
344, 345; *70–71*
Patson, George *09–19,* 439
Patten, Gilbert   (see Burt L.
Standish)
Patterson, Ada *09–19,* 626
Patterson, Haywood *63–64,* 351
Patterson, Joseph Medill *09–19,* 402,
407, 452
Pauker, John *59–60,* 295
Paul, Cedar & Eden *38–39,* 455
Paul, Charles *61–62,* 275
Paul, Isaac *31–32,* 509
Paul, Louis *47–48,* 400
Paul, M. Cooper *39–40,* 437
Paulding, Frederick *94–99,* 148;
99–09, 514, 571
Paulding, William Irving *94–99,* 148
Paull, H.M. *99–09,* 414
Paulsen, Paul M. *09–19,* 539
Paulson, Arvid *09–19,* 564
Paulson, Edward *19–20,* 434
Paulton, Edward A. *94–99,* 84, 106,
140, 188; *99–09,* 519, 530, 543;
09–19, 459, 494, 505, 522, 527,
554, 558, 602, 617; *20–21,* 439;
22–23, 446; *28–29,* 448

Paulton, Harry *94–99,* 106, 140, 188, 202; *99–09,* 441, 446, 543; *09–19,* 494; *20–21,* 418

Paumier, Alfred *09–19,* 530

Paver, Charles *43–44,* 414

Paver, C(K)haver *35–36,* 510; *38–39,* 482; *39–40,* 474

Pavi, Leon *09–19,* 467

Paxton, Glenn *58–59,* 331

Payne, B. Iden *22–23,* 470

Payne, John Howard *36–37,* 496

Payson, W.F. *25–26,* 496

Payton, Lew *24–25,* 442

Peabody, Josephine Preston *09–19,* 438; *19–20,* 438

Pearn, Violet *09–19,* 584

Pears, Peter *62–63,* 334

Pearson, Bud *42–43,* 471; *44–45,* 430

Pearson, Humphrey *29–30,* 520

Pearthree, Jonathan *70–71*

Pease, Nelson & Dodge *56–57,* 333

Peaslee, Richard *65–66,* 393, 422; *66–67,* 380; *67–68,* 387, 392, 409; *68–69,* 391; *69–70,* 300, 370, 376; *70–71*

Peck, Charles K. Jr. *59–60,* 339; *69–70,* 308

Peck, George *94–99,* 95

Peck, Raymond W. *99–09,* 507; *09–19,* 470; *20–21,* 436; *26–27,* 374

Peglar, Arthur James *39–40,* 468

Peile, F. Kinsey *99–09,* 365

Pelletier, Louis Jr. *36–37,* 455

Peluso, Emanuel *65–66,* 422

Peluso, Tom *31–32,* 502

Pember, Clifford *28–29,* 366

Pemberton, Murdoch *09–19,* 547; *31–32,* 430

Pemberton, T. Edgar *94–99,* 177

Pen, John *43–44,* 460

Penella, Manuel *21–22,* 467

Penfield, Roderic C. *99–09,* 478, 534

Penn, W.H. *99–09,* 446

Penny, Martin *46–47,* 491

Penon, Agustin *67–68,* 342

Pepin, Clermont *57–58,* 330

Peple, Edward *99–09,* 494, 524, 546; *09–19,* 418, 458, 479, 523, 602

Pepys, Samuel *27–28,* 448

Percival, Julie Helene *24–25,* 513

Percival, Walter C. *09–19,* 636; *22–23,* 475

Percy, Edward *26–27,* 437; *39–40,* 449, 454; *48–49,* 407

Percy, William Alexander *54–55,* 58

Percyval, T. Wigney *09–19,* 515, 591; *32–33,* 458; *40–41,* 432

Perelman, Laura *33–34,* 467; *40–41,* 423

Perelman, S.J. *32–33,* 433; *33–34,* 467; *40–41,* 423; *43–44,* 417; *62–63,* 291

Peretti, Hugo *68–69,* 386

Peretz, Isaac Loeb *35–36,* 479; *45–46,* 460; *46–47,* 497; *63–64,* 351

Perez, J. *68–69,* 416

Performance Group, The *70–71*

Pergament, Lola *61–62,* 310

Pergolesi, Giovanni Batista *37–38,* 412; *42–43,* 487; *43–44,* 479; *45–46,* 453; *47–48,* 426

Perinque, Eugene F. *99–09,* 547

Perkins, Grace *41–42,* 450

Perkins, Kenneth *27–28,* 410; *34–35,* 388; *47–48,* 339

Perkins, Ray *27–28,* 536

Perkinson, Coleridge-Taylor *67–68,* 396; *68–69,* 440, 441; *69–70,* 336

Perlet, Herman *94–99,* 158, 199, 201, 226; *99–09,* 363, 376

Perlman, William J. *26–27,* 364, 470; *28–29,* 471; *33–34,* 511

Perlmutter, A. *99–09,* 458

Perr, Harvey *63–64,* 371; *67–68,* 406

Perrie, Ernestine *63–64,* 353

Perrin & Palacios *68–69,* 416

Perrin, Margaret *63–64,* 355

Perrin, Sam *45–46,* 405

Perry, John *38–39,* 436

Personaggi, Signor *36–37,* 500

Pertwee, Michael *38–39,* 404
Pertwee, Roland *25–26,* 559; *27–28,*
432; *30–31,* 492; *32–33,* 436
Perutz, Leo *34–35,* 470; *35–36,* 456
Peter, Rene *25–26,* 493
Peterkin, Julia *30–31,* 460
Peters, Paul *33–34,* 516; *34–35,* 383,
478; *35–36,* 436, 510; *50–51,* 374
Peters, Robert *69–70,* 373
Peters, William Frederick *99–09,*
423, 503; *09–19,* 449, 499, 518,
553
Petersen, Don *68–69,* 407
Peterson, Louis *53–54,* 306; *56–57,*
55; *61–62,* 328
Petit, Roland *64–65,* 315
Petronius *49–50,* 379
Petrova, (Mme.) Olga *21–22,* 483;
23–24, 372; *27–28,* 473
Pettitt, Henry *94–99,* 83, 94, 98,
153, 164, 257, 258
Pettitt, Wilfred H. *42–43,* 459
Pezet, Washington (A.W.) *09–19,*
524; *30–31,* 459; *33–34,* 487;
35–36, 473
Pfeiffer, Jack *55–56,* 361
Pflueger, Carl *94–99,* 103
Pfoutz, S.F. *60–61,* 357
Phelps, Lyon *61–62,* 263; *70–71*
Phelps, Merridan (Richard
Mansfield) *94–99,* 228; *99–09,* 355
Phelps, Pauline *99–09,* 547; *19–20,*
426
Phelps, Robert *69–70,* 367; *70–71*
Philipp, Adolf(ph) *09–19,* 505, 522,
554, 558; *33–34,* 435, 487
Philips, Anita *35–36,* 407
Philips, F.C. *94–99,* 84, 164
Phillipe, Pierre *57–58,* 330
Phillips, David Graham *99–09,* 558;
09–19, 462, 464
Phillips, Rev. Forbes (see Rev.
Forbes-Phillips)
Phillips, H.I. *23–24,* 337; *31–32,*
379; *33–34,* 476; *34–35,* 432;
50–51, 309
Phillips, Irving *57–58,* 299

Phillips, Jonas B. *94–99,* 250
Phillips, Nancie *67–68,* 377
Phillips, Peggy *43–44,* 443
Phillips, Stephen *99–09,* 437, 520;
09–19, 403; *24–25,* 498; *28–29,*
484
Phillips, Watts *94–99,* 132, 248
Phillpotts, Adelaide *27–28,* 400
Phillpotts, Eden *09–19,* 564; *21–22,*
538; *24–25,* 468; *27–28,* 400;
51–52, 276
Phipps, (Hon.) Edmund *99–09,* 520
Phipps, Thomas W. *57–58,* 286
Piave, Francesco Maria *45–46,* 388,
391
Piazza, Ben *68–69,* 449
Picard, André *99–09,* 521; *21–22,*
470; *22–23,* 502; *24–25,* 501;
30–31, 463
Picasso, Pablo *51–52,* 333
Pickett, George *27–28,* 505; *32–33,*
417
Pickow, George *68–69,* 428
Picon, Molly *42–43,* 435
Pidgin, Charles Felton *94–99,* 95;
99–09, 413
Pier, Garrett Chatfield *26–27,* 395
Pierce, G.A. *94–99,* 177
Pierce, Nat *59–60,* 40
Pierce, Noel *32–33,* 501
Pierson, Arthur *41–42,* 448; *43–44,*
426
Pigott, J. Smyth *99–09,* 576
Pilditch, Charles R. *66–67,* 408
Pilhofer, Herbert *68–69,* 399; *70–71*
Pillott, Eugene *23–24,* 429
Pimentel, J. Garcia *09–19,* 612
Pincus, Irvin *39–40,* 453; *40–41,*
375; *41–42,* 395
Pine, Les *52–53,* 307
Pineda, José *67–68,* 401
Pinelli, Tullio *65–66,* 395
Pinero, (Sir) Arthur Wing *94–99,*
102, 114, 159, 160, 194, 216, 234,
246, 260; *99–09,* 361, 379, 403,
404, 417, 419, 465, 477, 480, 518,
557; *09–19,* 412, 430, 435, 458,

Pinero, (Sir) Arthur Wing *(cont.)*
466, 475, 493, 500, 614, 651;
22–23, 549; *24–25,* 477, 598;
26–27, 471; *55–56,* 58; *61–62,* 332;
62–63, 339; *69–70,* 377; *70–71*
Ping(u)et, Robert *60–61,* 44; *69–70,*
363
Pinillos, José Lopez *25–26,* 599;
27–28, 540
Pink, Wal *21–22,* 503
Pinkard, Maceo *22–23,* 494; *28–29,*
505
Pinkham, Daniel *56–57,* 361
Pinski, David *20–21,* 391; *28–29,*
407
Pinter, Harold *61–62,* 258; *62–63,*
320, 322; *63–64,* 354, 358; *64–65,*
349; *66–67,* 380; *67–68,* 342,
68–69, 429; *69–70,* 345, 348;
70–71
Piotrowski, Andrew *68–69,* 455
Piper, Will *31–32,* 402
Pippin, Donald *54–55,* 406
Pirandello, Luigi *22–23,* 482; *23–24,*
324, 388, 396; *24–25,* 474; *26–27,*
421, 436, 486; *30–31,* 484, 516;
46–47, 485; *47–48,* 425; *50–51,*
373; *55–56,* 366; *56–57,* 58; *60–61,*
44; *62–63,* 328, 329, 330; *63–64,*
359; *66–67,* 371, 418; *68–69,* 451
Pironti, Tarquin C. *39–40,* 469
Pirosh, Robert *44–45,* 402
Piscator, Erwin *35–36,* 494; *40–41,*
432; *41–42,* 458; *64–65,* 348;
66–67, 371
Pitcher, Mears *38–39,* 486
Pitot, Genevieve *32–33,* 496; *34–35,*
460; *38–39,* 483; *41–42,* 459;
47–48, 401; *50–51,* 336; *56–57,*
313, 371; *57–58,* 312; *59–60,* 310;
65–66, 375
Pitou, Augustus *94–99,* 97, 119,
192, 249; *99–09,* 385, 390, 420
Pitt, George Dibdin *24–25,* 431
Pittaluga, Senor *44–45,* 440
Pittinger, Martha *37–38,* 464
Pittman, Arthur *68–69,* 437

Pixley & Luders *09–19,* 485
Pixley, Frank S. *99–09,* 363, 379,
383, 410, 430, 474, 537, 570;
29–30, 478
Planchon, Roger *68–69,* 374
Planquette, Robert *09–19,* 437;
31–32, 421
Plant, Michael *57–58,* 308
Plante, J. *69–70,* 314
Plato *68–69,* 455
Platter, Thomas *63–64,* 314
Plautus *61–62,* 297
Playfair, Nigel *28–29,* 384
Pleininger, Carl *94–99,* 178, 238
Pleydell, George *09–19,* 424, 566
Ploner, George *63–64,* 355
Plumptre, Edward Hayes *09–19,*
621
Pockriss, Lee *59–60,* 359; *62–63,*
302; *64–65,* 362
Podrecca, Vittorio *32–33,* 439
Poe, Edgar Allen *99–09,* 485; *46–47,*
490
Pogodin, Nikolai *64–65,* 323
Pohl, Frederick *34–35,* 411
Pohle, Lawrence *35–35,* 374
Pokrass, Samuel *33–34,* 476
Pola, Edward *29–30,* 467
Pollack (Pollock), Lew *20–21,* 425,
453; *21–22,* 397
Polesie, Herbert *31–32,* 516
Polis, Daniel *52–53,* 306
Politis, Photos *52–53,* 272
Pollard, Percival *99–09,* 537
Pollitt, Josephine *34–35,* 411
Pollock, Mr. *53–54,* 306
Pollock, Alice Leal *09–19,* 573
Pollock, Arthur *30–31,* 517; *31–32,*
412
Pollock, Channing *99–09,* 454, 508,
519, 534, 553; *09–19,* 398, 457,
476, 511, 526, 537, 553, 616, 645,
646; *19–20,* 401; *21–22,* 388;
22–23, 476; *25–26,* 478; *28–29,*
398; *30–31,* 504
Pollock, John *36–37,* 484
Pollock, Muriel *28–29,* 469

Pollock, Walter *94–99*, 120
Polnareff, Michel *69–70*, 329
Ponchielli, Mr. *56–57*, 333
Pond, Anson *94–99*, 253; *99–09*, 408
Ponzi, Joe *70–71*
Poole, Ernest *09–19*. 413, 498
Popkin, Larry *63–64*, 343
Popovic, Alexander *68–69*, 425; *69–70*, 375
Popp, Andre *64–65*, 331
Poquelin, Jean-Baptiste (see Molière)
Porcelain, Syd *39–40*, 469
Porche, François *26–27*, 463
Pordes-Milo, Signor *19–20*, 406
Porter, Cole *09–19*, 572; *19–20*, 366; *24–25*, 454; *28–29*, 390; *29–30*, 452, 473; *30–31*, 465; *32–33*, 431; *34–35*, 412; *35–36*, 418; *36–37*, 424; *38–39*, 406, 425; *39–40*, 398, 420; *40–41*, 390; *41–42*, 407; *42–43*, 423, 458; *43–44*, 451; *44–45*, 402; *45–46*, 448; *48–49*, 405; *50–51*, 336; *51–52*, 303; *52–53*, 303; *53–54*, 306; *54–55*, 386, 400, 407; *55–56*, 59, 388; *59–60*, 48; *61–62*, 300, 330; *62–63*, 295, 339; *64–65*, 331, 334, 357; *65–66*, 428; *68–69*, 379; *69–70*, 377
Porter, Eleanor H. *09–19*, 582
Porter, Gene Stratton (see Gene Stratton-Porter)
Porter, H.T. *35–36*, 479
Porter, Henry *36–37*, 497
Porter, Jessie *09–19*, 646
Porter, Katherine Anne *60–61*, 48
Porter, Olive *09–19*, 396
Porter, Paul W. *25–26*, 487; *26–27*, 364
Porter, Rose Albert *32–33*, 421
Porter, Stephen *63–64*, 360
Porterfield, Gordon *69–70*, 372
Portnoff, Mischa & Wesley *49–50*, 366
Posner, Lee *31–32*, 502

Post, Melville Davisson *44–45*, 417
Post, William H. *99–09*, 407; *09–19*, 484, 572; *20–21*, 444; *25–26*, 451; *27–28*, 480
Potter, Mr. (see Leigh & Potter)
Potter, Paul M. *94–99*, 85, 100, 121, 132, 158, 220, 235; *99–09*, 387, 395, 406, 463, 486, 491, 522, 555, 558, 574, 577; *09–19*, 438, 493, 549, 657; *26–27*, 445
Pottle, Sam *61–62*, 316; *62–63*, 317, 324; *63–64*, 344; *64–65*, 343; *67–68*, 377, 378
Poulenc, Francis *49–50*, 368; *50–51*, 329; *52–53*, 270; *56–57*, 353
Pound, Ezra *60–61*, 347; *62–63*, 322
Powel, Robert Hare *33–34*, 477
Powell, Mr. *34–35*, 460
Powell, Dawn *32–33*, 451; *33–34*, 521; *41–42*, 427
Powell, Jerry *62–63*, 329; *63–64*, 358, 359, 371, 372; *64–65*, 342, 359; *66–67*, 404; *67–68*, 377
Powers, Charles Eugene *24–25*, 584
Powers, Francis *94–99*, 211
Powers, Gudrun *63–64*, 352
Powers, James T. *99–09*, 577; *09–19*, 471; *22–23*, 522
Powers, Tom *34–35*, 391
Powys, Stephen *37–38*, 380; *39–40*, 466; *48–49*, 404
Poynter, Beulah *09–19*, 565; *28–29*, 439
Praga, Marco *99–09*, 536; *23–24*, 366
Prager, Jacob *36–37*, 500
Praskins, Leonard *21–22*, 537
Pratt, Theodore *22–23*, 570; *38–39*, 478
Pratt, William W. *31–32*, 467
Pray, Isaac C. *94–99*, 218
Preble, Ed *31–32*, 420
Premise, The *62–63*, 333, 334; *63–64*, 343, 367
Presbrey, Eugene W. *94–99*, 218, 223, 246; *99–09*, 348, 375, 398,

Rachleff, Owen *66–67,* 407
Rachmaninoff, Sergei *25–26,* 515;
    32–33, 502; *40–41,* 427; *44–45,*
    439; *45–46,* 452; *56–57,* 333;
    65–66, 387
Racine, Jean *94–99,* 163; *09–19,*
    432; *60–61,* 326; *63–64,* 310, 326,
    345, 359; *65–66,* 430, 438
Radano, Gene *61–62,* 306
Raddock, Charles *47–48,* 350
Rado, James *67–68,* 374, 389
Radok, Alfred *64–65,* 297
Radok, Emil *64–65,* 297
Raeburn, Henzie *63–64,* 368
Ragni, Gerome *67–68,* 374, 389
Railey, Thomas T. *09–19,* 446
Raine, Norman Reilly *32–33,* 467
Rainsford, Jill *35–36,* 421
Raisbeck, Kenneth *22–23,* 574;
    30–31, 486
Raison, Milton *31–32,* 378
Raksin, David *46–47,* 446
Raleigh, Cecil *94–99,* 99, 139, 216,
    240, 253; *99–09,* 362, 390, 441;
    09–19, 397, 486, 494, 558
Raleigh, (Sir) Walter *63–64,* 314
Ralston, Bob *69–70,* 372
Rameau, Mons. *46–47,* 491
Ramer, Jack *69–70,* 358
Ramin, Sid *66–67,* 376
Ramsey, Alicia *99–09,* 519; *09–19,*
    609
Ranck, Carty *33–34,* 431
Rand, Ayn *35–36,* 404; *39–40,* 436,
    470
Randall, Dudley *68–69,* 433
Randall, F.J. *09–19,* 578
Randall, John 38–39, 488
Randau, Carl *44–45,* 389
Randole, Leo *25–26,* 573; *33–34,*
    532
Randolph, Clemence *22–23,* 483;
    24–25, 443; *34–35,* 451; *44–45,*
    397; *47–48,* 428
Randolph, Forbes *31–32,* 392
Randolph, John *61–62,* 331
Raney, Jim *59–60,* 324; *60–61,* 289
Ranger, Ralph *32–33,* 499–500

Ranken, Frederic M. *99–09,* 358,
    412, 428, 446, 497, 504, 529
Rankin, McKee *94–99,* 189
Raoul, Mons. *28–29,* 475
Raphael, Alice *60–61,* 323
Raphael, John N. *99–09,* 554;
    09–19, 413, 599; *27–28,* 387;
    30–31, 514
Raphael, Lennox *68–69,* 456
Raphaelson, Samson *25–26,*
    443; *26–27,* 511; *28–29,* 405;
    33–34, 475; *34–35,* 430; *36–37,*
    419; *39–40,* 401; *41–42,* 429;
    44–45, 392; *50–51,* 323; *68–69,*
    455
Raposo, Joseph *61–62,* 315; *62–63,*
    314; *66–67,* 415; *69–70,* 295
Rapp, William Jourdan *28–29,* 472;
    29–30, 426, 456; *35–36,* 422;
    36–37, 439
Rastede, Hans *34–35,* 420
Rastegar-Nejad, Nasser *69–70,* 366
Rath, E.J. *23–24,* 331; *26–27,* 402
Rath, Frederick *30–31,* 461; *32–33,*
    481
Rathbone, Basil *28–29,* 461
Rathbone, Ouida *53–54,* 314
Rattigan, Terence *34–35,* 372;
    37–38, 372; *39–40,* 459; *42–43,*
    453; *44–45,* 384; *45–46,* 424;
    47–48, 362; *49–50,* 357; *52–53,*
    266; *56–57,* 327, 330; *61–62,* 275;
    63–64, 313, 315
Rau, Santha Rama *61–62,* 283
Rauch, Maurice *39–40,* 474, 475;
    65–66, 423
Raucher, Herman *62–63,* 290
Rauh, Stanley *26–27,* 368
Ravel, Maurice *31–32,* 475; *40–41,*
    428; *42–43,* 484, 485; *44–45,* 437;
    45–46, 452; *47–48,* 416; *48–49,*
    429; *51–52,* 331
Ravitch, Melach *45–46,* 460; *46–47,*
    497
Rawlings, Marjorie Kinnan *65–66,*
    390
Ray, Anje *67–68,* 407
Raye, Don *55–56,* 337

Rayfiel, David *62–63*, 317; *65–66*, 399

Rayman, Sylvia *51–52*, 311

Raynal, Paul (see Paul Reynal)

Raynes, J.A. *99–09*, 555

Raynolds, Robert *37–38*, 462

Razaf, Andy *27–28*, 518; *29–30*, 376; *30–31*, 438

Reach, James *38–39*, 488

Read, Edward C.K. *39–40*, 473

Read, Opie *99–09*, 363, 431

Reade, Charles *94–99*, 150, 151; *99–09*, 353, 354, 436, 520, 532, 534

Reade, Leslie *33–34*, 509; *44–45*, 417

Reardon, Dennis J. *69–70*, 376; *70–71*

Reardon, Frank *57–58*, 299; *63–64*, 363

Reardon, Leo F. *33–34*, 510

Reavey, Jean *63–64*, 366; *65–66*, 437

Recht, Charles *09–19*, 445; *25–26*, 505; *26–27*, 505

Reckord, Barry *70–71*

Redd, Freddie *59–60*, 350

Reddie, Milton *37–38*, 447

Redgrave, Michael *61–62*, 288

Redman, George *33–34*, 454

Redmond, Johanna *09–19*, 459

Redwine, Skip *70–71*

Reece, Robert *94–99*, 131

Reed, Allan *94–99*, 183

Reed, Charles *94–99*, 98

Reed, Daniel *30–31*, 460

Reed, Dave Jr. *99–09*, 376, 381, 492

Reed, Henry *55–56*, 350; *63–64*, 347

Reed, John *09–19*, 547

Reed, Luther *20–21*, 421

Reed, Mark *19–20*, 349; *28–29*, 454; *34–35*, 460; *36–37*, 462; *67–68*, 410

Reed, Ramon *40–41*, 428

Reed, Stuart *99–09*, 349

Reel, Arthur *65–66*, 425

Reese, Trevor *68–69*, 429

Reeves, Arnold *99–09*, 458

Reeves, Theodore *45–46*, 401; *54–55*, 376

Regan, Sylvia *39–40*, 456; *49–50*, 376; *52–53*, 283; *68–69*, 409

Regener, Eric *62–63*, 314

Reich, John *46–47*, 485; *57–58*, 290

Reich, Richard *68–69*, 452; *70–71*

Reicher, Edward *68–69*, 433

Reichert (Reichart), Heinz *25–26*, 564; *30–31*, 500; *34–35*, 377; *38–39*, 438; *43–44*, 410

Reichert, James *67–68*, 391; *68–69*, 431; *69–70*, 363, 371

Reichner, S. Bickley *35–36*, 507; *38–39*, 491; *39–40*, 472; *41–42*, 460

Reid, Hal *94–99*, 136, 252

Reid, James Halleck *09–19*, 441

Reid, Nat *29–30*, 429

Reif, Ada *47–48*, 417

Reif, Paul *63–64*, 329

Reilly, Frank C. *27–28*, 396

Reinbrack, Mons. *99–09*, 547

Reine, Bella *46–47*, 499

Reiner, Carl *62–63*, 301; *67–68*, 353

Reines, Bernard *48–49*, 409

Reinhardt, Gottfried *42–43*, 441; *43–44*, 470; *45–46*, 396

Reinhardt, Heinrich *09–19*, 434, 499

Reinhardt, Max *23–24*, 385; *42–43*, 441; *43–44*, 470

Reinhardt, Robert *33–34*, 534

Reisch, Walter *31–32*, 379

Reisel, Zvi *70–71*

Reisenfeld, Hugo *19–20*, 450; *32–33*, 377

Reiser, Allan *69–70*, 351

Reizenstein, Elmer L. (see Elmer Rice)

Reizner, June *62–63*, 317; *63–64*, 355; *64–65*, 343; *65–66*, 422; *66–67*, 404

Rella, Ettore *57–58*, 56

Relonde, Maurice *09–19*, 561

Remail(l)y, Robin *69–70*, 305; *70–71*

Remington, Frederic *99–09*, 443

Renard, Joseph *70–71*
Renard, Jules *99–09*, 418
Renauld, Charles *94–99*, 165
Renault, Francis *47–48*, 429
Renavent, Georges *26–27*, 460
René, Mr. *53–54*, 305
Renyi, Aladar *09–19*, 538
Reoyo, Enrique *42–43*, 490
Reparaz, Sr. *53–54*, 322
Resnick, L. *34–35*, 471
Resnik, Muriel *63–64*, 326
Respighi, Ottorino *40–41*, 428
Revel, Harry *31–32*, 377, 487;
   32–33, 382; *45–46*, 405
Revil, Rudi *40–41*, 411, 422
Revuers, The (Betty Comden,
   Adolph Green, Judy Holliday,
   John Frank & Alvin Hammer)
   58–59, 315
Rex, Laurel *38–39*, 486
Reyher, Ferdinand *40–41*, 393
Reynal (Raynal), Paul *28–29*, 404;
   31–32, 416
Reynolds, Alfred *38–39*, 491
Reynolds, Bruce *27–28*, 470
Reynolds, Herbert *09–19*, 547, 554,
   630
Reynolds, Timothy *68–69*, 445, 456
Rhodes, Harrison *99–09*, 436, 569;
   09–19, 442, 451, 467, 567, 596,
   636; *26–27*, 499; *29–30*, 413
Rhodes, Shirley *70–71*
Ribman, Ronald *64–65*, 358, 362;
   65–66, 433; *67–68*, 391; *69–70*,
   349
Ricardel, Molly *32–33*, 398
Ricciardi, William *22–23*, 536
Rice, Alice Hegan *99–09*, 463
Rice, Andy *19–20*, 456; *26–27*, 499
Rice, Cale Young *09–19*, 649
Rice, Edmund *49–50*, 379
Rice, Edward E. *94–99*, 141, 154,
   178, 226; *99–09*, 359
Rice (Reizenstein), Elmer L. *09–19*,
   202, 595, 612; *19–20*, 400; *20–21*,
   420; *22–23*, 443, 496, 544; *24–25*,
   496, 505; *27–28*, 489; *28–29*, 453,

462; *29–30*, 406; *31–32*, 402, 424;
   32–33, 385, 400, 453; *34–35*, 370,
   397; *38–39*, 435; *39–40*, 431;
   40–41, 407; *42–43*, 445; *43–44*,
   413; *45–46*, 414; *46–47*, 454;
   47–48, 424; *48–49*, 425, 426;
   50–51, 350, 369; *51–52*, 297;
   53–54, 341; *58–59*, 54, 306; *65–66*,
   371, 384; *70–71*
Rice, (Lieut.) Gitz *09–19*, 625, 637;
   20–21, 447; *26–27*, 364
Rich, Max *34–35*, 362
Richard, Charles *46–47*, 499
Richard, Gaston Charles *09–19*, 509
Richards, Lexford *51–52*, 311, 334
Richards, Stanley *45–46*, 408; *70–71*
Richardson, Abby Sage *94–99*, 104,
   244, 255; *99–09*, 364
Richardson, Anna Steese *09–19*,
   511; *33–34*, 473
Richardson, Claibe *62–63*, 317;
   65–66, 422
Richardson, Howard *44–45*, 421;
   49–50, 369; *56–57*, 348; *57–58*, 56;
   62–63, 326; *69–70*, 362
Richardson, Jack *59–60*, 353; *60–61*,
   360; *61–62*, 323; *62–63*, 298;
   65–66, 383; *67–68*, 412
Richardson, Roy S. *69–70*, 335
Richardson, Willis *22–23*, 567
Riche, Robert *68–69*, 456
Richepin, Jean *99–09*, 447, 468;
   09–19, 432
Richman, Arthur *19–20*, 449;
   21–22, 439; *22–23*, 442, 454;
   24–25, 462; *25–26*, 439, 479, 502;
   26–27, 427; *28–29*, 367; *35–36*,
   451; *43–44*, 463
Richman, Charles *09–19*, 399
Richman, Sol *66–67*, 418
Richman, Stanley *66–67*, 418
Richter, Carolyn *70–71*
Rickett, Edmond W. *27–28*, 437;
   33–34, 442
Rickman, Carl *30–31*, 427
Rideamus, Edward *22–23*, 526
Rideout, Ransom *28–29*, 361

Ridley, Arnold *26–27*, 369; *27–28*, 517

Ridley, Michael *69–70*, 372

Riegger, Wallingford *37–38*, 458; *38–39*, 483; *41–42*, 457

Rieti, Vittorio *34–35*, 460; *44–45*, 439; *50–51*, 360

Riewerts, J.P. *29–30*, 509

Rifkin, Leo *41–42*, 440

Riggs, Eva Foster *99–09*, 367

Riggs, Lynn *26–27*, 506; *30–31*, 421, 481; *35–36*, 460; *40–41*, 412; *42–43*, 471; *47–48*, 424; *50–51*, 313, 372; *51–52*, 333; *53–54*, 299; *57–58*, 325; *62–63*, 298, 308; *65–66*, 392; *69–70*, 295

Riggs, T. Lawrason *09–19*, 572

Rightmire, William H. *94–99*, 247

Rigsby, Howard *43–44*, 445

Riley, Edna & Edward P. *32–33*, 460

Riley, James Whitcomb *09–19*, 644

Riley, Lawrence *34–35*, 393; *40–41*, 391

Rilke, Rainer Maria *68–69*, 407

Rimbaud, Arthur *69–70*, 378

Rimsky-Korsakoff, Nikolai *37–38*, 468; *42–43*, 485; *43–44*, 440; *44–45*, 437; *45–46*, 452, 453, 455; *47–48*, 414

Rinehart, Mary Roberts (Rinehart Roberts) *99–09*, 529; *09–19*, 404, 490; *20–21*, 366, 371, 397; *23–24*, 302; *36–37*, 486; *52–53*, 281

Rinehart, Patricia *67–68*, 366

Rines, Robert *60–61*, 352; *61–62*, 321; *66–67*, 403

Rinn, Joseph F. *23–24*, 308

Rising, Lawrence *09–19*, 509, 528, 577

Riskin, Robert *27–28*, 475; *29–30*, 486

Risque, W.H. *99–09*, 420

Ritterman, H. *70–71*

Rittman, Trude(i) *50–51*, 336; *52–53*, 268; *54–55*, 369, 374; *63–64*, 310

Ritz, Robert *24–25*, 479

Rivas, Linares *53–54*, 322

Rivers, Joan *64–65*, 342

Rives, Amelie (Princess Pierre Troubetskoy) *09–19*, 569, 632; *20–21*, 400; *25–26*, 582; *28–29*, 353

Rives, Hallie Erminie *99–09*, 438

Rivgauche, Michel *62–63*, 294

Rivkin, Allen *34–35*, 480

Rivoire, Andre *09–19*, 506

Rizzo, Gino 65–66, 416

Roach, James C. *94–99*, 120

Robbins, Jerome *44–45*, 406; *47–48*, 379, 418; *57–58*, 286; *59–60*, 336; *63–64*, 333; *68–69*, 373

Robbins, Leo *39–40*, 474

Robbins, Sam *59–60*, 40

Robe, Alice *26–27*, 436

Robert, Jerrold *31–32*, 522

Roberts, Al(l)an *42–43*, 420; *48–49*, 408

Roberts, Ben *43–44*, 405, 448, 477; *44–45*, 375; *46–47*, 480; *56–57*, 365

Roberts, C. Luckyeth (Luckey) *22–23*, 542; *23–24*, 358; *26–27*, 360

Roberts, Edward *32–33*, 470; *37–38*, 371

Roberts, George N. *25–26*, 591

Roberts, John *09–19*, 488

Roberts, Katherine *31–32*, 405

Roberts, Lee *69–70*, 371

Roberts, Les *64–65*, 342

Roberts, Meade *58–59*, 50

Roberts, Rhoda *69–70*, 360

Roberts, Rinehart (see Mary Roberts Rinehart)

Roberts, Walter Charles *36–37*, 475

Robertson, T.W. *94–99*, 146, 160, 235; *99–09*, 472; *09–19*, 418, 516, 568

Robertson, Willard *19–20*, 419; *25–26*, 430; *27–28*, 417; *29–30*, 507

Robi, Armand *23–24*, 441

Robin, Leo *26–27,* 516; *27–28,* 390,
    429; *28–29,* 406; *32–33,* 499;
    49–50, 363; *53–54,* 343; *55–56,*
    347; *62–63,* 295; *64–65,* 331;
    66–67, 414
Robins, Elizabeth *99–09,* 579
Robinson, A. *31–32,* 379
Robinson, Armin *37–38,* 405
Robinson, Bertrand *26–27,* 457;
    29–30, 442; *30–31,* 400, 459;
    33–34, 425; *35–36,* 423
Robinson, Charles *33–34,* 437, 481;
    34–35, 477; *36–37,* 419; *40–41,*
    406; *45–46,* 425
Robinson, Earl *35–36,* 476; *36–37,*
    497; *37–38,* 450; *38–39,* 482;
    42–43, 433; *44–45,* 431; *54–55,*
    376
Robinson, Edward G. *28–29,* 469
Robinson, Lennox *09–19,* 459, 494;
    19–20, 384; *21–22,* 419; *23–24,*
    432; *32–33,* 404, 407; *33–34,* 456;
    34–35, 407, 409; *35–36,* 511;
    37–38, 375, 378, 463; *38–39,* 484;
    47–48, 426
Robinson, Percy *28–29,* 467; *39–40,*
    462
Robinson, Phyllis *69–70,* 325
Robinson, Richard *66–67,* 404
Robinson, Thomas P. *21–22,* 388;
    23–24, 306; *24–25,* 503; *28–29,*
    465
Robison, Willard *29–30,* 548; *32–33,*
    500
Roblès, Emmanuel *49–50,* 358
Robson, Cecil *49–50,* 377
Robson, E.M. *94–99,* 124
Robson, Eleanor *23–24,* 364
Robson, May *09–19,* 456
Robyn, Alfred G. *94–99,* 106;
    99–09, 455, 530, 541; *09–19,* 490,
    532
Roc, John *68–69,* 403
Rochberg, George *66–67,* 363
Roche, Arthur Somers *09–19,* 607;
    29–30, 397
Roche, Jack *49–50,* 379

Roche, P. *69–70,* 314
Rock, Charles *09–19,* 515
Rodale, J.I. *59–60,* 40; *61–62,* 313;
    62–63, 326, 338; *65–66,* 427
Rodansky, R. (see Robert Bodansky)
Rodda, Violet *38–39,* 484
Rodell, John *37–38,* 465
Rodgers, Bob *59–60,* 289; *61–62,*
    253
Rodgers, Lou *68–69,* 452
Rodgers, Mary *58–59,* 335; *59–60,*
    335; *62–63,* 306; *65–66,* 428;
    66–67, 413, 422
Rodgers, Richard (C.) *20–21,* 359;
    24–25, 602; *25–26,* 448, 572, 598;
    26–27, 447, 450; *27–28,* 445, 486,
    546; *28–29,* 381, 478; *29–30,* 439,
    497; *30–31,* 488, 502; *35–36,* 435,
    499; *36–37,* 446, 479; *37–38,* 369,
    385, 445; *38–39,* 429; *39–40,* 404,
    453, 471; *40–41,* 375, 404; *41–42,*
    391, 455; *42–43,* 471; *43–44,* 428;
    44–45, 428; *46–47,* 433; *47–48,*
    359; *48–49,* 409, 418; *50–51,* 360,
    372; *51–52,* 301; *52–53,* 304;
    53–54, 299; *54–55,* 359, 366, 412;
    55–56, 364, 384; *56–57,* 369;
    57–58, 285, 325; *58–59,* 306;
    59–60, 303, 340; *60–61,* 337, 343;
    61–62, 291; *62–63,* 295, 298, 308,
    311, 332; *63–64,* 302; *64–65,* 296,
    330, 331, 362; *65–66,* 366, 368,
    392; *66–67,* 378, 386, 410; *67–68,*
    339, 379, 409; *69–70,* 295, 374;
    70–71
Roeder, Ralph *09–19,* 579; *25–26,*
    515; *30–31,* 470
Roerick, William *48–49,* 420; *70–71*
Roethke, Theodore *52–53,* 306;
    68–69, 407
Roffey, Jack *65–66,* 398
Roger, Victor *94–99,* 242
Rogers, Alex(ander) C. *99–09,* 509,
    556; *09–19,* 403; *22–23,* 542;
    23–24, 358; *26–27,* 360
Rogers, David *56–57,* 357; *60–61,*
    292; *61–62,* 284; *67–68,* 402

Rogers, Howard Emmett *21–22*, 552; *30–31*, 413

Rogers, John W. Jr. 27–28, 549

Rogers, Merrill *27–28*, 394; *31–32*, 515

Rogers, Robert *63–64*, 369

Rogers, (Maj.) Robert *69–70*, 371

Rogers, William R. Jr. *23–24*, 431

Rogge, Florence *38–39*, 490

Rohac, Jan *64–65*, 297

Rohe, Alice *26–27*, 436

Rohman, Richard *38–39*, 464

Rolfe, (Fr.) Frederick William (Baron Corvo) *68–69*, 401

Rolland, Romain *29–30*, 447; *31–32*, 459

Rollins, Pierce *63–64*, 345

Rollins, Sherwood Jr. *38–39*, 491; *39–40*, 473; *40–41*, 433

Rollit(t), George *99–09*, 482; *09–19*, 532

Rollo, Walter *22–23*, 479

Rolt, Bernard *99–09*, 519

Rolvaag, O.E. *50–51*, 375

Romains, Jules *27–28*, 516; *37–38*, 469; *56–57*, 353; *60–61*, 44

Roman, Lawrence *60–61*, 307; *63–64*, 366; *64–65*, 315

Romberg, Sigmund *09–19*, 519, 527, 534, 546, 553, 554, 562, 567, 571, 576, 579, 585, 588, 589, 600, 602, 603, 610, 615, 622, 631, 649, 652; *19–20*, 385; *20–21*, 435; *21–22*, 437, 506, 523; *22–23*, 479, 582; *23–24*, 439; *24–25*, 432, 446, 474, 500, 552–3; *25–26*, 485, 565; *26–27*, 435, 499; *27–28*, 402, 424, 437, 488; *28–29*, 376–7; *30–31*, 415, 485, 500; *31–32*, 417; *32–33*, 462; *35–36*, 446; *36–37*, 425; *38–39*, 438; *41–42*, 418; *42–43*, 424, 475; *43–44*, 410, 442; *44–45*, 413; *45–46*, 393; *46–47*, 413; *48–49*, 390; *53–54*, 343; *61–62*, 304, 332

Rome, Harold J. *37–38*, 395; *38–39*, 407, 470; *39–40*, 394; *41–42*, 460;

42–43, 420, 433, 471; *45–46*, 438; *49–50*, 367; *50–51*, 309, 334; *52–53*, 253; *54–55*, 373; *57–58*, 291; *58–59*, 334; *61–62*, 294; *65–66*, 383, 391

Romero, Ramon *45–46*, 446

Romilli, G. *28–29*, 466

Romoff, Colin *56–57*, 357

Ronell, Ann *42–43*, 434; *43–44*, 439

Roos, Audrey *56–57*, 346

Roos, William *41–42*, 449; *45–46*, 424; *48–49*, 394; *50–51*, 309; *51–52*, 276; *56–57*, 346

Root, Ivy Ashton *99–09*, 511

Root, Lin S. *35–36*, 442

Root, Lynn *33–34*, 526; *36–37*, 412; *40–41*, 388; *42–43*, 476; *63–64*, 357

Rorem, Ned *62–63*, 302; *63–64*, 318, 346

Rosa, Dennis *65–66*, 434

Rose, Billy *27–28*, 386, 460; *30–31*, 454, 529; *44–45*, 402, 435; *62–63*, 295; *66–67*, 414

Rose, Carl *46–47*, 487

Rose, David *43–44*, 429

Rose, Edward E. *94–99*, 133, 190, 228, 248–9; *99–09*, 349, 370, 381, 398, 400, 405, 433, 439, 554, 568; *09–19*, 428, 635, 649; *21–22*, 494; *24–25*, 580

Rose, Norman S. *19–20*, 442

Rose, Philip *69–70*, 318

Rose, Reginald *61–62*, 325

Rose, William *29–30*, 421

Rosebrook, Leon *20–21*, 358

Rosemont, Walter L. *23–24*, 330

Rosen, Arnie *56–57*, 357

Rosen, Julius *94–99*, 128

Rosen, Lew *94–99*, 116

Rosen, Sam *55–56*, 335

Rosen, Samuel *39–40*, 402

Rosen, Zvi *63–64*, 322

Rosenberg, Israel *45–46*, 460

Rosenberg, J.B. *42–43*, 453

Rosenberg, James N. *26–27*, 515

Rosenberg, L. *46–47*, 497

Rosenberg, Michael *39–40*, 475
Rosenblum, Robert (Bob) *64–65*, 358; *68–69*, 436
Rosendahl, Henry *34–35*, 386; *35–36*, 421
Rosener, George *27–28*, 414; *28–29*, 475; *34–35*, 434, 476
Rosenfeld, Morris *66–67*, 367
Rosenfeld, Sydney *94–99*, 86, 119, 162, 170, 171, 186, 202, 224, 245, 252, 257; *99–09*, 381, 392, 401, 405, 421, 490, 503, 507, 513, 531, 546, 569; *09–19*, 414, 439, 440, 464, 465, 515, 527, 611, 623; *23–24*, 327
Rosenthal, Andrew *39–40*, 440; *42–43*, 419; *52–53*, 296; *63–64*, 343
Rosenthal, Laurence *58–59*, 318; *59–60*, 299; *60–61*, 299; *63–64*, 320; *66–67*, 385; *67–68*, 370; *69–70*, 299
Rosenthal, Raymond *65–66*, 435
Rosey, Joseph *99–09*, 463
Rosmer, Ernst *99–09*, 421
Rosoff, Charles *39–40*, 429
Ross, Adrian *94–99*, 149, 201, 207, 219; *99–09*, 357, 373, 395, 403, 417, 471, 522, 538, 548, 577; *09–19*, 409, 445, 455, 476, 479, 507, 517, 524, 583; *21–22*, 412; *42–43*, 423; *43–44*, 405; *44–45*, 375; *56–57*, 365
Ross, Arthur *40–41*, 403
Ross, Ben *36–37*, 498
Ross, Carmel *61–62*, 306, 328; *62–63*, 325, 338
Ross, Charles J. *99–09*, 512
Ross, Don *43–44*, 424
Ross, Donald *68–69*, 445
Ross, Eliza *62–63*, 324
Ross, George *44–45*, 405; *62–63*, 284
Ross, George Maxim *60–61*, 39
Ross, J.A. *65–66*, 403
Ross, Jerry *53–54*, 326, 354; *54–55*, 413; *56–57*, 375; *66–67*, 422

Ross, Michael *60–61*, 292
Ross, Robert *09–19*, 478
Ross, Sam *70–71*
Ross, Terry *66–67*, 414
Rossell, Levy *68–69*, 456
Rossen, Robert *35–36*, 429; *59–60*, 320
Rossett, Alan *70–71*
Rossini, Gioacchino *34–35*, 460; *42–43*, 444; *47–48*, 343, 417, 418; *64–65*, 315
Rossler, Carl *09–19*, 496
Rost, Martin *38–39*, 486
Rostand, Edmond *94–99*, 240; *99–09*, 349, 355, 376, 380, 403; *09–19*, 432, 437, 446, 467, 589 (and 605); *23–24*, 345; *24–25*, 474; *25–26*, 492, 556; *27–28*, 478; *28–29*, 439; *32–33*, 440; *34–35*, 401; *35–36*, 504; *46–47*, 422; *53–54*, 318, 322; *59–60*, 358; *63–64*, 367; *67–68*, 348
Rostand, Maurice *09–19*, 491
Rosten, Leo *67–68*, 369
Rosten, Norman *39–40*, 471; *40–41*, 408; *55–56*, 382; *63–64*, 367; *66–67*, 422
Rostova, Mira *53–54*, 353
Rota, Nino *61–62*, 287
Roth, Don *09–19*, 420
Rothenberg, Jerome *63–64*, 327
Rothfield, Tom *64–65*, 361
Rothstein, Raphael *67–68*, 346
Rotter, Fritz *41–42*, 422
Roulston, Allison *62–63*, 317; *63–64*, 358, 359
Rourke, M.E. *99–09*, 522, 583; *09–19*, 409
Roussin, André *51–52*, 296; *53–54*, 309; *64–65*, 315
Rouverol, Aurania *27–28*, 556; *29–30*, 445; *31–32*, 448; *33–34*, 460; *37–38*, 389
Roux, Noel *62–63*, 294; *64–65*, 331, 332
Rouzaud, Rene *62–63*, 295; *64–65*, 331

Rowan, Irwin *40–41*, 431
Rowe, Bolton *94–99*, 109
Rowe, Saville *94–99*, 109
Rowley, William *64–65*, 309
Rox, John *40–41*, 405; *53–54*, 326; *56–57*, 314
Roxlo, Conrado Nale *61–62*, 329
Roy, William *52–53*, 289; *61–62*, 286; *62–63*, 317; *63–64*, 355; *64–65*, 343; *66–67*, 408
Royal, Matthew J. *99–09*, 363
Royall, W. Allen *29–30*, 536
Royle, Edwin Milton *94–99*, 129, 190, 195; *99–09*, 207, 434, 499, 517, 545; *09–19*, 435, 436, 495; *21–22*, 420, 484; *24–25*, 428; *27–28*, 480
Rubber Duck *70–71*
Ruben, Jose *35–36*, 480
Rubens, Mauri(c)e *24–25*, 551; *25–26*, 420, 427, 527, 600, 604; *27–28*, 452, 501, 536; *28–29*, 373, 486, 506; *29–30*, 379
Rubens, Paul A.N. *99–09*, 417, 435, 519, 524–5, 542, 548, 554; *09–19*, 438, 445, 494, 529, 542, 552, 583; *19–20*, 443
Rubin, Daniel N. *25–26*, 553; 571; *27–28*, 400; *29–30*, 445; *31–32*, 485; *32–33*, 475; *33–34*, 447
Rubinstein, Mr. *44–45*, 440
Rubinstein, Arthur *68–69*, 446
Rubinstein, Eli *70–71*
Rubinstein, H.F. *09–19*, 533
Rubio, Emery *51–52*, 328
Rublee, George *09–19*, 417
Ruby, Harry *23–24*, 293; *24–25*, 433; *25–26*, 475; *26–27*, 382–3, 429, 495; *27–28*, 427, 486; *28–29*, 368, 402; *29–30*, 467; *41–42*, 408
Rudd, Enid *64–65*, 322
Rudd, Eric *63–64*, 363
Ruderman, Mikhail *42–43*, 461
Rudley, Sarett & Herbert *49–50*, 365
Rudsten, Daniel *47–48*, 427
Ruesch, Hans *68–69*, 437

Ruffin, Hank & Gary *70–71*
Rukeyser, Muriel *68–69*, 407
Rumshinsky, Joseph *31–32*, 389; *38–39*, 493; *39–40*, 474; *42–43*, 435; *43–44*, 490; *44–45*, 443; *45–46*, 460; *46–47*, 497
Rumshinsky, Murray *61–62*, 312; *70–71*
Runkle, Bertha *99–09*, 400
Runyon, Damon *35–36*, 403; *50–51*, 329; *54–55*, 407; *64–65*, 334; *66–67*, 351
Rusk, James *62–63*, 324; *64–65*, 342; *66–67*, 404, 416
Ruskay, Everett *99–09*, 530
Ruskin, Harry *29–30*, 382; *30–31*, 468
Ruskin, John *38–39*, 490
Ruslander, Daniel *63–64*, 345
Russell, A.J. *61–62*, 299; *67–68*, 395; *68–69*, 437; *70–71*
Russell, Andrew *38–39*, 486
Russell, Anna *51–52*, 333; *53–54*, 300; *64–65*, 340
Russell, Bill *55–56*, 336
Russell, Charlie L. *69–70*, 341
Russell, Franklin L. *30–31*, 494
Russell, Robert *59–60*, 299; *64–65*, 336
Russell, S.K. *40–41*, 405
Russotto, Leo *45–46*, 421
Rustin, Dan *70–71*
Rutenborn, Guenter *60–61*, 44
Rutherford, Forrest *21–22*, 469
Rutman, Leo *65–66*, 437
Ryan, Benny *29–30*, 377
Ryan, Donald J. *28–29*, 500
Ryan, Elaine *49–50*, 374
Ryan, Marah Ellis *99–09*, 533
Ryan, Terry *56–57*, 316
Ryder, Arthur William *24–25*, 502; *26–27*, 419
Ryer, George W. *94–99*, 116, 173; *99–09*, 465
Ryerson, Florence *40–41*, 394; *42–43*, 466; *44–45*, 375; *47–48*, 376

Rylands, George *58–59,* 316; *62–63,* 305

Ryley, Madeleine Lucette *94–99,* 145, 201, 208, 211; *99–09,* 386, 387, 419, 423, 426; *09–19,* 509

Ryskind, Morrie *26–27,* 363, 531; *28–29,* 402, 457; *29–30,* 479; *30–31,* 493; *31–32,* 451; *32–33,* 496; *33–34,* 445; *39–40,* 465; *51–52,* 322; *68–69,* 447, 455

Saavedra, Miguel de Cervantes (see Cervantes)

Sabatini, Rafael *23–24,* 342; *25–26,* 486; *30–31,* 451

Sabine, Lillian *19–20,* 389

Sacher, Toby *41–42,* 438

Sachs, Mary Parmly Koues *29–30,* 540

Sack, Charles *47–48,* 428

Sack, Louis *39–40,* 469

Sackheim, Jerome *31–32,* 479

Sackler, Howard *68–69,* 380

Saffird, Mary J. *09–19,* 417

Safranski, Eddie *52–53,* 307

Sahl, Mort *57–58,* 329

Sager, Sidney *66–67,* 383

Said, Boris *39–40,* 464

Saidy, Fred *44–45,* 387; *46–47,* 411, 455; *50–51,* 370; *54–55,* 414; *57–58,* 297; *59–60,* 338; *60–61,* 332; *63–64,* 368; *66–67,* 386

Sainer, Arthur *63–64,* 365–6; *64–65,* 357; *70–71*

St. Albin, Mons. *09–19,* 616

St. Clair, Stewart *26–27,* 456

St. Cyr, Dirce *99–09,* 539

St. John, Adela Rogers *27–28,* 490

St. John, Christopher *99–09,* 532

St. John, Theodore *31–32,* 453; *34–35,* 455

St. Joseph, Ellis *39–40,* 443

St. Maur, Harry *94–99,* 193, 199; *99–09,* 362

Saint-Saëns, Charles Camille *47–48,* 414, 418; *56–57,* 333

Saisson, Pierre (see also Guy Bolton and George C. Middleton) *19–20,* 412

Saker, Annie *09–19,* 530

Saki (Hector Hugh Munro) *47–48,* 425

Salacrou, Armand *56–57,* 353

Sal(d)amando, Peter *62–63,* 324; *63–64,* 343

Salsburg, Lewis S. *70–71*

Salt, Waldo *54–55,* 376; *66–67,* 413

Salt(n)ikov-Shchedrin, Mikhail *23–24,* 356

Saltz, Amy *70–71*

Salvador, Henri *64–65,* 332

Salvatore, George *38–39,* 485

Sammis, Edward R. *38–39,* 473

Sampaio, Silveira *64–65,* 349

Samuels, Arthur *23–24,* 313

Samuels, Gertrude *70–71*

Samuels, Lesser *59–60,* 327; *70–71*

Samuels, Maurice V. *99–09,* 580; *09–19,* 593; *23–24,* 422; *26–27,* 531

Samuels, Walter G. *28–29,* 457

Sand, L. *29–30,* 477

Sand, Paul *64–65,* 358

Sandberg, Sara *36–37,* 462

Sandburg, Carl *60–61,* 294

Sanders, Mr. (see Carlo & Sanders)

Sanders, Alma *47–48,* 339

Sanders, Carlo *21–22,* 391

Sanders, Robert *44–45,* 440

Sandrich, Mark Jr. *64–65,* 308

Sands, Dorothy *31–32,* 501; *32–33,* 454; *33–34,* 457

Sanford, Gerald *60–61,* 39

Sanford, Stephen *32–33,* 377

Sanford, Walter *94–99,* 104, 108, 244

Sanger, Margo *33–34,* 534

Sanguinetti, Eduardo *70–71*

Sankey, Ira D. *99–09,* 418

Sankey, Tom *66–67,* 411; *68–69,* 432

Santley, Joseph *27–28,* 429

Santoni, Reni *62–63,* 313

Sapin, Louis *68–69,* 421
Sapper *21–22,* 486
Sardou, Victorien *94–99,* 104, 109, 111, 115, 117, 126, 156, 163, 169, 195, 196, 199, 217, 222, 244; *99–09,* 353, 380, 391, 411, 412, 442, 468, 482, 491, 505, 522, 539; *09–19,* 424, 432, 499, 527, 535; *21–22,* 508; *24–25,* 474; *27–28,* 558; *43–44,* 438; *44–45,* 378; *45–46,* 387
Sarg, Tony *32–33,* 439
Saroyan, William *38–39,* 469, 487; *39–40,* 406, 458, 471; *40–41,* 380, 424, 429; *41–42,* 459; *42–43,* 425, 431; *43–44,* 431; *46–47,* 495, 498; *49–50,* 384, 385; *54–55,* 392; *55–56,* 58, 59; *57–58,* 295; *61–62,* 309, 310, 332; *69–70,* 303
Sarros, Dimitrios *64–65,* 298; *68–69,* 434
Sartene, Jean *26–27,* 460
Sartre, Jean-Paul *46–47,* 443, 497; *47–48,* 390, 424, 426; *48–49,* 398, 426; *61–62,* 268; *63–64,* 365; *65–66,* 378; *67–68,* 392
Sassoon, Siegfried *64–65,* 303
Satie, Erik *34–35,* 460
Sauguet, Henri *52–53,* 270
Saul, Oscar *39–40,* 455
Saunders, Mr. (see Carlo & Sanders)
Saunders, James *63–64,* 352; *67–68,* 410; *68–69,* 454; *69–70,* 344
Saunders, John Monk *31–32,* 398
Saunders, Lillian *25–26,* 507; *27–28,* 433
Sauter, Edward *55–56,* 392
Sauter, Joe *62–63,* 337; *63–64,* 361
Sauvajon, Marc-Gilbert *54–55,* 360
Savacool, John K. *46–47,* 461; *64–65,* 348
Savage, (Col.) *94–99,* 134
Savage, Courtenay *24–25,* 534; *26–27,* 402; *27–28,* 528; *29–30,* 524; *34–35,* 446
Savage, Robert Cosmos *66–67,* 418; *67–68,* 403

Savery, James *09–19,* 593
Saville, Mari *69–70,* 362
Savin, M. *20–21,* 376
Savo, Jimmy *40–41,* 399
Savoir, Alfred *21–22,* 421; *22–23,* 458; *23–24,* 410; *25–26,* 471; *26–27,* 396; *31–32,* 394; *35–36,* 511
Savory, Gerald *37–38,* 369; *44–45,* 401
Sawyer, Lucile *09–19,* 457
Sawyer, Michael *63–64,* 361; *70–71*
Sawyer, Ruth *09–19,* 639
Saxe, Alfred *35–36,* 475; *41–42,* 460
Sayers, Dorothy L. *47–48,* 428
Sayers, Henry J. *94–99,* 205
Sayers, Michael *47–48,* 380
Saylor, Oliver *58–59,* 55
Sayre, H.T. *94–99,* 256
Sayre, Theodore Burt *94–99,* 188; *99–09,* 390, 393, 428, 497, 523, 551; *09–19,* 407, 606
Scarborough, George *09–19,* 503, 511, 523, 532, 571; *19–20,* 358, 387, *20–21,* 373; *21–22,* 457; *26–27,* 491
Schack, William *31–32,* 443
Schaeffer, Mary *35–36,* 430
Schafer, Milton *61–62,* 299; *65–66,* 375
Schanzer, Rudolph *09–19,* 459, 473, 517; *22–23,* 468, 479; *24–25,* 485; *26–27,* 378
Schapiro, Herb *65–66,* 423; *69–70,* 368, 369; *70–71*
Schappert, Edna *70–71*
Schary, Dore *37–38,* 389; *57–58,* 313; *59–60,* 302; *60–61,* 329; *64–65,* 318; *69–70,* 312
Schauffler, Elsie *35–36,* 433, 506
Schdanoff, Georg *34–35,* 443
Schechner, Richard *69–70,* 377; *70–71*
Schechtman, Saul *56–57,* 330; *58–59,* 292
Scheffauer, Herman *09–19,* 561
Scheglov, Dmitry *28–29,* 503

Schenck, Leopold *94–99*, 245
Schenker, Joel W. *35–36*, 449
Schertzinger, Victor *64–65*, 332
Schickele, Peter *63–64*, 368
Schifferes, (Dr.) Justus *39–40*, 468
Schiffman, Samuel *99–09*, 516
Schiller (Friedrich von Schiller)
  94–99, 146, 147; *99–09*, 363, 486;
  57–58, 290; *59–60*, 50; *61–62*, 324;
  63–64, 345; *64–65*, 317; *67–68*,
  367
Schilling, Carl *94–99*, 239
Schindler, Paul *99–09*, 462
Schisgal, Murray *62–63*, 325; *64–65*,
  312; *67–68*, 387; *68–69*, 396, 418;
  69–70, 318
Schizzano (see Mandel & Schizzano)
Schlein, Hap *64–65*, 342
Schlick, Frederick *31–32*, 498
Schlitt, Robert *61–62*, 281
Schmidt, Godfrey *24–25*, 583
Schmidt, Harvey *59–60*, 358; *63–64*,
  311; *65–66*, 422; *66–67*, 375;
  68–69, 402; *69–70*, 367; *70–71*
Schmidt, Max *99–09*, 506
Schmidtbonn, Wilhelm *09–19*,
  593
Schmiedel, Hans *34–35*, 387
Schnee, Charles *42–43*, 468
Schnee, Thelma *46–47*, 473
Schneider, Frank *65–66*, 382
Schneider, Monroe *61–62*, 316
Schneir, Walter & Miriam *69–70*,
  327
Schnibble, Harry *39–40*, 473
Schnitzler, Arthur *99–09*, 533, 534;
  09–19, 417, 480, 560, 579, 628;
  25–26, 469; *30–31*, 427, 480;
  53–54, 358; *61–62*, 270; *67–68*,
  367, 411; *69–70*, 345
Schochen, Seyril *60–61*, 41; *62–63*,
  290
Schoeberg-Reif, Mr. *47–48*, 414
Schoenberg, Mr. *41–42*, 456; *47–48*,
  417
Schoenberg, Edgar M. *26–27*, 493;
  27–28, 458

Schoenfeld, Bernard C. *32–33*, 501;
  36–37, 478
Schofield, Thomas *35–36*, 461
Scholz, August *28–29*, 419
Schomer, Abraham S. *09–19*, 510,
  603
Schonberg, James *94–99*, 204, 246
Schoner (Schoenherr), Carl *20–21*,
  404; *21–22*, 440
School, Jack *34–35*, 362
Schorr, Anschel *38–39*, 493
Schrader, Frederick E. (F.) *94–99*,
  201; *09–19*, 468
Schrank, Joseph *34–35*, 415; *38–39*,
  427, 470; *44–45*, 402
Schroeder, Robert *68–69*, 456;
  69–70, 373
Schroeder, William *09–19*, 542, 600,
  630
Schubart, William H. Jr. *41–42*, 461
Schubert, Bernard S. *25–26*, 541
Schubert, Franz *21–22*, 427; *23–24*,
  438; *25–26*, 564–5; *30–31*, 500;
  38–39, 438; *41–42*, 456; *43–44*,
  410; *46–47*, 488; *47–48*, 418;
  56–57, 333
Schuchardt, Emile *61–62*, 308;
  65–66, 429
Schulberg, Budd *58–59*, 308; *61–62*,
  333; *63–64*, 327
Schulberg, Stuart *63–64*, 327
Schulman, Arnold *56–57*, 356;
  63–64, 308; *67–68*, 361, 362
Schulman, Howard *64–65*, 358
Schulman, Joseph *50–51*, 354
Schultz, Willy *94–99*, 198
Schulz, Charles M. *66–67*, 415
Schuman, Howard *68–69*, 436
Schuman, William *44–45*, 439;
  47–48, 416
Schumann, J.A. *41–42*, 461
Schumann, Peter *70–71*
Schumann, Robert *40–41*, 428
Schumann, Walter *52–53*, 288;
  54–55, 403
Schumer, Leo *50–51*, 352
Schutz, Herb *55–56*, 338

Schwab, Charles M. *26–27,* 362, 492; *29–30,* 548

Schwab, Laurence *23–24,* 390, *25–26,* 438; *26–27,* 376; *27–28,* 399; *28–29,* 376, 451; *31–32,* 387; *32–33,* 430; *42–43,* 424; *43–44,* 442

Schwartz, Arthur *25–26,* 605; *26–27,* 492; *28–29,* 498, 499; *30–31,* 407, 429, 432, 532; *32–33,* 387; *34–35,* 418; *35–36,* 406; *36–37,* 446; *37–38,* 367, 404; *38–39,* 458; *46–47,* 434; *47–48,* 401; *50–51,* 363; *53–54,* 349; *61–62,* 270; *63–64,* 308; *65–66,* 437

Schwartz, Ben *26–27,* 531

Schwartz, Jean (Eugene) *99–09,* 427, 432, 436, 446, 457, 489, 490, 491, 493, 498, 499, 524, 540, 541, 544–5; *09–19,* 397, 421, 494, 503, 631, 652; *19–20,* 366; *20–21,* 416, 425; *21–22,* 397, 534; *22–23,* 582; *23–24,* 358, 439; *24–25,* 446; *26–27,* 525; *27–28,* 505; *46–47,* 434

Schwartz, Jerome J. *65–66,* 423

Schwartz, Maurice *33–34,* 472; *37–38,* 470; *39–40,* 474; *45–46,* 460; *46–47,* 497

Schwartz, Owen Gibson *63–64,* 345

Schwartz, Sid *37–38,* 401

Schwartz, Sidney *63–64,* 345

Schwartz, Stephen *70–71*

Schwarz, Eugene *62–63,* 331

Schwarzwald, Milton *09–19,* 581; *24–25,* 447

Schweikert, Ernest G. *57–58,* 299

Schwerd, Mark *37–38,* 470

Schwerin, Doris *60–61,* 42; *63–64,* 321

Schwob, Marcel *99–09,* 380

Scibilia, Anton *27–28,* 446

Scibor, Maria *64–65,* 357

Scolari, Camillo *27–28,* 499

Scollay, J. Fred *58–59,* 51

Scott (see Mills & Scott)

Scott, Mr. *47–48,* 417

Scott, A.C. *65–66,* 435

Scott, Allan *32–33,* 443; *37–38,* 380; *43–44,* 425; *47–48,* 391; *55–56,* 386

Scott, Bobby *60–61,* 298; *62–63,* 280

Scott, Clement *94–99,* 141, 156

Scott, Ed *55–56,* 335, 336; *64–65,* 358

Scott, Fred Newton *09–19,* 580

Scott, John *70–71*

Scott, Kenyon *29–30,* 384

Scott, Leroy *09–19,* 555

Scott, Raymond *39–40,* 471; *40–41,* 429; *45–46,* 426; *50–51,* 309; *58–59,* 54, 329

Scott, Reginald *63–64,* 314

Scott, Robert *49–50,* 384

Scott, Thomas Jefferson *38–39,* 430

Scott, (Sir) Walter *94–99,* 197

Scribe, Eugene *94–99,* 163; *99–09,* 363, 403, 417, 557; *19–20,* 450; *29–30,* 506

Scrysmour, Ella and John *25–26,* 458

Scudder, George *34–35,* 479

Scudder, William *47–48,* 344

Scudmore, F.A. *94–99,* 123, 225

Scully, Daniel H. *94–99,* 112

Sears, Zelda *20–21,* 411; *22–23,* 507; *23–24,* 325, 389; *25–26,* 425, 570

Seaton, George *43–44,* 467; *63–64,* 306

Seawell, Molly Elliott *99–09,* 380

Sebastian, John *68–69,* 397

Sebesi, Herr (see Lothar & Sebesi)

Sebree, Charles *54–55,* 379

Second City *61–62,* 255, 318, 331; *62–63,* 330; *63–64,* 345, 356, 363; *64–65,* 341; *65–66,* 434; *69–70,* 343; *70–71*

Secter, David *68–69,* 444

Secunda, Sholo(e)m *38–39,* 493; *39–40,* 474; *42–43,* 490; *44–45,* 444; *51–52,* 281; *61–62,* 310; *64–65,* 344

Sedgwick, Anne Douglas *09–19,* 512

Seebohm, E.V. *94–99*, 229
Seeger-Hays *65–66*, 402
Seelen, Jerry *42–43*, 420, 429, 471
Seff, Manuel *31–32*, 477; *42–43*, 455
Seff, Richard *69–70*, 311
Segal, Erich *61–62*, 315; *67–68*, 372
Segal, Lynda *60–61*, 354
Segáll, Bernardo *52–53*, 296; *57–58*,
   295; *69–70*, 304
Segall, Harry *27–28*, 531; *34–35*,
   392; *44–45*, 385; *46–47*, 449
Segil, Jackson *37–38*, 464
Seidelman, Arthur A. *63–64*, 366
Seidman, Stanley *70–71*
Seigel (Eli, William; see Siegel)
Seiger, Marvin *59–60*, 317
Seiler, Conrad *36–37*, 496; *37–38*,
   427
Seitz, Dran & Tani *64–65*, 361
Selden, Mr. *99–09*, 540
Selden, Albert W. *41–42*, 461;
   48–49, 380
Selden, Edgar *94–99*, 110, 207, 244
Selden, Neil *68–69*, 449
Seldes, Gilbert *25–26*, 518; *29–30*,
   548; *39–40*, 417; *46–47*, 428
Seletsky, Harold *66–67*, 411
Self, Edwin B. *26–27*, 456; *32–33*,
   449; *41–42*, 397
Sellar, W.C. *38–39*, 491
Seller, Thomas *43–44*, 490
Selling, C.M. *27–28*, 499
Selser, Maxwell *37–38*, 443
Seltzer, Dov *68–69*, 385
Seltzer, Thomas *09–19*, 547
Selver, Paul *38–39*, 471; *42–43*, 450
Selwyn, Edgar *99–09*, 511, 569, 570;
   09–19, 422, 431, 451, 470, 506,
   555, 645; *20–21*, 389; *22–23*, 535;
   24–25, 432, 458; *25–26*, 426;
   28–29, 387
Semos, Murray *70–71*
Semple, Lorenzo Jr. *54–55*, 398;
   59–60, 296
Senghor, Léopold Sédar *69–70*, 353,
   354
Sergel, Christopher *57–58*, 316

Serly, Tibor *47–48*, 360
Serrano, J. *68–69*, 416
Settle, Mary Lee *64–65*, 362
Sevilla, V. & Carreño *68–69*, 416
Severance, John *99–09*, 498
Sexton, Anne *69–70*, 341
Seymour, Tot *23–24*, 439
Seymour, William *94–99*, 105
Sgoyanov, Racho *37–38*, 461
Searelle, Luscombe *99–09*, 520
Shaffer, Anthony *70–71*
Shaffer, Peter *59–60*, 307; *63–64*,
   307, 350; *65–66*, 382; *66–67*, 381;
   68–69, 455
Shah, Krishna *63–64*, 330
Shairp, Mordaunt *25–26*, 494;
   33–34, 445; *50–51*, 346
Shakespeare, William *94–99*, 88, 92,
   105, 107, 113, 120, 125, 127, 130,
   145, 146, 147, 150, 167, 184, 189,
   193, 200, 214, 221, 222, 226, 239,
   246, 257, 259; *99–09*, 350, 353,
   363, 370, 374, 380, 392, 402, 407,
   423, 428, 442, 443, 452, 454, 456,
   469, 470, 471, 476, 477, 480, 486,
   523, 534, 536, 558; *09–19*, 404,
   410, 412, 413, 416, 430, 433, 443,
   447, 448, 471, 478, 483, 485, 486,
   492, 494, 505, 508, 509, 521, 523,
   539, 545, 546, 565, 570, 572, 573,
   575, 589 (and 605), 592, 599, 620,
   622, 625, 626–7, 642, 645, 646,
   650; *19–20*, 363, 435, 436; *20–21*,
   428, 443; *21–22*, 445, 446, 496,
   497; *22–23*, 490, 503, 514, 524,
   539, 560; *23–24*, 327, 328, 361,
   401, 408; *24–25*, 482–3, 520;
   25–26, 469, 491, 523, 602; *26–27*,
   444, 532; *27–28*, 438, 454, 455,
   492, 529, 530; *28–29*, 417, 440;
   29–30, 460, 515, 527; *30–31*, 426,
   431, 464, 471; *31–32*, 423, 433,
   520; *32–33*, 423, 424; *34–35*, 424,
   428; *35–36*, 412, 413, 415, 452,
   474, 512; *36–37*, 415, 429, 449,
   460, 498; *37–38*, 368, 383, 386,
   388, 438, 455, 468; *38–39*, 414,

Shakespeare, William *(cont.)*
429, 454; *39–40,* 417, 418, 435,
451, 461; *40–41,* 394, 432; *41–42,*
404, 412, 418; *42–43,* 469; *43–44,*
418, 488; *44–45,* 383, 412; *45–46,*
392, 413, 421, 441, 442, 458;
46–47, 407, 408, 435, 465, 466,
468; *47–48,* 365, 392; *48–49,* 406,
411, 428; *49–50,* 355, 370; *50–51,*
309, 337, 343, 356, 365; *51–52,*
299, 321, 333; *52–53,* 273, 284,
291; *53–54,* 325, 337, 358; *54–55,*
56, 361, *55–56,* 55, 341, 343, 369;
56–57, 55, 324, 350, 356; *57–58,*
53, 53–4, 324; *58–59,* 52, 310, 316;
59–60, 43, 44, 291, 324, 333;
60–61, 46, 331; *61–62,* 286, 321,
324, 327, 333, 338, 343; *62–63,*
295, 305, 319, 322, 326, 327, 331,
334, 335, 354; *63–64,* 314, 334,
336, 345, 347, 353, 360, 361, 368,
369, 387; *64–65,* 74, 76, 344, 351,
361; *65–66,* 95, 97; *66–67,* 106,
107, 382; *67–68,* 93, 345, 385, 389,
397, 398, 401, 408; *68–69,* 383,
390, 414, 422, 455, 457; *69–70,*
305, 337, 376, 377; *70–71*
Shalleck, Joseph *44–45,* 368
Shane, Margaret *41–42,* 399
Shangold, Mark *69–70,* 374
Shantl, Susan *67–68,* 412
Shapiro, Dan(ny) *43–44,* 424, 466;
50–51, 309; *54–55,* 405; *55–56,*
339, 341
Shapiro, Stanley *69–70,* 329
Sharkey, Jack *67–68,* 377
Sharp, Margery *39–40,* 449
Sharpe, R. Farquharson *61–62,* 306;
62–63, 325
Shattuck, Richard *43–44,* 408
Shavelson, Melville *69–70,* 302
Shaw & Silva *68–69,* 416
Shaw, Barnett *69–70,* 297
Shaw, David *41–42,* 440; *58–59,*
319; *62–63,* 302; *67–68,* 410
Shaw, George Bernard *94–99,* 91,
93; *99–09,* 355, 382, 383, 447, 467,
481, 494, 495, 512, 524, 532, 535,
547; *09–19,* 399, 458, 477, 479,
494, 509, 518, 534, 545, 549, 550,
552, 553, 559, 560, 586, 590, 608,
612, 652; *20–21,* 404; *21–22,* 476,
516, 517, 530; *22–23,* 561; *23–24,*
336, 378; *24–25,* 504, 570; *25–26,*
442, 493, 499; *26–27,* 426; *27–28,*
455; *28–29,* 418; *29–30,* 483, 500;
30–31, 509; *31–32,* 395, 501, 502;
33–34, 523; *34–35,* 453; *35–36,*
476, 492; *36–37,* 470, 497; *37–38,*
442, 453, 458, 463, 468; *38–39,*
479, 482, 484; *39–40,* 433; *40–41,*
418; *41–42,* 448; *42–43,* 419, 489;
43–44, 488; *45–46,* 417, 437;
46–47, 437, 470; *47–48,* 358, 381,
389, 429; *48–49,* 423; *49–50,* 364,
370, 384, 385; *50–51,* 321, 338,
367, 374; *51–52,* 284, 294, 298,
319, 333; *52–53,* 262, 292, 307,
308; *53–54,* 359; *54–55,* 391;
55–56, 55, 58, 378; *56–57,* 58, 317,
318, 324, 329; *57–58,* 326; *59–60,*
43, 297, 329; *60–61,* 46; *61–62,*
286, 306, 314, 326; *62–63,* 300,
312, 322, 327, 334, 339; *63–64,*
338, 364, 367; *64–65,* 348, 361;
65–66, 427, 436; *66–67,* 422;
67–68, 344, 348, 384, 409; *68–69,*
373, 386, 447, 457; *69–70,* 324,
373; *70–71*
Shaw, Howard *61–62,* 299
Shaw, Irwin *35–36,* 502, 510; *37–38,*
400; *38–39,* 445, 487; *40–41,* 400;
42–43, 474; *45–46,* 399; *47–48,*
424; *49–50,* 384; *58–59,* 300;
62–63, 304; *70–71*
Shaw, Kerry *35–36,* 437; *36–37,* 497
Shaw, Percy *32–33,* 458
Shaw, Robert *68–69,* 378
Shaw, Si(y)dney *55–56,* 391; *67–68,*
378
Shaw, Larry *64–65,* 331
Shdanoff, George *39–40,* 405
Shea, (Dr.) Evan *37–38,* 462
Shecter, Louis E. *38–39,* 437

Sheean, Vincent *39–40,* 452
Sheehan, Peter *42–43,* 486
Sheekman, Arthur *40–41,* 411;
   41–42, 399
Sheffer, Isaiah *63–64,* 351
Shelby, Ann *29–30,* 544
Sheldon, Edward *99–09,* 572; *09–19,*
   118, 405, 437, 485, 540, 541;
   19–20, 149; *20–21,* 430; *21–22,*
   502; *24–25,* 463; *25–26,* 549;
   27–28, 424; *29–30,* 415, 487;
   48–49, 390
Sheldon, Ernie *64–65,* 307
Sheldon, H.S. *09–19,* 436, 657;
   22–23, 499
Sheldon, Sidney *43–44,* 405, 448,
   477; *44–45,* 375, 414; *56–57,* 365;
   58–59, 319; *59–60,* 316; *67–68,*
   410
Shelley, Elsa *43–44,* 476; *44–45,*
   432; *49–50,* 377
Shelley, Gladys *64–65,* 343
Shelley, Percy Bysshe *62–63,* 322
Shelly, Gladys *45–46,* 427
Shelton, James *33–34,* 507; *37–38,*
   429; *39–40,* 400; *49–50,* 368;
   54–55, 379; *55–56,* 335
Shelton, Sidney (see Sidney Sheldon)
Shepard, Drey *66–67,* 404
Shepard, Lionel *59–60,* 48
Shepard, Sam *64–65,* 354; *65–66,*
   433; *66–67,* 421; *67–68,* 405, 413;
   69–70, 303, 305, 335, 362, 375,
   376; *70–71*
Shepard, Mrs. Sam (see O-lan)
Shephard, Esther *41–42,* 459
Shepherd, Jean *61–62,* 284
Shepp, Archie *69–70,* 355, 372
Sheppard, J.T. *31–32,* 461
Sheppard, Madelyn *21–22,* 529
Shepperd, Dray *65–66,* 424
Sher, Ben *47–48,* 351
Sher, Jack *62–63,* 282
Sheridan, Richard Brinsley *94–99,*
   122, 135, 155, 239; *99–09,* 350,
   351, 405, 452, 478; *09–19,* 408,
   410, 488, 544; *21–22,* 555; *22–23,*

568, 581; *24–25,* 590; *25–26,* 481,
   508; *28–29,* 482; *29–30,* 511;
   31–32, 428; *37–38,* 468; *41–42,*
   428; *45–46,* 444; *61–62,* 312, 326;
   62–63, 294; *66–67,* 371, *68–69,*
   407
Sheriff, Noam *66–67,* 402
Sherman, Allan *68–69,* 400
Sherman, Arthur *61–62,* 316
Sherman, Charles *09–19,* 531;
   34–35, 482; *39–40,* 394; *42–43,*
   471; *43–44,* 414; *44–45,* 402;
   47–48, 350; *48–49,* 407; *52–53,*
   275
Sherman, Harold M. *30–31,* 523;
   32–33, 442; *45–46,* 403
Sherman, Henry *54–55,* 415
Sherman, Hiram *33–34,* 503
Sherman, Nathan (see also Jor
   Marcy) *33–34,* 519; *38–39,* 464;
   43–44, 471
Sherman, Robert J. *24–25,* 599
Sherman, Susan *69–70,* 375
Sherriff, R.C. *28–29,* 482; *36–37,*
   414; *38–39,* 487; *39–40,* 399;
   68–69, 457
Sherry, Edna *29–20,* 463
Sherry, Gordon *36–37,* 429
Sherry, John *63–64,* 326
Sherwin, Albert *41–42,* 461
Sherwin, Manning *25–26,* 589;
   47–48, 356
Sherwood, Robert Emmet *26–27,*
   471; *27–28,* 472, 497, 557; *29–30,*
   474; *30–31,* 462; *31–32,* 432;
   34–35, 435; *35–36,* 494; *36–37,*
   403, 418; *38–39,* 417; *39–40,* 457;
   40–41, 376; *43–44,* 423; *45–46,*
   406; *49–50,* 354; *50–51,* 339, 371;
   51–52, 324; *56–57,* 348; *62–63,*
   302, 323
Shevelove, Burt *61–62,* 297; *63–64,*
   356
Shewell, L.R. *94–99,* 258
Shi, K.L. *25–26,* 569
Shiebler, Howard A. *35–36,* 453
Shields (see Cobb & Shields)

Sifton, Paul *27–28*, 436; *30–31*, 474; *31–32*, 446; *35–36*, 510

Sigman, Carl *47–48*, 368; *68–69*, 383

Sigurjonsson, Johann *20–21*, 432

Sikola, Zdenek *64–65*, 297

Sill, L.M. *22–23*, 510

Sillman, June *33–34*, 507; *34–35*, 429; *35–36*, 507; *37–38*, 429; *40–41*, 405

Sillman, Leonard *33–34*, 507; *37–38*, 429; *57–58*, 284; *67–68*, 376

Sills, Paul *70–71*

Silone, Ignazio *35–36*, 495

Silva (see Shaw & Silva)

Silver, Milton *26–27*, 493

Sil-Vara *28–29*, 446

Silver, Fred *63–64*, 371, 372; *65–66*, 422; *67–68*, 402

Silverman, Stanley *65–66*, 381; *66–67*, 363; *67–68*, 349, 350; *69–70*, 305

Silverman, Triva *62–63*, 316; *63–64*, 355, 358, 359; *64–65*, 342

Silvernail, Clarke *28–29*, 458

Silvers, Sid *30–31*, 480; *32–33*, 430; *41–42*, 408; *56–57*, 317

Silving, Bert *39–40*, 437

Simak, Clifford *60–61*, 321

Simckes, Seymour *69–70*, 351

Simenon, Georges *64–65*, 315

Simkhovitch, Ben K. *42–43*, 488

Simmon, Louis *67–68*, 412

Simmons, Willard Earl *29–30*, 518

Simon, Charles *94–99*, 250; *99–09*, 373, 472

Simon, Danny *55–56*, 338; *56–57*, 315

Simon, Henry *94–99*, 229

Simon, John *63–64*, 355, 372

Simon, Louis M. *26–27*, 460; *29–30*, 548

Simon, Max *27–28*, 388, 461; *33–34*, 487

Simon, Mayo *67–68*, 394

Simon, Nat *67–68*, 377

Simon, Neil *55–56*, 338; *56–57*, 315; *60–61*, 326; *62–63*, 287; *63–64*, 311; *64–65*, 329; *65–66*, 395; *66–67*, 379; *67–68*, 363; *68–69*, 395; *69–70*, 310, 374; *70–71*

Simon, Robert A. *28–29*, 392; *30–31*, 493; *33–34*, 434, 441

Simon, S. Sylvan *39–40*, 470

Simon, Ted *64–65*, 342

Simonov, Konstantin(e) *42–43*, 455; *46–47*, 473

Simonson, Jules *09–19*, 555

Simpson, Alan *68–69*, 389

Simpson, Harold *23–24*, 328; *25–26*, 526

Simpson, J. Palgrave *94–99*, 114, 115; *99–09*, 384

Simpson, Kenneth *37–38*, 416

Simpson, N.F. *60–61*, 44; *61–62*, 306

Simpson, Reginald *34–35*, 437

Sims, George Robert *94–99*, 83, 99, 140, 152, 235; *99–09*, 350; *09–19*, 445, 515; *36–37*, 488

Sinclair, Upton *28–29*, 432; *34–35*, 483; *60–61*, 46

Singer, André *39–40*, 437; *47–48*, 342, 365, 426

Singer, Campbell *62–63*, 284

Singer, Dolf *27–28*, 428; *35–36*, 500

Singer, Gerard *68–69*, 422

Singer, I.J. *33–34*, 472; *37–38*, 470; *39–40*, 474; *43–44*, 490; *46–47*, 497

Singer, Morris *38–39*, 489

Sirmay (Szirmai), (Dr.) Albert *09–19*, 517; *24–25*, 429; *29–30*, 491; *30–31*, 429

Sirovich, (Dr.) William Irving *24–25*, 452

Sissle & Blake (see Noble Sissle and Eubie Blake)

Sissle, Noble *20–21*, 442; *22–23*, 552; *24–25*, 442; *32–33*, 441; *51–52*, 323; *68–69*, 446

Sitwell, Edith *62–63*, 322

Six, Jack *59–60*, 324; *60–61*, 289

Skariatina, Irina *43–44,* 450; *44–45,* 380

Skeel, Adelaide *99–09,* 392

Skelton, Geoffrey *65–66,* 393; *66–67,* 379

Skinner, Charles M. *99–09,* 468

Skinner, Constance Lindsay *09–19,* 617

Skinner, Cornelia Otis *31–32,* 432; *32–33,* 429; *33–34,* 471; *34–35,* 467; *36–37,* 498; *37–38,* 400; *51–52,* 312; *58–59,* 298

Skinner, Maud *19–20,* 417

Skinner, Otis *99–09,* 368

Skinner, Ralph M. *99–09,* 514; *09–19,* 395

Sklar, George *31–32,* 507; *33–34,* 465, 516; *34–35,* 383, 478; *35–36,* 510; *38–39,* 481; *47–48,* 341

Slade, Susan *64–65,* 318

Slaughter, Walter *94–99,* 161, 209; *99–09,* 452

Slitr, Jiri *64–65,* 297

Sloan, Anthony *69–70,* 377

Sloane, A. Baldwin *94–99,* 154, 182; *99–09,* 360, 363, 372, 378, 381, 382, 392, 405, 407, 421, 427, 453, 478, 504, 507, 515, 517, 531, 540; *09–19,* 409, 419, 420, 438, 453, 465, 473, 486, 487, 497, 641; *20–21,* 374; *24–25,* 527

Sloane, Everett *59–60,* 335

Sloane, Mae Anwerda *99–09,* 392, 405

Sloane, Robert *36–37,* 455

Sloane, Sydney *61–62,* 324

Slowacki, Julius *69–70,* 343

Small, Paul *44–45,* 384

Small, (Dr.) Victor R. *37–38,* 435

Smetana, Bedrich *45–46,* 389; *46–47,* 409; *47–48,* 415

Smiddie, Robert *64–65,* 362

Smit, Leo *46–47,* 490; *65–66,* 435

Smith, Alice M. *99–09,* 513

Smith, Anthony Patrick *61–62,* 329

Smith, Arden *94–99,* 88

Smith, Art(hur) *34–35,* 483; *37–38,* 461, 466; *38–39,* 485; *39–40,* 469

Smith, Ben *55–56,* 347

Smith, Betty *50–51,* 363; *65–66,* 437

Smith, Boyd *29–30,* 448

Smith, Burrell *43–44,* 488

Smith, Carl Beitell *30–31,* 525

Smith, Catharine Cook *37–38,* 468; *38–39,* 491

Smith, Conrad S. *47–48,* 363

Smith, Dodie (see also C.L. Anthony) *35–36,* 465; *38–39,* 449; *43–44,* 431

Smith, Edgar *94–99,* 110, 126, 137, 180, 226, 242, 248, 259; *99–09,* 350, 354, 369, 380, 394, 416, 437, 452, 471, 506, 529, 546, 562, 564, 575; *09–19,* 405, 419, 421, 442, 451, 465, 473, 486, 487, 506, 513, 547, 553, 554, 562, 571, 575, 578, 602, 627, 649; *19–20,* 342, 366; *20–21,* 453; *21–22,* 552; *29–30,* 396; *30–31,* 453

Smith, Edgar Valentine *27–28,* 551

Smith, Edward C. *25–26,* 590

Smith, Edward Percy (see Edward Percy)

Smith, Esther *45–46,* 410

Smith, F. Hopkinson *94–99,* 191; *99–09,* 370

Smith, George Jay *09–19,* 547

Smith, George Totten *99–09,* 367, 483; *09–19,* 426, 428

Smith, Gerald *68–69,* 422

Smith, Glenn Allen *68–69,* 451

Smith, H. Greenbough *94–99,* 93

Smith. H.S. (see W.H.S. Smith)

Smith, Harry B. *94–99,* 101, 117, 135, 152, 176, 177, 180, 182, 198, 213, 218, 238, 239, 251; *99–09,* 346, 349, 350, 352, 355, 364, 367, 372, 379, 391, 392, 393, 396, 398, 405, 409, 416, 425, 428, 434, 443, 445, 448, 464, 473, 479, 493, 499, 513, 524, 526, 534, 540, 556, 559, 563, 570, 571, 573, 584; *09–19,* 403, 420, 426, 429, 434, 437, 442,

445, 446, 448, 454, 455, 461, 462,
470, 471, 473, 481, 502, 504, 506,
507, 537, 538, 540, 541, 558, 567,
575, 593, 606, 641, 658; *19–20,*
407, 450; *22–23,* 526; *23–24,* 294;
24–25, 524, 542; *25–26,* 485, 531;
26–27, 378, 380, 459, 499, 517;
27–28, 403, 437, 538; *28–29,* 370;
29–30, 400, 434, 444, 505, 523,
535; *31–32,* 471, 487; *44–45,* 396;
46–47, 419, 457
Smith, Harry James *09–19,* 40, 491,
604, 621; *28–29,* 486; *29–30,* 426
Smith, Helen Zenna *30–31,* 425
Smith, Henry Clapp *22–23,* 572
Smith, Jeffrey *65–66,* 402
Smith, J. Augustus *32–33,* 467;
36–37, 496
Smith, Joe Bates *38–39,* 411
Smith, Lena R. *99–09,* 487, 516
Smith, Lillian *45–46,* 410
Smith, Mary Stafford *09–19,* 653
Smith, Michael *69–70,* 375; *70–71*
Smith, Paul Gerard *23–24,* 440;
27–28, 386, 428, 457, 547; *29–30,*
382, 439; *51–52,* 323
Smith, Robert B. *99–09,* 364, 376,
416, 473, 482, 491, 504, 508, 526,
552; *09–19,* 401, 434, 437, 445,
446, 454, 462, 470, 473, 502, 506,
537, 540, 558, 575, 588, 658;
19–20, 407; *46–47,* 457
Smith, Robert Paul *54–55,* 368
Smith, S. Theyre *94–99,* 159
Smith, Samuel W. *94–99,* 94
Smith, Sarah B. *34–35,* 429
Smith, Thorne *37–38,* 417; *70–71*
Smith, W.H.S. *33–34,* 505; *69–70,*
365
Smith, Wallace *35–36,* 446
Smith, Walt *70–71*
Smith, Winchell *99–09,* 530, 572;
09–19, 398, 421, 422, 454, 516,
554, 578, 634; *21–22,* 403, 430;
25–26, 456, 483; *38–39,* 405
Smolin, Dmitry *25–26,* 514
Smollett, Tobias George *29–30,* 387

Snegoff, Leonid *28–29,* 503
Sneider, Vern J. *53–54,* 310; *56–57,*
332; *70–71*
Snellings, Roland *68–69,* 433
Snitt, A.E. *29–30,* 477
Snow, C.P. *62–63,* 277
Snow, Davis *50–51,* 364
Snyder, Mr. *99–09,* 554
Snyder, Burton *67–68,* 409
Snyder, (Rev.) John M. *99–09,*
503
Snyder, Ted *23–24,* 294
Snyder, William *62–63,* 313
Sobell, Jack *38–39,* 409
Sobol, Louis *27–28,* 552
Society of Illustrators, The *35–36,*
463
Soffer, Sam *62–63,* 321
Solano, Solita *21–22,* 485
Solms, Kenny *65–66,* 417, 424;
67–68, 378
Solomon, Frederick *99–09,* 398, 427,
446, 473, 492
Solomon, Louis *44–45,* 391
Solorzano, Carlos *69–70,* 374
Somerfeld, Robert *68–69,* 454
Somin, W.O. *38–39,* 462
Sommer, Edith *55–56,* 354
Sondheim, Stephen *56–57,* 337;
57–58, 286; *58–59,* 337; *59–60,*
336; *60–61,* 303; *61–62,* 297;
63–64, 330, 333; *64–65,* 330, 331;
65–66, 419; *68–69,* 373; *69–70,*
328; *70–71*
Sophocles *99–09,* 536, 557; *09–19,*
448, 493, 621; *23–24,* 343; *27–28,*
463; *30–31,* 472; *31–32,* 461;
40–41, 432; *45–46,* 428, 444, 458;
46–47, 410; *47–48,* 432; *52–53,*
269, 272; *56–57,* 55; *58–59,* 52;
60–61, 45, 347; *61–62,* 255; *62–63,*
322; *63–64,* 368; *64–65,* 74, 298;
66–67, 410; *68–69,* 456; *69–70,*
377; *70–71*
Sosin, Jean *41–42,* 461
Sothern, E.H. *99–09,* 453; *09–19,*
596

Sour, Robert *38–39,* 481; *39–40,*
456; *45–46,* 381

Sousa, John Philip *94–99,* 172, 227,
237; *99–09,* 358, 513; *09–19,* 496,
633

Soussanin, Nicholas *33–34,* 511

Soutello & Vert *42–43,* 490

Souvaine, Henry *26–27,* 363, 531

Sowande, Fela *63–64,* 330

Sowerby, K. G(itha) *09–19,* 489;
26–27, 507

Soyfer, Jura *39–40,* 394

Soyinka, Wole *67–68,* 393, 396;
69–70, 353

Spaak, Charles *53–54,* 301

Spalding, Charles *48–49,* 380

Spark, Muriel *67–68,* 358

Spaulding, Bruce *30–31,* 498

Spears, Patti *43–44,* 481

Spedelieri, Dennis *70–71*

Speirs, Ruth *68–69,* 391; *69–70,* 296

Spence, Eulalie *26–27,* 522

Spence, Ralph *21–22,* 388, 555;
24–25, 589; *31–32,* 383

Spence, Wall *29–30,* 414; *35–36,*
511

Spencer, Anne *66–67,* 355

Spencer, Colin *68–69,* 446

Spencer, Edward *94–99,* 251

Spencer, Franz *59–60,* 46

Spencer, R.E. *40–41,* 407

Spencer, T.J. *67–68,* 385

Spenser, Edmund *63–64,* 314

Spenser, Willard *94–99,* 141

Spewack, Bella *28–29,* 379, 438;
32–33, 386; *34–35,* 381; *35–36,*
442; *38–39,* 425, 460; *39–40,* 398;
43–44, 401; *45–46,* 437; *48–49,*
405; *51–52,* 303; *52–53,* 295;
54–55, 392; *55–56,* 388; *59–60,* 40;
64–65, 334

Spewack, Samuel *28–29,* 379, 438;
32–33, 386; *34–35,* 381; *35–36,*
442; *38–39,* 425, 460; *39–40,* 398;
43–44, 401; *45–46,* 437; *48–49,*
405, 414; *50–51,* 331; *51–52,* 303;
52–53, 295; *54–55,* 392; *55–56,*

388; *59–60,* 40, 355; *60–61,* 323;
64–65, 334

Speyer, Wilhelm *33–34,* 490

Spialek, Hans *38–39,* 475

Spielman, Fred *44–45,* 409

Spier, Larry *56–57,* 359

Spiering, Frank (Jr.) *63–64,* 352;
68–69, 453

Spigelgass, Leonard *58–59,* 323;
62–63, 299; *68–69,* 408; *69–70,*
321

Spink, Alfred H. *94–99,* 122

Spink, George A. *99–09,* 512

Spitzer, Robert *36–37,* 499

Spollen, Patricia *39–40,* 473

Spottiswoode, Sybil *09–19,* 623

Sprigge, Elizabeth *63–64,* 353

Springer, Fleta Campbell *19–20,* 362

Springer, Philip *56–57,* 357; *62–63,*
302; *65–66,* 423

Springer, Thomas Grant *19–20,* 362;
21–22, 404

Srnec, Jiri *66–67,* 368

Stackpole, Paul *36–37,* 497

Stagg, Elizabeth *94–99,* 112

Stahl, Richard *94–99,* 161, 214, 236

Stallings, Laurence *24–25,* 448;
25–26, 447, 459; *26–27,* 392;
28–29, 423; *30–31,* 416; *37–38,*
367; *44–45,* 398; *48–49,* 426

Stambler, Bernard *61–62,* 310

Stamer, Fred *52–53,* 259

Stamford, Paul *45–46,* 403

Stammers, Frank *19–20,* 374

Stamper, David *09–19,* 502, 527,
553, 576, 601; *19–20,* 361; *20–21,*
355; *21–22,* 388, 464, 555; *23–24,*
340; *24–25,* 429; *27–28,* 457, 484;
31–32, 377; *35–36,* 430; *36–37,*
482

Stampfel, Peter *69–70,* 305

Standish, Burt L. (Gilbert Patten)
70–71

Stanford, C. Villers *94–99,* 191

Stanford, Frederick *99–09,* 370

Stangé, Hugh Stanislaus *94–99,* 125,
166, 182, 200, 245, 258; *99–09,*

352, 366, 382, 404, 424, 457, 468, 474, 488, 529, 532, 550; *09–19,* 405, 418, 428, 601, 620; *21–22,* 476; *26–27,* 502; *28–29,* 409; *29–30,* 441, 457, 482; *30–31,* 409; *31–32,* 382, 394; *33–34,* 480, 523; *35–36,* 434; *42–43,* 419; *46–47,* 470

Stanley, (Prof.) A.A. *99–09,* 549

Stanley, Martha M. *19–20,* 348; *20–21,* 364; *21–22,* 389; *24–25,* 455; *25–26,* 540; *27–28,* 439; *29–30,* 545

Stanton, Frank *70–71*

Stapleton, John *94–99,* 206; *09–19,* 448

Starbuck, Wilson *39–40,* 409

Starer, Ronald *62–63,* 319

Stark, Sheldon *53–54,* 359

Starkie, Martin *68–69,* 404

Starkweather, David *62–63,* 327; *69–70,* 372

Starling, Lynn *23–24,* 360; *24–25,* 471; *25–26,* 472; *27–28,* 431; *33–34,* 471; *40–41,* 392

Starr, Ben *64–65,* 323

Stavis, Barrie *47–48,* 426; *58–59,* 51

Staw, Sala *63–64,* 345

Stayton, Frank *09–19,* 411; *26–27,* 518

Steele, Wilbur Daniel *24–25,* 586; *26–27,* 522; *34–35,* 420; *35–36,* 443

Steell, Willis *99–09,* 490

Steen, Jan *68–69,* 444

Stein, Gertrude *33–34,* 498; *46–47,* 498; *49–50,* 383; *51–52,* 319, 333; *52–53,* 308; *62–63,* 327; *63–64,* 346; *67–68,* 393; *68–69,* 325; *69–70,* 350

Stein, Joseph *48–49,* 400, 422; *49–50,* 367; *54–55,* 394; *55–56,* 380; *57–58,* 311; *58–59,* 326; *59–60,* 299; *62–63,* 301; *63–64,* 368; *64–65,* 302; *68–69,* 393

Stein, Leo *99–09,* 386, 548; *09–19,* 398, 448, 458, 480, 502, 504, 547,

554; *29–30,* 456; *31–32,* 385; *42–43,* 423; *43–44,* 405; *44–45,* 375; *64–65,* 297, 299

Stein, Sol *57–58,* 306

Steinbeck, John *37–38,* 395; *37–38,* 416; *41–42,* 445; *50–51,* 320; *51–52,* 333; *55–56,* 364; *58–59,* 53; *63–64,* 368; *67–68,* 365

Steinberg, Harold *67–68,* 351

Steinbrecher, Alexander *67–68,* 367

Steiner, Emma *94–99,* 112

Steiner, Robert *37–38,* 441

Steinert, Alexander *39–40,* 461; *53–54,* 315

Steininger, Franz *47–48,* 355

Stellman, M. *69–70,* 314

Stephani, Frederick *43–44,* 476

Stephens, Hal *09–19,* 396

Stephens, Leona *25–26,* 421

Stephens, Nan Bagby *23–24,* 379

Stephens, Robert Neilson *94–99,* 89, 144, 161, 176, 232; *99–09,* 446

Stephens, Wilford *94–99,* 254

Stephenson, B.C. *94–99,* 115, 134, 138; *99–09,* 480

Stept, Samuel H. *33–34,* 421; *39–40,* 395; *50–51,* 309

Sterk, Wilhelm *31–32,* 455

Sterling, Ada *25–26,* 537

Sterling, George *40–41,* 433

Stern, Alan *69–70,* 351; *70–71*

Stern, Arthur *26–27,* 379

Stern, August L. *31–32,* 519

Stern, Charles H. 40–41, 433

Stern, G.B. *29–30,* 513

Stern, Harold *29–30,* 550

Stern, Philip Van Doren *39–40,* 430

Sternberg, Ann *69–70,* 350

Sternheim, Carl *66–67,* 412; *68–69,* 458

Sterni, (Commendatore) Giuseppe *35–36,* 511; *37–38,* 470

Steuer, Arthur *55–56,* 362

Stevens, D.K. *99–09,* 409, 490

Stevens, David *09–19,* 514

Stevens, Jerry *46–47,* 494; *54–55,* 405

Stevens, John *37–38,* 462

Stevens, John A. *94–99,* 226

Stevens, Leslie *53–54,* 356–8; *54–55,* 404; *55–56,* 390; *58–59,* 300

Stevens, Thomas Wood *23–24,* 432

Stevenson, Janet *42–43,* 461

Stevenson, Philip *35–36,* 510; *37–38,* 465; *42–43,* 461

Stevenson, Robert Louis *94–99,* 91; *99–09,* 355, 368, 486, 521; *09–19,* 566, 595; *28–29,* 490; *29–30,* 532; *31–32,* 449; *37–38,* 460

Steward, Nella   (see Anthony Baird)

Steward, Ron *67–68,* 407; *69–70,* 345; *70–71*

Stewart, Charles Conger *30–31,* 533

Stewart, Donald Ogden *27–28,* 469; *29–30,* 487; *30–31,* 417; *47–48,* 354

Stewart, Fred *35–36,* 503; *39–40,* 468

Stewart, Grant *94–99,* 255; *99–09,* 382, 427, 514, 530; *09–19,* 395, 415, 518, 583

Stewart, Michael (Mike) *49–50,* 367; *50–51,* 352; *55–56,* 341, 391; *59–60,* 331; *60–61,* 336; *63–64,* 319; *66–67,* 373; *67–68,* 370; *68–69,* 397

Stewart, Philip & Aimee *30–31,* 421

Stickney, Dorothy *59–60,* 316; *63–64,* 357

Stillman, (Al)bert *37–38,* 367; *40–41,* 384; *42–43,* 420, 421; *46–47,* 482; *48–49,* 377, 424

Stillman, Henry *24–25,* 543; *26–27,* 479; *30–31,* 525

Stirling, Edward *38–39,* 450

Stobitzer, Heinrich *94–99,* 111; *99–09,* 351

Stock, E. Cecil *99–09,* 492

Stockbridge, Dorothy *22–23,* 575

Stockton, Frank R. *66–67,* 364

Stoddard, George E. *99–09,* 462, 463; *09–19,* 647; *19–20,* 381; *20–21,* 391; *22–23,* 542; *23–24,* 358; *24–25,* 527; *25–26,* 510

Stoddard, Haila *62–63,* 309; *69–70,* 371

Stoddard, Lorimer *94–99,* 91, 170, 196; *99–09,* 383, 409

Stoeber, Orville *68–69,* 431; *69–70,* 334

Stoker, Bram *27–28,* 422; *30–31,* 515; *70–71*

Stokes, Leslie & Sewell *38–39,* 413; *56–57,* 58

Stokes, Rose Pastor *09–19,* 547

Stokowski, Leopold *44–45,* 376

Stoller, Maurice *38–39,* 485

Stolz, Robert *24–25,* 551; *31–32,* 379; *40–41,* 409; *43–44,* 405; *44–45,* 375; *45–46,* 381

Stone, Irving *28–29,* 414; *35–36,* 458

Stone, Mary *94–99,* 145, 235

Stone, Mimi *63–64,* 355

Stone, Peter *61–62,* 268; *65–66,* 384; *68–69,* 410; *70–71*

Stone, Sydney *23–24,* 348; *27–28,* 481; *32–33,* 427

Stone, William *22–23,* 580

Stonehill, Maurice J. *99–09,* 442

Stoppard, Tom *67–68,* 344; *70–71*

Storer, Edward *30–31,* 516

Storey, David *70–71*

Storey, Fabian *37–38,* 413

Storm, (Miss) Lesley *39–40,* 424; *41–42,* 439; *50–51,* 316; *63–64,* 339

Stothart, Herbert P. *19–20,* 411; *20–21,* 367, 406; *22–23,* 441, 529; *23–24,* 374, 413; *24–25,* 432, 445; *25–26,* 526; *26–27,* 467; *27–28,* 462; *28–29,* 368, 451

Stow, John *62–63,* 295

Stowe, Harriet Beecher *94–99,* 134; *99–09,* 389; *32–33,* 498; *36–37,* 423

Stowell, Thomas C. *29–30,* 537

Stradley, John (Duff) *38–39,* 466; *59–60,* 40

Straight, Willard *58–59,* 322; *63–64,* 356

Strange, John Stephen *39–40,* 460
Strange, Michael *20–21,* 442; *35–36,* 512
Stratton, Mike *41–42,* 438
Stratton-Porter, Gene *09–19,* 488
Stratz, Rudolph *94–99,* 221
Straus(s), Oscar *99–09,* 556; *09–19,* 400, 502, 602; *20–21,* 449; *21–22,* 476; *29–30,* 482; *33–34,* 523; *37–38,* 405; *42–43,* 419; *46–47,* 470
Strauss (undesignated composer) *45–46,* 452; *47–48,* 415, 417
Strauss, Johann *(fils)* *99–09,* 386; *09–19,* 474; *29–30,* 431; *33–34,* 441; *34–35,* 377; *35–36,* 400; *37–38,* 405; *40–41,* 428; *42–43,* 441, 490; *44–45,* 379, 439, 444; *45–46,* 390, 453; *47–48,* 417; *53–54,* 355; *54–55,* 386; *64–65,* 299
Strauss, Johann, *pere* *34–35,* 377; *35–36,* 400; *37–38,* 405
Strauss, John *55–56,* 391
Strauss, Marcel *26–27,* 489
Strauss, Richard *43–44,* 485; *44–45,* 437; *45–46,* 453; *46–47,* 409, 412; *47–48,* 343
Stravinsky, Igor *34–35,* 460; *40–41,* 427, 428; *41–42,* 456; *42–43,* 483, 484; *44–45,* 402, 437; *45–46,* 453, 454; *46–47,* 410; *47–48,* 420, 421; *48–49,* 429; *51–52,* 330; *69–70,* 375
Strawn, Arthur *44–45,* 372
Street, James *52–53,* 286
Street, Julian *99–09,* 485; *09–19,* 605; *22–23,* 534
Stribling, T.S. *27–28,* 515
Strickland, Mr. *56–57,* 333
Strimer, Joseph *46–47,* 499
Strindberg, Mme. *27–28,* 409
Strindberg, August *09–19,* 470, 497, 498, 501, 579; *23–24,* 382; *25–26,* 533, 573; *26–27,* 524; *27–28,* 549, 553; *31–32,* 406; *37–38,* 422; *47–48,* 379; *49–50,* 360, 382, 384; *53–54,* 359; *55–56,* 376; *56–57,* 55; *60–61,* 45, 348; *61–62,* 298, 321; *63–64,* 353; *65–66,* 425; *66–67,* 36; *67–68,* 413; *70–71*
Stringer, Robert *56–57,* 317
Strode, Hudson *27–28,* 549; *28–29,* 503
Stromberg, John *94–99,* 179, 180; *99–09,* 350, 369, 394, 416; *09–19,* 465
Strong, Austin *99–09,* 510, 552, 574; *09–19,* 491, 531, 568, 642; *22–23,* 481; *26–27,* 521; *28–29,* 424; *29–30,* 546; *35–36,* 489; *54–55,* 416
Strong, Jay *36–37,* 497
Strouse, Charles *55–56,* 391; *56–57,* 322; *59–60,* 331; *61–62,* 292; *64–65,* 307; *65–66,* 405; *69–70,* 323; *70–71*
Strunk, William Jr. *37–38,* 386
Stuart, Aimee *29–30,* 525; *34–35,* 430; *37–38,* 402; *51–52,* 280
Stuart, Clinton *99–09,* 363
Stuart, Don *54–55,* 53
Stuart, Eddie *62–63,* 318
Stuart, Frank S. *68–69,* 429
Stuart, J. Marberger *68–69,* 452
Stuart, Leslie *99–09,* 379, 420, 463, 528, 578; *09–19,* 435, 460; *19–20,* 443
Stuart, Marjorie L. *68–69,* 452
Stuart, Mike (see Michael Stewart)
Stuart, Philip *29–30,* 525; *34–35,* 430; *37–38,* 402
Stuart-Clark, Chris *64–65,* 305
Stubbes, Philip *63–64,* 314
Stucky, William *52–53,* 283
Sturges, Preston *28–29,* 449; *29–30,* 397, 484; *30–31,* 448; *31–32,* 486; *50–51,* 362; *53–54,* 301; *60–61,* 318
Sturgess, Arthur *94–99,* 212, 242
Sturm, Justin *39–40,* 415; *54–55,* 379
Stutchkoff, Nathan (Nuchim) *38–39,* 494; *39–40,* 474

Stutz, Richard *48–49*, 406–7

Styne, Jule *47–48*, 358; *49–50*, 363; *50–51*, 309; *51–52*, 278; *52–53*, 286; *54–55*, 369; *56–57*, 339; *57–58*, 289, 327; *58–59*, 315, 324, 337; *60–61*, 315; *61–62*, 276; *63–64*, 313, 329, 339; *64–65*, 331; *65–66*, 436; *66–67*, 391; *67–68*, 360; *69–70*, 321

Subotnick, Morton *65–66*, 381

Sudermann, Hermann *94–99*, 147, 153, 166, 169; *99–09*, 403, 420, 470, 474, 475, 557, 560; *09–19*, 541; *25–26*, 539

Suesse, Dana *40–41*, 411; *46–47*, 458; *52–53*, 271; *59–60*, 296

Suga, Sensuke *65–66*, 403

Sullivan, Alan *28–29*, 504

Sullivan, (Sir) Arthur Seymour (see also Gilbert & Sullivan) *94–99*, 142; *99–09*, 369, 414; *34–35*, 364; *36–37*, 401; *43–44*, 456; *52–53*, 308

Sullivan, Charles *94–99*, 197

Sullivan, Dan J. *99–09*, 549

Sullivan, Ed *41–42*, 450

Sullivan, Henry *29–30*, 382; *34–35*, 432; *53–54*, 326

Sullivan, T.R. *94–99*, 91; *99–09*, 355, 486

Sully, Daniel *94–99*, 135

Sully, Ruby *55–56*, 372

Sultan, Arnie *61–62*, 286

Summers, Robert N. *65–66*, 428

Summers, Sam *29–30*, 467

Sumner, Charles *09–19*, 550

Sunday, Billy *47–48*, 421

Sundgaard, Arnold *38–39*, 442; *39–40*, 468; *41–42*, 424; *44–45*, 399; *46–47*, 463; *50–51*, 375; *52–53*, 306; *60–61*, 42, 350; *62–63*, 312; *64–65*, 363; *66–67*, 383

Susa, Conrad *60–61*, 354; *61–62*, 326; *63–64*, 359, 360; *64–65*, 349; *66–67*, 373; *67–68*, 354; *68–69*, 384; *70–71*

Susann, Jacqueline *46–47*, 447

Suskind, Milton *25–26*, 487

Sutherland, (Mrs.) Evelyn Greenleaf *94–99*, 165; *99–09*, 400, 406, 417, 530, 538; *09–19*, 467

Sutro, Alfred *94–99*, 185; *99–09*, 482, 496, 507, 517, 553; *09–19*, 403, 475, 545, 561; *22–23*, 530; *24–25*, 588; *28–29*, 501; *29–30*, 483

Sutton, Mr. (see Lenox & Sutton)

Sutton, George W. Jr. *24–25*, 585; *28–29*, 502

Svitacek, Vladimir *64–65*, 297

Svoboda, Josef *64–65*, 297

Swan, Jon *66–67*, 359; *69–70*, 334

Swan, Mark E. *94–99*, 229, 253; *99–09*, 502, 548; *09–19*, 425, 449, 473, 501, 502, 505, 528, 578, 594, 618, 632, 648; *19–20*, 351; *22–23*, 522; *24–25*, 465; *26–27*, 441, 478

Swann, Donald *57–58*, 328; *59–60*, 294; *66–67*, 379

Swann, Francis *40–41*, 416; *62–63*, 313

Swanstrom, Arthur *20–21*, 374; *21–22*, 407; *29–30*, 451; *33–34*, 434; *36–37*, 484

Swarthout, Glendon *46–47*, 461

Swartz, Jean (see Jean Schwartz)

Swenson, May *65–66*, 436

Swerling, Jo(seph) *09–19*, 636; *26–27*, 492; *28–29*, 469; *50–51*, 329; *54–55*, 407; *64–65*, 334; *66–67*, 351

Swete, E. Lyall *99–09*, 446; *09–19*, 640

Swickard, Charles *99–09*, 466

Swift, Kay *29–30*, 548; *30–31*, 417; *34–35*, 459; *51–52*, 312

Swift, Michael *27–28*, 510

Swinarski, Arthur Marya *61–62*, 329

Swingle, Ward *64–65*, 315

Swinnerton, Frank *24–25*, 543

Sydenham, Lewis *46–47*, 409

Sydney, Thomas *09–19*, 593

Sydorick, Tom *67–68*, 408

Sydow, Jack 60–61, 348
Sylvane, Mons. 94–99, 259
Sylvaine, Vernon 41–42, 401
Sylvestre, Armand 94–99, 163
Sylvia, Kenneth 56–57, 58
Sylvon, Jerry 44–45, 368
Symons, Arthur 99–09, 557
Synge, John Millington 09–19, 458,
    459, 494; 20–21, 441; 29–30, 473;
    31–32, 468; 32–33, 407; 34–35,
    408, 409, 410, 411; 36–37, 497;
    37–38, 376, 463; 46–47, 430;
    48–49, 427; 49–50, 384; 56–57, 55;
    57–58, 56; 58–59, 325; 63–64, 369;
    67–68, 409; 70–71
Szczepkowska, Marja M. 33–34, 455
Szilasi, Alix 42–43, 486
Szirmai, (Dr.) Albert (see Sirmay)
Szajna-Lewandowska, Jadwiga
    64–65, 322
Szogyi, Alex 59–60, 360; 61–62,
    326; 63–64, 360; 66–67, 422;
    68–69, 453
Szomory, Dezso 35–36, 480

Taber, Richard 24–25, 517
Tabori, George 51–52, 313; 52–53,
    285; 55–56, 376; 59–60, 40; 61–62,
    317, 331; 62–63, 296; 63–64, 312,
    344, 365; 67–68, 387; 68–69, 398,
    430; 69–70, 335; 70–71
Tachibana, Sahomi 68–69, 406
Taggart, Alexander L. III 47–48,
    428
Taggart, Tom 38–39, 488
Tagore, Rabindranath 60–61, 44
Taitchevitch, Marko 44–45, 437
Takeda, Izumo 65–66, 403
Talbot, F. Story 66–67, 412
Talbot, Hayden 09–19, 466
Talbot, Howard 94–99, 226; 99–09,
    412, 463, 525, 546, 576; 09–19,
    404, 410, 651
Taliaferro, Hugh 63–64, 343
Tamayo y Baus, Manuel 25–26,
    599
Tannen, Julius 25–26, 420

Tanner, James T. 94–99, 183, 201,
    207, 219; 99–09, 395, 403, 417,
    471, 538; 09–19, 422, 445, 455,
    517, 529
Tanner, Tony 68–69, 427
Tansman, Alexander 41–42, 431;
    46–47, 492
Taradash, Daniel 48–49, 398; 59–60,
    324
Tarbe, Edmond 94–99, 140
Tarbox, Russell 30–31, 453
Tardieu, Jean 61–62, 321
Targioni-Tozetti, G. 43–44, 441;
    44–45, 377; 45–46, 387
Tarkington, Booth 99–09, 303, 400;
    09–19, 402, 406, 408, 429, 467,
    487, 582, 605, 620, 635; 19–20,
    346, 354, 398; 20–21, 381; 21–22,
    437, 454; 22–23, 508, 571; 23–24,
    298, 309, 428; 25–26, 529; 29–30,
    450, 499; 30–31, 477; 51–52, 277;
    61–62, 333
Tarloff, Frank 41–42, 440; 62–63,
    298
Tarr, Yvonne 60–61, 42
Tarver, Ben 66–67, 406
Tate, Carroll 37–38, 464
Tate, James W. 09–19, 637
Tate, Neal 69–70, 345; 70–71
Tattersall, Viva 29–20, 490
Taube, Theodore 94–99, 102
Taubenslag, Elliott 67–68, 403
Tauber, Chaim 38–39, 493; 64–65,
    344
Tauber, Doris 42–43, 420
Taubert, Karl 94–99, 200
Tauritz, Frank 55–56, 366
Tavel, Ronald 66–67, 35, 418;
    67–68, 409, 411; 68–69, 430, 456;
    70–71
Taylor, C.W. 94–99, 134
Taylor, Charles A. 99–09, 463;
    09–19, 539
Taylor, Charles H. 99–09, 492,
    550
Taylor, Charles M. 99–09, 504
Taylor, Charles S. 94–99, 84, 255

Taylor, Deems *09–19*, 422; *23–24*, 395; *32–33*, 438; *39–40*, 448; *47–48*, 348; *58–59*, 53

Taylor, Douglas *68–69*, 399; *69–70*, 372

Taylor, Dwight *32–33*, 431; *50–51*, 336; *62–63*, 339

Taylor, Ethel *31–32*, 440

Taylor, Howard P. *94–99*, 116

Taylor, James *68–69*, 424

Taylor, Jeremy *65–66*, 402

Taylor, Ken *63–64*, 368

Taylor, Leila *21–22*, 528

Taylor, Marie Zane *09–19*, 532

Taylor, Marvin *09–19*, 654

Taylor, Matt *37–38*, 415

Taylor, Noel *34–35*, 454

Taylor, Raymond *55–56*, 335

Taylor, Renee *68–69*, 377

Taylor, Robert Lewis *61–62*, 292

Taylor, Rosemary *43–44*, 465

Taylor, Sam *37–38*, 415

Taylor, Samuel *49–50*, 370; *51–52*, 296; *53–54*, 319; *58–59*, 298; *61–62*, 274, 291; *64–65*, 306; *67–68*, 358, 361

Taylor, Simon Watson *68–69*, 428

Taylor, Tom *94–99*, 99, 100, 114, 127, 235; *99–09*, 385, 470, 471, 534; *09–19*, 565; *34–35*, 383; *61–62*, 316

Taylor, William C. *09–19*, 628

Tayor, Hilda *52–53*, 307

Tazewell, Charles *31–32*, 451

Tchaikowsky, Modeste *42–43*, 487

Tchaikovsky, Peter Ilich *24–25*, 542; *34–35*, 459, 460; *40–41*, 427; *42–43*, 483, 485, 487; *44–45*, 437, 438; *45–46*, 452, 453, 454; *46–47*, 409, 486; *47–48*, 343, 355, 414, 418, 420; *62–63*, 316

Tchekhov, Anton (see Anton Chekhov)

Tcherepnin, Mr. *45–46*, 455

Tcherepnine, Serge *63–64*, 352

Teal, Ben *94–99*, 181; *09–19*, 518

Tearle, David *26–27*, 458

Tebelak, John-Michael *70–71*

Tees, Levin C. *94–99*, 193

Teichmann, Howard (M.) *53–54*, 316; *57–58*, 288; *58–59*, 297; *60–61*, 320; *63–64*, 310

Teifer, Jerry *58–59*, 319

Teitel, Nathan R. *67–68*, 402; *69–70*, 371

Teitelbaum, Maurice *65–66*, 432

Telfer, Ronald *48–49*, 402

Tell, P. William *30–31*, 454

Tellegen, Lou *09–19*, 616

Temple, Edward P. *99–09*, 528, 551

Temple, Richard *20–21*, 450

Tenniel, (Sir) John *46–47*, 439

Tennyson, Alfred (Lord) *94–99*, 150; *99–09*, 449; *29–30*, 506

Teplitsky, Grigory *63–64*, 306

Terkel, Studs *66–67*, 423

Terry, Daniel *94–99*, 197

Terry, J.E. Harold *09–19*, 546, 618, 626; *25–26*, 486; *30–31*, 410

Terry, Megan *66–67*, 407; *68–69*, 431

Tesich, Steven *70–71*

Thackeray, William Makepeace *99–09*, 348; *09–19*, 436, 586, 599; *28–29*, 509

Thane, Elswyth *37–38*, 387; *38–39*, 486

Thayer, Sigourney *25–26*, 492

Theater Workshop (see Joan Littlewood)

Thenstead, Adolph *47–48*, 367

Theodore, Lee *68–69*, 378

Thery, Jacques *27–28*, 501

Theuriet, Andre *09–19*, 446

Thie, Sharon *67–68*, 406

Thiriet, Maurice *64–65*, 315

Thom, Robert *63–64*, 303

Thoma, Ludwig *25–26*, 505

Thomas, Mr. *53–54*, 305; *54–55*, 386

Thomas, A.E. *09–19*, 419, 451, 459, 468, 539, 585, 592, 640; *20–21*, 399, 417; *21–22*, 417, 513; *22–23*, 497; *23–24*, 312; *24–25*, 495;

25–26, 521, 542; *26–27*, 500;
27–28, 429; *28–29*, 360, 450;
29–30, 413; *32–33*, 498; *33–34*,
484; *34–35*, 367; *37–38*, 398;
45–46, 459
Thomas, Ambroise *09–19*, 638
Thomas, Augustus *94–99*, 95, 125,
142, 191, 212, 221, 228, 237;
99–09, 271, 365, 369, 388, 399,
407, 430, 450, 452, 484, 493, 510,
543; *09–19*, 402, 440, 474, 486,
500, 512, 573, 623; *19–20*, 378;
20–21, 439; *24–25*, 585; *25–26*,
560; *27–28*, 437
Thomas, Berte *99–09*, 367; *09–19*,
633
Thomas, Brandon *94–99*, 86, 165;
99–09, 511; *24–25*, 600; *40–41*,
386; *48–49*, 388; *50–51*, 346;
53–54, 331; *61–62*, 333; *65–66*,
407; *70–71*
Thomas, Dylan *57–58*, 289, 291;
60–61, 48, 359; *62–63*, 320, 322;
69–70, 311
Thomas, E.D. *26–27*, 487
Thomas, Edward *68–69*, 439
Thomas, Hugh *52–53*, 289
Thomas, Leo *54–55*, 53
Thomas, Millard *30–31*, 427
Thomas, Milo *67–68*, 404
Thomas, Robert *64–65*, 329
Thomashefsky, Bores & Harry
31–32, 389
Thompson, A.M. *99–09*, 504, 542,
550; *09–19*, 410
Thompson, Charlotte *09–19*, 400,
426; *37–38*, 467
Thompson, Denman *94–99*, 116,
173; *99–09*, 465
Thompson, Dorothy *39–40*, 439
Thompson, Francis *62–63*, 322
Thompson, Fred *09–19*, 542, 651;
20–21, 402; *23–24*, 413; *24–25*,
432, 497, 574; *25–26*, 525; *26–27*,
475; *27–28*, 427, 457, 547; *28–29*,
411; *29–30*, 451; *41–42*, 427;
43–44, 466; *45–46*, 403

Thompson, Frederic *99–09*, 489
Thompson, Hallem *20–21*, 419
Thompson, Harlan *23–24*, 301;
24–25, 494; *25–26*, 454; *26–27*,
429
Thompson, J. Lee *43–44*, 408
Thompson, Jay *58–59*, 335; *59–60*,
40, 335; *60–61*, 358; *62–63*, 336;
66–67, 422
Thompson, Julian F. *23–24*, 430;
31–32, 493; *33–34*, 440; *41–42*,
455; *64–65*, 362; *66–67*, 410
Thompson, Lewis S. *94–99*, 138
Thompson, Maravene *09–19*, 651
Thompson, Maurice *99–09*, 400
Thompson, Randall *25–26*, 605
Thompson, Robert J. *68–69*, 432
Thompson, Sydney *34–35*, 484
Thompson, Mrs. Vance *99–09*, 487,
516
Thompson, W.J. *94–99*, 205
Thompson, William C. *66–67*, 423
Thomson, Virgil *33–34*, 498; *37–38*,
387; *38–39*, 475; *46–47*, 498;
51–52, 317, 319; *53–54*, 342;
56–57, 351
Thorne, David *25–26*, 603; *27–28*,
556
Thorne, Francis *61–62*, 317
Thorne, T. Pearsall *94–99*, 148
Thornton, Marianne *62–63*, 295
Thuna, Lee *66–67*, 384; *69–70*, 360
Thurber, James *39–40*, 427; *44–45*,
439; *47–48*, 416, 417, 430; *51–52*,
321; *59–60*, 322; *60–61*, 289;
62–63, 309, 322; *64–65*, 345;
65–66, 436
Thurman, Wallace *28–29*, 472;
29–30, 426
Thurner, Georges *09–19*, 421
Thurschwell, Harry T. *39–40*, 469;
46–47, 477
Thurston, E. Temple *09–19*, 541;
21–22, 449; *24–25*, 561; *26–27*,
474
Thurston, Katherine Cecil *09–19*,
606

Ti, Yang (see Yang Ti)
Tichborne, Chidiock *63–64*, 314
Tiercelin, Louis *99–09*, 442; *09–19*, 509
Tierney, Harry *09–19*, 643; *19–20*, 386; *20–21*, 355, 453; *22–23*, 484, 513; *23–24*, 381; *24–25*, 429; *28–29*, 375
Tierney, Harry Jr. *60–61*, 47; *61–62*, 304
Tietjens, Eunice *25–26*, 478
Tietjens, Paul *99–09*, 427
Tiffault, Leighton *50–51*, 326
Tighe, Harry *30–31*, 410
Tilden, Freeman *19–20*, 372
Tillman, Sen. *63–64*, 350–1
Tillotson, J.K. *94–99*, 256; *99–09*, 347
Tilton, George *24–25*, 597; *29–30*, 385; *31–32*, 506
Timber(g), Sam *25–26*, 604; *29–30*, 379, 396
Timberg, Herman *09–19*, 585, 610, 615; *19–20*, 431; *42–43*, 456
Timoney, Alice *27–28*, 539
Tintore, Sr. *53–54*, 322
Tiomkin, Dmitri *31–32*, 377
Titcomb, Caldwell *56–57*, 318
Titheradge, Dion *26–27*, 417
Titzell, Josiah *29–30*, 548
Tobias, Charles *29–30*, 377; *34–35*, 482; *38–39*, 407; *39–40*, 395; *67–68*, 377
Tobias, Fred *63–64*, 355; *64–65*, 343; *65–66*, 403, 422; *69–70*, 315
Tobias, Henry H. *27–28*, 387
Tobin, John *94–99*, 129
Tompkins, Juliet Wilbor *23–24*, 433
Todd, Clarence *27–28*, 518
Todd, Michael *42–43*, 420
Tokatyan, Leon *60–61*, 327
Tokonogy, Gertrude (see Gertrude Tonkonogy)
Tokyo Kid Brothers *70–71*
Toler, Sidney *21–22*, 453; *22–23*, 556; *24–25*, 437; *29–30*, 490
Tolkien, J.R.R. *66–67*, 379

Tolkin, Mel *41–42*, 438–9; *49–50*, 379; *57–58*, 312
Toller, Ernest (Ernst) *23–24*, 419; *31–32*, 443; *36–37*, 448; *37–38*, 454
Tolson, Melvin *66–67*, 354
Tolstoy, (Count) Alexis *99–09*, 455, 486; *22–23*, 517; *23–24*, 356
Tolstoy, (Count) Leo N. *99–09*, 429, 543; *09–19*, 639; *19–20*, 415; *27–28*, 455; *28–29*, 419; *29–30*, 458; *41–42*, 458; *42–43*, 489; *59–60*, 42; *60–61*, 45; *64–65*, 348; *66–67*, 371
Tomasson, Verna *63–64*, 348
Tomaszewski, Henryk *64–65*, 322
Tomer, Ben-Zio *63–64*, 322
Tompkins, Elizabeth Knight *99–09*, 376
Tonkonogy, Gertrude *32–33*, 477; *48–49*, 383
Toohey, John Peter *22–23*, 475; *28–29*, 491
Toombs, Alfred *56–57*, 359
Topa, John A. *67–68*, 392
Torn, Jesse *61–62*, 303
Torn, Rip *69–70*, 376
Toronto Workshop Company *69–70*, 369
Torrance, Ridgely *09–19*, 524, 598
Tortajada *09–19*, 442
Totheroh, Dan *23–24*, 431; *24–25*, 568; *31–32*, 464; *33–34*, 513; *34–35*, 426; *35–36*, 485; *45–46*, 395
Totten, Joseph Byron *09–19*, 491, 520; *25–26*, 441; *29–30*, 547
Touchstone *70–71*
Tourneur, Cyril *68–69*, 455; *69–70*, 373
Tours, Frank A. *99–09*, 542; *09–19*, 442, 620
Towne, Charles Hanson *39–40*, 466
Towne, Edward Owings *94–99*, 139
Towner, Wesley *39–40*, 446
Townsend, Edward W. *94–99*, 162, 210, 239

Townsend, Horace *94–99,* 147, 153
Townsend, Margaret *09–19,* 501
Townsend, Stephen *94–99,* 213
Townsend, Stuart Richard *63–64,*
  371
Tracey, Andrew & Paul *65–66,* 402
Tracy, George Lowell *94–99,* 154
Trader, George Henry *99–09,* 393
Traill, Peter *22–23,* 546
Train, Elizabeth Phipps *94–99,* 145,
  235
Trainer, David *68–69,* 430
Trapp, Maria Augusta *59–60,* 303;
  66–67, 386
Trask, Katrina *09–19,* 410
Travers, Ben *49–50,* 385
Traversi, Camillo Antona *35–36,*
  511
Traversi, Humbert *46–47,* 499
Treadwell, Sophie *22–23,* 500;
  24–25, 578; *28–29,* 369; *29–30,*
  410; *32–33,* 475; *36–37,* 428;
  41–42, 417; *59–60,* 42
Trebitsch, Siegfried *22–23,* 520
Tree, Jonathan *48–49,* 426
Treichler, Paul F. *39–40,* 406
Tremayne and Hall *99–09,* 507
Tremayne, W.A. *94–99,* 140
Trent, Jo *27–28,* 388; *31–32,* 451
Tretyakov, S. *30–31,* 440
Trevelyan, H.B. *24–25,* 538
Trevor, Leo *99–09,* 359; *09–19,* 397
Treynor, Blair *20–21,* 388
Triana, Jose *69–70,* 359; *70–71*
Tridon, Andre *09–19,* 560, 579
Trilling, Ilia *38–39,* 493
Trimble, Jessie *09–19,* 406
Tristram, W. Outram *94–99,* 120
Trivas, Victor *34–35,* 443
Trivers, Barry *31–32,* 377; *48–49,*
  380
Trollope, Anthony *37–38,* 396
Trotter, Monroe *63–64,* 351
Troubetzkoy, (Prince) Pierre *09–19,*
  632
Troubetzkoy, Princess Pierre (see
  Amelie Rives)

Trouille, Clovis *69–70,* 335
Trovaioli, Armando *63–64,* 323
True Brethren, The *70–71*
Truesdell, Frederick *09–19,* 535
Truman, Garrick *26–27,* 422
Trumbo, Dalton *37–38,* 442; *48–49,*
  416
Truth, Sojourner *63–64,* 350; *68–69,*
  433
Trzcinski, Edmund *50–51,* 368, 374
Tschaikowsky, Peter Ilich (see
  Tchaikowsky)
Tubby, Gertrude Ogden *45–46,* 382
Tucci, Niccolo *66–67,* 421
Tuchman, Barbara *64–65,* 303
Tuck, Edward H. *47–48,* 428
Tucker, Carl *53–54,* 327
Tucker, Don *68–69,* 403
Tucker, Norman *63–64,* 364
Tugend, Harry *33–34,* 476; *65–66,*
  394
Tulane, Paul *26–27,* 403
Tull, Maurice C. *26–27,* 523
Tully, Jim *26–27,* 395; *28–29,* 378
Tully, May *09–19,* 602
Tully, Richard Walton *99–09,* 527;
  09–19, 462, 519, 581; *30–31,* 413
Tumarin, Boris *60–61,* 348
Tunbridge, Joseph *32–33,* 411
Tunkel, Joseph *37–38,* 470
Tunney, Kieran *58–59,* 325
Tuotti, Joseph Dolan *68–69,* 439;
  69–70, 307
Tupper, Edith Sessions *09–19,* 486
Turgenev (Turgenieff), Ivan *22–23,*
  517; *29–30,* 511; *55–56,* 383;
  62–63, 338; *65–66,* 433
Turk, Roy *24–25,* 479
Turnbull, Hector *09–19,* 640
Turnbull, Margaret *99–09,* 543;
  09–19, 520
Turnbull, McPherson *99–09,* 533
Turner, David *63–64,* 306
Turner, John Hastings (J.H.) *24–25,*
  548, 592; *29–30,* 473
Turner, Nat *63–64,* 350
Turner, W.J. *23–24,* 411

Turney, Catherine *39–40,* 434
Turney, Robert *36–37,* 417; *40–41,* 431; *45–46,* 403
Tutt, Homer *28–29,* 449
Tuttle, Day *37–38,* 465; *64–65,* 361
Twain, Mark *94–99,* 131, 231; *20–21,* 400; *27–28,* 445; *31–32,* 449; *39–40,* 471; *43–44,* 428; *56–57,* 371; *58–59,* 50; *63–64,* 348, 369; *65–66,* 404, 436; *66–67,* 364
Twomey, Kay *45–46,* 403
Twomey, Neil *09–19,* 488; *19–20,* 356; *26–27,* 363, 494
Tyler, Cornelia Osgood *99–09,* 460
Tyler, Ed *62–63,* 314
Tyler, Franklin J. *39–40,* 473; *40–41,* 433
Tyler, Royall *33–34,* 457
Tynan, Brandon *99–09,* 413, 414; *09–19,* 570
Tynan, Kenneth *69–70,* 335
Tynan, Leonard J. *32–33,* 378
Tyrrell, Henry *99–09,* 485

Udell, Peter *69–70,* 318
Uhl, Richard *37–38,* 468; *38–39,* 491
Uhry, Alfred *67–68,* 365
Unamuno, Miguel (see Miguel de Unamuno)
Underhill, John Garrett *09–19,* 612, 655; *19–20,* 415; *26–27,* 466; *29–30,* 417; *34–35,* 448
Underwood, Franklin *64–65,* 342; *66–67,* 404; *67–68,* 402; *70–71*
Unger, Gladys B. *99–09,* 539, 547, 566; *09–19,* 401, 424, 460, 474, 507, 583; *21–22,* 474, 535; *22–23,* 544; *23–24,* 369; *24–25,* 437, 440, 547, 553; *25–26,* 465, 523; *26–27,* 377; *27–28,* 484, 501; *31–32,* 388, 455; *32–33,* 395, 494
Unger, Robert *65–66,* 434
Unger, Stella *54–55,* 416
Untermeyer, Louis H. *23–24,* 419
Unkelbach, Kurt *37–38,* 408; *46–47,* 495
Upham, T.C. *31–32,* 459

Upright, Blanche *24–25,* 525
Urbont, Jack (Jacques) *56–57,* 371; *61–62,* 312; *65–66,* 396; *66–67,* 422; *70–71*
Uris, Leon *70–71*
Urvantzov, Leo *25–26,* 553
Ussachevsky, Vladimir *55–56,* 369; *63–64,* 365
Ustinov, Peter *52–53,* 280; *57–58,* 291; *62–63,* 297; *67–68,* 340, 352

Vaccaro, John *67–68,* 413
Vachell, Horace Annesley *09–19,* 562, 565, 592, 597, 637
Vail, Amanda *57–58,* 329
Vajda, Ernest *23–24,* 404; *24–25,* 457, 459, 499; *26–27,* 497; *31–32,* 449
Valcourt, Gaston *35–36,* 506
Vale, Eugene *45–46,* 383
Vale, Martin *43–44,* 405; *44–45,* 369
Valency, Maurice *48–49,* 403; *49–50,* 368; *50–51,* 308; *53–54,* 342; *57–58,* 332; *59–60,* 326; *61–62,* 307; *67–68,* 410; *68–69,* 405; *69–70,* 361
Valenti, Michael *68–69,* 429; *69–70,* 319, 373
Valentine, Mr. *09–19,* 637
Valentine, B.B. *94–99,* 206; *99–09,* 347
Valentine, John *99–09,* 573
Valentini, Vincent *27–28,* 507
Valerio, Frederico *54–55,* 380
Vall, Seymour *67–68,* 357
Vallabreque, Albin *99–09,* 355, 361, 536
Valmiki *30–31,* 478
Valverde (see Chueca & Valverde)
Valverde, J. *09–19,* 611
Valverde, Quinito *09–19,* 616
Van Alsteyne, Egbert *09–19,* 396, 420
Van Antwerp, John Van Ostend (John Krimsky) *36–37,* 457; *37–38,* 449; *38–39,* 422; *46–47,* 429

van Beethoven, Ludwig (see
   Beethoven)
Vanbrugh, (Sir) John *50–51,* 328
Vance, Elmer E. *94–99,* 87
Vance, Kermit *37–38,* 462
Vandair, Maurice *64–65,* 331
Van Doren, Mark *64–65,* 361
Van Druten, John *25–26,* 484;
   27–28, 489; *31–32,* 442, 478;
   32–33, 412; *34–35,* 378, 468;
   35–36, 414; *39–40,* 440; *40–41,*
   403; *41–42,* 436, 460; *42–43,* 439;
   43–44, 434; *44–45,* 389; *45–46,*
   410; *47–48,* 361; *48–49,* 401;
   50–51, 325; *51–52,* 295; *52–53,*
   274; *56–57,* 58; *66–67,* 370
van Dyke, Philip *47–48,* 425
Vane, Norman *56–57,* 321
Vane, Sutton *94–99,* 102, 108, 123,
   152, 192, 238; *23–24,* 383; *38–39,*
   437
Van Gluck, Stephen *36–37,* 463
Van Heusen, Jimmy (James) *39–40,*
   417; *45–46,* 422; *53–54,* 301;
   62–63, 278, 279; *65–66,* 384;
   66–67, 374
van Itallie, Jean-Claude *63–64,* 370;
   65–66, 432–3; *66–67,* 405; *67–68,*
   406; *68–69,* 457; *69–70,* 369
Van Loan, H.H. *26–27,* 407; *27–28,*
   394
Van Loan, Paul *42–43,* 421
Vanloo, Mons. *94–99,* 177, 225
Vanloo, Albert *99–09,* 499, 532
Vann, R. *94–99,* 223
Van Ronkel, Alford *35–36,* 505
Van Ross, Rhyissa *45–46*
Van Scoyk, Bob *55–56,* 391
Van Sickle, Raymond *32–33,* 384;
   36–37, 471
Van Vechten, Carl *60–61,* 41
van Zandt, Roland *69–70,* 330
Van Zile, Edward S. *99–09,* 492
Vann, Dorothy *70–71*
Vardi, David *31–32,* 512
Varesi, Gilda *20–21,* 366
Vari, John *60–61,* 296
Varney, Louis *94–99,* 195

Vaszary, Johann *33–34,* 454; *37–38,*
   445
Vaucaire, Maurice *09–19,* 424, 538
Vaughn, James *66–67,* 355
Vaupel, Louise *38–39,* 484
Vaux, Henry Allen *37–38,* 464
Vazov, Ivan *37–38,* 461
Veber, Pierre *99–09,* 475, 555, 577;
   09–19, 453, 507; *24–25,* 433;
   26–27, 443; *27–28,* 505; *28–29,*
   386
Vecsey, Armand *09–19,* 612; *19–20,*
   390; *21–22,* 526; *26–27,* 454
Veiller, Anthony *45–46,* 396
Veiller, Bayard *99–09,* 539; *09–19,*
   475, 482, 505, 564, 587; *27–28,*
   407, 521; *29–30,* 472; *30–31,*
   407
Vein, Norm *53–54,* 359
Velasco, E. *09–19,* 611
Velone, Tony *56–57,* 359
Vencill, Cornelia C. *23–24,* 428
Venneri, Darwin *60–61,* 42
Veran, T. *69–70,* 314
Verdi, Francis M. *31–32,* 483
Verdi, Giuseppe *42–43,* 487; *43–44,*
   442, 473; *44–45,* 378; *45–46,* 388,
   391, 440; *46–47,* 409; *47–48,* 343,
   418; *52–53,* 264
Verdier, Paul *70–71*
Verga, Giovanni *94–99,* 166
Verne, Jules *94–99,* 173; *45–46,* 448;
   63–64, 343; *64–65,* 341
Verneuil, Louis *09–19,* 643; *22–23,*
   544; *25–26,* 428, 509; *26–27,* 420;
   28–29, 400, 463; *30–31,* 476;
   36–37, 431; *44–45,* 380; *46–47,*
   421; *50–51,* 315; *51–52,* 288
Vernon, Frank & Virginia *29–30,*
   462
Vernon, Harry M. *09–19,* 534
Vernon, Margaret *26–27,* 385
Vershinin, Ilya *42–43,* 461
Vert, Senor (see Soutello & Vert)
Vessella, Oreste *09–19,* 572
Vian, Boris *64–66,* 316; *68–69,* 428
Viana, Sr. *36–37,* 499
Victor, Leon *09–19,* 589

Victor, Victor *20–21*, 394; *28–29*, 470; *38–39*, 432
Victoria I (Queen) *62–63*, 295; *67–68*, 365
Vidal, Gore *56–57*, 354; *59–60*, 330; *61–62*, 281; *67–68*, 367
Vidalin, Maurice *66–67*, 367; *68–69*, 383
Vidrac, Charles *21–22*, 488
Viele, Herman Knickerbocker *99–09*, 508
Viereck, George Sylvester *99–09*, 576
Viertel, Joseph M. *36–37*, 409
Viertel, Peter *47–48*, 378
Vigoda, Bob *63–64*, 346
Vila, Sr. *53–54*, 322
Vildrac, Charles *24–25*, 555; *25–26*, 492; *37–38*, 463; *38–39*, 492
Viller, Louise *94–99*, 124
Villa-Lobos, Heitor *48–49*, 381
Villetard, Mons. *94–99*, 132
Vinaver, Chemjo *38–39*, 455
Vinaver, Stephen *58–59*, 53; *62–63*, 336; *63–64*, 350; *65–66*, 428
Vincent, Allen *41–42*, 422
Vincent, Charles T. *94–99*, 87, 94, 113, 152, 186
Vincent, Claude *51–52*, 325
Vincent, Nat *22–23*, 494
Vincent, Sean *41–42*, 458
Vincent, Walter *94–99*, 213; *99–09*, 350
Vine, Sam *68–69*, 415
Violett, Ellen *57–58*, 293; *63–64*, 346
Violinsky, Mr. *29–30*, 377
Vitrac, Roger *68–69*, 425
Vittes, Louis *41–42*, 453
Vittonet, Mons. *55–56*, 347
Vivaldi, Antonio *47–48*, 416
Vivanco, Moises *50–51*, 371
Vivas, Nelly *68–69*, 454
Voegtlin, Arthur *09–19*, 442, 505, 530
Vogel, Arthur *42–43*, 479; *60–61*, 39

Vogel, S.J. *67–68*, 411
Voight, B. *25–26*, 588
Vokes, Harry *94–99*, 220
Volanakis, Minos *67–68*, 394
Vollmer, Lula *22–23*, 579; *23–24*, 335; *24–25*, 566; *27–28*, 468; *28–29*, 403; *29–30*, 519, 537; *31–32*, 450; *37–38*, 432
Vollmoeller, Karl *23–24*, 385
Volodin, Alexander *62–63*, 336
Voltaire (François Marie Arouet) *32–33*, 496; *56–57*, 340; *70–71*
Vomacka, Jaromir *64–65*, 297
Von Bakonyi, Karl *09–19*, 395
Von Barre, J.W. *29–30*, 419
von Flotow, Friedrich *09–19*, 638; *43–44*, 439
Von Gatti, Emerich *09–19*, 537
von Goethe, Johann Wolfgang (see Goethe)
von Gluck, Christoph Willibald *43–44*, 485
von Hessen, Giza H. *32–33*, 379
von Hoffmannsthal(stahl), Hugo *99–09*, 557; *27–28*, 455, 466; *30–31*, 472; *40–41*, 433; *46–47*, 409
von Kleist, Heinrich *57–58*, 326; *70–71*
von Moser, Gustav *99–09*, 536, 552
Von Orbok, Attila *30–31*, 439
von Ottenfeld, Eddison *38–39*, 480
Von Reznich, E.H. *22–23*, 505
von Schiller, Friedrich (see Schiller)
von Schlieffen, (Field Marshal Graf) *64–65*, 303
von Schonthan, Franz *94–99*, 85, 119, 164; *48–49*, 427
von Scho(e)nthan, Fritz *99–09*, 462, 536, 552; *09–19*, 402
von Schonthan, Paul *94–95*, 85, 90; *48–49*, 427
Von Sterk, Herr *99–09*, 569
von Stroheim, Eric *35–36*, 446
Von Suppé, Franz *99–09*, 479; *42–43*, 486

Von Tilzer, Albert *99–09,* 463, 517; *09–19,* 439–40, *19–20,* 448; *22–23,* 443, 580
Von Tilzer, Harry *99–09,* 438, 519
Von Waldberg, H. *09–19,* 465
von Weber, Carl Maria *40–41,* 427; *44–45,* 437
von Wildenbruch, Ernst *99–09,* 426
von Zadora, Michael *37–38,* 422
Vonnegut, Kurt Jr. *70–71*
Voorhees, Don *39–40,* 418
Vorse, (Mary) Heaton *27–28,* 436, 492
Vosper, Frank *27–28,* 450; *29–30,* 391; *36–37,* 411
Voss, Richard *94–99,* 217
Voteur, Ferdinand *38–39,* 487
Voysey, Michael *67–68,* 344
Vozzo, Tony *70–71*
Vroom, Edward *99–09,* 562
Vroom, Lodevick *37–38,* 463
Vulpius, Paul *36–37,* 489
Vyner, Leslie *09–19,* 653

Waber, Bernard *69–70,* 361
Wachthausen, Rene *30–31,* 470
Waddell, Helen *70–71*
Wagenheim, Charles *31–32,* 469
Wager, Michael *55–56,* 366
Waggoner, George *32–33,* 500
Wagman, Benny *62–63,* 312
Wagner, John H. *99–09,* 466
Wagner, Richard *39–40,* 470; *40–41,* 427; *43–44,* 440; *44–45,* 439; *45–46,* 390; *46–47,* 488; *65–66,* 434
Wagner, Thomas *65–66,* 401; *69–70,* 375
Wagstaff, Samuel J. *41–42,* 461
Wainer, Lee *35–36,* 472; *36–37,* 492; *37–38,* 468; *38–39,* 481; *39–40,* 456, 473
Wakatake, Fuemi *65–66,* 403
Wakeman, Frederic *44–45,* 423
Walberg, Betty *64–65,* 326; *65–66,* 377
Walcott, Derek *68–69,* 440; *70–71*

Walden, Stanley *67–68,* 388; *69–70,* 370, 376; *70–71*
Walden, William *49–50,* 363
Waldman, Robert *67–68,* 365
Waldron, Georgia *99–09,* 395
Waldron, W.R. *94–99,* 225
Wales, Amy *28–29,* 495
Walker, David *70–71*
Walker, Dolores *68–69,* 455
Walker, Don *43–44,* 469; *44–45,* 432; *51–52,* 276; *53–54,* 344; *62–63,* 292
Walker, Joseph A. *67–68,* 407; *69–70,* 352; *70–71*
Walker, Laura *33–34,* 455; *35–36,* 482
Walker, Margaret *66–67,* 354, 355
Walker, Mildred *54–55,* 397
Walker, Stuart *09–19,* 588, 636, 650
Walker, Sydney *61–62,* 327
Walkes, W.R. *94–99,* 178
Wall, Fred *24–25,* 557
Wall, Harry *24–25,* 439
Wallace, David *27–28,* 515
Wallace, Edgar *09–19,* 497, 535; *21–22,* 503; *28–29,* 433; *30–31,* 443; *31–32,* 509; *32–33,* 396
Wallace, (Gen.) Lew *99–09,* 357, 520; *09–19,* 461, 586
Wallace, Morgan *28–29,* 499
Wallach, Ira *54–55,* 409; *58–59,* 293; *60–61,* 360; *63–64,* 302; *64–65,* 359
Wallach, Michael *35–36,* 417
Wallack, Lester *94–99,* 104; *09–19,* 500
Waller, Henry *99–09,* 423
Waller, "Fats" *27–28,* 518
Waller, Jack *32–33,* 411
Waller, Lewis *26–27,* 425, 460
Waller, Thomas *29–30,* 376; *43–44,* 400
Walling, Roy *43–44,* 422
Wallis, Eva *62–63,* 295
Wallis, Keene *34–35,* 423
Wallo, K.M. *64–65,* 297

Wallop, Douglass *54–55,* 413; 66–67, 422
Wallowitch, John *63–64,* 371
Wallsten, Robert *40–41,* 409
Walpole, Horace *62–63,* 295
Walpole, Hugh *28–29,* 412; *34–35,* 473; *35–36,* 403, 432; *40–41,* 376
Walsh, Joseph Lee *37–38,* 431
Walsh, Maurice *60–61,* 339
Walsh, Thomas deWitt *67–68,* 396
Walsh, Townsend *94–99,* 197
Walsh, William *32–33,* 500
Walter, Cy *61–62,* 308; *63–64,* 343
Walter, Eugene *99–09,* 559, 561, 576; *09–19,* 1, 413, 464, 491, 569, 599, 619, 627; *19–20,* 343; *21–22,* 413, 463; *28–29,* 400
Walter, Serge *27–28,* 558; *28–29,* 499; *32–33,* 392
Walters, Lou *43–44,* 424
Walton, Georgina Jones *28–29,* 393
Walzer, W. *25–26,* 475
Wanshel, Jeff *69–70,* 348
Warburg, Edward M.M. *34–35,* 459
Ward, Artemus *94–99,* 235
Ward, David *70–71*
Ward, Douglas Turner *65–66,* 426; *69–70,* 339, 352
Ward, Edward *32–33,* 499
Ward, Happy *94–99,* 220
Ward, Harrison *99–09,* 359
Ward, Mrs. Humphrey *99–09,* 445, 501
Ward, Robert *61–62,* 310
Ward, Theodore *40–41,* 387; *46–47,* 495; *47–48,* 352
Warde, Shirley *30–31,* 475; *31–32,* 481
Warden, Gentry *38–39,* 472, 480
Ware, Alice Holdship *37–38,* 464
Waren, Helen *47–48,* 429; *61–62,* 323
Warfield, Ruth White *25–26,* 478
Warhol, Andy *70–71*
Waring, Richard *62–63,* 316
Warner, Anne *99–09,* 550

Warnick, Clay *43–44,* 477; *44–45,* 432; *49–50,* 379
Warren, Edna *29–30,* 537
Warren, Harry *31–32,* 420; *56–57,* 313; *62–63,* 295; *64–65,* 331
Warren, Jane *52–53,* 308
Warren, Robert Penn *59–60,* 42; 66–67, 422
Warren, Rod *62–63,* 316; *63–64,* 343, 355, 358, 359; *64–65,* 342; *65–66,* 417, 424; *66–67,* 400, 403
Warshavsky, M.M. *66–67,* 393; *67–68,* 339
Warshawsky, Samuel Jesse *23–24,* 343; *35–36,* 469
Warwick, James *35–36,* 409; *40–41,* 385
Washburn, Charles (S.) *36–37,* 444; *39–40,* 468
Washburn, Deric *62–63,* 324
Washburne, John *32–33,* 494
Washburn-Freund, Dr. *09–19,* 621
Washburn-Freund, Mrs. F.E. *09–19,* 579, 598
Washington, Booker T.
Washington, Ned *33–34,* 430, 466
Wasserman, Dale *56–57,* 371; *63–64,* 313; *65–66,* 386; *70–71*
Waterhouse, Keith *63–64,* 359; *64–65,* 356; *66–67,* 358
Waters, Mr. *94–99,* 236
Waters, Ethel *53–54,* 306
Waters, Hadley *29–30,* 430, 528
Waters, Marianne Brown *33–34,* 428; *37–38,* 413
Waters, Safford *99–09,* 420, 423, 554
Waters, Tom *65–66,* 431
Wathall, Alfred G. *99–09,* 425
Watkin, Lawrence Edward *37–38,* 421; *52–53,* 286
Watkins, Gordon *67–68,* 392
Watkins, Maurine *26–27,* 452; *27–28,* 401
Watson, Donald *57–58,* 308; *59–60,* 356; *63–64,* 366; *67–68,* 353, 402
Watson, Macdonald *22–23,* 449

Watson, Morris *35–36,* 471
Watson, Nan Marriott *24–25,* 519
Watson, Simon *70–71*
Watt, Hannah *60–61,* 46
Watt, (Prof.) W.W. *49–50,* 366
Watters, George Manker *27–28,*
    396; *46–47,* 448
Watts, Schuyler *36–37,* 430
Waxman, Percy *25–26,* 555
Wayburn, Ned *09–19,* 447
Wayne, Bernie *55–56,* 340; *66–67,*
    417
Wayne, Chuck *56–57,* 363
Wayne, Fredd *69–70,* 344
Wayne, Sid *60–61,* 328
Wead, Frank *34–35,* 469
Weatherly, Tom *35–36,* 463
Weaver, Harriett *46–47,* 463
Weaver, John V.A. *25–26,* 546;
    46–47, 463
Weaver, Neal *68–69,* 450
Webb, Denis *57–58,* 308
Webb, Kenneth *09–19,* 631; *25–26,*
    519; *28–29,* 444; *30–31,* 400;
    31–32, 476; *32–33,* 431
Webb, Roy K. *09–19,* 616, 631
Webb, Sherrill *26–27,* 361
Webber, James Plaisted *28–29,* 440
Weber (see Carl Maria von Weber)
Weber (& Hennequin) (see Pierre
    Veber)
Weber, Amy L. *26–27,* 524; *27–28,*
    549
Weber, Steve *69–70,* 305
Webster, Charles *25–26,* 513
Webster, Henry Kitchell *09–19,* 478
Webster, Jean *09–19,* 532, 644
Webster, John *46–47,* 426, 485;
    54–55, 52; *56–57,* 362; *65–66,* 427,
    438
Webster, Margaret *43–44,* 418;
    44–45, 383, 412; *45–46,* 392;
    50–51, 365; *63–64,* 353, 367
Webster, Paul Francis *33–34,* 430;
    49–50, 367; *55–56,* 338; *59–60,*
    339
Webster, Tony *56–57,* 373

Wedekind, Frank *09–19,* 560;
    24–25, 591; *50–51,* 373; *63–64,*
    366; *69–70,* 362
Weed, Robert Lewis *99–09,* 391
Weeden, Bill *65–66,* 422, 424;
    66–67, 404; *67–68,* 372
Weeks, Al *20–21,* 415
Weenolsen, Robert *26–27,* 361
Weidman, Charles *32–33,* 496
Weidman, Jerome *59–60,* 305;
    60–61, 301; *61–62,* 294; *62–63,*
    277; *65–66,* 403; *68–69,* 403
Weigel, Hans *39–40,* 394
Weil, Robert *39–40,* 446
Weil, Simone *69–70,* 343
Weill, Gus *66–67,* 420; *68–69,* 443
Weill, Kurt *32–33,* 483; *36–37,* 432,
    449; *38–39,* 419; *40–41,* 412;
    41–42, 392, 460; *42–43,* 465;
    43–44, 417; *44–45,* 424; *46–47,*
    417, 454; *48–49,* 386; *49–50,* 358;
    52–53, 306; *53–54,* 358; *58–59,* 54;
    61–62, 317; *62–63,* 342, 365;
    64–65, 363; *65–66,* 371; *66–67,*
    366; *67–68,* 410; *69–70,* 335, 366;
    70–71
Weille, Blair *63–64,* 343
Weiman, Rita *09–19,* 573; *19–20,*
    410
Weinberg, Charles *31–32,* 517
Weinberg, Edwin *63–64,* 343
Weinberg, Lawrence *65–66,* 435;
    69–70, 365
Weinberger, Jaromir *41–42,* 456
Weine, Max G. *62–63,* 317
Weiner, Leslie *62–63,* 291
Weiners, John *63–64,* 346
Weinstein, Arnold *61–62,* 303, 317,
    325; *63–64,* 360; *66–67,* 416;
    69–70, 335, 366; *70–71*
Weinstein, Sol *64–65,* 343
Weinstock, Jack *61–62,* 261; *62–63,*
    306; *64–65,* 329; *65–66,* 407
Weiser, Jacob A. *38–39,* 464
Weisfisch, Shlomo *66–67,* 393;
    67–68, 339
Weisgall, Hugo *63–64,* 359

Weiss, Ernest Raoul *30–31*, 446
Weiss, George David *68–69*, 387
Weiss, George *55–56*, 380; *58–59*, 331; *60–61*, 311
Weiss, Peter *65–66*, 393; *66–67*, 359, 379; *67–68*, 396, 401; *68–69*, 421
Weissman, José A. *34–35*, 449
Weitzel, Edward *94–99*, 94
Weitzenkorn, Louis *29–30*, 416; *30–31*, 475
Welch, Eddie *31–32*, 383
Welch, Ken *66–67*, 417
Welch, William *60–61*, 321
Welisch, Ernest (Ernst) *22–23*, 468; *24–25*, 485; *26–27*, 378
Welles, Benjamin *36–37*, 499; *37–38*, 469
Welles, Halstead *47–48*, 395
Welles, Orson *35–36*, 474; *45–46*, 448; *62–63*, 290
Wellman, Rita *09–19*, 647
Wells, Billy K. *50–51*, 309; *53–54*, 326
Wells, Carolyn *99–09*, 554; *09–19*, 523
Wells, Charlotte E. *09–19*, 641
Wells, Eleanor *41–42*, 403
Wells, Emma *33–34*, 485
Wells, John *29–30*, 421
Wells, H.G. *23–24*, 399; *64–65*, 333
Wells, Leigh Burton *34–35*, 399
Wells, Robert *54–55*, 403
Wells, William K. *23–24*, 293; *24–25*, 431, 574; *25–26*, 419, 604; *27–28*, 412, 460; *28–29*, 353; *29–30*, 401; *32–33*, 428; *35–36*, 453; *41–42*, 403; *42–43*, 471
Wellwarth, George *61–62*, 321
Welsh, Robert Gilbert *09–19*, 548
Welty, Eudora *55–56*, 376, 391
Welty, Jeanne *46–47*, 499
Welty, Ruth *30–31*, 411; *32–33*, 436
Wendel, Beth *57–58*, 305
Wendell, Dorothy Day *37–38*, 403
Wenrich, Percy *09–19*, 523; *20–21*, 436; *21–22*, 534; *26–27*, 374; *30–31*, 400

Werbing, Teja *28–29*, 501
Werfel, Franz *25–26*, 535, 575; *26–27*, 398; *36–37*, 449; *43–44*, 462; *44–45*, 393; *45–46*, 434
Werner, Fred *68–69*, 379
Wernher, Hilda *59–60*, 339
Wernick, Richard *62–63*, 316
Werris, Sam E. *40–41*, 411
Wertenbaker, Lael Tucker *61–62*, 289
Wertimer, Sidney Jr. *41–42*, 460
Wesker, Arnold *60–61*, 359; *63–64*, 305; *64–65*, 362; *65–66*, 437; *66–67*, 399; *67–68*, 403
Weslyn, Louis *20–21*, 358
Wesson, Gene *61–62*, 338
West, Clarence *09–19*, 536
West, Mae *27–28*, 536; *28–29*, 385; *31–32*, 390; *44–45*, 367; *48–49*, 410; *51–52*, 281
West, Morris L. *60–61*, 329; *61–62*, 273
West, Nathanael *38–39*, 427; *57–58*, 288
West, Paul *99–09*, 420, 423, 460, 463, 492, 524, 534, 540, 554, 562, 580; *09–19*, 484
West, Roland *09–19*, 637
Westbay, Annette *26–27*, 491
Westcott, Edward Noyes *99–09*, 372
Westervelt, Conrad *22–23*, 579; *27–28*, 421, 481; *44–45*, 384
Westervelt, Leonidas *99–09*, 477; *23–24*, 409; *24–25*, 462
Westheimer, David *66–67*, 376
Westman, Bernard *60–61*, 349
Westman, Theodore Jr. *25–26*, 497
Weston & Lee (see R.P. Weston and Bert Lee)
Weston, R.P. *09–19*, 615; *32–33*, 411
Wette, Adelheid *94–99*, 146
Wettin, Albert (see Albert, Prince Consort)
Wettin, Ernest *62–63*, 295
Wetzel, Donald *54–55*, 363
Wexler, Norman *65–66*, 436

Wexley, John *29–30,* 494; *31–32,*
    435; *33–34,* 499; *35–36,* 510;
    36–37, 497; *39–40,* 397; *49–50,*
    383
Weyman, Stanley *94–99,* 190; *99–09,*
    402; *28–29,* 441
Whalen, (Rev.) Will W. *42–43,* 488
Wharton, Anthony P. *99–09,* 555;
    09–19, 540, 631
Wharton, Edith *99–09,* 420, 523;
    28–29, 428; *34–35,* 436; *35–36,*
    462
Whedon, John *35–36,* 406; *49–50,*
    361
Whedon, Tom *61–62,* 316; *62–63,*
    317; *63–64,* 344; *64–65,* 343
Wheeler, A.C. *94–99,* 141, 194
Wheeler, Hugh *60–61,* 330; *61–62,*
    266; *66–67,* 365
Wheeler, Post *35–36,* 511
Wheeler, Roger *30–31,* 503
Whelen, Christopher *56–57,* 325
Whipper, Leigh *31–32,* 517
Whistler, James McNeill *66–67,* 423
Whitcomb, Joyce *67–68,* 410
White, Alfred Henri *30–31,* 454;
    35–36, 479
White, Arthur Corning *25–26,* 558;
    26–27, 526; *27–28,* 435
White, Dan *42–43,* 471
White, E.B. *31–32,* 379; *62–63,* 322
White, Edgar *70–71*
White, Edmund *62–63,* 335
White, G. Harris *69–70,* 371
White, George (1) *09–19,* 657;
    19–20, 456; *21–22,* 388; *22–23,*
    443; *23–24,* 293; *24–25,* 431;
    25–26, 419, 604; *27–28,* 412;
    28–29, 353; *29–30,* 401; *31–32,*
    390; *32–33,* 428; *35–36,* 453;
    39–40, 397
White, George (2) *62–63,* 332, 339;
    63–64, 328
White, Henry C. *26–27,* 366
White, Hervey *09–19,* 560
White, Hugh *46–47,* 456
White, Irving *34–35,* 439
White, Jessie Graham *09–19,* 483

White, John *65–66,* 426; *68–69,* 437
White, Josh *44–45,* 438
White, Kenneth *40–41,* 407; *44–45,*
    389; *48–49,* 427; *49–50,* 378
White, Leonard *29–30,* 539
White, Les *42–43,* 471; *44–45,* 430
White, Lyman *39–40,* 469
White, Nat *70–71*
White, Sheldon *24–25,* 602
White, Stewart Edward *99–09,* 565
White, T.H. *60–61,* 310
White, Walter *63–64,* 351
Whitehouse, Frances *09–19,* 501,
    539
Whiting, Arthur *37–38,* 468; *38–39,*
    491
Whiting, John *59–60,* 45; *65–66,*
    385
Whiting, Richard A. *09–19,* 656,
    658; *31–32,* 387; *32–33,* 430;
    55–56, 347; *62–63,* 295; *64–65,*
    331
Whiting, William *47–48,* 424
Whitlock, Bache McEvers *68–69,*
    452
Whitman, Lawrence *09–19,* 556,
    584, 624
Whitman, Walt *40–41,* 430; *65–66,*
    436; *66–67,* 371, 402
Whitney (Whitney & Tutt), Mr.
    28–29, 449
Whitney, John *63–64,* 368
Whittier, Robert *27–28,* 553
Whittington, Bob *38–39,* 483
Whorf, Richard *34–35,* 429; *47–48,*
    345
Whytal, Russ *94–99,* 136, 248;
    99–09, 469
Wiberg, Knud *26–27,* 489
Wiborg, Mary Hoyt *21–22,* 531
Wicheler, Fernand *09–19,* 434, 522
Wied, Gustav *27–28,* 459
Wieder, Hardy *52–53,* 306
Wiener, Sally Dixon *69–70,* 374
Wieniawski, Henri *44–45,* 439
Wiernik, Bertha *32–33,* 379
Wiers-Jenssen (Jensen), H. *09–19,*
    414; *26–27,* 429

Wiggin, Kate Douglas *09–19,* 426, 608; *37–38,* 467

Wight, Frederic Colt *99–09,* 460

Wightman, Marian *25–26,* 440

Wilbraham, Edward *24–25,* 563

Wilbur, Herr *09–19,* 454

Wilbur, Crane *19–20,* 441; *22–23,* 436; *25–26,* 452; *28–29,* 358; *31–32,* 497; *32–33,* 460; *33–34,* 474, 517

Wilbur, Richard *56–57,* 340; *64–65,* 309; *65–66,* 419; *68–69,* 383; *70–71*

Wilcox, Ella Wheeler *99–09,* 520

Wilde, Frank Lee *70–71*

Wilde, Hagar *41–42,* 435; *46–47,* 429

Wilde, Oscar *94–99,* 127, 133; *99–09,* 408; *09–19,* 415, 430, 478, 512, 525, 574, 588, 612, 637; *20–21,* 422; *21–22,* 550; *22–23,* 566; *25–26,* 595; *26–27,* 526; *27–28,* 556; *31–32,* 470, 501; *36–37,* 397, 398; *38–39,* 450; *45–46,* 450, 459; *46–47,* 424, 468; *47–48,* 343; *53–54,* 328, 358; *59–60,* 359; *60–61,* 42, 330; *62–63,* 326, 327; *63–64,* 344; *67–68,* 411

Wilde, Percival *19–20,* 352; *20–21,* 361; *34–35,* 441; *42–43,* 489

Wilde, R. *31–32,* 465

Wilder, Alec *49–50,* 374; *52–53,* 275; *60–61,* 350; *62–63,* 317

Wilder, Billy *68–69,* 395

Wilder, Clinton E. *41–42,* 461

Wilder, Robert *30–31,* 440; *45–46,* 432

Wilder, Sally *45–46,* 432

Wilder, Thornton (N.) *26–27,* 439; *32–33,* 438; *37–38,* 406, 421, 465; *38–39,* 441, 487; *42–43,* 443; *43–44,* 437; *46–47,* 485; *47–48,* 390, 426; *49–50,* 384; *55–56,* 337, 365; *58–59,* 49; *61–62,* 318; *62–63,* 321, 328; *63–64,* 319; *66–67,* 401; *67–68,* 369; *69–70,* 306

Wilderman, Louis *38–39,* 485

Wildeur, A. *94–99,* 243

Wildman, Carl *37–38,* 464; *62–63,* 322

Wiley, Kent (Samuel Ruskin Golding) *37–38,* 371

Wilhelm II (Kaiser) *64–65,* 303

Wilhelm, Julius *09–19,* 471, 519; *29–30,* 484

Wilk, Max *48–49,* 380; *57–58,* 318

Wilkes, Allene Tupper *25–26,* 559

Wilkes, Ernest *09–19,* 611

Wilkes, McElroy *49–50,* 384

Wilkinson, Dudley *22–23,* 473

Wilkinson, Marc *65–66,* 382; *67–68,* 345

Willard, Bassett *94–99,* 139

Willard, John *19–20,* 437; *21–22,* 507; *24–25,* 445; *26–27,* 477; *27–28,* 474; *28–29,* 380; *36–37,* 487; *64–65,* 352

Willard, Ruth *70–71*

Wille, Frank *62–63,* 312

Willemetz, Albert *23–24,* 363; *28–29,* 475; *53–54,* 306; *62–63,* 295; *64–65,* 331

Willeminsky, J.M. *32–33,* 427

Willems, Paul *50–51,* 373

Williams, Alan *29–30,* 489

Williams, Alexander *31–32,* 379

Williams, Bert A. *99–09,* 509; *09–19,* 403; *68–69,* 446

Williams, Charles *59–60,* 40; *62–63,* 323

Williams, Clarence *27–28,* 386

Williams, E. Harcourt *09–19,* 437

Williams, Emlyn *36–37,* 410; *39–40,* 468; *40–41,* 396; *41–42,* 447; *42–43,* 428, 473; *49–50,* 367, 383; *51–52,* 308; *52–53,* 300; *55–56,* 374, 383; *57–58,* 289; *61–62,* 332; *68–69,* 455; *70–71*

Williams, Espy *94–99,* 226

Williams, Harry *99–09,* 489; *09–19,* 396, 412, 420

Williams, Heathcote *69–70,* 345; *70–71*

Williams, Herbert *25–26,* 509

Williams, Herschel *42–43*, 427; *47–48*, 377

Williams, Hugh & Margaret *63–64*, 303; *68–69*, 385

Williams, Jay *38–39*, 485; *39–40*, 468

Williams, Jesse *94–99*, 259

Williams, Jesse Lynch *99–09*, 521; *09–19*, 315; *22–23*, 511; *25–26*, 474

Williams, Louise Alice *35–36*, 512

Williams, Malcolm *99–09*, 449

Williams, Margery *27–28*, 432

Williams, Mary Lou *44–45*, 438

Williams, Pauline *46–47*, 494

Williams, Richard *66–67*, 364

Williams, Tennessee (Thomas Lanier) *44–45*, 427; *45–46*, 385; *47–48*, 366; *48–49*, 386; *49–50*, 380; *50–51*, 347; *51–52*, 334; *52–53*, 295, 306; *54–55*, 53, 402, 406; *55–56*, 375; *56–57*, 337, 362, 363; *57–58*, 53; *58–59*, 50, 328, 333; *59–60*, 42, 49; *60–61*, 307; *61–62*, 278; *62–63*, 293; *63–64*, 318; *64–65*, 336, 362; *65–66*, 399; *66–67*, 358, 422; *67–68*, 369; *68–69*, 452; *69–70*, 303

Williams, Valentine *31–32*, 455

Williams, William Carlos *58–59*, 50; *61–62*, 305

Williamson, A.M. & C.N. *09–19*, 411

Williamson, Bruce *62–63*, 317; *63–64*, 343

Willimore, Carl *99–09*, 549

Willingham, Calder *53–54*, 303

Willis, Harold *64–65*, 355

Willner, (Dr.) A.M. *09–19*, 399, 448, 468, 471, 490, 502, 504, 562; *25–26*, 564; *29–30*, 496; *30–31*, 500; *34–35*, 377; *38–39*, 438; *43–44*, 410

Wills, Freeman *99–09*, 349, 422

Wills, W.G. *94–99*, 105, 150, 151; *99–09*, 353, 521

Willson, A. Leslie *65–66*, 434; *66–67*, 411

Willson, Meredith *57–58*, 306; *60–61*, 304; *63–64*, 306; *65–66*, 366

Wilm(n)er, Sidney *94–99*, 213; *99–09*, 350

Wilmurt, Arthur *31–32*, 405; *34–35*, 451; *39–40*, 433

Wilner, Sis *42–43*, 420

Wilson, Al *31–32*, 517

Wilson, Alma *30–31*, 517

Wilson, Don *42–43*, 486

Wilson, Earl Jr. *70–71*

Wilson, Edmund *24–25*, 469; *50–51*, 366

Wilson, Forrest *31–32*, 443, 477

Wilson, Francis *09–19*, 407, 498

Wilson, Frank *27–28*, 504; *35–36*, 466

Wilson, H. Crownin *09–19*, 627

Wilson, Harry Leon *99–09*, 303, 439; *09–19*, 402, 406, 408, 429, 567, 583; *19–20*, 346; *22–23*, 485; *23–24*, 298; *29–30*, 450

Wilson, (Gen. Sir) Henry *64–65*, 303

Wilson, Jack *60–61*, 292

Wilson, John *66–67*, 416

Wilson, John Fleming *09–19*, 580

Wilson, John P. *99–09*, 502; *09–19*, 505, 530

Wilson, Lanford *64–65*, 354; *65–66*, 432; *66–67*, 413; *67–68*, 406, 411; *68–69*, 413; *69–70*, 368; *70–71*

Wilson, Nathaniel *29–30*, 383

Wilson, Robert *70–71*

Wilson, Sandy *54–55*, 363; *60–61*, 349; *65–66*, 436; *69–70*, 326

Wilson, Will R. *94–99*, 131, 175

Wilson, (Pres.) Woodrow *63–64*, 351; *69–70*, 330

Wilstach, Paul *94–99*, 209; *09–19*, 441, 529

Wiltshire, David *38–39*, 486

Wiman, Dwight Deere *30–31*, 407, 530

Wimperis, Mr. (see Martos, Wimperis & Wylie)
Wimperis, Arthur *09–19*, 410, 438, 521; *19–20*, 420; *24–25*, 552
Wincelberg, Shimon *58–59*, 332
Windham, Donald *45–46*, 385
Wing, Tom *66–67*, 413
Winsloe, Christa *32–33*, 445; *39–40*, 397, 473
Winslow, Charles Edward Amory *25–26*, 539
Winslow, Herbert Hall *94–99*, 175, 243; *99–09*, 433, 464; *09–19*, 651; *21–22*, 521; *23–24*, 326; *24–25*, 575; *26–27*, 528
Winter, Keith *33–34*, 495; *37–38*, 465; *47–48*, 399
Winter, Louise *99–09*, 410
Winter, William *94–99*, 93; *09–19*, 574
Winters, Shelley *70–71*
Winterberg, Robert *09–19*, 579, 657
Wiren, Myra *09–19*, 526
Wirtz, Arthur M. *40–41*, 384; *42–43*, 421; *46–47*, 482
Wise, James *62–63*, 336; *63–64*, 372; *66–67*, 35; *68–69*, 441; *70–71*
Wise, Thomas A. *99–09*, 569; *09–19*, 442, 636
Wishart, Peter *63–64*, 337
Wishengrad, Morton *57–58*, 302
Wister, Owen *99–09*, 451
Witherspoon, Frances *27–28*, 552
Witmark, Isidore *99–09*, 412
Witney, Frederick *26–27*, 476
Witt, Fred *47–48*, 420
Witte, Max H. *99–09*, 495
Wittlinger, Karl *61–62*, 262; *62–63*, 329; *66–67*, 412
Wittman, Morris *20–21*, 445
Wode, Ed *67–68*, 409; *69–70*, 367, 374
Wodehouse, P.G. *09–19*, 448, 593, 595, 605, 607, 613, 621, 638, 645; *19–20*, 390; *23–24*, 418; *26–27*, 419, 420, 454, 494; *27–28*, 486, 488, 526, 537; *29–30*, 408; *34–35*,

412; *47–48*, 400, 403; *59–60*, 48; *60–61*, 355; *61–62*, 330; *66–67*, 353; *67–68*, 400
Woess, Carl *09–19*, 575
Wohl, H. *99–09*, 458
Wolas, Eva *47–48*, 390, 426
Wolf, Daisy *27–28*, 496
Wolf, Eugene *39–40*, 446
Wolf, Friedrich *34–35*, 423; *36–37*, 493
Wolf, (Dr.) N. *47–48*, 420
Wolf, Rennold *09–19*, 444, 457, 476, 511, 526, 537, 553, 616, 626, 631
Wolf, Richard R. *63–64*, 352
Wolf, Tommy *58–59*, 336
Wolfe, Harrison J. *99–09*, 382
Wolfe, Ian *32–33*, 496
Wolfe, Jacques *39–40*, 428
Wolfe, Michael *70–71*
Wolfe, Thomas *57–58*, 303
Wolff, Edgar Allan (see Edgar Allan Woolf
Wolff, Egon *70–71*
Wolff, Leon *64–65*, 303
Wolff, Pierre *99–09*, 453; *09–19*, 407, 460; *25–26*, 542
Wolff, William Almon *33–34*, 518
Wolf-Ferrari, Mr. *43–44*, 479
Wolfit, Donald *55–56*, 370
Wolfson, John *64–65*, 347; *66–67*, 423
Wolfson, Victor *34–35*, 443; *35–36*, 495; *36–37*, 479; *39–40*, 407; *42–43*, 470; *50–51*, 326; *53–54*, 358; *54–55*, 416
Wolheim, Louis *21–22*, 442, 478
Wolpe, Stefan *41–42*, 457; *64–65*, 361
Wood, Allan *39–40*, 441
Wood, Cyrus *09–19*, 649; *21–22*, 506; *22–23*, 448, 468, 479, 576; *24–25*, 561; *25–26*, 424; *27–28*, 484; *29–30*, 396, 467; *44–45*, 410
Wood, G. *56–57*, 58; *62–63*, 336; *63–64*, 355
Wood, Mrs. Henry *94–99*, 213; *25–26*, 565

Wood, J. Hickory *99–09*, 398, 427, 446, 473, 499

Wood, Joseph *41–42*, 418; *43–44*, 414

Wood, Maxine *45–46*, 445

Wood, Metcalfe *99–09*, 356

Wood, Philip *36–37*, 414

Woodgate, (Maj.) Herbert *21–22*, 410

Woodhouse, Frederick *37–38*, 412

Woodruff, Helen S. *21–22*, 529

Woodward, Eugenie *24–25*, 548

Woodward, Matthew C. *94–99*, 198; *99–09*, 427, 434, 446, 540, 556; *09–19*, 451, 562, 615; *22–23*, 479

Woodward, Ruth M. *21–22*, 544; *44–45*, 441

Woolf, B.E. *94–99*, 213

Woolf (Wolff), Edgar Allan *99–09*, 515, 576; *09–19*, 456, 624, 630, 634; *19–20*, 357; *20–21*, 435

Woolf, Virginia *60–61*, 48; *67–68*, 410

Woolfenden, Guy *63–64*, 337

Wooll, Edward *35–36*, 450

Woollcott, Alexander *29–30*, 421; *33–34*, 462

Wormeley, Katherine Prescott *09–19*, 597

Wormser, Andre *09–19*, 581

Worrall, Lechmere *09–19*, 433, 546, 626

Worth, Marvin *61–62*, 286

Wotanna, Onoto *99–09*, 445

Wouk, Herman *48–49*, 417; *53–54*, 338; *57–58*, 293; *69–70*, 374

Wray, John *27–28*, 449; *29–30*, 475

Wright, Bruce McM. *66–67*, 355

Wright, David *64–65*, 344

Wright, Grace Latimer *09–19*, 612

Wright, Richard *40–41*, 421; *42–43*, 439; *59–60*, 318; *66–67*, 355; *68–69*, 421, 433

Wright, Robert *44–45*, 370; *48–49*, 381; *53–54*, 324; *61–62*, 268; *63–64*, 367; *65–66*, 368, 387

Wright, William H. *58–59*, 300

Wulff, Derick *25–26*, 475; *27–28*, 388

Wulp, John *58–59*, 51

Wunderlich, Lawrence *63–64*, 371

Wupperman, Carlos *21–22*, 401

Wyatt, Frank *99–09*, 483

Wycherly, Margaret *99–09*, 488

Wycherley, William *94–99*, 224; *36–37*, 439; *57–58*, 303; *65–66*, 378

Wyckoff, Eugene Thomas *21–22*, 395

Wylie, Mr. (see Martos, Wimperis & Wylie)

Wylie, Elinor *30–31*, 496

Wylie, Laurie *53–54*, 326

Wyman, Joel *51–52*, 291

Wyner, Yehudi *64–65*, 346

Wyngate, Valerie *26–27*, 494

Wynick, Don *37–38*, 469

Wynn, Ed *19–20*, 444; *21–22*, 457; *24–25*, 467; *29–30*, 382, 497; *30–31*, 502; *31–32*, 420; *40–41*, 382; *42–43*, 418

Wynne, Anna *09–19*, 565

Wynne-Tyson, Esme *28–29*, 484

Wyspianski, Stanislaw *69–70*, 343

XL   (see Julian Field)

X, Marvin *69–70*, 371

Xanrof, Leon *99–09*, 485; *09–19*, 657

Yablokoff, Herman *45–46*, 460

Yablonsky, Yabo *68–69*, 439

Yaffe, James *59–60*, 315; *62–63*, 299; *65–66*, 430

Yamada, Kagashi *65–66*, 403

Yang Ti *68–69*, 407

Yankowitz, Susan *69–70*, 369, 376; *70–71*

Yantis, Luther *28–29*, 508

Yaray, Hans *46–47*, 496

Yarborough, Barton *47–48*, 412

Yardley, W. *99–09*, 480

Yardley, William *94–99*, 134

Yarno & Fischer *94–99*, 171

Yates, Edmund *94–99*, 103
Yates, Ray B. *47–48*, 425
Yeatman, R.J. *38–39*, 491
Yeats, William Butler *99–09*, 375,
  377, 378, 458, 488, 547, 555;
  09–19, 458, 494; *23–24*, 336;
  32–33, 407; *34–35*, 410, 411;
  45–46, 444, 458; *58–59*, 52; *62–63*,
  322; *68–69*, 443; *69–70*, 372, 375,
  378
Yellen, Jack *19–20*, 439; *27–28*, 506;
  29–30, 382; *30–31*, 480; *35–36*,
  453; *39–40*, 397; *40–41*, 382;
  41–42, 417; *42–43*, 471
Yellen, Sherman *69–70*, 335; *70–71*
Yellin, Gleb *43–44*, 407
Yerby, Frank *66–67*, 354
Yerby, Lorees *62–63*, 335; *63–64*,
  371
Yomen, Ben *34–35*, 471
Yordan, Philip *40–41*, 432; *43–44*,
  489; *44–45*, 372; *47–48*, 351,
  432
York, Vincent *34–35*, 411
Yorke, John Merrick *23–24*, 430
Youmans, Vincent *20–21*, 446;
  22–23, 529; *23–24*, 374, 389;
  25–26, 446; *26–27*, 517; *29–30*,
  421; *30–31*, 455; *31–32*, 471;
  32–33, 430; *54–55*, 386, 407;
  69–70, 371; *70–71*
Young, Mr. *53–54*, 306
Young, Anthony *32–33*, 410
Young, (Sir) Charles L. *94–99*, 196,
  234, 236; *09–19*, 419
Young, Clarence III *70–71*
Young, Cy *64–65*, 342
Young, Effie *54–55*, 53
Young, Emily *19–20*, 366; *21–22*,
  552
Young, Franklin B. *41–42*, 461
Young, Harry *42–43*, 471; *47–48*,
  340
Young, Howard Irving *25–26*, 540;
  29–30, 394; *33–34*, 461
Young, Joseph (Joe) *26–27*, 510;
  33–34, 466

Young, Rida Johnson *99–09*, 510,
  538, 552, 568; *09–19*, 405, 430,
  452, 484, 493, 511, 521, 542, 587,
  589, 600, 603, 639, 643; *20–21*,
  380; *24–25*, 436, 472; *29–30*, 425;
  31–32, 433
Young, Stanley *37–38*, 392; *38–39*,
  439; *42–43*, 462; *52–53*, 255
Young, Stark *24–25*, 469; *37–38*,
  436; *54–55*, 56; *62–63*, 326
Young, Victor *33–34*, 430, 466;
  50–51, 317; *54–55*, 416; *63–64*,
  343; *64–65*, 341
Young, William *99–09*, 357, 380,
  445
Younin, Sylvia *70–71*
Younin, Wolf *66–67*, 367, 393, 394;
  67–68, 339; *70–71*
Yradier *46–47*, 490
Yung, Wang *44–45*, 444
Yurka, Blanche *33–34*, 447
Yushny, Yascha *24–25*, 516; *31–32*,
  507
Yvain, Maurice *23–24*, 363; *28–29*,
  373; *53–54*, 306

Zagoren, Marc Alan *70–71*
Zahn, Curtis *66–67*, 422
Zakrzweski, Paul *70–71*
Zamacois, Miguel *99–09*, 554;
  09–19, 432
Zangwill, Israel *94–99*, 160; *99–09*,
  351, 375, 449, 465, 489, 521;
  09–19, 399; *23–24*, 407
Zapolska, Gabryela *21–22*, 395
Zappa, Frank *66–67*, 421
Zaret, Hy *42–43*, 433
Zavin, Benjamin Bernard *67–68*, 369
Zelinka, Sidney *48–49*, 379
Zeller, Robert *47–48*, 418
Zeller, Wolfgang *28–29*, 389
Zeno, Norman *34–35*, 429, 482;
  46–47, 494
Ziehrer, (E.) (C.) M. *99–09*, 569;
  09–19, 451
Ziegfeld, Florenz *31–32*, 377
Ziffer, Frances *52–53*, 306

Zilahy, Lajos *32–33*, 425
Zilber, Jacob *69–70*, 373
Zilboorg, Gregory *21–22*, 492; *67–68*, 410
Ziman, Edward A. *27–28*, 491
Zimbalist, Efrem *20–21*, 377
Zimmer, B. *53–54*, 301
Zimmerman, Charles *94–99*, 236
Zimmerman, Edward J.P. *40–41*, 433
Zimmerman, Ralph C. *28–29*, 503
Zinberg, Len *45–46*, 435
Zindel, Paul *63–64*, 363; *69–70*, 363; *70–71*
Zink, Ralph Spencer *36–37*, 482
Zipser, Arthur *41–42*, 438

Ziskin, Victor *60–61*, 42; *61–62*, 292
Zoffer, G. *69–70*, 339
Zogott, Seymour *62–63*, 317
Zola, Emile *94–99*, 124; *99–09*, 436; *45–46*, 397
Zor(r)illa, José *25–26*, 599; *31–32*, 500; *53–54*, 321
Zuckerman, Lew *37–38*, 469
Zuckmayer, Carl *64–65*, 317
Zugsmith, Leane *44–45*, 389
Zur, Menachem *69–70*, 356
Zwar, Charles *53–54*, 329; *59–60*, 336
Zweig, Max *47–48*, 432
Zweig, Stefan *27–28*, 535; *29–30*, 509; *38–39*, 455; *56–57*, 353
Zwetkoff, Peter *65–66*, 407

Titles of Shows and Sources
1894–1971

———————◦———————

Here are the titles of all Broadway, off-Broadway, off-off-Broadway and other productions listed in the 52 *Best Plays* volumes dated 1919–20 to 1970–71, plus the three retrospective *Best Plays* volumes dated 1894–99, 1899–1909 and 1909–19. This Directory also includes the titles of all literary and musical sources mentioned in the *Best Plays* listings. This is a *complete* compilation of title data contained in the statistical "Plays Produced in New York" sections of all the volumes covering 77 years of American theater; plus the title data available in *Best Plays* articles during the years, for example, when the off-Broadway theater was covered in the form of a report rather than a listing; plus a few entries from other sections of the volumes which add to the general fund of information about titles.

Titles are alphabetized in the order of their words, not counting articles (a, an, the; le, la, un; die, los, etc,) in all languages. Each title appears in roman (regular) type, and opposite it is the abbreviated date of the *Best Plays* volume (in *italics*) and number of the page (again in roman) on which the title appears or the show's cast-and-credits entry starts, as follows:

Mourning Becomes Electra *31–32,* 417

The hypenated number *31–32* in *italics* refers to the volume in which the title appears (in this case it is *The Best Plays of 1931–32*). The number 417 following the comma is the number of the 1931–32 volume's page on which the *Mourning Becomes Electra* entry starts. (Entries compiled from the 1970–71 *Best Plays* volume do not have page numbers, because this Directory went to press before that yearbook was paged.)

This Directory contains an entry for each time a title is mentioned as a production or source in the *Best Plays* listings, so that a play produced several times will have several volume entries, each separated by a semicolon. And a play produced more than once in a single theater season will have more than one page number after a volume number, as follows:

American Dream, The *60–61,* 356;
61–62, 306, 323; *62–63,* 313, 337;
63–64, 364; *68–69,* 379

To facilitate identification, unrelated entries with identical titles are differentiated by numbers in parentheses following the title. For example, there are

"South Pacific (1)" and "South Pacific (2)" entries—the former a play and the latter the famous musical.

Different adaptations of the same non-theatrical literary source, such as two dramatizations of the same novel, are considered unrelated and also appear with differentiating numbers. For example, there are four numbered versions of *Alice in Wonderland*. But different adaptations of the same theater work—such as the various translations of *Cyrano de Bergerac*—are considered versions of the same play and are listed in one entry.

A play and a musical with a common source and identical titles appear, for example, as "Street Scene (p)" for the straight-play version and "Street Scene (m)" for the musical version.

In a few cases where a literary source has been the subject of different dramatizations under the original title, the source itself is listed and identified separately for easy differentiation. Thus, this Directory carries four separate *Don Quixote* entries, as follows: "Don Quixote (source)," "Don Quixote (p 1)," "Don Quixote (p 2)" and "Don Quixote (m)," indicating that this Cervantes novel (entered under "source" whenever it is mentioned) has been dramatized twice and musicalized once under its *own* title. The volume and page reference to the *Man of La Mancha* musicalization appears within the "Don Quixote (source)" entry.

Song numbers were included consistently in the *Best Plays* cast-and-credits entries starting in the late 1940s, but often an older musical's list of songs was not placed on the record in the series until several revivals after its first production. Pages on which the titles of a show's songs appear—usually in a complete listing—are designated with an "s" as in the following example:

> Oklahoma! *42–43*, 471; *50–51*, 372;
> *53–54*, 299; *57–58*, 325; *62–63*,
> 298s, 308; *65–66*, 392; *69–70*, 295s

Oklahoma's list of song numbers will be found, therefore, in entries beginning on page 298 of *The Best Plays of 1962–63* and page 295 of *The Best Plays of 1969–70*, as indicated by "s" above.

Other special designations used with titles in this Directory are (mn) denoting marionette programs which are usually listed under both the title of the program and the marionette company comprising it. Works originally written and principally performed for grand opera carry the notation (opera rep)—opera productions were included in a few of the volumes at the discretion of the individual editor.

Dance programs were also included occasionally, at individual editorial discretion, and they are indicated by the parenthetical notation (dance program). The Directory includes titles of ballet programs and the title of the corps de ballet (example: "Ballet Russe de Monte Carlo") or soloists (example: "Ruth St. Denis & Ted Shawn"), but not the titles of individual ballets. Titles of works from which ballets were derived are included when they appear in the *Best Plays* listings.

Stars' names are used as titles only when there is no other title for a production (example: "Maurice Chevalier" appears as a title alphabetized by the first, not the last, name; but Richard Mansfield's vehicles are listed as titles, not his name, even though his troupe appeared under the portmanteau title *Richard Mansfield*).

One-act plays are separately entered in the Directory, as are literary sources

as brief as a sonnet or letter—but sketches within shows or scraps of a complete literary work are not listed separately. Monodrama program titles and the names of their solo performers (for example, "Cornelia Otis Skinner" alphabetized under her first name) are indexed, but not the titles of individual sketches; nor, in the case of pantomine, are individual mine vignettes included.

Where a source is mentioned in the *Best Plays* listing but not named (example: references to musical scores which contain "folk music" or "sea chanteys") it is indexed as a general subject within the title directory, but only when it is actually mentioned, not merely deduced from the description of the show.

Foreign plays are entered under the English translation of their titles whenever one is given in the course of the *Best Plays* record. Thus Molière's *L'Avare* appears under the title *The Miser* in each case, whether it played under its French or English title, with the French version cross-referenced as "Avare, L' (see *The Miser*)." (And speaking of Molière, accent marks are used in the Directory's list of names, but not in its list of titles.)

Cross-references have been used sparingly, for a translation or common abbreviation (such as "Marat/Sade" for the longer version of its title) or to flag a title change. Variations of spelling, wording or general usage over the decades are indicated in parentheses in such entries as "Alice('s Adventures) in Wonderland" or "Grand Vizir (Vizier), The."

Titles of Shows and Sources
1894–1971

AC/DC 70–71

A.E.F. 60–61, 295

A la Broadway 09–19, 448

A la Carte 27–28, 392

Aaron Slick From Punkin Crick 47–48, 428

Abanico de Lady Windermere, El 31–32, 501

Abe and Mawruss 09–19, 563

Abe Lincoln in Illinois 38–39, 417; 46–47, 485; 62–63, 323

Abel Hermant's Dialogues 24–25, 553

Abelard & Heloise 70–71

Abide With Me 35–36, 438

Abie's Irish Rose 21–22, 550; 36–37, 483; 54–55, 375

Abigail 99–09, 484

Abortion 59–60, 49

About Town 99–09, 517

Above the Clouds 21–22, 491

Abraham 44–45, 441

Abraham Cochrane 63–64, 326

Abraham Lincoln 19–20, 399; 29–30, 424

Absence of a Cello 64–65, 302

Absent Father 32–33, 402

Absolutely Free 66–67, 421

Abyssinia 99–09, 509

Academy, The 62–63, 339; 70–71

Accent on Youth 34–35, 430; 68–69, 455

Accomplices, The *(Die Mitschuldigen)* 65–66, 406

According to Law 39–40, 444, 445; 43–44, 480

Accused 25–26, 458

Achilles Had a Heel 35–36, 419

Acquisition, The 68–69, 430

Acquittal, The 19–20, 410

Acrobats (and Line) 70–71

Acropolis 69–70, 343

Across the Board on Tomorrow Morning 41–42, 459; 42–43, 425; 61–62, 310

Across the Border 09–19, 535

Across the Street 23–24, 411

Actress, The 37–38, 465

Ada Beats the Drum 29–30, 542

Adam and Eva 19–20, 351

Adam and Eve 65–66, 405

Adam Had Two Sons 31–32, 467

Adam Solitaire 25–26, 489

Adam's Apple 28–29, 511

Adams' Wife 31–32, 453

Adaptation 68–69, 445

Adding Machine, The 22–23, 544; 47–48, 424; 48–49, 426; 70–71

Adelante 38–39, 483

Adele 09–19, 505

Adelgitha 33–34, 457

Adieux, Les 56–57, 353

Admirable Bashville, The 55–56, 58

Admirable Crichton, The 99–09, 445; 30–31, 501

Admiral, The 23–24, 425

Adonis 94–99, 260

Adorable Liar, The 26–27, 371

Adrea *99–09*, 481

Adrienne *22–23*, 580

Adrienne Lecouvreur *94–99*, 163; *99–09*, 557

Advent *37–38*, 460

Adventure *28–29*, 380

Adventure of Lady Ursula, The *94–99*, 236; *09–19*, 547

Adventure of the Empty House, The *64–65*, 328

Adventurer, The *35–36*, 511

Aventures of Ola, The *33–34*, 534

Adventures of Huckleberry Finn, Sherlock Holmes, Tom Sawyer, etc., The (see *Huckleberry Finn, Sherlock Holmes, Tom Sawyer,* etc.)

Adventurous Age, The *26–27*, 476

Advertising of Kate, The *21–22*, 543

Advise and Consent (source) *60–61*, 308; *62–63*, 323

Advise and Consent *60–61*, 308

Advocate, The *63–64*, 308

Aero, Club, The *99–09*, 531

Affair, The *62–63*, 277

Affair of Honor *55–56*, 383

Affair of State, An *30–31*, 458

Affaires Sont Affaires (see also *Business Is Business*) *23–24*, 406

Affairs of Anatol, The (see also *Anatol*) *09–19*, 480; *45–46*, 451

Affairs of State *50–51*, 315

Affinity, The (see also *The Incubus*) *09–19*, 408

Afgar *20–21*, 402

African Academy of Arts and Research (dance programs) *43–44*, 486; *44–45*, 440; *45–46*, 456; *46–47*, 487

African folk chants, songs, dances, tales *63–64*, 330; *65–66*, 401, 402, 403, 436; *66–67*, 369; *67–68*, 364; *69–70*, 352, 375

African Millionaire, An *99–09*, 457

Africana *27–28*, 388; *34–35*, 414

Africanella *35–36*, 511

After All *31–32*, 442

After Dark *94–99*, 170

After Five *09–19*, 512

After Office Hours *99–09*, 382

After Such Pleasures *33–34*, 493

After the Angels *60–61*, 39

After the Fall *63–64*, *321*

After the Opera *99–09*, 547

After the Rain *67–68*, 343

After Tomorrow *31–32*, *383*

After You, My Dear Alphonse *60–61*, 48

Aftermath *27–28*, 549

Afternoon of a Faun *38–39*, 486

Afternoon of Poetry, An *60–61*, 47

Afternoon Storm *47–48*, 397

Agamemnon *68–69*, 398, 399

Agatha Dene *99–09*, 469

Agatha Sue I Love You *66–67*, 376

Aged 26 *36–37*, 443

Age of Innocence, The *28–29*, 428

Age of Reason, The *09–19*, 561

Agee *68–69*, 454

Ages of Man *58–59*, 316; *62–63*, 305

Agnes (1) *94–99*, 217, 244

Agnes (2) *99–09*, 570

Agrippino Manteo Marionettes *37–38*, 467

Ah, Wilderness! *33–34*, 438; *41–42*, 401; *46–47*, 485; *52–53*, 309; *59–60*, 299

Aida (opera rep) *43–44*, 473; *44–45*, 443; *45–46*, 440; *46–47*, 480; *47–48*, 399; *52–53*, 264

Aiglon, L' *99–09*, 376, 380; *09–19*, 432, 446, 589 (and 605); *24–25*, 474; *27–28*, 478; *34–35*, 401; *46–47*, 484

Ain't Goin' to Study War No Mo' *60–61*, 295

Air and Variations (dance program) *38–39*, 476

Air Minded *31–32*, 475

Air Ship, The *94–99*, 254

Airborne *45–46*, 392

Akokawe (see *Initiation*)

Aladdin (mn) *35–36*, 512

Aladdin and His Wonderful Lamp *34–35*, 484

Aladdin and His Wonderful Lamp (mn) (1) *47–48*, 431

Aladdin and His Wonderful Lamp (mn) (2) *63–64*, 305

Aladdin, Jr., *94–99*, 129

Alarm Clock, The *23–24*, 373

Alarums and Excursions *61–62*, 331

Alaskan, The *99–09*, 541

Alcalde de Zalamea, El (see *The Mayor of Zalamia*)

Alcestis Comes Back *61–62*, 329

Alchemist, The *47–48*, 348; *50–51*, 373; *57–58*, 56; *64–65*, 342; *66–67*, 361

Alcide Pepie *23–24*, 333

Alderman, The *94–99*, 202

Aleko *25–26*, *515*

Alexandra *94–99*, 216

Alfie! *64–65*, 320

Algeria *99–09*, 566; *09–19*, 400

Ali Baba and the 40 Thieves *70–71*

Alias Jimmy Valentine *09–19*, 411; *21–22*, 475

Alias the Deacon *25–26*, 503

Alibi Bill *09–19*, 491

Alice at the Mad Hatter's Tea Party (mn) *36–37*, 498

Alice Dudley (dance programs) *46–47*, 486

Alice in Arms *44–45*, 414

Alice in Wonder *52–53*, 308

Alice ('s Adventures) in Wonderland (source) *09–19*, 548; *32–33*, 434; *46–47*, 439; *69–70*, 369; *70–71*

Alice in Wonderland (1) *09–19*, 548

Alice in Wonderland (2) *32–33*, 434; *46–47*, 439

Alice in Wonderland (3) *35–36*, 512

Alice in Wonderland (4) *70–71*

Alice in Wonderland (mn) *33–34*, 534; *36–37*, 498; *37–38*, 466; *38–39*, 489, 490

Alice My Wife *45–46*, 458

Alice of Old Vincennes *99–09*, 400

Alice Sit-by-the-Fire *99–09*, 503; *09–19*, 439; *31–32*, 489

Alice Takat *35–36*, 480

Alicia Markova & Anton Dolin (dance programs) *45–46*, 453; *47–48*, 414, 418, 423

Alien Corn *32–33*, 465

Alison's House *30–31*, 464

Alive and Kicking *49–50*, 367s

All Aboard *09–19*, 502

All About Eve *69–70*, 323

All American *61–62*, 292s

All Around the Town *38–39*, 491

All by Myself *64–65*, 340

All Dressed Up *25–26*, 439

All Editions *36–37*, 444

All for a Girl *99–09*, 565

All for All *43–44*, 415

All for Her *94–99*, 114; *99–09*, 384

All for Love (1) *45–46*, 451; *69–70*, 373

All for Love (2) *48–49*, 408s

All for the Ladies *09–19*, 490

All Good Americans *33–34*, 467

All in a Lifetime *48–49*, 430

All in Favor *41–42*, 428

All in Fun *40–41*, 405

All in Good Time *64–65*, 328

All in Love *61–62*, 312s; *66–67*, 422

All in One *54–55*, 406

All Kinds of Giants *61–62*, 316s

All Men Are Alike *41–42*, 401

All My Pretty Ones *63–64*, 358

All My Sons *46–47*, 458; *49–50*, 384; *68–69*, 455

All on Account of Eliza *99–09*, 368

All Over *70–71*

All Rights Reserved (1) *34–35*, 404

All Rights Reserved (2) *47–48*, 428

All Soul's Eve *19–20*, 453

All Star Variety Jubilee *09–19*, 517

All Summer Long *54–55*, 363

All That Glitters *37–38*, 416

All the Comforts of Home *19–20*, 380; *41–42*, 453

All the Dark and Beautiful Women *68–69*, 442

All the King's Horses *33–34,* 489
All the King's Men (1) *28–29,* 465
All the King's Men (2) *59–60,* 42;
    66–67, 422
All the Living *37–38,* 435
All the Way Home *60–61,* 308
All Wet *25–26,* 421
All Women Are One *64–65,* 352
All You Need Is One Good Break
    49–50, 373
Allah Be Praised! *43–44,* 469
Allegiance *09–19,* 632
Allegro *47–48,* 359
Alleluia (Alleluja) *99–09,* 536
Allergic Summer *37–38,* 462
Alley Cat *34–35,* 374
Alley of the Sunset *59–60,* 40
Allez-Oop *27–28,* 390
Alligation, The *70–71*
Alligators, The *60–61,* 38
All-of-a-Sudden Peggy *99–09,* 533
Alloy *24–25,* 479
All's Well That Ends Well *66–67,*
    106
Allure *34–35,* 399
Alma, Where Do You Live? *09–19,*
    425
Almanac (see *John Murray
    Anderson's Almanac*)
Almost a Husband *32–33,* 377
Almost Crazy *55–56,* 335s
Aloma of the South Seas *24–25,* 579
Alone at Last *09–19,* 562
Alone in London *94–99,* 248
Along Came a Spider *62–63,* 337
Along Came Ruth *09–19,* 522
Along Fifth Avenue *48–49,* 406s
Alt Heidelberg *99–09,* 424, 439
Altar of Friendship, The *99–09,* 423
Alternate Current *39–40,* 469
Altruism *09–19,* 579
Alvin Joslin *94–99,* 110
Always On Time *94–99,* 215
Always You *19–20,* 411
Amante Anglaise, L' *70–71*
Amazing Dr. Clitterhouse, The
    36–37, 468

Amazons, The *94–99,* 102; *09–19,*
    500
Ambassador, The *99–09,* 361
Amber Empress, The *09–19,* 582
Amber Heart, The *99–09,* 353
Ambition *94–99,* 148
Ambitious Mrs. Alcott, The *99–09,*
    537
Ambush *21–22,* 439
Ameer, The *99–09,* 358
Amelia Goes to the Ball (opera rep)
    47–48, 347
Amen Corner, The *64–65,* 332
America *09–19,* 505
America Hurrah *66–67,* 405
America Sings *38–39,* 485
American Ace, An *09–19,* 626
American Ballad Singers, The
    43–44, 437
American Ballet Caravan (dance
    programs) *39–40,* 471
American Ballet Company, The
    (dance programs) *34–35,* 459
American Beauty, An *94–99,* 189
American Born *25–26,* 461
American Caravan *38–39,* 484
American Cartoon *38–39,* 486
American Citizen, An *94–99,* 211
American Concert Ballet (dance
    programs) *43–44,* 486
American Dream *32–33,* 465
American Dream, The *60–61,* 356;
    61–62, 306, 323; *62–63,* 313, 337;
    63–64, 364; *68–69,* 379
American Gothic *53–54,* 358
American Hamburger League, The
    69–70, 340
American Hero, An *94–99,* 259
American Holiday *35–36,* 468
American Idea, The *99–09,* 570
American Indian dances (untitled
    dance programs) *47–48,* 415
American Invasion, An *99–09,*
    419
American Landscape *38–39,* 435
American Legend *40–41,* 431
American Lord, The *99–09,* 512

American Lyric Theater (dance
   programs) *38–39*, 475, 476, 477;
   53–54, 359
American Mime Theater *67–68*, 410
American Maid, The *09–19*, 496
American musical theater (unnamed
   selections) *67–68*, 395; *68–69*, 446
American Reasons *43–44*, 490
American songs of the 1960s
   (unnamed selections) *68–69*, 436
American Tragedy, An (source)
   26–27, 399; *30–31*, 495; *35–36*,
   494
American Tragedy, An *26–27*, 399;
   30–31, 495
American—Very Early *33–34*, 488
American Way, The *38–39*, 452;
   39–40, 396
American Widow, An *09–19*, 399
Americana (1926) *26–27*, 363
Americana (1928) *28–29*, 406
Americana (1932) *32–33*, 395s
Americana (2) *45–46*, 458
Americana Pastoral *68–69*, 439
Americans at Home *94–99*, 255
Americans in France, The *20–21*,
   363
America's Sweetheart *30–31*, 488
Among the Married *29–30*, 411
Among Those Present *99–09*, 421
Among Those Sailing *35–36*, 482
Amor *36–37*, 499
Amores de la Nati, Los *31–32*, 501
Amores y Amorios *31–32*, 500
Amorous Antic, The *29–30*, 455
Amorous Flea, The *63–64*, 359s
Amour et Sucre D' Erable (see *Love
   and Maple Syrup*)
Amour Qui ne Finit Pas, L' *64–65*,
   315
Amourette *33–34*, 436
Amoureuse *99–09*, 472; *24–25*, 474
Amphitryon (1) *52–53*, 270; *69–70*,
   313; *70–71*
Amphitryon (2) *69–70*, 348
Amphitryon 38 *37–38*, 384
Anastasia *54–55*, 388; *65–66*, 387

Anathema *22–23*, 557
Anatol (see also *The Affairs of
   Anatol*) *30–31*, 480; *61–62*, 270
Anatomist, The *32–33*, 408
Ancient Mariner, The *23–24*, 415
And Be My Love (1) *33–34*, 482
And Be My Love (2) *44–45*, 418
And I Met a Man *69–70*, 365
. . . And in This Corner *63–64*,
   358s; *66–67*, 400
And Miss Reardon Drinks a Little
   70–71
And Now Good-Bye *36–37*, 457
And Puppy Dog Tails *67–70*, 343
And So They Perish *49–50*, 385
And So to Bed *27–28*, 448
And Stars Remain *36–37*, 416
And Things That Go Bump in the
   Night *64–65*, 334
And Whose Little Boy Are You?
   70–71
Andersonville Trial, The *59–60*, 312
Andorra *62–63*, 296
Andre Charlot's Revue of 1924 (see
   Charlot's Revue)
Andrea *94–99*, 217, 244
Andrea Chenier *46–47*, 412
Androcles and the Lion *09–19*, 545;
   25–26, 499; *37–38*, 468; *38–39*,
   479; *46–47*, 437; *61–62*, 314
Andromaque *63–64*, 326
Angel Face *19–20*, 407
Angel in the House, The *09–19*, 564
Angel in the Pawnshop *50–51*, 343
Angel in the Wings *47–48*, 368s
Angel Island *37–38*, 382
Angel Street *(Gaslight)* *41–42*, 419;
   46–47, 485; *47–48*, 346, 425
Angel With Red Hair *50–51*, 374
Angela (1) *28–29*, 430
Angela (2) *69–70*, 306
Angela Maria *26–27*, 520
Angelic Doctor *52–53*, 308
Angeline Moves In *31–32*, 506
Angelo Herndon *35–36*, 510
Angels Don't Kiss *31–32*, 503
Angels Kiss Me *50–51*, 362

Angels of Anadarko 62–63, 315

Anglais tel Qu'on Parle, L' 09–19, 589 (and 605)

Anglo-Saxon Chronicle, The 62–63, 295

Angna Enters (dance programs) 39–40, 472; 42–43, 485; 51–52, 330

Animal Crackers 28–29, 402

Animal Kingdom, The 31–32, 463; 44–45, 436; 45–46, 451

Anita Zahn & Duncan Dancers (dance programs) 47–48, 415

Ankles Aweigh 54–55, 405s

Ann Adams, Spinster 32–33, 498

Ann Boyd 09–19, 499

Anna 27–28, 555

Anna and the King of Siam 50–51, 360; 55–56, 384; 59–60, 340; 63–64, 302; 64–65, 296; 67–68, 379

Anna Ascends 20–21, 384

Anna Christie 21–22, 454; 31–32, 501; 45–46, 451; 51–52, 304; 56–57, 373; 62–63, 339; 70–71

Anna Karenina 99–09, 543

Anna Lucasta 43–44, 489; 44–45, 372; 47–48, 351, 432

Anna Russell 51–52, 333

Anna Russell's Little Show 53–54, 300s

Annajanska, the Bolshevik Empress 67–68, 409

Anne Frank: The Diary of a Young Girl 55–56, 350

Anne of England 41–42, 402

Anne of the Thousand Days 48–49, 399

Annie Dear 24–25, 480

Annie Get Your Gun 45–46, 447; 57–58, 319; 65–66, 413; 66–67, 356s

Anniversary, The 60–61, 45

Anniversary Waltz 53–54, 348

Annonce Fait a Marie, L' (see *The Tidings Brought to Mary*)

Another Chance 69–70, 333

Another City, Another Land 68–69, 428

Another Evening With Harry Stoones 61–62, 310

Another Interior 09–19, 547

Another Language 31–32, 508; 32–33, 492; 47–48, 389; 51–52, 333

Another Love 33–34, 507

Another Love Story 43–44, 418

Another Man's Shoes 09–19, 637

Another Part of the Forest 46–47, 443

Another Room for Rent 28–29, 500

Another Sun 39–40, 439

Another Way Out 09–19, 579; 22–23, 575

Anselma 94–99, 217

Answered the Flute 59–60, 40

Anthony in Wonderland 09–19, 611

Antick, The 09–19, 560

Antigone (1) 45–46, 428; 55–56, 59; 59–60, 43; 66–67, 410; 70–71

Antigone (2) 62–63, 322

Antigone and the Tyrant 45–46, 176

Antigone of Sophokles, The 68–69, 456

Anti-Masque 61–62, 314

Anti-Matrimony 09–19, 425

Anton Dolin (dance programs; see *Alicia Markova & Anton Dolin*)

Antonia 25–26, 479

Antonio (dance programs; (see *Rosario & Antonio*)

Antony and Cleopatra 09–19, 404; 23–24, 401; 37–38, 386; 47–48, 365; 51–52, 299; 58–59, 52; 63–64, 387

Anvil, The 62–63, 317

Any Day Now 40–41, 432

Any House 09–19, 570

Any Moment Now 39–40, 472

Any Night 09–19, 497

Any Resemblance to Persons Living or Dead . . . 70–71

Any Wednesday 63–64, 326

Anya 65–66, 387s

Anybody's Game *32–33*, 438
Anybody Home *48–49*, 414
Anyone Can Whistle *63–64*, 330s
Anything Goes *34–35*, 412; *61–62*, 330s
Anything Might Happen *22–23*, 535
Aoi-No-Ue (see *Lady Aoi*)
Apache, The *22–23*, 569
Apartment, The *68–69*, 395
Apartment 12-K *09–19*, 528
Aphrodite *19–20*, 391
Apocalypsis Cum Figuris *69–70*, 343
Apocrypha *36–37*, 493
Apology *42–43*, 468
Apollo of Bellac, The *(L'Apollon de Bellac)* *62–63*, 325
Apothecary, The *25–26*, 569
Apotheker, Der *25–26*, 569
Apparition Theater of Prague, The *66–67*, 368
Appearances *25–26*, 473; *28–29*, 487
Applause *69–70*, 323s
Apple, The *61–62*, 305, 315
Apple Cart, The *29–30*, 500; 56–57, 324
Apple Blossoms *19–20*, 367
Apple of His Eye *45–46*, 425
Apple Tree, The *66–67*, 364s
Applesauce *25–26*, 457
Applicant *69–70*, 345
Appraisal of a Ghost, The *62–63*, 335
Apprentice Theater of the American Theater Council (untitled sketches) *38–39*, 488
April *09–19*, 627
Apron Strings *29–30*, 495
Arah, The *09–19*, 451
Arab Fantasia, An *23–24*, 336
Arabesque *25–26*, 478
Arabian, The *27–28*, 442
Arabian Girl and Forty Thieves, An *94–99*, 259
Arabian Nightmare *26–27*, 458
Arcadians, The *09–19*, 410

archie and mehitabel stories *56–57*, 367; *62–63*, 322
Architruc *69–70*, 363
Ardele *57–58*, 52, 53
Arden of Faversham *69–70*, 375
Are You a Crook? *09–19*, 501
Are You a Mason? *99–09*, 390
Are You Decent *33–34*, 517
Are You My Father? *99–09*, 439
Are You With It? *45–46*, 405
Arena Conta Zumbi *69–70*, 339
Arena Tells About Bolivar *(Arena Conte Bolivar)* *69–70*, 339
Arenas of Lutetia *68–69*, 456
Aren't We All? *22–23*, 577; *24–25*, 576; *49–50*, 384
Arf! *66–67*, 423; *68–69*, 453
Argentinita (dance programs) *39–40*, 471; *41–42*, 457; *42–43*, 485; *43–44*, 485, 486; *44–45*, 440
Argyle Case, The *09–19*, 489
Ari *70–71*s
Aria da Capo *24–25*, 583; *58–59*, 50
Ariadne *24–25*, 546
Ariadne auf Naxos (opera rep) *46–47*, 409, 412; *47–48*, 343
Aries Is Rising *39–40*, 413
Aristocrat, The *28–29*, 501
Aristocrats *34–35*, 472
Arithmetic *60–61*, 295
Arizona *99–09*, 369; *09–19*, 500; *27–28*, 437
Arlecchino, Servitore di due Padroni (see *Servant of Two Masters*)
Arlequin Poli par L'Armour (see *Love Teaches Harlequin*)
Arlesienne, L' *94–99*, 198
Arm of the Law *94–99*, 166
Armour Medecin, L' *63–64*, 327
Arms and the Girl (1) *09–19*, 583
Arms and the Girl (2) *49–50*, 372s
Arms and the Man *94–99*, 91, 92, 93; *99–09*, 355, 512; *09–19*, 399, 552; *21–22*, 476; *25–26*, 442; *29–30*, 483, *31–32*, 395; *33–34*, 523; *42–43*, 419; *46–47*, 470, 485;

Arms and the Man *(cont.)*
  50–51, 321; *56–57,* 55; *63–64,* 364;
  65–66, 436; *67–68,* 384
Arms for Venus *36–37,* 472
Army Play-by-Play, The *42–43,* 477;
  43–44, 404
Army With Banners, The *09–19,*
  627
Around the Corner *36–37,* 447
Around the Map *09–19,* 563
Around the World (1) *09–19,* 449
Around the World (2) *45–46,* 448
Around the World in Dance and
  Song (dance programs) *47–48,*
  415
Around the World in 80 Days
  (source) *45–46,* 448; *63–64,* 343;
  64–65, 341
Around the World in 80 Days
  63–64, 343s; *64–65,* 341s
Arrah-Na-Pogue *99–09,* 435
Arrest That Woman *36–37,* 407
Arrow Maker, The *09–19,* 440
Arsene Lupin *09–19,* 397
Arsenic and Old Lace *40–41,* 410;
  41–42, 459
Art and Mrs. Bottle *30–31,* 457;
  45–46, 457
Art and Opportunity *09–19,* 615
Artef Variety Show *35–36,* 510
Arthur Mahoney & Thalia Mara
  (dance programs) *44–45,* 381
Arthur Whittemore & Jack Lowe
  47–48, 423
Article 47 *94–99,* 143, 144
Artie *99–09,* 549
Artistic Temperament *24–25,* 503
Artists and Models (1923) *23–24,*
  306
Artists and Models (1924) *24–25,*
  474
Artists and Models (1925) *25–26,*
  420
Artists and Models (1927) *27–28,*
  452
Artists and Models (1930) *29–30,*
  550
Artists and Models (1943) *43–44,*
  424
Artist's Model, An *94–99,* 158
Artists' Theater (unnamed programs)
  53–54, 359
Art's Rejuvenation *09–19,* 631
Arturo Ui (see *The Resistible Rise of*
  Arturo Ui)
As a Man Thinks *09–19,* 440
As Good as New *30–31,* 446
As Happy as Kings *67–68,* 412
As Husbands Go *30–31,* 501; *32–33,*
  451; *37–38,* 462; *43–44,* 489
As I Lay Dying *48–49,* 429
As I Remember You *24–25,* 587
As the Girls Go *48–49,* 394s
As Thousands Cheer *33–34,* 438
As We Forgive Our Debtors *46–47,*
  462
As We Love *32–33,* 377
As Ye Mould *21–22,* 444
As Ye Sow *99–09,* 503
As You Desire Me *30–31,* 484;
  44–45, 436
As You Like It *94–99,* 147, 167,
  184, 214, 221; *99–09,* 407, 534;
  09–19, 413, 433, 443, 447, 478,
  508, 523, 622, 650; *22–23,* 560;
  29–30, 516; *30–31,* 471; *32–33,*
  424; *37–38,* 383; *41–42,* 404;
  45–46, 457; *46–47,* 466; *49–50,*
  370; *52–53, 308–9; 55–56,* 55;
  58–59, 316; *62–63,* 305; *63–64,*
  314, 353, 387; *64–65,* 361; *68–69,*
  455; *70–71*
As You Like It (m) *64–65,* 361
As You Were *19–20,* 420
Ascent of F 6, The *38–39,* 487;
  49–50, 383
Ashes *24–25,* 475
Ashes of Love *25–26,* 574
Ask Me Another *41–42,* 461
Ask My Friend Sandy *42–43,* 462
Aspern Papers, The (source) *47–48,*
  423; *61–62,* 288
Aspern Papers, The (1) *47–48,* 423
Aspern Papers, The (2) *61–62,* 288

Asphodel, in Hell's Despite *63–64,* 346

Assassin, The *45–46,* 399

Assault Upon Charles Sumner, The *63–64,* 369

Asses *70–71*

Assomoir, L' *99–09,* 436

Assorted Nuts *39–40,* 473

Assumption of Hannele, The (see also *Hannele*) *23–24,* 400

Astonished Heart, The *36–37,* 435

Astrakham Coat, The *66–67,* 380

At Bay *09–19,* 511

At Dead Rat, Room No. 6 *(Au Rat Mort, Cabinet No. 6)* *23–24,* 333

At Fort Bliss *94–99,* 229

At Gay Coney Island *94–99,* 193

At Home Abroad *35–36,* 406

At Home With Ethel Waters *53–54,* 305s

At Mrs. Beam's *25–26,* 586

At 9:45 *19–20,* 337

At Piney Ridge *94–99,* 195

At Sea *61–62,* 329

At the Barn *09–19,* 540

At the Bottom *29–30,* 476

At the Drop of a Hat *59–60,* 294s

At the Drop of Another Hat *66–67,* 379s

At the French Ball *94–99,* 201

At the Gate of the Kingdom *27–28,* 468

At the Stroke of Eight *39–40,* 462

At the Telephone *99–09,* 417

At the Threshold *99–09,* 484

At the White Horse Tavern *94–99,* 252

At War With the Army *48–49,* 415

Athaliah *63–64,* 359

Athenian Touch, The *63–64,* 356s

Atlas and Eva *27–28,* 503

Atta Boy *09–19,* 646

Attack, The *09–19,* 477

Attentat *38–39,* 462

Au Coin Joli *23–24,* 333

Au Rat Mort, Cabinet No. 6 (see *At Dead Rat, Room No. 6*)

Aucassin and Nicolette *46–47,* 484, 499

Auctioneer, The *99–09,* 395; *09–19,* 510, 643

Audiences *60–61,* 295

Auditions (public perfs) *38–39,* 488

Audrey *99–09,* 423

Augustus Does His Bit *09–19,* 652

Aunt From England, The *38–39,* 486

Aunt Hannah *99–09,* 363

Aunt Jeannie *99–09,* 417

Auntie Mame (source) *56–57,* 329; *58–59,* 291; *65–66,* 412

Auntie Mame *56–57,* 329; *58–59,* 291; *65–66,* 412

Aupres de Ma Blonde *49–50,* 359

Auto Race, The *99–09,* 551

Autobiography (dance program) *56–57,* 319

Autograph Hound, The *68–69,* 439

Automobile Graveyard, The *61–62,* 313

Autumn Crocus *32–33,* 425

Autumn Fire *26–27,* 412

Autumn Garden, The *50–51,* 355

Autumn Hill *41–42,* 446

Autumn's Here! *66–67,* 404s

Avanti! *67–68,* 361

Avare, L' (see *The Miser*)

Aventuriere, L' *22–23,* 488; *26–27,* 434

Avenue, The *09–19,* 612

Averil Tam (dance programs) *47–48,* 415

Aviator, The *09–19,* 433, 618

Awake and Sing *34–35,* 454; *35–36,* 402; *38–39,* 463; *38–39,* 482; *46–47,* 485, 494; *69–70,* 370

Awakening, The (1) *99–09,* 557

Awakening, The (2) *09–19,* 639

Awakening of Helena Ritchie, The *09–19,* 400

Awakening of Spring, The *63–64,* 366

Away! *62–63,* 322

Awful Truth, The *22–23*, 454
Aztec Romance, An *09–19*, 476

Baal *64–65*, 344, 359; *69–70*, 378
Bab *20–21*, 397
Babbling Brookes *26–27*, 487
Babes and the Baron, The *99–09*, 504
Babes Don't Cry Anymore *67–68*, 408
Babes in Arms *36–37*, 479; *50–51*, *374; 67–68*, 409
Babes in the Wood *64–65*, 351s
Babes in Toyland *99–09*, 440; *29–30*, 466; *30–31*, 467
Babette *99–09*, 445
Babies a la Carte *27–28*, 391; *28–29*, 355
Babushka *46–47*, 496
Baby Cyclone *27–28*, 402
Baby Mine *09–19*, 422; *26–27*, 534; *47–48*, 425
Baby Pompadour *34–35*, 432
Baby Want a Kiss *63–64*, 335
Baby With a Knife *68–69*, 452
Bacchae, The *68–69*, 457
Bachelor, The *99–09*, 579
Bachelor Belles, The *09–19*, 429
Bachelor Born *37–38*, 418
Bachelor Father, The *27–28*, 519
Bachelors and Benedicts *09–19*, 482
Bachelor's Baby, A *94–99*, 204
Bachelor's Baby, The *09–19*, 407
Bachelors Brides *24–25*, 597
Bachelor's Honeymoon, A *94–99*, 206
Bachelor's Night, A *21–22*, 443
Bachelors Romance, A *94–99*, 208
Back Bog Beast Bait *70–71*
Back Fire *31–32*, 522
Back Here *28–29*, 427
Back Home *09–19*, 564
Back Pay *21–22*, 405
Back Seat Drivers *28–29*, 445
Back to Earth *09–19*, 647
Back to Methuselah *21–22*, 517; *57–58*, 326; *59–60*, 43; *62–63*, 322

Backfire *09–19*, 583
Backslapper, The *24–25*, 569
Bad Bad Jo-Jo *68–69*, 448
Bad Boy Sketches, The *94–99*, 95
Bad Girl *30–31*, 425
Bad Habits of 1926 *25–26*, 589
Bad Habits of '71 *70–71*
Bad Man, The *20–21*, 374
Bad Manners *32–33*, 455
Bad Place to Get Your Head, A *70–71*
Bad Samaritan, The *99–09*, 496
Bad Seed *54–55*, 381
Bad Seed, The (source) *54–55*, 120, 381
Baden School Play, The *63–64*, 365
Badges *24–25*, 501
Bag of Flies, A *70–71*
Bagels and Yox *51–52*, 281
Baggage Check, A *94–99*, 224
Baird Marionette Theater (Bil and Cora Baird's Marionettes) *66–67*, 413; *67–68*, 395; *68–69*, 436; *69–70*, 351; *70–71*
Bajaders, Die *22–23*, 467
Bajour *64–65*, 316s
Baker Street *64–65*, 327s
Baker's Dozen *63–64*, 355s
Baker's Dozen, A *63–64*, 367
Bal des Voleurs, Le (see *Thieves' Carnival*)
Bal Negre (dance Program) *46–47*, 440
Balcony, The *59–60*, 355
Bald Soprano, The *58–59*, 51; *63–64*, 345
Balieff's Chauve-Souris (see *Chauve-Souris* 1929)
Balkan Princess, The *09–19*, 438
Ball in Old Vienna, A (dance program) *41–42*, 431
Ballad for a Firing Squad *68–69*, 439
Ballad for Bimshire *63–64*, 348s
Ballad of Reading Gaol, The *09–19*, 478
Ballad Monger, The *94–99*, 120, 121

Ballad of Davy Crockett, The
  35–36, 479
Ballad of Jazz Street *59–60*, 40
Ballad of Johnny Pot, The *70–71*
Ballad of the Sad Cafe, The *63–64*,
  312
Ballads (unnamed verses and songs)
  62–63, 295; *67–68*, 365
Ballet Ballads *47–48*, 397; *60–61*, 45
Ballet Caravan, The (dance
  programs) *38–39*, 476
Ballet Girl, The *94–99*, 219
Ballet International (dance programs)
  44–45, 439
(Colonel de Basil's Original) Ballet
  Russe (dance programs) *40–41*,
  427–8
(S. Hurok's Original) Ballet Russe
  (dance programs) *46–47*, 488–9
Ballet Russe de Monte Carlo (dance
  programs) *33–34*, 519–20; *34–35*,
  459–60; *39–40*, 470–1; *40–41*, 427;
  41–42, 456; *42–43*, 483–5; *43–44*,
  440; *44–45*, 437; *45–46*, 387, 453,
  454; *46–47*, 408, 411; *46–47*, 490;
  47–48, 342, 420, 421; *48–49*, 428,
  429; *49–50*, 386
Ballet Russe Highlights (dance
  programs) *45–46*, 452
Ballet Society, The (dance programs)
  46–47, 487–8; *47–48*, 421–2
Ballet Theatre (dance programs)
  39–40, 471; *40–41*, 428–9; *41–42*,
  456; *42–43*, 483–4; *43–44*, 485–6;
  44–45, 438; *45–46*, 454, 455;
  46–47, 413, 489–90, 491; *47–48*,
  343, 419, 421; *48–49*, 429; *49–50*,
  386; *51–52*, 330
Ballets Africains, Les (dance
  program) *66–67*, 369; *67–68*, 364
(Roland Petit's) Ballets de Paris, Les
  (dance programs) *49–50*, 385
Balls *64–65*, 354
Ballyhoo (1) *26–27*, 455
Ballyhoo (2) *30–31*, 468
Ballyhoo of 1932 *32–33*, 383s
Bamboo Cross *54–55*, 52–3

Bamboola *29–30*, 377
Bananas *68–69*, 437
Band Wagon, The *30–31*, 532
Bandanna Land *99–09*, 556
Banco *22–23*, 458
Banjo Eyes *41–42*, 422; *63–64*, 357
Banker's Daughter, The (1) *94–99*,
  230
Banker's Daughter, The (2) *61–62*,
  320s
Banquet for the Moon, A *60–61*, 39
Banshee, The *27–28*, 466
Baptism, The *63–64*, 364
Baptiste *52–53*, 267
Bar Kochba *46–47*, 497; *47–48*, 432
Barbara *09–19*, 613
Barbara Frietchie *99–09*, 1, 352;
  27–28, 403
Barbara's Millions *99–09*, 522
Barbara's Wedding *31–32*, 406
Barber Had Two Sons, The *42–43*,
  461
Barber of New Orleans, The *99–09*,
  575
Barber of Seville, The (*Le Barbier de
  Seville;* p) *42–43*, 444; *55–56*, 357
Barber of Seville, The (opera rep)
  42–43, 444; *45–46*, 441; *46–47*,
  480; *47–48*, 343, 399
Barbizon Tuesdays (dance programs)
  46–47, 486, 493
Barchester Towers *37–38*, 396
Bare Facts of 1926 *26–27*, 362
Barefoot *25–26*, 477
Barefoot Boy With Cheek *46–47*,
  474
Barefoot in Athens *51–52*, 289
Barefoot in the Park *63–64*, 311;
  69–70, 374
Bargain, The (1) *09–19*, 561
Bargain, The (2) *39–40*, 470
Barker, The *26–27*, 462
Barnabetta *09–19*, 569
Barnum Was Right *22–23*, 541
Baron Trenck *09–19*, 468
Baroness Fiddlesticks, The *99–09*,
  473

Barretts of Wimpole Street, The
  30–31, 487; 34–35, 456; 44–45,
  424
Barrier, The (1) 09–19, 409
Barrier, The (2) 49–50, 384; 50–51,
  323; 52–53, 306
Barrister, The 32–33, 427
Barroom Monks, The 61–62,
  331
Bartered Bride, The (opera rep)
  45–46, 389; 46–47, 409
Bartleby 60–61, 356
Barton Mystery, The 09–19, 609
Basement, The (1) 67–68, 387
Basement, The (2) 68–69, 429
Basic Training of Pavlo Hummel,
  The 70–71
Basker, The 09–19, 586
Bassa Mona 36–37, 496
Bat, The 20–21, 371; 36–37, 486;
  52–53, 281
Bat Theater of Moscow, the 21–22,
  504; 43–44, 407
Bath Comedy, The 99–09, 448
Bathing Girl, The 94–99, 140
Bathsheba 46–47, 472
Bathtub 69–70, 376
Battle, The 99–09, 574
Battle Cry, The 09–19, 537
Battle for Heaven 47–48, 412
Battle Hymn 35–36, 477
Battle of Port Arthur, The 99–09,
  551
Battle of the Butterflies, The 99–09,
  560
Battling Buttler 23–24, 330
Battleship Gertie 34–35, 442
Bauble Shop, The 94–99, 90
Bavu 21–22, 516
Bawdy Party (La Remolienda)
  67–68, 401
Baxter's Partner 09–19, 446
Be Calm, Camilla 09–19, 642
Be Happy 42–43, 490
Be Proud if You Want To 60–61,
  294–5
Be So Kindly 36–37, 462

Be Your Age (1) 28–29, 465
Be Your Age (2) 52–53, 280
Be Yourself 24–25, 447
Bead-Tangle 70–71
Bear, A (The) 09–19, 547, 579;
  47–48, 346
Beard, The 67–68, 389
Beast in Me, The 62–63, 309s
Beast's Story, A 68–69, 434
Beat the Band 42–43, 436
Beaten Track, The 25–26, 548
Beatrice Herford 36–37, 498
Beau Brummell 94–99, 91, 92, 93;
  99–09, 355, 455, 486, 487; 09–19,
  573
Beau Gallant 25–26, 580
Beau James 69–70, 302
Beaucaire (see also Monsieur
  Beaucaire) 99–09, 400, 455
Beau-Strings 25–26, 587
Beautiful Adventure, The 09–19,
  529
Beautiful Bait, The (Tiao Ch'an)
  62–63, 285
Beautiful Dreamer 60–61, 42
Beautiful Legend of Pokey, The
  09–19, 612
Beautiful People, The 40–41, 424;
  55–56, 58; 59–60, 43
Beauty and the Barge 99–09, 494;
  09–19, 514
Beauty and the Beast (1) 35–36, 512
Beauty and the Beast (2) 64–65, 362
Beauty and the Jacobin 09–19, 487;
  23–24, 428
Beauty Part, The 62–63, 291
Beauty Shop, The 09–19, 526
Beauty Spot, The 99–09, 580
Beaux' Stratagem, The 27–28, 559;
  38–39, 492; 57–58, 56; 58–59, 323;
  65–66, 437
Because of Helen (see Merchants of
  Venus)
Because She Loved Him So 94–99,
  250
Becket (1) 94–99, 150
Becket (2) 60–61, 298, 299

Becky Sharp *99–09*, 348; *09–19*, 441; *28–29*, 509
Beclch *68–69*, 439
Bedfellows *29–30*, 379
Bedford's Hope *99–09*, 508
Bedtime Story *58–59*, 333
Beekman Place *64–65*, 306
Bees and the Flowers, The *46–47*, 420
Beethoven *09–19*, 417
Beffa, La *09–19*, 432
Before and After *99–09*, 502
Before Breakfast *28–29*, 477
Before I Wake *68–69*, 429
Before Morning *32–33*, 460
Before Sundown *61–62*, 325
Before You Go *67–68*, 358
Before You're 25 *28–29*, 494
Beg, Borrow or Steal *59–60*, 317s;
Beggar on Horseback *23–24*, 398; *24–25*, 560; *48–49*, 425; *69–70*, 303
Beggar Student, The *09–19*, 498; *42–43*, 486
Beggars Are Coming to Town *45–46*, 401
Beggar's Holiday *46–47*, 451
Beggar's Opera, The *20–21*, 416; *25–26*, 468; *27–28*, 533; *32–33*, 484; *34–35*, 483; *46–47*, 451; *50–51*, 373; *56–57*, 360s; *64–65*, 362; *66–67*, 366
Behavior of Mrs. Crane, The *27–28*, 531
Behind Red Lights *36–37*, 454
Behind the Wall *60–61*, 39
Behold the Bridegroom *27–28*, 475
Behold! Cometh the Vanderkellans *70–71*
Behold This Dreamer *27–28*, 442
Bei Mir Bist du Schoen *61–62*, 310
Believe Me Xantippe *09–19*, 504
Believers, The *67–68*, 407
Belinda *09–19*, 629
Bell, Book and Candle *50–51*, 325
Bell for Adano, A *44–45*, 402
Bella *61–62*, 313s

Bella Donna *09–19*, 484
Bella Reine *46–47*, 499
Bellamy Trial, The *30–31*, 519
Belle Helene, La *94–99*, 250; *43–44*, 470
Belle Marie, La, or A Woman's Revenge *94–99*, 129
Belle Marseillaise, La *99–09*, 501
Belle of Bohemia, The *99–09*, 372
Belle of Bond Street, The *09–19*, 524
Belle of Bridgeport, The *99–09*, 378
Belle of Brittany, The *09–19*, 404
Belle of Broadway, The *99–09*, 407
Belle of London Town, The *99–09*, 532
Belle of Mayfair, The *99–09*, 528
Belle of New York, The *94–99*, 210; *20–21*, 453; *48–49*, 425–6
Belle Paris, La *09–19*, 442
Bells, The (1) *94–99*, 150, 151; *99–09*, 353, 442; *25–26*, 584; *39–40*, 470; *40–41*, 432; *42–43*, 489; *43–44*, 490
Bells Are Ringing *56–57*, 339s
Belmont Varieties (Vanities) *32–33*, 392
Below the Belt *66–67*, 400
Belt, The *27–28*, 436
Ben Bagley's Shoestring Revues *70–71*
Ben Franklin in Paris *64–65*, 308s
Ben Hur (Ben-Hur) *99–09*, 357; *09–19*, 461, 586
Bench, The *67–68*, 402
Bendita Seas *27–28*, 468
Benedict Arnold *94–99*, 160
Benefit of the Doubt, The *94–99*, 160
Benificent Bear, The *(Il Burbero Benefico)* *99–09*, 536
Benito Cerino (source) *63–64*, 369; *64–65*, 346
Benito Cerino *64–65*, 346
Benkei in the Boat *(Funa-Benkei)* *70–71*
Ben-My-Cree *94–99*, 105

Beppo's Circus (mn) *35–36*, 512

Bereft *62–63*, 322

Berenice *63–64*, 310

Berkeley Square *29–30*, 432

Berlin *31–32*, 455

Berlin stories (untitled sources; see also *Sally Bowles*) *51–52*, 295; *66–67*, 370

Bernard Shaw Story, The *65–66*, 427, 436

Bernardine *52–53*, 260

Bertha, the Sewing Machine Girl *35–36*, 431

Bessarabia *45–46*, 460

Best Foot Forward *41–42*, 400; *62–63*, 330s

Best House in Naples, The *56–57*, 328

Best Laid Plans, The *65–66*, 405

Best Man, The *59–60*, 330

Best of Friends, The *99–09*, 441

Best People, The *24–25*, 435; *32–33*, 476

Best Plays of Chekhov *62–63*, 326

Best Sellers *32–33*, 490

Best Sellers, The *09–19*, 631

Best Years *32–33*, 384

Bet Your Life *36–37*, 476, 486

Betrothal, The *09–19*, 644

Betsy (1) *09–19*, 460

Betsy (2) *26–27*, 450

Better Luck Next Time *65–66*, 429

Better 'Ole, The *09–19*, 641; *26–27*, 424

Better Times *22–23*, 447

Betty (1) *09–19*, 583

Betty (2) *70–71*

Betty at Bay *09–91*, 646

Betty, Be Careful *30–31*, 521

Betty Be Good *19–20*, 450

Betty Lee *24–25*, 512

Between the Devil *37–38*, 404

Between Two Thieves *59–60*, 46

Between Two Worlds *34–35*, 397

Between Whisky and Vodka *61–62*, 308

Beverly Hills *40–41*, 392

Beverly's Balance *09–19*, 551

Beware of Dogs *21–22*, 429

Beware of Widows *25–26*, 506

Bewitched *24–25*, 463

Beyond *24–25*, 530

Beyond Desire *67–68*, 387

Beyond Evil *25–26*, 603

Beyond Help *38–39*, 486

Beyond Human Power *99–09*, 403

Beyond the Fringe *62–63*, 283

Beyond the Fringe 1964 *63–64*, 318

Beyond the Fringe '65 *64–65*, 320

Beyond the Horizon *19–20*, 420; *26–27*, 435; *46–47*, 485

Bianca (opera rep) *09–19*, 638

Bible (source; see also Genesis, Esther, St. Luke, etc., titles of Books) *42–43*, 487, 488; *44–45*, 376; *46–47*, 473; *47–48*, 357, 417, 429; *60–61*, 44; *62–63*, 321; *63–64*, 314, 354; *64–65*, 322; *65–66*, 431; *66–67*, 36; *69–70*, 343; *70–71*

Bible Salesman, The *59–60*, 40; *60–61*, 358s

Bichon *36–37*, 499

Bicycle Girl, The *94–99*, 153

Bicycle Ride to Nevada *63–64*, 303

Bidding High *32–33*, 393

Biedermann und die Brandstifter (see *The Firebugs*)

Biff! Bang! *09–19*, 630

Biff! Bing! Bang! *20–21*, 448

Big Blow, The *38–39*, 478

Big Boy *24–25*, 518; *25–26*, 431

Big Chance, The *09–19*, 642

Big City, The (dance program) *41–42*, 431

Big Fight, The *28–29*, 375

Big Fish, Little Fish *60–61*, 330

Big Game *19–20*, 419

Big Hearted Herbert *33–34*, 473

Big Hotel *66–67*, 35

Big Idea, The *09–19*, 539

Big Ideal, The *52–53*, 308

Big Jim Garrity *09–19*, 535

Big Knife, The *48–49*, 413

Big Lake *26–27*, 506

Big Man *65–66*, 435
Big Mogul, The *24–25*, 593
Big Move, The *63–64*, 369
Big Night *32–33*, 451
Big Nose Mary Is Dead *67–68*, 412
Big Pond, The *28–29*, 360
Big Scene, The *09–19*, 628
Big Shot, The (1; see *Nigger Rich*)
Big Shot, The (2) *47–48*, 431
Big Show, The *09–19*, 580
Big Time Buck White *68–69*, 439;
    69–70, 307
Big Two, The *46–47*, 453
Big White Fog *40–41*, 387
Bigfoot *70–71*
Biggest Thief in Town, The *48–49*,
    416
Bil and Cora Baird's Marionettes
    (see *Baird Marionette Theater*)
Bil Baird's Variety *70–71*
Bilbea *60–61*, 295
Bill and Coo *64–65*, 336
Bill of Divorcement, A *21–22*, 438
Billeted *09–19*, 618; *21–22*, 545
Billie *28–29*, 385
Billion Dollar Baby *45–46*, 415
Billionaire, The *99–09*, 425
Billy (1) *09–19*, 395
Billy (2) *68–69*, 411s
Billy (Billie) Barnes People, The
    61–62, 253s
Billy Barnes Revue *59–60*, 46, 289s
Billy Budd (source) *48–49*, 427;
    50–51, 349; *68–69*, 411
Billy Budd *50–51*, 349; *54–55*, 57;
    58–59, 53
Billy Draws a Horse *39–40*, 424
Billy Liar *64–65*, 356
Billy Noname *69–70*, 359s
Billy Rose's Crazy Quilt *30–31*, 529
Billy the Kid *51–52*, 332
Billy the Kid (dance program)
    38–39, 477
Billygoat Eddie *63–64*, 364
Biography *32–33*, 434; *33–34*, 492
Bird Cage, The (1) *24–25*, 600
Bird Cage, The (2) *49–50*, 374

Bird Center *99–09*, 471
Bird in Hand *28–29*, 489; *30–31*,
    449; *42–43*, 437
Bird in the Cage, The *99–09*, 426
Bird of Paradise, The *09–19*, 462;
    30–31, 413
Birdbath *65–66*, 432; *70–71*
Birthday *34–35*, 430
Birthday of the Infanta, The *09–19*,
    588; *43–44*, 490
Birthday Party, The (1; mn) *35–36*,
    479, 513
Birthday Party, The (2) *67–68*, 342;
    70–71
Birthright (1) *09–19*, 458, 494;
    32–33, 407
Birthright (2) *33–34*, 460
Biscuit *65–66*, 435
Bishop, The (see *The Bishop's Move*)
Bishop Misbehaves, The *34–35*, 454;
    36–37, 497; *43–44*, 489; *47–48*,
    425
Bishop of Munster, The *37–38*, 464
Bishop's Move, The *99–09*, 429
Bit of Love, A *24–25*, 593
Bit of Old Chelsea, A *94–99*, 169,
    228
Bitch of Waverly Place, The *63–64*,
    365–6; *64–65*, 357; *70–71*
Bits and Pieces, XIV *64–65*, 343s
Bitter Oleander *(Blood Wedding)*
    34–35, 449
Bitter Stream *35–36*, 495
Bitter Sweet *29–30*, 435; *33–34*, 524
Black Ace *32–33*, 377
Black Boy *26–27*, 395
Black Cat, The *36–37*, 498
Black Chiffon *50–51*, 316
Black Comedy *66–67*, 381
Black Crook, The *94–99*, 95
Black Cockatoo *26–27*, 452
Black Diamond *32–33*, 466
Black Flag, The *94–99*, 153
Black Limelight *36–37*, 429
Black Mask, The *09–19*, 509
Black Messiah, The *38–39*, 487
Black Monday *61–62*, 325

Black Nativity *61–62*, 315s; *68–69*, 454

Black Pit *34–35*, 463

Black Quartet, A *68–69*, 455; *69–70*, 338

Black Rhythm *36–37*, 443

Black Sheep *32–33*, 400

Black Sheep and How It Came to Washington, A *94–99*, 161

Black Souls *31–32*, 499

Black Tower, The *31–32*, 462

Black Velvet *27–28*, 417

Black Widow *35–36*, 483

Blackberries of 1932 *31–32*, 502

Blackbirds *09–19*, 491

Blackbirds of 1928 *27–28*, 553

Blackbirds (Lew Leslie's, 1930) *30–31*, 438

Blackbirds of 1933 *33–34*, 466

Blackbirds of 1939 (Lew Leslie's) *38–39*, 459

Black-Eyed Susan *54–55*, 385

Blackfriars' Guild, The (unnamed productions) *55–56*, 59; *60–61*, 48

Blackouts of 1949 (see *Ken Murray's Blackouts of 1949*)

Blacks, The *60–61*, 361

Blacksmith's Daughter, The *48–49*, 430

Blanchette *23–24*, 406

Blancs, Les *68–69*, 442; *70–71*

Blastoma City *64–65*, 347

Bleak House (source) *28–29*, 447; *52–53*, 300

Bleak House *52–53*, 300

Bless You All *50–51*, 334s

Bless You, Sister *27–28*, 475

Blessed Are the Debonair *37–38*, 462

Blessed Event *31–32*, 477

Blind Alley *35–36*, 409; *40–41*, 385; *45–46*, 451

Blind Alleys (1) *09–19*, 612

Blind Alleys (2) *24–25*, 490

Blind Angel, The *64–65*, 357

Blind Heart, The *26–27*, 520

Blind Law *40–41*, 432

Blind Men, The *63–64*, 352

Blind Mice *30–31*, 432

Blind Monster, The *44–45*, 368

Blind Youth *09–19*, 616

Blindness of Virtue, The *09–19*, 481

Blithe Spirit *41–42*, 410; *43–44*, 410; *45–46*, 450; *51–52*, 333; *63–64*, 333

Blitzstein! *66–67*, 408

Block, The *70–71*

Blonde in Black, The *99–09*, 434

Blonde Sinner, The *26–27*, 361

Blood *70–71*s

Blood and Sand *21–22*, 422

Blood Bugle, The *61–62*, 304

Blood Knot, The *63–64*, 359

Blood Money *27–28*, 394

Blood Red Roses *69–70*, 319s

Blood, Sweat and Stanley Poole *61–62*, 258

Blood Wedding *48–49*, 427; *57–58*, 53

Bloodstream *31–32*, 498

Bloody Laughter *31–32*, 443

Bloomer Girl *44–45*, 387; *46–47*, 411; *49–50*, 384

Blossom Time *21–22*, 427; *23–24*, 438; *25–26*, 564; *30–31*, 500; *38–39*, 438; *43–44*, 410

Blot in the 'Scutcheon, A *99–09*, 488

Blow Ye Winds *37–38*, 370

Bludgeon, The *09–19*, 530

Blue Angel, The *65–66*, 404

Blue Bandanna, The *24–25*, 427

Blue Bird, The (1) *09–19*, 426, 451; *23–24*, 376

Blue Bird, The (2) (1924) *24–25*, 516

Blue Bird, The (2) (1932) *31–32*, 507

Blue Bonnet *20–21*, 373

Blue Boy in Black, The *62–63*, 335

Blue Denim *57–58*, 321

Blue Envelope, The *09–19*, 572

Blue Eyes *20–21*, 428

Blue Flame, The *19–20*, 437

Blue Ghost, The *29–30,* 509
Blue Grass *99–09,* 572
Blue Holiday *44–45,* 431
Blue Jeans *94–99,* 116
Blue Kitten, The *21–22,* 494
Blue Lagoon, The *21–22,* 418
Blue Monday *31–32,* 519
Blue Moon, The *99–09,* 524
Blue Mouse, The *99–09,* 573; *19–20,* 382
Blue Paradise, The *09–19,* 554
Blue Pearl, The *09–19,* 632
Blue Peter, The *24–25,* 561
Blue Pierrots, The *09–19,* 568
Blue Widow, The *33–34,* 428
Bluebeard (1) (see *Mr. Bluebeard*)
Bluebeard (2) *70–71*
Bluebeard's Eighth Wife *21–22,* 421; *35–36,* 511
Blueprints: Projections and Perspectives *68–69,* 407
Blues, Ballads and Sin-Songs *(see Libby Holman's "Blues, Ballads and Sin-Songs")*
Blues for Mister Charlie *63–64,* 335
Bluffing Bluffers *24–25,* 507
Bluffs *99–09,* 560
Blushing Bride, The *21–22,* 506
Bob and Ray the Two and Only *70–71*
Bobby Burnit *09–19,* 422
Boccaccio *99–09,* 479
Boccaccio's Untold Tale *22–23,* 570
Bodies in Our Cellar *(Arsenic and Old Lace)* *40–41,* 165
Body Beautiful, The (1) *35–36,* 429
Body Beautiful, The (2) *57–58,* 311s
Boeing-Boeing *64–65,* 323
Boesman and Lena *70–71*
Boheme, La (*The Bohemian Girl;* opera rep) *09–19,* 638; *33–34,* 423; *34–35,* 360; *43–44,* 441, 474; *44–45,* 377; *45–46,* 388, 441, 457; *46–47,* 409, 480, 493; *47–48,* 343, 347, 399
Bohemia *94–99,* 167
Bohikee Creek *65–66,* 434

Bold Sojer Boy, The *99–09,* 428
Bolero (dance program) *47–48,* 416
Bombo *21–22,* 437
Bon Garcon, Un *28–29,* 373
Bond, The *67–68,* 413
Bond Between, The *38–39,* 488
Bonds of Interest, (The) *09–19,* 655; *29–30,* 417
Bondsman, The *94–99,* 125
Bonehead, The *19–20,* 445
Bonheur, Le *23–24,* 333
Bonheur, Mesdames, Le *99–09,* 522
Bonnie Briar Bush, The *99–09,* 396
Bonnie Scotland *94–99,* 158
Book, The *64–65,* 322
Book of Adventures *99–09,* 556
Book of Charm, The *25–26,* 435; *29–30,* 455
Book of Job, The (1) *09–19,* 650
Book of Job, The (2) *61–62,* 322
Boom *38–39,* 488
Boom Boom *28–29,* 463
Boom-Boom Clopper *39–40,* 469
Boomerang, The *09–19,* 554
Booster, The *29–30,* 429
Bootleggers, The *22–23,* 493
Borak *60–61,* 353
Border-Land *31–32,* 497
Borderline *36–37,* 500
Borderside *99–09,* 367
Born Yesterday *45–46,* 425
Borned in Texas *50–51,* 313
Borrowed Love *29–30,* 376
Borscht Capades *51–52,* 282
Borstal Boy *69–70,* 324
Boshibari (see *Tied to a Stick*)
Bosom Friends *09–19,* 598
Boss, The *09–19,* 437
Both Your Houses *32–33,* 472, 473
Bottled *27–28,* 539
Bottom of the Cup, The *26–27,* 470
Bottomland *27–28,* 386
Boubouroche *21–22,* 468
Boudoir *40–41,* 415
Bouffons, Les (see *The Jesters 1*)
Bough Breaks, The *37–38,* 393

Bought and Paid For *09–19*, 452; *21–22*, 475

Boule de Suif *29–30*, 421

Bound East for Cardiff *24–25*, 480; *37–38*, 451, 452; *47–48*, 349; *51–52*, 333

Bound for Mexico *41–42*, 459

Bound to Happen *38–39*, 486

Boundary Line, The *29–30*, 488

Bourgeois Gentleman, The (*The Would-Be Gentleman, Le Bourgeois Gentilhomme;* p) *24–25*, 483; *28–29*, 383; *29–30*, 393, 403; *44–45*, 436, 437; *45–46*, 420; *49–50*, 383; *55–56*, 356; *63–64*, 327

Bourgeois Gentleman, The (*The Would-Be Gentleman, Le Bourgeois Gentilhomme;* m) *45–46*, 420; *69–70*, 313

Bowery Girl, A *94–99*, 155

Box *68–69*, 379

Box of Watercolors, A *56–57*, 58

Box Seats *27–28*, 543

Box-Mao-Box *68–69*, 380

Boy and the Girl, The *99–09*, 583

Boy David, The *40–41*, 431

Boy Friend, The (1) *31–32*, 521

Boy Friend, The (2) *54–55*, 363s; *57–58*, 53; *65–66*, 436; *69–70*, 326

Boy Growing Up, A *57–58*, 289

Boy Meets Girl *35–36*, 442; *43–44*, 401

Boy on the Straight-Back Chair *68–69*, 430

Boy Tramp, The *94–99*, 122

Boy Wanted, A *94–99*, 192

Boy Who Lived Twice, A *45–46*, 382

Boyd's Daughter *40–41*, 384

Boys and Betty, The *99–09*, 571

Boys and Girls Together *40–41*, 382

Boys From Syracuse, The *38–39*, 429; *62–63*, 331s

Boys in the Band, The *67–68*, 404

Boys of Company "B", The *99–09*, 538

Boys of Kilkenny, The *94–99*, 197

Boys Will Be Boys *19–20*, 370

Brace of Partridges, A *94–99*, 237

Bracelet, The *24–25*, 588

Brain Sweat (Mississippi Rainbow) *33–34*, 513; *37–38*, 460

Brains *25–26*, 590

Braisley Diamond, The *99–09*, 507

Brand *09–19*, 415; *70–71*

Branded *09–19*, 607

Brass Ankle *30–31*, 520

Brass Bottle, The *09–19*, 421

Brass Butterfly, The *69–70*, 372

Brass Buttons *27–28*, 464

Brass Doorknob, The *25–26*, 594

Brass Ring, The *51–52*, 317

Brat, The *09–19*, 596

Brave and the Blind, The *36–37*, 497; *37–38*, 464

Bravo! *48–49*, 393

Bravo Giovanni *61–62*, 299s

Brazilian folklore (untitled source) *46–47*, 488

Breadwinner, The *31–32*, 395

Breakfast at Tiffany's *66–67*, 395s

Breakfast in Bed *19–20*, 424

Breaking Point, The *23–24*, 302

Breaking Wall, The *59–60*, 41

Breaks, The *27–28*, 541

Breasts of Tiresias, The *67–68*, 411

Brecht on Brecht: His Life and Art *61–62*, 317, 331; *63–64*, 344

Brewster's Millions *99–09*, 530

Brian Boru *94–99*, 181

Brickdust Man, The *37–38*, 412

Bridal Crown, The *37–38*, 422

Bridal Night, The *66–67*, 407

Bridal Path, The *09–19*, 495

Bridal Quilt *34–35*, 391

Bridal Wise *31–32*, 517

Bride, The (1) *09–19*, 509

Bride, The (2) *23–24*, 426

Bride Comes to Yellow, Sky, The *70–71*

Bride Elect, The *94–99*, 227

Bride of the Lamb *25–26*, 577

Bride of Torozko, The *34–35*, 371

Bride Retires, The *24–25,* 594

Bride the Sun Shines On, The
  31–32, 452

Bridge, The (1) *09–19,* 399

Bridge, The (2) *29–30,* 533

Bridge of Distances *25–26,* 458

Bridge to the Sun *43–44,* 488

Bridges *20–21,* 431

Brief Lives *67–68,* 357

Brief Moment *31–32,* 426

Brig, The *62–63,* 337; *63–64,* 353

Brigadier Gerard *99–09,* 525

Brigadoon *46–47,* 471; *49–50,* 379;
  56–57, 363; *61–62,* 301s; *62–63,*
  296; *64–65,* 321; *67–68,* 356

Bright Boy *43–44,* 461

Bright Eyes *09–19,* 415

Bright Honor *36–37,* 409

Bright Lights of 1944 *43–44,* 414

Bright Rebel *38–39,* 439

Bright Star *35–36,* 420

Brighten the Corner *45–46,* 412

Brighter Side, The *99–09,* 384

Brightower *69–70,* 312

Bring Me a Warm Body *61–62,* 329

Bringing up Father *24–25,* 564

Bringers of Offerings, The (see *The
  Choephori*)

Britannicus *60–61,* 326

British songs (unnamed) *60–61,* 42

Brittle Heaven *34–35,* 411

Brixton Burglary, The *99–09,* 392

Broadway *26–27,* 381; *50–51,* 373

Broadway and Buttermilk *09–19,*
  577

Broadway Boy *31–32,* 509

Broadway Brevities 1920 *20–21,* 388

Broadway Chapel Players (unnamed
  productions) *55–56,* 59

Broadway Interlude *33–34,* 518

Broadway Jones *09–19,* 477; *28–29,*
  385

Broadway Nights *29–30,* 379

Broadway Shadows *29–30,* 518

Broadway Sho-Window *35–36,* 500

Broadway to Paris *09–19,* 485

Broadway to Tokio *99–09,* 360

Broadway Whirl, The *20–21,* 453

Broken Branches *21–22,* 521

Broken Chain, The *28–29,* 471

Broken Dishes *29–30,* 436

Broken Hearts of Broadway *43–44,*
  490

Broken Idol, A *09–19,* 396

Broken Journey *42–43,* 419

Broken Jug, The *57–58,* 326

Broken Melody, The *94–99,* 183

Broken Threads *09–19,* 611

Broken to Harness *94–99,* 103

Broken Wing, The *20–21,* 409

Broken Wings *(Con las Alas Rotas)*
  27–28, 467

Brontes, The *63–64,* 353, 367

Bronx Express, The *21–22,* 538

Brooding Angel, The *59–60,* 40

Brook *23–24,* 306

Brooklyn Biarritz *40–41,* 418

Brooklyn, U.S.A. *41–42,* 420

Broomsticks, Amen! *33–34,* 493

Brother Cain *41–42,* 395

Brother Elks *25–26,* 444

Brother for Brother *94–99,* 187

Brother Jacques *99–09,* 475

Brother John *94–99,* 111

Brother Nothings *60–61,* 294

Brother Officers *99–09,* 359

Brother Rat *36–37,* 441

Brotherhood *69–70,* 352

Brothers *28–29,* 442

Brothers Ashkenazi, The *37–38,* 470

Brothers Karamazov(ff), The
  (source) *22–23,* 517; *23–24,* 356;
  26–27, 453

Brothers Karamazov, The (1) *23–24,*
  356

Brothers Karamazov, The (2) *26–27,*
  453

Brothers Karamazov, The (3; undesignated adaptation) *57–58,*
  53

Brouhaha *59–60,* 40

Brown Buddies *30–31,* 427

Brown Danube *38–39,* 473

Brown of Harvard *99–09,* 510

Brown Sugar *37–38*, 397
Brownies, The *94–99*, 103
Browning Version, The *49–50*, 357;
  60–61, 48
Brownings in the Foot on the Stairs,
  The *64–65*, 361
Brown's in Town *94–99*, 253
Brownstone Urge, The *69–70*, 351
Bruno and Sidney *48–49*, 427
Brute, The *09–19*, 480
Bubble, The *09–19*, 550
Bublitchki *37–38*, 470
Buccaneer, The *25–26*, 459
Buck White *69–70*, 307s
Buckaroo *28–29*, 480
Buddies *19–20*, 379
Buddy Hackett at the Palace (see
  *Eddie Fisher-Buddy Hackett at the
  Palace*)
Budget, The *32–33*, 389
Bufano Marionettes (see *Remo
  Bufano Marionettes*)
Buffalo Skinner, The *58–59*, 50
Buffoon *23–24*, 336
Bugle Call, The *99–09*, 365
Bugs (1) *60–61*, 294
Bugs (2) *65–66*, 426
Builder of Bridges, A *40–41*, 432
Builder of Bridges, The *09–19*, 403
Builders, The *99–09*, 540
Building Fund, The *09–19*, 458
Building 222 *49–50*, 384
Bulldog Drummond *21–22*, 486
Bullfight *53–54*, 358
Bulls, Bears and Asses *31–32*, 510
Bully, The *24–25*, 513
Bumble Bee Prince, The *37–38*, 468
Bunch and Judy, The *22–23*, 495
Bunch of Violets, A *94–99*, 120,
  121
Bundle of Lies, A *94–99*, 128
Bunk of 1926 *25–26*, 555
Bunny *09–19*, 568
Bunraku (mn) *65–66*, 403
Bunty, Bulls and Strings *09–19*, 465
Bunty Pulls the Strings *09–19*, 453
Buoyant Billions *59–60*, 43

Burbero Benefico, II (see *The
  Beneficent Bear*)
Burger Schippel *66–67*, 412
Burglar, The *94–99*, 212
Burgomaster, The *99–09*, 383
Burgomaster of Belgium, A *09–19*,
  653
Burgomaster of Stilemonde *23–24*,
  343
Burial Committee, The *65–66*, 437
Burial of Esposito, The *69–70*, 349
Buried Alive *67–68*, 360
Burlesca *43–44*, 485
Burlesque *27–28*, 396; *46–47*, 448
Burmah *94–99*, 164
Burmese Pwe, A *25–26*, 569
Burn Me to Ashes! *63–64*, 352
Burning, The *63–64*, 353
Burning Bright (source) *50–51*, 321
Burning Bright *50–51*, 320; *51–52*,
  333
Burning Bush, The *49–50*, 384
Burning Deck, The *39–40*, 440
Burning Glass, The *53–54*, 342
Burr Oaks *94–99*, 230
Bursting the Barriers *29–30*, 533
Bury the Dead *35–36*, 502, 510;
  49–50, 384; *70–71*
Bus Stop *54–55*, 402
Bushido *09–19*, 579
Business Before Pleasure *09–19*, 603
Business Is Business (see also *Affaires
  Sont Affaires*) *99–09*, 466
Business of Good Government, The
  70–71
Business Widow, The *23–24*, 369
Buskers, The *61–62*, 312
Buster Brown *99–09*, 483
Busybody, The *24–25*, 461
But for the Grace of God *36–37*,
  453
But for Whom Charlie *63–64*, 321
But Not for Love *34–35*, 414
—But Not Goodbye *43–44*, 467
But, Seriously . . . *68–69*, 408
Butter and Egg Man, The *25–26*,
  453; *66–67*, 403

Butterflies Are Free *69–70,* 301
Butterfly, The *62–63,* 322
Butterfly Dream, The *65–66,* 435;
    70–71
Butterfly on the Wheel, A *09–19,*
    463
Button, Button (1) *29–30,* 428
Button, Button (2) *70–71*
Button Your Lip *42–43,* 477; *43–44,*
    404
Buttrio Square *52–53,* 259
Buy, Buy, Baby *26–27,* 397
Buy Me Blue Ribbons *51–52,* 287
Buzzard, The *27–28,* 528
Buzzin' Around *20–21,* 356
By George *67–68,* 344
By Jupiter *41–42,* 455; *64–65,* 362;
    66–67, 410s
By Pigeon Post *09–19,* 645
By Request *28–29,* 382
By the Beautiful Sea *53–54,* 349s
By the Sad Sea Waves *94–99,* 253
By the Way *25–26,* 526
By Your Leave *33–34,* 485
Bye, Bye, Barbara *24–25,* 437
Bye Bye Birdie *59–60,* 331s
Bye Bye, Bonnie *26–27,* 460
By'm By *60–61,* 295

C.O.D. *09–19,* 484
Cabalgata *49–50,* 354
Cabaret *66–67,* 370s
Cabin in the Sky *40–41,* 388; *63–64,*
    357s
Cactus Flower *65–66,* 390
Cadet Girl, The *90–09,* 368
Caesar and Cleopatra *99–09,* 524;
    09–19, 509; *24–25,* 570; *49–50,*
    364; *51–52,* 298; *62–63,* 327;
    68–69, 386
Caesar's Wife *19–20,* 388
Cafe *30–31,* 405
Cafe Crown (p) *41–42,* 434
Cafe Crown (m) *63–64,* 334s
Cafe de Danse *28–29,* 458
Cafe Univers *66–67,* 423
Cage, The (1) *60–61,* 39

Cage, The (2) *70–71*
Cage, The (3) *70–71*
Cages *63–64,* 343
Cain *24–25,* 568
Caine Mutiny, The (source) *53–54,*
    338
Caine Mutiny Court-Martial, The
    53–54, 338; *69–70,* 374
Cajun, The *25–26,* 592
Calculated Risk *62–63,* 284
Caleb Stone's Death Watch *23–24,*
    429
Caleb West *99–09,* 370
Caliban of the Yellow Sands *09–19,*
    575
Calico Wedding *44–45,* 419
Caligula *59–60,* 319
Caliph, The *94–99,* 176
Call It a Day *35–36,* 465
Call It Virtue *62–63,* 329
Call Me By My Rightful Name
    60–61, 357
Call Me Madam *50–51,* 319s
Call Me Mister *45–46,* 438
Call Me Ziggy *36–37,* 464
Call of Life, The *25–26,* 469
Call of the Cricket, The *09–19,* 418
Call of the North, The *99–09,* 565
Call on Kuprin, A *60–61,* 342
Call the Doctor *20–21,* 375
Calling All Stars *34–35,* 424
Calling in Crazy *69–70,* 341
Camel Through the Needle's Eye
    28–29, 493
Camel's Back, The *23–24,* 353
Cambridge Circus *64–65,* 305, 346
Camelot *60–61,* 310s
Camelot, Le *94–99,* 256
Camels Are Coming, The *31–32,*
    401
Cameo Kirby *09–19,* 406
Camera Obscura *67–68,* 407
Camille *(La Dame aux Camelias)*
    94–99, 100, 143, 144, 146, 147,
    148, 156, 163, 166, 226, 234, 249;
    99–09, 380, 459, 472, 557; *09–19,*
    432, 444, 446, 589 (and 605), 618;

Camille *(cont.)*
  26–27, 434; *30–31*, 482; *32–33*,
  414; *35–36*, 446; *37–38*, 470;
  47–48, 418, 430; *56–57*, 55; *62–63*,
  303
Camille *(La Dame aux Camelias;*
  novel) *62–63*, 303
Camino Real *52–53*, 295; *59–60*, 42;
  69–70, 303
Can You Make Baby Poems? *60–61*,
  294
Canaries Sometimes Sing *30–31*, 434
Canary, The *09–19*, 643
Canary Cottage *09–19*, 594
Canary Dutch *25–26*, 437
Can-Can *52–53*, 303s; *61–62*, 300
Cancion de Cuna *31–32*, 500
Cancionera *25–26*, 599
Candaules, Commissioner *69–70*,
  371, 372
Candida *99–09*, 447, 467, 495, 547;
  09–19, 553; *21–22*, 530; *24–25*,
  504; *25–26*, 493; *31–32*, 501;
  36–37, 470; *37–38*, 463; *41–42*,
  448; *45–46*, 437; *51–52*, 319, 333;
  55–56, 58; *63–64*, 367; *68–69*, 457;
  69–70, 324
Candidates, The *69–70*, 371
Candide (source) *32–33*, 496; *56–57*,
  340; *70–71*
Candide (1) *32–33*, 496
Candide (2) *56–57*, 340s; *65–66*, 418
Candide (3) *70–71*
Candle in the Wind *41–42*, 405
Candle Light *29–30*, 408; *45–46*, 450
Candy Shop, The *99–09*, 582
Candy Store *48–49*, 426
Candyapple, The *70–71*
Cannibals, The *68–69*, 430
Canterbury Tales *68–69*, 404s
Canterbury Tales, The (source)
  68–69, 404, 444
Cantilevered Terrace, The *61–62*,
  320
Cantor's Melody, The *47–48*, 431
Cantor's Wife, The *47–48*, 432
Cape Cod Folks *99–09*, 522

Cape Cod Follies *29–30*, 398
Cape Smoke *24–25*, 541
Capitan, El *94–99*, 172
Capitol, The *94–99*, 142
Caponsacchi *26–27*, 413; *28–29*,
  421; *29–30*, 437
Cappy Ricks *09–19*, 649
Capriccio Brilliante *51–52*, 330
Caprice *28–29*, 446
Caprice, Un *24–25*, 474; *37–38*, 469;
  55–56, 358
Captain Applejack *21–22*, 487
Captain Barrington *99–09*, 445
Captain Brassbound's Conversion
  99–09, 532; *09–19*, 560; *50–51*,
  338
Captain Dieppe *99–09*, 436
Captain Fantastic Meets the
  Ectomorph *65–66*, 437
Captain Impudence *94–99*, 190
Captain Jack's Revenge *69–70*, 375
Captain Jinks *25–26*, 438
Captain Jinks of the Horse Marines
  99–09, 387; *33–34*, 457; *37–38*,
  453, 454; *48–49*, 425
Captain Kidd, Jr. *09–19*, 587
Captain Lettarblair *94–99*, 131
Captain Molly *99–09*, 415
Captain of Koepenick, The *64–65*,
  317
Captain of the Nonsuch, The *94–99*,
  207
Captain Paul *94–99*, 133
Captain Swift *94–99*, 120, 121, 234
Captains and the Kings, The *61–62*,
  278
Captain's Mate, The *94–99*, 97
Captive, The *26–27*, 390
Caravan *28–29*, 366
Cardinal, The *(El Cardenal)* *99–09*,
  384; *35–36*, 511; *53–54*, 322
Cardinal's Edict, The *99–09*, 485
Career (1) *43–44*, 488
Career (2) *56–57*, 58
Career Angel *43–44*, 479, 480
Carefree Tree, The *55–56*, 353
Careless Love *60–61*, 294

Caretaker, The *61–62*, 258; *63–64*, 358

Carib Song *45–46*, 386

Caribbean Carnival *47–48*, 367

Carmen (source) *94–99*, 156; *99–09*, 503, 557; *43–44*, 432; *44–45*, 382; *45–46*, 394; *55–56*, 393

Carmen (opera rep) *09–19*, 638; *32–33*, 443; *43–44*, 439, 472, 474; *44–45*, 443; *45–46*, 389, 440; *46–47*, 409, 479; *47–48*, 343, 347, 399; *49–50*, 385

Carmen (p) *94–99*, 156; *99–09*, 503, 557

Carmen Jones *43–44*, 432; *44–45*, 382; *45–46*, 394; *55–56*, 393s

Carmencita and the Soldier *25–26*, 514–5

Carmencita Maracci (dance programs) *45–46*, 455–6

Carmilla *70–71*

Carnival (1) *19–20*, 406

Carnival (2) *24–25*, 514

Carnival (3) *27–28*, 548

Carnival (4) *28–29*, 497

Carnival! (5) *60–61*, 336s; *68–69*, 397

Carnival in Flanders *53–54*, 301s

Caroline (1) *09–19*, 582

Caroline (2) *22–23*, 526

Carolinian, The *25–26*, 486

Carousel *44–45*, 428; *48–49*, 409; *54–55*, 359; *57–58*, 285; *59–60*, 43; *65–66*, 368; *66–67*, 378s

Carpenters, The *70–71*

Carpetbagger, The *99–09*, 363

Carricknabauna *66–67*, 416s

Carrots *99–09*, 418

Carry Me Back to Morningside Heights *67–68*, 364

Carry Nation *32–33*, 412

Carry On *27–28*, 496

Carving a Statue *67–68*, 406

Casanova *23–24*, 322

Cascando *70–71*

Case History *38–39*, 420

Case of Arson, A *99–09*, 506

Case of Becky, The *09–19*, 479

Case of Clyde Griffiths *35–36*, 494

Case of Frenzied Finance, A *99–09*, 488

Case of Lady Camber, The *09–19*, 597

Case of Libel, A *63–64*, 308

Case of Philip Lawrence, The *36–37*, 494

Case of Rebellious Susan, The *94–99*, 113; *99–09*, 481

Case of Youth, A *39–40*, 446

Casey Jones *37–38*, 426

Cashel Byron (1) *99–09*, 382

Cashel Byron (2) *99–09*, 383

Casino Girl, The *99–09*, 364

Caspar's Circus (mn) *38–39*, 490

Caste (1) *94–99*, 160; *09–19*, 418

Caste (2) *27–28*, 473

Castle, The *(Das Schloss)* *68–69*, 433

Castle Sombras *94–99*, 93

Castles in the Air *26–27*, 374

Castro Complex, The *70–71*

Cat and the Canary, The *21–22*, 507; *36–37*, 487; *64–65*, 352

Cat and the Cherub, The *94–99*, 208; *09–19*, 535

Cat and the Fiddle, The *31–32*, 411s

Cat on a Hot Tin Roof *54–55*, 402

Cat Screams, The *42–43*, 418

Cat That Hated Christmas, The *50–51*, 374

Cat-Bird, The *19–20*, 427

Catch a Star! *55–56*, 338s

Catch Me if You Can *64–65*, 329

Catch of the Season, The *99–09*, 492

Catherine (1) *94–99*, 180

Catherine (2) *94–99*, 243

Catherine Goulden *23–24*, 333

Catherine Was Great *44–45*, 367

Cats' Pajamas, The *61–62*, 331s

Catskill Dutch *23–24*, 433

Caucasian Chalk Circle, The *65–66*, 378

Caudal de los Hijos, El *25–26*, 599; *27–28*, 540

Caught *25–26*, 462
Caught in the Rain *99–09*, 530;
  20–21, 388
Caught Wet *31–32*, 423
Caukey *43–44*, 458
Cause Celebre, Une *94–99*, 149, 234
Cause of It All, The *42–43*, 489
Cavalier, The *99–09*, 424
Cavalier of France, A *94–99*, 226
Cavalleria Rusticana (p) *94–99*, 166
Cavalleria Rusticana (opera rep)
  43–44, 441, 474; *44–45*, 377, 443;
  45–46, 387, 441; *46–47*, 409, 480;
  47–48, 343, 347, 399
Cave at Machpelah, The *59–60*, 41
Cave Dwellers, The *57–58*, 295;
  58–59, 53; *61–62*, 309
Cave Girl, The *20–21*, 369
Cave Man, The *09–19*, 456
Cave of Salamanca, The *36–37*, 497
Cavern, The *67–68*, 409; *68–69*, 455
Caviar *33–34*, 532
Cayenne Pepper *61–62*, 332
Cecilia Loftus *37–38*, 466; *38–39*,
  488
Ceiling Zero *34–35*, 469
Celebrate Me *70–71*
Celebrated Case, A *94–99*, 149, 234;
  09–19, 550
Celebration (1) *47–48*, 397
Celebration (2) *68–69*, 402s
Celebration, The *67–68*, 413
Celebrity *27–28*, 476
Celestina, La *66–67*, 36
Cellar and the Well, The *50–51*, 332
Cena Delle Beffe, La *09–19*, 655;
  19–20, 353
Cenci, The *46–47*, 485; *70–71*
Cendres D'Opium *09–19*, 589 (and
  605)
Censor and the Dramatists, The
  09–19, 504
Censored *37–38*, 427
Centuries *27–28*, 461
Century Girl, The *09–19*, 586
Century Revue, The *20–21*, 359
'Ception Shoals *09–19*, 592

Ceremonies in Dark Old Men
  68–69, 440, 451
Ceremony of Innocence, The *67–68*,
  391
Certain Party, A *09–19*, 444
Certain Young Man, A *67–68*, 396
Cesar *54–55*, 373
Cesarine *94–99*, 169
Chad Mitchell's Counterpoint *68–69*,
  436
Chain of Destiny *94–99*, 247
Chains (1) *09–19*, 488
Chains (2) *23–24*, 319
Chains (3) *36–37*, 497
Chains of Dew *21–22*, 540
Chair, The *54–55*, 53
Chair Endowed *54–55*, 56
Chairs, The *(Les Chaises)* *57–58*,
  308; *58–59*, 51; *69–70*, 363
Chalk Dust *35–36*, 470
Chalk Garden, The *55–56*, 358
Chalked Out *36–37*, 473
Challenge, The *19–20*, 343
Challenge of Youth, The *29–30*, 482
Chamberlain Brown stock company
  (unnamed programs) *35–36*, 511
Chamberlain Brown's Scrap Book
  32–33, 380
Chameleon *48–49*, 427
Chameleon, The *32–33*, 379
Champagne Complex *54–55*, 404
Champagne, Sec *33–34*, 441
Champion, The *20–21*, 417
Chance du Mari, La *09–19*, 589
  (and 605)
Change *09–19*, 521
Change Alley *94–99*, 206
Change Your Luck *29–30*, 549
Changeling, The *64–65*, 309
Changelings, The *23–24*, 317
Channel Road, The *29–30*, 421
Chantecler *09–19*, 437
Chaparral *58–59*, 50
Chapeau de Paille D'Italie, Le
  64–65, 342
Chaperon, The *99–09*, 575
Chaperons, The *99–09*, 412

Character Intrudes, A *34–35*, 483
Characters and Caricatures *36–37*, 498
Charity Girl, The *09–19*, 479
Charlatan, The (1) *94–99*, 237
Charlatan, The (2) *21–22*, 537
Charlatans *61–62*, 329
Charles I *94–99*, 151; *99–09*, 353, 521
Charles Aznavour *65–66*, 377s; *69–70*, 314s
Charles Laughton *51–52*, 333
Charles Weidman (dance programs; see also *Doris Humphrey & Charles Weidman*) *47–48*, 416, 417
Charley's Aunt *94–99*, 86; *99–09*, 511; *24–25*, 600; *40–41*, 386; *48–49*, 388; *50–51*, 346; *53–54*, 311; *61–62*, 333; *65–66*, 408; *70–71*
(Andre) Charlot's Revue of 1924 *23–24*, 384
Charlot('s) Revue, 1926 *25–26*, 494
Charlotte Corday *94–99*, 124
Charm *20–30*, 455
Charm of Isabel, The *09–19*, 527
Charm School, The *20–21*, 362; *25–26*, 424
Charming Rascal *32–33*, 377
Chas. Abbott & Son *70–71*
Chase, The *51–52*, 318
Chasseur de Chez Maxim's, Le *21–22*, 494
Chastening, The *22–23*, 531
Chattanooga *94–99*, 250
Chauve-Souris (1922) *21–22*, 504
Chauve-Souris (1925) *24–25*, 526
Chauve-Souris (1927) *27–28*, 426
Chauve-Souris (1929) *28–29*, 460
(New) Chauve-Souris (1931) *31–32*, 413
Chauve-Souris 1943 *43–44*, 407
Chaver Nachman *39–40*, 474
Che! *68–69*, 456
Che Guevara *70–71*
Cheaper to Marry *23–24*, 419
Cheapside *37–38*, 464

Cheat, The *09–19*, 640
Cheater, The *09–19*, 421
Cheating Cheaters *09–19*, 577
Checkerboard, The *20–21*, 369
Checkers *99–09*, 437, 438; *19–20*, 448
Chee-Chee *28–29*, 381
Cheer Up (1) *09–19*, 490
Cheer Up (2) *09–19*, 604
Chekhov Carnival, A *45–46*, 450
Chekhov Sketchbook, A *61–62*, 323
Chemineau, Le *99–09*, 468
Cheri *59–60*, 295
Cherokee Night *36–37*, 495
Cherry Blossoms *26–27*, 499
Cherry Orchard, The *22–23*, 517; *23–24*, 356; *27–28*, 521; *28–29*, 396; *29–30*, 402; *32–33*, 474; *43–44*, 450; *44–45*, 380; *45–46*, 451; *49–50*, 376; *54–55*, 396; *59–60*, 50; *62–63*, 319; *64–65*, 323; *67–68*, 353; *69–70*, 329; *70–71*
Cherry Pickers, The *94–99*, 180
Chevalier au Masque, Le *19–20*, 409
Chiaroscuro *63–64*, 342
Chicago (1) *26–27*, 452; *51–52*, 334
Chicago (2) *65–66*, 433
Chicago 70 *69–70*, 369
Chicken Every Sunday *43–44*, 465
Chicken Feed *23–24*, 321
Chief, The *09–19*, 565
Chief Thing, The *25–26*, 573; *62–63*, 335
Chieftain, The *94–99*, 142
Chien du Jardinier, Le (see *The Gardener's Dog*)
Chiffon Girl, The *23–24*, 402
Child and the Dragon, The *66–67*, 400
Child Buyer, The *64–65*, 350
Child of Fortune *56–57*, 334
Child of Manhattan *31–32*, 486
Child of Nature, A *99–09*, 560
Childhood *61–62*, 318
Children *09–19*, 560
Children Come Home *47–48*, 431

Children From Their Games *62–63*, 304

Children in the Rain *70–71*

Children of Darkness *29–30*, 475; *57–58*, 52, 53

Children of Destiny *09–19*, 414

Children of Earth *09–19*, 544

Children of Kings, The *99–09*, 421

Children of the Ghetto *99–09*, 351

Children of the Moon *23–24*, 303

Children of the Shadows *63–64*, 322

Children of the Sun, The *99–09*, 560

Children of Today *09–19*, 515

Children Without a Home *46–47*, 497; *47–48*, 431

Children's Christmas Story *44–45*, 376

Children's Hour, The *34–35*, 412; *44–45*, 436; *52–53*, 279

Children's Repertory Ballet *38–39*, 490

Children's Tragedy, The *21–22*, 440

Child's Christmas in Wales, A *60–61*, 48

Child's Play *69–70*, 316

Chili Widow, The *94–99*, 185

Chimes of Normandy, The *31–32*, 421

Chimmie Fadden *94–99*, 162

China Doll, A *99–09*, 473

China Rose *24–25*, 527

Chin-Chin *09–19*, 535

Chinese (and Dr. Fish), The *69–70*, 318

Chinese Honeymoon, A *99–09*, 412

Chinese legends, anecdotes, etc. (untitled sources) *55–56*, 353; *62–63*, 318

Chinese Love *20–21*, 432

Chinese Nightingale, The *34–35*, 387

Chinese O'Neill *28–29*, 506

Chinese plays, stories, etc. (unnamed programs & sources) *44–45*, 444; *46–47*, 496; *50–51*, 373; *65–66*, 435

Chinese Prime Minister, The *63–64*, 318

Chip, The *59–60*, 40

Chip Woman's Fortune, The *22–23*, 567

Chippies *28–29*, 508

Chips With Everything *63–64*, 305

Chivalry *25–26*, 517

Chocolate Dandies, The *24–25*, 442

Chocolate Soldier, The *09–19*, 399; *21–22*, 476; *29–30*, 482; *31–32*, 394; *33–34*, 523; *42–43*, 419; *46–47*, 470

Chocolates *66–67*, 418

Choephori, The *(The Libation Pourers)* *61–62*, 255; *68–69*, 398, 399

Choice, The *29–30*, 537

Choir Rehearsal, The *20–21*, 431

Choir Singer, The *33–34*, 256

Chorus Lady, The *99–09*, 518

Chosen People, The *09–19*, 469

Chris and the Wonderful Lamp *99–09*, 358

Christian *36–37*, 499

Christian, The *94–99*, 242

Christian Pilgrim, The *99–09*, 550

Christine *59–60*, 339s

Christmas Carol, A *47–48*, 425

Christmas Eve *39–40*, 427

Christmas Rappings *69–70*, 375

Christmas songs *59–60*, 328; *61–62*, 315

Christmas Stories *52–53*, 301

Christmas Story, A *94–99*, 150

Christmas Turkey *67–68*, 409

Christophe Colombe *56–57*, 353

Christopher Blake *46–47*, 444

Christopher Columbus *63–64*, 352

Christopher Comes Across *31–32*, 518

Christopher, Jr. *94–99*, 145

Christy *63–64*, 369

Chronicles *62–63*, 295

Chronicles of King Henry VI, Part 1 *70–71*

Chronicles of King Henry VI, Part 2 *70–71*

Chrysalis *32–33*, 421

Chu Chin Chow *09–19,* 610

Chuck *67–68,* 406

Church Mouse, A *31–32,* 408;
32–33, 33–34, 421; *46–47,* 485

Church Street *34–35,* 409; *47–48,*
426

Chushingura (see *The Treasury of
Loyal Retainers*)

Cicero *60–61,* 46

Cid, Le *58–59,* 295; *65–66,* 397

Cigarette Maker's Romance, A
99–09, 422

Cinderelative *30–31,* 414

Cinderella (source) *46–47,* 446

Cinderella (mn) *34–35,* 484; *35–36,*
512; *36–37,* 498; *37–38,* 467;
38–39, 489

Cinderella Man, The *09–19,* 569

Cinderella on Broadway *20–21,*
356

Cinderella's Brother *32–33,* 498

Cinders *22–23,* 554

Cindy *63–64,* 361s

Cingalee, The *99–09,* 471

Cipher Code, The *99–09,* 396

Circle, The *21–22,* 416; *37–38,* 440;
46–47, 485

Circle of Chalk, The *40–41,* 432

Circus Events *99–09,* 527, 551

Circus Girl, The *94–99,* 201

Circus Princess, The *26–27,* 517

Cities in Bezique *68–69,* 434

Citizen Pierre *94–99,* 257

Citizen's Home, A *09–19,* 401

Citta Morta, La *99–09,* 421; *23–24,*
366

City, The *09–19,* 406

City Chap, The *25–26,* 483

City Haul *29–30,* 470

City Madam, The *49–50,* 384

City of Kings *48–49,* 426

City of Pleasure, The *94–99,* 140

Civilian Clothes *19–20,* 349

Claim, The *09–19,* 609

Clair de Lune *20–21,* 442

Claire Adams *29–30,* 445

Claire and the Forgemaster *94–99,*
212

Clandestine Marriage, The *54–55,*
52

Clandestine on the Morning Line
61–62, 311

Clansman, The *99–09,* 506

Clara's Ole Man *67–68,* 391; *69–70,*
371

Clarence *19–20,* 354

Clarice *99–09,* 522

Clarissa's Troublesome Baby *99–09,*
492

Clash by Night *41–42,* 423

Class of '29 *35–36,* 477

Classmates *99–09,* 543

Claudia *40–41,* 417; *45–46,* 457

Claudian *94–99,* 105

Claudia's Husband *94–99,* 248

Claudine *68–69,* 456

Claw, The (1) *21–22,* 442

Claw, The (2) *26–27,* 460

Claw, The (3) *26–27,* 460

Clean Beds *38–39,* 477

Clean Slate, A *99–09,* 444

Cleaning Solution, The *70–71*

Clear All Wires *32–33,* 386

Clearing House *70–71*

Clearing in the Woods, A *56–57,*
349; *58–59,* 52

Cleopatra (1) *94–99,* 222

Cleopatra (2) *25–26,* 515

Clerambard *57–58,* 53; *63–64,* 368

Clever Ones, The *09–19,* 545

Cliche, U.S.A. *63–64,* 369

Climax, The *99–09,* 581; *09–19,*
419, 650; *25–26,* 599; *32–33,* 502

Climate of Eden, The *52–53,* 268;
53–54, 359

Climbers, The *99–09,* 30, 386

Clinging Vine, The *22–23,* 507

Clinton Street *39–40,* 474

Clock, The *22–23,* 573

Clock on the Stairs *36–37,* 496

Clod, The *09–19,* 560

Close Harmony *24–25,* 496

Close Quarters *38–39,* 462

Close Shave, A *94–99,* 216

Closing Door, The *49–50,* 362

Clothes *99–09,* 519

Clothes Moth and the Luna Moth, The *59–60*, 323

Cloud 7 *57–58*, 318

Cloud Shadow *62–63*, 322

Clouds *25–26*, 434

Clouds, The *09–19*, 445

Cloudy With Showers *31–32*, 384

Club Bedroom, The *67–68*, 408

Clubs Are Trumps *24–25*, 472

Clutching Claw, The *27–28*, 509

Clutterbuck *49–50*, 362

Coach With the Six Insides, The *62–63, 320;* *66–67*, 420

Coastwise *31–32*, 441

Coat of Many Colors, A *94–99*, 208

Coats *09–19*, 494

Coat-tales *09–19*, 576

Cobra *23–24*, 423

Cock o' the Roost *24–25*, 472

Cock o' the Walk *09–19*, 567

Cock Robin *27–28*, 489

Cock-a-Doodle Dandy *58–59*, 52; *68–69*, 383

Cockeyed Kite *61–62*, 305

Cocktail Party, The *49–50*, 369; *68–69*, 383

Coco *69–70*, 309s

Cocoanuts, The *25–26*, 511

Coffee Lace, The *69–70*, 348

Coffin Room, The *44–45*, 368

Coggerers, The *38–39*, 451; *59–60*, 49

Cohan and Harris Minstrels *99–09*, 564; *09–19*, 396

Cohan Revue of 1916, The *09–19*, 570

Cohan Revue of 1918, The *09–19*, 619

Coiner, The *34–35*, 410

Col. Carter of Cartersville *94–99*, 191

Cold Feet *22–23*, 578

Cold in Sables *31–32*, 448

Cold Wind and the Warm, The *58–59*, 309

Colette *69–70*, 367; *70–71*

Colin and His Wife *37–38*, 412

Colinette *94–99*, 256

Collection, The *62–63*, 320

Collector's Item *51–52*, 309

Colleen Bawn, The *94–99*, 168

College Widow, The *99–09*, 466; *09–19*, 605

College Sinners *34–35*, 372

Colliere de la Reine, Le *94–99*, 141

Collision *31–32*, 478

Collision Course *67–68*, 406

Colombe (see also *Mademoiselle Colombe*) *64–65*, 355

Colonel de Basil's Original Ballet Russe (see *Ballet Russe*)

Colonel Newcome *09–19*, 599

Colonel Satan *30–31*, 477

Colonial Girl, A *94–99*, 244

Color of Darkness *63–64*, 346

Colorado *99–09*, 399

Columbyre *50–51*, 374

Come Across (1) *36–37*, 499

Come Across (2) *38–39*, 404

Come Along *09–19*, 655

Come Angel Band *35–36*, 484

Come Back Laughter *47–48*, 425

Come Back, Little Sheba *49–50*, 373; *65–66*, 436

Come Back on Tuesday *49–50*, 383

Come Blow Your Horn *60–61*, 326

Come Easy *33–34*, 428

Come Live With Me *66–67*, 381

Come Marching Home *45–46*, 401

Come of Age *33–34*, 479; *45–46*, 436; *51–52*, 307

Come on Strong *62–63*, 279

Come Out, Carlo! *61–62*, 330

Come Out of the Kitchen *09–19*, 585; *24–25*, 495

Come Seven *20–21*, 358

Come Share My House *59–60*, 41

Come Slowly, Eden *66–67*, 422

Come Summer *68–69*, 411s

Come to Bohemia *09–19*, 574

Come to the Palace of Sin *63–64*, 367

Come What May (1) *33–34*, 528

Come What May (2) *49–50*, 385

Comedian, The 22–23, 542

Comedienne, The 24–25, 476

Comedy and Tragedy 94–99, 159, 199

Comedy in Music 53–54, 308

Comedy in Music Opus 2 64–65, 311

Comedy of Errors, The 32–33, 424; 37–38, 469; 38–39, 429; 62–63, 331; 63–64, 337; 67–68, 93

Comedy of Good and Evil, A 37–38, 464; 48–49, 391

Comedy of Women, A 29–30, 392

Comforter, The 64–65, 363

Come-on Charlie 09–19, 654

Come-on Man, The 28–29, 495

Comes a Day 58–59, 302

Comes the Revelation 41–42, 453

Comet, The 99–09, 553

Comforts of Ignorance, The 09–19, 643

Comic, The 26–27, 513

Comic Artist, The 32–33, 486

Comic Strip 57–58, 56; 61–62, 329

Comin' Thro' the Rye 99–09, 507

Coming Forth by Day of Osiris Jones, The 60–61, 48

Coming of Mrs. Patrick, The 99–09, 550

Coming Woman, The 94–99, 103

Command Decision 47–48, 354

Command Performance 66–67, 400

Command Performance, The 28–29, 387

Command to Love, The 27–28, 409

Commander Macmillan 34–35, 484

Commanding Officer, The 09–19, 407

Commedia Dell' Arte 26–27, 504; 38–39, 487; 51–52, 333; 68–69, 407

Committee, The 64–65, 300

Commodore Marries, The 29–30, 387

Common Clay 09–19, 555

Common Ground 44–45, 430

Common Sense Bracket 99–09, 478

Common Sin, The 28–29, 397

Commune 70–71

Commuters, The 09–19, 421

Company 69–70, 328s

Company's Coming 30–31, 517

Complaisant Lover, The 61–62, 268

Complex, The 24–25, 552

Compulsion 57–58, 296

Comte Obligado 28–29, 476

Comtesse Coquette 99–09, 539

Con & Co. 09–19, 424

Con las Alas Rotas (see *Broken Wings*)

Concerning the Effects of Methyl-Chloride 70–71

Concert, The *(Das Konzert)* 09–19, 427; 67–68, 367

Concert Varieties 44–45, 435

Concerto for Fun 48–49, 428

Con-curers, The 94–99, 180

Condemned of Altona, The 65–66, 378

Condesa, Maria, La 25–26, 599

Conditioned Reflex 66–67, 422

Conduct Unbecoming 70–71

Conerico Was Here to Stay 63–64, 371; 64–65, 354; 68–69, 448

Coney Island Play 70–71

Confession 26–27, 522

Confession, The (1) 09–19, 441

Confession, The (2) 70–71

Confession of an Ignorant 67–68, 412

Confidential Clerk, The 53–54, 340

Conflict 28–29, 477

Conflict, The 99–09, 580

Confusion 94–99, 207, 234

Congai 28–29, 428

Congratulations 28–29, 499

Congressional petitions, speeches, etc. (untitled sources) 63–64, 350

Conjur Man Dies 35–36, 470

Conjuror's House 99–09, 565

Connecticut Yankee in (at) King Arthur's Court, A (source) 27–28, 445, 43–44, 428

Connecticut Yankee, A *27–28*, 445;
  43–44, 428s
Connecticut Yankee, A (mn) *35–36*,
  512
Connection, The *59–60*, 350; *60–61*,
  37; *61–62*, 305; *62–63*, 314
Connie Goes Home *23–24*, 313
Conquering Hero, The *60–61*, 318s
Conquerors, The *94–99*, 220
Conquest *32–33*, 464
Conquest of Granada, The *31–32*,
  501
Conquest of the Universe *67–68*,
  413
Conscience (1) *24–25*, 452
Conscience (2) *51–52*, 325
Consequences *09–19*, 533
Consider the Lilies *65–66*, 437
Conspiracy, The *09–19*, 488
Constant Nymph, The *26–27*, 438;
  46–47, 485
Constant Prince, The *69–70*, 343
Constant Sister, The *31–32*, 390,
  391
Constant Wife, The *26–27*, 433;
  51–52, 296
Consul, The (1) *99–09*, 426
Consul, The (2) *49–50*, 375; *65–66*,
  371; *66–67*, 361
Conte de Noel *94–99*, 150
Contented Woman, A *94–99*, 190;
  09–19, 641
Continental Varieties (1) *34–35*, 385
Continental Varieties (2) *35–36*, 454
Contrast, The *33–34*, 457
Contribution *68–69*, 440; *69–70*, 361
Contributions *69–70*, 361
Controleur des Wagon-Lits, Le
  94–99, 243
Conversation at Midnight *64–65*,
  313
Conversation Piece *34–35*, 396
Cook for Mr. General, A *61–62*,
  263
Cool World, The *59–60*, 320
Cooler Near the Lake *70–71*
Coon Hollow *94–99*, 84

Coop, The *65–66*, 431
Cop-Out *68–69*, 412
Copper and Brass *57–58*, 293s
Copperhead, The *09–19*, 623
Coquette *27–28*, 448; *45–46*, 450
Coquin de Printemps *99–09*, 522
Coralie and Company, Dressmakers
  99–09, 361
Cordelia Blossom *09–19*, 529
Co-respondent, The *09–19*, 573
Co-respondent Unknown *35–36*,
  481; *44–45*, 436
Coriolanus *37–38*, 453, 455; *53–54*,
  337; *65–66*, 95
Corn Is Green, The *40–41*, 396;
  42–43, 473; *49–50*, 367; *53–54*,
  358; *61–62*, 332
Cornelia Otis Skinner *31–32*, 432;
  32–33, 429; *33–34*, 471; *34–35*,
  467; *36–37*, 498; *37–38*, 400;
  51–52, 312
Corner Grocery, The *94–99*, 135
Corner of the Bed, A *68–69*, 446
Cornered *20–21*, 410
Coronet of the Duchess, The *99–09*,
  467
Corrins for Butterflies *70–71*
Corrupters, The *70–71*
Corruption in the Palace of Justice
  63–64, 347
Cortez *29–30*, 432
Cosi fan Tutte *68–69*, 436
Cosi Sia *23–24*, 366
Cosmo Vanities *32–33*, 392
Cosmonaute Agricole, Le *69–70*,
  363
Cossacks Beyond the Danube *36–37*,
  500
Cottage in the Air, The *09–19*, 404
Cotton King, The *94–99*, 108
Cotton Spinner, The *94–99*, 174
Counsellor-at-Law *31–32*, 424;
  32–33, 385; *42–43*, 445
Counsel's Opinion *32–33*, 436
Count Me In *42–43*, 434
Count of Luxembourg, The *09–19*,
  476; *29–30*, 496

Count of Monte Cristo, The (see *Monte Cristo*)

Count That Day Lost *70–71*

Counterattack *42–43*, 461

Countess Cathleen, The *99–09*, 488; *09–19*, 494; *69–70*, 378

Countess Chiffon, The *99–09*, 362

Countess Gucki, The *94–99*, 164

Countess Julia *09–19*, 501

Countess Maritza *26–27*, 380; *27–28*, 538

Countess Valeska, The *94–99*, 221

Country Boy, The *09–19*, 422

Country Circus, The *94–99*, 101

Country Cousin, The *09–19*, 605

Country Folk *60–61*, 295

Country Girl, A *99–09*, 417; *09–19*, 445

Country Girl, The (1) *94–99*, 224

Country Girl, The (2) *50–51*, 325; *60–61*, 48; *66–67*, 358; *67–68*, 403

Country Mouse, A *99–09*, 418

Country Scandal, A *59–60*, 360

Country Sport, A *94–99*, 112

Country Wife, The *94–99*, 224; *36–37*, 439; *57–58*, 303; *58–59*, 53; *65–66*, 378

County Chairman, The *99–09*, 140, 446; *35–36*, 507

County Fair, The *94–99*, 157

Courage *28–29*, 391

Courier de Lyon, Le *94–99*, 150, 247

Courier of Lyons, The (see *The Lyons Mail*)

Court Circuit, Le (see *The Short Circuit*)

Court Comedy, A *38–39*, 488

Court Street *39–40*, 469

Courted Into Court *94–99*, 189

Courtesan *29–30*, 531

Courtin' Time *51–52*, 376s

Courting *25–26*, 441

Courtship of Al and Arthur, The *47–48*, 417

Courtship of Kevin and Roxanne, The *70–71*

Courtship of Leonie, The *94–99*, 185

Courtship of Then, Now and Tomorrow, The *09–19*, 565

Courtyard *59–60*, 41

Cousin Billy *99–09*, 480

Cousin Kate *99–09*, 441; *09–19*, 465

Cousin Louisa *99–09*, 514

Cousin Lucy *09–19*, 556

Cousin Sonia *25–26*, 509

Couturierre de Lunéville, La *23–24*, 410

Coventry Cathedral Porch Plays *63–64*, 368

Cowboy and the Lady, The *99–09*, 358

Cox and Box *34–35*, 364; *36–37*, 401; *38–39*, 447; *41–42*, 458; *43–44*, 456; *47–48*, 373, 375; *50–51*, 353

Crabbed Youth and Age *23–24*, 432; *32–33*, 407

Cracks *63–64*, 346

Cradle Snatchers, (The) *25–26*, 436; *32–33*, 423; *41–42*, 407, 408; *42–43*, 423

Cradle Song, The *26–27*, 466, 520; *29–30*, 393, 403; *30–31*, 427; *34–35*, 403; *38–39*, 492; *55–56*, 59

Cradle Will Rock, The *37–38*, 411, 461; *38–39*, 484; *47–48*, 343, 370; *59–60*, 48; *63–64*, 363; *64–65*, 347

Craig's Wife *25–26*, 470; *45–46*, 459; *46–47*, 464

Cranks *56–57*, 338s

Cranmer of Canterbury *59–60*, 40

Crashing Through *28–29*, 405

Crazy Quilt (see *Billy Rose's Crazy Quilt*)

Crazy With the Heat *40–41*, 411

Creaking Chair, The *25–26*, 559

Cream in the Well, The *40–41*, 412

Creditors, The *49–50*, 384; *61–62*, 321; *70–71*

Creeping Fire *34–35*, 439

Creoles *27–28*, 410; *47–48*, 339

Crescendo *32–33*, 447

Cretan Woman, The *54–55*, 52

Cricket on the Hearth, The (source)
 94–99, 147; *37–38*, 461

Cricket on the Hearth, The (1)
 94–99, 147

Cricket on the Hearth, The (2)
 37–38, 461

Crier by Night, The *09–19*, 588

Crime *26–27*, 485

Crime, The *35–36*, 510

Crime and Crime *63–64*, 353

Crime and Punishment (source)
 94–99, 92; *99–09*, 470; *26–27*, 402;
 34–35, 443; *47–48*, 369

Crime and Punishment (1) *34–35*,
 443

Crime and Punishment (2) *47–48*,
 369

Crime in the Whistler Room, The
 24–25, 469

Crime Marches On *35–36*, 423

Crime of Giovanni Venturi, The
 61–62, 299

Crimes of Passion *69–70*, 344

Criminal at Large *32–33*, 396

Criminal Code, The *29–30*, 410

Criminals, The (1) *41–42*, 458

Criminals, The (2) *69–70*, 359;
 70–71

Crimson Alibi, The *19–20*, 339

Crinoline Girl, The *09–19*, 523

Crisis, The *99–09*, 422, 568

Criss Cross *26–27*, 400

Criss-Crossing *69–70*, 312

Cristo, El *25–26*, 594

Critic, The *94–99*, 122; *09–19*, 544;
 24–25, 590; *45–46*, 444, 445;
 68–69, 407

Critic as Artist, The *62–63*, 327

Critic's Choice *60–61*, 313

Critic's Comedy, The *09–19*, 612

Crooked Friday, The *25–26*, 466

Crooked Gamblers *20–21*, 361

Crooked Square, The *23–24*, 314

Crooks' Convention, The *29–30*, 397

Crops and Croppers *09–19*, 637

Cross My Heart *28–29*, 375

Cross Road of Life, The *94–99*, 86

Cross Roads *29–30*, 438

Cross Ruff *34–35*, 454

Crossing, The *99–09*, 505

Cross-Town *36–37*, 472

Cross-Ways, The *99–09*, 425

Crowded Hour, The *09–19*, 645

Crown Colony *46–47*, 498

Crown Prince, The (1) *99–09*, 460

Crown Prince, The (2) *26–27*, 497

Crown, the Ring and the Roses, The
 62–63, 339

Crowsnest, The *22–23*, 572

Cruce de Vias *69–70*, 374

Crucible *33–34*, 429

Crucible, The (p) *52–53*, 282; *56–57*,
 58; *57–58*, 52, 53; *63–64*, 332

Crucible, The (m) *61–62*, 310

Crucifies, Les *23–24*, 333

Cruelest Month, The *51–52*, 332

Cruising Speed 600 M.P.H. *69–70*,
 372

Cruiskeen Lawn, The *94–99*, 168

Crust of Society, The *94–99*, 105

Cry for Us All *69–70*, 325s

Cry Havoc *42–43*, 454

Cry of Players, A *68–69*, 391

Cry of the Peacock *49–50*, 377;
 57–58, 52

Cry of the Raindrop *60–61*, 38

Cry, the Beloved Country *49–50*,
 358

Crystal Heart, The *59–60*, 354s

Cuando los Hijos de Eva No Son los
 Hijos de Adam *31–32*, 500;
 36–37, 499

Cub, The *09–19*, 429

Cuba Si *68–69*, 454

Cuban Thing, The *68–69*, 377

Cuban's Vendetta, The *94–99*, 230

Cuba's Vow *94–99*, 194

Cuckoo, The *94–99*, 256

Cuckoo Song *62–63*, 322

Cuckoos on the Hearth *41–42*, 396

Cue for Passion *40–41*, 401; *58–59*,
 306

Cuisine des Anges, La *52–53*, 295

Cumberland '61 *94–99*, 212

Cup, The *23–24*, 351

Cup of Trembling, The *47–48*, 400
Cupid Outwits Adam *99–09*, 370
Cure for Curables, A *09–19*, 624
Cure for Matrimony *39–40*, 406
Curious Accident, A *(Un Curioso
    Accidente)* *99–09*, 536
Curious Evening With Gypsy Rose
    Lee, A *60–61*, 48
Curiosity *19–20*, 400
Curious Savage, The *50–51*, 321
Curley McDimple *67–68*, 395s
Curtain Call *36–37*, 481
Curtain Rises, The *33–34*, 444
Curtain Time *38–39*, 487
Curve, The *(Die Kurve)* *70–71*
Customs Director in Baggy Pants,
    The *63–64*, 369
Cut of the Axe *59–60*, 315
Cyanamide *53–54*, 359
Cyclone Lover, The *27–28*, 560
Cymbeline *94–99*, 193; *99–09*, 523;
    23–24, 327; *62–63*, 326; *63–64*,
    360
Cynara *31–32*, 420
Cynthia *99–09*, 430
Cyrano de Bergerac (p) *94–99*, 240;
    99–09, 355, 380; *23–24*, 345;
    25–26, 556; *28–29*, 439; *32–33*,
    440; *35–36*, 504; *46–47*, 422;
    53–54, 318, 322; *63–64*, 367;
    67–68, 348
Cyrano de Bergerac (m) *99–09*, 349
Cyrano de Bergerac (opera rep)
    46–47, 423
Cyranose de Bricabrac *94–99*, 180
Czar Paul I *09–19*, 469
Czarina, The *21–22*, 502

D.M.Z. Revue *67–68*, 409
Dada *69–70*, 373
Daddies *09–19*, 635
Daddy Dufard *09–19*, 433
Daddy Dumplins *20–21*, 406
Daddy Goodness *68–69*, 421
Daddy Long-Legs *09–19*, 532, 644
Daddy's Gone A-Hunting *21–22*,
    408

Daffy Dill *22–23*, 441
Dagger, The *25–26*, 440
Dagger and the Cross, The *99–09*,
    476
Dagmar *22–23*, 521
Daily Express (London) *64–65*, 303
Dairy Farm, The *99–09*, 348
Dairymaids, The *99–09*, 542
Daisy Mayme *26–27*, 410
Daisy Miller *62–63*, 337
Dakota *52–53*, 306
Damaged Goods *09–19*, 497; *36–37*,
    484
Damask Cheek, The *42–43*, 439;
    45–46, 458
Damask Drum, The *60–61*, 44
Dame aux Camelias, La (see
    Camille)
Dame Nature *38–39*, 408
Damer's Gold *09–19*, 494
Dames at Sea (or Golddiggers
    Afloat) *66–67*, 35; *68–69*, 441s;
    70–71
Damn the Tears *26–27*, 465
Damn Yankees *54–55*, 413s; *66–67*,
    422
Damn You, Scarlett O'Hara *63–64*,
    358
Damn Your Honor *29–30*, 472
Damnation of Faust *46–47*, 489;
    47–48, 418
Dance Below, The *27–28*, 549
Dance Me a Song *49–50*, 368s
Dance Night *38–39*, 416
Dance of Death, The (1) *35–36*,
    479
Dance of Death, The (2; *Dodsdan-
    cen*) *47–48*, 379; *60–61*, 348;
    70–71
Dance Players, Inc. (dance
    programs) *41–42*, 457
Dance program (undesignated)
    60–61, 38
Dance Ways From Spain to the
    Philippines (dance programs)
    47–48, 415
Dance With Your Gods *34–35*, 388

Dancer, The (1) *19–20*, 359
Dancer, The (2) *46–47*, 414
Dancers, The *23–24*, 337
Dancing Around *09–19*, 534
Dancing Duchess, The *09–19*, 528
Dancing Girl, The (1) *94–99*, 121
Dancing Girl, The (2) *22–23*, 524
Dancing Mothers *24–25*, 432
Dancing Partner *30–31*, 401
Dancing Princess, The *99–09*, 499
Dandy Dick *55–56*, 58
Danger *21–22*, 479
Dangerfield *63–64*, 303
Dangerfield '95 *94–99*, 223
Dangerous Age, The *20–21*, 427
Dangerous Corner *32–33*, 410;
33–34, 423; *45–46*, 450; *50–51*,
374
Dangerous Maid, A. *94–99*, 245
Dangers of a Great City *94–99*,
220
Danites, The *94–99*, 202
Danny Kaye *62–63*, 304
Danny Larkin *47–48*, 412
Dans le Noir *36–37*, 499
Dante (1) *99–09*, 442
Dante (2) *61–62*, 311
Danton's Death *(Danton's Tod)*
27–28, 455, 471; *38–39*, 424;
65–66, 378
Daphne in Cottage D *67–68*, 344
Daphne Laureola *50–51*, 314
D'Arcy of the Guards *99–09*, 401
Dark, The (1) *26–27*, 473
Dark, The (2) *69–70*, 148
Dark Angel, The *24–25*, 538
Dark at the Top of the Stairs, The
57–58, 305
Dark Chapter, The *26–27*, 402
Dark Clouds *37–38*, 465
Dark Corners *63–64*, 365
Dark Eyes *42–43*, 459
Dark Fire *65–66*, 436
Dark Hammock *44–45*, 403
Dark Hours, The *32–33*, 418
Dark Is Light Enough, The *54–55*,
400

Dark Lady of the Sonnets, The
59–60, 43; *61–62*, 314
Dark Legend *51–52*, 332
Dark Mirror, The *28–29*, 414
Dark of the Moon *44–45*, 421;
50–51, 374; *57–58*, 56; *59–60*, 43;
69–70, 362
Dark Rosaleen *09–19*, 656
Dark Tower, The *33–34*, 462
Dark Victory *34–35*, 404
Darker Flower, A *62–63*, 328
Darkest America *94–99*, 188
Darkest Russia *94–99*, 87
Darkness at Noon *50–51*, 341;
62–63, 339
Darling of the Day *67–68*, 360s
Darling of the Gallery Gods, The
99–09, 434
Darling of the Gods, The *99–09*,
107, 424
Darwin's Theories *60–61*, 42
Date With April, A *52–53*, 300
Daughter of Cuba, a *94–99*, 238
Daughter of Heaven, The *09–19*,
480
Daughter of Silence *61–62*, 273
Daughter of the Regiment, The
(opera rep) *09–19*, 638
Daughter of the Revolution, A
94–99, 135
Daughter of the Tumbrils, The
99–09, 508
Daughters of Atreus *36–37*, 417
Daughters of Eve *94–99*, 100
Daughters of Men, The *99–09*, 525
Daughters of the Late Colonel, The
51–52, 333
Daughters of the Poor *94–99*, 250
David and Esther *47–48*, 431
David Copperfield *09–19*, 536
David Garrick (1) *94–99*, 146;
99–09, 384, 385, 472; *09–19*,
568
David Garrick (2) *99–09*, 497
David Garrick on the Art of Acting
99–09, 469
David Harum *99–09*, 372

David Show, The *68–69*, 432;
  69–70, 334
David's Crown *47–48*, 432
Davy Jones' Locker (mn) *66–67*,
  413; *67–68*, 396
Dawn *24–25*, 493
Dawn of a Tomorrow, The *99–09*,
  576
Dawn of Freedom, The *94–99*,
  238
Day After Tomorrow, The *50–51*,
  322
Day and a Night in New York, A
  94–99, 236
Day Before, The *99–09*, 515
Day Before Spring, The *45–46*, 409
Day by the Sea, A *55–56*, 343
Day in the Death of Joe Egg, A
  67–68, 361
Day in the Life Of, A *68–69*, 457
Day in the Life of Just About
  Everyone, A *70–71*
Day in the Sun *38–39*, 473
Day of Absence *65–66*, 426; *69–70*,
  352
Day of Dupes, The *09–19*, 523
Day the Money Stopped, The *57–58*,
  320
Day the Whores Came Out to Play
  Tennis, The *64–65*, 356
Day Will Come, The *44–45*, 374
Daybreak *09–19*, 603
Daylight and Dark *37–38*, 462
Days and Nights of Beebee
  Fenstermaker, The *62–63*, 313
Days of Duveen, The *62–63*, 288
Days of Our Youth, The *41–42*, 458
Days to Come *36–37*, 441
Days Without End *33–34*, 478
De Lancey *99–09*, 493
De Luxe *34–35*, 461
De Luxe Annie *09–19*, 606
De Muy Buena Familia *31–32*, 500
De Nature Rerum *63–64*, 327
De Profundis *60–61*, 330; *62–63*,
  327
De Sade Illustrated *68–69*, 452

Deacon and the Lady, The *09–19*,
  426
Dead End *35–36*, 426; *60–61*, 48
Dead Pigeon *53–54*, 332
Dead Souls *64–65*, 323
Dead to Rights *46–47*, 498
Deadfall *55–56*, 359
Deadlock, The *09–19*, 520
Deadly Art, The *66–67*, 422
Deadly Game, The *59–60*, 315;
  65–66, 430
Deafman Glance *70–71*
Dear Barbarians *51–52*, 311, 334
Dear Brutus *09–19*, 647; *46–47*, 494
Dear Charles *54–55*, 360
Dear Departed Mother-in-Law *(Feu
  la Mere de Madame)* *56–57*, 353
Dear Fool, The *09–19*, 521
Dear Jane *32–33*, 420
Dear Janet Rosenberg, Dear Mr.
  Kooning *69–70*, 363
Dear Judas *47–48*, 356
Dear Liar *59–60*, 329; *61–62*, 326
Dear Love *29–30*, 550
Dear Me *20–21*, 421
Dear Me, the Sky Is Falling *62–63*,
  299
Dear Octopus *38–39*, 449
Dear Old Charlie *09–19*, 470
Dear Old Darling *35–36*, 490
Dear Old England *29–30*, 517
Dear Ruth *44–45*, 404
Dear Sir *24–25*, 458
Dear Unfair Sex, The *99–09*, 519
Dear World *68–69*, 405s
Dearest Enemy *25–26*, 448
Death in the Family, A *60–61*, 308;
  63–64, 369
Death of a Man *61–62*, 289
Death of a Salesman *48–49*, 412;
  67–68, 401
Death of Bessie Smith, The *60–61*,
  356; *61–62*, 306; *68–69*, 379
Death of Cuchulain, The *58–59*, 52
Death of Pazukhin, The *23–24*, 356
Death of Satan, The *59–60*, 357
Death of Spring *37–38*, 466

Death of the Well-Loved Boy, The 66–67, 420

Death of Tintagiles, The 09–19, 579

Death Sounds the Trumpet 39–40, 469

Death Takes a Holiday 29–30, 469; 30–31, 492; 44–45, 436

Deathwatch 58–59, 51; 61–62, 323

Deborah (1) 94–99, 208

Deborah (2) 94–99, 218

Deborah Bertonoff 47–48, 430

Debtors, The 09–19, 402

Deburau 20–21, 414

Debut 55–56, 377

Debutante, The 09–19, 540

Decameron, The (source) 34–35, 484; 60–61, 42

Decameron, The 60–61, 42

Decay of Lying, The 62–63, 327

Deceased, The 61–62, 326

Decision (1) 28–29, 508

Decision (2) 43–44, 452; 51–52, 334

Declassee 19–20, 363

Decline and Fall of the Entire World as Seen Through the Eyes of Cole Porter Revisited, The 64–65, 357s

Decorating Clementine 09–19, 424

Decoy, The 31–32, 501

Dedale, Le 99–09, 501

Deep Are the Roots 45–46, 386; 52–53, 309

Deep Blue Sea, The 52–53, 266

Deep Channels 29–30, 419

Deep Harlem 28–29, 449

Deep Mrs. Sykes, The 44–45, 423

Deep Purple, The 09–19, 436

Deep River 26–27, 392

Deep Tangled Wildwood, The 23–24, 346

Deer Kill, The 69–70, 378

Deer Park, The 66–67, 412

Defender, The 99–09, 413

Degenerates, The 99–09, 359

Deirdre of the Sorrows 49–50, 384

Dejeuner D'Amoureux, Un 36–37, 499

Dejeuner de Soleil 27–28, 484

Del Monte 47–48, 430

Delicate Balance, A 66–67, 357

Delicate Story 40–41, 398

Delightful Season, A 60–61, 42

Delmar's Revels 27–28, 460

Delmonico's at Six 94–99, 134

Delta Wife, The 26–27, 524

Deluge, The (1) 09–19, 603; 21–22, 499; 34–35, 453

Deluge, The (2) 26–27, 440

Demi Monde, Le 26–27, 434

Demi-God, The (see The Black Messiah)

Demi-Virgin, The 21–22, 443

Democracy's King 09–19, 623

Demon, The 44–45, 440

Denial, The 09–19, 535

Denise 94–99, 156

Dens and Palaces, or Two Lives (see A Young Wife)

Depths, The 24–25, 530

Depths of Purity, The 09–19, 565

Deputy, The 63–64, 327

Deputy of Paris, The 46–47, 495

Derby Mascot, The 94–99, 84

Derby Winner, The 94–99, 122

Derryowen 46–47, 431

Desert Flower, The 24–25, 491

Desert Incident, A 58–59, 332

Desert Sands 21–22, 510

Desert Song, The 26–27, 435; 45–46, 393

Deserters, The 09–19, 425

Design for a Stained Glass Window 49–50, 369

Design for Laughter 44–45, 441

Design for Living 32–33, 454

Desire 51–52, 333

Desire to Live 38–39, 485

Desire Under the Elms 24–25, 485; 51–52, 306, 333; 62–63, 323; 70–71

Desk Set, The 55–56, 355

Desperate Hours, The 54–55, 397

Destruction 32–33, 379

Destry Rides Again 58–59, 334s

Detective Sparks 09–19, 396

Detective Story *48–49*, 416; *51–52*, 332; *53–54*, 358; *60–61*, 48

Detour, The *21–22*, 400; *46–47*, 485

Deuces Wild *61–62*, 329

Deux Gosses, Les *94–99*, 184

Devi Dja (dance programs) *47–48*, 415

Devil, The (1) *99–09*, 564, 565

Devil, The (2) *31–32*, 300

Devil and Daniel Webster, The *38–39*, 474, 475; *70–71*

Devil in Boston, The *52–53*, 308

Devil in the Cheese *26–27*, 450

Devil in the Mind *30–31*, 521

Devil Is a Good Man, The *39–40*, 444, 445

Devil of Pei-Ling, The *35–36*, 486

Devil Passes, The *31–32*, 458; *38–39*, 487

Devil Takes a Bride, The *38–39*, 411

Devil to Pay, The (1) *25–26*, 507

Devil to Pay, The (2) *47–48*, 428

Devil Within, The *24–25*, 558

Devils *25–26*, 571

Devils, The *65–66*, 385

Devil's Advocate, The *60–61*, 329

Devil's Daughter, The *32–33*, 377

Devil's Deputy, The *94–99*, 87

Devil's Disciple, The *94–99*, 93; *99–09*, 335; *22–23*, 561; *49–50*, 370; *62–63*, 339

Devil's Dream, The *99–09*, 382

Devils Galore *45–46*, 383

Devil's Garden, The *09–19*, 568

Devil's Host, The *31–32*, 437

Devil's Island *94–99*, 233

Devil's Little Game, The *32–33*, 380

Devils of Loudun, The *65–66*, 385

Dew Drop Inn *22–23*, 576

Dial "M" for Murder *52–53*, 266

Dialogues of Plato *68–69*, 455

Diamond Breaker, The *94–99*, 116

Diamond Lil *27–28*, 536; *48–49*, 410, 411; *51–52*, 281

Diamond Orchid *64–65*, 326

Diana *29–30*, 459

Diana of Dobson's *99–09*, 567

Diary of a Madman (source) *63–64*, 363; *65–66*, 423; *66–67*, 416

Diary of a Madman *63–64*, 363

Diary of a Madman, The *66–67*, 416

Diary of a Scoundrel *56–57*, 331

Diary of a Superfluous Man *65–66*, 433

Diary of Adam and Eve, The (see also *Extracts From Adam's Diary*) *66–67*, 364

Diary of Anne Frank, The *55–56*, 350

Dice of the Gods, The *22–23*, 555

Dick Whittington and His Cat *34–35*, 484

Dickey Bird, The *09–19*, 540

Dictator, The *99–09*, 457; *09–19*, 443; *19–20*, 447

Did I Say No? *31–32*, 396

Difference in Gods *09–19*, 598, 622, 646; *38–39*, 485; *43–44*, 490; *51–52*, 332

Difficult Woman, The *61–62*, 329s

Diff'rent *20–21*, 417; *37–38*, 453; *61–62*, 309

Difunta, La *69–70*, 374

Digb(e)y's Secretary (see *The Private Secretary*)

Digging for Apples *62–63*, 315

Dime a Dozen *62–63*, 317s

Dindon, Le *60–61*, 326

Dinner at Eight *32–33*, 407; *66–67*, 357

Dinner for One *70–71*

Dinner Is Served *29–30*, 382

Dinny and the Witches *59–60*, 352

Dinosaur Wharf *51–52*, 291

Dionysus in '69 *68–69*, 457

Diplomacy *94–99*, 109; *99–09*, 391; *09–19*, 424, 535; *27–28*, 558

Diplomat, The *99–09*, 408

Dirtiest Show in Town, The *69–70*, 375; *70–71*

Dirty Ferdie Comes Clean *70–71*

Dirty Old Man, The *63–64*, 365

Disasters of War *38–39,* 486

Discontent of a Russian Prince, The *61–62,* 311

Discover America *70–71*

Discovering America *09–19,* 475

Disenchanted, The *58–59,* 308; *61–62,* 333

Disengaged *99–09,* 579

Dishonored Lady *29–30,* 487

Disintegration of James Cherry, The *69–70,* 348

Dishwasher, The *45–46,* 460

Displaced Person, The *66–67,* 409

Disraeli *09–19,* 79, 451, 471, 598; *26–27,* 522

Distaff Side, The *34–35,* 378

Distant Bell, A *59–60,* 314

Distant City, The *41–42,* 397

Distant Drum, A *27–28,* 495

Distant Drums *31–32,* 464

Distant Shore, The *34–35,* 455

District Attorney, The *94–99,* 118

District Leader, The *99–09,* 514

Diversion *27–28,* 489

Diversions *58–59,* 53

Divided by Three *34–35,* 383

Divided Honors *29–30,* 409

Divine Drudge, A *33–34,* 450

Divine Moment, A *33–34,* 477

Division Street: America *66–67,* 423

Divorce *09–19,* 405

Divorce a la Carte *27–28,* 532

Divorce Cure, A *94–99,* 199

Divorce Me, Dear *31–32,* 405

Divorcons *94–99,* 126, 169, 186, 196, 199; *99–09,* 411, 538, 578; *09–19,* 499

Dixie to Broadway *24–25,* 479

Do I Dare Disturb the Universe? *63–64,* 371

Do I Hear a Waltz? *64–65,* 330s

Do It Again! *70–71*

Do Not Pass Go *64–65,* 358

Do Re Mi *60–61,* 315s

Do You Know the Milky Way? *(Kennen Sie die Milchstrasse?)* *61–62,* 262; *62–63,* 329; *66–67,* 412

Dock Brief, The *61–62,* 314

Dockstader's Minstrels (see *Lew Dockstader's Minstrels*)

Doctor: titles abbreviated Dr. are in alphabetical order under DR

Doctor Faustus *(The Tragical History of Doctor Faustus)* *09–19,* 410; *36–37,* 491; *52–53,* 309; *64–65,* 343

Doctor Faustus Lights the Lights *51–52,* 333

Doctor Herzl *45–46,* 460; *46–47,* 497

Doctor in Spite of Himself, The *(Le Medecin Malgre Lui)* *37–38,* 469; *43–44,* 489; *45–46,* 451; *50–51,* 373; *56–57,* 55; *63–64,* 327

Doctor Monica *33–34,* 455

Doctor Sganarelle *43–44,* 489

Doctor Social *47–48,* 383

Doctor X *30–31,* 488

Doctored Wife, The *50–51,* 373

Doctor's Dilemma, The *09–19,* 549; *27–28,* 455; *40–41,* 418; *54–55,* 391

Doctors Disagree *43–44,* 444

Dodo Bird, The *67–68,* 396

Dodsdancen (see *The Dance of Death*)

Dodsworth *33–34,* 501; *34–35,* 361

Does a Tiger Wear a Necktie? *68–69,* 407

Dog Beneath the Skin, The *47–48,* 425

Dog Years *65–66,* 434

Dog's Love, A *70–71*

Doigt's de Fee, Les *99–09,* 403

Doing Nicely *40–41,* 431

Doing Our Bit *09–19,* 610

Dolce *99–09,* 513

Doll Girl, The *09–19,* 504

Dollar Mark, The *09–19,* 396

Dollar Princess, The *09–19,* 399

Dolle Hans *30–31,* 410

Doll's Home, A *62–63,* 325

Doll's House, A *(Maison de Poupee; Thora; A Doll's Home)* *94–99,* 126, 136, 169; *99–09,* 410, 411,

560; *09–19*, 629; *37–38*, 406;
43–44, 488; *45–46*, 450; *55–56*, 55;
62–63, 325; *70–71*
Dolly Jordan *22–23*, 470
Dolly Varden *99–09*, 404, 405
Dolores, La *31–32*, 501
Dom Juan (see *Don Juan* 2)
Dombey and Son *52–53*, 301
Dominant Sex, The *34–35*, 466
Dominic's Lover *70–71*
Domino *32–33*, 381
Dominos Roses, Les *94–99*, 230
Don *09–19*, 408
Don Caesar *99–09*, 393
Don Caesar de Bazan *99–09*, 393
Don Caesar's Return *99–09*, 393,
394
Don Carlos *99–09*, 486; *61–62*, 324;
64–65, 317
Don Cossack Chorus & Dancers
(dance programs) *43–44*, 486
Don Giovanni (opera rep) *47–48*,
343, 347, 425
Don Juan (1) *21–22*, 414
Don Juan (2; *Dom Juan*) *55–56*, 59;
58–59, 295; *63–64*, 327; *69–70*,
313
Don Juan in Hell *51–52*, 294;
60–61, 46; *62–63*, 312; *64–65*, 349;
69–70, 373; *70–71*
Don Juan Tenorio *25–26*, 599;
31–32, 500–1; *53–54*, 321
Don Q., Jr. *25–26*, 541
Don Quixote (de la Mancha) (source)
94–99, 151; *99–09*, 470; *23–24*,
359; *65–66*, 386
Don Quixote (p 1) *94–99*, 151
Don Quixote (p 2) *99–09*, 470
Don Quixote (m) *37–38*, 412
Dona Maria la Brava *25–26*, 599
Dona Rosita la Soltera *69–70*,
374
Done on a Shoestring *40–41*, 433
Donkey and His Friends, The (mn)
35–36, 512
Donnybrook! *60–61*, 339s
Donogoo *60–61*, 44
Donovan Affair, The *26–27*, 369

Don't Bother Me, I Can't Cope
70–71
Don't Bother Mother *24–25*, 534
Don't Call Me by My Right Name
63–64, 346
Don't Drink the Water *66–67*, 369
Don't George *44–45*, 394
Don't Listen, Ladies *48–49*, 404
Don't Look Now *36–37*, 426
Don't Shoot Mable It's Your
Husband *68–69*, 431
Don't Tell *20–21*, 387
Don't Throw Glass Houses *38–39*,
440
Don't Weaken *09–19*, 520
Don't Worry *45–46*, 460
Don't You Want to be Free *37–38*,
464
Doodle Dandy of the U.S.A. *42–43*,
488
Doormat, The *22–23*, 499
Dope *50–51*, 375
Dora *94–99*, 109; *27–28*, 559
Dora Mobridge *29–30*, 526
Dorcas *94–99*, 188
Dori, Shoshanah Bat *39–40*, 469
Dorian Gray (1) *27–28*, 556
Dorian Gray (2) *36–37*, 397, 398
Doris *94–99*, 117, 235
Doris Humphrey (& Charles
Weidman; dance programs) *38–39*,
483; *41–42*, 457; *42–43*, 485
Dorothy *94–99*, 138
Dorothy Crawford *38–39*, 489
Dorothy Gordon *36–37*, 498
Dorothy Sands *32–33*, 454; *33–34*,
457
Dorothy Vernon of Haddon Hall
99–09, 448
Dostigayev *34–35*, 472
Double Axe, The *68–69*, 454
Double Bill (portmanteau title)
61–62, 304, 305, 314, 315, 330,
331
Double Life, The *99–09*, 529
Double Door *33–34*, 433
Double Dublin *63–64*, 318s
Double Dummy *36–37*, 430

Double Entry 60–61, 358s
Double Exposure 09–19, 634
Double in Hearts 56–57, 323
Double Play 67–68, 408
Doubles and Opposites 65–66, 436
Doubletalk 63–64, 364
Doughgirls, The 42–43, 457
Douleureuse, La 99–09, 472
Dove, The (1) 24–25, 539; 25–26, 432
Dove, The (2) 25–26, 593
Dove of Peace, The 09–19, 482
Dover Road, The 21–22, 480
Dowerless Bride, The 99–09, 560
Down in Dixie 94–99, 115
Down in the Valley 52–53, 306; 62–63, 312s; 64–65, 363
Down on the Farm 94–99, 243
Down on the Suwanee River 94–99, 164
Down Stream 25–26, 528
Down to Miami 44–45, 384
Downfall of Haman 45–46, 460
Downward Path to Wisdom, The 60–61, 48
Dozens, The 68–69, 409
Dr. Belgraff 94–99, 200
Dr. Claudius 94–99, 193
Dr. Cook's Garden 67–68, 341
Dr. David's Dad 24–25, 434
Dr. De Luxe 09–19, 443
Dr. Faustus (see Doctor Faustus)
Dr. Fish 69–70, 318
Dr. Galley 69–70, 356
Dr. Herzl (see Doctor Herzl)
Dr. Jekyll and Mr. Hyde (source) 94–99, 91; 99–09, 355, 486
Dr. Jekyll and Mr. Hyde 94–99, 91, 92, 93; 99–09, 355, 455, 486, 487; 51–52, 334
Dr. Knock 27–28, 516; 37–38, 469
Dr. Pygmalion 62–63, 293
Dr. Raymond Ditmars 34–35, 484
Dr. Syntax 94–99, 83
Dr. Wake's Patient 99–09, 551
Dracula 27–28, 422; 30–31, 515; 43–44, 489; 70–71

Dracula Sabbat 70–71
Dragon, The (1) 28–29, 483
Dragon, The (2) 62–63, 331
Dragon Zne Zee, The (mn) 35–36, 479, 513; 37–38, 466
Dragon's Claw, The 09–19, 531
Dragon's Mouth 55–56, 58
Drama at Inish (see also Is Life Worth Living?) 34–35, 407; 37–38, 378
Drat! The Cat! 65–66, 375s
Dream Child 34–35, 379
Dream City 99–09, 529
Dream Girl 45–46, 414; 50–51, 369; 65–66, 384
Dream Girl, The 24–25, 436
Dream House 49–50, 383
Dream Maker, The 21–22, 466
Dream of a Blacklisted Actor 69–70, 372
Dream of Denang 70–71
Dream of Swallows, A 63–64, 363
Dream on Monkey Mountain, The 70–71
Dream Out of Time, A 70–71
Dream Play, The 25–26, 533; 60–61, 45
Dream With Music 43–44, 477
Dreams for Sale 22–23, 453
Dreamy Kid, The 24–25, 540; 27–28, 551
Dress Parade, The 99–09, 434
Drift, The 35–36, 510
Drifting (1) 09–19, 434
Drifting (2) 21–22, 490
Drink 99–09, 436
Drink to Me Only 58–59, 293
Drinking Gourd, The 68–69, 442
Drinking Party, The 68–69, 455
Driven 09–19, 541
Drone, The 09–19, 490
Druid Circle, The 47–48, 361
Drums Begin, The 33–34, 461
Drums in the Night 66–67, 420
Drums of Jeopardy, The 21–22, 553
Drums of Oude, The 26–27, 521

Drums Under the Windows *60–61,* 351

Drunkard, The (or The Fallen Saved; p) *33–34,* 505; *37–38,* 462; *45–46,* 450; *69–70,* 365

Drunkard, The (m) *69–70,* 365s

Du Barry *99–09,* 402, 481

Du Barry Was a Lady *39–40,* 420; *64–65,* 357

Du Theatre au Champ D'Honneur *09–19,* 589 (and 605)

DuBarry, The *32–33,* 427s

Duchess, The *09–19,* 454

Duchess Misbehaves, The *45–46,* 427

Duchess of Dantzic, The *99–09,* 482

Duchess of Malfi, The *46–47,* 426; *56–57,* 362; *65–66,* 438

Duel, The *99–09,* 509

Duel of Angels *59–60,* 334

Duet for Solo Voice *69–70,* 341

Duet for Three *65–66,* 435

Duet for Two Hands *47–48,* 357

Duet in a Dark Forest *38–39,* 486

Duffy's Blunders *94–99,* 112

Duke in Darkness, The *43–44,* 449

Duke of Duluth, The *99–09,* 495

Duke of Killicrankie, The *99–09,* 464; *09–19,* 557

Dulcy *21–22,* 393

Dumb and the Blind, The *09–19,* 541

Dumb Luck *32–33,* 377

Dumb-Bell *23–24,* 362

Dumbbell People in a Barbell World *61–62,* 323

Dumbwaiter, The *62–63,* 320; *70–71*

Dummy, The *09–19,* 526

Duncan Dancers (dance programs; see *Anita Zahn*)

Duncan Noble (dance programs) *47–48,* 415

Dunce Boy, The *24–25,* 566

Dunnigan's Daughter *45–46,* 416

Due Gemelli Veneziani, I (see *The Venetian Twins*)

Dust Heap, The *23–24,* 424

Dutchman *63–64,* 362, 364, 370

Duty *37–38,* 463

Dybbuk, The *25–26,* 517; *26–27,* 440, 442; *46–47,* 485, 497; *47–48,* 432; *54–55,* 56; *63–64,* 322

Dylan *63–64,* 320; *70–71*

Dynamite Tonight *63–64,* 360; *66–67,* 416

Dynamo *28–29,* 467

Dynasty, The *37–38,* 462

E & O E *35–36,* 397

E Equals mc Squared *47–48,* 412

Each Had Six Wings *63–64,* 322

Eagle Has Two Heads, The *46–47,* 472; *56–57,* 58

Eagle's Nest, The *94–99,* 232

Earl and the Girl, The *99–09,* 499

Earl Carroll's Sketch Book (1929) *29–30,* 378

Earl Carroll('s) Sketch Book (1935) *34–35,* 482

(Earl Carroll's) Vanities of 1923 *23–24,* 294

Earl Carroll's Vanities (1924) *24–25,* 451

Earl Carroll('s) Vanities (1925) *25–26,* 420

Earl Carroll('s) Vanities (1926) *26–27,* 368

(Earl Carroll's) Vanities (1928) *28–29,* 355

Earl Carroll's Vanities (1930) *30–31,* 399

Earl Carroll's Vanities (1931) *31–32,* 383s

Earl Carroll('s) Vanities (1932) *32–33,* 392s

Earl Carroll('s) Vanities (1940) *39–40,* 429

Earl of Essex, The, or The Unhappy Favorite *29–30,* 512

Earl of Pawtucket, The *99–09,* 430

Earl of Ruston *70–71*

Early American Primitives (source) *46–47,* 490

Early Havoc *63–64,* 317

Early Morning 70–71
Early to Bed 43–44, 400
Earth 26–27, 492
Earth, The 09–19, 559
Earth Between, The 28–29, 476
Earth Journey 43–44, 474
Earth Spirit 50–51, 373; 69–70, 362
Earthly Paradise 69–70, 367; 70–71
Easiest Way, The 99–09, 576;
    09–19, 1; 21–22, 413; 33–34, 457
East Is West 09–19, 648
East Lynne 94–99, 213, 234; 25–26,
    31–32, 467
East of Broadway 31–32, 469
East of Eden (1) 39–40, 474
East of Eden (2) 67–68, 365
East of Suez 22–23, 459
East Side Professor, The 37–38, 470
East Wind 31–32, 417s
East Wind, The 66–67, 361
Easter (One Day More) 25–26, 573;
    56–57, 55
Easterner, The 99–09, 559
Eastward in (of) Eden 47–48, 365;
    55–56, 59
Easy Come, Easy Go 25–26, 482;
    28–29, 463
Easy Dawson 99–09, 492
Easy Mark, The 24–25, 438
Easy Street 24–25, 434
Easy Terms 25–26, 452
Easy Virtue 25–26, 509
Ebb Tide 30–31, 534
Eben Holden 99–09, 398
Eccentricities of Davy Crockett, The
    47–48, 398
Ecclesiazusae 69–70, 367, 374
Echo, The 09–19, 422
Echo's Bones 70–71
Ecole des Cocottes, L' 64–65, 343
Ecole des Femmes, L' (see The
    School for Wives)
Ecole des Maris, L' (see The School
    for Husbands 2)
Ed Wynn Carnival 19–20, 444
Eddie Fisher at the Winter Garden
    62–63, 278

Eddie Fisher-Buddy Hackett at the
    Palace 67–68, 341
Eden End 35–36, 422
Edgar Allen Poe 25–26, 461
Edge of the Sword, The 49–50, 384
Edith, or The Earl's Daughter (see
    East Lynne)
Edith Paif 47–48, 362
Editha's Burgler (1; see The Bur-
    glar)
Editha's Burglar (2) 09–19, 591
Edmund Burke 99–09, 497
Edna 28–29, 503
Edna His Wife 37–38, 400
Education of Hyman Kaplan, The
    67–68, 369s
Education of Mr. Pipp, The 99–09,
    484
Edward II 47–48, 429; 57–58, 56
Edward and Agrippina 61–62, 326
Edward, My Son 48–49, 385
Edwin Booth 58–59, 305
Edwina Black 50–51, 327
Eenie, Meenie, Minie, Moe 69–70,
    373
Effect of Gamma Rays on
    Man-in-the-Moon Marigolds, The
    69–70, 363
Egg, The 61–62, 281
Egg and I, The 58–59, 53
Egghead,.The 57–58, 290
Egmont 48–49, 426
Egoists, The 59–60, 46
Egotist, The 22–23, 513
Eh? 66–67, 403, 421
Ehe des Herrn Mississippi, Die (see
    The Marriage of Mr. Mississippi)
Eight Bells (1) 94–99, 101
Eight Bells (2) 33–34, 452
Eight O'Clock Tuesday 40–41,
    408
1860, or An Interrupted Festival
    31–32, 414
Eileen 09–19, 597
Eileen Alannah, Eileen Asthore
    99–09, 523
Eileen Asthore 99–09, 523

Einen Jux Will Er Sich Machen (see *He Wants to Have a Good Time*)

Elder Miss Blossom, The 99–09, 356

Elder Son, The 09–19, 531

Eldest, The 34–35, 450

Electra (author unnamed) 09–19, 513; 50–51, 373; 58–59, 52

Electra (Euripides) 50–51, 374; 61–62, 326

Electra (Sophocles) 99–09, 557; 09–19, 621; 27–28, 463; 30–31, 472; 31–32, 461; 52–53, 269; 60–61, 45; 61–62, 255; 64–65, 74, 298

Electric Map, a Melodrama, The 69–70, 354

Electrician, The 94–99, 210

Electricity 09–19, 428

Electronic Nigger, The 67–68, 391

Electronic Nigger and Others, The 67–68, 391

Elephant Calf, The 62–63, 314s

Elevating a Husband 09–19, 464

Elevation, L' 09–19, 614

Elevator, The 68–69, 454

Elisha, Story of (see *Kings II*)

Eliza Comes to Stay 09–19, 519

Elizabeth and Essex 30–31, 29

Elizabeth Sleeps Out 35–36, 503

Elizabeth the Queen (see also *Elizabeth and Essex*) 30–31, 445; 46–47, 485; 62–63, 339; 66–67, 358

Elizabeth Umpstead 60–61, 295

Ellen Van Volkenburg Marionettes 36–37, 498

Elliott Murphy's Aquashow 51–52, 332

Elmer Gantry (source) 28–29, 356; 69–70, 315

Elmer Gantry 28–29, 356

Elmer the Great 28–29, 377

Elsa Lanchester—Herself 60–61, 42

Elsie 22–23, 552

Elsie Janis (and Her Gang) 19–20, 392; 21–22, 495; 38–39, 489

Elton Case, The 21–22, 415

Embarrassment of Riches, The 99–09, 514

Embassy Ball, The 99–09, 510

Embers (1) 25–26, 542

Embers (2) 60–61, 47; 70–71

Embezzled Heaven 44–45, 393

Emerald Isle, The 99–09, 414

Emerald Slippers, The 70–71

Emily Dickinson 34–35, 411

Emlyn Williams as Charles Dickens 51–52, 308; 52–53, 300; 70–71

Emmanuel 60–61, 44

Emperor, The 62–63, 332

Emperor and the Barmaid 62–63, 286

Emperor Jones, The 20–21, 399; 24–25, 540; 25–26, 556; 26–27, 424; 44–45, 441

Emperor Jones, The (mn) 33–34, 534

Emperor's Clothes, The 52–53, 285; 53–54, 359

Emperor's New Clothes, The 35–36, 479; 36–37, 495; 37–38, 467

Empire Builders, The 68–69, 428

Empress Eugenie, The 34–35, 467; 36–37, 498

Empress of Destiny 37–38, 431

Empty Room, The 63–64, 370

En Attendant Godot *(Waiting for Godot)* 67–68, 405

En Deshabile 09–19, 509

Enchanted, The 49–50, 368; 51–52, 332

Enchanted April, The 25–26, 429

Enchanted Cottage, The 22–23, 549; 45–46, 450

Enchanted Forest, The 34–35, 485

Enchanted Isle 27–28, 408

Enchanting Melody 64–65, 347

Enchantment 26–27, 519

Enchantress, The 09–19, 455

Encore 63–64, 346

End as a Man 53–54, 303

End of a Cycle 37–38, 466

End of All Things Natural, The, or
A Drama of Contemporary Russia
69–70, 339
End of Summer *35–36,* 483
End of the Dance, The *28–29,* 503
End of the "Tiger" General, The
29–30, 497
End of the World, The (1) *62–63,*
322
End of the World, The (2) *69–70,*
378
Endecott and the Red Cross (source)
63–64, 369
Endecott and the Red Cross *67–68,*
391
Endgame *57–58,* 53; *61–62,* 323;
69–70, 370, 376; *70–71*
Endless Chain, The *22–23,* 448
Enemies (1) *34–35,* 453
Enemies (2) *65–66,* 421
Enemy, The *25–26,* 478
Enemy, The *(Kataki)* *58–59,* 255
Enemy of the People, An *94–99,*
121; *23–24,* 356; *27–28,* 419;
28–29, 410; *36–37,* 465; *50–51,*
339; *57–58,* 56; *58–59,* 52; *67–68,*
410; *70–71*
Enemy to the King, An *94–99,* 175,
206
Enemy Within *31–32,* 402
Engaged *46–47,* 484
Engagement, The *63–64,* 371
Engagement Baby, The *69–70,* 329
Engineer, The *94–99,* 139
English Daisy, An *99–09,* 452
Englishman's Home, An *99–09,* 579
Enigma, The *99–09,* 557
Enough Stupidity in Every Wise
Man *23–24,* 356
Ensign, The *94–99,* 100, 233
Enter Laughing *62–63,* 301
Enter Madame *20–21,* 366
Enter the Hero *09–19,* 612
Entertain a Ghost *61–62,* 328
Entertainer, The *57–58,* 317
Entertaining Mr. Sloane *65–66,* 376
Epiphany *63–64,* 343

Episode *24–24,* 536
Epitaph for George Dillon *58–59,*
301, 317; *60–61,* 45
Equity Library Theater (unnamed
revivals) *54–55,* 57; *55–56,* 59;
57–58, 56
Erdgeist *24–25,* 592
Ergo *67–68,* 389
Erminie *94–99,* 202; *99–09,* 441;
20–21, 418
Ernest in Love *59–60,* 359s; *64–65,*
362
Erpingham Camp, The *69–70,* 344
Errant Lady *34–35,* 373
Erratic Trains *60–61,* 295
Erstwhile Susan *09–19,* 569
Escapade *53–54,* 321
Escape *27–28,* 440
Escape, The *09–19,* 507
Escape Me Never *34–35,* 442;
44–45, 436; *59–60,* 43
Escape This Night *37–38,* 441
Escurial *60–61,* 44; *67–68,* 402
Esmeralda *94–99,* 111
Espoir, L' (see *Promise*)
Essential Lenny Bruce, The *70–71*
Establishment, The *62–63,* 323;
63–64, 350s
Esther (Book of) *99–09,* 520; *68–69,*
385
Eternal Cage *44–45,* 442
Eternal City, The *99–09,* 423
Eternal Jew, The *26–27,* 440
Eternal Magdalene, The *09–19,* 563
Eternal Mother *46–47,* 497
Eternal Mystery, The *09–19,* 509
Eternal Road, The *36–37,* 449
Eternal Sabbath *63–64,* 368
Eternal Triangle *66–67,* 407
Ethan Frome *35–36,* 462; *47–48,*
424–5
Ethel Waters *58–59,* 53
Etienne Decroux *59–60,* 48
Eugene Hari (dance programs; see
Ruth Mata & Eugene Hari)
Eugene Onegin (opera rep) *46–47,*
409; *47–48,* 343

Eugenia *56–57*, 353
Eugenically Speaking *09–19*, 547, 579
Eumenides, The *(The Furies)* *61–62*, 255; *68–69*, 398, 399
Europeans, The *56–57*, 353
Eurydice *51–52*, 300
Eva *09–19*, 490
Eva Lorraine & Ted Montague *47–48*, 429
Eva the Fifth *28–29*, 364
Evangeline (source) *09–19*, 510; *47–48*, 429
Evangeline (p) *09–19*, 510
Evangeline (m) *94–99*, 178
Evangeline (opera rep) *47–48*, 429
Evangelist, The *99–09*, 546
Eve of St. Mark, The *42–43*, 434
Evening for Merlin Finch, An *68 69*, 437
Evening in Cathay, An (1939) *38–39*, 493
Evening in Cathay (1947) *46–47*, 496
Evening of Brecht, An *61–62*, 322
Evening of One Acts, An *68–69*, 440
Evening of Three Farces, An *57–58*, 330
Evening of Two Plays, An *47–48*, 426
Evening With Beatrice Lillie, An *52–53*, 256s
Evening With Max Morath at the Turn of the Century, An *68–69*, 446
Evening With Mike Nichols and Elaine May, An *60–61*, 229
Evening With Sue & Pugh, An *66–67*, 423
Evening With the Times Square Two, An *66–67*, 421
Evening With Yves Montand, An *61–62*, 266s
Evening's Frost, An *65–66*, 422
Evenings in Dixie *35–36*, 512
Evensong *32–33*, 456

Ever Green Lady, The *22–23*, 474
Every Maid Her Own Mistress *37–38*, 412
Every Man for Himself *40–41*, 400
Every Other Evil *60–61*, 39
Every Thursday *33–34*, 528
Everybody Loves Opal *61–62*, 260
Everybody's Welcome *31–32*, 409s
Everyday *21–22*, 463
Everyman *(Jedermann)* *99–09*, 419, 534; *09–19*, 410, 496, 619; *27–28*, 455, 466; *40–41*, 433; *53–54*, 358
Everything *09–19*, 633
Everything in the Garden *67–68*, 353
Everything Under the Sun *63–64*, 346
Everything's Jake *29–30*, 480
Everywhere I Roam *38–39*, 442; *39–40*, 468
Everywoman *09–19*, 440
Eve's Daughter *09–19*, 609
Eve's Leaves *24–25*, 562
Evidence *09–19*, 533
Evil Eye, The *94–99*, 250
Exceeding Small *28–29*, 401
Excelsior, Jr. *94–99*, 154
Exception and the Rule, The *61–62*, 322; *64–65*, 360
Excess Baggage *27–28*, 479
Exchange *69–70*, 357
Exchange of Wives, An *19–20*, 357
Exciters, The *22–23*, 460
Excursion *36–37*, 479
Excuse Me *09–19*, 439, 624
Executioners, The *59–60*, 46
Exercise, The *67–68*, 373
Exhaustion of Our Son's Love, The *65–66*, 422
Exhibition *68–69*, 453
Exile, The *22–23*, 556
Exiles *24–25*, 545; *46–47*, 485; *56–57*, 55
Exit the King *67–68*, 353
Exodus *70–71*
Experience *09–19*, 536, 620
Experience Unnecessary *31–32*, 455

Experiment, The *66–67*, 419

Experiments in Dance-Theater *66–67*, 423

Experiments With the Great God Brown 70–71

Explainers, The *63–64*, 369

Explorer, The *09–19*, 472

Expressing Willie *23–24*, 420

Extra *22–23*, 523; *25–26*, 463

Extracts From Adam's Diary (see also *The Diary of Adam and Eve*) *65–66*, 405

Eye on the Sparrow *37–38*, 443

Eyes *29–30*, 538

Eyes of the Heart, The *99–09*, 487, 513

Eyes of Youth *09–19*, 604

Eyes Upon the Cross *61–62*, 327

Eyvind of the Hills *20–21*, 432

Fabio Romani *94–99*, 138

Fables for Our Time(s) *47–48*, 416, 417; *59–60*, 226; *62–63*, 309

Fabulous Invalid, The *38–39*, 412

Fabulous Miss Marie, The *70–71*

Face of a Hero *60–61*, 302

Face the Music *31–32*, 480s; *32–33*, 457s

Face Value *21–22*, 485

Facing the Music *99–09*, 433

Factory Waif, A *94–99*, 238

Fad and Folly *99–09*, 423

Fade Out—Fade In *63–64*, 339s

Fads and Fancies *09–19*, 548

Failures, The *23–24*, 355

Fair and Warmer *09–19*, 564

Fair at Sorochinsk, The (opera rep) *42–43*, 485, 487

Fair Circassian, The *21–22*, 474

Fair Co-ed, The *99–09*, 577

Fair Enough *38–39*, 491, 492

Fair Exchange, A *99–09*, 502

Fair Game *57–58*, 299

Fair Game for Lovers *63–64*, 324

Fair in Midgettown, The *94–99*, 209

Faiseur, Le *38–39*, 492

Faith *40–41*, 430

Faith and Prudence *52–53*, 308

Faith Healer, The *09–19*, 411; *69–70*, 371

Faithful, The *19–20*, 369

Faithful Heart, The *22–23*, 472

Faithfully Yours *51–52*, 287

Fake, The *24–25*, 466

Fakir Rahman Bey *25–26*, 601

Fall and Rise of Susan Lenox *19–20*, 457

Fall Guy, The *24–25*, 558

Fall of Eve, The *25–26*, 433

Fallen Among Thieves *94–99*, 133

Fallen Angels *27–28*, 463; *55–56*, 370; *68–69*, 457

Fallen Idol, The *09–19*, 544

Falote, La *94–99*, 195

False Confession, The *(Les Fausses Confidences)* *52–53*, 267; *62–63*, 340; *70–71*

False Dreams, Farewell *33–34*, 480

Falsely True *09–19*, 459

Falstaff *28–29*, 440

Fam and Yam *60–61*, 47

Fame *69–70*, 376

Familiar Pattern *43–44*, 488

Family, The (1) *09–19*, 427

Family, The (2) *42–43*, 470

Family Affair, A (1) *46–47*, 444

Family Affair, A (2) *61–62*, 283s

Family Affairs *29–30*, 461

Family Album *36–37*, 438; *47–48*, 385

Family Carnovsky, The *43–44*, 490

Family Cupboard, The *09–19*, 504

Family Exit, The *09–19*, 607; *32–33*, 436

Family Failing *09–19*, 494

Family Failing, The *24–25*, 603

Family Portrait *38–39*, 463; *45–46*, 451

Family Reunion, (The) *47–48*, 425; *50–51*, 373; *58–59*, 297; *67–68*, 410

Family Upstairs, The *25–26*, 427; *33–34*, 451; *43–44*, 489

Family Versus the Universe *62–63,* 335

Family Way, The *64–65,* 323

Famous Mrs. Fair, The *19–20,* 404

Fan, The *21–22,* 434

Fanatics, The *27–28,* 447

Fanchon *94–99,* 243

Fancy Free (1) *09–19,* 497; *28–29,* 501

Fancy Free (2) *09–19,* 627

Fancy Meeting You Again *51–52,* 305

Fanny (1) *26–27,* 384

Fanny (2; p) *54–55,* 373

Fanny (2; m) *54–55,* 373s

Fanny Hawthorn *21–22,* 546

Fanny's First Play *09–19,* 477

Fanshastics *23–24,* 386

Fantana *99–09,* 482

Fantasia *32–33,* 447

Fantasio *37–38,* 469

Fantasma *94–99,* 88

Fantastic Fricassee, A *22–23,* 452

Fantasticks, The *59–60,* 358s

Far Country, A *60–61,* 333

Far Cry, The *24–25,* 462

Far-Away Horses *32–33,* 478

Farewell, Farewell, Eugene *60–61,* 296

Farewell Summer *36–37,* 474

Farewell to Arms, A *30–31,* 416

Farm of Three Echoes *39–40,* 416

Farmer Takes a Wife, The *34–35,* 400

Farmer's Wife, The *24–25,* 468; *51–52,* 276

Far-Off Hills, The *32–33,* 404; *34–35,* 407; *35–36,* 511; *36–37,* 497; *37–38,* 375; *38–39,* 492

Fascinating Flora *99–09,* 540

Fascinating Mr. Vanderveldt, The *99–09,* 507

Fascinating Widow, The *09–19,* 450

Fashion *23–24,* 395; *58–59,* 53

Fashions for Men *22–23,* 498

Fashions of 1924 *23–24,* 294

Fast and Furious *31–32,* 392

Fast and Grow Fat *09–19,* 580

Fast Life *28–29,* 381

Fast Mail, The *94–99,* 219

Fast Service *31–32,* 434

Fata Morgana *23–24,* 404; *31–32,* 449; *46–47,* 485

Fatal Alibi, The *31–32,* 474

Fatal Beauty *67–68,* 412

Fatal Card, The *94–99,* 115

Fatal City *94–99,* 191

Fatal Weakness, The *46–47,* 442

Fatal Wedding, The *99–09,* 398; *23–24,* 441

Father, The *09–19,* 470; *27–28,* 553; *31–32,* 406; *49–50,* 360, 382, 383; *61–62,* 298

Father and Son *99–09,* 569

Father and the Boys *99–09,* 559

Father Malachy's Miracle *37–38,* 391

Father of His Country, The *94–99,* 236

Father Returns, The *28–29,* 500

Father Sees a Son Nearing Manhood, A *60–61,* 294

Father Uxbridge Wants to Marry *67–68,* 391

Father's Day *70–71*

Father's Sons, The *40–41,* 432

Fatinitza *99–09,* 479; *42–43,* 486

Fatted Calf, The *09–19,* 466

Faun, The *09–19,* 436

Fausses Confidences, Les (see *The False Confession)*

Faust (source) *94–99,* 119, 150, 205; *09–19,* 410; *21–22,* 501; *28–29,* 389; *38–39,* 475; *39–40,* 468; *45–46,* 390; *60–61,* 323

Faust (p) *94–99,* 119, 150; *28–29,* 389; *45–46,* 390, 450; *60–61,* 322

Faust (opera rep) *43–44,* 473; *45–46,* 390, 441; *46–47,* 409, 480; *47–48,* 399

Faust Foutu *59–60,* 40

Faust, Part I *60–61,* 322

Faustina *51–52,* 334

Faux Modele, La *09–19*, 589 (and 605)

Fear *09–19*, 497, 509

Fear Market, The *09–19*, 569

Feast of Panthers *60–61*, 39

Feathers in a Gale *43–44*, 443

Federal Theater Project dance programs *36–37*, 496; *37–38*, 459, 460, 467; *38–39*, 483

Federal Theater Project Marionettes *35–36*, 479, 513; *37–38*, 460, 466; *38–39*, 483, 489

Fedora *94–99*, 163, 222; *99–09*, 491; *21–22*, 508

Felice *09–19*, 509

Felicia Sorel (dance programs) *42–43*, 485

Felines, Les *24–25*, 475

Female Drummer, A *94–99*, 248

Femme de Claude, La *94–99*, 163, 169

Femme de Tabarin, La *99–09*, 485

Femme X, La (see *Madame X*)

Femmes Savantes, Les (see *The Learned Ladies*)

Ferdinand (see *The Story of Ferdinand*)

Fermiere, Le (sic) *94–99*, 182

Fern Hill *62–63*, 322

Festival (1; *Matsuri*) *29–30*, 506

Festival (2) *54–55*, 392

Fétards, Les *99–09*, 576

Feu la Mere de Madame (see *Dear Departed Mother-in-Law*)

Feudalism or the Lowland *36–37*, 500

Few Are Chosen *35–36*, 405

Few of the Usual Nudes, A *66–67*, 423

Few Wild Oats, A *31–32*, 494

Fickle Women *37–38*, 402

Fiddle-dee-dee *99–09*, 369

Fiddler on the Roof *64–65*, 302s

Fiddler's House, The *40–41*, 431

Fiddlers Three *09–19*, 635

Field God, The *26–27*, 514

Field of Ermine *34–35*, 448

Fields Beyond, The *35–36*, 491

Fiesta *29–30*, 395

Fiesta in Madrid *68–69*, 415s

Fifth Column, The *39–40*, 442

Fifth Commandment, The *65–66*, 426

Fifth Horseman, The *49–50*, 383

Fifth Season, The *52–53*, 283

Fifty Miles From Boston *99–09*, 557

Fifty Million Frenchmen *29–30*, 452; *64–65*, 357

Fifty-Fifty *37–38*, 468

Fifty-Fifty, Ltd. *19–20*, 380

57 Bowery *27–28*, 498

Fig Leaf in Her Bonnet, A *61–62*, 303

Fig Leaves Are Falling, The *68–69*, 400s

Fight, The *09–19*, 482, 505

Fight for Honor, A *94–99*, 204

Fighting Cock, The *59–60*, 310

Figuro in the Night *62–63*, 338

Fighting Hope, The *99–09*, 569

Fil a la Patte, Un *65–66*, 397

Filling Station (dance program) *38–39*, 475

Fils de Famille, Le *94–99*, 115

Fils Surnaturel, Le *09–19*, 538

Final Balance, The *28–29*, 407

Final Problem, The *64–65*, 328

Find Daddy *25–26*, 564

Find the Fox *30–31*, 398

Fine and Dandy *30–31*, 417

Fine Feathers *09–19*, 491

Fine Old Wine of Monsieur Nuche, The *50–51*, 373

Fingers (1) *37–38*, 464

Fingers (2) *60–61*, 294

Finian's Rainbow *46–47*, 455; *52–53*, 309; *54–55*, 414; *59–60*, 338; *66–67*, 386s

Finis for Oscar Wilde *63–64*, 368

Finish of Mr. Fresh, The *94–99*, 245

Finnegan's 400 *94–99*, 257

Finnegans Wake *62–63*, 320; *66–67*, 420; *68–69*, 458

Fiole, La *23–24*, 333

Fiorello! *59–60,* 305s; *62–63,* 277

Fioretta *28–29,* 466

Fire! *68–69,* 403

Fire and Water *09–19,* 560

Fire Patrol, The *94–99,* 243

Firebird *32–33,* 425

Firebrand, The *24–25,* 473; *44–45,* 424; *65–66,* 436

Firebrand of Florence, The *44–45,* 424

Firebugs, The *(Biedermann und die Brandstifter) 62–63,* 325; *68–69,* 426; *69–70,* 347

Fire-Eaters, The *63–64,* 371

Firefly, The *09–19,* 487; *31–32,* 441

Fireman's Flame, The *37–38,* 449

Fires of Fate, The *09–19,* 408

Fires of St. John, The *99–09,* 475, 560

Fireworks (for a Hot Fourth) *69–70,* 334

Fireworks on the James *39–40,* 446

Firm of Cunningham, The *99–09,* 490

First, The *64–65,* 344

First American Dictator *38–39,* 464

First Apple, The *33–34,* 471

First Born, The *94–99,* 211

First Cousins *42–43,* 477; *43–44,* 404

First Crocus, The *41–42,* 424

First Episode *34–35,* 372

First Fifty Years, The *21–22,* 525

First Flight *25–26,* 447

First Gentleman, The *56–57,* 370

First Gentleman of Europe, The *94–99,* 192

First Impressions *58–59,* 331s

First Is Last *19–20,* 352

First Lady *35–36,* 440; *51–52,* 328

First Lady in the Land, The *09–19,* 460

First Law, The *28–29,* 503

First Legion, The *34–35,* 382

First Love (1) *26–27,* 420; *46–47,* 497

First Love (2) *52–53,* 307

First Love (3) *61–62,* 274

First Man, The *21–22,* 519

First Million, The *42–43,* 472

First Mortgage *29–30,* 416

First Mrs. Fraser, The *29–30,* 470; *47–48,* 364

First Night *30–31,* 461

First One Asleep, Whistle *65–66,* 400

First Stone, The *27–28,* 492

First Stop to Heaven *40–41,* 408

First Violin, The *94–99,* 228; *99–09,* 355

First Wife, The *45–46,* 458

First Year, The *20–21,* 398; *46–47,* 485

Firstborn, The *57–58,* 331

Fisher Maiden, The *99–09,* 438

Fisherman, The (1) *48–49,* 426

Fisherman, The (2) *64–65,* 352

Fisherman's Vengeance *62–63,* 286

Fishing for Wives (mn) *65–66,* 403

Fitz *65–66,* 435

Five Alarm Waltz *40–41,* 420

Five Evenings *62–63,* 336

Five Finger Exercise *59–60,* 307; *68–69,* 455

Five Frankforters, The *09–19,* 496

Five Fridays *09–19,* 580

Five Little Peppers, The *33–34,* 534

Five Million, The *19–20,* 338

Five O'Clock *19–20,* 372

5 O'Clock Girl *27–28,* 427

Five on the Black Hand Side *69–70,* 341

Five Posts in the Market Place *60–61,* 39

Five Queens *63–64,* 345

Five Star Final *30–31,* 475

Five Star Saint *69–70,* 372

Fixing Sister *09–19,* 584

Flag Is Born, A *46–47,* 417; *47–48,* 431

Flag Lieutenant, The *09–19,* 397

Flag of Truce, A *94–99,* 86

Flag Station, The *99–09,* 539, 547

Flahooley *50–51,* 370s; *63–64,* 368

Flambee, La *09–19*, 492
Flame, The *09–19*, 581
Flame of Love *23–24*, 422
Flamenco music & dance (dance programs) *63–64*, 353
Flamingo Road *45–46*, 432
Flams, The *94–99*, 106
Flandes se ha Puesto el Sol, El *31–32*, 500
Flare Path *42–43*, 453
Flashing Stream, The *38–39*, 467
Flea in Her Ear, A *69–70*, 297
Fledermaus, Die *29–30*, 431; *33–34*, 441; *42–43*, 441; *53–54*, 355
Fledgling *40–41*, 397
Flesh *24–25*, 589
Fleur de Lis *94–99*, 139
Flies, The *46–47*, 497
Flight *28–29*, 470; *36–37*, 496
Flight Into Egypt *51–52*, 313
Flight 13 *39–40*, 469
Flight to the West *40–41*, 407
Flip Side, The *68–69*, 385
Flo-Flo *09–19*, 617
Floor, The *65–66*, 436
Flora Bella *09–19*, 581
Flora, the Red Menace *64–65*, 336s
Floradora *19–20*, 443
Floradora sextette (mn) *38–39*, 489
Floriani's Wife *23–24*, 324
Florida Enchantment, A *94–99*, 181
Florida Girl *25–26*, 487
Florist Shop, The *09–19*, 396
Florizel and Perdita (see *The Winter's Tale*)
Florodora *99–09*, 379
Flossie *23–24*, 441
Flower Drum Song *58–59*, 306s
Flower in Drama, The *62–63*, 326
Flower of the Palace of Han, The *09–19*, 469
Flower of the Ranch, The *99–09*, 561
Flower of Yamato, The *99–09*, 558
Flowering Cherry *59–60*, 298
Flowering Peach, The *54–55*, 387; *70–71*

Flowers & Moonlight of the Spring River *68–69*, 407
Flowers of the Forest *34–35*, 468
Flowers of Virtue, The *41–42*, 438
Fluffy Ruffles *99–09*, 567
Fly Away Home *34–35*, 439
Fly Blackbird *61–62*, 322s
Fly by Night *32–33*, 500
Flying Blind *29–30*, 540
Flying Colors *32–33*, 387
Flying Dutchman, The *45–46*, 390
Flying Gerardos, The *40–41*, 406
Flying High *29–30*, 503
Foenix in Choir *58–59*, 50
Fog (1) *26–27*, 477
Fog (2) *60–61*, 294
Fog, The *09–19*, 535
Fog-Bound *26–27*, 502
Fol-de-rol *37–38*, 468
Folies Bergere (1939) *39–40*, 425
Folies Bergere (1964) *64–65*, 294s
Folk songs, dances, tales (sources & untitled programs) *33–34*, 519; *36–37*, 499; *37–38*, 460, 467; *42–43*, 485; *44–45*, 406; *45–46*, 454; *46–47*, 488, 496; *47–48*, 344–5, 415, 423; *49–50*, 354; *54–55*, 360, 386; *57–58*, 329; *63–64*, 323, 330, 354, 356; *64–65*, 316, 361; *65–66*, 401, 402, 403; *66–67*, 353, 354, 355, 357, 369; *67–68*, 363, 364; *68–69*, 413; *70–71*
Follies *70–71*
Follies Burlesque '67 *66–67*, 418s
Follies of 1910 *59–60*, 46
Follow Me *09–19*, 588
Follow the Girl *09–19*, 624
Follow the Girls *43–44*, 466
Follow Thru *28–29*, 451
Following the Equator *65–66*, 404
Fontamara *35–36*, 495
Fool, The *22–23*, 476
Fool and His Money, A *99–09*, 431
Fool Hath Said: "There Is No God", The *99–09*, 470

Fool of Fortune, The (A) *94–99*, 186; *09–19*, 463
Fool There Was, A (1) *99–09*, 580
Fool There Was, A (2) *34–35*, 444
Foolhardy Mouse and the Cautious Cat, The *62–63*, 310
Foolish Notion *44–45*, 420
Foolish Virgin, The *09–19*, 433
Fools Are Passing Through *(The Marriage of Mr. Mississippi)* *57–58*, 56, 244
Fool's Bells *25–26*, 521
Fool's Errand, The *26–27*, 522
Fools Errant *22–23*, 440
Fool's Revenge, The *94–99*, 127; *99–09*, 385
Fools Rush In *34–35*, 429
Foolscap *32–33*, 449
Football *69–70*, 334
Footlights *27–28*, 393
Footloose *19–20*, 452
Footsteps *45–46*, 459
Footsteps of Doves, The *66–67*, 384
For All of Us *23–24*, 334
For Better or Worse *26–27*, 472
For Bonnie Prince Charlie *94–99*, 194
For Distinguished Service *24–25*, 583
For Fair Virginia *94–99*, 136
For Goodness Sake *21–22*, 514
For Heaven's Sake, Mother! *48–49*, 395
For Keeps *43–44*, 483
For Liberty and Love *94–99*, 211
For Love or Money *47–48*, 364
For Love's Sweet Sake *99–09*, 430
For Men Only *36–37*, 454
For One Sweet Grape *49–50*, 361
For Services Rendered *32–33*, 482
For the Crown *94–99*, 165
For the Defense *19–20*, 400
For Valor *35–36*, 435
For Value Received *22–23*, 568
For Your Pleasure *42–43*, 463
Forbidden (1) *19–20*, 403
Forbidden (2) *23–24*, 327

Forbidden Fruit *09–19*, 547
Forbidden Guests, The *09–19*, 523
Forbidden Melody *36–37*, 425
Forbidden Roads *27–28*, 540
Foreign Affairs *31–32*, 506
Foreigners *39–40*, 419
Forensic and the Navigators *67–68*, 413; *69–70*, 362
Foreplay *70–71*
Forest Lovers, The *99–09*, 394
Forest of Happy Dreams, The *09–19*, 535
Forever After *09–19*, 636
Forget-Me-Not *94–99*, 109, 136; *19–20*, 452
Forsaking All Others *32–33*, 470
Fortress of Glass *52–53*, 306
Fortuna *61–62*, 317s
Fortunatus (see *The Purse of Fortunatus)*
Fortune *94–99*, 132
Fortune and Men's Eyes *66–67*, 414; *69–70*, 344
Fortune Hunter, The *09–19*, 398; *25–26*, 483
Fortune Teller, The (1) *94–99*, 239; *29–30*, 434; *46–47*, 419
Fortune Teller, The (2) *09–19*, 652
Fortunes of the King, The *99–09*, 477
Forty Carats *68–69*, 400
Forty Winks *38–39*, 492
Forty-Five Minutes From Broadway *99–09*, 505; *09–19*, 468
'49ers, The *22–23*, 485
49th Cousin, The *60–61*, 303
41 in a Sack *59–60*, 48
Forward the Heart *48–49*, 409
Foundling, The *94–99*, 124
Fountain, The (1) *09–19*, 509
Fountain, The (2) *25–26*, 512
Fountain, The (3) *25–26*, 515
Fountain of Youth, The *09–19*, 626
Four in Hand *60–61*, 39
Four Minute Mile, The *63–64*, 371
Four No Plays *68–69*, 456
Four O'Clock *32–33*, 461

Four on a Garden *70–71*
Four Saints in Three Acts *33–34*,
    498; 51–52, 319
Four Seasons, The (1) *99–09*, 551
Four Seasons, The (2) *67–68*, 403
417 *60–61*, 39
Four Twelves Are 48 *50–51*, 342
Four Walls *27–28*, 406
Four Winds *57–58*, 286
Fourberies de Scapin, Les (see
    Scapin)
Fourflusher, The *24–25*, 571
Fourposter, The *51–52*, 288; *54–55*,
    391; *66–67*, 375
1492 up to Date *94–99*, 103
4th Avenue North *61–62*, 308s
Fourth Estate, The *09–19*, 402
Fourth Kingdom, The *36–37*, 498;
    37–38, 467
Fourth Pig, The *64–65*, 352
Fourth Wall, The *68–69*, 426
Foxhole in the Parlor *44–45*, 432
Foxy *63–64*, 325s
Foxy Grandpa *99–09*, 406
Foxy Quiller *99–09*, 379
Fra Diavolo (opera rep) *09–19*, 638
Fragile Fox *54–55*, 367
Fragments *67–68*, 387
Francesca da Rimini *99–09*, 403,
    421; *24–25*, 499; *28–29*, 485
Francillon *94–95*, 124
Francis Renault *47–48*, 429
Frank Fay's Fables *21–22*, 507
Frank Gagliano's City Scene *68–69*,
    448s
Frank Merriwell, or Honor
    Challenged *70–71*
Frank Merriwell's School Days
    70–71
Frankenstein *68–69*, 456
Frankie and Johnny (1) *30–31*, 420
Frankie and Johnny (2) *52–53*, 307
Frauenfresser, Die *09–19*, 480
Freak In *70–71*
Freaking Out of Stephanie Blake,
    The *67–68*, 380
Freckles *09–19*, 488

Freddy *29–30*, 379
Frederico Rey (dance programs; see
    *Maria Teresa Acuna & Frederico
    Rey)*
Frederika *36–37*, 459
Free for All *31–32*, 387s
Free Lance, The *99–09*, 513
Free Soul, A *27–28*, 490
Freedom *09–19*, 640
Freedom for Clemens *67–68*, 414
Freedom of Suzanne, The *99–09*,
    490
Freiburg Passion Play *28–29*, 497
Freight *48–49*, 427; *49–50*, 378
French Doll, The *21–22*, 513
French Leave *20–21*, 402
French Maid, The *94–99*, 209
French plays, music (unnamed
    programs) *35–36*, 511; *44–45*, 444
French Touch, The *45–46*, 411
French Way, The *61–62*, 326
French Without Tears *37–38*, 372;
    39–40, 470
Frenesie *45–46*, 460
Frere Jacques *68–69*, 422
Fresh Fields *35–36*, 480
Friday Bench, The *70–71*
Friday Night *64–65*, 353
Friend Indeed, A *25–26*, 588
Friend Martha *09–19*, 602
Friendly Enemies *09–19*, 631
Friends (1) *94–99*, 129
Friends (2) *65–66*, 421
Friends Invited *24–25*, 587
Friendship *31–32*, 384
Friquet *99–09*, 483
Frisky Mrs. Johnson, The *99–09*,
    428
Fritz in a Madhouse *94–99*, 90
Fritz in Love *94–99*, 171
Fritz in Tammany Hall *99–09*, 498
Frivolities of 1920 *19–20*, 414
Frocks and Frills *99–09*, 403
Frogs of Spring, The *53–54*, 311
From a Clear Sky *94–99*, 221
From A to Z *59–60*, 334s
From an Abandoned Work *70–71*

From Distant Rooms *66–67*, 423
From Morn Till Midnight *21–22*,
    548; *22–23*, 432
From Sire to Son *94–99*, 84
From the Second City *61–62*, 255
From the Second City (1969) *69–70*,
    343
From the Two Coony Lemels to
    Lovka Molodetz *46–47*, 497
From Vienna *39–40*, 394
Front Page, The *28–29*, 358; *34–35*,
    477; *44–45*, 436; *46–47*, 416;
    60–61, 48; *68–69*, 414; *69–70*, 301
Frou-Frou (Frou Frou) (1) *94–99*,
    156, 169; *99–09*, 412
Frou-Frou (2) *09–19*, 469
Fruit Salad *66–67*, 36
Frying Pan, The *66–67*, 407
Fuerza Ciega, La *27–28*, 468
Fugitive, The *09–19*, 597
Fugitives *38–39*, 488
Full House, A *09–19*, 552
Fully Guarenteed Fuck-Me Doll,
    The *69–70*, 374
Fulton of Oak Falls *36–37*, 463
Fumed Oak *36–37*, 436; *47–48*, 384;
    66–67, 393
Fun City *67–68*, 402s
Fun Couple, The *62–63*, 283
Fun To Be Free *41–42*, 460
Funabashi *99–09*, 554
Funa-Benkei (see *Benkei in the
    Boat*)
Funny Face *27–28*, 457
Funny Girl *63–64*, 329s
Funny Thing Happened on the Way
    to the Forum, A *61–62*, 297s
Funnyhouse of a Negro *63–64*, 356
Furies, The (1) *27–28*, 523
Furies, The (2; see *The Eumenides*)
Furnished Rooms *33–34*, 530
Furs, and Frills *09–19*, 609
Futz! *66–67*, 36; *68–69*, 425

G.B.Essence of Women, The *64–65*,
    361
Gabrielle *40–41*, 422

Gaby *09–19*, 445
Gadfly, The *99–09*, 349
Gaiety Girl, A *94–99*, 94
Gala Night *29–30*, 501
Galician Wedding, The *47–48*, 431
Galileo *47–48*, 393; *61–62*, 318;
    66–67, 361
Gallant Lady *41–42*, 459
Galley Slave, or The Blind Boy and
    His Dog *94–99*, 158
Galloper, The *99–09*, 507, 541
Galloping Sheik, The (see *Arabian
    Nightmare*)
Gallops *99–09*, 509
Gallows Humor *60–61*, 360; *61–62*,
    323
Gambler, The *52–53*, 258; *68–69*,
    458
Gamblers, The *09–19*, 428
Gamblers All *09–19*, 592
Gambling *29–30*, 384
Gambling Chaplain, The *22–23*, 451
Game Is Up, The (1964) *64–65*,
    342s; *66–67*, 400
Game Is Up, The (1965) *65–66*,
    417s; *66–67*, 400
Game of Chess, The *23–24*, 433
Game of Love, The *99–09*, 583
Game of Love and Chance, The *(Le
    Jeu de L'Amour et du Hasard)*
    55–56, 358
Game of Love and Death, The
    29–30, 447
Gammer Gurton's Needle *09–19*,
    588
Gandhi *70–71*
Gang War *28–29*, 359
Gang's All Here, The (1) *30–31*,
    493
Gang's All Here, The (2) *59–60*,
    292
Gantry *69–70*, 315s
Gaol Gate, The *09–19*, 458, 494
Garden District *57–58*, 53
Garden of Allah, The *09–19*, 455,
    624
Garden of Eden, The *27–28*, 416

Garden of Paradise, The *09–19*, 540
Garden of Sweets, The *61–62*, 267
Garden of Weeds *23–24*, 425
Gardener's Dog, The *(Le Chien du Jardinier)* *56–57*, 353
Gardiens de Phare *23–24*, 333
Garrett O'Magh *99–09*, 385
Garrick Gaieties (1925) *24–25*, 602
Garrick Gaieties (1926) *25–26*, 598
Garrick Gaieties (1930) *29–30*, 548
Garrick Gaieties (Second Edition) (1930) *30–31*, 433
Garry Owen *94–99*, 128
Gas *43–44*, 488; *47–48*, 425
Gaslight *(Angel Street)* *41–42*, 282
Gasoline Gypsies *30–31*, 533
Gay Apprentice, The *59–60*, 49
Gay Deceiver, The *94–99*, 209
Gay Divorce *32–33*, 431s; *59–60*, 48; *64–65*, 357
Gay Hussars, The *09–19*, 395
Gay Life, The (1) *99–09*, 582
Gay Life, The (2) *61–62*, 270s
Gay Lord Quex, The *99–09*, 379; *09–19*, 614
Gay Mr. Lightfoot, The *94–99*, 188
Gay Musician, The *99–09*, 562
Gay Paree (1925) *25–26*, 427
Gay Paree (1926) *26–27*, 422
Gay Parisians, The *94–99*, 144
Gay White Way, The *99–09*, 546
Gayden *48–49*, 422
Gayest Manhattan, or Around New York in Ninety Minutes *94–99*, 198
Gazebo, The *58–59*, 313
Geese *68–69*, 443
Geezer, The *94–99*, 179
Geisha, The *94–99*, 176; *09–19*, 498; *31–32*, 403
General John Regan *09–19*, 513; *29–30*, 485
General Kumagai's Battle Camp *(Kumagai Jinya)* *69–70*, 296
General Post *09–19*, 618
General Returns From One Place to Another, The *63–64*, 364

General Seeger *61–62*, 290
General's Daughter, The (mn) *65–66*, 403
Generation *65–66*, 374
Genesee of the Hills *99–09*, 533
Genesis (Book of) *09–19*, 491; *29–30*, 492; *64–65*, 322
Geneva *39–40*, 433
Genio Alegre, El *31–32*, 500
Genius, The *99–09*, 521
Genius and the Crowd *20–21*, 377
Genius and the Goddess, The *57–58*, 305
Gentile Wife, The *09–19*, 647
Gentle Art of Making Enemies, The *66–67*, 423
Gentle Grafters *26–27*, 414
Gentle People, The *38–39*, 445; *47–48*, 424
Gentleman Caller, The *69–70*, 338
Gentleman From Athens, The *47–48*, 367
Gentleman From Mississippi, A *99–09*, 569
Gentleman From Number 19, The *09–19*, 501
Gentleman Jack *94–99*, 87
Gentleman Joe, the Hansom Cabby *94–99*, 161
Gentleman of France, A *99–09*, 402
Gentleman of Leisure, A *09–19*, 448
Gentlemen, Be Seated! *63–64*, 348s
Gentlemen of the Press *28–29*, 362
Gentlemen Prefer Blondes (p) *26–27*, 388
Gentlemen Prefer Blondes (m) *49–50*, 363s
Gentlemen, the Baby Is Born *34–35*, 484
Gentlewoman *33–34*, 509
Gently Does It *53–54*, 313
George and Margaret *37–38*, 369
George Barnwell, or The London Merchant *28–29*, 384
George Dandin *23–24*, 416; *63–64*, 327; *68–69*, 374
George Washington *19–20*, 432

George Washington Crossing the Delaware *61–62*, 325

George M! *67–68*, 370s

George Washington, Jr. *99–09*, 509

George Washington Slept Here *40–41*, 387

George White's Music Hall Varieties *32–33*, 428

(George White's) Scandals of 1919 *09–19*, 657

(George White's) Scandals of 1920 *19–20*, 456

George White's Scandals (1921) *21–22*, 388

George White's Scandals of 1922 *22–23*, 443

George White's Scandals (1923) *23–24*, 293

George White's Scandals (1924) *24–25*, 431

George White's Scandals (1925) *25–26*, 419

George White's Scandals (1926) *25–26*, 604

George White's Scandals (1928) *28–29*, 353

George White's Scandals (1929) *29–30*, 401

George White's Scandals (1931) *31–32*, 390s

George White's Scandals (1935) *35–36*, 453

George White's Scandals (1939) *39–40*, 397

Georgie-Porgie *68–69*, 455; *70–71*

Georgy *69–70*, 317s

Georgy Girl *69–70*, 317

Geranium Hat, The *58–59*, 51

Geraniums in My Window *34–35*, 398

Gertie (1) *26–27*, 427

Gertie (2) *51–52*, 307

Gertrude *70–71*

Gertrude Stein's First Reader *69–70*, 350s

Gertrude's Wrong Choice *62–63*, 335

Get Away Old Man *43–44*, 431

Get Me in the Movies *27–28*, 555

Get Thee to Canterbury *68–69*, 444s

Get Together *21–22*, 411

Get-Rich-Quick Wallingford *09–19*, 424, 600

Getting a Polish *09–19*, 429

Getting and Spending *62–63*, 338

Getting Even *29–30*, 383

Getting Gertie's Garter *21–22*, 390

Getting Married *09–19*, 586; *30–31*, 509; *49–50*, 385; *50–51*, 367; *52–53*, 308; *59–60*, 43; *69–70*, 373

Getting Together *09–19*, 625

Gettysburg *94–99*, 228

Getzel at the Ball Game *48–49*, 430

Ghetto, The *99–09*, 348

Ghost Between, The *20–21*, 436

Ghost Breaker, The *09–19*, 496

Ghost for Sale *41–42*, 398

Ghost of Jerry Bundler, The *09–19*, 515

Ghost of Yankee Doodle, The *37–38*, 394

Ghost Parade, The *29–30*, 430

Ghost Sonata, The *70–71*

Ghost Train, The *26–27*, 369

Ghost Writer, The *33–34*, 420

Ghosts *99–09*, 430; *09–19*, 468; 551, 579, 651; *21–22*, 516; *23–24*, 366 *25–26*, 570; *26–27*, 458; *32–33*, 498; *34–35*, 483; *35–36*, 450, 512; *36–37*, 499; *45–46*, 450, 460; *47–48*, 386; *51–52*, 332, 333; *61–62*, 306

Gianni Schicchi *68–69*, 407

Giants' Dance, The *64–65*, 347

Giants in the Earth *50–51*, 375

Giants, Sons of Giants *61–62*, 280

Giants' Stair, The *24–25*, 586; *26–27*, 522

Giddy Throng, The *99–09*, 381

Gideon *61–62*, 270

Gift, The *23–24*, 392

Gift of the Magi, The *45–46*, 454

Gift of Time, A *61–62*, 289

Gigi *51–52*, 295

Gigolette *94–99*, 140
Gil Blas *57–58*, 56
Gilbert Becaud on Broadway *66–67*, 367s
Gilbert Becaud Sings Love *68–69*, 382s
Gilbert's Engaged *25–26*, 418
Gilded Fool, A *94–99*, 143, 236
Ginger *23–24*, 337
Ginger Man, The *63–64*, 352; *70–71*
Gingerbread Lady, The *70–71*
Gingerbread Man, The *99–09*, 504
Gingham Dog, The *68–69*, 413
Gingham Girl, The *22–23*, 443
Gioconda, La *99–09*, 421
Gioconda Smile, The *50–51*, 318
Gipsy Trail, The *09–19*, 616
Girl and the Cat, The *26–27*, 520
Girl and the Governor, The *99–09*, 533
Girl and the Judge, The *99–09*, 400
Girl and the Kaiser, The *09–19*, 431
Girl and the Pennant, The *09–19*, 511
Girl and the Wizard, The *09–19*, 401
Girl Behind the Counter, The *99–09*, 546; *09–19*, 575
Girl Behind the Gun, The *09–19*, 638
Girl Can Tell, A *53–54*, 313
Girl Could Get Lucky, A *64–65*, 302
Girl Crazy *30–31*, 430
Girl Friend, The *25–26*, 572
Girl From Brazil, The *09–19*, 578
Girl From Brighton, The *09–19*, 474
Girl From Child's, A *34–35*, 483
Girl From Dixie, The *99–09*, 448
Girl From Home, The *19–20*, 447
Girl From Kay's, The *99–09*, 442; *09–19*, 524
Girl From Maxim's, The *99–09*, 346
Girl From Montmartre, The *09–19*, 473

Girl From Nantucket, The *45–46*, 403
Girl From Paris, The *94–99*, 187
Girl From Rector's The *99–09*, 577
Girl From Up There, The *99–09*, 385
Girl From Utah, The *09–19*, 529
Girl From Wyoming, The *38–39*, 422
Girl He Couldn't Leave Behind Him, The *09–19*, 415
Girl I Left Behind Me, The *94–99*, 95
Girl in Pink Tights, The *53–54*, 343s
Girl in the Barracks, The *99–09*, 351
Girl in the Coffin, The *09–19*, 612
Girl in the Freudian Slip, The *66–67*, 394
Girl in the Limousine, The *19–20*, 365
Girl in the Spotlight, The *20–21*, 357
Girl in the Taxi, The *09–19*, 428
Girl in the Train, The *09–19*, 426
Girl o' Mine *09–19*, 620
Girl of My Dreams, The *09–19*, 447
Girl of the Golden West, The *99–09*, 500; *57–58*, 56
Girl on the Film, The *09–19*, 517
Girl on the Via Flaminia, The *53–54*, 340, 358
Girl Outside, The *32–33*, 408
Girl Patsy, The *99–09*, 514
Girl Question, The *99–09*, 564
Girl Trouble *28–29*, 404
Girl Wanted, A *94–99*, 161
Girl Who Came to Supper, The *63–64*, 315s
Girl Who Has Everything, The *99–09*, 528
Girl Who Smiles, The *09–19*, 554
Girl With the Carmine Lips, The *20–21*, 366
Girl With the Green Eyes, The *99–09*, 424

Girl With the Ring on Her Nose, The *70–71*

Girl With the Whooping Cough, The *09–19*, 418

Girlies *09–19*, 420

Girls *99–09*, 560

Girls Against the Boys, The *59–60*, 300s

Girls in 509, The *58–59*, 297

Girls in Uniform *32–33*, 445; *39–40*, 397, 473; *43–44*, 489

Girls of Gottenburg, The *99–09*, 567

Girls of Holland, The *99–09*, 550

Girls of Summer *56–57*, 336

Girls Will Be Girls *99–09*, 462

Girofle-Girofla *99–09*, 479

Gismonda *94–99*, 111, 163

Give and Take *22–23*, 521; *43–44*, 415

Give Me Yesterday *30–31*, 499

Give Us This Day *33–34*, 450

Gizmo Does the Audition *68–69*, 456

Glad Hand, The *94–99*, 180

Glad of It *99–09*, 449

Glad Tidings *51–52*, 286

Gladiator, The (see also *Spartacus*) *94–99*, 226; *70–71*

Gladys Laubin (dance programs; see *Reginald & Gladys Laubin*)

Glamour *62–63*, 326

Glamour Preferred *40–41*, 394

Glass *60–61*, 294

Glass Bottom Boat, The *63–64*, 371

Glass Menagerie, The *44–45*, 427; *52–53*, 308; *56–57*, 337; *64–65*, 336

Glass of Water, A *29–30*, 506

Glass Slipper, The *25–26*, 476

Glencairn (see *S.S. Glencairn*)

Glimpse of the Domesticity of Franklin Barnabas, A *59–60*, 43

Glimpse of the Gay White Way, A *09–19*, 511

Glittering Gloria *99–09*, 454

Gloria and Esperanza *69–70* 314

Gloria Mundi *24–25*, 587

Gloriana *38–39*, 430

Glorianna *09–19*, 641

Glorious Betsy *99–09*, 568

Glorious Morning *38–39*, 451

Glorious Ruler, The *69–70*, 336

Glory *22–23*, 513

Glory Hallelujah *25–26*, 580

Glory in the Flower, The *59–60*, 49

Glowing Bird, The (mn) *35–36*, 512

Gluck Bei Frauen *09–19*, 396

Gnadiges Fraulein *65–66*, 399

Go Easy, Mabel *21–22*, 545

Go Fight City Hall *61–62*, 312

Go Fly a Kite *69–70*, 344

Go, Go, Go, God Is Dead! *66–67*, 423

Go Show Me a Dragon *61–62*, 311

Go to It *09–19*, 585

Go West, Young Man *23–24*, 352

Goa *67–68*, 402

Goal, The *09–19*, 535; *40–41*, 432

Goat Alley *21–22*, 387; *26–27*, 514

Goat Song, The *25–26*, 535; *53–54*, 358

Gobi Curse, The *44–45*, 368

God and Kate Murphy *58–59*, 325

God and My Father *39–40*, 142

God Bless America *63–64*, 371

God Bless Us, Every One *67–68*, 412

God Bless You, Harold Fineberg *68–69*, 449

"God Is a (Guess What?)" *68–69*, 440s

God Loves Us *26–27*, 405

God, Man & You, Baby! *63–64*, 350

God of Vengeance, The *22–23*, 501

God Sends Sunday *45–46*, 436

God Strikes Back *42–43*, 489

Goddess of Liberty, The *09–19*, 406

Goddess of Reason, The *99–09*, 578

Goddess of Truth, The *94–99*, 166

Godefroi and Yolande *94–99*, 151

Gods Are Wise, The *29–30*, 533

Gods of the Lightning *28–29*, 402; *61–62*, 332

Gods of the Mountain, The *09–19*, 588, 650

God's Trombone *63–64*, 354; *68–69*, 413

Gods We Make, The *33–34*, 475

Godspell *70–71*

Go-Getters, The *26–27*, 406

Go-Go *22–23*, 542

Gogo Loves You *64–65*, 343

Goin' Home *28–29*, 361

Going Gay *33–34*, 424

Going Some *99–09*, 581; *24–25*, 513

Going to the Races *94–99*, 242

Going Up *09–19*, 618

Gold *20–21*, 452

Gold Braid *29–30*, 544

Gold Bug, The *94–99*, 177

Gold Diggers, The 19–20, 360

Gold Eagle Guy *34–35*, 417

Gold in the Hills *45–46*, 457

Gold Mine, A *94–99*, 235

Golden Age, The (1) *27–28*, 545

Golden Age, The (2) *63–64*, 314s

Golden Apple, The *53–54*, 346s; *60–61*, 48; *61–62*, 323

Golden Bat *70–71s*

Golden Boy (p) *37–38*, 386; *44–45*, 436; *45–46*, 450; *51–52*, 312; *64–65*, 307

Golden Boy (m) *64–65*, 307s

Golden Bride, The *47–48*, 431

Golden Bull of Boredom, The *63–64*, 371

Golden Butterfly, The *99–09*, 570

Golden Cage, The *37–38*, 468; *38–39*, 491

Golden Dawn *27–28*, 462

Golden Days *21–22*, 453

Golden Doom, The *09–19*, 588, 649

Golden Falcon, The *47–48*, 427

Golden Fleece, The *69–70*, 334

Golden Fleecing *59–60*, 296

Golden Horseshoe, The *94–99*, 238

Golden Journey, The *36–37*, 405

Golden Land, The *43–44*, 490

Golden Rainbow *67–68*, 361s

Golden Screw, The *66–67*, 411s

Golden Six, The *58–59*, 55

Golden State, The *50–51*, 331

Golden Wedding, The *48–49*, 430

Golden Wings *41–42*, 420

Goldfische *94–99*, 119

Goldfish, The *21–22*, 535

Goldfish Bowl, The *42–43*, 486

Goldilocks *58–59*, 294s

Golem, The *47–48*, 432

Gondoliers, The (or The King of Barataria) *09–19*, 639; *30–31*, 531; *31–32*, 461; *34–35*, 364; *35–36*, 399, 400; *36–37*, 400; *38–39*, 447; *39–40*, 470; *40–41*, 381; *41–42*, 433, 458; *43–44*, 456; *45–46*, 457; *46–47*, 494; *47–48*, 374, 375; *50–51*, 350; *61–62*, 332; *62–63*, 286; *63–64*, 328, 367; *64–65*, 359; *67–68*, 388

Gone Tomorrow *47–48*, 404

Good, The *38–39*, 411

Good as Gold *56–57*, 359

Good Bad Woman, A (1) *09–19*, 654

Good Bad Woman, A (2) *24–25*, 536; *25–26*, 419

Good Boy *28–29*, 368

Good Companions, The *31–32*, 400

Good Day *65–66*, 422

Good Earth, The *32–33*, 401

Good Fairy, The *31–32*, 439; *32–33*, 424; *46–47*, 485; *50–51*, 362

Good Fellow, The *26–27*, 394

Good Girl in the Kitchen, A *38–39*, 488

Good Gracious Annabelle *09–19*, 281, 586

Good Hope, The *99–09*, 532; *27–28*, 433; *45–46*, 450

Good Hunting *38–39*, 427

Good Little Devil, A *09–19*, 491

Good Luck *64–65*, 344

Good Men and True *35–36*, 425

Good Men Do, The *09–19*, 630

Good Morning Corporal *44–45*, 368

Good Morning Dearie *21–22*, 452

Good Morning, Judge *09–19*, 651

Good Morning, Rosamond *09–19,*
  617

Good Mr. Best, The *94–99,* 205

Good Neighbor *41–42,* 405

Good News (1) *27–28,* 399

Good News (2) *44–45,* 443

Good Night, Ladies *44–45,* 410

Good Night, Paul *09–19,* 605

Good Old Days, The *23–24,* 299;
  30–31, 450

Good Place to Raise a Boy, A
  58–59, 50

Good Soldier Schweik (Sweik), The
  (source) *37–38,* 470; *62–63,* 331

Good Soldier Schweik, The (1)
  37–38, 470

Good Soldier Schweik, The (2)
  62–63, 331

Good Soup, The *59–60,* 325

Good Thing, A *94–99,* 181

Good Times *20–21,* 365

Good Woman of Setzuan, The
  56–57, 345; *61–62,* 318; *62–63,*
  340; *70–71*

Good Woman, Poor Thing, A
  32–33, 447

Goodbye *94–99,* 238

Goodbye Again *32–33,* 443; *43–44,*
  425; *55–56,* 386

Goodbye, Charlie *59–60,* 311

Goodbye in the Night *39–40,* 443

Goodbye, My Fancy *48–49,* 395;
  50–51, 375

Goodbye People, The *68–69,* 396

Good-bye Please *34–35,* 397

Goofyisms *60–61,* 295

Goose, The *59–60,* 40

Goose for the Gander, A *44–45,* 411

Goose Hangs High, The *23–24,* 393

Gordon Reilly *52–53,* 306

Gorilla, The *24–25,* 589

Gorilla Queen *66–67,* 418s

Goslings, The *38–39,* 486

Gospel of St. Luke, The *09–19,* 593

Gospels (source; see *St. Matthew, St.*
  Luke, etc., titles of Books)

Gossip *94–99,* 127

Gossipy Sex, The *26–27,* 512

Gotami the Frail *62–63,* 318

Government Inspector, The (see *The*
  Inspector General)

Governor of Kentucky, The *94–99,*
  164

Governors, The *94–99,* 220

Governor's Boss, The *09–19,* 525

Governor's Lady, The *09–19,* 475

Governor's Son, The *99–09,* 388

Goya drawings (dance program
  source) *43–44,* 485

Grab and Grace *62–63,* 323

Grab Bag, The (1) *24–25,* 467

Grab Bag, The (2) *68–69,* 432

Graduation (1) *64–65,* 361

Graduation (2) *70–71*

Graham Crackers *62–63,* 324s

Grand Street Follies *23–24,* 439

Grain of Dust, The *09–19,* 462

Gramercy Ghost *50–51,* 366

Gran Galeoto, El *99–09,* 355;
  31–32, 500

Grand Army Man, A *99–09,* 547

Grand Duchess, The *94–99,* 110

Grand Duchess and the Waiter, The
  25–26, 471

Grand Duke, The *21–22,* 451

Grand Duke, The (or The Statutory
  Duel) *61–62,* 332

Grand Guignol Horror Plays *35–36,*
  397

Grand Hotel *30–31,* 452

Grand Kabuki, The *69–70,* 296

Grand Mal Crick *70–71*

Grand Mogul, The *99–09,* 537

Grand Music Hall of Israel *67–68,*
  362s *69–70,* 298

Grand Opening *40–41,* 431

Grand Panic Circus, Le *68–69,* 456

Grand Prize, The *54–55,* 393

Grand Street Follies, The (1924)
  23–24, 439

Grand Street Follies (1925) *25–26,*
  418

Grand Street Follies (1926) *25–26,*
  605

Grand Street Follies (1927) *26–27*, 529

Grand Street Follies (1928) *27–28*, 558

Grand Street Follies of (1929) *28–29*, 499

Grand Tarot, The *70–71*

Grand Tour, The *51–52*, 297

Grand Vizier, The 94–99, 126

Grand Vizir (Vizier), The *61–62*, 326, 332; *69–70*, 363

Grandma's Diary *48–49*, 383

Grandma's Sweetheart *47–48*, 431

Granite *26–27*, 480; *35–36*, 459

Granny *99–09*, 471

Granny Maumee *09–19*, 524, 598

Grass Harp, The *51–52*, 317; *52–53*, 306; *60–61*, 48

Grass Widow, The *09–19*, 616

Grasshopper *09–19*, 598

Gratefully Yours *41–42*, 460

Gray Shadow *30–31*, 503

Great Adventure, The *09–19*, 511; *26–27*, 445

Great Airplane Snatch, The *68–69*, 453

Great Barrington, The *30–31*, 494

Great Big Doorstep, The *42–43*, 447; *49–50*, 382, 384

Great Brooklyn Handicap, The *94–99*, 90

Great Broxopp, The *21–22*, 462

Great Campaign, The *46–47*, 463

Great Career, A *68–69*, 437

Great Catherine, (The) *09–19*, 590; *35–36*, 476

Great Day *29–30*, 421

Great Day in the Morning *61–62*, 295

Great Decide, The *99–09*, 518

Great Diamond Robbery, The *94–99*, 141

Great Divide, The *99–09*, 242, 521; *09–19*, 594

Great Dumb Show, The *62–63*, 335

Great Gatsby, The *25–26*, 545

Great, Git-Away, The *68–69*, 428

Great God Brown, The *25–26*, 535; *46–47*, 485; *59–60*, 292

Great Goodness of Life *69–70*, 338

Great Guns *39–40*, 472

Great Indoors, The *65–66*, 396

Great John Ganton, The *99–09*, 582

Great Lady *38–39*, 434

Great Lover, The *09–19*, 564; *32–33*, 398

Great Magician, The *38–39*, 487; *51–52*, 333

Great Magoo, The *32–33*, 432

Great Man, The *30–31*, 513

Great Music *24–25*, 464

Great Name, The *09–19*, 453

Great Necker, The *27–28*, 523

Great Northwest, The *94–99*, 175

Great Power, The *28–29*, 371

Great Pursuit, The *09–19*, 572

Great Question, The *99–09*, 571

Great Ruby, The *94–99*, 253

Great Scot! *65–66*, 424s

Great Scott *29–30*, 386

Great Sebastians, The *55–56*, 368

Great Suggestion, The *38–39*, 488

Great Temptations *25–26*, 600

Great to Be Alive! *49–50*, 376s

Great Train Robbery, The *94–99*, 182

Great Waltz, The *34–35*, 377; *35–36*, 400

Great Way, The *21–22*, 456

Great Western Union, The *64–65*, 353

Great White Hope, The *68–69*, 380

Greater Love *30–31*, 498

Greater Love, The *99–09*, 511

Greatest Man Alive!, The *56–57*, 373

Greatest Nation, The *09–19*, 571

Greatest Show on Earth, The *37–38*, 413

Greatest Thing in the World, The *99–09*, 374

Greed for Gold *34–35*, 483

Greek Slave, A *99–09*, 357

Greeks Had a Word for It, The
  30–31, 419
Green Bay Tree, The (1) 27–28, 418
Green Bay Tree, The (2) 33–34,
  445; 45–46, 450; 50–51, 346
Green Beetle, The 24–25, 445
Green Bundle, The 35–36, 510
Green Carnation, The 60–61, 330
Green Cockatoo, The 09–19, 417;
  30–31, 427
Green Goddess, The 20–21, 422;
  46–47, 485
Green Grow the Lilacs 30–31, 481;
  42–43, 471; 50–51, 372; 53–54,
  299; 57–58, 325; 62–63, 298, 308;
  65–66, 392; 69–70, 295
Green Hat, The 25–26, 445
Green Man and Red Lady in the
  Red and Green, The 70–71
Green Pastures, The 29–30, 502;
  34–35, 457; 50–51, 358s
Green Ring, The 21–22, 532
Green Stick 34–35, 391
Green Stockings 09–19, 452
Green Stone Mountain 29–30, 497
Green Table, The (dance program)
  41–42, 430
Green Waters 36–37, 427
Greengrocer's Daughter, The (mn)
  65–66, 403
Greenwich Village Follies (1919)
  19–20, 339
Greenwich Village Follies of 1920,
  The 20–21, 374
Greenwich Village Follies (1921)
  21–22, 407
Greenwich Village Follies, The
  (1922) 22–23, 452
Greenwich Village Follies (1923)
  23–24, 320
Greenwich Village Follies (1924)
  24–25, 454
Greenwich Village Follies (1925)
  25–26, 522
Greenwich Village Follies (1928)
  27–28, 536
Greenwich Village U.S.A. 60–61, 42

Greenwillow 59–60, 327s; 70–71
Grenadier, The 37–38, 412
Gretna Green 99–09, 425
Grey Farm 39–40, 459
Grey Fox, The 28–29, 400
Grey Lady Cantata, The 70–71
Grey-Eyed People, The 52–53, 279
Greyhound, The 09–19, 467
Grierson's Way 99–09, 507
Griffe, La 23–24, 333
Grime's Cellar Door 94–99, 133
Grimm's Fairy Tales 94–99, 146;
  99–09, 499; 09–19, 483; 38–39,
  490; 70–71
Grin and Bare It! 69–70, 319
Gringa, La 27–28, 502
Gringo 22–23, 500
Gringoire 94–99, 120
Grip, The 94–99, 214
Grip of Steel, A 94–99, 246
Grobe Hemd, Das 99–09, 352
Grosse Valise, La 65–66, 391s
Grosse Wut des Philipp Hotz, Die
  (see Philipp Hotz)
Grounds for Divorce 24–25, 457
Growing Pains 33–34, 460; 37–38,
  467
Grumpy 09–19, 515; 40–41, 432
Grune Kakadu, Der 67–68, 411
g-II 47–48, 427
Guardsman, The (see also Where
  Ignorance Is Bliss) 24–25, 3, 470
Guernica 68–69, 450
Guest in the House 41–42, 435
Guest of Honor, The 20–21, 383
Guest Room The 31–32, 405
Guests of the Nation 58–59, 50
Guide, The 67–68, 366
Guidelines 66–67, 36
Guilty Conscience, The 09–19, 500
Guilty Man, The 09–19, 577
Guilty Mother, A 94–99, 217
Guilty One, The 22–23, 546
Guimpes and Saddles 67–68, 408
Guinea Pig, The 28–29, 449
Guitar 59–60, 40
Gulliver's Travels (mn) 34–35, 484

Gum *70–71*

Guns *28–29,* 356

Guns of Carrar *68–69,* 454

Gunter Grass's Selected Poems
  65–66, 434

Guv'nor, The *94–99,* 236

Guy Mannering *94–99,* 197

Guys and Dolls *50–51,* 329s; *54–55,*
  407; *64–65,* 334; *66–67,* 351

Gypsies *42–43,* 483

Gypsy (p) (1) *99–09,* 450

Gypsy (p) (2) *28–29,* 455

Gypsy (m) *58–59,* 337s

Gypsy, The *09–19,* 485

Gypsy Aza *46–47,* 497

Gypsy Baron, The *42–43,* 486, 490;
  44–45, 379; *45–46,* 390

Gypsy Blonde *34–35,* 360

Gypsy Fires *25–26,* 511

Gypsy Jim *23–24,* 384

Gypsy Lady *46–47,* 419s

Gypsy Love *09–19,* 454

H.M.S. Pinafore (or The Lass That
  Loved a Sailor) *94–99,* 174;
  09–19, 445, 472, 501, 525, 551,
  639; *25–26,* 581; *30–31,* 527;
  31–32, 380; *32–33,* 485; *33–34,*
  515; *34–35,* 365; *35–36,* 400, 498;
  36–37, 401; *38–39,* 447; *41–42,*
  430, 458; *43–44,* 455; *44–45,* 434;
  45–46, 458; *46–47,* 493, 494;
  47–48, 373, 375; *49–50,* 356;
  50–51, 347; *52–53,* 263; *55–56,*
  346; *60–61,* 291; *61–62,* 332;
  62–63, 286, 339; *63–64,* 328;
  64–65, 313, 359; *66–67,* 367, 399;
  67–68, 373, 388; *68–69,* 390

Habima, Dybbuk *25–26,* 517

Habit *09–19,* 612

Habitual Husband, The *24–25,* 512

Hadrian VII *68–69,* 401

Hadrian the Seventh *68–69,* 401

Hail and Farewell (1) *22–23,* 533

Hail and Farewell (2) (see *Tomorrow
  and Tomorrow*)

Hail Scrawdyke! *66–67,* 375

Hail, the Conquering Hero *60–61,*
  318

Hair *67–68,* 374s, 389s

Hairpin Harmony *43–44,* 416

Hairy Ape, The *21–22,* 524

Haiti *37–38,* 456

Hajj Malik, El *70–71*

Half a King *94–99,* 177

Half a Sixpence *64–65,* 333s

Half a Widow *27–28,* 403

Half an Hour *09–19,* 508; *25–26,*
  593

Half Gods *29–30,* 464

Half Horse Half Alligator *65–66,*
  432

Half Moon, The *20–21,* 401

Half Naked Truth, The *25–26,*
  603

Half-Caste, The *25–26,* 576

Half-Delivered Gift, The *(Kirokuda)*
  70–71

Half-Past Wednesday *61–62,* 327s

Halfway to Hell *33–34,* 474

Halfway up the Tree *67–68,* 352

Hall of Fame, The *99–09,* 405

Hallams, The *47–48,* 389

Hallelujah, Baby! *66–67,* 391s

Hallowe'en *35–36,* 486

Ham Tree, The *99–09,* 493; *19–20,*
  367

Hamilton *09–19,* 607

Hamlet *94–99,* 88, 105, 120, 121,
  127, 133, 145, 226, 239; *99–09,*
  370, 371, 380, 469, 470, 471, 476,
  477, 536; *09–19,* 413, 433, 443,
  447, 448, 471, 478, 485, 494, 508,
  509, 545, 599, 642, 645; *19–20,*
  363; *22–23,* 490; *23–24,* 328, 343,
  361; *25–26,* 469, 491; *29–30,* 515;
  30–31, 471; *31–32,* 423, 433;
  32–33, 424; *34–35,* 428, 483;
  36–37, 415, 429; *37–38,* 414;
  39–40, 418; *44–45,* 436; *45–46,*
  413; *46–47,* 407, 468; *48–49,* 426;
  49–50, 386; *52–53,* 273; *53–54,*
  359; *56–57,* 55; *58–59,* 51, 310,
  316; *59–60,* 43; *60–61,* 331; *62–63,*

305, 335; *63–64*, 334; *64–65*, 74; *66–67*, 382; *67–68*, 345, 389; *68–69*, 383, 414; *70–71*
Hamlet and His Father *62–63*, 335
Hamlet and Ophelia *62–63*, 335
Hamlet and the World *62–63*, 335
Hamlet Is an Army *62–63*, 335
Hamlet of Stepney Green, The *58–59*, 51
Hamlet Revisited *62–63*, 335
Hamlet's Enemies Contrive *62–63*, 335
Hammerstein's 9 O'Clock Revue (see *Nine O'Clock Revue*)
Hamp (see also *King and Country*) *66–67*, 416
Hand in Glove *44–45*, 401
Hand Is on the Gate, A *66–67*, 353
Hand of the Potter, The *21–22*, 473
Handful of Fire *58–59*, 292
Hands Across the Sea (1) *94–99*, 257
Hands Across the Sea (2) *36–37*, 435; *45–46*, 450; *47–48*, 384
Hands Up *09–19*, 553
Handy Man, The *24–25*, 557
Hang Down Your Head and Die *64–65*, 344
Hangman's House *26–27*, 441
Hangman's Whip *32–33*, 467
Hanjo *60–61*, 47
Hanky Panky *09–19*, 473
Hannele (see also *The Assumption of Hannele*) *09–19*, 417
Hans Brinker *35–36*, 512
Han's Crime *60–61*, 44
Hans, the Flute Player *09–19*, 424
Hansel and Gretel (source) *94–99*, 146; *47–48*, 430
Hansel and Gretel (p) *34–35*, 484; *36–37*, 498; *37–38*, 467; *38–39*, 491
Hansel and Grete(a)l (m) *94–99*, 146; *34–35*, 485; *47–48*, 425, 426
Happiest Days, The *38–39*, 468
Happiest Girl in the World, The *60–61*, 332s

Happiest Millionaire, The *56–57*, 337
Happiest Night of His Life, The *09–19*, 439
Happiest Years, The *48–49*, 420
Happily Ever After *44–45*, 422
Happily Never After *65–66*, 403
Happiness (1) *09–19*, 523, 619
Happiness (2) *67–68*, 394
Happiness Cage, The *69–70*, 376; *70–71*
Happiness Is Just a Little Thing Called a Rolls Royce *67–68*, 378
Happy (1) 27–28, 465
Happy (2) 70–71
Happy Alienist, The *35–36*, 446
Happy as Larry *49–50*, 366s; *60–61*, 46
Happy Birthday *46–47*, 433
Happy Birthday, Wanda June *70–71*
Happy Days (1) *19–20*, 346
Happy Days (2; *Oh! Les Beaux Jours*) *61–62*, 305; *65–66*, 420; *68–69*, 379; *69–70*, 363
Happy Days, The *40–41*, 425
Happy End *63–64*, 342; *69–70*, 335
Happy Ending *65–66*, 426
Happy Ending, The *09–19*, 578
Happy Faculty, The *66–67*, 423
Happy Go Lucky *26–27*, 391
Happy Hunting *56–57*, 343s
Happy Husband, The *27–28*, 548
Happy Hypocrite, The (source) *99–09*, 404; *68–69*, 427
Happy Hypocrite, The (p) *99–09*, 404
Happy Hypocrite, The (m) *68–69*, 427s
Happy Journey to Trenton and Camden, The *38–39*, 486; *42–43*, 490; *44–45*, 436; *47–48*, 390, 426; *66–67*, 401
Happy Landing *31–32*, 495
Happy Little Home, A *94–99*, 154
Happy Marriage, The *99–09*, 581

Happy Prince, The 60–61, 330;
62–63, 327

Happy Time, The (source) 49–50,
370

Happy Time, The (p) 49–50, 370

Happy Time, The (m) 67–68, 358s

Happy Town 59–60, 293s

Happy-Go-Lucky 20–21, 372

Happyland 99–09, 497

Harald Kreutzberg (dance programs)
47–48, 415; 48–49, 428

Harangues, The 69–70, 352

Harbor Lights (1) 94–99, 83

Harbor Lights (2) 56–57, 321

Hard Man, The 09–19, 509

Harem, The 24–25, 499

Hari-Kari 09–19, 509

Harlem 28–29, 472; 29–30, 426

Harlem Cavalcade 41–42, 450

Harlequinade 49–50, 357

Harold (1) 62–63, 290

Harold (2) 66–67, 420

Harold Arlen Songbook, The 66–67,
414s

Harp of Life, The 09–19, 588

Harriet 42–43, 466; 44–45, 375

Harriet's Honeymoon 99–09, 450

Harry Lauder (see Sir Harry
Lauder)

Harry, Noon and Night 64–65, 358,
362

Harvest (1) 09–19, 459

Harvest (2) 25–26, 449

Harvest Moon, The 09–19, 402

Harvest of Years 47–48, 375

Harvester, The 99–09, 468

Harvey 44–45, 394; 69–70, 316

Hassan 24–25, 455

Hassard Short's Ritz Revue 24–25,
454

Haste Me to Know It 62–63, 335

Hastings Marionettes (see Sue
Hastings Marionettes)

Hasty Heart, The 44–45, 408;
45–46, 451; 53–54, 358; 56–57, 58;
59–60, 43

Hat, a Coat, a Glove, A 33–34,
490

Hatful of Rain, A 55–56, 360;
69–70, 374

Hats off to Ice 44–45, 365

Haunch, Paunch and Jowl 35–36,
510

Haunted, The 31–32, 417, 511

Haunted Host, The 69–70, 344

Haunted House, The 24–25, 444

Havana 99–09, 577

Have a Heart 09–19, 593

Have I Got a Girl for You! 63–64,
315

Have I Got One for You 67–68, 398

Have You Seen Smith? 94–99, 242

Haven, The 46–47, 441

Haven in the Dark 53–54, 359

Having Wonderful Time 36–37, 467;
52–53, 253

Havoc 24–25, 439

Havoc, The 09–19, 436; 32–33, 377

Hawk, The (1) 09–19, 532

Hawk, The (2) 67–68, 405

Hawk Island 29–30, 394

Hawkshow the Detective (see The
Ticket of Leave Man)

Hawthorne of the U.S.A 09–19, 483

Hay Fever 25–26, 460; 31–32, 453;
45–46, 450; 70–71

Haydee Morini (dance programs)
47–48, 417

Hayride 54–55, 360

Hazel Flagg 52–53, 286s

Hazel Kirke 94–99, 237

He 31–32, 394

He and She 19–20, 425; 70–71

He Came From Milwaukee 09–19,
425

He Comes up Smiling 09–19, 531

He Didn't Want to Do It 09–19,
633

He Is to Blame for Everything
27–28, 455, 485

He Loved the Ladies 26–27, 528

He Understood Women 28–29, 357

He Walked in Her Sleep 28–29, 489

He Wants to Have a Good Time
(Einen Jux Will Er Sich Machen)
67–68, 367

He Was Like a Continent *37–38,* 464

He Who Gets Slapped *21–22,* 492; *45–46,* 432; *55–56,* 59; *67–68,* 410

Head First *25–26,* 527

Head of the Family, The *94–99,* 247

Head or Tail *26–27,* 422

Head Over Heels *09–19,* 634

Headquarters *29–30,* 457

Heads or Tails *46–47,* 478

Heads Up *29–30,* 439

Hear That Trumpet *46–47,* 422

Heart of a City *41–42,* 439

Heart of a Thief, The *09–19,* 533

Heart of Chicago *94–99,* 221

Heart of Maryland, The *94–99,* 149

Heart of Ruby, The *94–99,* 118

Heart of the Klondike, The *94–99,* 214

Heart of Wetona, The *09–19,* 571

Heartbreak House *20–21,* 404; *37–38,* 442; *49–50,* 384; *55–56,* 58; *59–60,* 297

Hearts Aflame *99–09,* 410

Hearts and Masks *09–19,* 553

Hearts Are Trumps (1) *99–09,* 362

Hearts Are Trumps (2) *26–27,* 504

Hearts Courageous *99–09,* 438

Heartsease *94–99,* 191

Heat Lightning *33–34,* 432

Heat Wave *30–31,* 492

Heather Field, The *99–09,* 367

Heaven Grand in Amber Orbit *69–70,* 375

Heaven on Earth *48–49,* 380s

Heaven Tappers, The *26–27,* 491

Heaven Trees *62–63,* 326

Heavenly Express *39–40,* 456; *53–54,* 358

Heavenly Rackets *34–35,* 483

Heavy Duty Radio Theater *70–71*

Heavy Traffic *28–29,* 367

Heaven Mother, The *70–71*

Heavenly Twins, The *55–56,* 359

Hebrew sketches (untitled program) *33–34,* 534

Hecube *09–19,* 589 (and 605)

Hedda Gabler *94–99,* 227; *99–09,* 404, 438, 439; *09–19,* 627; *23–24,* 437; *25–26,* 538; *27–28,* 532; *28–29,* 464; *34–35,* 403; *36–37,* 432; *41–42,* 437; *46–47,* 485; *47–48,* 386; *50–51,* 373; *55–56,* 55; *60–61,* 353; *69–70,* 355; *70–71*

Heidelberg (see also *Old Heidelberg*) *99–09,* 424

Heidi *35–36,* 512

Heigh-Ho, Everybody *31–32,* 516

Heights, The *09–19,* 412

Heir to the Hoorah, The *99–09,* 489

Heiress, The *47–48,* 353; *49–50,* 372

Held by the Enemy *09–19,* 432

Helen *64–65,* 350

Helen Goes to Troy *43–44,* 470s

Helen Howe *34–35,* 484; *36–37,* 498; *37–38,* 466; *39–40,* 472

Helen of Troy, New York *23–24,* 293

Helen Waren *47–48,* 429

Helena's Boys *23–24,* 416

Helena's Husband *09–19,* 560

Helena's Room *47–48,* 424

Hell *09–19,* 444

Hell Freezes Over *35–36,* 455

Hell Is Other People *63–64,* 365

Hell-Bent for Heaven *23–24,* 382; *59–60,* 43

Hello, Alexander *19–20,* 366

Hello and Goodbye *68–69,* 454; *69–70,* 340

Hello Broadway *09–19,* 542

Hello Charlie *65–66,* 423

Hello Daddy *28–29,* 445

Hello, Dolly! *63–64,* 319s; *67–68,* 369

Hello, Franco *37–38,* 464

Hello, Lola *25–26,* 529

Hello, Out There *42–43,* 431; *44–45,* 436; *46–47,* 484; *55–56,* 59

Hello, Paris (1) *09–19,* 447

Hello, Paris (2) *30–31,* 453

Hello, Solly! *66–67,* 386

Hello Yourself *28–29,* 406

Hell's Bells *24–25,* 529

Hell's Half Acre *38–39,* 487

Hellzapoppin *38–39*, 407

Helmet of Navarre, The *99–09*, 400

Heloise *58–59*, 51; *70–71*

Help Stamp Out Marriage! *66–67*, 358

Help Wanted *09–19*, 522

Help Yourself *36–37*, 489

Helter Skelter *94–99*, 180

Hen-Pecked Husband, The *94–99*, 258

Hen-Pecks, The *09–19*, 438

Henrietta, The *09–19*, 517

Henry IV (Pirandello; see also *The Living Mask*) *23–24*, 388; *46–47*, 485; *47–48*, 425

Henry IV (Shakespeare; part undesignated) *94–99*, 167; *25–26*, 602

Henry IV, Part 1 *38–39*, 454, 455; *45–46*, 441, 442; *55–56*, 343; *58–59*, 316; *59–60*, 324; *62–63*, 305; *63–64*, 360; *68–69*, 422

Henry IV, Part 2 *45–46*, 442, 443; *58–59*, 316; *59–60*, 333; *62–63*, 305; *63–64*, 360; *68–69*, 422

Henry V *99–09*, 374; *09–19*, 478; *27–28*, 529; *46–47*, 408; *58–59*, 310; *60–61*, 46; *62–63*, 305; *63–64*, 353, 360, 361; *65–66*, 97; *69–70*, 305

Henry V (movie) *46–47*, 408

Henry VI (part undesignated) *19–20*, 436; *63–64*, 361

Henry VI, Part 1 *70–71*

Henry VI, Part 2 *70–71*

Henry VI, Part 3 *58–59*, 316; *62–63*, 305; *70–71*

Henry VIII *09–19*, 572; *46–47*, 435, 436; *59–60*, 43; *63–64*, 360

Henry L. Scott *48–49*, 428

Henry-Behave *26–27*, 367

Henry, Sweet Henry *67–68*, 347s

Henry of Navarre *09–19*, 431

Henry's Harem *26–27*, 379

Her Atonement *94–99*, 253

Her Cardboard Lover *26–27*, 494

Her Country *09–19*, 623

Her Family Tree *20–21*, 415

Her Father's Melody *48–49*, 430

Her First Affaire *27–28*, 394

Her First Appearance *94–99*, 140

Her First Divorce *09–19*, 501

Her First Roman *668–69*, 386s

Her Friend the King *29–30*, 413

Her Great Match *99–09*, 493

Her Great Mistake *39–40*, 474

Her Great Secret *47–48*, 431

Her Honor, the Mayor *09–19*, 630

Her Husband's Wife *09–19*, 419, 592; *45–46*, 459

Her Little Highness *09–19*, 511

Her Lord and Master *99–09*, 406

Her Majesty, the Girl Queen of Nordenmark *99–09*, 376

Her Majesty the King *39–40*, 470

Her Majesty the Widow *34–35*, 360

Her Man of Wax *33–34*, 440

Her Master's Voice *33–34*, 446; *64–65*, 351

Her Own Money *09–19*, 505

Her Own Way *99–09*, 438

Her Regiment *09–19*, 614

Her Salary Man *21–22*, 469

Her Sister *99–09*, 553

Her Soldier Boy *09–19*, 589

Her Supporting Cast *30–31*, 523

Her Temporary Husband *22–23*, 446

Her Tin Soldier *32–33*, 481

Her Unborn Child *27–28*, 522

Her Way Out *24–25*, 428

Here Are Ladies *70–71*

Here Be Dragons *70–71*

Here Come the Clowns *38–39*, 436; *60–61*, 45; *65–66*, 437

Here Comes Mr. Jordon *46–47*, 450

Here Comes the Bride *09–19*, 608

Here Goes the Bride *31–32*, 422s

Here Today *32–33*, 383

Here's Hoping *37–38*, 461

Here's Howe *27–28*, 547

Here's Love *63–64*, 306s

Here's the Pitch *47–48*, 344s

Here's Where I Belong *67–68*, 365s

Heritage *70–71*
Heritage, L' *48–49*, 427
Heritage, The *09–19*, 619
Hermit's Cock, The *69–70*, 376
Hero *70–71*
Hero, The *20–21*, 434; *21–22*, 412
Hero Is Born, A *37–38*, 448
Hero of Santa Maria, The *09–19*, 579
Hero Worship *27–28*, 551
Herod *09–19*, 403
Heroes, The *52–53*, 308
Heroine, The *62–63*, 298
Herschel, the Jester *48–49*, 429
Heure du Berger, L' *36–37*, 499
Heure H, L' (see *The Hour*)
Hey Nonny Nonny! *31–32*, 520
Hey, You *52–53*, 307
Hey You, Light Man! *62–63*, 327
Hi Ho Figaro *47–48*, 424
Hi, Paisano! *61–62*, 308s
Hiatus *67–68*, 413
Hickory Stick *43–44*, 476
Hidden *27–28*, 422
Hidden Horizon *46–47*, 420
Hidden House *50–51*, 373
Hidden River, The *56–57*, 351
Hidden Stranger *62–63*, 293
Hide and Seek *56–57*, 364
Hiding a Prince *37–38*, 467
Higgledy-Piggledy *99–09*, 471
High Born Lady, A *94–99*, 243
High Button Shoes *47–48*, 358s
High Cost of Loving, The *09–19*, 529
High Gear *27–28*, 424
High Ground, The *50–51*, 353
High Hatters, The *27–28*, 552
High Jinks *09–19*, 516
High Kickers *41–42*, 408
High Named Today *54–55*, 56
High Road, The (1) *09–19*, 485
High Road, The (2) *28–29*, 369
High Spirits *63–64*, 333s
High Stakes *24–25*, 450
High Tor *36–37*, 452; *45–46*, 450

High Wind in Jamaica, A *43–44*, 355
Higher and Higher *39–40*, 453; *40–41*, 375
Highest Bidder, The *94–99*, 131
Highest Tree, The *59–60*, 302
Highland Fling, A *43–44*, 475
Highway of Life, The *09–19*, 536
Highwayman, The *94–99*, 218; *09–19*, 600
Hilarities *48–49*, 379
Hilda Cassidy *32–33*, 490
Hilda Crane *50–51*, 323
Hill Between, The *37–38*, 432
Him *27–28*, 541
Hindle Wakes (see also *Fanny Hawthorn*) *09–19*, 487
Hindu, The *21–22*, 528
Hip! Hip! Hooray! *99–09*, 546
Hip-Hip-Hooray *09–19*, 560
Hipper's Holiday *34–35*, 394
Hippolytus *48–49*, 426; *68–69*, 434
Hired Girl, A *94–99*, 221
Hired Husband *31–32*, 519
Hirondelle, L' *99–09*, 472
Hirsch Lekert *35–36*, 510
His Absent Boy *94–99*, 171
His and Hers *53–54*, 335
His Bridal Night *09–19*, 577
His Children *25–26*, 590
His Chinese Wife *19–20*, 454
His Excellency *94–99*, 147
His Excellency the Governor *94–99*, 260; *99–09*, 419
His Honor, Abe Potash *19–20*, 374
His Honor, the Barber *09–19*, 445
His Honor the Mayor (1) *94–99*, 229
His Honor the Mayor (2) *99–09*, 514
His House in Order *99–09*, 518
His Last Appearance *94–99*, 223
His Little Dodge *94–99*, 216
His Little Widows *09–19*, 600
His Majesty *99–09*, 511
His Majesty Bunker Bean *09–19*, 583

His Majesty's Car *30–31,* 439
His Name on the Door *09–19,* 405
His Queen *24–25,* 592
His Royal Highness *37–38,* 463
His Widow's Husband *09–19,* 612
His Wife by His Side *09–19,* 490
His Wife's Family *99–09,* 570
His Wife's Father *94–99,* 125, 235
History as Was *26–27,* 523
Hit the Deck *26–27,* 516
Hit the Trail *54–55,* 380s
Hitch Your Wagon *36–37,* 478
Hitchy-Koo *09–19,* 601
Hitchy-Koo of 1918 *09–19,* 630
Hitchy-Koo, 1919 *19–20,* 366
Hitchy-Koo 1920 *20–21,* 397
Hit-the-Trail-Holiday *09–19,* 557
Hobby Horse, The *94–99,* 160
Hobo (1) *30–31,* 490
Hobo (2) *60–61,* 41
Hoboes in Heaven *47–48,* 427
Hobohemia *09–19,* 651
Hoboken Blues *27–28,* 511
Hobson's Choice *09–19,* 564; *52–53,*
    309; *66–67,* 374
Hocus Pocus *34–35,* 485
Hodge, Podge & Co. *99–09,* 376
Hogan's Alley *94–99,* 181
Hogan's Goat *65–66,* 425; *69–70,*
    325
Hoity Toity *99–09,* 394
Hokey-Pokey *09–19,* 465
Hold Everything *28–29,* 395
Hold It! *47–48,* 402s
Hold on to Your Hats *40–41,* 378
Hold Your Horses *33–34,* 433
Hole, The *60–61,* 44
Hole in the Head, A *56–57,* 356;
    67–68, 362
Hole in the Wall, The *19–20,* 440
Holiday *28–29,* 424; *44–45,* 436
Holiday for Lovers *56–57,* 355
Holiday in Paris *49–50,* 384
Holiday on Strings (mn) *70–71*
Holka Polka *25–26,* 475
Hollow Crown, The *62–63,* 295
Holly Golightly *66–67,* 396

Hollywood Ice Revue *42–43,* 489
Hollywood Ice Revue (1944) *43–44,*
    489
Hollywood Ice Revue (1945) *44–45,*
    442
Hollywood Ice Revue (1947) *46–47,*
    495
Hollywood Ice Revue (1948) *47–48,*
    424
Hollywood Ice Revue (1949; Sonja
    Henie) *48–49,* 427
Hollywood Pinafore *44–45,* 434
Holmeses of Baker Street, The
    36–37, 439
Holocauste, L' *09–19,* 589 (and 605)
Holy Night *36–37,* 496
Holy Terror, A *25–26,* 456
Homage to Shakespeare *63–64,* 360
Home *70–71*
Home Again *09–19,* 644
Home Away From, A *68–69,* 451
Home Fires (1) *23–24,* 304
Home Fires (2) *68–69,* 412
Home Folks *99–09,* 478
Home for Mother, A *48–49,* 430
Home Free! *64–65,* 354
Home Is the Hero (1) *44–45,* 395
Home Is the Hero (2) *54–55,* 362
Home Is the Hunter *45–46,* 414
Home Life of a Buffalo *47–48,* 404
Home Movies *63–64,* 365s
Home of the Brave *45–46,* 418;
    46–47, 485, 495
Home of the Free, The *09–19,* 612
Home Secretary, The *94–99,* 155
Home Towners, The *26–27,* 367
Homecoming (1) *31–32,* 417, 511
Homecoming (2) *42–43,* 488
Homecoming, The *66–67,* 380;
    70–71
Homecoming Game, The *58–59,* 318
Homeward Look *54–55,* 53
Homme a la Rose, L' *21–22,* 414
Homme et Ses Fantomes, L' *24–25,*
    483
Homme Qui Assassina, L' *24–25,*
    482

Hon. John Grigsby *99–09*, 405
Honest Abe (see *Lincoln*)
Honest Jim Blunt *09–19*, 476
Honest Liars *26–27*, 361
Honest-to-God Schnozzola, The
    68–69, 451
Honey Girl *19–20*, 448
Honeydew *20–21*, 377
Honeymoon *32–33*, 440; *47–48*, 430
Honeymoon, The (1) *94–99*, 129
Honeymoon, The (2) *09–19*, 495
Honeymoon Express, The *09–19*,
    494
Honeymoon Lane *26–27*, 383
Honeymooners, The (see *Running
    for Office*)
Honeys, The *54–55*, 411
Honor Be Damned! *26–27*, 469
Honor Code, The *30–31*, 528
Honor of the Family, The *99–09*,
    558; *09–19*, 653; *26–27*, 445
Honorable Lover, The *09–19*, 560
Honors Are Even *21–22*, 392
Honour *94–99*, 153
Hoodman Blind *94–99*, 217
Hoofers, The *69–70*, 338
Hook'n' Ladder *51–52*, 320
Hook-up, The *34–35*, 477
Hooray for What! *37–38*, 397
Hooray! It's a Glorious Day . . .
    and All That *65–66*, 432
Hoosier Doctor, The *94–99*, 228
Hop o' My Thumb *09–19*, 515
Hop, Signor *61–62*, 330
Hope for a Harvest *41–42*, 417
Hope for the Best *44–45*, 415
Hope Is the Thing With Feathers
    47–48, 396, 404
Hope's the Thing *47–48*, 404
Horrible Experience, L' *23–24*, 333
Horse Eats Hat *36–37*, 496
Horse Fever *40–41*, 395
Horse Play *37–38*, 460
Horseman, Pass By *68–69*, 443s
Horses in Midstream *52–53*, 296
Hospitality *22–23*, 486
Hoss and Hoss *94–99*, 98

Hostage, The *60–61*, 295; *61–62*,
    315; *66–67*, 422
Hostile Witness *65–66*, 398
Hot Chocolates *29–30*, 376
Hot Corner, The *55–56*, 372
Hot Mikado, The *38–39*, 466
Hot Money *31–32*, 425
Hot Old Time, A *94–99*, 207
Hot Pan *27–28*, 510
Hot Rhythm *30–31*, 403
Hot Spot *62–63*, 306s
Hot Water *28–29*, 460
Hotbed *28–29*, 413
Hot-Cha! *31–32*, 491s
Hotel Alimony *33–34*, 487
Hotel Mouse, The *21–22*, 526
Hotel Paradiso *56–57*, 366; *59–60*,
    43
Hotel Passionato *65–66*, 423
Hotel Topsey Turvey *94–99*, 242
Hotel Universe *29–30*, 522; *46–47*,
    485; *52–53*, 308
Hottentot, The *19–20*, 433
Hour, The (*L'Heure H*) *37–38*, 465
Hour Glass, The *99–09*, 378, 458,
    547
House Afire *29–30*, 518
House Beautiful, The *30–31*, 504
House by the Stable, The *62–63*,
    323
House in Berlin, A *50–51*, 374
House in Paris, The *43–44*, 463
House in the Country, A *36–37*, 452
House Next Door, The *99–09*, 581
House of a Thousand Candles, The
    99–09, 554
House of Atreus, The *68–69*, 398
House of Bernarda Alba, The *48–49*,
    426; *50–51*, 340
House of Blue Leaves, The *70–71*
House of Bondage, The *09–19*, 520
House of Burnside, The *99–09*, 480
House of Cantrell, The *37–38*, 462
House of Cards, A *94–99*, 170
House of Connelly, The *31–32*, 398
House of Doom, The *31–32*, 469
House of Dunkelmayer *70–71*

House of Fear, The (1) *22–23,* 477

House of Fear, The (2) *29–30,* 414

House of Flowers *54–55,* 389s; *67–68,* 399s

House of Glass, The *09–19,* 556

House of Hate *32–33,* 377

House of Judgement, The *62–63,* 327

House of Leather, The *69–70,* 361

House of Mirth, The *99–09,* 523

House of Mystery, A *94–99,* 177

House of Remsen *33–34,* 511

House of Shadows *26–27,* 516

House of Silence, The *99–09,* 508

House of Ussher, The *25–26,* 529

House of Women, The *27–28,* 418

House Possessed, A *47–48,* 427

House That Jack Built, The *99–09,* 382

House Unguarded *28–29,* 457

House With the Twisty Windows, The *28–29,* 501; *29–39,* 535

Houseboat on the Styx *28–29,* 444

Houseparty *29–30,* 389

Houses of Sand *24–25,* 544

Housewarming *31–32,* 503

How a Nice Girl Named Janet Contracted Syphilis *70–71*

How Beautiful With Shoes *35–36,* 443

How Come? *22–23,* 558

How Come, Lawd? *37–38,* 373, 460

How Do I Love Thee *68–69,* 407

How Green Was My Valley *65–66,* 410

How He Lied to Her Husband *99–09,* 467, 495, 512, 547; *09–19,* 590; *70–71*

How I Wonder *47–48,* 354

How Long Till Summer *49–50,* 365

How Much? *62–63,* 303

How Much, How Much? *69–70,* 366

How Now, Dow Jones *67–68,* 355s

How the Other Half Loves *70–71*

How to be a Jewish Mother *67–68,* 357s

How to Get Tough About It *37–38,* 423

How to Make a Man *60–61,* 321

How to Steal an Election *68–69,* 428s

How to Succeed in Business Without Really Trying *61–62,* 261s; *65–66,* 407

Howdy, King *26–27,* 441

Howdy, Mr. Ice! *48–49,* 377

Howdy Mr. Ice of 1950 *48–49,* 424

Howdy Stranger *36–37,* 455

Howie *58–59,* 292

How's the World Treating You? *66–67,* 365

How's Your Health *29–30,* 450

Hoyden, The *99–09,* 548

Huck Finn (mn) *36–37,* 498

(The Adventures of) Huckleberry Finn (source) *56–57,* 371; *65–66,* 405

Hughie *64–65,* 321

Hughie Roddis *44–45,* 401

Human Hearts (see *Logan's Luck*)

Human Nature *25–26,* 455

Humanity *94–99,* 123

Humble, The *26–27,* 402

Humbug, The *29–30,* 452

Humming Bird, The *22–23,* 519

Humming Sam *32–33,* 482

Humoresque *22–23,* 537

Humpty Dumpty (1) *99–09,* 473

Humpty Dumpty (2) *09–19,* 637

Humpty Dumpty up to Date *94–99,* 90

Hunchback, The *94–99,* 167; *99–09,* 412

Hundred, A (see also *One Hundred*)

Hundred Years Ago, A *60–61,* 295

Hundred Years Old, A *29–30,* 409

Hundredth Man, The *09–19,* 495

Hunky Dory *22–23,* 449

Hunted, The *31–32,* 417, 511

Hunter, The *68–69,* 457

Hunter College Make-Up Box (mn) *37–38,* 466; *38–39,* 492

Hunting the Jingo Bird *64–65,* 354

Hurdy-Gurdy Girl, The *99–09,* 545

Hurly Burly *94–99,* 180

Hurricane *23–24,* 372

Husband and Wife *09–19*, 558
Husbands of Leontine, The *99–09*, 369
Hush! *09–19*, 584
Hush Money *25–26*, 568
Hustler, The *94–99*, 116
Huui, Huui *68–69*, 434
Hyacinth Halvey *09–19*, 459
Hymn to the Rising Sun *35–36*, 510; *36–37*, 496; *37–38*, 459
Hyphen, The *09–19*, 551
Hypocrites, The *99–09*, 518

I Am a Camera *51–52*, 295; *56–57*, 58; *66–67*, 370
I Am My Youth *37–38*, 430
I Can Get It for You Wholesale *61–62*, 294s
I Can't Sleep *34–35*, 483; *67–68*, 409
I Did But Jest *24–25*, 583
I Do! I Do! *66–67, 375s*
I Dreamt I Dwelt in Bloomingdale's *69–70*, 358
I Feel Wonderful *54–55*, 56
I Forgot *34–35*, 453
I Got Shoes *62–63*, 324
I Gotta Get Out *47–48*, 351
I Had a Ball *64–65*, 319s
I Had My Bitter and Lonely Hours *60–61*, 295
I Have Been Here Before *38–39*, 415
I Hear America Singing *40–41*, 430
I Hear It Kissing Me Ladies *70–71*
I Killed the Count *42–43*, 426
I Knew 3000 Lunatics *37–38*, 435
I Knock at the Door *57–58*, 288; *64–65*, 347
I Know My Love *49–50*, 359
I Know What I Like *39–40*, 415
I Like It Here *45–46*, 433
I Love an Actress *31–32*, 393
I Love You *09–19*, 656; *23–24*, 394
I Loved You Wednesday *32–33*, 398
I Made Iron *37–38*, 469
I Married an Angel *37–38*, 445

I Must Be Talking to My Friends *67–68*, 394
I Must Love Someone *38–39*, 457
I, Myself *33–34*, 527
I Never Sang for My Father *67–68*, 359
I.O.U. *09–19*, 640
I Only Want an Answer *67–68*, 401
I.Q. *40–41*, 431
I Remember Foxtrot *67–68*, 408
I Remember Mama *44–45*, 389
I Rise in Flame Cried the Phoenix *58–59*, 50
I Saw a Monkey *68–69*, 432
ITUCH Anthology *67–68*, 401
I Want a Child *48–49*, 430
I Want a Policeman *35–36*, 460
I Want My Wife *29–30*, 514
I Want You *61–62*, 305s
I Was Born Ten Thousand Years Ago *60–61*, 294
I Was Dancing *64–65*, 311
I Was the Red Hot Pepper Queen *63–64*, 370
I Was Waiting for You *33–34*, 457
Ib and Little Christina *99–09*, 369
Ice Follies of 1942 *41–42*, 459
Ice Follies of 1944 *43–44*, 489
Ice Follies of 1946, The *45–46*, 458
Ice Follies of 1947 *46–47*, 494
Ice Follies of 1948 *47–48*, 424
Ice Follies (1949) *48–49*, 426
Icebound *22–23*, 530
Iceman Cometh, The *46–47*, 424; *55–56*, 55
Icetime *46–47*, 414
Icetime of 1948 *46–47*, 482
I'd Rather Be Right *37–38*, 385
Ideal Husband, An *94–99*, 127; *09–19*, 637; *62–63*, 327
Idiot, The (source) *60–61*, 348; *70–71*
Idiot, The *60–61*, 348
Idiots a la Mode *39–40*, 469
Idiot's Delight *35–36*, 494; *36–37*, 403; *49–50*, 384; *50–51*, 371; *56–57*, 58
Idiot's First *63–64*, 364

Idle Inn, The *21–22,* 478
Idler, The *94–99,* 235
Idols *09–19,* 403
Idol's Eye, The *94–99,* 213
Idylls of the King *21–22,* 420;
29–30, 506
If (1) *09–19,* 594
If (2) *27–28,* 437
If a Body *34–35,* 476
If Booth Had Missed *30–31,* 525;
31–32, 473
If Five Years Pass *44–45,* 442;
61–62, 330
If I Was Rich *26–27,* 373
If I Were King *99–09,* 66, 398, 470,
471; *09–19,* 508, 574; *25–26,* 451;
43–44, 402
If I Were Rothschild *39–40,* 474
If I Were You (1) *31–32,* 396
If I Were You (2) *37–38,* 417
If in the Greenwood *46–47,* 431
If Love Were All *31–32,* 431
If Only We Might Live as We Chose
62–63, 322
If the Shoe Fits *46–47,* 446
If the Shoe Pinches *38–39,* 488
If This Be Treason *35–36,* 408
If Winter Comes *22–23,* 551
If You Hate a Man *60–61,* 294
Ignorants Abroad, The *59–60,* 40
Ihre Ideale *94–99,* 111
Ikkaku Sennin *64–65,* 362
Il ne Faut Jurer de Rien *23–24,* 406
'Ile *09–19,* 628; *24–25,* 587
I'll Be Hanged if I Do *09–19,* 431
I'll Be Home for Christmas *66–67,*
384
I'll Say She Is *23–24,* 437
I'll Take the High Road *43–44,* 424
Illustrators' Show, The *35–36,* 463
Illya Darling *66–67,* 390s
I'm Herbert *66–67,* 384
I'm in Love *46–47,* 497
I'm Solomon *67–68,* 372s
Im Weissen Roess'l *94–99,* 252
Image, The *09–19,* 459
Imaginary Invalid, The *(Le Malade
Imaginaire) 09–19,* 597; *43–44,*

489; *57–58,* 330; *61–62,* 313;
63–64, 327; *66–67,* 392; *69–70,*
313, 360
Immaculate Misconception, The
70–71
Immodest Violet *20–21,* 370
Immoral Isabella? *27–28,* 441
Immoralist, The *53–54,* 339; *63–64,*
351
Immortal Beloved, The *26–27,* 523
Immortal Husband, The *54–55,* 56
Immortal Seed *47–48,* 429
Immortal Shadows *62–63,* 326
Immortal Thief, The *26–27,* 391
Imperfect Lover, An *31–32,* 420–1
Imperfect Soliloquy, The *62–63,*
335
Importance of Being Earnest, The
94–99, 133; *99–09,* 408; *09–19,*
430; *20–21,* 422; *25–26,* 595;
26–27, 526; *38–39,* 450; *44–45,*
436, 450; *46–47,* 468; *59–60,* 359;
62–63, 326, 327
Importance of Being Oscar, The
60–61, 330
Importance of Coming and Going,
The *09–19,* 549
Impossible Years, The *65–66,* 376
Impostor, The (1) *09–19,* 433
Impostor, The (2; see *Tartuffe)*
Impromptu at Versailles
(L'Impromptu de Versailles)
60–61, 325; *63–64,* 327, 360
Improvisations in June *27–28,*
520
Imprudence *99–09,* 422
Impudent Wolf, An *65–66,* 427
Impulse *94–99,* 115
In a Balcony *99–09,* 375, 378
In a Cold Hotel *63–64,* 367
In a Garden *25–26,* 495
In a Jewish Grocery *39–40,* 474
In a Season *94–99,* 136
In a Train *37–38,* 376
In Abraham's Bosom *26–27,* 453;
27–28, 398
In Any Language *52–53,* 257
In April *09–19,* 547

In April Once *54–55*, 58
In Atlantic City *94–99*, 232
In Bed We Cry *44–45*, 397
In Circles *67–68*, 393; *68–69*, 425
In Clover *37–38*, 380
In Dahomey *99–09*, 429
In der Sache J. Robert Oppenheimer
  68–69, 234
In for the Night *09–19*, 593
In Gay New York *94–99*, 173
In Gay Paree *94–99*, 255; *99–09*,
  354
In Glass Houses *61–62*, 317
In God's Country *94–99*, 206
In Good King Charles's Golden
  Days *56–57*, 58
In Greater New York (see *Mrs.
  Radley Barton's Ball*)
In Hayti *09–19*, 397
In Heaven and Earth *35–36*, 473
In His Arms *24–25*, 471
In Love With Love *23–24*, 295;
  27–28, 554
In New England Winter *70–71*
In Newport *99–09*, 478
In Old Kentucky *94–99*, 97; *32–33*,
  482
In Paradise *99–09*, 347
In Sight of St. Paul's *94–99*, 152
In Spite of All (see also *Alexandra*)
  94–99, 217, 244
In Splendid Error *54–55*, 57
In the Bag *36–37*, 442
In the Bar of a Tokyo Hotel *68–69*,
  452
In the Best of Families *30–31*, 486
In the Big City *94–99*, 152
In the Bishop's Carriage *99–09*,
  534
In the Circus Parade (mn) *36–37*,
  498
In the Claws of Life *23–24*, 356
In the Counting House *62–63*, 291
In the Darkness *23–24*, 431
In the First Place *61–62*, 332
In the Groove *37–38*, 469
In the Heart of the Storm *94–99*,
  175

In the Jungle of Cities *60–61*, 355;
  61–62, 305
In the Long Run *09–19*, 405
In the Matter of J. Robert
  Oppenheimer *68–69*, 391; *69–70*,
  296
In the Name of the Czar *94–99*,
  83
In the Near Future *24–25*, 557
In the Next Room *23–24*, 364
In the Nick of Time *67–68*, 384
In the Night Watch *20–21*, 423
In the Palace of the King *99–09*,
  383
In the Penal Colony *61–62*, 330
In the Shadow of the Glen (see *The
  Shadow of the Glen*)
In the Summer House *53–54*, 333;
  63–64, 362
In the Tenderloin *94–99*, 111
In the Trenches *94–99*, 258
In the Zone *09–19*, 612; *24–25*, 480;
  37–38, 451; *47–48*, 349; *51–52*,
  333
In Time to Come *41–42*, 424
In Times Square *31–32*, 439
In Town *94–99*, 207
In White America *63–64*, 350;
  64–65, 359
Inadmissible Evidence *65–66*, 389
Inca of Jerusalem, The *09–19*, 590
Incident at Vichy *64–65*, 309
Incog *99–09*, 563
Incognito *99–09*, 472
Inconstant George *09–19*, 401
Increased Difficulty of Concentration,
  The *69–70*, 348
Incubator *32–33*, 415
Incubus, The *99–09*, 582
Indestructible Wife, The *09–19*, 621
Indian, The *94–99*, 207
Indian Summer (1) *94–99*, 211
Indian Summer (2) *09–19*, 512
Indian Wants the Bronx, The *67–68*,
  398
Indians *69–70*, 299
Indira Gandhi's Daring Device
  66–67, 35

Indiscretion *28–29,* 474
Indiscretion of Truth, The *09–19,* 487
Indoor Circus *34–35,* 484
Infancy *61–62,* 318
Infantry, The *66–67,* 408
Inferior Sex, The *09–19,* 411
Infernal Machine, The *37–38,* 464; *45–46,* 451; *53–54,* 359; *57–58,* 314
Infidel Caesar *61–62,* 338
Infinite Jest, or The Mortuary Songster *62–63,* 335
Infinite Shoeblack, The *29–30,* 494
Information Bureau, The *61–62,* 321
Information Please *09–19,* 639
Informer, The *38–39,* 486
Ingomar *94–99,* 214; *99–09,* 461
Inherit the Wind *54–55,* 409
Inheritors *26–27,* 490
Initiation *(Akokawe)* *69–70,* 352
Injun *70–71*
Injunction Granted *36–37,* 495
Injury Sustained *40–41,* 430
Ink *27–28,* 443
Inner Journey, The *68–69,* 437
Inner Man, The *09–19,* 603
Innkeepers, The *55–56,* 373
Innocent *09–19,* 531
Innocent Eyes *23–24,* 439
Innocent Idea, An *19–20,* 455
Innocent Party, The *68–69,* 455
Innocent Sinner, An *94–99,* 183
Innocent Voyage, The *43–44,* 427
Innocents, The *49–50,* 371; *58–59,* 52
Inquest *69–70,* 327
Insect Comedy, The *22–23,* 480; *48–49,* 376
Inside Story *42–43,* 486
Inside Story, The *31–32,* 483
Inside the Lines *09–19,* 546
Inside Track, The *94–99,* 225
Inside U.S.A. *47–48,* 401s
Insolent Breed, The *66–67,* 376
Inspector Calls, An *47–48,* 361

Inspector General (Inspector-General), The *(The Government Inspector; Revisor)* *22–23,* 563; *30–31,* 469; *34–35,* 452; *46–47,* 485
Inspector Kennedy *29–30,* 463
Instant Theater *60–61,* 36
Insult *30–31,* 410
Interesting People *60–61,* 295
Interference *27–28,* 432
Interior *09–19,* 547, 560
Interlock *57–58,* 317
Intermezzo *49–50,* 294; *56–57,* 353; *67–68,* 413
International, The *27–28,* 491
International Cup, the Ballet of Niagara and the Earthquake, The *09–19,* 423
International Incident, An *39–40,* 452
International Marriage, An *99–09,* 575
International Review, The *29–30,* 500
Interrupted Honeymoon, The *99–09,* 365
Interview (1) *66–67,* 405
Interview (2) *69–70,* 345
Interview With Mark Twain, An *43–44,* 490
Intimate Relations (1) *31–32,* 497
Intimate Relations (2) *62–63,* 318
Intimate Strangers, The *21–22,* 454
Intruder, The (1) *09–19,* 400
Intruder, The (2) *09–19,* 583
Intruder, The (3) *28–29,* 355
Invaders, The *70–71*
Investigation, The *66–67,* 359
Invincible! *70–71*
Invisible Foe, The *09–19,* 648
Invitation au Voyage, L' *28–29,* 388
Invitation to a Beheading *68–69,* 434
Invitation to a March *60–61,* 303; *66–67,* 423
Invitation to a Murder *33–34,* 529
Invitation to an Inquest *69–70,* 327

Iolanthe (or The Peer and the Peri) *09–19*, 502, 551, 639; *25–26*, 585; *27–28*, 452; *31–32*, 378; *33–34*, 520; *34–35*, 365; *35–36*, 498; *36–37*, 400; *38–39*, 447; *39–40*, 469; *40–41*, 430; *41–42*, 432, 458; *43–44*, 457, 488; *45–46*, 458; *46–47*, 494; *47–48*, 373, 375; *50–51*, 351; *52–53*, 264; *55–56*, 344; *62–63*, 286, 339; *63–64*, 328; *64–65*, 313, 359; *67–68*, 388; *68–69*, 390

Iole *09–19*, 518

Iphigenia in Aulis *20–21*, 440; *67–68*, 394; *68–69*, 434

Iphigenie auf Tauris *69–70*, 347

Irato ou L'Importo, L' *46–47*, 498

Irene *19–20*, 386

Irene Hawthorne *56–57*, 319

Irene Wycherley *99–09*, 555

Iris *99–09*, 417

Iris Mabry (dance programs) *47–48*, 415

Irish Artist, The *94–99*, 97

Irish Gentleman, An *94–99*, 217

Irish Inspiration *94–99*, 116

Irish literature, folk songs (unnamed sources) *67–68*, 394; *70–71*

Irish Minstrel, The *94–99*, 166

Irma La Douce *60–61*, 296s

Iron Cross, The *09–19*, 595

Iron Men *36–37*, 420

Iron Will, An (see *Hazel Kirke*)

Ironmaster, The *94–99*, 114, 115, 234

Irregular Verb To Love, The *63–64*, 303

Is Geraldine an Angel? *46–47*, 496

Is Life Worth Living? (see also *Drama at Inish*) *33–34*, 456

Is Matrimony a Failure? *09–19*, 397

Is Sex Necessary? *62–63*, 322

Is Zat So? *24–25*, 517

Isabel *24–25*, 522

Isaiah (Book of) *62–63*, 321

Island of Goats *55–56*, 350

Isle o' Dreams, The *09–19*, 493

Isle of Champagne *94–99*, 230

Isle of Children *61–62*, 292

Isle of Gold, The *94–99*, 201

Isle of Spice, The *99–09*, 462

Israel *09–19*, 403

Istanboul *70–71*

It All Depends *25–26*, 425

It Can Be Done *09–19*, 509

It Can't Happen Here *36–37*, 490

It Doesn't Happen Here *36–37*, 499

It Happened in Nordland *99–09*, 475

It Happened Tomorrow *32–33*, 491

It Happens on Ice (1940) *40–41*, 384

It Happens on Ice (1941) *41–42*, 391

It Happens to Everybody *09–19*, 657

It Is the Law *22–23*, 496

It Is to Laugh *27–28*, 478

It Never Rains *29–30*, 445; *31–32*, 448

It Pays to Advertise *09–19*, 530

It Pays to Sin *33–34*, 454

It Takes Two *46–47*, 458

"It's a Bird   It's a Plane   It's SUPERMAN" *65–66*, 405s

It's a Boy! *22–23*, 455

It's a Gift *44–45*, 419

It's a Grand Life *29–30*, 489

It's a Great Life *45–46*, 459

It's a Small World (mn) *38–39*, 489

It's a Wise Child *29–30*, 381; *32–33*, 497

It's About Time *41–42*, 459

It's All Your Fault *99–09*, 511

It's All Yours *61–62*, 329

It's Called the Sugar Plum *67–68*, 398

It's Up to You *20–21*, 439

It's You I Want *34–35*, 448

It's Your Move *46–47*, 494

Iva Kitchell (dance programs) *47–48*, 416; *56–57*, 333

Ivan the Terrible (p) *99–09*, 455, 486

Ivan the Terrible (opera rep) *43–44*, 440

Ivanov (Ivanoff) *23–24*, 356; *58–59*, 49; *65–66*, 410

I've Got Sixpence *52–53*, 274

I've Got the Tune *38–39*, 485; *39–40*, 468

Ivory Door, The *27–28*, 434

,Ivy Green, The *48–49*, 418

Ivy Leaf, The *94–99*, 109

Izeyl *94–99*, 163

Izzy *24–25*, 453

J.B. *58–59*, 312; *61–62*, 333

Jabberwocky *68–69*, 407

Jacinta *94–99*, 106

Jack *58–59*, 51

Jack and Jill *22–23*, 547

Jack and the Beanstalk (1) *94–99*, 182

Jack and the Beanstalk (2) *31–32*, 447

Jack and the Beanstalk (3) *37–38*, 467; *47–48*, 430

Jack and the Beanstalk (mn) *34–35*, 484; *38–39*, 489

Jack Benny *62–63*, 299

Jack in the Pulpit *24–25*, 518

Jack Lowe (see *Arthur Whittemore & Jack Lowe*)

Jack MacGowran in the Works of Samuel Beckett *70–71*

Jack O'Lantern *09–19*, 610

Jack Straw *99–09*, 568

Jackass, The *59–60*, 46

Jackdaw, The *09–19*, 459, 494

Jackhammer, The *61–62*, 322

Jackknife, a Truck Stop *58–59*, 51

Jackpot *43–44*, 448

Jack's Little Surprise *99–09*, 462

Jackson White *34–35*, 472

Jacob and the Angel *64–65*, 322

Jacob Slovak *27–28*, 423

Jacobowsky and the Colonel *43–44*, 462; *53–54*, 358

Jacobs Pillow Dance Festival Troupe (dance programs) *48–49*, 429

Jacques Brel Is Alive and Well and Living in Paris *67–68*, 399s

Jacques Cartier *46–47*, 493

Jade God, The *28–29*, 504

Jail for Sale *38–39*, 486

Jakey Fat Boy *69–70*, 363

Jalousie *94–99*, 250

Jalousie du Barbouille, La *37–38*, 469; *57–58*, 330

Jamaica *57–58*, 297s

Jamboree *32–33*, 429

Jane (1) *94–99*, 103

Jane (2) *51–52*, 308

Jane Clegg *19–20*, 431

Jane Eyre *57–58*, 331

Jane, Our Stranger *25–26*, 467

Janice Meredith *99–09*, 381

Janie *42–43*, 427

January Thaw *45–46*, 424

Janus *55–56*, 363

Japan at Night *99–09*, 413

Japanese Doll, A *99–09*, 547

Japanese Lady, A *99–09*, 547

Japanese Nightingale, A *99–09*, 445

Japanese Ophelia, A *99–09*, 547

Jar, The *68–69*, 451

Jarnegan *28–29*, 378

Jaselka *64–65*, 322

Jashiwara, The *99–09*, 547

Jason *41–42*, 429; *45–46*, 450

Javelin *66–67*, 407

Jay Walker, The *25–26*, 548

Jayhawker *34–35*, 403

Jazz and Minuet *26–27*, 523

Jazz Fantasia *60–61*, 295

Jazz Singer, The *25–26*, 443; *26–27*, 511

Jazznite *70–71*

Jealous Moon, The *28–29*, 421

Jealous Sister, The *37–38*, 467

Jealousy *28–29*, 400; *46–47*, 421

Jean de la Lune *37–38*, 469

Jean Marie *09–19*, 446

Jeanne d'Arc *99–09*, 470

Jeanne d'Arc au B(o)ucher *47–48*, 423; *63–64*, 346

Jeanne Welty *46–47*, 499

Jeannette *59–60,* 357

Jeb *45–46,* 428

Jedermann (see *Everyman*)

Jeff Chandler *70–71*

Jefferson Davis *35–36,* 467

Jeffrey Does a Book *37–38,* 465

Jennie *63–64,* 308s

Jenny *29–30,* 415

Jenny Kissed Me *48–49,* 401

Jeremiah *38–39,* 455

Jeremiah (Book of) *38–39,* 456

Jerico-Jim Crow *63–64,* 356s

Jerry *09–19,* 524

Jerry-for-Short *29–30,* 381

Jersey Lily, The *99–09,* 436

Jest, The *09–19,* 655; *19–20,* 353;
    25–26. 547

Jesters, The *(Les Bouffons)* (1)
    99–09, 554; *09–19,* 432

Jesters, The (2) *37–38,* 470

Jesus Christ (Biblical story of)
    38–39, 483

Jeu de L'Amour et du Hasard, Le
    (see *The Game of Love and
    Chance*)

Jeune Fille a Marier, La *69–70,* 363

Jeunesse *99–09,* 521

Jew! *67–68,* 406

Jewel of Asia, The *99–09,* 428

Jewel Robbery *31–32,* 464

Jeweled Tree, The *26–27,* 395

Jewess, The *47–48,* 432

Jewish King Lear, The *46–47,* 497

Jewish Wife, The *63–64,* 365

Jezebel *33–34,* 468

Jigsaw *33–34,* 521

Jilt, The *94–99,* 234

Jim Bludso of the Prairie Belle
    99–09, 425

Jim Jam Jems *20–21,* 391

Jim the Penman *94–99,* 196, 234;
    09–19, 419

Jim, the Westerner (see *The
    Westerner*)

Jimmie *20–21,* 406

Jimmie's Women *27–28,* 415

Jimmy *69–70,* 302s

Jimmy Savo *40–41,* 399

Jimmy Shine *68–69,* 396

Jinny, the Carrier *99–09,* 489

Jitta's Atonement *22–23,* 520

Jo *63–64,* 358s

Joan *94–99,* 222

Joan o' the Shoals *99–09,* 406

Joan of Arc *35–36,* 453

Joan of Lorraine *46–47,* 442; *60–61,*
    48

Job, Book of *61–62,* 322

Joe Egg (see *A Day in the Death of
    Joe Egg*)

Johannes Kreisler *22–23,* 505

John *27–28,* 444

John Brown *33–34,* 483

John Brown's Body *52–53,* 288;
    60–61, 45; *68–69,* 433, 455

John Bull's Other Island *99–09,*
    495; *47–48,* 381

John Ermine of the Yellowstone
    99–09, 443

John Ferguson *09–19,* 351, 657;
    33–34, 422, 423; *46–47,* 485

John Gabriel Borkman *94–99,* 216;
    09–19, 549; *25–26,* 541; *26–27,*
    423; *46–47,* 437

John Gladye's Honour *99–09,* 553

John Hawthorne *20–21,* 422

John Henry (1) *99–09,* 433

John Henry (2) *39–40,* 428

John Hudson's Wife *99–09,* 519

John Ingerfield *94–99,* 256

John Loves Mary *46–47,* 459

John Martin's Secret *94–99,* 238

John Murray Anderson's Almanac
    (see also *Murray Anderson's
    Almanac*) *53–54,* 326s

John the Baptist *99–09,* 470

John-a-Dreams *94–99,* 127

Johnny Belinda *40–41,* 379

Johnny Doodle *41–42,* 460

Johnny, Get Your Gun *09–19,*
    595

Johnny Johnson *36–37,* 432; *40–41,*
    431; *56–57,* 58; *63–64,* 342; *69–70,*
    335; *70–71*

Johnny No-Trump *67–68*, 343;
  70–71
Johnny on a Spot *41–42*, 426
Johnny on the Spot *94–99*, 254
Johnny 2 x 4 *41–42*, 444
Joint Owners in Spain *28–29*, 500
Joker, The *25–26*, 496
Jolly Bachelors, The *09–19*, 409
Jolly Musketeer, The *94–99*, 245
Jolly Roger, The *23–24*, 312
Jolly's Progress *59–60*, 308
Jonah (1) *65–66*, 430
Jonah! (2) *67–68*, 385
Jonathan Makes a Wish *09–19*, 636
Jonesy *28–29*, 491
Jonica *29–30*, 520
Jooss Ballet (dance programs)
  33–34, 520; *41–42*, 430–32, 456;
  46–47, 410, 491–2
José Greco's Spanish Ballet (dance
  programs) *51–52*, 330
José Limon (dance programs) *46–47*,
  487; *47–48*, 415, 416
Josef Suss *29–30*, 481
Joseph *29–30*, 492
Joseph (Biblical story of; see *Gene-
  sis*)
Joseph and His Brethren *09–19*, 491
Joseph Entangled *99–09*, 468
Josephine *09–19*, 621
Josephine Baker *63–64*, 323s
Josephine Premice (dance programs)
  44–45, 438
Joshua Whitcomb (see *The Old
  Homestead*)
Journey by Night, A *34–35*, 470
Journey of Snow White, The *70–71*
Journey of the Fifth Horse, The
  65–66, 433
Journey to Bahia *70–71*
Journey to Jerusalem *40–41*, 383
Journey to the Day *63–64*, 351
Journeyman *37–38*, 419
Journey's End *28–29*, 482; *38–39*,
  487; *39–40*, 399; *68–69*, 457
Journeys End in Lovers' Meeting
  94–99, 151

Jours Heureux, Les *40–41*, 425
Joy *69–70*, 357s
Joy Forever, A *45–46*, 419
Joy of Living *30–31*, 512
Joy of Living, The *99–09*, 420
Joy to the World *47–48*, 391
Joyce Grenfell (Requests the Pleasure
  . . .) *55–56*, 352s; *57–58*, 328s
Joyful Noise, A *66–67*, 376s
Joyous Season, The *33–34*, 486;
  39–40, 470
Juan Jose *31–32*, 500
Juana la Loca *64–65*, 362
Juarez and Maximilian *26–27*, 398
Jubilee (1) *27–28*, 550
Jubilee (2) *35–36*, 418
Judas (1) *09–19*, 432
Judas (2) *28–29*, 461
Judge and the Jury, The *99–09*, 518
Judge Lynch *23–24*, 431
Judgement Day *70–71*
Judges, The *63–64*, 342
Judgment Day *34–35*, 370
Judge's Husband, The *26–27*, 387
Judgment of Bolivas Plain, The
  94–99, 177
Judith (1) *24–25*, 547
Judith (2) *47–48*, 432
Judith (3) *64–65*, 348
Judith of Bethulia *99–09*, 475
Judith Zaraine *09–19*, 437
Judith Zaraine *09–19*, 436
Judy *26–27*, 478
Judy Drops In *24–25*, 465; *26–27*,
  478
Judy Forgot *09–19*, 427
Judy Garland at Home at the Palace
  67–68, 340
Juif Polonais, Le (see *The Polish
  Jew*)
Julie *26–27*, 526
Julie Bonbon *99–09*, 505
Julia, Jake and Uncle Joe *60–61*,
  320
Julius Caesar *94–99*, 127, 226, 239,
  257; *99–09*, 423, 476, 477, 534;
  09–19, 410, 443, 483, 521, 545,

599, 625; *21–22*, 496; *26–27*, 532; *29–30*, 516; *30–31*, 471; *31–32*, 433; *32–33*, 424; *37–38*, 388, 468; *50–51*, 309; *58–59*, 316; *59–60*, 44; *61–62*, 324, 338; *62–63*, 305

Julius Caesar's Circus (mn) *35–36*, 512

Jumbo *35–36*, 435

Jumping Fool, The *69–70*, 357

Jumping Jupiter *09–19*, 440

June Days *25–26*, 424

June Love *20–21*, 444

June Madness *09–19*, 478

June Moon *29–30*, 416; *32–33*, 495

Jungle, The *37–38*, 465

Junior Miss *41–42*, 415

Junk *26–27*, 456

Juno *58–59*, 326s

Juno and the Paycock *25–26*, 567; *27–28*, 469; *32–33*, 407; *34–35*, 411; *35–36*, 511; *37–38*, 377; *39–40*, 430; *46–47*, 494; *47–48*, 424; *54–55*, 57; *58–59*, 326

Jupiter Laughs *40–41*, 377

Just a Minute (1) *19–20*, 381

Just a Minute (2) *28–29*, 391

Just a Wife *09–19*, 413

Just a Woman *09–19*, 569

Just Around the Corner *09–19*, 651

Just as Well *09–19*, 523

Just Because *21–22*, 529

Just Beyond *25–26*, 507

Just Boys *09–19*, 557

Just Fancy *27–28*, 429

Just for Love *68–69*, 429

Just for Openers *65–66*, 424s; *66–67*, 400

Just Herself *09–19*, 542

Just Life *26–27*, 379

Just Like John *09–19*, 473

Just Married *20–21*, 445

Just My Luck *47–48*, 431

Just Out of College *99–09*, 497

Just Outside the Door *09–19*, 556

Just Say You're Sorry *60–61*, 39

Just Suppose *20–21*, 399; *27–28*, 430

Just to Get Married *09–19*, 461

Just to Remind You *31–32*, 386

Justice (1) *09–19*, 573; *46–47*, 485

Justice (2) *38–39*, 486

K Guy, The *28–29*, 397

Kaaka-Makaakoo *70–71*

Kabuki theater (see also *The Grand Kabuki*) *70–71*

Kagami-Jishi (see *The Mirror Lion Dance)*)

Kage-No-Chikara (see *The Shadow Man*)

Kama Sontra, Le *23–24*, 333

Kanjincho *67–68*, 411

Karen *09–19*, 619

Karl and Anna *29–30*, 412; *46–47*, 485

Kassa *99–09*, 576

Kataki *(The Enemy)* *58–59*, 332; *59–60*, 43

Kate Kip, Buyer *94–99*, 244

Katerina *28–29*, 473

Katherine Dunham (dance programs) *43–44*, 486; *44–45*, 440; *49–50*, 377

Kathleen *47–48*, 380

Kathleen ni Houlihan *99–09*, 378, 547; *09–19*, 458, 494; *34–35*, 411

Katie Roche *37–38*, 374

Katinka *09–19*, 566

Katja *26–27*, 406

Katy Did *26–27*, 527

Katya Kabanova *63–64*, 364

Katy's Kisses *19–20*, 356

Kean (or Disorder and Genius) (*Kean, ou Desordre et Genie;* see also *The Royal Box;* p 1) *99–09*, 536, 537; *28–29*, 422; *61–62*, 268

Kean (p 2) *61–62*, 268

Kean (m) *61–62*, 268s

Keep Cool *23–24*, 440

Keep 'Em Laughing *41–42*, 448

Keep Her Smiling *09–19*, 632

Keep It Clean *29–30*, 377

Keep It in the Family *67–68*, 341

Keep It to Yourself *09–19*, 648

Keep Kool *23–24*, 440

Keep Moving *34–35*, 362
Keep Off the Grass *39–40*, 463
Keep Shufflin' *27–28*, 518
Keeper of the Keys *33–34*, 444
Keeping Expenses Down *32–33*, 406
Keeping up Appearances (1) *94–99*, 124
Keeping up Appearances (2) *09–19*, 428, 587, 619
Kelly *64–65*, 325s
Kempy *21–22*, 547; *26–27*, 527
Ken Murray's Blackouts of 1949 *49–50*, 355
Ken Murray's Hollywood *64–65*, 336
Kendo, or The Way of the Sword *62–63*, 319
Kennen Sie die Milchstrasse? (see *Do You Know the Milky Way?*)
Kept *26–27*, 381
Kermesse Heroique, La *53–54*, 301
Kernel and the Shell, The *64–65*, 322
Kerry Gow *94–99*, 99
Key Largo *39–40*, 416
Keyhole, The *61–62*, 321
Khaki Blue *68–69*, 449
Kibitzer *28–29*, 469
Kick Back, The *36–37*, 397
Kick In *09–19*, 534
Kicking the Castle Down *66–67*, 410
Kid, The *60–61*, 48
Kid Boots *23–24*, 381
Kidding Kidders *27–28*, 544
Kidnapped *94–99*, 258
Kiki *21–22*, 470
Kill That Story *34–35*, 374
Kill the One-Eyed Man *65–66*, 423
Killarney *94–99*, 122
Killarney and the Rhine *94–99*, 239
Killer, The *59–60*, 356; *61–62*, 323
Killers *27–28*, 527
Killing of Sister George, The *66–67*, 360
Kind Lady *34–35*, 473; *35–36*, 403; *40–41*, 376

Kind Sir *53–54*, 316
Kindling *09–19*, 460
Kindred *39–40*, 426
King, The *09–19*, 615
King and Country *66–67*, 190
King and I, The *50–51*, 360s; *55–56*, 384s; *59–60*, 340; *63–64*, 302; *64–65*, 296; *67–68*, 379
King Argimenes (and the Unknown Warrior) *09–19*, 588, 650
King Arthur *94–99*, 150, 151
King Can Do No Wrong, The *27–28*, 453
King Dodo *99–09*, 410
King Henry IV, V, VI, VIII (see *Henry*)
King Heroin *70–71*
King Highball *99–09*, 415
King John *99–09*, 477; *09–19*, 545; *37–38*, 463; *67–68*, 93
King Lear *99–09*, 476, 477, 536; *09–19*, 443, 545, 599, 642; *22–23*, 539; *29–30*, 516; *30–31*, 471; *32–33*, 424; *40–41*, 432; *46–47*, 465, 497; *50–51*, 337, 373; *55–56*, 369; *58–59*, 52, 316; *62–63*, 305, 354; *63–64*, 336, 353, 360; *68–69*, 390, 457
King Midas and the Golden Touch *48–49*, 426
King of Cadonia, The *09–19*, 409
King of Friday's Men, The *50–51*, 354
King of Hearts *53–54*, 348
King of Nowhere, A *09–19*, 572
King of Peru, The *94–99*, 92
King of the Dark Chamber *60–61*, 44
King of the Golden River, The *38–39*, 490
King of the Opium Ring, The *94–99*, 255
King of the Whole Damn World *61–62*, 328s
King Rene's Daughter *99–09*, 520
King Richard II, III (see *Richard*)

King Solomon and the Cobbler *67–68*, 372

King Washington *99–09*, 391

Kingdom of God, The *28–29*, 436

Kingdom of 137 *37–38*, 461

Kings II, Book of *30–31*, 74

King's Arrowmaker, The *37–38*, 467

King's Carnival, The *99–09*, 392

King's Darling, The *51–52*, 332

Kings in Nomania *42–43*, 489

King's Musketeer, The *94–99*, 254

King's Parting With His Favorite, The *29–30*, 497

Kingsland Marionettes *35–36*, 512

Kino-Konigin, Die *09–19*, 519

Kipps *64–65*, 333

Kirokuda (see *The Half-Delivered Gift*)

Kismet (1) *94–99*, 138

Kismet (2; p) *09–19*, 461; *53–54*, 324; *63–64*, 367; *65–66*, 368

Kismet (2; m) *53–54*, 324s; *63–64*, 367; *65–66*, 368

Kiss and Tell *42–43*, 467

Kiss Burglar, The *09–19*, 629, 653

Kiss for Cinderella, A *09–19*, 591; *41–42*, 442; *66–67*, 409

Kiss in a Taxi, A *25–26*, 433

Kiss in the Dark, The *09–19*, 509

Kiss in Xanadu, A *23–24*, 398; *37–38*, 468

Kiss Mama *64–65*, 342

Kiss Me *27–28*, 388

Kiss Me, Kate *48–49*, 405s; *51–52*, 303; *53–54*, 358; *55–56*, 388s; *64–65*, 334

Kiss Me Quick *09–19*, 504

Kiss Now *70–71*

Kiss of Importance, A *30–31*, 463

Kiss the Boys Good-bye *38–39*, 409

Kiss Them for Me *44–45*, 423; *46–47*, 484

Kiss Waltz, The *09–19*, 451

Kissing Time *20–21*, 392

Kit, the Arkansas Traveller *94–99*, 251

Kitchen, The *65–66*, 437; *66–67*, 399

Kitchenette *66–67*, 35

Kith and Kin *29–30*, 539

Kittiwake Island *60–61*, 350s

Kitty Clive, Actress *94–99*, 186

Kitty Darlin' *09–19*, 613

Kitty Grey *99–09*, 576

Kitty, I Hardly Knew You *63–64*, 342

Kitty Mackay *09–19*, 519; *19–20*, 445

Kitty's Kisses *25–26*, 597

Klara *70–71*

Kleinburgerhochzeit, Die (see *The Wedding Feast*)

Knack, The *63–64*, 366

Knack With Horses, A *70–71*

Knave of Hearts *37–38*, 468

Knickerbocker Girl, The *99–09*, 367

Knickerbocker Holiday *38–39*, 419; *63–64*, 342

Knife, The *09–19*, 599

Knight for a Day, A *99–09*, 552

Knight of Olmedo, The *62–63*, 340

Knight of the Burning Pestle, The *53–54*, 356

Knights of Song *38–39*, 418

Knobs of Tennessee *94–99*, 252

Knock (see *Dr. Knock*)

Knock on Wood *34–35*, 480

Know Thyself *09–19*, 407

Koi-No-Yozakura (see *Romance in Cherry Blossom Lane*)

Komedie *25–26*, 534

Kongi's Harvest *67–68*, 396

Kongo *25–26*, 578

Konzert, Das (see *The Concert*)

Korb'n *44–45*, 441

Koreans, The *94–99*, 229

Kosher Kitty Kelly *24–25*, 604

Krapp's Last Tape *59–60*, 352; *61–62*, 305; *65–66*, 416; *68–69*, 379; *70–71*

Kremlin Chimes *64–65*, 323

Kreutzer Sonata, The (1) *99–09*, 516

Kreutzer Sonata, The (2) *99–09*,
516; *23–24*, 436
Kreutzer Sonata, The (3) *60–61*, 45
Kuan Yin *25–26*, 569
Kukla, Burr and Ollie (mn) *60–61*,
48
Kultur *33–34*, 435
Kumagai Jinya (see *General
Kumagai's Battle Camp*)
Kumquat in the Persimmon Tree,
The *62–63*, 312
Kurt Jooss Ballet (see *Jooss Ballet*)
Kurve, Die (see *The Curve*)
Kwamina *61–62*, 264s
Kykundor *33–34*, 533; *34–35*, 483
Kyogen Theater *70–71*

La, La, Lucille *09–19*, 657
La Perichole (see *Perichole*)
Labor Sings *40–41*, 430
Laboratoire des Hallucinations, Le
23–24, 333
Laburnum Grove *34–35*, 438
Labyrinth, The (1) *99–09*, 501
Labyrinth, The (2) *64–65*, 322
Lace on Her Petticoat *51–52*, 280
Lace Petticoat *26–27*, 456
Lacune, La *69–70*, 363
Ladder, The *26–27*, 409; *51–52*, 332
Ladder of Life, The *94–99*, 221
Ladies All *30–31*, 400
Ladies and Gentlemen *39–40*, 403
Ladies' Battle, The *99–09*, 363
Ladies Don't Lie *29–30*, 417
Ladies First *09–19*, 641
Ladies in Retirement *39–40*, 449;
44–45, 436, 441
Ladies in Waiting *70–71*
Ladies Leave *29–30*, 410
Ladies' Money *34–35*, 400
Ladies Night *20–21*, 364; *44–45*,
410
Ladies' Night in a Turkish Bath
49–50, 384; *60–61*, 46
Ladies of Creation *31–32*, 388
Ladies of the Corridor, The *53–54*,
311
Ladies of the Evening *24–25*, 510

Ladies of the Jury *29–30*, 423
Ladies Paradise, The *99–09*, 394
Ladies' Voices *51–52*, 333
Lady, The *23–24*, 367
Lady Across the Hall, The *99–09*,
485
Lady Akane, The *60–61*, 47
Lady Alone *26–27*, 464
Lady Aoi *(Aoi-No-Ue)* *70–71*
Lady Baltimore *39–40*, 468
Lady, Be Good *24–25*, 497
Lady, Behave *43–44*, 427
Lady Beyond the Moon *30–31*, 510
Lady Billy *20–21*, 411
Lady Bookie, The *99–09*, 485
Lady Bug *21–22*, 536
Lady Butterfly *22–23*, 522
Lady Clancarty *94–99*, 114
Lady Clara *29–30*, 525
Lady Comes Across, The *41–42*,
427
Lady Cristilinda, The *22–23*, 511
Lady Dedlock *28–29*, 447
Lady Detained, A *34–35*, 436
Lady Do *26–27*, 510
Lady Fingers *28–29*, 463
Lady for a Night, A *27–28*, 539
Lady Frederick *99–09*, 572
Lady From Alfaqueque, The *28–29*,
455; *30–31*, 427
Lady From Lane's, The *99–09*, 542
Lady From Lobster Square, The
09–19, 416
Lady From Maxim's *69–70*, 377
Lady From Oklahoma, The *09–19*,
499
Lady From the Provinces, The
22–23, 517
Lady From the Sea, The *09–19*,
457; *23–24*, 366; *28–29*, 481;
33–34, 522; *50–51*, 312; *56–57*, 55
Lady Gay's Garden Party *99–09*,
551
Lady Godiva *66–67*, 35
Lady Has a Heart, The *37–38*, 371
Lady Huntworth's Experiment
99–09, 381
Lady in Danger *44–45*, 426

Lady in Ermine, The *22–23*, 468
Lady in Love, A *26–27*, 481
Lady in Red, The *09–19*, 657
Lady in the Dark *40–41*, 412;
  41–42, 392; *42–43*, 465; *51–52*,
  333; *63–64*, 342
Lady in Waiting *39–40*, 449
Lady Is a Tramp, Geraldine, The
  63–64, 367
Lady Jane *34–35*, 368
Lady Jim *99–09*, 517
Lady Killer, The *23–24*, 407
Lady Lee's Widowhood *94–99*, 104
Lady Lies, The *28–29*, 426
Lady Luck *35–36*, 501
Lady Luxury *09–19*, 542
Lady Madcap (see *My Lady's Maid*)
Lady Margaret *99–09*, 405
Lady of Coventry, The *09–19*, 459
Lady of Dreams, The *09–19*, 467
Lady of Fatima *47–48*, 427
Lady of Letters *34–35*, 466
Lady of Lyons. The *94–99*, 167,
  206, 207; *99–09*, 410
Lady of Quality, A (The) *94–99*,
  213, 214
Lady of the Camellias (see also
  Camille) *62–63*, 303
Lady of the Lamp, The *20–21*, 368
Lady of the Legs, The *62–63*, 310
Lady of the Orchids, The *28–29*,
  435
Lady of the Rose *24–25*, 595
Lady of the Slipper, The *09–19*,
  481
Lady of the Weeping Willow Tree,
  The *09–19*, 588
Lady or the Tiger?, The *66–67*, 364
Lady Patricia *09–19*, 466
Lady Precious Stream *35–36*, 464;
  50–51, 374
Lady Refuses, The *32–33*, 474
Lady Remembers, The *31–32*, 512
Lady Rose's Daughter *99–09*, 445
Lady Says Yes, A *44–45*, 409
Lady Screams, The *26–27*, 520
Lady Shore, The *99–09*, 487
Lady Slavey, The *94–99*, 164

Lady Teazle *99–09*, 478
Lady Who Came to Stay, The
  40–41, 407
Lady Windermere's Fan *09–19*, 525;
  31–32, 470, 501; *45–46*, 459;
  46–47, 425; *60–61*, 42
Lady With a Lamp, The *31–32*, 436
Lady's Name, A *09–19*, 575
Lady's Not for Burning, The *50–51*,
  324; *56–57*, 58
Lady's Virtue, A *25–26*, 500
Laff That Off *25–26*, 488
Laffing Room Only *44–45*, 404
L'Aiglon (see *Aiglon*)
Lake, The *33–34*, 470
Lally *26–27*, 479
Lamentation of the Virgin Mary, The
  32–33, 458
Lamp at Midnight *47–48*, 426
Lamplight *23–24*, 432
Lancashire Lass, The *31–32*, 457
Lancelot and Elaine (see *Launcelot
  and Elaine*)
Lancers, The *99–09*, 552
Land Beyond the River, A *56–57*,
  58
Land Is Bright, The *41–42*, 406
Land of Fame *43–44*, 414
Land of Heart's Desire, The *99–09*,
  375, 377, 378
Land of Joy, The *09–19*, 611
Land of Nod, The *99–09*, 537
Land of Promise, The *09–19*, 517
Land of Smiles *46–47*, 418
Land of the Free, The *09–19*, 609
Land of the Living, The *94–99*, 144
Land of the Midnight Sun, The
  94–99, 125
Land's End *46–47*, 447
Landscape *69–70*, 348; *70–71*
Lange Preusse, Der *94–99*, 221
Langusten *67–68*, 401
Lark, The *55–56*, 362
Larry Adler (see *Paul Draper and
  Larry Adler*)
Lash of a Whip, The *99–09*, 389
Lass o' Laughter *24–25*, 519
Lassie *19–20*, 444

Lassoo, The *09–19,* 602

Last Analysis, The *64–65,* 305

Last Appeal, The *99–09,* 409

Last Chapter, The *94–99,* 254

Last Christmas, The *39–40,* 446

Last Dance, The *47–48,* 379

Last Days of Lincoln, The *64–65,* 361

Last Enemy, The *30–31,* 443

Last Generation, The *42–43,* 488

Last Laugh, The *09–19,* 554

Last Letters From Stalingrad *65–66,* 382

Last Man In, The *25–26,* 592; *29–30,* 535

Last Mile, The *29–30,* 494; *39–40,* 397; *45–46,* 450

Last Minstrel, The *62–63,* 335

Last Night of Don Juan *25–26,* 492

Last of Cheri, The *59–60,* 295

Last of His Race, The *94–99,* 227

Last of Mrs. Cheyney, The *25–26,* 491

Last of the Lowries, The *26–27,* 524

Last of the Red Hot Lovers *69–70,* 310

Last of the Rohans, The *99–09,* 346

Last Resort, The *09–19,* 523

Last Savage, The *63–64,* 321

Last Shift, The *50–51,* 328

Last Stand *70–71*

Last Stop *44–45,* 373

Last Straw, The (1) *09–19,* 579

Last Straw, The (2) *69–70,* 341

Last Stroke, The *94–99,* 170

Last Sweet Days of Isaac, The *69–70,* 356s

Last to Go *69–70,* 345

Last Toast, The *09–19,* 526

Last Torture, The *26–27,* 460

Last Triangle, The *67–68,* 403

Last Waltz, The *20–21,* 449

Last Warning, The *22–23,* 477

Last Word, The *60–61,* 295

Late Arrival *53–54,* 359

Late Christopher Bean, The *32–33,* 413; *44–45,* 436

Late George Apley, The *44–45,* 399

Late Late Show, The *68–69,* 432

Late Love *53–54,* 309

Late Mr. Castello, The *94–99,* 188

Late One Evening *32–33,* 448

Late Wisdom *33–34,* 519

Later On *94–99,* 98

Laterna Magika *64–65,* 297

Latin Liturgy *62–63,* 321

Laugh, Clown, Laugh! (1) *23–24,* 364

Laugh, Clown, Laugh (2) *45–46,* 459

Laugh Parade, The *31–32,* 420

Laugh Time *43–44,* 411

Laugh, Town, Laugh! *42–43,* 418

Laughing Husband, The *09–19,* 521

Laughing Lady, The *22–23,* 530

Laughing Woman, The *36–37,* 417

Laughs and Other Events *60–61,* 299s

Laughs, Etc. *68–69,* 448

Laughter of the Gods, The *09–19,* 649

Laughwind *65–66,* 431

Launcelot and Elaine *21–22,* 420; *29–30,* 506

Laundry, The *62–63,* 326

Launzi *23–24,* 332

Laura *47–48,* 341; *51–52,* 333

Laurette *63–64,* 308

Law and the Man, The *99–09,* 529

Law Breaker, The *21–22,* 505

Law of Tayhol, The *39–40,* 473

Law of the Land, The (1) *94–99,* 171

Law of the Land, The (2) *09–19,* 533

Law Takes Its Toll, The *29–30,* 175

Lawful Larceny *21–22,* 489

Lawyer, The *45–46,* 450

Lawyer's Dilemma, The *28–29,* 354

Lazarus *62–63,* 330

Lazarus Laughed *47–48,* 428

Lazybones *24–25,* 456

Le Meri & Natya Dancers (dance programs) *41–42,* 457; *44–45,*

438; *45–46*, 452, 455; *46–47*, 486;
47–48, 414, 415
Leader *68–69*, 451
Leading Lady, The *48–49*, 389
Leaf and Bough *48–49*, 408
Leah *94–99*, 218
Leah Kleschna *99–09*, 169, 477;
23–24, 421
Leah the Forsaken *94–99*, 208, 218
Lean Harvest *31–32*, 408
Leaping Sword, The *35–36*, 511
Learned Ladies, The *(Les Femmes
Savantes) 09–19*, 457; *66–67*, 412;
69–70, 313
Leave Her to Heaven *39–40*, 440
Leave It to Charlie *48–49*, 429
Leave It to Jane *09–19*, 605; *59–60*,
48
Leave It to Me (1) *38–39*, 425;
39–40, 398; *64–65*, 357
Leave It to Me (2) *46–47*, 497
Leavenworth Case, The *43–44*, 489
Lebende Leichman, Der *27–28*, 485
Led Astray *94–99*, 209
Leda Had a Little Swan *67–68*, 381
Ledge, A *29–30*, 443
Left Bank, The *31–32*, 402
Left Fork, The *24–25*, 584
Legal Murder *33–34*, 498
Legataire Universel, Le *23–24*, 406
Legend *29–30*, 533
Legend of Leonora, The *09–19*, 518;
26–27, 501
Legend of Lizzie, The *58–59*, 321
Legend of Lovers *51–52*, 300;
52–53, 308
Legend of Sarah *50–51*, 318
Legend of Sleepy Hollow *66–67*, 404
Legend of the Dance *24–25*, 565
Lem Kettle *94–99*, 95
Lemon Sky *69–70*, 368
Lemonade *68–69*, 439
Lemonade Boy, The *99–09*, 539
Lend an Ear *48–49*, 400s; *59–60*,
46; *69–70*, 373
Lend Me Five Shillings *94–99*, 146
Lend Me Your Ears! *36–37*, 414

Lenin's Dowry *31–32*, 512
Lenny *70–71*
Lenten plays (untitled programs)
61–62, 327
Leonard Bernstein's Theater Songs
65–66, 418s
Leonard Sillman's New Faces (see
New Faces)
Leonardo *94–99*, 148
Leonce and Lena *68–69*, 455
Leopard's Spots, The *99–09*, 506
Lesson, The *57–58*, 308; *63–64*, 345
Lesson for Today, A *62–63*, 322
Lesson in Dead Language *70–71*
Lesson in Love, A *23–24*, 320
Let and Sub-let *29–30*, 545
Let 'Em Eat Cake *33–34*, 445
Let Freedom Ring *35–36*, 431
Let Freedom Sing *42–43*, 433
Let It Ride! *61–62*, 260s
Let Them Down, Gently *67–68*, 408
Let Us Be Gay *28–29*, 471
Let Us Now Praise Famous Men
63–64, 369
Lethe *94–99*, 124
Let's Face It *41–42*, 407; *42–43*,
423; *64–65*, 357
Let's Go *09–19*, 624
Let's Make an Opera *50–51*, 333
Let's Sing Yiddish *66–67*, 367
Lettarblair, or Loves Me, Loves Me
Not (see *Captain Lettarblair*)
Letter, The *27–28*, 411; *45–46*, 450
Letter of the Law, The *19–20*, 430
Letter to the President, A *35–36*,
510
Letters From the Earth *65–66*, 405
Letters to Father Flye *63–64*, 369
Letters to Lucerne *41–42*, 422;
44–45, 436
Lettre Morte *69–70*, 363
Letty *99–09*, 465
Letty Pepper *21–22*, 533
Lew Dockstader's Minstrels *99–09*,
450, 529
Lew Leslie's Blackbirds (see
Blackbirds 1930)

Lewisohn Stadium (dance programs) 44–45, 437

Leyenda del Beso, La 42–43, 490

Liar, The (1) 94–99, 176

Liar, The (2) 49–50, 380s

Liars, The 94–99, 240; 09–19, 559

Libation Pourers (Bearers), The (see *The Choephori*)

Libby Holman's "Blues, Ballads and Sin-Songs" 54–55, 365s

Libel 35–36, 450

Liberated Woman, A 70–71

Liberte Provisoire 34–35, 425

Liberty Belles, The 99–09, 396

Liberty Hall 09–19, 497

Liberty Jones 40–41, 414

License, The 68–69, 451

Licensed 09–19, 547

Lido Girl, The 28–29, 362

Lie, The 09–19, 542

Lied von der Erde, Das 47–48, 419

Lieber Augustin 09–19, 506

Lifar Dancers (see *Serge Lifar Russian Dancers*)

Life (1) 99–09, 408

Life (2) 09–19, 536

Life and Death of an American 38–39, 481

Life and Loves of Dorian Gray, The 36–37, 398

Life and Times of J. Walter Smintheus, The 70–71

Life Begins 31–32, 496

Life Begins at 8:40 34–35, 362

Life Begins in '40 39–40, 473

Life Guard, The 94–99, 84

Life in the Day of a Secretary, A 38–39, 485; 39–40, 468

Life Is a Dream *(La Vida es Sueno)* 53–54, 322; 63–64, 362

Life Is Like That 30–31, 469

Life Line, The 30–31, 473

Life Marches On 39–40, 474

Life of Galileo, The (see *Galileo*)

Life of Juanita Castro, The 66–67, 35

Life of Man, The 09–19, 580

Life of Reilly, The 41–42, 449

Life on the Mississippi 65–66, 405

Life Sentence 47–48, 425

Life With Father (source) 39–40, 142; 48–49, 391; 67–68, 346

Life With Father 39–40, 410; 67–68, 346

Life With Mother (source) 39–40, 142; 48–49, 391

Life With Mother 48–49, 391

Lifeline 42–43, 449

Life's Too Short 35–36, 406

Lifting the Lid 99–09, 491

Light Eternal, The 99–09, 528

Light Fantastic, The 39–40, 250

Light From St. Agnes, A (The) 94–99, 169; 99–09, 487, 513

Light, Lively and Yiddish 70–71s

Light of Asia, The 28–29, 393

Light of the World, The 19–20, 412

Light That Failed, The 99–09, 444; 09–19, 509–10

Light That Lies in Woman's Eyes, The 99–09, 453

Light Up the Sky 48–49, 397

Light Wines and Beer 30–31, 450

Lightnin' 09–19, 634; 38–39, 405

Lights o' London (The) 94–99, 152, 235; 09–19, 445; 36–37, 488

Lights Out 22–23, 439

'Lijah 27–28, 551

Like a King 21–22, 431

Likes o' Me, The 99–09, 566

Li'l Abner 56–57, 335s

Lilac Domino, The 09–19, 537

Lilac Room, The 99–09, 538

Lilac Time 09–19, 594

Lili Tse 94–99, 224

Lilies of the Field (1) 21–22, 433

Lilies of the Field (2) 69–70, 321

Liliom 20–21, 443; 32–33, 409; 39–40, 448; 44–45, 428; 48–49, 409; 54–55, 359; 65–66, 368; 66–67, 378

Lilliput Theater (dance programs) 37–38, 468

Lilliput Theater Puppets 37–38, 468

Lilly Turner *32–33*, 388
Lily, The *09–19*, 407
Lily and the Prince, The *09–19*, 443
Lily of the Valley *41–42*, 436
Lily Sue *26–27*, 428
Lima Beans *24–25*, 586
Limb of Snow *67–68*, 408
Lime Green (Khaki Blue) *68–69*,
    449
Limited Mail, The *94–99*, 87
Lincoln (at the White House) *99–09*,
    511, 574
Lincoln: The Prairie Years *60–61*,
    295
Linden Tree, The *47–48*, 388
Line *67–68*, 412; *70–71*
Line of Least Existence, The *67–68*,
    411
Linger Longer Letty *19–20*, 388
Lingering Past, The *32–33*, 378
Lion and the Mouse, The *99–09*,
    501
Lion Hunters, The *51–52*, 334
Lion in Love, The *62–63*, 334
Lion in Winter, The *65–66*, 400
Lion Tamer, The *26–27*, 396
Lion's Heart, A *94–99*, 171
Listen Lester *09–19*, 647
Listen, Professor! *43–44*, 443
Listen Sean to the Silhouettes of
    Raindrops *70–71*
Listen to the Quiet *58–59*, 51
Listening In *22–23*, 497
Literature *09–19*, 560, 579
Literary Sense, The *99–09*, 534
Little A *46–47*, 456
Little Accident *28–29*, 394
Little Angel, The *24–25*, 459
Little Bit of Everything, A *99–09*,
    461
Little Bit of Fluff, A *09–19*, 578
Little Black Book, The *32–33*, 442
Little Black Sambo (mn) *36–37*,
    498; *37–38*, 467
Little Blue Deveil, The *19–20*, 381
Little Blue Light, The *50–51*, 366
Little Boxes *69–70*, 348

Little Boy Blue *09–19*, 459
Little Brother, The *09–19*, 645
Little Brother of the Rich, A *09–19*,
    407
Little Brown Jug *45–46*, 430
Little Cafe, The *09–19*, 514
Little Cherub, The *99–09*, 516
Little Christopher Columbus (Little
    Christopher) *94–99*, 99
Little Clay Cart, The *24–25*, 502;
    26–27, 419; *53–54*, 356
Little Corporal, The *94–99*, 238
Little Damozel, The *09–19*, 425
Little Dark Horse *41–42*, 414
Little Darling *42–43*, 440
Little Duchess, The *99–09*, 398
Little Duke, The *94–99*, 171
Little Eyolf *09–19*, 418; *25–26*, 545;
    45–46, 459; *63–64*, 361
Little Face *09–19*, 535
Little Father of the Wilderness, The
    99–09, 510; *29–30*, 546
Little Foxes, The *38–39*, 460; *49–50*,
    359; *63–64*, 364; *67–68*, 348
Little Girl and the Wolf, The *59–60*,
    323; *60–61*, 289
Little Glass Clock *55–56*, 381
Little Gray Lady, The *99–09*, 508
Little Host, The *94–99*, 248
Little Hussar, The *94–99*, 112
Little Hut, The *53–54*, 309; *61–62*,
    304
Little Italy *94–99*, 169; *99–09*, 411;
    27–28, 550
Little Jessie James *23–24*, 301
Little Johnny Jones *99–09*, 472
Little Journey, A *09–19*, 648
Little Lady in Blue *09–19*, 591
Little Lord Fauntleroy *94–99*, 229;
    99–09, 431
Little Malcolm and His Struggle
    Against the Eunuchs *66–67*, 375
Little Man, The *09–19*, 595
Little Mary *99–09*, 450
Little Mary Sunshine *59–60*, 351s;
    69–70, 373
Little Mazel, A *47–48*, 432

Little Me *62–63,* 287s
Little Mermaid, The *09–19,* 540
Little Michus, The *99–09,* 532
Little Millionaire, The *09–19,* 452
Little Minister, The *94–99,* 209;
  99–09, 478; *09–19,* 569; *24–25,*
  559
Little Miss Bluebeard *23–24,* 310
Little Miss Brown *09–19,* 474
Little Miss Charity *20–21,* 376
Little Miss Fix-It *09–19,* 442
Little Moon of Alban *60–61,* 309
Little Murders *66–67,* 391; *68–69,*
  442
Little Nell and the Marchioness
  99–09, 365; *33–34,* 457
Little Nellie Kelly *22–23,* 487
Little Nemo *99–09,* 571
Little Ol' Boy *32–33,* 487
Little Old New York *20–21,* 380
Little Orchid Annie *29–30,* 528
Little Poor Man, The *25–26,* 423
Little Princess, The *99–09,* 426;
  38–39, 490
Little Private World of Arthur
  Fenwick, The *67–68,* 392
Little Racketeer, A *31–32,* 465
Little Ray of Sunshine, A *99–09,*
  346
Little Red Riding Hood (source)
  23–24, 349
Little Red Riding Hood (1) *99–09,*
  359
(Little) Red Riding Hood (2) *36–37,*
  498; *37–38,* 467; *38–39,* 490;
  47–48, 430
Little Shot *34–35,* 441
Little Show, The (see also *The
  Second Little Show, The Third
  Little Show*) *28–29,* 498
Little Simplicity *09–19,* 643
Little Spitfire, The *26–27,* 365
Little Stone House, The *22–23,* 573
Little Stranger, The *99–09,* 492
Little Teacher, The *09–19,* 621
Little Theater Tournament *22–23,*
  570; *23–24,* 428; *24–25,* 583;

25–26, 590; *26–27,* 521; *27–28,*
  548; *28–29,* 500; *29–30,* 532
Little Town of Bethlehem *09–19,*
  410
Little Trooper, The *94–99,* 85
Little Water on the Side, A *09–19,*
  518
Little Whopper, The *19–20,* 371
Little Women (source) *09–19,* 480,
  590; *31–32,* 444; *38–39,* 390;
  44–45, 379; *45–46,* 393; *63–64,*
  358
Little Women *09–19,* 480, 590;
  31–32, 444; *32–33,* 405; *38–39,*
  490; *44–45,* 379; *45–46,* 393
Littlest Girl, The *94–99,* 140
Littlest Rebel, The *09–19,* 458
Littlest Revue, The *55–56,* 391s
Liturgy (see *Latin Liturgy*)
Live and Learn *29–30,* 521
Live Life Again *45–46,* 395, 450
Live Like Pigs *65–66,* 416
Live Wire, The *50–51,* 313
Lives of the Poets *99–09,* 387
Livin' the Life *56–57,* 371s
Living Corpse, The (see also
  Redemption) *09–19,* 639; *29–30,*
  458
Living Dangerously *34–35,* 437
Living Mask, The (see also *Henry
  IV*) *23–24,* 388
Living Newspaper, The *35–36,* 471;
  36–37, 495; *37–38,* 452, 459;
  39–40, 455
Living Premise, The *63–64,* 343
Living Room, The *54–55,* 374;
  62–63, 320
Liz the Mother *09–19,* 408
Liza *22–23,* 494
Lo and Behold *51–52,* 297
Local Stigmatic, The *69–70,* 345
Locandiera, La (Locondiera) (see
  The Mistress of the Inn)
Locked Door, The *24–25,* 426
Locked Room, The *33–34,* 469
Loco *46–47,* 427
Locura de Amor *25–26,* 599

Lodger, The *09–19*, 592
Logan's Luck *94–99*, 136
Loggerheads *24–25*, 537
Lola From Berlin *99–09*, 544
Lollipop *23–24*, 389
Lolly *29–30*, 420
Lolotte *94–99*, 126; *99–09*, 472
Lombardi, Ltd. *09–19*, 608; *26–27*, 533
London Assurance *94–99*, 109, 185; *99–09*, 488; *36–37*, 467
London Calling *30–31*, 434
London Follies *09–19*, 443
London Life *94–99*, 256
Lone Valley *32–33*, 475
Lonely Romeo, A *09–19*, 658
Lonely Steeple, The *53–54*, 358
Lonesome Like *09–19*, 526, 612
Lonesome Town *99–09*, 555
Long and the Short and the Tall, The *61–62*, 327
Long Christmas Dinner, The *62–63*, 328; *66–67*, 401
Long Dash, The *09–19*, 643
Long Days, The *50–51*, 364
Long Day's Journey Into Night *56–57*, 332; *61–62*, 298; *67–68*, 401; *70–71*
Long Dream, The *59–60*, 318
Long Goodbye, The *46–47*, 484
Long Live America *38–39*, 494
Long Road, The *30–31*, 409
Long Strike, The *94–99*, 176
Long Voyage Home, The *24–25*, 480; *37–38*, 451, 452; *47–48*, 349; *51–52*, 333; *61–62*, 310
Long Watch, The *51–52*, 315
Long Way From Home, A *47–48*, 395
Long-Play Tournament *29–30*, 538; *30–31*, 524
Look After Lulu *58–59*, 325; *64–65*, 362
Look at Any Man *63–64*, 367
Look at the Heffernans *34–35*, 408
Look at Us *62–63*, 312s

Look Back in Anger *57–58*, 288; *58–59*, 53
Look Homeward, Angel *57–58*, 303
Look in Your Glass *46–47*, 205
Look, Ma, I'm Dancin' *47–48*, 379s
Look to the Lilies *69–70*, 321s
Look: We've Come Through *61–62*, 266
Look Where I'm At *70–71*
Look Who's Here *19–20*, 434
Loose Ankles *26–27*, 365
Loose Ends *26–27*, 417
Loose Moments *34–35*, 446
Loot *67–68*, 367
Lord and Lady Algy *94–99*, 253; *99–09*, 351, 352; *09–19*, 617
Lord Blesses the Bishop, The *34–35*, 416
Lord Chumley *94–99*, 96, 131, 206, 207
Lord Dundreary *99–09*, 470
Lord Pengo *62–63*, 288
Lorelei *38–39*, 433
Lorenzaccio *58–59*, 295; *64–65*, 362
Lorenzo *62–63*, 298
Los Angeles *27–28*, 469
Losers *68–69*, 375
Losing Eloise *09–19*, 614
Loss of Roses, A *59–60*, 307
Lost *26–27*, 500
Lost Boy *31–32*, 459
Lost Bride, The *48–49*, 430
Lost Co-respondent, The *09–19*, 552
Lost Horizons (1) *34–35*, 392
Lost Horizons (2) *56–57*, 313
Lost in Siberia *94–99*, 247
Lost in the Stars *49–50*, 358; *63–64*, 343; *67–68*, 410
Lost Leader, The *19–20*, 384
Lost Paradise, The *94–99*, 201
Lost River *99–09*, 374
Lost Sheep *29–30*, 541
Lost Sister, The *39–40*, 468
Lost, Strayed or Stolen *94–99*, 177
Lost, Twenty-Four Hours *94–99*, 140

Lotte Goslar (dance programs)
42–43, 485
Lottery Man, The 09–19, 405
Lottery of Love, The 94–99, 134
Lou Gehrig Did Not Die of Cancer
69–70, 374
Loud Red Patrick, The 56–57, 320
Loud Speaker 26–27, 490
Louder, Please 31–32, 429
Louie the 14th 24–25, 552
Louis XI 94–99, 88, 150, 151;
99–09, 353, 442, 477, 536; 09–19,
443, 545, 642; 39–40, 470; 40–41,
432
Louise Alice Williams 35–36, 512
Louisiana 32–33, 467
Louisiana Lady 47–48, 339s
Louisiana Purchase 39–40, 465
Love Among the Lions 09–19, 421
Love and Babies 33–34, 426
Love and Death 25–26, 515
Love and Intrigue 59–60, 50
Love and Kisses 63–64, 316
Love and Let Love (1) 51–52, 288
Love and Let Love (2) 67–68, 397
Love and Libel, or The Ogre of the
Provincial World 60–61, 312
Love and Maple Syrup (Amour et
Sucre D'Erable) 69–70, 354
Love and the Man 99–09, 484
Love Birds 20–21, 435
Love Call, The 27–28, 437
Love Chase, The 94–99, 145
Love Child, The 22–23, 489
Love City, The 25–26, 537
Love Comes First 46–47, 493
Love Cure, The 09–19, 398
Love Dreams 21–22, 441
Love Drive, The 09–19, 611
Love Duel, The 28–29, 493
Love 'Em and Leave 'Em 25–26,
546
Love Expert, The 29–30, 402
Love Finds the Way 94–99, 169,
228
Love for Love 24–25, 564; 25–26,
444; 39–40, 466; 46–47, 481
Love From a Stranger 36–37, 411

Love Goes to Press 46–47, 453
Love Habit, The 22–23, 544
Love, Honor and Betray 29–30, 510
Love in a Coffee Cup 37–38, 412
Love in a Mist 25–26, 582; 28–29,
353
Love in E-Flat 66–67, 382
Love in Humble Life 36–37, 496
Love in Idleness 99–09, 480
Love in My Fashion 37–38, 399
Love in Our Time 52–53, 306
Love in the Tropics 27–28, 435
Love Is a Simple Thing 38–39,
484
Love Is a Time of Day 69–70, 310
Love Is Just Around the Corner
64–65, 336
Love Is Like That 26–27, 509
Love Is No Heaven 42–43, 488
Love Kills 33–34, 521
Love Laughs 09–19, 657
Love Leash, The 09–19, 511
Love Letter, The (1) 99–09, 522
Love Letter, The (2) 21–22, 435
Love Life 48–49, 386s
Love Match, The 99–09, 397
Love Me Little 57–58, 329
Love Me Long 49–50, 360
Love Mill, The 09–19, 622
Love Nest, The (1) 27–28, 472
Love Nest, The (2) 62–63, 324
Love o' Mike 09–19, 593
Love of Four Colonels, The 52–53,
280
Love of One's Neighbor 09–19, 547
Love of Two Hours, The 62–63, 317
Love of Women 37–38, 402
Love on Crutches 94–99, 111
Love on Leave 44–45, 364
Love on the Dole 35–36, 488
Love on the Farm 62–63, 322
Love Only Me 47–48, 432
Love Route, The 99–09, 524
Love Scandal, A 23–24, 348
Love Set, The 22–23, 545
Love Song, The 24–25, 524
Love Song of J. Alfred Prufrock, The
62–63, 322

Love Teaches Harlequin *(Arlequin Poli par L'Amour)* 55–56, 357
Love Thief, The 26–27, 466
Love Watches 99–09, 566
Love Your Crooked Neighbor 69–70, 352
Lovely Ladies, Kind Gentlemen 70–71s
Lovely Lady (1) 25–26, 474
Lovely Lady (2) 27–28, 484
Lovely Light, A 59–60, 316; 63–64, 357
Lovely Me 46–47, 447
Lover, The 63–64, 354
Lover and His Lass, The 62–63, 310
Lovers 68–69, 375
Lovers, The 55–56, 390
Lovers and Enemies 27–28, 409
Lovers and Friends 43–44, 431
Lovers and Other Strangers 68–69, 377
Lovers in the Metro, The 61–62, 321
Lovers' Lane 99–09, 388
Lover's Luck 09–19, 579
Love's Call 25–26, 441
Love's Labour's Lost 52–53, 284; 63–64, 353; 65–66, 95
Love's Lightning 09–19, 626
Love's Lottery 99–09, 468
Loves of Cass McGuire, The 66–67, 360
Loves of Charles II, The 33–34, 471; 34–35, 467; 36–37, 498
Loves of Lulu, The 24–25, 591
Love's Old Sweet Song 39–40, 458; 61–62, 332
Love's Pilgrimage 99–09, 459
Lovey 64–65, 354
Lovey Mary 99–09, 463
Low Bridge 32–33, 459
Lower Depths, The 22–23, 517; 23–24, 356; 29–30, 477; 38–39, 487; 42–43, 490; 46–47, 485, 498; 47–48, 395; 56–57, 55; 63–64, 360; 69–70, 373
Lower North 44–45, 371

Lower Than the Angels 64–65, 362
Loyalties 22–23, 464
Luana 30–31, 413
Luck in Pawn 09–19, 654
Luck of MacGregor, The 99–09, 562
Luck of the Navy, The 19–20, 373
Luckee Girl 28–29, 373
Lucky 26–27, 495
Lucky Break, A 25–26, 425, 571
Lucky Durham 99–09, 384
Lucky Fool, The 47–48, 431; 48–49, 430
Lucky Miss Dean 99–09, 508
Lucky One, The 22–23, 491
Lucky O'Shea 09–19, 606
Lucky Sam McCarver 25–26, 480; 49–50, 382
Lucky Sambo 24–25, 601
Lucky Star, A 09–19, 411
Lucrece 32–33, 438
Ludlow Fair 65–66, 432
Lullaby 53–54, 339
Lullaby, The 23–24, 316
Lullaby Go to Sleepy 60–61, 294
Lulu 69–70, 362
Lulu Belle 25–26, 549
Lulu's Husbands 09–19, 418
Lunatic View, The 62–63, 338
Lunatics and Lovers 54–55, 382
Lunch Break 70–71
Lure, The 09–19, 503
Lusmore 19–20, 347
Lute Song 45–46, 426; 58–59, 55, 329
Luther 63–64, 304
Luthier de Cremone, Le 94–99, 93
Luv 64–65, 312
Lydia Gilmore 09–19, 465
Lyle 69–70, 361
Lyons Mail, The (see also *Chain of Destiny*) 94–99, 150, 151; 99–09, 354, 520
Lyric Drama 26–27, 503
Lysistrata 25–26, 514; 29–30, 548; 39–40, 469; 46–47, 428; 59–60, 306; 60–61, 332

Ma Cousine *94–99,* 126, 260; *99–09,* 472

Macbeth *94–99,* 147, 150, 151, 239; *99–09,* 350, 363, 476, 477, 534, 536; *09–19,* 410, 433, 443, 447, 448, 478, 508, 545, 570, 599, 642, 646; *20–21,* 428, 443; *21–22,* 496; *23–24,* 408; *28–29,* 417; *29–30,* 515; *30–31,* 471; *31–32,* 501; *32–33,* 424; *34–35,* 428; *35–36,* 415, 474; *36–37,* 495; *37–38,* 462; *41–42,* 412; *43–44,* 488–9; *47–48,* 392; *51–52,* 333; *55–56,* 55; *56–57,* 324; *58–59,* 316; *61–62,* 286; *62–63,* 305, 319; *63–64,* 345, 353, 360, 368; *66–67,* 107, 414; *67–68,* 401; *69–70,* 377; *70–71*

Macbeth (mn) *37–38,* 467

Macbeth (opera rep) *42–43,* 487

MacBird! *66–67,* 414

Machine, Yes, the Machine, The *60–61,* 295

Machinal *28–29,* 369; *49–50,* 384; *59–60,* 42

Mackerel Skies *33–34,* 484

Mackey of Appalachia *65–66,* 437

Mad Dog, The *21–22,* 457

Mad Dog Blues *70–71*

Mad Honeymoon, The *23–24,* 297

Mad Hopes, The *32–33,* 432

Mad Magazine *65–66,* 428

Mad Show, The *65–66,* 428s

Mad Whirl, The *36–37,* 499

Madam Moselle *09–19,* 527

Madam President *09–19,* 507

Madam, Will You Walk *53–54,* 323

Madame X *(La Femme X)* *09–19,* 413, 432, 446; *27–28,* 387

Madame Butterfly (see *Madame Butterfly*)

Madame (titles abbreviated Mme. are in alphabetical order under MM)

Madame *94–99,* 170

Madame Aphrodite *61–62,* 317s

Madame Bovary *37–38,* 390

Madame Butterfly (source) *99–09,* 359; *45–46,* 391

Madame Butterfly (p) *99–09,* 359; *45–46,* 391

Madame (Madama) Butterfly (opera rep) *09–19,* 638; *45–46,* 391, 440; *46–47,* 408, 479; *47–48,* 343, 347, 399, 423

Madame Capet *38–39,* 421

Madame Is Served *48–49,* 427

Madame Lafayette *59–60,* 40

Madame Pierre *21–22,* 511

Maggie *52–53,* 289s

Maggie Flynn *68–69,* 387s

Madame Sand *09–19,* 615

Madame Sans Gene (Mme. Sans-Gene) *94–99,* 117, 126; *99–09,* 353, 482; *24–25,* 474

Madame Sherry *09–19,* 423

Madame Troubadour *09–19,* 427

Madcap, The *27–28,* 501

Madcap Duchess, The *09–19,* 514

Madcap Princess, A *99–09,* 464

Made for Each Other *24–25,* 462

Made in America *25–26,* 475

Made in France *30–31,* 450

Made in Heaven! *46–47,* 429

Madeleine (opera rep) *09–19,* 638

Madeleine and the Movies *21–22,* 520

Madeleine, or The Magic Kiss *94–99,* 125

Madeline *99–09,* 505

Madeline of Fort Reno *94–99,* 217

Mademoiselle (titles abbreviated Mlle. are in alphabetical order under ML)

Mademoiselle *32–33,* 404

Mademoiselle Bourrat *29–30,* 413

Mademoiselle Colombe (see also *Colombe*) *53–54,* 334

Mademoiselle Fifi *94–99,* 220, 252

Mademoiselle Marni *99–09,* 485

Madge Smith, Attorney *99–09,* 381

Madness at Noon *69–70,* 377

Madness of Lady Bright, The *65–66,* 432

Madonna of the Future, The *09–19,*
620
Madras House, The *21–22,* 450
Madrigal of Shakespeare, A *67–68,*
408
Madwoman of Chaillot, The *48–49,*
403; *50–51,* 308; *51–52,* 334;
53–54, 358; *68–69,* 405; *69–70,*
361
Maedchen in Uniform *44–45,* 436
Magda *94–99,* 147, 166, 169; *99–09,*
403, 404, 474, 557; *25–26,* 539
Magdalen, The *32–33,* 458
Magdalena *48–49,* 381s
Magdalene, The *94–99,* 215
Maggie French Understands *63–64,*
342
Maggie Pepper *09–19,* 449; *21–22,*
533
Maggie the Magnificent *29–30,* 422
Magic *09–19,* 595; *42–43,* 431
Magic and Hypnotism *47–48,* 430
Magic and the Loss, The *53–54,* 351
Magic Barrel, The *63–64,* 364
Magic Melody, The *19–20,* 385
Magic Ring, The *23–24,* 325
Magic Skin, The *99–09,* 580
Magic Touch, The *47–48,* 350
Magical City, The *09–19,* 561
Magistrate, The *94–99,* 194; *09–19,*
651; *62–63,* 339
Magnanimous Lover, The *09–19,*
494
Magnificent Hugo, The *60–61,* 44
Magnificent Yankee, The *45–46,* 423
Magnolia *23–24,* 309
Magnolia Alley *48–49,* 420
Magnolia Lady, The *24–25,* 495
Mahagonny *69–70,* 366
Mahogany Hall *33–34,* 481
Maid and the Millionaire, The
99–09, 540
Maid and the Mummy, The *99–09,*
462
Maid as Mistress, The (*La Serva
Padrone;* opera rep) *42–43,* 487;
43–44, 479; *47–48,* 426

Maid in America *09–19,* 546
Maid in Japan *38–39,* 485
Maid in the Ozarks *46–47,* 415
Maid Marian *99–09,* 405
Maid of All Work *26–27,* 460
Maid of France, The *09–19,* 628
Maid of the Mountains, The *09–19,*
636
Maidens and Mistresses at Home at
the Zoo *58–59,* 50
Maid-Mistress, The (see also *The
Maid as Mistress*) *42–43,* 487
Maids, The *63–64,* 351
Maids of Athens *09–19,* 523
Mail Call *42–43,* 478; *43–44,* 404
Main Line, The *23–24,* 412
Main Street *21–22,* 436
Maine Avenged, The *94–99,* 236
Mainly for Lovers *35–36,* 487
Maison de Danse, Le *28–29,* 458
Maison de Poupee *94–99,* 126
Maison du Marie, La *94–99,* 115
Maitre de Forges, Le *94–99,* 114,
212, 234
Maitresse de Roi *26–27,* 434
Major, The *94–99,* 123
Major André *99–09,* 444
Major Barbara *09–19,* 559; *28–29,*
418; *50–51,* 374; *54–55,* 57; *56–57,*
329
Major Pendennis *09–19,* 586
Majority of One, A *58–59,* 323
Makbeth *69–70,* 377
Make a Million *58–59,* 299
Make a Wish *50–51,* 362s
Make It Snappy *21–22,* 534
Make Like a Dog *65–66,* 431
Make Me Disappear *68–69,* 452
Make Me Know It *29–30,* 433
Make Mine Manhattan *47–48,* 377s
Make Mine Mink *70–71*
Make Way for Lucia *48–49,* 401
Make Way for the Ladies *99–09,*
355
Make Yourself at Home *45–46,* 384
Maker of Dreams, The *09–19,* 548
Maker of Men, A *99–09,* 482

Makers of Light *21–22*, 551
Making Good *09–19*, 465
Making of Moo, The *58–59*, 51
Makropoulos Secret, (The) *25–26*, 534; *57–58*, 304
Malade Imaginaire, Le (see *The Imaginary Invalid*)
Malcochon *68–69*, 440
Malcolm *65–66*, 394
Male Animal, The *39–40*, 427; *51–52*, 321
Malone Dies *70–71*
Malquerida, La *25–26*, 599; *31–32*, 500
Malvaloca, (La) *22–23*, 466; *31–32*, 501
Mama Loves Papa *25–26*, 557
Mama's Baby Boy *09–19*, 472
Mama's Bank Account *44–45*, 389
Mama's Boy *48–49*, 430
Mamba's Daughters *38–39*, 443; *39–40*, 447; *52–53*, 309
Mame *65–66*, 412s
Mamma's Affair *19–20*, 418
Mam'selle 'Awkins *99–09*, 363
Mam'selle Napoleon *99–09*, 447
Mamselle Sallie *99–09*, 526
Mamzelle Champagne *99–09*, 515
Man, The *49–50*, 368
Man and Boy *63–64*, 313
Man and His Angel *99–09*, 519
Man and His Gods, A *39–40*, 469
Man and His Wife, A *94–99*, 196; *99–09*, 365, 366
Man and Superman *99–09*, 494; *09–19*, 479; *47–48*, 358; *48–49*, 423; *51–52*, 294; *52–53*, 309; *60–61*, 46; *62–63*, 327; *64–65*, 348; *67–68*, 409; *69–70*, 373; *70–71*
Man and the Masses *23–24*, 419
Man and Wife *09–19*, 487
Man Better Man *69–70*, 336s
Man Bites Dog *32–33*, 488
Man Crazy *32–33*, 377
Man for All Seasons, A *61–62*, 272; *63–64*, 322

Man From Blankley's, The *99–09*, 437
Man From Cairo, The *37–38*, 444
Man From China, The *99–09*, 460
Man From Cook's, The *09–19*, 469
Man From Home, The *99–09*, 303, 564
Man From Mexico, The *94–99*, 200; *99–09*, 583
Man From Now, The *99–09*, 519
Man From Toronto, The *26–27*, 359
Man Goin' Roun' *60–61*, 295
Man Hunt *40–41*, 431
Man in Evening Clothes, The *24–25*, 501
Man in Possession, The *30–31*, 444
Man in the Bowler Hat, The *23–24*, 428
Man in the Dog Suit, The *58–59*, 300
Man in the Glass Booth, The *68–69*, 378
Man in the Making, The *21–22*, 423
Man in the Moon (mn) *62–63*, 331s
Man in the Moon, The *94–99*, 258
Man in the Stalls, The *28–29*, 501
Man Inside, The *09–19*, 514
Man Is Man *62–63*, 314
Man of Destiny, The *99–09*, 448, 467, 495; *25–26*, 499; *36–37*, 497; *42–43*, 489; *55–56*, 58; *62–63*, 327
Man of Forty, The *99–09*, 380
Man of Honor, A (1) *94–99*, 188
Man of Honor, A (2) *09–19*, 450
Man of La Mancha *65–66*, 386s
Man of the Hour, The *99–09*, 528
Man of the People, A *20–21*, 379
Man on Stilts, The *31–32*, 388
Man on the Box, The *99–09*, 497
Man on the Case, The *99–09*, 544
Man or Devil *24–25*, 596
Man Out Loud, Girl Quiet *61–62*, 327
Man Proposes *99–09*, 455
Man That Corrupted Hadleyburg, The *63–64*, 369s

Man Upstairs, The *94–99*, 125; *24–25*, 585

Man Who Ate the Popomack, The *23–24*, 411

Man Who Came Back, The *09–19*, 580

Man Who Came to Dinner, The *39–40*, 402; *66–67*, 385

Man Who Changed His Name, The *31–32*, 509

Man Who Died at Twelve O'Clock, The *28–29*, 503

Man Who Had All the Luck, The *44–45*, 400

Man Who Killed Lincoln, The *39–40*, 430

Man Who Laughed, The *20–21*, 442

Man Who Married a Dumb Wife, The *09–19*, 545; *22–23*, 573; *29–30*, 536; *46–47*, 488; *67–68*, 411

Man Who Never Died, The (1) *25–26*, 513

Man Who Never Died, The (2) *58–59*, 51

Man Who Never Gave Up, The *44–45*, 444

Man Who Never Lived, The *46–47*, 494

Man Who Owns Broadway, The *09–19*, 402

Man Who Reclaimed His Head, The *32–33*, 384

Man Who Stayed at Home, The *09–19*, 626

Man Who Stole the Castle, The *99–09*, 432

Man Who Stood Still, The *99–09*, 571

Man Who Was, The *99–09*, 385

Man Who Washed His Hands, The *66–67*, 423

Man With a Load of Mischief (m) *66–67*, 406s

Man With a Load of Mischief, The (p) *25–26*, 483

Man With a Past, A *94–99*, 140

Man With Blond Hair, The *41–42*, 409

Man With Red Hair, A *28–29*, 412

Man With the Flower in His Mouth, The *68–69*, 451

Man With the Iron Mask, The *94–99*, 223

Man With Three Wives, The *09–19*, 493

Man Without a Country, The *94–99*, 100

Mancha Que Limpia *31–32*, 500

Mandarin, The (1) *94–99*, 182

Mandarin, The (2) *20–21*, 403

Mandigo *60–61*, 341

Mandragola *45–46*, 450; *67–68*, 411

Manhattan *22–23*, 437

Manhattan Nocturne *43–44*, 422

Manhattan Mary *27–28*, 412

Manhattan Vanities *32–33*, 392

Manhatters, The *27–28*, 389

Manicure, The *94–99*, 259

Manikin and Minikin *26–27*, 522

Manoeuvres of Jane, The *99–09*, 356

Manon Lescaut (source) *99–09*, 390; *44–45*, 377

Manon Lescaut (p) *99–09*, 390

Manon Lescaut (opera rep) *44–45*, 377

Man-o-War's Man *94–99*, 155

Man's a Man, A *62–63*, 314; *70–71*

Man's Estate *28–29*, 485

Man's Friends, A *09–19*, 498

Man's House, A *42–43*, 487

Man's Man, A *25–26*, 472; *30–31*, 533

Man's Name, The *21–22*, 463

Man's Reach, A *40–41*, 431

Man's World, A *09–19*, 414

Mansion on the Hudson *34–35*, 467; *36–37*, 498

Manteo Marionettes (see *Agrippino Manteo Marionettes*)

Many a Slip (1) *29–30*, 486

Many a Slip (2) *40–41*, 433

Many Happy Returns *44–45*, 408

Many Loves *58–59*, 50; *61–62*, 305

Many Mansions *37–38*, 382
Many Moons *47–48*, 430
Many Things *39–40*, 445
Many Waters *29–30*, 404
Manxman, The *94–99*, 105
Maple Leaf-Viewing Picnic, The
  (Momiji-Gari) 69–70, 296
Marat/Sade (see *The Persecution
  and Assassination of Marat*, etc.)
Marathon *32–33*, 455
Marathon '33 *63–64*, 317
Marc Blitzstein Memorial Concert
  63–64, 363
Marcel Marceau *55–56*, 341, 373;
  57–58, 309; *60–61*, 290; *62–63*,
  292; *65–66*, 386; *69–70*, 325
Marcelle (1) *99–09*, 375
Marcelle (2) *99–09*, 570
March Hares *21–22*, 392; *27–28*,
  534
March Heir, The *32–33*, 436
March of Drama Repertory *45–46*,
  459; *46–47*, 498
Marchand de Venise, Le *(The
  Merchant of Venice) 24–25*, 482
Marchande de Sourires, La *94–99*,
  118
Marching By *31–32*, 487
Marching Song (1) *36–37*, 466
Marching Song (2) *59–60*, 45
Marco Millions *27–28*, 487; *29–30*,
  504; *63–64*, 321
Marco Millions (mn) *38–39*, 489
Marcus in the High Grass *60–61*, 39
Mardi Gras! *65–66*, 417s; *66–67*,
  401
Margaret Schiller *09–19*, 570
Margery Daw *09–19*, 589
Margin for Error *39–40*, 409
Margo Sanger *33–34*, 534
Mari de la Debutante, Le *94–99*,
  229
Maria and the Captain *55–56*, 377
Maria Golovin *58–59*, 302
Maria Stuart (see *Mary Stuart* 1)
Maria Teresa Acuna & Frederico
  Rey (dance programs) *46–47*, 486

Maria Rosa *09–19*, 520; *35–36*, 511
Mariage de Figaro, Le (see *The
  Marriage of Figaro*)
Mariage Force, Le *63–64*, 327
Mariana *99–09*, 404
Mariana of the Moated Grange
  99–09, 449
Marie Antoinette (1) *99–09*, 363
Marie Antoinette (2) *21–22*, 465
Marie Deloche *94–99*, 169
Marie Dressler's All Star Gambol
  09–19, 497
Marie Galante *63–64*, 342
Marie Marchowsky *47–48*, 417
Marie Tudor *58–59*, 295
Marie-Odile *09–19*, 544
Marietta *99–09*, 458
Marigold *30–31*, 428
Marilyn's Affairs *32–33*, 477
Mariners *26–27*, 498
Marinka *45–46*, 380
Marionette Carnival, The (mn)
  37–38, 466
Marionette Guild Marionettes
  33–34, 534; *38–39*, 489
Marionettes, The *09–19*, 460
Mariposa Que Volo Sombre el Mar,
  La *31–32*, 500
Mariquilla Terremoto *31–32*, 500
Marius *54–55*, 373
Marjolaine *21–22*, 498
Majorie *24–25*, 432
Majorie Daw *69–70*, 374
Mark of the Beast, The *09–19*, 563
Mark of Zorro *66–67*, 36
Mark Twain Tonight! *58–59*, 50;
  65–66, 404
Mark Twain's Articles,
  Autobiography, Essays, Notebook,
  Short Stories, Sketches, Speeches
  65–66, 404, 405
Markheim *99–09*, 521
Marlene Dietrich *67–68*, 343s;
  68–69, 382s
Marquis de Priola, The *09–19*, 650
Marquis of Michigan, The *94–99*,
  239

Marquise, The 27–28, 450
Mariage Force, Le 57–58, 330
Marriage (1) 94–99, 165; 32–33, 377
Marriage (2) 34–35, 453
Marriage, The 36–37, 497
Marriage à la Carte 09–19, 435
Marriage Bed, The 28–29, 448
Marriage d'Olympe, Le 99–09, 401
Marriage for Three 31–32, 429
Marriage Game, The (1) 99–09, 401
Marriage Game, The (2) 09–19, 512
Marriage Is for Single People 45–46, 408
Marriage Market, The 09–19, 507
Marriage of a Star, The 09–19, 421
Marriage of Cana, The 31–32, 472
Marriage of Columbine, The 09–19, 538
Marriage of Convenience, A 94–99, 215; 09–19, 629
Marriage of Figaro, The (Le Mariage de Figaro; p) 63–64, 326
Marriage of Figaro, The (opera rep) 48–49, 428
Marriage of Kitty, The 99–09, 446; 09–19, 541; 22–23, 457
Marriage of Mr. Mississippi, The (Fools Are Passing Through; Die Ehe des Herrn Mississippi) 57–58, 244; 69–70, 347
Marriage of Reason, A 99–09, 538
Marriage of William Ashe, The 99–09, 501
Marriage on Approval 27–28, 520
Marriage Proposal, The (A) 38–39, 488; 42–43, 489; 52–53, 308
Marriage-Go-Round, The 58–59, 300
Marriage-not, The 09–19, 472
Marriages Are Made 09–19, 631
Married—and How! 27–28, 560
Married Not Mated 94–99, 132
Married Woman, The 09–19, 590; 21–22, 482
Marry the Man 28–29, 496
Marry the Poor Girl 20–21, 385
Marrying Maiden, The 60–61, 347

Marrying Mary 99–09, 517
Marrying Money 09–19, 524
Marsa Van 94–99, 165
Marseillaise, La 99–09, 422
Marseilles 30–31, 453
Marshal 29–30, 537
Marsyas, the Faun 24–25, 584
Marta of the Lowlands 99–09, 440, 441
Martha (opera rep) 09–19, 638; 43–44, 439
Martha Graham (dance programs) 41–42, 457; 43–44, 486–7; 44–45, 440; 45–46, 456; 46–47, 487; 47–48, 416; 51–52, 331
Martin Chuzzlewit 99–09, 384
Martine 27–28, 534; 36–37, 499
Martin(i)que 19–20, 446
Marty Malone 94–99, 175
Mary 20–21, 396
Mary Adelaide 38–39, 492
Mary Agnes Is Thirty-Five 64–65, 353
Mary and John 99–09, 495
Mary Goes First 09–19, 538
Mary Jane McKane 23–24, 374
Mary Jane's Pa 99–09, 511, 574
Mary Magdalene 09–19, 431
Mary, Mary 60–61, 329
Mary, Mary Quite Contrary (1) 99–09, 505
Mary, Mary, Quite Contrary (2) 23–24, 315
Mary of Magdala (1) 99–09, 422
Mary of Magdala (2) 45–46, 400
Mary of Scotland 33–34, 463
Mary Pennington 94–99, 178
Mary Rose 20–21, 414; 44–45, 436; 50–51, 355
Mary (Maria) Stuart (1) 94–99, 146, 147; 99–09, 363; 57–58, 290; 63–64, 345; 67–68, 367
Mary Stuart (2) 20–21, 437; 44–45, 436
Mary the 3d 22–23, 528
Mary's Ankle 09–19, 602
Mary's Lamb 99–09, 562

Mary's Little Lamb *39–40*, 470
Mary's Manoeuvres *09–19*, 496
Maschera e Il Volto, La *24–25*, 450
Mascot, The *99–09*, 581
Mask and Gown *57–58*, 284s
Mask and the Face, The *24–25*, 450; *32–33*, 493
Mask of Hamlet, The *21–22*, 399
Masked Woman, The *22–23*, 504
Maskers, The *37–38*, 461
Masks and Faces (1) *99–09*, 534
Masks and Faces (2) *32–33*, 478
Masque *61–62*, 314
Masque of Kings, The *36–37*, 461
Masque of Reason, A *59–60*, 49
Masque of Venice, The *25–26*, 561
Masquerade *58–59*, 330
Masquerader, The *09–19*, 606
Masqueraders, The *94–99*, 109
Master, The (1) *94–99*, 225
Master, The (2) *09–19*, 589, 623
Master Builder, The *99–09*, 360, 560; *25–26*, 490; *26–27*, 418; *29–30*, 393, 403; *40–41*, 432; *50–51*, 373; *53–54*, 358; *54–55*, 401
Master Key, The *09–19*, 401
Master Mind, The *09–19*, 495
Master of Solitaire *35–36*, 479
Master of the House, The *09–19*, 474
Master of the Inn, The *25–26*, 520
Mata & Hari (dance programs; see *Ruth Mata & Eugene Hari*)
Matador, El *70–71*
Match Play (Match-Play) *63–64*, 371; *66–67*, 402
Matchmaker, The *55–56*, 365; *58–59*, 53; *63–64*, 319; *67–68*, 369
Mater *99–09*, 569
Maternity *09–19*, 543
Matilda *99–09*, 530
Matinee Girl, The *25–26*, 544
Matinee Hero, The *09–19*, 640
Matinee Idol, A *09–19*, 419
Matinee Wife, (The) *35–36*, 511; *47–48*, 432

Matinees of Magic *33–34*, 534
Mating Dance *65–66*, 383
Mating Season, The *27–28*, 389
Matriarch, The *29–30*, 513
Matrimonial Bed, The *27–28*, 431
Matrimony Pfd. *36–37*, 431
Matsuri (see *Festival*)
Matter of Like Life and Death, A *63–64*, 346
Matty and the Moron and Madonna *64–65*, 356
Maud's Peril *94–99*, 132
Maurice Chevalier *29–30*, 517s; *31–32*, 475; *46–47*, 470; *47–48*, 388; *55–56*, 347s; *62–63*, 294s
Maurice Chevalier at 77 *64–65*, 331s
Maurice Chevalier in Songs and Impressions *55–56*, 347s
Maurice Harte *09–19*, 494
Mauricette *99–09*, 521
Mavourneen *94–99*, 147
May Blossom, or Two Loves *94–99*, 233
May Night *25–26*, 591
May Wine *35–36*, 446
Maya *27–28*, 514; *53–54*, 356
Maya legends *09–19*, 612
Maybe Tuesday *57–58*, 312
Mayfair *29–30*, 513
Mayflower, The *94–99*, 196
Mayflowers *25–26*, 502
Mayhem at Mayhew *70–71*
Mayor of Tokio, The *99–09*, 502
Mayor of Za(o)lamia, The *(El Alcalde de Zalamia)* *45–46*, 458; *53–54*, 321
Maytime *09–19*, 603
Mazel Tov Mama *45–46*, 460
Mazel Tov, Rabbi! *38–39*, 493
McCarthy's Mishaps *94–99*, 200
McChesney stories (see *Our Mrs. McChesney*)
McFadden's Elopement *94–99*, 101
McFadden's Row of Flats *94–99*, 210
McKenna's Flirtation *94–99*, 110

McSorley's Twins *94–99*, 213
Me *25–26*, 500
Me and Harry *41–42*, 459
Me and Juliet *52–53*, 304s; *69–70*,
374
Me and Molly *47–48*, 387
Me and Thee *65–66*, 390
Me, Candido *56–57*, 58
Me Nobody Knows, The *69–70*,
368s; *70–71*
Me, the Sleeper *48–49*, 428
Meanest Man in the World, The
20–21, 395
Measure for Measure *94–99*, 146,
147; *29–30*, 460; *44–45*, 436;
56–57, 350; *58–59*, 316; *59–60*, 43;
60–61, 46; *62–63*, 305; *63–64*, 369;
66–67, 106, 382
Measure of a Man, The *99–09*,
523
Mecca *20–21*, 390
Medal and the Maid, The *99–09*,
451
Meddler, The *94–99*, 237
Medea *19–20*, 439; *47–48*, 360;
48–49, 421; *64–65*, 298; *65–66*,
427
Medecin Malgre Lui, Le (see *The
Doctor in Spite of Himself*)
Medicine Show *38–39*, 487; *39–40*,
455
Medico Delle Pazze, Il *37–38*, 470
Meditation on Forms of Love *60–61*,
295
Medium, The *45–46*, 459; *46–47*,
477; *48–49*, 399; *50–51*, 311
Meek Mose *27–28*, 504
Meet a Body *44–45*, 388
Meet My Sister *30–31*, 476
Meet Peter Grant *60–61*, 41
Meet the People *40–41*, 403
Meet the Prince *28–29*, 474
Meet the Wife *23–24*, 360
Meeting, A *42–43*, 489
Meeting, The *63–64*, 371; *67–68*,
408
Meg Merrilies *94–99*, 197

Megilla of Itzik Manger, The *68–69*,
385s
Mei Lan-Fang *29–30*, 496
Melo *30–31*, 517; *31–32*, 412
Melody *32–33*, 462s
Melody Man, The *23–24*, 434
Melody of Youth, The *09–19*, 570
Melting of Molly, The *09–19*, 648
Melting Pot, The *09–19*, 399
Melville and Stetson *99–09*, 382
Member of the Wedding, The
49–50, 366; *59–60*, 43
Memento Mori *62–63*, 338
Memorandum, The *67–68*, 389
Memorial Tribute to Stark Young, A
62–63, 326
Memory Bank, The *69–70*, 354
Memory of Two Mondays, A *55–56*,
347; *64–65*, 362
Memphis Bound! *44–45*, 432
Men and Dreams *66–67*, 402
Men and Women *94–99*, 84
Men in Shadow *42–43*, 467
Men in White *33–34*, 435
Men Must Fight *32–33*, 401
Men of Distinction *52–53*, 302
Men to the Sea *44–45*, 386
Menace *26–27*, 493
Mendel, Inc. *29–30*, 448
Mensajero de Paz *31–32*, 500
Menschen im Hotel *(Grand Hotel)*
30–31, 355
Men We Marry, The *47–48*, 377
Mercedes *94–99*, 214
Mercenary Mary *24–25*, 575
Merchant of Venice, The *94–99*, 88,
92, 93, 150, 151, 246, 257; *99–09*,
353, 392, 442, 452, 469, 470, 476,
477, 486, 534, 536, 558; *09–19*,
410, 413, 443, 447, 448, 478, 492,
508, 509, 545, 575, 589 (and 605),
599, 620, 627, 642; *21–22*, 446;
22–23, 503; *23–24*, 328; *24–25*,
482; *25–26*, 523; *27–28*, 492;
29–30, 516; *30–31*, 464, 471;
31–32, 433; *32–33*, 424; *42–43*,
489; *44–45*, 436; *46–47*, 466, 496;

Merchant of Venice, *(cont.)*
50–51, 374; *52–53*, 291; *54–55*, 56;
58–59, 316; *61–62*, 321; *62–63*,
305, 354; *63–64*, 353
Merchant of Yonkers, The *38–39*,
441
Merchants of Glory *25–26*, 515
Merchants of Venus *20–21*, 386
Mercy Street *69–70*, 341
Mere Man *09–19*, 486
Merely Mary Ann *99–09*, 499, 531
Merely Murder *37–38*, 398
Mermaids Singing, The *45–46*, 410
Merrily We Roll Along *34–35*, 380;
39–40, 397; *49–50*, 383
Merry Andrew *28–29*, 459
Merry Christmas, Daddy! *09–19*,
591
Merry Countess, The (1) *94–99*, 153
Merry Countess, The (2) *09–19*,
474; *29–30*, 431
Merry Death, A *09–19*, 579
Merry Malones *27–28*, 413
Merry, Merry *25–26*, 454
Merry Tramps, The *94–99*, 178
Merry Whirl, The *09–19*, 420
Merry Widow, The *99–09*, 548;
21–22, 412; *29–30*, 456; *31–32*,
385; *42–43*, 423; *43–44*, 405;
44–45, 375; *56–57*, 365s; *61–62*,
332; *64–65*, 297s
Merry Widow Burlesque, The
99–09, 554
Merry Wives of Gotham *23–24*, 386
Merry Wives of Windsor, The
94–99, 120, 121, 222; *09–19*, 430,
575, 592; *27–28*, 530; *32–33*, 424;
37–38, 438; *61–62*, 333; *63–64*,
360
Merry World, The (1) *94–99*, 137
Merry World, The (2) *25–26*, 604
Merry-Go-Round (1) *26–27*, 531
Merry-Go-Round (2) *31–32*, 507
Merry-Go-Round (3) *52–53*, 309
Merry-Go-Round, The (see
The-Merry-Go-Round)
Merton of the Movies *22–23*, 485
Message for Margaret *46–47*, 475

Message From Cougar, A *67–68*,
412
Message From Mars, A *99–09*, 397
Message From the Grassroots
68–69, 456
Messenger Boy, The *99–09*, 395
Messin' Around *28–29*, 496
Metamorphoses (see *Ovid's*
Metamorphoses)
Metaphors *67–68*, 407
Meteor *29–30*, 465
Metropole *49–50*, 363
Mexican dances (untitled dance
programs) *47–48*, 415
Mexican Hayride *43–44*, 451; *64–65*,
357
Mexican Mural *41–42*, 459
Mexicana (1) *99–09*, 508
Mexicana (2) *38–39*, 471
Meyer & Son *99–09*, 578
Mia Moglie Non Ha Chic (see *My*
Wife Is Not Stylish)
Mice and Men *99–09*, 426; *09–19*,
509
Michael and His Lost Angel *94–99*,
162
Michael and Mary (see also *This*
Flower) *29–30*, 462
Michael Drops In *38–39*, 440
Michael Strange *35–36*, 512
Michael Strogoff *94–99*, 173
Michael Todd's Peep Show *50–51*,
309s
Michel Auclair *24–25*, 555
Mickey Mouse Circus (mn) *37–38*,
467
Microbe Hunters, The *33–34*, 505;
46–47, 439
Mid-channel *09–19*, 412
Middle of the Night *55–56*, 374
Middle Watch, The *29–30*, 419
Middle-Aged Man on the Flying
Trapeze, The *59–60*, 226
Middleman, The *94–99*, 186, 187;
99–09, 384, 385
Midgie Purvis *60–61*, 321
Midnight *30–31*, 474
Midnight Bell, A *94–99*, 194

Midnight Flood, The *94–99*, 232
Midnight Girl, The *09–19*, 522
Midnight Rounders, The (1920) *20–21*, 357
Midnight Rounders of 1921, The *20–21*, 425
Midnight Sons, The *99–09*, 583
Midnight Trust, A *94–99*, 225
Mid-Summer *52–53*, 281
Midsummer Night's Dream, A *94–99*, 130; *99–09*, 443; *09–19*, 410, 546; *27–28*, 454; *32–33*, 423; *39–40*, 417; *46–47*, 498; *49–50*, 384; *54–55*, 361; *55–56*, 55; *58–59*, 316; *61–62*, 343; *62–63*, 305, 334; *63–64*, 353; *64–65*, 76, 351; *67–68*, 385; *70–71*
Midsummer Night's Dream, A (m) *62–63*, 334
Mid-West *35–36*, 457
Mighty Conlon, The *32–33*, 498
Mighty Man Is He, A *59–60*, 313
Mighty Nimrod, The *30–31*, 524
Mighty Wind a Blowin' *37–38*, 464
Mignon (opera rep) *09–19*, 638
Mikado, The (or The Town of Titipu) *99–09*, 413; *09–19*, 419, 472, 500, 551, 639; *24–25*, 569; *27–28*, 406; *30–31*, 522; *31–32*, 381; *32–33*, 485; *33–34*, 512; *34–35*, 366; *35–36*, 398, 400, 496; *36–37*, 398; *38–39*, 446, 466, 472, 480; *40–41*, 381; *41–42*, 431, 458; *42–43*, 486; *43–44*, 455, 488; *45–46*, 458; *46–47*, 494; *47–48*, 372, 375; *49–50*, 356; *50–51*, 345; *52–53*, 262; *55–56*, 344; *60–61*, 48; *61–62*, 332; *62–63*, 286, 339; *63–64*, 328, 367; *64–65*, 313, 359; *66–67*, 367, 399; *67–68*, 373, 388; *68–69*, 390
Mikado, The (mn) *36–37*, 498; *38–39*, 490
Mike Angelo *22–23*, 516
Mike Downstairs *67–68*, 371
Mikhail Mordkin Dancers (dance programs) *34–35*, 485
Milady's Boudoir *09–19*, 537

Mildred Klinghoffer *60–61*, 294
Mile-a-Minute Kendall *09–19*, 588
Milestones *09–19*, 477; *29–30*, 545; *46–47*, 485
Milgrim's Progress *24–25*, 508
Military Mad *99–09*, 462
Military Maid, The *99–09*, 375
Milk and Honey *61–62*, 259s
Milk Train Doesn't Stop Here Anymore, The *62–63*, 293; *63–64*, 318
Milk White Flag, A *94–99*, 98; *09–19*, 585
Milky Way, The *33–34*, 526; *42–43*, 476; *46–47*, 484
Million, The *09–19*, 455
Million Dollars, A *99–09*, 372
Million Torments, A *35–36*, 510
Millionairess, The *52–53*, 262; *68–69*, 447
Mills of the Gods, The *99–09*, 535
Mima *28–29*, 434
Mime and Me, The *59–60*, 48–9
Mime's Eye View, A *62–63*, 312
Mimic and the Maid, The *99–09*, 531
Mimic World, The (1) *99–09*, 564
Mimic World, The (2) *21–22*, 397
Mimie Scheller *36–37*, 412
"Mind-the-Paint" Girl, The *09–19*, 475
Mineral Workers, The *09–19*, 458
Minick *24–25*, 459
Minister in Hell *32–33*, 377
Minister of Police, The *09–19*, 486
Minna von Barnhelm *68–69*, 433
Minnie and Mr. Williams *48–49*, 391
Minnie Field *40–41*, 431
Minnie's Boys *69–70*, 320s
Minor Adjustment, A *67–68*, 342
Minor Miracle *65–66*, 374
Minstrel Boy, The *48–49*, 425
Minstrel of Clare, The *94–99*, 166
Miracle, The (1) *23–24*, 385
Miracle, The (2) *60–61*, 39
Miracle at Verdun *30–31*, 505
Miracle in Brooklyn *66–67*, 400

Miracle in the Mountains *46–47*, 476

Miracle Man, The *09–19*, 532

Miracle of St. Anthony, The (A) *99–09*, 560; *09–19*, 547, 579

Miracle of the Warsaw Ghetto, The *44–45*, 444

Miracle on 34th Street *63–64*, 306

Miracle plays (untitled sources) *62–63*, 321

Miracle Worker, The *59–60*, 297

Miracles: Poems by Children of the English-Speaking World *68–69*, 407

Miraculous Birth and the Midwives, The *32–33*, 458

Miraculous Mandarin, The *51–52*, 330

Mirage, The *20–21*, 389

Miranda *50–51*, 374

Miranda of the Balcony *99–09*, 396

Mirasoles, Los *27–28*, 468

Mirele Efros *67–68*, 345

Miriam Elgas *33–34*, 534

Mirror Lion Dance, The *(Kagami-Jishi)* *69–70*, 296

Mirrors *27–28*, 494

Mis' Nelly of N'Orleans *09–19*, 650

Misalliance *09–19*, 608; *50–51*, 373; *52–53*, 292; *61–62*, 306

Misanthrope, The (Le) *99–09*, 486; *26–27*, 434; *56–57*, 55, 353; *59–60*, 50; *63–64*, 327; *68–69*, 383

Miser, The *(L'Avare)* *23–24*, 406; *35–36*, 475; *49–50*, 384; *65–66*, 397; *68–69*, 391; *69–70*, 313

Miserables, Les *99–09*, 529

Misguided Tour *59–60*, 46

Misleading Lady, The *09–19*, 515

Mismates *24–25*, 572

Miss Daisy *09–19*, 531

Miss Dolly Dollars *99–09*, 493

Miss Dynamite *94–99*, 102

Miss Elizabeth's Prisoner *99–09*, 446

Miss Emily Adam *59–60*, 47

Miss Francis of Yale *94–99*, 215

Miss Geo. Washington Jr. *19–20*, 371

Miss Gulliver Travels *31–32*, 440

Miss Hobbs *99–09*, 347

Miss Hook of Holland *99–09*, 554

Miss Information *09–19*, 561

Miss Innocence *99–09*, 573

Miss Innocence Abroad *94–99*, 84

Miss Isobel *57–58*, 308

Miss Jack *09–19*, 449

Miss Julie(a) *53–54*, 359; *55–56*, 376; *61–62*, 298; *65–66*, 425

Miss Liberty *49–50*, 354s

Miss Lonelyhearts *57–58*, 288

Miss Lulu Bett *20–21*, 415

Miss Manhattan *94–99*, 199

Miss Marlowe at Play *39–40*, 470

Miss Millions *19–20*, 396

Miss Multon *94–99*, 143, 144

Miss 1917 *09–19*, 613

Miss Patsy *09–19*, 422

Miss Phoenix *09–19*, 513

Miss Pocahontas *99–09*, 549

Miss Princess *09–19*, 489

Miss Prinnt *99–09*, 382

Miss Quis *36–37*, 477

Miss Simplicity *99–09*, 406

Miss Springtime *09–19*, 583

Miss Swan Expects *38–39*, 460

Mississippi Rainbow (see *Brain Sweat*)

Missouri Legend *38–39*, 405; *50–51*, 373, 374

Mistakes Will Happen *99–09*, 514; *09–19*, 415

Mister: titles abbreviated Mr. are in alphabetical order under MR

Mister Antonio *09–19*, 582

Mister Johnson *55–56*, 382; *63–64*, 367

Mister Malatesta *22–23*, *536*

Mister Punch at Home (mn) *34–35*, 484

Mister Roberts *47–48*, 383; *56–57*, 343; *62–63*, 339

Mister Romeo *27–28*, 398

Mistletoe Bough, The *22–23*, 575

Mistress: titles abbreviated Mrs. are
in alphabetical order under MRS
Mistress Betty *94–99*, 146; *99–09*,
502
Mistress Nell *99–09*, 375, 406
Mistress of the Inn, The *(La
Locandiera) 94–99*, 166; *23–24*,
356; *26–27*, 432; *46–47*, 485
Mitschuldigen, Die (see *The
Accomplices*)
Mixed Bill (1) *25–26*, 569
Mixed Bill (2) *52–53*, 301
Mixed Doubles (1) *26–27*, 518
Mixed Doubles (2) *66–67*, 403s
Mixed Marriage *09–19*, 459, 494;
20–21, 412
Mix-up, A *09–19*, 542
Mizpah *99–09*, 520
Mille. Ma Mere *28–29*, 463
Mlle. Mischief *99–09*, 569
Mlle. Modiste *99–09*, 504; *09–19*,
502; *29–30*, 414
Mme. Flirt *99–09*, 428
Mme. Mongodin *99–09*, 562
Mme. Pompadour *24–25*, 485
Mme. Sans-Gene *(see Madame Sans
Gene)*
Moby Dick (source) *60–61*, 48;
62–63, 290, 322; *69–70*, 336, 373;
70–71
Moby Dick (1) *60–61*, 48
Moby Dick (2) *62–63*, 290
Moby Dick (3) *69–70*, 373; *70–71*
Mocking Bird, The *99–09*, 421, 422
Mod Donna *69–70*, 345s
Model, The *09–19*, 474
Modern Eve, A *09–19*, 552
Modern Girl, A *09–19*, 531
Modern Magdalen, A *99–09*, 408
Modern Marriage *09–19*, 451
Modern Statuary *67–68*, 408
Modern Virgin, A *30–31*, 529
Modest Suzanne *09–19*, 462
Modiste Shop, The *09–19*, 511
Moishe's Wedding *47–48*, 431
Molehills *46–47*, 494
Moliere *09–19*, 653

Molloy *70–71*
Mollusc, The *99–09*, 566; *40–41*,
432; *43–44*, 490; *49–50*, 384
Molly Darling *22–23*, 446
Molly Dolly *47–48*, 431
Molly May *09–19*, 417
Molly O' *09–19*, 575
Moloch *09–19*, 558
Moment Musical *42–43*, 487
Moment of Death, The *99–09*, 375
Moment With Mandy, A *62–63*,
310
Momiji-Gari *(see The Maple Leaf
Viewing Picnic)*
Mom's Boy *44–45*, 441
Mon Cure Chez les Riche *26–27*,
447
Monday's Heroes *52–53*, 307
Money *63–64*, 344s
Money Business *25–26*, 532
Money From Home *26–27*, 488
Money in the Air *31–32*, 490
Money Lender, The *28–29*, 363
Money Mad *36–37*, 486
Money Makers, The (1) *99–09*, 482
Money Makers, The (2) *09–19*, 533
Mongolia *27–28*, 481
Mongrel, The *24–25*, 505
Monique *57–58*, 295
Monkey *31–32*, 476
Monkey of Stars *60–61*, 295
Monkey Talks, The *25–26*, 523
Monkey's Paw, The *99–09*, 539;
22–23, 575; *28–29*, 502
Monks of Malabar, The *99–09*, 370
Monna Vanna *99–09*, 498
Monopoly *65–66*, 431
Monsieur Beaucaire (see also
Beaucaire) (1) *09–19*, 467
Monsieur Beaucaire (2) *19–20*, 398
Monsieur Brotonneau *23–24*, 406
Monsieur de Pourceaugnac *69–70*,
313
Monsieur le Directeur *94–99*, 185
Monsignor's Hour *38–39*, 492
Monster, The *22–23*, 436; *32–33*,
460

Monte Carlo *94–99*, 226

Monte Carlo Ballet Russe (see *Ballet Russe de Monte Carlo*)

(Count of) Monte Cristo (source) *94–99*, 185; *99–09*, 377

Monte Cristo *94–99*, 185; *99–09*, 377

Monte Cristo, Jr. *09–19*, 652

Month in the County, A *29–30*, 511; *55–56*, 383; *62–63*, 338

Month of Sundays *68–69*, 428

Montjoye *94–99*, 120

Montmartre *21–22*, 509

Montserrat *49–50*, 358; *53–54*, 358; *60–61*, 45

Moon Besieged, The *62–63*, 290

Moon Dreamers, The *67–68*, 412; *69–70*, 350

Moon for the Misbegotten, A *56–57*, 372; *68–69*, 424

Moon in Capricorn *53–54*, 356

Moon in the Yellow River, The *31–32*, 485; *44–45*, 436; *60–61*, 357

Moon Is a Gong, The *25–26*, 566

Moon Is Blue, The *50–51*, 356; *61–62*, 304

Moon Is Down, The *41–42*, 445

Moon of the Caribbees, The *24–25*, 480; *37–38*, 451; *47–48*, 348

Moon on a Rainbow Shawl *61–62*, 319; *70–71*

Moon Over Mulberry Street *35–36*, 401, 402

Moon Over Taurus *62–63*, 338

Moon Shines on Kylenamoe, The *62–63*, 338

Moon Vine, The *42–43*, 463

Moonbirds *59–60*, 295

Moondown *09–19*, 547

Moon-Flower, The *23–24*, 403

Moonlight *23–24*, 394

Moonlight and Honeysuckle *19–20*, 358

Moonlight File, The *69–70*, 376

Moonlight Mary *09–19*, 570

Moon-Peddler, The *37–38*, 464

Moonshine *99–09*, 499

Moor Born *33–34*, 513

Moral Fabric *32–33*, 426

Morals *25–26*, 505

Morals of Marcus, The *99–09*, 551

Mordkin Dancers (see *Mikhail Mordkin Dancers*)

More Stately Mansions *67–68*, 351

More Than Queen *99–09*, 352, 375

More Than We Know *42–43*, 479

More the Merrier, The *41–42*, 395

Mormon Wife, The *99–09*, 393

Morning *68–69*, 394

Morning After, The *25–26*, 421

Morning, Noon and Night *68–69*, 394

Morning Star *39–40*, 456

Morning Star, The *42–43*, 428

Morning Sun *63–64*, 347s

Morning's at Seven *39–40*, 418; *55–56*, 58

Morphia *22–23*, 539

Morris Carnovsky *37–38*, 464

Morris Dance, The *09–19*, 595

Morris Gest Midnight Whirl *19–20*, 407

Mort de Cleopatre, La *09–19*, 589 (and 605)

Morte Civile, La (see *The Outlaw*)

Morte d'Arthur *62–63*, 296

Morton: The Patient *70–71*

Mosquitos, Los *31–32*, 500

Most Happy Fella, The *55–56*, 387; *58–59*, 322; *65–66*, 407

Most Immoral Lady, A *28–29*, 426

Most of the Game *35–36*, 414

Motel *66–67*, 405

Moth and the Flame, The *94–99*, 228

Moth and the Star, The *62–63*, 310

#*%!&#! Mother! *69–70*, 373

Mother (1) *09–19*, 423

Mother (2) *35–36*, 436

Mother, The *38–39*, 471

Mother Carey's Chickens *09–19*, 608

Mother Commands and Is Rebuked,
  A *62–63*, 335
Mother Courage and Her Children
  (A Chronicle of the Thirty Years
  War) *61–62*, 318; *62–63*, 190,
  304; *67–68*, 345
Mother Goose (1) *94–99*, 259
Mother Goose (2) *99–09*, 446
Mother Holle(a) *37–38*, 467; *38–39*,
  490
Mother Lode *34–35*, 426
Mother Lover, The *68–69*, 403
Mother of Us All, The *46–47*, 498
Mother Sings *35–36*, 434
Mother's Liberty Bond *09–19*, 632
Moths, The *69–70*, 367
Motor Chaperon, The *09–19*, 411
Motor Girl, The *09–19*, 395
Moumou *62–63*, 311
Mountain, The *33–34*, 431
Mountain Climber, The *99–09*, 510
Mountain Fury *29–30*, 406
Mountain Man, The *21–22*, 477
Mountebank, The *22–23*, 566
Mourner's Bench, The *50–51*, 373
Mourning Becomes Electra *31–32*,
  417, 511
Mousetrap, The *60–61*, 44
Move On *25–26*, 530
Move On, Sister *33–34*, 447
Movers, The *99–09*, 544
Movie Man, The *59–60*, 49
Mozart *26–27*, 430, 446
Mr. Adam *48–49*, 423
Mr. and Mrs. Daventry *09–19*, 415
Mr. and Mrs. Lyman *67–68*, 408
Mr. and Mrs. North *40–41*, 410
Mr. and Mrs. Phipps *46–47*, 494
Mr. Banks of Birmingham *38–39*,
  453
Mr. Barnes of New York *94–99*,
  234
Mr. Barnum *09–19*, 636
Mr. Barry's Etchings *49–50*, 371
Mr. Big *41–42*, 399
Mr. Bluebeard *99–09*, 427
Mr. Buttles *09–19*, 411

Mr. Chops *52–53*, 301
Mr. Faust *21–22*, 501
Mr. Gilhooley *30–31*, 424
Mr. Grossman *63–64*, 365
Mr. Hamlet of Broadway *99–09*,
  575
Mr. Hopkinson *99–09*, 509
Mr. Jiggins of Jigginstown *36–37*,
  496
Mr. Lazarus *09–19*, 581
Mr. Lode of Koal *09–19*, 403
Mr. Moneypenny *28–29*, 398
Mr. Myd's Mystery *09–19*, 555
Mr. Noah (mn) *35–36*, 512–3
Mr. Peebles and Mr. Hooker *46–47*,
  424
Mr. Pickwick (1) *99–09*, 427
Mr. Pickwick (2) *52–53*, 255
Mr. Pim Passes By *20–21*, 430;
  26–27, 511
Mr. Pitt *23–24*, 391
Mr. Potter of Texas *94–99*, 254
Mr. Preedy and the Countess *09–19*,
  429
Mr. President *62–63*, 280s
Mr. Sampson *26–27*, 524
Mr. Samuel *30–31*, 448
Mr. Simian *63–64*, 349
Mr. Smooth *99–09*, 347
Mr. Strauss Goes to Boston *45–46*,
  381
Mr. Sycamore *42–43*, 442
Mr. Thing *51–52*, 40
Mr. Winkle's Holiday *46–47*, 494
Mr. Wix of Wickham *99–09*, 466
Mr. Wonderful *55–56*, 380s
Mr. Wu *09–19*, 534
Mrs. Avery *09–19*, 455
Mrs. Battle's Bath *99–09*, 490
Mrs. Black Is Back *99–09*, 472
Mrs. Boltay's Daughters *09–19*,
  563
Mrs. Bumpstead-Leigh *09–19*, 40,
  442; *28–29*, 486
Mrs. Christmas Angel *09–19*, 485
Mrs. Dakon *09–19*, 406
Mrs. Dally *65–66*, 370

Mrs. Dally Has a Lover *62–63*, 315; *65–66*, 370; *70–71*

Mrs. Dane's Defense *99–09*, 383; *27–28*, 503

Mrs. Deering's Divorce *99–09*, 435

Mrs. Dot *09–19*, 412

Mrs. Gibbon's Boys *48–49*, 422

Mrs. Gorringe's Necklace *99–09*, 477

Mrs. Jack *99–09*, 415

Mrs. January and Mr. X *43–44*, 463

Mrs. Jimmie Thompson *19–20*, 442

Mrs. Kimball Presents *43–44*, 460

Mrs. Leffingwell's Boots *99–09*, 482

Mrs. McThing *51–52*, 310

Mrs. Moonlight *30–31*, 423; *52–53*, 309

Mrs. O'Brien Entertains *38–39*, 457

Mrs. Partridge Presents *24–25*, 516

Mrs. Patterson *54–55*, 379s

Mrs. Peckham's Carouse *99–09*, 566; *09–19*, 500

Mrs. Ponderbery's Past *94–99*, 162

Mrs. Radley Barton's Ball, or In Greater New York *94–99*, 198

Mrs. Richard Mansfield *35–36*, 512; *36–37*, 498

Mrs. Smith's Husband *94–99*, 100

Mrs. Snow *69–70*, 372

Mrs. Temple's Telegram *99–09*, 483

Mrs. Thing *51–52*, 40

Mrs. Warren's Profession *99–09*, 496, 535; *09–19*, 612; *21–22*, 516; *50–51*, 374; *62–63*, 334

Mrs. Wiggs of the Cabbage Patch *99–09*, 463

Mrs. Wilson, That's All *(Mrs. Wilson-Andrews)* *99–09*, 525

Much Ado About Nothing *94–99*, 150, 189; *99–09*, 363, 456, 469, 534; *09–19*, 478, 486, 505, 508; *27–28*, 455; *32–33*, 424; *46–47*, 485; *51–52*, 321; *55–56*, 55; *58–59*, 316; *59–60*, 291; *61–62*, 343; *62–63*, 305; *63–64*, 314

Mud Turtle, The *25–26*, 429

Muddy Doorsteps *32–33*, 377

Muffled Report, The *63–64*, 363s

Muggins *09–19*, 631

Mujer Desconocida, Una *27–28*, 468

Mulatto *35–36*, 424; *50–51*, 324

Mulberry Bush, The *27–28*, 440

Mummers and Men *61–62*, 327

Mummy, The *94–99*, 183

Mummy and the Humming Bird, The *99–09*, 415

Mum's the Word *40–41*, 399

Mundy Scheme, The *69–70*, 308

Murder at Mrs. Loring's *39–40*, 470

Murder at the Vanities *33–34*, 430

Murder Has Been Arranged, A *49–50*, 383

Murder in the Cathedral *35–36*, 472; *37–38*, 425; *38–39*, 492; *47–48*, 429; *50–51*, 374

Murder in the Old Red Barn *35–36*, 512

Murder of Roger Ackroyd, The *31–32*, 474

Murder on the Nile *46–47*, 420

Murder on the Second Floor *29–30*, 391

Murder Sails at Midnight *37–38*, 463

Murder Without Crime *43–44*, 408; *45–46*, 457

Murderer Among Us, A *63–64*, 329

Murderers, The *61–62*, 150

Murray Anderson's Almanac (see also *John Murray Anderson's Almanac*) *29–30*, 382

Murray Hill *27–28*, 418; *35–36*, 504

Mushrooms *67–68*, 412

Music Box Revue (1921) *21–22*, 426

Music Box Revue (1922) *22–23*, 477

Music Box Revue (1923) *23–24*, 320

Music Box Revue (1924) *24–25*, 496

Music Hall Varities (see *George White's Music Hall Varieties*)

Music Hath Charms *34–35*, 434

Music in May *28–29*, 486

Music in My Heart *47–48*, 355s

Music in the Air *32–33*, 416s; *51–52*, 285

Music Man, The *57–58*, 306s;
  65–66, 366
Music Master, The *99–09*, 467, 547;
  09–19, 584
Music Shop, The *61–62*, 324
Musical Timepiece, A *70–71*
Musk *19–20*, 436
Musketeers, The *94–99*, 255
Mutilated, The *65–66*, 399
Muzeeka *67–68*, 405
My Aunt Bridget *94–99*, 93
My Aunt From Ypsilanti *22–23*,
  564
My Baby's Wedding *38–39*, 493
My Beginning *61–62*, 321
My Best Girl *09–19*, 476
My Boys *94–99*, 217
My Colleen *94–99*, 252
My Country *26–27*, 364
My Darlin' Aida *52–53*, 264s
My Daughter, Your Son *68–69*, 415
My Daughter-in-Law *99–09*, 363
My Dear Children *39–40*, 434
My Dear Public *43–44*, 411
My Fair Ladies *40–41*, 420
My Fair Lady *55–56*, 378s; *63–64*,
  338; *68–69*, 373
My Friend From India *94–99*, 179,
  235
My Friend Yossel *44–45*, 444
My Girl *24–25*, 494
My Girl Friday *28–29*, 468
My Golden Girl *19–20*, 422
My Heart's in the Highlands *38–39*,
  469, 487; *49–50*, 382, 384; *60–61*,
  48
My House Is Your House *70–71*
My Indian Family *59–60*, 339
My Innocent Boy *99–09*, 350
My Kinsman, Major Molyne(a)ux
  (source) *63–64*, 369; *64–65*, 346
My Kinsman, Major Molyneux
  64–65, 346
My Lady *99–09*, 388
My Lady Dainty *99–09*, 386
My Lady Dreams *23–24*, 429
My Lady Friends *19–20*, 394; *70–71*

My Lady Molly *99–09*, 451
My Lady Peggy Goes to Town
  99–09, 432
My Lady's Dress *09–19*, 534
My Lady's Garter *09–19*, 557
My Lady's Glove *09–19*, 602
My Lady's Honor *09–19*, 547
My Lady's Lord *99–09*, 358
My Lady's Maid *99–09*, 519
My Life in Court *63–64*, 308
My Life Is Yours *47–48*, 429
My Little Friend *09–19*, 502
My Magnolia *26–27*, 360
My Malkele *37–38*, 470
My Man *09–19*, 425
My Maryland *27–28*, 402
My Milliner's Ball *99–09*, 458
My Mother, My Father and Me
  62–63, 303
My Name Is Aquilon *48–49*, 411
My Official Wife *94–99*, 134
My Partner *94–99*, 113, 235
My Philadelphia Father *56–57*, 337
My Princess *27–28*, 424
My Romance *48–49*, 390
My Sister Eileen *40–41*, 405; *44–45*,
  436; *47–48*, 427; *52–53*, 290;
  57–58, 323; *62–63*, 297; *66–67*,
  389
My Son *24–25*, 455
My Sweet Charlie *66–67*, 376
My 3 Angels *52–53*, 295
My Wedding Night *45–46*, 460
My Wife *99–09*, 543
My Wife and I *66–67*, 402
My Wife Is Not Stylish *(Mia Moglie
  Non Ha Chic)* *99–09*, 536
My Wife Won't Let Me *99–09*,
  516
My Wife's Husbands *99–09*, 434,
  517
Myles Aroon *94–99*, 153
Myself—Bettina *99–09*, 570
Mysteries and Smaller Pieces *68–69*,
  456
Mysterious Mr. Bugle, The *94–99*,
  200

Mystery at Greenfingers, The *39–40*, 470

Mystery Man, The *27–28*, 498

Mystery Moon *30–31*, 399

Mystery of Theodosia Burr, The *46–47*, 499

Mystery Ship, The *26–27*, 493

Mystery Square *28–29*, 490

Myth of Sisyphus, The *62–63*, 322

Naboth's Vineyard *44–45*, 417

Nadrag, A *(The Trousers) 63–64*, 336

Naked *24–25*, 474; *26–27*, 421; *50–51*, 373; *53–54*, 358; *66–67*, 418

Naked Genius, The *43–44*, 419

Nan *09–19*, 492

Nance Oldfield *94–99*, 151; *99–09*, 353, 532

Nancy & Co. *94–99*, 128

Nancy Ann *23–24*, 414

Nancy Brown *99–09*, 428

Nancy Lee *09–19*, 627

Nancy Stair *99–09*, 486

Nancy's Private Affair *29–30*, 478

Napi *30–31*, 504

Napoleon *27–28*, 524

Napoleon Bonaparte *94–99*, 91, 92

Narrow Path, The *99–09*, 584

Narukami *60–61*, 45

Nat Turner *50–51*, 374

Nataraj Vashi & Pra-Veena (dance programs) *46–47*, 487

Nathan Hale *94–99*, 249

Nathan the Wise *(Nathan der Weise) 41–42*, 445, 458; *43–44*, 489; *61–62*, 325, 327; *66–67*, 412

Nathan Weinstein, Mystic, Connecticut *65–66*, 399

National Anthem, The *21–22*, 497

National Theater of the Deaf, The *68–69*, 406; *69–70*, 311

National Theaters of Japan *70–71*

Nationale 6 *37–38*, 469

Native Ground *36–37*, 492

Native Son *40–41*, 421; *42–43*, 439

Nativite, La *32–33*, 458

Nativity *37–38*, 460

Nativity, The *38–39*, 490

Natja *24–25*, 542

Natural Affection *62–63*, 296

Natural Law, The *09–19*, 550

Natural Look, The *66–67*, 384

Nature *94–99*, 204

Nature of the Crime *69–70*, 362

Nature's Nobleman *21–22*, 461

Nature's Way *57–58*, 293

Natya Dancers (see *Le Meri & Natya Dancers*)

Naughty Anthony *99–09*, 359

Naughty Cinderella *25–26*, 493

Naughty Marietta *09–19*, 430; *29–30*, 425; *31–32*, 433

Naughty Naught '00 *36–37*, 457; *38–39*, 423; *46–47*, 429

Naughty Riquette *26–27*, 378

Naughty Wife, The (see *Losing Eloise*)

Naval Cadet, A *94–99*, 186

Navy Relief Benefit Show *41–42*, 460

Near Santa Barbara *20–21*, 424

Nearly a Hero *99–09*, 559

Nearly Married *09–19*, 506

Necken, The *09–19*, 499

Ned McCobb's Daughter *26–27*, 433

Ned Wayburn's Gambols *28–29*, 457

Ned Wayburn's Town Topics *09–19*, 558

Ne'er-Do-Well, The *09–19*, 475

Neglected Lady, The *09–19*, 509

Neighborhood Playhouse Revue *34–35*, 484

Neighbors (1) *09–19*, 612

Neighbors (2) *23–24*, 377

Neighbors (3) *68–69*, 454

Nekros *60–61*, 47

Nell Go In *99–09*, 378

Nell Gwynn *99–09*, 378

Nellie Bly *45–46*, 422

Nemesis *20–21*, 439

Nemica, La *25–26*, 524

Neptune's Daughter *99–09*, 528
Nero *99–09*, 536
Nerves *24–25*, 441
Nervous Set, The *58–59*, 336s
Nervous Wreck, The *23–24*, 331;
    28–29, 431
Nest, The (1) *21–22*, 500
Nest, The (2) *69–70*, 364
Nest Egg, The *09–19*, 431
Net, The *09–19*, 651
Nether-World *38–39*, 485
Nettie *09–19*, 535
Never Again, or The Tricks of
    Seraphin *94–99*, 197
Never Homes, The *09–19*, 453
Never Live Over a Pretzel Factory
    63–64, 330
Never No More *31–32*, 460
Never on Sunday *66–67*, 390
Never Say Die *09–19*, 484; *25–26*,
    531
Never Say Never *51–52*, 294
Never Tell Isobel *68–69*, 456
Never Too Late *62–63*, 289
Nevertheless *09–19*, 588
New Blood *94–99*, 95
New Boy, The *94–99*, 94
New Brooms *24–25*, 488
New Cambridge Circus *64–65*, 346
New Chauve-Souris (see
    Chauve-Souris 1931)
New Clown, The *99–09*, 414
New Cole Porter Revue *65–66*, 428
New Dance Group Festival (dance
    programs) *47–48*, 422
New Dominion, The *94–99*, 199;
    99–09, 525
New England Folks *99–09*, 398
New Englander, The *23–24*, 397
New Faces *33–34*, 507
New Faces of 1936 *35–36*, 507
New Faces of 1943 *42–43*, 453
New Faces of 1952 *51–52*, 325s
New Faces of '56 *56–57*, 314s
New Faces of 1962 *61–62*, 284s
(Leonard Sillman's) New Faces of
    1968 *67–68*, 376s

New Freedom, The *29–30*, 539
New Gallantry, The *25–26*, 454
New Girl in Town *56–57*, 373s;
    62–63, 339
New Gossoon, The *32–33*, 406;
    34–35, 406; *37–38*, 377
New Henrietta, The *09–19*, 516
New Lady Bantock, The *99–09*, 577
New Life, A *43–44*, 413
New Magdalen, The *99–09*, 496
New Moon, The *28–29*, 376; *42–43*,
    424; *43–44*, 442
New Morality, The *20–21*, 424
New Music Hall of Israel, The
    69–70, 298
New Opera Company (dance
    programs) *42–43*, 485
New Poor, The *23–24*, 383
New Priorities of 1943 *42–43*, 429
New Secretary, The *09–19*, 493
New Show at the Premise, The
    62–63, 333
New Sin. The *09–19*, 481
New South, The *94–99*, 233
New Tenant, The *59–60*, 46; *63–64*,
    366
New Toys *23–24*, 401
New Way to Pay Old Debts, A
    45–46, 450
New Woman, The *94–99*, 103
New Word, The *09–19*, 601, 629
New York (1) *94–99*, 194
New York (2) *09–19*, 427
New York (3) *27–28*, 451
New York City Ballet Company, The
    (dance programs) *48–49*, 428-9,
    429; *49–50, 386; *51–52*, 330
New York City Center of Music and
    Drama (dedication ceremony)
    43–44, 435
New York City Dance Theater
    (dance programs) *49–50*, 386
New York City Symphony *43–44*,
    440; *44–45*, 376; *45–46*, 392;
    47–48, 342
New York Coloring Book *62–63*,
    329s

New York Day by Day *94–99*, 205
New York Exchange *26–27*, 451
New York Idea, The *99–09*, 526;
    09–19, 559; *32–33*, 480
New York to Cherbourg *31–32*, 482
New Yorker, A (see *Lost,*
    Twenty-Four Hours)
New Yorkers, The (1) *99–09*, 397
New Yorkers, The (2) *26–27*, 492
New Yorkers, The (3) *30–31*, 465;
    64–65, 357
Newcomers, The *23–24*, 298
Newcomes, The *09–19*, 599
Newlyweds and Their Baby, The
    99–09, 580
Newspapers *60–61*, 294
Next (1) *09–19*, 452
Next (2) *68–69*, 445
Next Half Hour, The *45–46*, 402
Next of Kin, The *09–19*, 407
Next President, The *57–58*, 329s
Next Time I'll Sing to You *63–64*,
    352; *67–68*, 410
Nic Nax of 1926 *26–27*, 364
Nica *25–26*, 537
Nice People *20–21*, 433
Nice Wanton *09–19*, 442
Nice Women *28–29*, 511
Nicholas Nickleby *28–29*, 384
Nicknames *60–61*, 294
Nicola (mn) *37–38*, 466
Nifties of 1923 *23–24*, 322
Nigger, The *09–19*, 405
Nigger Rich *(The Big Shot)* *29–30*,
    399
Niggerlovers, The *67–68*, 387
Night (1) *24–25*, 588
Night (2) *68–69*, 394
Night at an Inn, A *09–19*, 628;
    29–30, 537
Night at the Circus, A *94–99*, 104
Night Before Christmas, The *40–41*,
    423
Night Birds *29–30*, 431
Night Boat, The *19–20*, 421
Night Call, The *21–22*, 539
Night Circus, The *58–59*, 308

Night Clerk, The *94–99*, 153
Night Duel, The *25–26*, 553
Night Hawk *24–25*, 550; *26–27*, 446
Night Hostess *28–29*, 372
Night in a Den, A *(Une Nuit au*
    Bouge) *23–24*, 333
Night in Avignon, A *09–19*, 649
Night in Kankaz, A *46–47*, 497
Night in New York, A *94–99*, 185
Night in Paris, A *25–26*, 527
Night in Spain *09–19*, 616
Night in Spain, A *26–27*, 525
Night in the House *35–36*, 432
Night in Venice, A *28–29*, 506
Night Is Black Bottles, The *62–63*,
    321
Night Life *62–63*, 282
Night Little Girl Blue Made Her
    Social Debut, The *63–64*, 371
Night Lodging (see also *The Lower*
    Depths; At the Bottom) *19–20*,
    404; *29–30*, 476
Night Music *39–40*, 438; *50–51*,
    361
Night Must Fall *36–37*, 410; *39–40*,
    468; *45–46*, 450, 457; *47–48*, 425;
    68–69, 455
Night of January 16 *35–36*, 404;
    39–40, 470
Night of Love *40–41*, 409
Night of Love, A *46–47*, 497
Night of Snow, A *09–19*, 560
Night of the Auk *56–57*, 342;
    58–59, 53; *62–63*, 337
Night of the Dunce *66–67*, 409
Night of the Fourth, The *99–09*,
    386
Night of the Iguana, The *61–62*,
    278; *66–67*, 422
Night of the Party, The *99–09*, 418
Night Off, A *94–99*, 85; *99–09*, 536
Night Over Taos *31–32*, 492
Night Remembers, The *34–35*, 415
Night Session, A *94–99*, 211
Night Watch in Syria *42–43*, 488
Nightcap, The *21–22*, 394
Nightingale, The *26–27*, 454

Nightingale and the Rose, The
  53–54, 328
Nightmare, The *64–65*, 322
Nightpiece *70–71*
Nights of Cabiria *65–66*, 395
Nights of Fury *(Les Nuits de la
  Colere)* *56–57*, 353
Nightstick *27–28*, 449
Nighty-Night *19–20*, 348
Nihilists *94–99*, 183
Nikki *31–32*, 398s
Nina *51–52*, 296
Nina Boba, La *31–32*, 500
Nina Rosa *30–31*, 415
Nine Girls *42–43*, 459
(Hammerstein's) Nine (9) O'Clock
  Revue (1923) *23–24*, 328
Nine O'Clock Revue (1935) *35–36*,
  512
Nine O'Clock Revue (1936) *36–37*,
  497
Nine Pine Street *32–33*, 488
Nine Till Six *30–31*, 421
Nine to Five to Zero *63–64*, 371
Nine-Fifteen Revue *29–30*, 492
1999 *94–99*, 215
1935 *35–36*, 472
1931— *31–32*, 446
19th Hole, The *27–28*, 428
Nineteenth Hole of Europe, The
  48–49, 427
Ninety and Nine, The *99–09*,
  418
90 Horse Power *25–26*, 568
90 in the Shade *09–19*, 544
Ninety-Day Mistress, The *67–68*,
  352
Niniche *94–99*, 153
Ninotchka *54–55*, 400
9th Guest, The *30–31*, 404
Ninth Month Midnight *48–49*, 427
Nirvana *25–26*, 562
Nju *09–19*, 597
No Answer *37–38*, 465
No 'Count Boy, the *24–25*, 586;
  54–55, 56
No Edged Thing *37–38*, 465

No Exit *46–47*, 443; *47–48*, 424;
  52–53, 308; *56–57*, 58; *63–64*, 365;
  67–68, 392
No Foolin' *26–27*, 359
No for an Answer *40–41*, 430
No Laughter in Heaven *37–38*, 464
No More Blondes *19–20*, 413
No More Frontier *31–32*, 414
No More Ladies *33–34*, 484; 34–35,
  367; *44–45*, 436
No More Peace *37–38*, 453, 454
No More Women *26–27*, 363
No Mother to Guide Her *33–34*,
  534; 35–36, 512
No! No! Nanette! *25–26*, 446;
  *70–71*s
No Other Girl *24–25*, 433
No Place to Be Somebody *68–69*,
  434, 457; *69–70*, 310, 355
No Questions Asked *33–34*, 492
No Quiero, No Quiero *31–32*, 500
No Shoestrings *62–63*, 316s
No Strings *61–62*, 291s
No. 13 (33) Washington Square
  09–19, 555
No Time for Comedy *38–39*, 470
No Time for Sergeants *55–56*, 355
No Trespassing *26–27*, 375
No Way Out *44–45*, 392
Noah (author unnamed) *59–60*, 43
Noah (1) *34–35*, 451; *46–47*, 493;
  49–50, 384; *54–55*, 58
Noah (2) *36–37*, 496
Noah's Flood *09–19*, 442
Noble Experiment, The *30–31*, 441
Noble Rogue, A *29–30*, 384
Noble Spaniard, The *09–19*, 400
Nobody Hears a Broken Drum
  69–70, 361
Nobody Home *09–19*, 552
Nobody Loves an Albatross *63–64*,
  317
Nobody's Boy *38–39*, 490
Nobody's Business *23–24*, 340
Nobody's Daughter *09–19*, 439
Nobody's Girl *34–35*, 484
Nobody's Money *21–22*, 397

Nobody's Widow *09–19*, 430

Noces, D'Argent, Les *21–22*, 500

Nocturne (1) *09–19*, 631

Nocturne (2) *24–25*, 543

Noel Coward's Sweet Potato *68–69*, 378, 379s

Noh comedy (untitled source) *65–66*, 403

Noh Theater *70–71*

Noisy Passenger, The *70–71*

Nona *32–33*, 395

None Are So Blind *22–23*, 572

None So Blind *09–19*, 413

Noon *68–69*, 394

Noone *52–53*, 307

Noontide *61–62*, 303

Noose, The *26–27*, 407

Norman, Is That You? *69–70*, 316

Normandy Wedding, A *94–99*, 225

Northern Lights *94–99*, 158

Norths Meet Murder, The *40–41*, 301

Norwegian dances (untitled dance programs) *47–48*, 415

Not a Way of Life *66–67*, 416

Not Enough Rope *61–62*, 325

Not for Children *50–51*, 350

Not Herbert *25–26*, 540

Not in Our Stars *40–41*, 432

Not Now, Darling *70–71*

Not So Fast *22–23*, 579

Not So Long Ago *19–20*, 449

Not While I'm Eating *61–62*, 316

Not With My Money *09–19*, 641

Notes From Underground *59–60*, 49

Nothing but Lies *09–19*, 640

Nothing but Love *19–20*, 374

Nothing But the Truth (source) *09–19*, 582; *27–28*, 421; *32–33*, 411

Nothing But the Truth *09–19*, 582; *32–33*, 411

Nothing Sacred *52–53*, 286

Notoriety *94–99*, 110

Notorious Mrs. Ebbsmith, The *94–99*, 159; *99–09*, 404

Notre Dame *99–09*, 406

Notre Dame de Paris *99–09*, 406

Nounouche *23–24*, 333

Nouvelle Idole, La *23–24*, 406

Novellis Novellis *62–63*, 321

November 22nd *67–68*, 413

Novice and the Duke, The *29–30*, 460

Now *68–69*, 422s

Now I Lay Me Down to Sleep *49–50*, 374

Now Is the Time for All Good Men *67–68*, 386s; *70–71*

Now You See It *67–68*, 414

Now You've Done It *36–37*, 469

Now-a-days *29–30*, 380

Nowhere Bound *34–35*, 444

Nowhere to Go but Up *62–63*, 284s

Nude With Violin *57–58*, 301

Nuit au Bouge, Une (see *A Night in a Den*)

Nuit de Mai d'Alfred de Musset, La *23–24*, 406

Nuits de la Colere, Les (see *Nights of Fury*)

Number, The *51–52*, 288

Number Nine, or The Lady of Ostend *94–99*, 217

Number 7 *26–27*, 377

Nuns, The *70–71*

Nurse Marjorie *99–09*, 521

Nursery Maid of Heaven, The *23–24*, 432

Nut Farm, The *29–30*, 418

Nutmeg Tree, The *39–40*, 449

O Evening Star *35–36*, 457

O Marry Me *61–62*, 310s

O Mistress Mine *45–46*, 424

O, Nightingale *24–25*, 578

O, Oysters! *60–61*, 42

O Say Can You See! *62–63*, 315s

O Sweet Spontaneous *62–63*, 322

O Western Wind *62–63*, 322

Object—Matrimony *09–19*, 585

Objective Case *61–62*, 332

Obratsov Russian Puppet Theater *63–64*, 305

O'Brien Girl, The *21–22,* 432

Obsession *46–47,* 421

Occasion, L' *38–39,* 492

Occupe-Toi d'Amelie *52–53,* 271;
58–59, 325

Octoroon, The (or Life in Louisiana)
28–29, 479; *60–61,* 319

O'Daniel 46–47, 461

Odd Couple, The *64–65,* 329

Odd Man Out *24–25,* 597

Odds and Ends of 1917 *09–19,* 614

Odds on Mrs. Oakley, The *44–45,*
385

Ode to Liberty *34–35,* 425

Ode to the Nightingale *62–63,* 322

Ode to the West Wind *62–63,* 322

Ododo (see *Truth*)

Oedipus Rex (*Oedipus, Oedipus
Tyrannus;* p) *99–09,* 536; *09–19,*
448, 493; *23–24,* 343; *32–33,* 407;
40–41, 432; *45–46,* 444, 458;
47–48, 432; *52–53,* 272; *62–63,*
322; *69–70,* 377

Oedipus Rex (m) *46–47,* 410

Of Love Remembered *66–67,* 383

Of Mice and Men (p) *37–38,* 395;
63–64, 368

Of Mice and Men (m) *58–59,* 53

Of Thee I Sing *31–32,* 451; *32–33,*
496s; *33–34,* 446; *51–52,* 322;
68–69, 447s, 455

Of V We Sing *41–42,* 438

Ofay Watcher, The *69–70,* 339

Off Chance, The *09–19,* 622

Off Col'uh *26–27,* 524

Off the Earth *94–99,* 118

Off to Buffalo *38–39,* 461

Offenders, The *99–09,* 569

Offense, The *25–26,* 494

Office Boy, The *99–09,* 443

Officer 666 *09–19,* 465

Off-Key *26–27,* 479

O'Flaherty, V.C. *36–37,* 497

O'Flynn, The *34–35,* 431

Oh, Boy *09–19,* 595

Oh, Brother! *45–46,* 379

Oh! Calcutta! *69–70,* 335s

Oh Captain! *57–58,* 315s

Oh Dad, Poor Dad, Mamma's Hung
You in the Closet and I'm Feelin'
So Sad *61–62,* 324; *63–64,* 303

Oh, Ernest! *26–27,* 526

Oh, Henry *19–20,* 451

Oh, I Say! *09–19,* 513

Oh, James *70–71*

Oh, Kay(!) *26–27,* 420; *27–28,* 486;
59–60, 48

Oh, Lady! Lady! *09–19,* 621

Oh! Les Beaux Jours (see *Happy
Days* 2)

Oh, Look! *09–19,* 624

Oh Mama *25–26,* 428

Oh, Men! Oh, Women! *53–54,* 331

Oh, Mr. Meadowbrook! *48–49,* 402

Oh, My Dear! *09–19,* 645

Oh! Oh! Delphine *09–19,* 479

Oh! Oh! Oh! Nurse *25–26,* 510

Oh, Pioneers *69–70,* 372

Oh, Please *26–27,* 443

Oh, Professor! *29–30,* 531

Oh, Promise Me *30–31,* 459

Oh, Say Can You See L.A. *67–68,*
401

Oh, Susannah! *94–99,* 223

Oh, What a Girl! *19–20,* 342

Oh What a Lovely War *64–65,* 303s

Oklahoma! *42–43,* 471; *50–51,* 372;
53–54, 299; *57–58,* 325; *62–63,*
298s, 308; *65–66,* 392; *69–70,* 295s

Oktobertag *28–29,* 366

Ol' Man Adam an' His Chillun
34–35, 457; *50–51,* 358

Ol' Man Satan *32–33,* 394

Olathe Response, The *70–61*

Old Acquaintance *40–41,* 403

Old Adam *60–61,* 295

Old Bill, M.P. *26–27,* 423

Old Bucks and New Wings *62–63,*
318s

Old Coat, The *94–99,* 227

Old Country, The *09–19,* 611

Old Dutch *09–19,* 405

Old English *24–25,* 509

Old Firm, The *09–19,* 494

Old Foolishness, The *40–41,* 402

Old Friends *09–19,* 601

Old Gloary, The *63–64,* 369

Old Glory *94–99,* 94

Old Glory, The (see also *The Old Gloary*) *64–65,* 346, 362

Old Glory: Benito Cerino, The *64–65,* 347

Old Heidelberg (see also *Heidelberg*) *99–09,* 439, 455; *09–19,* 433; *24–25,* 500

Old Homestead, The *94–99,* 116; *99–09,* 465

Old Jed Prouty *94–99,* 112

Old Ladies, The *35–36,* 432

Old Lady Says "No!", The *47–48,* 382

Old Lady Shows Her Medals, The *09–19,* 601; *27–28,* 551; *31–32,* 489; *42–43,* 490

Old Lady 31 *09–19,* 586

Old Lavender *94–99,* 197

Old Limerick Town *99–09,* 420

Old Maid, The *34–35,* 436

Old Maid and the Thief, The (opera rep) *47–48,* 347

Old Man Murphy *30–31,* 527; *31–32,* 391

Old Money Bags *94–99,* 215

Old New Yorker, An *09–19,* 442

Old Rascal, The *29–30,* 516

Old Soak, The *22–23,* 441

Old Testament stories *36–37,* 452; *65–66,* 430

Old Town, The *09–19,* 409

Old Tune, The *60–61,* 44

Old Women, The *35–36,* 397

Oldest of the Ancients, The *60–61,* 294

Oldest Trick in the World, The *60–61,* 358s

Ole *58–59,* 53

Ole! Ole! *63–64,* 353

Olive Latimer's Husband *09–19,* 409

Oliver! *62–63,* 292s; *65–66,* 370

Oliver Goldsmith *99–09,* 365

Oliver Oliver *33–34,* 476

Oliver Twist (source) *94–99,* 129; *09–19,* 466; *62–63,* 292; *65–66,* 370

Oliver Twist (1) *94–99,* 129

Oliver Twist (2) *09–19,* 466

Olympe *99–09,* 452

Olympia *28–29,* 398

Omar, the Tentmaker *09–19,* 519

On a Clear Day You Can See Forever *65–66,* 377s

On an Open Roof *62–63,* 294

On and Off *94–99,* 243; *99–09,* 391

On Approval *26–27,* 404

On Borrowed Time *37–38,* 421; *52–53,* 286

On Broadway *94–99,* 181

On Call *28–29,* 413

On Circe's Island *61–62,* 329

On Land and Sea *94–99,* 244

On Location *37–38,* 371

On Parole *99–09,* 534

On Stage *35–36,* 426

On Strivers Row *45–46,* 415

On the Bench *(Sur le Banc)* *23–24,* 333

On the Bowery *94–99,* 89

On the Eve *09–19,* 401

On the Harmfulness (Hazards) of (Smoking) Tobacco *47–48,* 346; *58–59,* 333; *67–68,* 402; *68–69,* 407

On the High Road *60–61,* 45

On the Hiring Line *19–20,* 376

On the Make *31–32,* 514

On the Mississippi *94–99,* 122

On the Necessity of Being Polygamous *64–65,* 349

On the Quiet *99–09,* 388

On the Rocks *37–38,* 458

On the Seventh Day *46–47,* 432

On the Spot *30–31,* 443

On the Stairs *22–23,* 463

On the Town *44–45,* 406; *58–59,* 53; *65–66,* 418

On the Wabash *94–99,* 253

On to Fortune *34–35,* 447

On Trial *09–19,* 202, 528

On Vacation *67–68*, 408
On Vengeance Height *23–24*, 428
On Whitman Avenue *45–46*, 445
On With the Dance *09–19*, 611
On Your Toes *35–36*, 499; *54–55*, 366s
Once and Future King, The *60–61*, 310
Once for the Asking *63–64*, 314
Once in a Lifetime *30–31*, 418; *49–50*, 385; *63–64*, 357
Once Is Enough *37–38*, 424
Once More, With Feeling *58–59*, 298
Once Over Lightly (1) *38–39*, 491
Once Over Lightly (2) *42–43*, 444
Once There Was a Russian *60–61*, 323
Once Upon a Mattress *58–59*, 335s; *66–67*, 422
Once Upon a Tailor *54–55*, 415
Once Upon a Time (1) *99–09*, 480
Once Upon a Time (2) *09–19*, 628
Once Upon a Time (3) *39–40*, 423
Ondine *53–54*, 342; *60–61*, 48
One *20–21*, 382
One Bright Day *51–52*, 314
One by One *64–65*, 318
One Day More (see *Easter*)
One Every Minute *37–38*, 463
One Eye Closed *54–55*, 379
One Flew Over the Cuckoo's Nest *63–64*, 313; *70–71*
One for All *26–27*, 528
One for the Money *38–39*, 456
One Glorious Hour *26–27*, 508
One Good Year *35–36*, 442
One Helluva Night *23–24*, 442
One Hundred (see also *A Hundred*)
110 in the Shade *63–64*, 311s
One Is a Lonely Number *64–65*, 340
One Kiss *23–24*, 363
One Man's Woman *25–26*, 600
One More Honeymoon *33–34*, 510
One More River *59–60*, 329
One Night in Rome *19–20*, 393

One Night Stands of a Noisy Passenger *70–71*
One of the Family *25–26*, 519
One of Us *09–19*, 636
One on the House *40–41*, 433
One Perfect Rose *66–67*, 423
1 + 1 = 3, or The Sins of the Father *94–99*, 195
One Sabbath Afternoon *38–39*, 494
One Summer's Day *94–99*, 225
One Summer's Day (mn) *37–38*, 466
One Sunday Afternoon *32–33*, 463; *38–39*, 494
One Thing After Another *37–38*, 408
One Touch of Venus *43–44*, 417; *63–64*, 342
One, Two, Three *30–31*, 422
One Way Pendulum *61–62*, 306
One Way Street *28–29*, 439
One Wife or Another *32–33*, 458
One Woman's Way *38–39*, 485
One-Act Variety Theater *39–40*, 444
O'Neill of Derry *99–09*, 551
One-Man Show *44–45*, 416; *45–46*, 451
One-Man Theater *46–47*, 493
One-Third of a Nation *37–38*, 452
Only a Countess May Dance When She's Crazy *67–68*, 403
Only Game in Town, The *67–68*, 378
Only Girl, The *09–19*, 538; *33–34*, 530
Only in America *59–60*, 304
Only Jealousy of Emer, The *69–70*, 375
Only Law, The *09–19*, 395
Only Son, The *09–19*, 454
Only the Heart *42–43*, 488; *43–44*, 464
Only the Young *32–33*, 390
Only 38 *21–22*, 417
Only Way, The *99–09*, 349
Open Door, The *29–30*, 483
Open House (1) *25–26*, 516
Open House (2) *47–48*, 340

Open Season at the Second City *63–64*, 356

Open the Gates *45–46*, 459

Open 24 Hours *68–69*, 446

Opening Night *63–64*, 346

Opening of a Window, The *61–62*, 306

Opera Ball, The *09–19*, 465

Opera Cloak, The (opera rep) *42–43*, 487

Operation Sidewinder *69–70*, 303s

Ophelia Enclosed No Longer *62–63*, 335

Opium *70–71*

Opium-Journal of a Cure *70–71*

'Op-o'-Me-Thumb (Op o' Me Thumb) *99–09*, 479; *23–24*, 430

Opportunity *20–21*, 360

Optimist, The (1) *99–09*, 385

Optimist, The (2) *99–09*, 513

Optimists, The *27–28*, 500

Ora di Diana, L' *36–37*, 500

Orange Blossoms *22–23*, 456

Orange Souffle *66–67*, 366

Orchid, The *99–09*, 538, 539

Orchids Preferred *36–37*, 482

Order Please *34–25*, 390

Ordinary Man, An *68–69*, 427

Oresteia *68–69*, 398; *70–71*

Orient Express, The *94–99*, 121

Orientreise *94–99*, 121

Original Ballet Russe (see *Ballet Russe*)

Original Child Bomb *70–71*

Originals Only (unnamed one-acters) *53–54*, 359

Orlando Furioso *70–71*

Orlando Furioso (mn) *37–38*, 467

Orpheus *(Orphee)* *62–63*, 322, 325

Orpheus Descending *56–57*, 362; *58–59*, 53; *59–60*, 42

Oscar Wilde *38–39*, 413; *56–57*, 58

Ostriches *24–25*, 563

Othello *94–99*, 88, 105, 127, 226, 239, 257; *99–09*, 476, 477, 536; *09–19*, 443, 509, 521, 545, 642; *24–25*, 520; *32–33*, 424; *35–36*, 412; *36–37*, 449; *39–40*, 469; *43–44*, 418, 489; *44–45*, 383; *45–46*, 451; *51–52*, 333; *53–54*, 358; *55–56*, 341; *58–59*, 52, 316; *63–64*, 314, 353; *64–65*, 74, 344, 359; *70–71*

Other Fellow, The *09–19*, 428

Other Foot, The *52–53*, 308

Other Girl, The *99–09*, 450

Other Honor, The *(La Otra Honra)* *53–54*, 322

Other House, The *99–09*, 543

Other Man, The *67–68*, 401

Other Men's Wives *29–30*, 440

Other One, The (1) *32–33*, 393

Other One, The (2) *70–71*

Other People's Money *94–99*, 139

Other Room, The *27–28*, 552

Other Rose, The *23–24*, 371

Other Side of the Year, The *70–71*

Otra Honra, La (see *The Other Honor*)

Ouija Board, The *19–20*, 441

Our American Cousin *99–09*, 470; *09–19*, 565

Our Betters *09–19*, 596; *27–28*, 512

Our Boys *94–99*, 235; *99–09*, 536

Our Children *09–19*, 557

Our Lan' *46–47*, 495; *47–48*, 352

Our Little Wife *09–19*, 587

Our Man in Madras *67–68*, 408

Our Miss Gibbs *09–19*, 422

Our Mrs. McChesney *09–19*, 562

Our Mutual Friend *52–53*, 301

Our Nell *22–23*, 497

Our Pleasant Sins *09–19*, 656

Our Stage and Stars *33–34*, 457

Our Strategist *94–99*, 256

Our Town *37–38*, 421; *43–44*, 437; *46–47*, 484; *58–59*, 49; *69–70*, 306

Our Victory *45–46*, 459

Our Wife *32–33*, 471

Our Wives *09–19*, 482, 538; *33–34*, 530

Our World *09–19*, 438

Ours *94–99*, 235

Ourselves *09–19*, 514

Out at Sea *67–68*, 413
Out From Under (1) *39–40*, 459
Out From Under (2) *66–67*, 366
Out in the Streets *94–99*, 127
Out of a Blue Sky *29–30*, 489
Out of a Cave *37–38*, 467
Out of My House *41–42*, 459
Out of Step *24–25*, 532
Out of the Frying Pan *40–41*, 416
Out of the Night *27–28*, 432
Out of the Sea *27–28*, 464
Out of the Seven Seas *23–24*, 354
Out of This World (1) *41–42*, 460
Out of This World (2) *50–51*, 336s;
    55–56, 59; *62–63*, 339
Out of Windows Look Mother Faces
    60–61, 295
Out There *09–19*, 597, 630
Out West of Eighth *51–52*, 282
Outcast *09–19*, 537
Outcast, The *27–28*, 549
Outcasts of a Great City, The
    94–99, 256
Outhouse, The *70–71*
Outlaw, The *(La Morte Civile)*
    99–09, 536; *36–37*, 500; *37–38*,
    470
Outrageous Fortune *43–44*, 423
Outrageous Mrs. Palmer, The
    20–21, 395
Outside Looking In *25–26*, 436
Outside Man, The *64–65*, 362
Outside the Door *48–49*, 427
Outsider, The *23–24*, 405; *27–28*,
    537
Outward Bound *23–24*, 383; *38–39*,
    437; *45–46*, 450
Outward Room, The *39–40*, 413
Over a Welsh Rarebit *99–09*, 433,
    469
Over at Uncle Joe's *60–61*, 320
Over Here (1) *09–19*, 636
Over Here (2) *35–36*, 510
Over Night *09–19*, 435
Over the Hill to the Poorhouse
    68–69, 380
Over the 'Phone *09–19*, 607

Over the River *09–19*, 462
Over the Top *09–19*, 615
Over 21 *43–44*, 446
Overcoat, The *60–61*, 291
Overland Route (The) *94–99*, 100
Overruled *09–19*, 590; *59–60*, 43
Overtones *09–19*, 560
Overtons, The *44–45*, 415
Overture *30–31*, 465
Ovid's Metamorphoses *70–71*
Owl and the Pussycat, The *64–65*,
    314
Owl Answers, The *65–66*, 436;
    68–69, 434
Owl Who Was God, The *47–48*,
    416, 417; *59–60*, 323
Ox Cart, The *66–67*, 36, 408
Ox-Roast *68–69*, 455
Oy Is Dus a Leben! *42–43*, 435

P.S. I Love You *64–65*, 315
P.S. 193 *62–63*, 317
Pace That Kills, The *94–99*, 128
Pacific Mail, The *94–99*, 100
Pack up Your Troubles *42–43*, 478;
    43–44, 404
Paddy the Next Best Thing *20–21*,
    372
Padlocks of 1927 *27–28*, 386
Padre, The *26–27*, 447
Pagan Lady *30–31*, 435
Paganini *09–19*, 581
Pagans *20–21*, 419
Page Miss Glory *34–35*, 415
Page Pygmalion *32–33*, 381
Pageant of Puppetry (Puppet
    Variety), A (mn) *66–67*, 413;
    67–68, 396; *68–69*, 437; *69–70*,
    351; *70–71*
Paging Danger *30–31*, 497
Pagliacci, I (p) *99–09*, 557
Pagliacci (*I Pagliacci;* opera rep)
    99–09, 485, 557; *43–44*, 441, 474;
    44–45, 378, 443; *45–46*, 388, 441;
    46–47, 409, 480; *47–48*, 343, 347,
    399
Paid *25–26*, 504

Paid Companions *31–32*, 376
Paid in Full *99–09*, 559
Paint Your Wagon *51–52*, 292s;
  61–62, 333
Painted Days, The *60–61*, 39
Painted Woman, The *09–19*, 496
Pair of Paris, A *61–62*, 329
Pair of Petticoats, A *09–19*, 625
Pair of Queens, A *09–19*, 578
Pair of Silk Stockings, A *09–19*, 536
Pair of Sixes, A *09–19*, 523
Pair of Spectacles, A *94–99*, 159,
  160; *99–09*, 385
Pair of White Gloves, A *09–19*, 509
Paisley Convertible, The *66–67*, 381
Paix Chez Soi, La *09–19*, 589 (and
  605)
Pajama Game, The *53–54*, 353s;
  56–57, 375
Pajama Tops *62–63*, 311
Pal Joey *40–41*, 404; *41–42*, 391;
  51–52, 301s; *60–61*, 343; *62–63*,
  311
Palace of Truth, The *09–19*, 410
Palm Tree in a Rose Garden *57–58*,
  53
Palmy Days *19–20*, 378
Pals First *09–19*, 596
Pamela *94–99*, 166
Pan and the Young Shepherd *09–19*,
  625
Panama Hattie *40–41*, 390; *64–65*,
  357
Panic *34–35*, 462
Pansy *28–29*, 505
Pantagleize *67–68*, 353; *68–69*, 376
Pantaloon *99–09*, 503
Panthea *09–19*, 524
Paolo and Francesca *99–09*, 520;
  24–25, 498; *28–29*, 484
Papa *09–19*, 655
Papa Is All *41–42*, 425
Papa Joe *22–23*, 536
Papa Lebonnard *99–09*, 535, 536,
  562
Papa Martin *99–09*, 536
Papa's Darling *09–19*, 538

Papa's Wife *99–09*, 355
Papavert *31–32*, 454
Paper Chase, The *09–19*, 486
Papers *68–69*, 437
Papp *68–69*, 430
Paquebot Tenacity *38–39*, 492
Parade *34–35*, 478; *59–60*, 46
Paradis, Le *94–99*, 211
Paradise (1) *27–28*, 477
Paradise (2) *30–31*, 524
Paradise Alley *23–24*, 414
Paradise Gardens East *68–69*, 448s
Paradise Island *61–62*, 303s; *62–63*,
  313
Paradise Lost *35–36*, 448
Paradise Now *68–69*, 456
Paradise of Mahomet, The *09–19*,
  437
Paradise P M *37–38*, 462
Parasite, The *65–66*, 428
Parasites *24–25*, 492
Pardon My English *32–33*, 452
Pardon Our French *50–51*, 317s
Parents and Children *68–69*, 443
Parfumerie *62–63*, 307
Pariah *09–19*, 498, 579
Paris *28–29*, 390; *64–65*, 357
Paris Bound *27–28*, 483
Paris by Night *99–09*, 461
Paris Is Out! *69–70*, 311
Paris '90 *51–52*, 312
Parish Priest, The *99–09*, 368
Parisian Model, The *99–09*, 526
Parisian Romance, A *94–99*, 91, 92,
  93, 236; *99–09*, 355, 455, 486, 487
Parisiana *27–28*, 507
Parisienne *50–51*, 312
Parisienne, La *99–09*, 472; *24–25*,
  474
Park *69–70*, 327s
Park, The *67–68*, 414
Park Avenue *46–47*, 434
Park Avenue, Ltd. *31–32*, 488
Parlor, Bedroom and Bath *09–19*,
  618
Parlor Match, A *94–99*, 178
Parlor Story *46–47*, 469

Parnassus '63 62–63, 322
Parnell 35–36, 433, 506
Parnusseh 38–39, 494
Parson's Bride, The 28–29, 458
Partage de Midi 61–62, 303
Partie de Piquet, La 94–99, 159
Parting of the Angel's Child, The
    38–39, 493
Partners Again 21–22, 542
Party, A 33–34, 427
Party, A (With Betty Comden and
    Adolph Green) 58–59, 54, 315s
Party for Divorce, A 63–64, 370;
    66–67, 402
Party on Greenwich Avenue, The
    66–67, 420
Party's Over, The 32–33, 480
Pasquale Never Knew 37–38,
    437
Passage, Un 70–71
Passage to E.M. Forster, A 70–71
Passage to India, A 61–62, 283
Passant, Le 99–09, 367
Passe, Le 23–24, 410
Passenger to Bali, A 39–40, 443
Passerelle, La 99–09, 472; 22–23,
    456
Passers-by 09–19, 450
Passing of the Idle Rich, The 09–19,
    501
Passing of the Third Floor Back, The
    09–19, 401, 509; 47–48, 427
Passing Present, The 31–32, 444
Passing Regiment, The 99–09, 552
Passing Show, The 94–99, 86
Passing Show of 1912, The 09–19,
    473
Passing Show of 1913, The 09–19,
    503
Passing Show of 1914, The 09–19,
    527
Passing Show of 1915, The 09–19,
    553
Passing Show of 1916, The 09–19,
    576
Passing Show of 1917, The 09–19,
    600

Passing Show of 1918, The 09–19,
    631
Passing Show of 1919, The 19–20,
    377
Passing Show of 1921 20–21, 416
Passing Show of 1922 22–23, 457
Passing Show (1923) 22–23, 582
Passing Show of 1924, The 24–25,
    446
Passing Through From Exotic Places
    69–70, 349
Passion Flower, The 19–20, 415
Passion in the Suburb, A 99–09, 485
Passion of Jonathan Wade, The
    62–63, 316
Passion of Josef D., The 63–64, 324
Passion Play, The 28–29, 497
Passion, Poison and Putrefaction
    59–60, 43
Passionate Pilgrim, The 32–33, 405;
    62–63, 305
Passionella 66–67, 364
Passionnement 28–29, 476
Passport 64–65, 353
Passport, The 94–99, 134; 99–09,
    480
Past Midnight! Past the Morning
    Star! 66–67, 423
Pasteur 22–23, 540
Pastoral 39–40, 407
Pastrybaker, The 35–36, 510
Patate 58–59, 300
Path of Flowers, The 36–37, 495
Path of Glory 35–36, 411; 46–47,
    485; 60–61, 48
Patience (or Bunthorne's Bride)
    94–99, 174; 09–19, 471, 639;
    24–25, 515; 26–27, 530; 28–29,
    352; 30–31, 535; 32–33, 485;
    34–35, 367; 36–37, 401; 38–39,
    448; 41–42, 458; 42–43, 486;
    43–44, 457; 46–47, 494; 47–48,
    374, 375; 63–64, 328, 367; 66–67,
    367; 67–68, 373, 388; 68–69, 390
Patriarch, The 29–30, 448
Patrick—the First 64–65, 363
Patriot, The (1) 99–09, 573

Patriot, The (2) 27–28, 494
Patriot for Me, A 69–70, 299
Patriots 09–19, 494
Patriots, The (see also *Thomas Jefferson)* 42–43, 460; 43–44, 436
Patriots, Etc., The 70–71
Patsy, The 25–26, 522
Pattes de Mouche, Les 94–99, 115; 99–09, 505
Paul Draper (dance programs) 54–55, 386, 406, 407
Paul Draper and Larry Adler 43–44, 436; 44–45, 381; 45–46, 393; 46–47, 410; 47–48, 344
Paul Kauvar 94–99, 84
Paul Robeson 47–48, 423
Paul Sills' Story Theater 70–71s
Paul Swan (dance programs) 47–48, 414, 415
Pauvres de Paris, Les 94–99, 245
Paves du Ciel, Les 55–56, 359
Pavilion on the Links, The 29–30, 532
Pavillion, The 62–63, 326
Pawn, The 09–19, 606
Pawn Ticket 210 94–99, 97
Pay-day 09–19, 571
Paymaster, The 94–99, 251
Payment Deferred 31–32, 400; 50–51, 373
Peace 68–69, 445, 456
Peace and Plenty 37–38, 465
Peace Creeps, The 66–67, 423
Peace Interlude 37–38, 462
Peace on Earth 33–34, 465, 511
Peacemaker, The 46–47, 495
Peacock 32–33, 397
Peanuts 66–67, 415
Pearl and the Pumpkin, The 99–09, 492
Pearl Maiden, The 09–19, 464
Pearl of Great Price, The 26–27, 415
Pearl Primus (dance programs) 44–45, 438; 46–47, 486
Pearls of Wisdom 60–61, 295
Peasant Girl, The 09–19, 547

Peck's Bad Boy 94–99, 95
Peddler, The 67–68, 396
Pedestrian, The 65–66, 421
Peep Show (see *Michael Todd's Peep Show)*
Peepshow 43–44, 453
Peer Gynt 99–09, 487; 22–23, 527; 46–47, 485, 498; 50–51, 344; 59–60, 313; 69–70, 337
Peg o' My Heart (Peg-o'-My-Heart) 09–19, 488; 20–21, 426; 23–24, 427; 49–50, 384
Peggy 09–19, 460
Peggy From Paris 99–09, 436
Peggy Machree 99–09, 575
Peggy-Ann 26–27, 447
Peg-o'-My-Dreams 23–24, 427
Peh Shuh Tschuwan (see *The White Snake)*
Pelican, The 25–26, 450
Pelleas and Melisande (p) 99–09, 404; 23–24, 367
Pelleas and Melisande (opera rep) 47–48, 347
Penal Law 2010 29–30, 525
Penalty for Being Slow, The 67–68, 409
Penchant for Listening, A 63–64, 371
Pendennis (see *Major Pendennis)*
Penelope 09–19, 406
Penguin 53–54, 359
Penguin Island 27–28, 510
Penny Arcade 29–30, 508
Penny Change 63–64, 349
Penny Friend, The 66–67, 408s
Penny Wars, The 69–70, 300
Penny Wise (1) 09–19, 653
Penny Wise (2) 36–37, 480
Penrod 09–19, 635
People Don't Do Such Things 27–28, 458
People Is the Thing That the World Is Fullest Of (mn) 66–67, 413s; 67–68, 396
People Like Us 38–39, 485
People on the Hill 31–32, 397

People vs. Ranchman, The 68–69, 431
People Without Eyes 48–49, 430
Pepper Mill, The 36–37, 448
Pequod 69–70, 335
Peregrine Pickle 29–30, 387
Perfect Alibi, The 28–29, 429
Perfect Duel 60–61, 294
Perfect Fool, The 21–22, 457
Perfect Lady, A 09–19, 537
Perfect Marriage, The (1) 32–33, 422
Perfect Marriage, The (2) 44–45, 392
Perfect Match, The 70–71
Perfect Party, The 68–69, 449
Perfect Setup, The 62–63, 282
Perfectly Scandalous 30–31, 526
Perfumed Lady, The 33–34, 506
Pericas, Las 69–70, 374
Perichole, La (1) 94–99, 134
Perichole, La (2) 25–26, 514
Pericles, Prince of Tyre 70–71
Peril Jaune, Le 09–19, 616
Period of Adjustment 60–61, 307
Peripherie 27–28, 455, 485
Perkins 09–19, 641
Perplexed Husband, The 09–19, 475
Perro del Hortelano, El 31–32, 500
Perry's Mission 70–71
Persae 69–70, 365
Persecution and Assassination of (Jean-Paul) Marat as Performed by the Inmates of the Asylum of Charenton Under the Direction of the Marquis de Sade, The (Marat/Sade) 65–66, 393; 66–67, 379; 67–68, 401
Persians, The 69–70, 365
Personal 99–09, 544
Personal Appearance 34–35, 393; 40–41, 433
Personal Island 46–47, 494
Personalis 60–61, 295
Personality 21–22, 402
Persons Unknown 22–23, 478
Pert-Royal 59–60, 46

Peter Abelard 70–71
Peter Flies High 31–32, 427
Peter Hamilton (dance programs) 47–48, 414, 416
Peter Ibbetson 09–19, 599; 30–31, 514
Peter Pan (p) 99–09, 500; 09–19, 489, 566; 24–25, 481; 28–29, 425; 49–50, 378
Peter Pan (m) 54–55, 369s
Peter Rabbit (mn) 35–36, 512; 37–38, 467; 38–39, 489
Peter Stuyvesant 99–09, 350
Peter Weston 23–24, 318
Peterpat 64–65, 322
Peter's Mother 09–19, 642
Petit Cafe, Le 09–19, 514
Petite Bonne Serieuse 23–24, 333; 26–27, 460
Petite Fronde, La 94–99, 200
Petite Marquise, La 99–09, 472
Petites Oiseau, Les 94–99, 159
Petrified Forest, The 34–35, 435; 43–44, 423; 46–47, 485
Pets 68–69, 452
Petticoat Fever 34–35, 460
Petticoat Influence 30–31, 466
Peu de Musique, Un 23–24, 333
Peu Plus Tard, un Peu Plus Tot, Un 68–69, 258
Phaedra (see also Phedre) 66–67, 385
Phantom Lady, The 64–65, 362
Phantom Legion, The 19–20, 397
Phantom Lover, The 28–29, 366
Phantom Rival, The 09–19, 533; 21–22, 435; 25–26, 465
Phantoms 29–30, 477
Phedre (Phaedra) 94–99, 163; 09–19, 432; 63–64, 310, 345; 65–66, 430, 438
Philadelphia 29–30, 395
Philadelphia, Here I Come! 65–66, 398
Philadelphia Story, The 38–39, 467
Philanderer, The 09–19, 518; 55–56, 58

Philanthropist, The 70–71

Philharmonic-Symphony Orchestra 47–48, 423

Philip Goes Forth 30–31, 478

Philipp Hotz *(Die Grosse Wut des Philipp Hotz)* 69–70, 347

Philoctetes (1) 58–59, 52; 63–64, 368

Philoctetes (2) 58–59, 52

Philoktetes 60–61, 39

Philosopher in the Apple Orchard, The 09–19, 437

Philosophy in the Boudoir 68–69, 452, 453

Phipps 09–19, 509, 535

Phizzog 60–61, 295

Phoebe of Quality Street 20–21, 448

Phoenix, The 94–99, 247

Phoenix '55 54–55, 409s

Phoenix Too Frequent, A 49–50, 378; 70–71

Photo Finish 62–63, 297

Phroso 94–99, 248

Physician, The 94–99, 187

Physician in Spite of Himself, The (see *The Doctor in Spite of Himself*)

Physicists, The 64–65, 306

Piano Tuner, The 59–60, 40

Pick a Number XV 65–66, 422s

Picket Line 35–36, 510

Pick-up Girl 43–44, 476

Pickwick (see also *Mr. Pickwick*)

Pickwick (p) 27–28, 396

Pickwick (m) 65–66, 372s

Pickwick Papers, The (source) 99–09, 427; 27–28, 396; 52–53, 255, 301; 65–66, 372

Picnic (1) 33–34, 523

Picnic (2) 52–53, 290

Picnic on the Battlefield 59–60, 46; 61–62, 323

Picture of Dorian Gray, The (source) 27–28, 556; 36–37, 397, 398; 63–64, 344

Picture of Dorian Gray, The 63–64, 344

Pictures in the Hallway 56–57, 319; 59–60, 311; 64–65, 350; 70–71

Pie in the Sky 41–42, 421

Pied Piper, The 99–09, 574

Pied Piper of Hamelin (legend) 19–20, 438

Pierre and His People 99–09, 570

Pierre of the Plains 99–09, 570

Pierre Patelin 09–19, 561; 37–38, 467

Pierrot the Prodigal 09–19, 581; 24–25, 555

Pierrot's Journey 64–65, 297

Pieton de L'Air, Le 63–64, 326

Pietro 19–20, 417

Piff! Paff!! Pouf!!! 99–09, 457

Pig and the Pepper, The (mn) 36–37, 498

Pig Pen, The 69–70, 341

Pigeon, The 09–19, 468; 21–22, 503

Pigeons 63–64, 370; 64–65, 354

Pigeons and People 32–33, 450

Piggy 26–27, 459

Pigs 24–25, 440

Pike County Ballads 99–09, 425

Piker, The 24–25, 526

Pilate's Daughter 09–19, 539

Pile ou Face 26–27, 420

Pilgrim, The 37–38, 463

Pilgrimage, The 25–26, 492

Pilgrim's Progress (source) 99–09, 550

Pilgrim's Progress 61–62, 326

Pillar to Post 43–44, 434

Pillars of Society, (The) 99–09, 459; 09–19, 416; 31–32, 410; 50–51, 374

Pillow 61–62, 311

Pimpernel! 63–64, 354s

Pin to See the Peepshow, A 53–54, 304

Pin Up 66–67, 400

Pinafore (see *H.M.S. Pinafore*)

Pinch Hitter, A 21–22, 554

Pinion 69–70, 378

Pink and Patches 27–28, 551

Pink Dominos 94–99, 230

Pink Elephant, The *52–53*, 301
Pink Lady, The *09–19*, 441
Pink Slips on a Parade *36–37*, 497
Pinkville *70–71*
Pinocchio (source) *38–39*, 479
Pinocchio (1) *36–37*, 498
Pinocchio (2) *37–38*, 468
Pinocchio (3) *38–39*, 479; *39–40*, 472
Pinocchio (mn) *39–40*, 472
Pins and Needles (1) *21–22*, 503
Pins and Needles (2) *37–38*, 395; *66–67*, 36
Pins and Needles 1939 *38–39*, 470
Pinwheel (1) (see *Raymond Hitchcock's Pinwheel*)
Pinwheel (2) *26–27*, 475
Pioneer Days *99–09*, 527
Pi-Pa-Ki *45–46*, 426; *58–59*, 329
Pipe Dream *55–56*, 364s
Piper, The *09–19*, 438; *19–20*, 438
Piper Paid *34–35*, 429
Pipes of Pan, The *09–19*, 613
Pippa Passes *99–09*, 525
Pique *94–99*, 234
Pique-Nique en Campagne *68–69*, 450
Pirate, The *42–43*, 446
Pirates of Penzance, The (or The Slave of Duty) *09–19*, 472, 639; *26–27*, 436; *27–28*, 458; *31–32*, 377; *33–34*, 425, 514; *34–35*, 364; *35–36*, 398, 400, 497; *36–37*, 399; *38–39*, 446; *40–41*, 382; *41–42*, 431, 458; *43–44*, 456; *45–46*, 391, 457, 458; *46–47*, 408, 494; *47–48*, 373, 375; *49–50*, 356, 383; *50–51*, 353, 375; *51–52*, 334; *52–53*, 263; *55–56*, 345; *60–61*, 48; *61–62*, 304; *62–63*, 286; *63–64*, 328, 367; *64–65*, 313; *65–66*, 419; *66–67*, 367; *67–68*, 373; *68–69*, 390
Pit, The *99–09*, 454
Pitter Patter *20–21*, 387
Place for Chance, The *63–64*, 366
Place for Polly, A *69–70*, 327
Place in the Sun, A *09–19*, 646

Place of Our Own, A *44–45*, 427
Place Without Doors, A *70–71*
Place Without Twilight, A *62–63*, 291
Places Please! *37–38*, 389
Plan M *41–42*, 441
Plain and Fancy *54–55*, 394s; *63–64*, 367
Plain Jane *23–24*, 435
Plant in the Sun *37–38*, 464, 465; *38–39*, 485, 487
Plantation *69–70*, 361
Plantation Revue *22–23*, 434
Plantation Thomasin, La *94–99*, 107
Play *63–64*, 354, 362
Play, Genius, Play! *35–36*, 428
Play It Again, Sam *68–69*, 406
Play It for Comedy *37–38*, 465
Play of Daniel, The *58–59*, 52
Play of Elche, The *62–63*, 329
Play That on Your Old Piano *65–66*, 422
Play With a Tiger *64–65*, 352
Play With Fire (see *The Shop at Sly Corner*)
Play Without a Name, A *28–29*, 424
Playboy of Newark, The *42–43*, 488
Playboy of Seville, The *70–71*
Playboy of the Western World, The *09–19*, 458, 494; *20–21*, 441; *29–30*, 473; *32–33*, 407; *34–35*, 409; *37–38*, 376; *45–46*, 457; *46–47*, 430; *57–58*, 56; *63–64*, 369; *70–71*
Player Maid, The *99–09*, 498
Player Queen, The *23–24*, 336
Players From Japan, The *29–30*, 505
Playing the Game *27–28*, 470
Playroom, The *65–66*, 389
Plays for Bleecker Street *61–62*, 318
Play's the Thing, The *26–27*, 419; *27–28*, 537; *47–48*, 400
Playwrights Unit Musical Revue *63–64*, 371s
Plaza Suite *67–68*, 363

Please Get Married *09–19,* 651
Please Help Emily *09–19,* 577
Please, Mrs. Garibaldi *38–39,* 465
Pleasure Bound *28–29,* 469
Pleasure Man *28–29,* 385
Pleasure of His Company, The
 58–59, 298
Pleasure Seekers, The *09–19,* 513
Plot Against the Chase Manhattan
 Bank, The *63–64,* 352
Plot Thickens, The *22–23,* 450
Plots and Playwrights *09–19,* 579
Plough and the Stars, The *27–28,*
 459; *34–35,* 406; *37–38,* 375;
 49–50, 384, *52–53,* 308; *60–61,*
 312
Pluma en el Viento *31–32,* 500
Plumb Line, A *63–64,* 370
Plume de Ma Tante, La *58–59,* 303s
Plumes in the Dust *36–37,* 428
Plunger, The *94–99,* 213
Plutocrat, The *29–30,* 499
Plutus *63–64,* 344
Pocahontas *34–35,* 484
Pocahontas (dance program) *38–39,*
 476
Pocket Edition *39–40,* 446
Pocket Watch, The *65–66,* 428
Podrecca Marionettes (see *Teatro dei
 Piccoli*)
Poems in English (Beckett) *70–71*
Poetasters of Ispahan, The *09–19,*
 487
Point of Departure *67–68,* 412
Point of Honor, A *36–37,* 463
Point of No Return *51–52,* 298
Point of View, The *09–19,* 481
Point Valaine *34–35,* 440
Poisoned Flower, The *09–19,* 612
Poker Night, The *47–48,* 32
Poker Session, The *67–68,* 385
Poldekin *20–21,* 381
Police Inspector, The *94–99,* 130
Policeman, The *61–62,* 314
Policy Kings *38–39,* 486
Polish Jew, The *(Le Juif Polonais)*
 94–99, 150; *99–09,* 353, 442

Polish Mime Theater, The *64–65,*
 322
Polish Rabbi, The *38–39,* 494
Political Party, A *63–64,* 345
Politician, The *94–99,* 186
Polly (1) *25–26,* 468
Polly (2) *28–29,* 451
Polly of Hollywood *26–27,* 483
Polly of the Circus *99–09,* 553
Polly Preferred *22–23,* 518
Polly With a Past *09–19,* 606;
 28–29, 451
Pollyanna *09–19,* 582
Polonaise *45–46,* 396
Polygamy *09–19,* 540
Pomander Walk *09–19,* 434; *21–22,*
 498
Pomeroy's Past *25–26,* 585
Pom-pom *09–19,* 571
Ponder Heart, The *55–56,* 376
Ponteach *69–70,* 371
Poor, The *23–24,* 430
Poor Bitos *64–65,* 313; *69–70,* 373
Poor Fool, The *09–19,* 579
Poor Little Rich Girl, The *09–19,*
 492
Poor Little Ritz Girl *20–21,* 359
Poor Little Thing *09–19,* 541
Poor Nut, The *24–25,* 581
Poor of New York, The *94–99,*
 245
Poor Old Jim *28–29,* 502
Poor People *(Povera Gente)* *99–09,*
 536
Poor Richard *64–65,* 318
Pop Poems Pop Out *67–68,* 410
Poppa *28–29,* 438
Poppa Is Home *61–62,* 316
Poppy *23–24,* 313
Poppy, The *62–63,* 322
Poppy God, The *21–22,* 404
Popsy *40–41,* 415
Popularity *99–09,* 521; *09–19,* 402
Porgy *27–28,* 425; *29–30,* 391;
 35–36, 417; *41–42,* 434; *43–44,*
 412; *52–53,* 293; *60–61,* 338;
 63–64, 336

Porgy and Bess *35–36*, 416; *41–42*, 433; *43–44*, 412, 438; *52–53*, 293s; *60–61*, 338; *63–64*, 336

Pork *70–71*

Porphyria's Lover *70–71*

Port o' London *25–26*, 550

Porta Chiusa, La *23–24*, 366

Portofino *57–58*, 320s

Portofino P.T.A. *64–65*, 311

Portrait in Black *46–47*, 480

Portrait of a Lady *54–55*, 383

Portrait of a Madonna *58–59*, 333

Portrait of a Queen *67–68*, 365

Portrait of Gilbert *34–35*, 433

Portrait of the Artist *62–63*, 322

Portrait of the Artist as a Young Dog *57–58*, 289

Portrait of the Artist as a Young Man, A *61–62*, 331; *67–68*, 386

Possessed, The *39–40*, 405

Possession *28–29*, 387

Possibilities *68–69*, 437

Post Office, The *64–65*, 322

Post Road *34–35*, 420

Postcards *67–68*, 408; *69–70*, 319

Posterity for Sale *66–67*, 421

Postman Always Rings Twice, The *35–36*, 488

Postmark Zero *65–66*, 382

Pot Boiler, The *22–23*, 574

Pot Luck *21–22*, 428

Pot of Broth, A *99–09*, 378, 555

Potash and Perlmutter *09–19*, 503; *34–35*, 468

Potash and Perlmutter, Detectives *26–27*, 371

Potash and Perlmutter in Society *09–19*, 563

Potiphar's Wife *28–29*, 437

Potters, The *23–24*, 369

Potting Shed, The *56–57*, 352; *58–59*, 53; *62–63*, 339

Pound on Demand, (A) *46–47*, 438; *58–59*, 333

Poupee, La *94–99*, 212

Pour Lucrece (see *Duel of Angels*) *59–60*, 207

Pour Vivre Heureux *09–19*, 506

Pousse Cafe, or The Worst Born *94–99*, 180

Pousse-Cafe *65–66*, 403s

Povera Gente (see *Poor People*)

Poverty Is No Crime *34–35*, 453

Power (1) *29–30*, 481

Power (2) *36–37*, 492; *37–38*, 459

Power and the Glory, The *58–59*, 311

Power of Darkness, The *19–20*, 415; *59–60*, 42

Power of Gold, The *94–99*, 104

Power of the Press, The *94–99*, 119

Power Without Glory *47–48*, 376

Practical Ritual to Exorcise Frustration After Five Days of Rain, A *69–70*, 372

Praise of Folly *53–54*, 359

Pra-Veena (dance programs; see *Nataraj Vashi & Pra-Veena*)

Prayer Meeting, or the First Militant Minister *69–70*, 338

Praying Curve (see *The Love Thief*)

Precedent *30–31*, 515

Precieuses Ridicules, Les *38–39*, 492; *69–70*, 313

Precious *28–29*, 454

Pre-Honeymoon *35–36*, 505

Prelude *35–36*, 503

Prelude to Exile *36–37*, 438

Premise, The *62–63*, 334

Prenez Garde a la Peinture *32–33*, 238

Prenez Ma Dame *23–24*, 333

Prescott Proposals, The *53–54*, 330

Present Arms *27–28*, 546

Present Laughter *46–47*, 433; *57–58*, 302, 314; *70–71*

Preserving Mr. Panmure *09–19*, 466

Presidential letters, diaries, documents, statements, speeches, etc. (untitled or unnamed sources) *63–64*, 338, 350–1

President's Daughter, The *70–71*s

President's Jewish Friend, The *48–49*, 430

Press Agent, The 99–09, 502
Press Time 38–39, 485
Pressing Business 30–31, 454
Pretender, The 59–60, 41
Pretty Little Parlor 43–44, 468
Pretty Mrs. Smith 09–19, 532
Pretty Peggy 99–09, 431
Pretty Sister of Jose, The 99–09, 444
Pretty Soft 09–19, 657
Price, The (1) 09–19, 456
Price, The (2) 67–68, 363
Price of Money, The 99–09, 517
Price of Peace, The 99–09, 390
Pride 22–23, 564
Pride and Prejudice 35–36, 430; 58–59, 331
Pride of Jennico, The 99–09, 364
Pride of Mayo, The 94–99, 99
Pride of Race, The 09–19, 568
Pride's Crossing 50–51, 326
Priest's Vow, A (see *A Tale of Corsica*)
Prima Donna, The (1) 99–09, 391
Prima Donna, The (2) 99–09, 573
Prime of Miss Jean Brodie 67–68, 358
Primer for Lovers, A 29–30, 444
Primrose Path, The (1) 99–09, 539
Primrose Path, The (2) 38–39, 444
Prince Ananias 94–99, 104
Prince and the (Hob)goblins, The (mn) 35–36, 512; 38–39, 489
Prince and the Magic Sword, The (mn) 35–36, 512
Prince and the Pauper, The (source) 20–21, 400; 63–64, 348
Prince and the Pauper, The (1) 20–21, 400
Prince and the Pauper, The (2) 63–64, 348s
Prince Chap, The 99–09, 494
Prince Consort, The 99–09, 485
Prince Karl 94–99, 91, 92, 93; 99–09, 355
Prince of Bohemia, The 09–19, 409
Prince of India, The 99–09, 520

Prince of Liars, The 37–38, 465
Prince of Pilsen, The 99–09, 430; 29–30, 478
Prince Otto 99–09, 368
Prince There Was, A 09–19, 647
Prince's Secret, The 34–35, 485
Princess and the Butterfly, The 94–99, 216
Princess April 24–25, 497
Princess Beggar 99–09, 530
Princess Bonnie 94–99, 141
Princess Charming 30–31, 429
Princess Chic, The 99–09, 362
Princess Flavia 25–26, 485
Princess Ida 24–25, 573; 34–35, 367; 36–37, 402; 40–41, 430; 45–46, 458; 55–56, 345; 60–61, 48; 61–62, 332; 65–66, 419
Princess Ivona 70–71
Princess of Kensington, A 99–09, 435
Princess of Patches 94–99, 229
Princess Pat, The 09–19, 560
Princess Rebecca Birnbaum 65–66, 431
Princess Turandot 26–27, 425
Princess Virtue 20–21, 447
Priorities of 1942 41–42, 443
Prison Bars 27–28, 550
Prisoner, The 27–28, 484
Prisoner of Zenda, The (source) 94–99, 141, 258; 99–09, 568; 25–26, 485
Prisoner of Zenda, The (1) 94–99, 141, 142
Prisoner of Zenda, The (2) 99–09, 568
Prisonera, La (see *La Prisonniere*)
Prisoners of War 34–35, 445
Prisonniere, La 26–27, 390; 31–32, 501
Private Account, A 09–19, 579
Private Affair, A 35–36, 506
Private Ear, The 63–64, 307
Private Hicks 35–36, 510
Private Life of the Master Race, The 44–45, 443

Private Lives *30–31*, 483; *48–49*,
  385; *67–68*, 407; *69–70*, 307
Private Secretary, The *09–19*, 432
Privateer, The *94–99*, 204
Privilege Car *30–31*, 499
Proces, Le (see *The Trial*)
Proces de Jeanne d'Arc, Le (see *The
  Trial of Joan of Arc*)
Processional *24–25*, 521; *37–38*, 450
Procuteur Hallers, Le *24–25*, 483
Prodigal, The *59–60*, 353
Prodigal Daughter, The *94–99*, 98
Prodigal Father, The *94–99*, 85
Prodigal Husband, The *09–19*, 530
Prodigal Son, The (1) *99–09*, 494
Prodigal Son, The (2) *64–65*, 360s
Prodigal Son, The (dance program)
  41–42, 432
Prodigal Son, The (Parable of; see
  St. Luke)
Professional Men *38–39*, 484
Professor Bernhardi *67–68*, 367
Professor Fodorski *61–62*, 292
Professor Mamlock *36–37*, 493
Professor's Love Story, The *94–99*,
  186, 187; *99–09*, 384, 385; *09–19*,
  596
Profligate, The *94–99*, 260; *99–09*,
  361
Program of New American Plays, A
  66–67, 422
Progress of Bora, the Tailor, The
  68–69, 425
Projection Room, The *68–69*, 454
Prologue to Glory *37–38*, 457;
  38–39, 482; *49–50*, 384
Promenade *69–70*, 333s
Promessi Sposi, I *38–39*, 492
Promise *36–37*, 448
Promise, The *67–68*, 352
Promise at Dawn *61–62*, 274
Promises, Promises *68–69*, 395s
Proof Through the Night *42–43*,
  454
Proper Caper, The *94–99*, 211
Proposition, The *70–71*
Prospect of the Sea, A *57–58*, 289

Protective Custody *56–57*, 348
Proud Laird, The *99–09*, 490
Proud Prince, The *99–09*, 440
Proud Woman, A *26–27*, 427
Provincetown Follies *35–36*, 429
Prunella *09–19*, 512
Psalm 107 *63–64*, 314
Psyche *63–64*, 327
Psychedelic Follies *66–67*, 35
Psychodramatic Theater (untitled
  plays) *46–47*, 493
Public Eye, The *63–64*, 307
Public Relations *43–44*, 465
Pudd'nhead Wilson *94–99*, 131
Pullman Car Hiawatha *62–63*, 321
Punch and Judy shows (mn) *37–38*,
  466, 467
Punch, Judy & Co. *99–09*, 434
Punk, or The Amateur Rehearsal
  22–23, 572
Puppet Show *30–31*, 442
Puppet Theater of Don Cristobal,
  The *64–65*, 341
Puppet-Play, A *25–26*, 594
Puppets *24–25*, 556
Puppets of Passion *26–27*, 487
Puppy Love *25–26*, 540
Pure in Heart, The *33–34*, 508
Purification, The *59–60*, 49
Puritan, The *35–36*, 463
Purity *30–31*, 470
Purlie *69–70*, 318s
Purlie Victorious *61–62*, 256; *68–69*,
  455; *69–70*, 318
Purple Canary, The *62–63*, 334
Purple Dust *56–57*, 55
Purple Lady, The *94–99*, 257
Purple Mask, The *19–20*, 409
Purple Road, The *09–19*, 499
Purse of Fortunatus, The *37–38*,
  467; *38–39*, 490
Pursuit of Happiness, The *33–34*,
  439; *49–50*, 372; *51–52*, 333
Put It in Writing *62–63*, 336s
Puzzles of 1925 *24–25*, 534
Pygmalion *09–19*, 534; *26–27*, 426,
  520; *37–38*, 453; *45–46*, 417;

Pygmalion *(cont.)*
51–52, 333; 55–56, 378; 63–64,
338; 68–69, 373
Pygmalion and Galatea 94–99, 214
Pyramids 26–27, 362
Pyramus and Thisbe 68–69, 454

Quadrille 54–55, 372
Quaker Girl, The 09–19, 455
Quality Street 99–09, 399; 20–21,
448; 37–38, 467
Quarantine 24–25, 506
Quare Fellow, The 58–59, 49
Queen and the Rebels, The 64–65,
355
Queen at Home 30–31, 475
Queen Bee 29–30, 442
Queen High 26–27, 376
Queen o' Hearts 22–23, 473
Queen of Brilliants, The 94–99, 102
Queen of Liars, The 94–99, 169
Queen of Night 94–99, 130
Queen of Spades, The 31–32, 414
Queen of Spades, The (opera rep)
42–43, 487
Queen of the Moulin Rouge, The
99–09, 574
Queen of the Movies, The 09–19,
519
Queen Victoria 23–24, 353
Queen's Enemies, The 09–19, 590
Queen's Husband, The 27–28, 497
Queen's Necklace, The 94–99, 141
Queens of France 49–50, 384;
66–67, 401
Queen's Proctor, The 94–99, 186
Queen's Shilling, The 94–99, 115
Queer People 33–34, 497
Quentin Durward 94–99, 88; 40–41,
432
Question, A 62–63, 322
Question, The 09–19, 488
Quicksand 27–28, 508
Quiet City 38–39, 487
Quiet Don, The (opera rep) 44–45,
445
Quiet Man, The 60–61, 339

Quiet Please 40–41, 393
Quiet Rubber, A 94–99, 159, 160
Quincy Adams Sawyer 99–09, 413
Quinneys' 09–19, 562
Quintin Quintana 44–45, 441
Quite Early One Morning 57–58,
289
Quo Vadis (1) 99–09, 366
Quo Vadis (2) 99–09, 366
Quo Vadis (3) 35–36, 511
Quoat-Quoat 68–69, 450
Quotations From Chairman Mao
Tse-Tung 68–69, 379

R.U.R. 22–23, 471; 42–43, 450
Rabelais 69–70, 329
Rabenvater, Der 94–99, 171
Rabouilleuse, La (see also *The Honor
of the Family*) 99–09, 558; 26–27,
445
Race of Hairy Men!, A 64–65, 336
Races 34–35, 483
Rachel 09–19, 516
Rachel Cowan 28–29, 502
Rack, The 09–19, 450
Racket, The 27–28, 456
Racketty-Packetty House 09–19, 489
Radio City Music Hall (inaugural
program) 32–33, 443
Rafaga, La 31–32, 500
Raffles, the Amateur Cracksman
(Raffles) 99–09, 442; 09–19, 429
Ragged Army 33–34, 502
Ragged Earl, The 94–99, 251
Ragged Edge, The 35–36, 440
Ragged Regiment, The 94–99, 232
Ragina Devi (dance programs)
46–47, 486
Raiders, The 99–09, 489
Railroad of Love, The 94–99, 119
Rain (source) 22–23, 483; 34–35,
451; 44–45, 397
Rain (1) 22–23, 483; 24–25, 443;
34–35, 451; 44–45, 397; 45–46,
450; 47–48, 428; 51–52, 332;
69–70, 374
Rain (2) 28–29, 503

Rain From Heaven *34–35*, 427
Rain in the Doorway *70–71*
Rain or Shine *27–28*, 506
Rainbow *28–29*, 423
Rainbow, The *09–19*, 468
Rainbow Girl, The *09–19*, 626
Rainbow on the Road *68–69*, 411
Rainbow Rose *25–26*, 570
Rainbows for Sale *70–71*
Rainmaker, The *54–55*, 371; *63–64*, 311
Rainmakers, The *94–99*, 123
Rainy Day in Newark, A *63–64*, 310
Raisin' Hell in the Sun *62–63*, 313
Raisin in the Sun, A *58–59*, 328; *68–69*, 442, 456
Rajah's Diamond, The *28–29*, 490
Rake's Progress, The *49–50*, 386
Rambler Rose *09–19*, 606
Ramblers, The *26–27*, 382
Ram's Horn, The *63–64*, 367
Ramshackle Inn *43–44*, 446
Rang Tang *27–28*, 388
Ranger, The *99–09*, 543
Ransom's Folly *99–09*, 453
Rap, The *30–31*, 512
Rape of Lucretia, The *48–49*, 404
Rape of the Belt *60–61*, 306
Rape of the Sabine Women, The *48–49*, 427
Rapid Transit *26–27*, 505
Rapunzel (mn) *35–36*, 512
Raquel Meller *25–26*, 584; *26–27*, 412
Rashomon *58–59*, 317
Rat, The *24–25*, 538
Rat Race, The *49–50*, 364
Rate of Exchange *67–68*, 404
Rats *67–68*, 407
Rats, The *(Die Ratten)* *65–66*, 406
Rat's Mass, A *69–70*, 375
Rats of Norway, The *47–48*, 399
Ratten, Die (see *The Rats*)
Rattle of a Simple Man *62–63*, 306
Ratto Sabine, Il (see *The Seizure of the Sabines*)

Raub der Sabinerinnen, Der (see also *The Seizure of the Sabines*) *94–99*, 85; *48–49*, 427
Raveled Sleeve, The *38–39*, 488
Raw Meat *32–33*, 479
Raymond Duncan *46–47*, 499; *47–48*, 429
Raymond Hitchcock's Pinwheel *21–22*, 556
Raymonde *94–99*, 143, 144
Razzle Dazzle *50–51*, 352
Ready Money *09–19*, 473, 624
Ready When You Are, C.B.! *64–65*, 318
Real Reel *70–71*
Real Thing, The *09–19*, 447
Reaper, The *40–41*, 431
Reapers, The *35–36*, 510
Reason Why, The *69–70*, 376
Rebecca *44–45*, 411
Rebecca of Sunnybrook Farm *09–19*, 426; *37–38*, 467
Rebel, The *99–09*, 368
Rebellion *09–19*, 452
Rebels, The *37–38*, 461
Rebound *29–30*, 487
Recapture *29–30*, 484
Reckoning, The *99–09*, 533
Reckoning, The, or A Surreal Southern Fable *69–70*, 339
Reclining Figure *54–55*, 365
Recluse, The *65–66*, 433
Recorder, a History, The *69–70*, 354
Recount *38–39*, 485
Recruits *34–35*, 471; *35–36*, 510; *36–37*, 497
Rector's Garden, The *99–09*, 560
Red Blinds *26–27*, 390
Red Canary, The *09–19*, 525
Red Cat, The *34–35*, 376
Red Cloak, The *09–19*, 560
Red Cross *67–68*, 405
Red Dawn, The *19–20*, 344
Red Dust *27–28*, 485
Red Eye of Love *61–62*, 303
Red Falcon, The *24–25*, 467
Red Feather *99–09*, 444

Red Geranium, The *21–22*, 544
Red Gloves *48–49*, 398
Red Harvest *36–37*, 475
Red Horse Animation, The *70–71*
Red, Hot and Blue *36–37*, 424;
    64–65, 357
Red Kloof, The *99–09*, 395
Red Lamp, The *94–99*, 120
Red Light Annie *23–24*, 307
Red Lily, The *26–27*, 469
Red Mill, The (1) *99–09*, 520;
    45–46, 398
Red Mill, The (2) *28–29*, 434
Red Moon, The *99–09*, 583
Red Pepper *21–22*, 552
Red Peppers *36–37*, 435; *45–46*,
    450; *47–48*, 385; *60–61*, 48
Red Petticoat, The *09–19*, 484
Red Planet *32–33*, 437
Red Poppy, The *22–23*, 502
Red Rainbow, A *53–54*, 302
Red Riding Hood (see *Little Red
    Riding Hood*)
Red Robe, The *28–29*, 441
Red Rose, The *09–19*, 446
Red Roses for Me *55–56*, 367;
    61–62, 314
Red Rust *29–30*, 462
Red Velvet Goat, The *38–39*, 452
Red White and Black, The *70–71*
Red, White and Blue, The *94–99*,
    246
Red, White and Maddox *68–69*,
    403s
Red Widow, The *09–19*, 457
Redemption (see also *The Living
    Corpse*) *09–19*, 639; *28–29*, 419;
    29–30, 459
Redemption of David Corson, The
    99–09, 506
Redemptor, The *58–59*, 51
Redhead *58–59*, 319s; *67–68*, 410
Redskin, The *99–09*, 510
Redwoods *32–33*, 377
Re-echo *33–34*, 478
Reflected Glory *36–37*, 408
Refrigerators, The *70–71*

Regeneration, The *99–09*, 567
Regina *49–50*, 359; *63–64*, 363
Regina Devi (dance programs)
    44–45, 440; *45–46*, 455
Reginald & Gladys Laubin (dance
    programs) *47–48*, 415
Regular Feller, A *19–20*, 351
Regular Fix, A *36–37*, 496
Regular Guy, A *30–31*, 533
Rehearsal *38–39*, 485, 486, 487
Rehearsal, The *(La Repetition, ou
    L'Amour Puni)* *51–52*, 332;
    52–53, 273; *63–64*, 303
Reine Morte, La *65–66*, 397
Reinar Despues de Morir (see *Rule
    After Death*)
Rejuvenation of Aunt Mary, The
    99–09, 550
Relapse, The, or Virtue in Danger
    50–51, 328
Relations (1) *28–29*, 360
Relations (2) *70–71*
Release *25–26*, 590
Reluctant Debutante, The *56–57*,
    322
Remains To Be Seen *51–52*, 283
Remarkable Mr. Pennypacker, The
    53–54, 334
Remarkable Woman, A *94–99*, 129
Remember the Day *35–36*, 409
Remember the Maine *94–99*, 249
Remembrance of James Agee, The
    63–64, 369
Remnant *09–19*, 644
Remo Bufano Marionettes *35–36*,
    512; *36–37*, 498
Remolienda, La (see *The Bawdy
    Party*)
Remote Control *29–30*, 390
Renard *69–70*, 375
Rendezvous *32–33*, 399
Rendezvous at Senlis *60–61*, 44
Reno & Calvert's Punch & Judy
    Show *37–38*, 467
Rented Earl, The *09–19*, 546
Repetition, La, or L'Amour Puni
    (see *The Rehearsal*)

Report, The *69–70*, 334
Report for Duty *94–99*, 256
Reprisal *24–25*, 584
Reprise *34–35*, 476
Republic, The *69–70*, 367, 374
Request Stop *69–70*, 345
Requiem for a Nun *58–59*, 319
Rescuing Angel, The *09–19*, 609
Reserve Two for Murder *38–39*, 488
Resistible Rise of Arturo Ui, The *63–64*, 398; *68–69*, 398
Resounding Tinkle, The *60–61*, 44
Respect for Riches *19–20*, 453
Respectful Prostitute, The *47–48*, 390, 426; *49–50*, 384
Respectfully Yours *46–47*, 432
Restless Flame, The *51–52*, 334
Restless Women *27–28*, 481
Resurrection *99–09*, 429
Resurrection, The *34–35*, 410
Retour de Ma(e)lum, Le *94–99*, 99, 235
Retreat to Pleasure *40–41*, 400
Retrieved Reformation, A *09–19*, 411; *21–22*, 475
Return, The *62–63*, 339
Return Engagement *40–41*, 391
Return From Jerusalem, The *09–19*, 463
Return of Eve, The *99–09*, 579
Return of Peter Grimm, The *09–19*, 454; *21–22*, 424
Return of Second City in "20,000 Frozen Grenadiers" *65–66*, 434
Return of the Vagabond, The *39–40*, 462
Reuben, Reuben *67–68*, 357
Reunion *37–38*, 437
Reunion in New York *39–40*, 437
Reunion in Vienna *31–32*, 432
Rev. Griffith Davenport *94–99*, 251
Reveil, Le *99–09*, 557
Revelation *(There Shall Be No Night)* *39–40*, 29
Revellers, The *09–19*, 399
Revelry *27–28*, 401

Revenge of the Forty-seven Ronin, The (mn) *65–66*, 403
Revenge, or The Pride of Lillian Le Mar *09–19*, 496
Revenge With Music *34–35*, 418
Revenger's Tragedy, The *68–69*, 455; *69–70*, 373
Reverend Ferdinand and Bessie Mae *70–71*
Revisor *(The Inspector General)* *34–35*, 452
Revolt *28–29*, 408
Revolt, The *09–19*, 549
Revolt of the Beavers, The *36–37*, 496
Revolt of the Mummies, The *22–23*, 570
Revue of Revues, The *09–19*, 452
Revue Russe *22–23*, 471
Rhapsody *44–45*, 399
Rhapsody, The *30–31*, 412
Rhapsody in Black *30–31*, 523
Rhinoceros *60–61*, 316; *61–62*, 254
Rhyme of the Ancient Mariner, The (see *The Ancient Mariner*)
Rhythm of the City, The *28–29*, 500
Rich Full Life, The *45–46*, 404
Rich Man, Poor Man *09–19*, 584
Rich Man's Son, A (1) *99–09*, 352
Rich Man's Son, A (2) *09–19*, 482
Rich Mr. Hoggenheimer, The *99–09*, 524; *26–27*, 459
Rich Mrs. Repton, The *99–09*, 473
Rich Uncle, The *42–43*, 490
Richard II *36–37*, 460; *37–38*, 368; *39–40*, 451; *50–51*, 343; *56–57*, 324; *58–59*, 316; *61–62*, 343; *62–63*, 295, 305; *63–64*, 360
Richard III *94–99*, 88; *99–09*, 476, 477, 486, 558; *09–19*, 443, 545, 599, 642; *19–20*, 435; *29–30*, 516; *30–31*, 471; *34–25*, 428; *42–43*, 469; *48–49*, 411; *53–54*, 325; *58–59*, 316; *62–63*, 305; *63–64*, 353, 360; *66–67*, 106; *69–70*, 376; *70–71*
Richard Carvel *99–09*, 370

Richard Lovelace *99–09*, 394
Richard of Bordeaux *33–34*, 496
Richard Savage *99–09*, 387
Richelieu *94–99*, 88, 145; *99–09*,
   470, 476, 477; *09–19*, 443, 545,
   599, 642; *29–30*, 468; *34–35*, 428
Richest Girl, The *99–09*, 578
Richter's Wife *99–09*, 484
Riddle Me This *31–32*, 485; *32–33*,
   475
Riddle: Woman, The *09–19*, 641
Ride a Black Horse *70–71*
Ride for Life, A *94–99*, 98
Ride the Right Bus *51–52*, 333
Rider of Dreams, The *09–19*, 598
Riders to the Sea *09–19*, 458, 494;
   34–35, 411; *36–37*, 497; *37–38*,
   463; *48–49*, 427; *56–57*, 55
Ridi, Pagliaccio *23–24*, 364
Riding Hood Revisited *60–61*, 45
Riding to Lithend, The *24–25*, 585
Right Age to Marry, The *25–26*,
   552
Right Angle Triangle, A *38–39*, 487
Right Girl, The *20–21*, 436
Right Honorable Gentleman, The
   65–66, 378
Right Next to Broadway *43–44*, 459
Right of Happiness *30–31*, 510
Right of Possession *29–30*, 537
Right of Way, The *99–09*, 549
Right This Way *37–38*, 413
Right to Be Happy, The *09–19*, 470
Right to Dream, The *23–24*, 440
Right to Happiness, The *09–19*, 463
Right to Kill, The *25–26*, 553
Right to Love, The *24–25*, 602
Right to Strike, The *21–22*, 447
Right You Are if You Think You
   Are *26–27*, 486; *50–51*, 373;
   56–57, 58; *63–64*, 359; *66–67*, 371
Righteous Are Bold, The *55–56*, 366
Rights of the Soul, The *94–99*, 220
Rigoletto (opera rep) *43–44*, 474;
   45–46, 391, 440; *46–47*, 409, 479;
   47–48, 343, 347, 399
Rimers of Eldritch, The *66–67*, 413

Ring and the Book, The *26–27*, 413;
   28–29, 421; *29–30*, 437
Ring Around Elizabeth *41–42*, 414
Ring Round the Moon *50–51*, 329;
   59–60, 43
Ring Two *39–40*, 414
Ringmaster, The *09–19*, 396
Ringside *28–29*, 365
Ringside Seat *38–39*, 428
Rio Grande *09–19*, 573
Rio Rita *26–27*, 475
Riot *68–69*, 457
Riot Act, The *62–63*, 300
Rip Torn's Richard *69–70*, 376
Rip Van Winkle *94–99*, 129; *99–09*,
   497; *47–48*, 341
Ripples *29–30*, 491
Rise and Fall of the City of
   Mahagonny, The *63–64*, 342;
   69–70, 366
Rise of Rosie O'Reilly, The *23–24*,
   375
Rise of Silas Lapham, The *19–20*,
   389
Rising Generation, The *94–99*, 110
Rising of the Moon, The *99–09*,
   555; *09–19*, 458, 494; *32–33*, 407;
   36–37, 497; *37–38*, 463
Rising Son, The *24–25*, 478
Rita Coventry *22–23*, 534
Rites of Actuality, The *62–63*, 335
Ritornell *26–27*, 504
Ritual *70–71*
Ritz Revue (see *Hassard Short's Ritz
   Revue*)
Ritzy *29–30*, 490
Rivalry, The *58–59*, 321
Rivals, The *94–99*, 135; *99–09*, 351;
   09–19, 410, 488; *21–22*, 555;
   22–23, 568; *29–30*, 511; *41–42*,
   428; *52–53*, 307; *61–62*, 312
River, The *64–65*, 353
River Line, The *56–57*, 58
River Sumida, The (*Sumidagawa*)
   70–71
Riverside Drive *63–64*, 358
Riverwind *62–63*, 322s

Riviera Girl, The *09–19*, 607
Road Round Ireland, The *66–67*, 417
Road to Arcady, The *09–19*, 486
Road to Happiness, The (1) *09–19*, 556
Road to Happiness, The (2) *26–27*, 519
Road to Mandalay, The *09–19*, 572
Road to Rio, The *29–30*, 534
Road to Rome, The *26–27*, 471; *27–28*, 557
Road to Ruin, The *94–99*, 112
Road to Yesterday, The *99–09*, 530
Road Together, The *23–24*, 387
Roadhouse in Arden, 1616–1916, The *09–19*, 560
Roads and Rain *25–26*, 592
Roads of Destiny *09–19*, 646
Roadside *30–31*, 421; *47–48*, 424
Roar China *30–31*, 440
Roar Like a Dove *63–64*, 339
Roar of the Greasepaint—The Smell of the Crowd, The *64–65*, 338s
Roaring Dick and Co. *94–99*, 183
Rob Roy *94–99*, 101; *09–19*, 507
Robbery, The *20–21*, 432
Robe Rouge, La *99–09*, 472; *19–20*, 430
Robert Burns *99–09*, 483
Robert E. Lee *23–24*, 357
Robert Emmet *99–09*, 413, 414
Robert Molnar *66–67*, 423
Roberta *33–34*, 458
Robespierre *99–09*, 353
Robin Hood *94–99*, 117; *99–09*, 367, 405, 416; *09–19*, 471, 638; *29–30*, 444; *31–32*, 471; *35–36*, 512; *44–45*, 396
Robin Hood (mn) *36–37*, 498; *38–39*, 489
Robin Hood of Sherwood Forest *47–48*, 430
Robin Landing *37–38*, 392
Robinson Crusoe, Jr. *09–19*, 571
Rock Me, Julie *30–31*, 486
Rock-a-Bye Baby *09–19*, 630

Rockbound *28–29*, 495
Rockefeller and the Red Indians *68–69*, 389
Rocket to the Moon *38–39*, 430; *44–45*, 436; *46–47*, 485; *70–71*
Rodion the Student (see *The Story of Rodion the Student*)
Roger Bloomer *22–23*, 538
Rogers Brothers in Central Park, The *99–09*, 371
Rogers Brothers in Harvard, The *99–09*, 414
Rogers Brothers in Ireland, The *99–09*, 494
Rogers Brothers in London, The *99–09*, 435
Rogers Brothers in Panama, The *99–09*, 543
Rogers Brothers in Paris, The *99–09*, 464
Rogers Brothers in Wall Street, The *99–09*, 350
Rogers Brothers in Washington, The *99–09*, 393
Rogues and Vagabonds *29–30*, 535
Rogue's Comedy, The *94–99*, 186, 187
Roi Cerf, Le *37–38*, 469
Roland Petit (dance programs; see *Les Ballets de Paris*)
Roll, Sweet Chariot *34–35*, 384
Rollicking Girl, The *99–09*, 490
Rolling Stones *09–19*, 555
Rollo's Wild Oat *20–21*, 408
Roly Poly *09–19*, 486
Roly-Boly Eyes *19–20*, 357
Romainia That's the Old Country *68–69*, 457
Roman Candle *59–60*, 316
Roman Servant, A *34–35*, 419
Romance *09–19*, 118, 495; *20–21*, 430; *48–49*, 390
Romance and Arabella *09–19*, 610
Romance in a Toy Shop *34–35*, 485
Romance in Cherry Blossom Lane *(Koi-No-Yozakura) 29–30*, 505

Romance of Athlone, A *94–99*, 249;
  99–09, 390
Romancin' Round *27–28*, 421
Romanesques, The *99–09*, 403
Romanoff and Juliet *57–58*, 291
Romantic Age, The *22–23*, 488
Romantic Mr. Dickens *40–41*, 397
Romantic Young Lady, The *25–26*,
  596; *26–27*, 520
Romantiques, Les *59–60*, 358
Rome Haul *32–33*, 459; *34–35*, 400
Romeo and Jeannette *69–70*, 373
Romeo and Juliet *94–99*, 167, 194,
  226, 257, 259; *99–09*, 402, 428,
  469, 470, 477; *09–19*, 413, 433,
  443, 447, 478, 508, 545, 565, 627,
  642; *21–22*, 497; *22–23*, 514, 524;
  23–24, 328; *29–30*, 527; *30–31*,
  426; *32–33*, 424; *34–35*, 424;
  35–36, 452; *39–40*, 461; *49–50*,
  357; *50–51*, 356; *55–56*, 55; *56–57*,
  324; *58–59*, 316; *60–61*, 46; *61–62*,
  286, 327; *62–63*, 305; *65–66*, 97;
  66–67, 382; *68–69*, 422; *70–71*
Romeo From Brooklyn, The *48–49*,
  430
Romeo's First Love *94–99*, 124
Romulus *61–62*, 281
Ronde, La *59–60*, 43; *69–70*, 345
Rondelay *69–70*, 345
Roof, The *31–32*, 419
Rook, The *63–64*, 370
Room, The *64–65*, 349
Room in Hotel Babylon, A *63–64*,
  370
Room in Red and White, A *35–36*,
  461
Room of Dreams *30–31*, 446
Room Service *36–37*, 485; *52–53*,
  297; *62–63*, 339; *69–70*, 367
Room 349 *29–30*, 529
Roomful of Roses, A *55–56*, 354
Rooming House, The *69–70*, 356
Rooms *65–66*, 429
Roosty *37–38*, 424
Roots (1) *60–61*, 359; *64–65*, 362
Roots (2) *69–70*, 371
Roots in the Wasteland *50–51*, 374

Rope *27–28*, 515
Rope, The *65–66*, 436
Rope Dancers, The *57–58*, 302;
  58–59, 53
Ropes *24–25*, 586
Rope's End *29–30*, 399
Rory of the Hills *94–99*, 120
Rosa Machree *21–22*, 494
Rosalee Pritchett *70–71*
Rosalie (1) *09–19*, 589 (and 605)
Rosalie (2) *27–28*, 488
Rosalind *09–19*, 557
Rosalinda *42–43*, 441
Rosario & Antonio (dance programs)
  45–46, 456; *47–48*, 416, 418
Rosary, The *09–19*, 428
Rose *69–70*, 345
Rose, The *99–09*, 487
Rose and the Ring, The *47–48*, 430
Rose Bernd *22–23*, 463
Rose Briar *22–23*, 508
Rose Girl, The *20–21*, 426
Rose Maid, The *09–19*, 470
Rose Marionettes (see *Rufus Rose
  Marionettes*)
Rose Michel *94–99*, 218
Rose o' Plymouth-Town, A *99–09*,
  417
Rose of Algeria, The (see also
  Algeria) *09–19*, 400
Rose of Alhambra, The *99–09*, 533
Rose of China, The *19–20*, 390
Rose of Panama, The *09–19*, 464
Rose of Persia, The *99–09*, 369
Rose of Stamboul, The *21–22*, 523
Rose of the Rancho, The *99–09*, 527
Rose of the Wilderness *48–49*, 426
Rose Tattoo, The *50–51*, 347;
  66–67, 358
Roseanne *23–24*, 379
Rosedale *94–99*, 104; *09–19*, 500
Rose-Marie *24–25*, 445; *26–27*, 467
Rosemary (1) *94–99*, 175; *09–19*,
  543
Rosemary (2) *60–61*, 38
Rosemary and the Planet *59–60*, 47
Rosencrantz and Guildenstern
  67–68, 171

Rosencrantz and Guildenstern Are Dead *67–68*, 344; *70–71*

Rosmersholm *99–09*, 456; *24–25*, 582; *35–36*, 445; *46–47*, 484; *61–62*, 328

Ross *61–62*, 275

Rossum's Universal Robots (see *R.U.R.*)

Rothschilds, The *70–71*s

Rotters, The *21–22*, 549

Rouget De L'Isle *99–09*, 422

Roughing It *39–40*, 471; *65–66*, 404

Round of Pleasure, A *94–99*, 202

Round the Family Table *38–39*, 494

Round the Town *23–24*, 439

Round Trip *44–45*, 433

Round Up, The *99–09*, 542; *31–32*, 490

Round With Ring, A *69–70*, 371

Rounders, The *99–09*, 346

Route 1 *64–65*, 347

Royal Box, The *94–99*, 219; *99–09*, 536; *28–29*, 422

Royal Chef, The *99–09*, 463

Royal Family, A *99–09*, 369; *28–29*, 430

Royal Family, The *27–28*, 483; *50–51*, 341

Royal Fandango, A *23–24*, 350

Royal Gambit *58–59*, 51; *62–63*, 339

Royal Hunt of the Sun, The *65–66*, 382

Royal Mounted, The *99–09*, 561

Royal Peacock, The *26–27*, 520

Royal Rival, A *99–09*, 393

Royal Rogue, A *99–09*, 382

Royal Vagabond, The *09–19*, 652

Royal Virgin, The *29–30*, 512

Royalist, The *99–09*, 417

Rubicon, The *21–22*, 515

Ruddigore *26–27*, 530; *31–32*, 380; *34–35*, 366; *36–37*, 402; *41–42*, 458; *43–44*, 457, 488; *49–50*, 384; *55–56*, 346; *63–64*, 367; *64–65*, 313; *65–66*, 419; *66–67*, 367; *70–71*

Ruffian on the Stair, The *69–70*, 344

Rufus LeMaire's Affairs *26–27*, 499

Rufus Rose Marionettes *37–38*, 466

Rugantino *63–64*, 323s

Rugged Path, The *45–46*, 406

Ruggles of Red Gap *09–19*, 567

"Ruined" Lady, The *19–20*, 416

"Ruint" *24–25*, 567

Rule After Death *(Reinar Despues de Morir)* *53–54*, 322

Rule of Three, The *09–19*, 522

Rules of the Game, The *60–61*, 44

Ruling Power, The *99–09*, 456

Rumpelstiltskin (source) *61–62*, 328

Rumpelstiltskin *47–48*, 430

Rumple *57–58*, 299s

Run, Little Chillun *32–33*, 469; *43–44*, 406

Run on the Bank, A *94–99*, 117

Run Sheep Run *38–39*, 424

Runaway, The *09–19*, 453

Runaway Colt, A *94–99*, 157

Runaway Girl, The *94–99*, 233

Runaways, The *99–09*, 433

Runnin' Wild *23–24*, 344

Running Dogs *35–36*, 510

Running for Office *99–09*, 432

Rupert of Hentzau *94–99*, 258

Ruptured Duck, The *45–46*, 458

Ruse of the Empty City, The *29–30*, 497

Rush City *94–99*, 106

Russet Mantle *35–36*, 460

Russia *09–19*, 509

Russian plays (untitled program) *34–35*, 483

Russian Bank *39–40*, 464

Russian People, The *42–43*, 455

Rust *23–24*, 394

Rut, The *22–23*, 570

Ruth Draper *32–33*, 419; *34–35*, 430; *35–36*, 462; *36–37*, 498; *38–39*, 488; *40–41*, 433; *42–43*, 488; *46–47*, 464; *47–48*, 371; *53–54*, 338; *54–55*, 386; *56–57*, 347

Ruth Mata & Eugene Hari (dance programs) *46–47*, 486; *47–48*, 416

Ruth St. Denis & Ted Shawn (dance programs) *41–42*, 457; *44–45*, 440
Rutherford and (&) Son *09–19*, 489; *26–27*, 507
Ryan Girl, The *45–46*, 384

S.S. Glencairn *24–25*, 480; *28–29*, 452; *47–48*, 348
S.S. Tenacity, The *21–22*, 488
Sabine Women, The *46–47*, 485
Sabrina Fair *53–54*, 319
Sacco and Vanzetti *63–64*, 364
Sacco-Vanzetti! *68–69*, 455
Sacrament of Judas, The *99–09*, 442; *09–19*, 509
Sacred and Profane Love *19–20*, 429
Sacred Flame, The *28–29*, 418; *52–53*, 257
Sacrifice, The *20–21*, 445
Sacrifice of Isaac, The *47–48*, 432
Sadie Love *09–19*, 565
Sadie Thompson *44–45*, 397
Sadler's Wells Ballet (dance programs) *49–50*, 385–6
Sadler's Wells Theater Ballet (dance programs) *51–52*, 330–1
Sag Harbor *99–09*, 372
Sage of the Comstock Lode *39–40*, 471
Sail Away *61–62*, 257s
Sailor, Beware! *33–34*, 437; *34–35*, 477
Sailors of Cattaro *34–35*, 423
Saint: titles abbreviated St. are in alphabetical order under ST
Saint, The *24–25*, 469
Saint and the Fool, The (see *Joan*)
Saint Joan *23–24*, 378; *35–36*, 492; *43–44*, 488; *47–48*, 429; *49–50*, 382, 384; *51–52*, 284; *56–57*, 317; *61–62*, 286; *67–68*, 348
Saint Joan of the Stockyards *61–62*, 318; *63–64*, 369
Saint of Bleecker Street, The *54–55*, 387; *65–66*, 371
Saint Wench *32–33*, 446

Saintliness of Margery Kempe, The *58–59*, 51
Saints Alive *41–42*, 461
Sakura *28–29*, 443
Salad Days *58–59*, 53
Salad of the Mad Cafe, The *63–64*, 363
Salamander, The *09–19*, 536
Sally *20–21*, 413; *47–48*, 403s
Sally Bowles *51–52*, 83
Sally in Our Alley *99–09*, 414
Sally, Irene and Mary *22–23*, 448; *24–25*, 561
Sally Nusbaum Marionettes *45–46*, 458
Salome *09–19*, 512, 612; *21–22*, 550; *22–23*, 566; *67–68*, 411
Salome (opera rep) *46–47*, 412; *47–48*, 343
Salomy Jane *99–09*, 531
Salomy Jane's Kiss *99–09*, 531
Salon, The *68–69*, 454
Salt of the Earth, The *94–99*, 220
Salt Water *29–30*, 449
Salut a Moliere *63–64*, 326
Saluta *34–35*, 363
Salute to Negro Troops *41–42*, 460
Salvation (1) *27–28*, 501
Salvation (2) *39–40*, 474
Salvation (3) *69–70*, 340s
Salvation Nell *99–09*, 572
Sam Abramovitch *26–27*, 463
Sam Ego's House *49–50*, 385
Sam Houston *99–09*, 523
Samaritaine, La *09–19*, 432
Sambo *69–70*, 345s; *70–71*
Sam'l of Posen *94–99*, 110
Samson (1) *94–99*, 134
Samson (2) *99–09*, 571; *36–37*, 500
Samson and Delilah *20–21*, 405
San Toy *99–09*, 373
Sancho Panza *23–24*, 359
Sand *66–67*, 36
Sandalwood *26–27*, 386
Sandbar Queen, The *09–19*, 612
Sandbox, The *59–60*, 39; *60–61*, 38; *61–62*, 323

Sandhog *54–55*, 376s
Sandro Botticelli *22–23*, 548
Sans Famille *38–39*, 490
Sansone (see *Samson* 2)
Santa Maria *94–99*, 178
Sap, The *24–25*, 505
Sap From Syracuse (see *So Was Napoleon*)
Sap of Life, The *61–62*, 308s
Sap Runs High, The *35–36*, 479
Sapho (1) *94–99*, 126; *99–09*, 472; *09–19*, 432
Sapho (2) *99–09*, 361, 362, 501, 557
Sapphire King, The *24–25*, 577
Sappho *59–60*, 42
Sappho and Phaon *99–09*, 549
Sarah and the Sax *63–64*, 365
Sarah Simple *40–41*, 430
Saratoga *59–60*, 309s
Saratoga Trunk *59–60*, 309
Sarg Marionettes (see *Tony Sarg Marionettes*)
Sari *09–19*, 519; *29–30*, 484
Satellite *35–36*, 437
Satisfaction Guaranteed *68–69*, 446
Saturday Evening Post, The *09–19*, 503
Saturday It Rained *32–33*, 436
Saturday Night (1) *26–27*, 411
Saturday Night (2) *40–41*, 431
Saturday Night (3) *67–68*, 402
Saturday Night, A *32–33*, 468
Saturday to Monday *09–19*, 608
Saturday's Children *26–27*, 468; *27–28*, 538
Sauce for the Goose *09–19*, 443
Saucy Sally *99–09*, 458
Sauerkraut Seeds *46–47*, 493
Savage *70–71*
Savage Rhythm *31–32*, 457
Savages Under the Skin *26–27*, 497
Save It for Your Death Bed *68–69*, 432
Save Me a Place at Forest Lawn *62–63*, 335
Save Me the Waltz *37–38*, 428
Save the Pieces *46–47*, 493

Saved *70–71*
Saved From the Sea *94–99*, 161
Saving Grace, The (1) *09–19*, 638
Saving Grace, The (2) *62–63*, 333
Savoirs *09–19*, 547
Savonarola *41–42*, 459
Say, Darling *57–58*, 327s; *58–59*, 324; *65–66*, 436
Say It With Flowers *26–27*, 436
Say Nothing *64–65*, 353
Say When (1) *28–29*, 352
Say When (2) *34–35*, 405
Sayings of Mao Tse-Tung, The *67–68*, 411
Says and Ways Among the Hongdorshes *60–61*, 294
Scalawag *26–27*, 501
Scandal *19–20*, 350
Scandal, The *09–19*, 427
Scandal in Bohemia, A *64–65*, 328
Scandals (see *George White's Scandals*)
Scapegoat, The *49–50*, 385
Scapin *(Les Fourberies de Scapin)* *38–39*, 492; *52–53*, 270; *60–61*, 325; *63–64*, 327, 360; *66–67*, 419; *69–70*, 313
Scaramouche *23–24*, 342
Scarecrow, The *09–19*, 437; *53–54*, 356
Scarlet Fox, The *27–28*, 533
Scarlet Letter, The *94–99*, 91, 92, 93; *99–09*, 486, 487
Scarlet Lily, The *26–27*, 469
Scarlet Lullaby *67–68*, 403
Scarlet Man, The *21–22*, 398
Scarlet Pages *29–30*, 388
Scarlet Pimpernel, The *09–19*, 428; *63–64*, 354
Scarlet Sister Mary *30–31*, 460
Scenario, The *94–99*, 229
Scene of the Crime, The *39–40*, 450
Scenes From American Life *70–71*
Scent of Flowers, A *69–70*, 344
Schemers *24–25*, 452
Schloss, Das (see *The Castle*)
Schmendrick *47–48*, 431

School *09–19,* 516
School Days *99–09,* 568
School for Brides *44–45,* 366
School for Husbands, The (1) *99–09,* 488
School for Husbands, The (2; *L'Ecole des Maris*) *33–34,* 442; *63–64,* 327
School for Scandal, The *94–99,* 155, 239; *99–09,* 350, 405, 452, 478; *09–19,* 408; *22–23,* 581; *25–26,* 481, 508; *31–32,* 428; *53–54,* 356; *61–62,* 326; *62–63,* 294; *66–67,* 371
School for Virtue *30–31,* 519
School for Wives, The *(L'Ecole des Femmes)* *50–51,* 359; *63–64,* 327, 359; *69–70,* 313; *70–71*
School Girl, The (1) *94–99,* 160
School Girl, The (2) *99–09,* 463
Schoolgirl *30–31,* 459
Schoolhouse on the Lot *37–38,* 433
Schosskind, Das *94–99,* 157
Schwabenstreich, Der *94–99,* 90
Schwartze Mama *47–48,* 431
Schweiger *25–26,* 575
Science magazine (source) *47–48,* 383
Score *70–71*
Scorpion, The *33–34,* 464
Scotch Mist *26–27,* 382
Scotland Yard *29–30,* 407
Scoutcraft *39–40,* 473
Scrambled Wives *20–21,* 364
Scrap Book (see *Chamberlain Brown's Scrap Book*)
Scrap of Paper, A *94–99,* 115; *09–19,* 527
Scrap of Paper, The *09–19,* 607
Scrapbook *53–54,* 358
Scrape o' the Pen, A *09–19,* 478
Scratch *70–71*
Screen-Test *66–67,* 35
Scuba Duba *67–68,* 388
Scwartse Mamme *38–39,* 493
Sea and the Shore, The *62–63,* 309
Sea chanteys *46–47,* 491

Sea Dogs *39–40,* 409
Sea Is Boiling Hot, The *58–59,* 255
Sea Legs *36–37,* 484
Sea Woman, The *25–26,* 430
Seacoast of Bohemia *61–62,* 318s
Seagull (Sea Gull), The *09–19,* 560; *28–29,* 491; *29–30,* 393, 403, 501; *37–38,* 436; *44–45,* 436; *52–53,* 309; *53–54,* 353; *56–57,* 55; *61–62,* 326; *63–64,* 332
Seagulls Over Sorrento *52–53,* 255
Search Me *09–19,* 555
Searching for the Sun *35–36,* 485
Searching Wind, The *43–44,* 467
Season Changes, The *35–36,* 451
Season in Hell *50–51,* 374
Season in Hell, A *69–70,* 378
Season in the Sun *50–51,* 317
Season of Celebration *37–38,* 465
Season of Choice *58–59,* 51
Seats of the Mighty, The *94–99,* 121
Second Act, The *26–27,* 523
Second Best Bed *46–47,* 407
Second Comin', The *31–32,* 445
Second Door Left *69–70,* 375
Second Fiddle, The *99–09,* 474
Second Hurricane, The *36–37,* 499
Second in Command, The *99–09,* 394; *09–19,* 513
Second Lady Delcombe, The *99–09,* 538
Second Little Show *30–31,* 407
Second Man, The *26–27,* 507; *46–47,* 484
Second Mrs. Aarons, The *69–70,* 333
Second Mrs. Tanqueray, The *94–99,* 114, 115, 249; *99–09,* 361, 403, 404, 419, 557; *09–19,* 493; *24–25,* 477
Second String, A *59–60,* 331
Second Threshold *50–51,* 339
Secret, The *09–19,* 517
Secret Concubine, The *59–60,* 356
Secret Enemy, The *94–99,* 218
Secret Garden, The *35–36,* 512

Secret Life of Walter Mitty, The
    64–65, 345s
Secret of Polichinelle, The 99–09,
    453
Secret of Suzanne (opera rep) 43–44,
    479
Secret Orchard, The 99–09, 553
Secret Room, The 45–46, 403
Secret Service 94–99, 178; 09–19,
    432, 562
Secret Strings 09–19, 543
Secrets 22–23, 509
Security 28–29, 484
Seduction Scene From a Musical
    Play in Progress 63–64, 371
See America First 09–19, 572;
    64–65, 357
See My Lawyer (1) 09–19, 556
See My Lawyer (2) 39–40, 399
See Naples and Die 29–30, 406
See the Jaguar 52–53, 274
Seed of the Brute 26–27, 417
Seeds in the Wind 47–48, 405, 412
Seeing New York 99–09, 515
Seeing Things 20–21, 355
Seen But Not Heard 36–37, 406
Seeniaya Ptitza (see The Blue Bird
    2)
See-Saw (1) 19–20, 355
See-Saw (2) 63–64, 371
Seizure of the Sabines, The (Il Ratto
    Sabine; see also Der Raub der
    Sabinerinnen; A Night Off; The
    Rape of the Sabine Women)
    99–09, 536
Self and Lady 99–09, 375
Sellout, The 33–34, 430
Semele's Bar Mitzvah 45–46, 460
Semi-Detached (1) 59–60, 328
Semi-Detached (2) 63–64, 306
Senator, The 94–99, 111, 235
Senator Keeps House, The 09–19,
    459
Send Me No Flowers 60–61, 311
Sensations 70–71
Sentinels 31–32, 450
Separate Rooms 39–40, 447

Separate Tables 56–57, 327; 58–59,
    53
Septimus 09–19, 405
Sera del Sabato, La 36–37, 500
Seremonda 09–19, 592
Serena Blandish 28–29, 461
Serenade, The 94–99, 198; 99–09,
    367; 29–30, 505; 46–47, 419
Serge Lifar Russian Dancers (dance
    programs) 33–34, 520
Sergeant Brue 99–09, 490
Sergeant Kitty 99–09, 453
Serio-Comic Governess, The 99–09,
    465
Serjeant Musgrave's Dance 65–66,
    431
Sermon 63–64, 346
Serpent: A Ceremony, The 68–69,
    457; 69–70, 369
Serpent's Tooth, A 22–23, 442
Serpiente, La 27–28, 468
Serva Padrone, La (see The Maid as
    Mistress)
Servant in the House, The 99–09,
    561; 09–19, 628; 20–21, 446;
    24–25, 567; 25–26, 595
Servant of Two Masters (Arlecchino,
    Servitore di due Padroni) 27–28,
    455, 485; 41–42, 461; 45–46, 450;
    59–60, 43, 321; 64–65, 362
Service 09–19, 628
Service for Two 26–27, 370
Sesostra 09–19, 467
Set a Thief— 26–27, 483
Set My People Free 48–49, 392, 425
Set to Music 38–39, 451
Seul 23–24, 333
Seven 29–30, 469
Seven Against One 29–30, 534
Seven Ages of Bernard Shaw 66–67,
    422
Seven Ages of Man, No I, The
    61–62, 318
Seven Ages of Man, No II, The
    61–62, 318
7½ Cents 53–54, 353; 56–57, 375
Seven Chances 09–19, 576

Seven

Seven Days *09–19,* 404
Seven Days' Leave *09–19,* 619
Seven Days of Mourning *69–70,* 351
Seven Deadly Sins, The *58–59,* 54
Seven Deadly Sins, No. IV, The
    61–62, 318
Seven Descents of Myrtle, The
    67–68, 369
Seven Keys to Baldpate *09–19,* 166,
    507; *34–35,* 481
Seven Lively Arts *44–45,* 402;
    64–65, 357
Seven Mirrors *45–46,* 400
Seven Sisters *09–19,* 439
Seven Twenty-Eight *94–99,* 90
Seven Year Itch, The *52–53,* 270
Seventeen (source) *09–19,* 620;
    25–26, 529; *51–52,* 277
Seventeen (1) *09–19,* 620
Seventeen (2) *51–52,* 277s; *61–62,*
    333
1776 *68–69,* 410s
17th century music (unnamed
    sources) *58–59,* 295
Seventh Heart, The *26–27,* 521
Seventh Heaven (p) *22–23,* 481;
    54–55, 416
Seventh Heaven (m) *54–55,* 417s
Seventh Trumpet, The *41–42,* 416
70, Girls, 70 *70–71*
Severed Cord, The *28–29,* 501
Severed Head, A *64–65,* 309
Sex *25–26,* 587
Sex and the Single Dog *67–68,* 412
Sex Fable, The *31–32,* 412
Sextet *(Yes)* *70–71*
Sexual Practises in Heaven *70–71*
Seidman and Son *62–63,* 280
Sganarelle *09–19,* 579; *33–34,* 442;
    57–58, 330; *69–70,* 311
Sh, the Octopus *27–28,* 515
Shades of Night, The *99–09,* 389
Shadow, The (1) *09–19,* 544; *23–24,*
    370
Shadow, The (2) *21–22,* 538
Shadow and Substance *37–38,* 419;
    46–47, 494; *53–54,* 358

Shadow Man, The
    (Kage-No-Chikara) 29–30, 506
Shadow of a Gunman, (The) *51–52,*
    332; *58–59,* 305
Shadow of Heroes *(Stone and Star;*
    The Murderers) 61–62, 314
Shadow of My Enemy, A *57–58,*
    306
Shadow of the Glen, The *09–19,*
    459; *32–33,* 407; *34–35,* 408;
    56–57, 55
Shadow of the Rockies *28–29,* 459
Shadow Play *36–37,* 436; *47–48,*
    384
Shadow Years, The *56–57,* 58
Shadowed *09–19,* 508
Shadows *09–19,* 635
Shadows Move Among Them *52–53,*
    268
Shadows of a Great City, The
    94–99, 258
Shadows of the Past *94–99,* 231
Shady Lady *33–34,* 421
Shaft No. 2 *94–99,* 85
Shake Hands With the Devil *49–50,*
    383
Shakespeare Anthology *58–59,* 316;
    62–63, 305
Shakespeare in Harlem *59–60,* 49
Shakespeare readings (unnamed
    programs) *35–36,* 512; *36–37,* 498
Shakespeare sonnets (Nos. 11, 12, 18,
    29, 30, 73, 116, 129, 130, 138 &
    undesignated) *58–59,* 316; *62–63,*
    305, 322; *63–64,* 314, 360
Shakuntala *09–19,* 656; *59–60,* 42
Shall We Forgive Her? *94–99,* 205
Shall We Join the Ladies? *24–25,*
    522; *28–29,* 501
Sham *99–09,* 580
Sham Battles *99–09,* 560
Shame Woman, The *23–24,* 335
Shameen Dhu *09–19,* 521
Shamus O'Brien *94–99,* 191
Shanghai Gesture *25–26,* 543;
    27–28, 507
Shango *69–70,* 375

Shangri-La *56–57*, 313s
Shan-Kar Dancers (see *Uday
    Shan-Kar Hindu Dancers*)
Shannon of the Sixth *94–99*, 220
Shannons of Broadway *27–28*, 414
Sharkey, or The Shadow Detective
    94–99, 251
Sharlee *23–24*, 358
Sharon's Grave *61–62*, 312
Shatter'd Lamp, The *33–34*, 509
Shaughraun, The *94–99*, 96
Shaun Rhue *94–99*, 100
Shavings *19–20*, 426
Shawn (dance programs; see *Ted
    Shawn*)
She Couldn't Say No *26–27*, 372
She Gave Him All She Had With
    Free Beer and Pretzels *39–40*, 468
She Got What She Wanted *28–29*,
    475
She Had to Know *24–25*, 533
She Lived Next to the Firehouse
    30–31, 489
She Loves Me *62–63*, 307s; *68–69*,
    455
She Loves Me Not *33–34*, 459
She Means Business *30–31*, 483
She Shall Have Music *58–59*, 53
She Stoops to Conquer (or The
    Mistakes of a Night) *94–99*, 167;
    99–09, 474, 489; *09–19*, 410, 484;
    23–24, 443; *27–28*, 554; *49–50*,
    365; *60–61*, 304; *61–62*, 310;
    70–71
She Walked in Her Sleep *09–19*, 632
She Went to Town *38–39*, 484
She Would and She Did *19–20*, 349
Sheep on the Runway *69–70*, 312
Sheila *70–71*
Sheila Barrett *36–37*, 498
Shelf, The *26–27*, 386
Shenandoah *94–99*, 86
Shepherd in the Distance, The
    09–19, 547
Shepherd King, The *99–09*, 458
Shepherd of Avenue B, The *69–70*,
    368

Shepherd's Chameleon, The *60–61*,
    47
Sheppey *43–44*, 469
Shepsel Schlemiel *47–48*, 431
Sherlock Holmes (1) *99–09*, 354,
    355; *09–19*, 432, 562; *27–28*, 513;
    29–30, 446
Sherlock Holmes (2) *53–54*, 314
Sherman Was Right *09–19*, 563
Sherry! *66–67*, 385s
She's a Good Fellow *09–19*, 656
She's in Again *09–19*, 552
She's My Baby *27–28*, 486
Shewing-up of Blanco Posnet, The
    (see *The Showing-up of Blanco
    Posnet*)
Shidohogaku *(Shidohogaku the
    Horse)* *70–71*
Shinbone Alley *56–57*, 367s
Shining Hour, The *33–34*, 495;
    44–45, 436; *46–47*, 484
Ship Comes In, A *34–35*, 375
Shipwrecked *24–25*, 487
Shirkers, The *99–09*, 547
Shirley Kaye *09–19*, 591
Shoe Store *70–71*
Shock of Recognition, The *66–67*,
    384
Shoemaker and the Peddler, The
    60–61, 352s
Shoemakers' Holiday (m) *66–67*,
    415
Shoemaker's Holiday, The (p)
    37–38, 409; *63–64*, 314; *66–67*,
    414
Shoemaker's Prodigious Wife, The
    49–50, 383; *64–65*, 341
Shoes *69–70*, 361
Shoestring '57 *56–57*, 58
Shoestring Revue (see also *Ben
    Bagley's Shoestring Revues*) *54–55*,
    56
Sho-gun, The *99–09*, 468
Shoo-Fly Regiment, The *99–09*, 541
Shoot Anything With Hair That
    Moves *68–69*, 445
Shoot the Works *31–32*, 378

Shooting Shadows *24–25*, 430

Shooting Star *32–33*, 501

Shop at Sly Corner, The *48–49*, 407

Shop Girl, The *94–99*, 149

Shore Acres *94–99*, 154

Shore and the Sea, The *62–63*, 310

Shore Leave (source) *44–45*, 423

Shore Leave *22–23*, 435; *26–27*, 516

Short Circuit, The *(Le Court Circuit)* *23–24*, 333

Short Novels *60–61*, 295

Short Story *39–40*, 469

Shot in the Dark, A *61–62*, 263

Shout From the Rooftops *64–65*, 346

Show Boat *27–28*, 482; *31–32*, 513s; *45–46*, 418; *48–49*, 378; *53–54*, 352; *60–61*, 334s; *66–67*, 352s

Show Girl (1) *29–30*, 378

Show Girl (2) *60–61*, 317s

Show Girl, The *99–09*, 409

Show Is On, The *36–37*, 446; *37–38*, 369

Show Me Where the Good Times Are *69–70*, 360s

Show of Wonders, The *09–19*, 585

Show Party for Easter Week *46–47*, 493

Show Shop, The *09–19*, 543

Show Time *42–43*, 429

Shower *67–68*, 411

Showing Off *37–38*, 460

Showing-up of Blanco Posnet, The *09–19*, 458, 494; *23–24*, 336; *59–60*, 43

Showman's Tale, The *46–47*, 496

Show-Off, The *23–24*, 396; *32–33*, 436; *36–37*, 496; *49–50*, 381, 385; *67–68*, 353; *68–69*, 376

Shrike, The *51–52*, 305; *53–54*, 322; *63–64*, 367

Shrike and the Chipmunks, The *47–48*, 416, 417

Shrinking Bride, The *70–71*

Shropshire Lad, A *67–68*, 277

Shubert Gaieties 1919 *19–20*, 340

Shuffle Along *20–21*, 450

Shuffle Along of 1933 *32–33*, 441

Shuffle Along (1952) *51–52*, 323s

Shulamite, The *99–09*, 524

Shunned *60–61*, 39

Shy and the Lonely, The *44–45*, 436

Shylock *09–19*, 589 (and 605)

Shylock '47 *46–47*, 496

Shylock's Daughter *47–48*, 431

Si Je Voulais *36–37*, 499

Siberia *99–09*, 482

Sick-a-Bed *09–19*, 623

Sickness of Youth *32–33*, 377

Side Show *94–99*, 112

Side Tracked *94–99*, 204

Sideshow *30–31*, 525

Sideshows *54–55*, 52

Sidewalks of New York *27–28*, 420

Sidewalks of New York, The *94–99*, 157

Siege *37–38*, 400

Siegfried *30–31*, 436

Sightseers *28–29*, 500

Sigmund Spaeth *34–35*, 484

Sign in Sidney Brustein's Window, The *64–65*, 307; *68–69*, 442

Sign of Jonah *60–61*, 44

Sign of the Cross, The *94–99*, 183

Sign of the Leopard *28–29*, 433

Sign of the Rose, The *09–19*, 453

Sign of Winter *57–58*, 56

Sign on the Door, The *19–20*, 401

Signal Man, The *52–53*, 301

Signature *44–45*, 417

Signora Dalle Camelie, La *(Camille)* *37–38*, 470

Signs Along the Cynic Route *61–62*, 316s

Silence (1) *24–25*, 486

Silence (2) *69–70*, 348; *70–71*

Silent Assertion, The *09–19*, 617; *43–44*, 490

Silent Call, The *09–19*, 435

Silent House, The *27–28*, 505; *32–33*, 417

Silent Night, Lonely Night *59–60*, 308; *67–68*, 413

Silent Voice *41–42*, 459

Silent Voice, The *09–19*, 543
Silent Witness, The (1) *09–19*, 577
Silent Witness, The (2) *30–31*, 508
Silent Woman, The *38–39*, 492
Silhouettes *69–70*, 339
Silk Stockings *54–55*, 400s
Silks and Satins *20–21*, 358
Silver Box, The *99–09*, 537; *27–28*, 493
Silver Cord, The *26–27*, 444; *45–46*, 450
Silver Fox, The *21–22*, 411
Silver Girl, The *99–09*, 546
Silver Grey Toy Poodle *68–69*, 452
Silver King, The *94–99*, 105, 234; *31–32*, 501
Silver Lake, The *63–64*, 342
Silver Mask, The *40–41*, 376
Silver Slipper, The *99–09*, 420
Silver Star, The *09–19*, 403
Silver Swan, The *29–30*, 453
Silver Tassie, The *29–30*, 429; *49–50*, 383
Silver Wedding, The *09–19*, 503
Silver Whistle, The *48–49*, 397
Sim Sala Bim *40–41*, 378
Simon Called Peter *24–25*, 483
Simon the Cyrenian *09–19*, 598
Simon's Hour *25–26*, 592
Simon's Wife *44–45*, 395
Simple Simon *29–30*, 497; *30–31*, 502
Simpleton of the Unexpected Isles, The *34–35*, 453; *53–54*, 359
Simply Heavenly *56–57*, 58; *57–58*, 283s
Sin of Pat Muldoon, The *56–57*, 360
Sinbad *09–19*, 622
Sing and Whistle *33–34*, 494
Sing Before Breakfast *40–41*, 431
Sing for Your Supper *38–39*, 481
Sing High, Sing Low *31–32*, 430
Sing Israel Sing *66–67*, 393s; *67–68*, 339
Sing Me No Lullaby *54–55*, 369
Sing Muse! *61–62*, 315s
Sing Out Sweet Land *44–45*, 406

Sing Out the News *38–39*, 407
Sing Till Tomorrow *53–54*, 332
Sing to Me Through Open Windows *64–65*, 356
Singapore *32–33*, 420
Singin' Hare Krishna *70–71*
Singin' the Blues *31–32*, 392
Singing Bridegroom, The *48–49*, 430
Singing Girl, The *99–09*, 352
Singing Jailbirds *28–29*, 432; *34–35*, 483
Singing Rabbi, The *31–32*, 389
Single Man, A *09–19*, 449
Sinner *26–27*, 476
Sinners *09–19*, 543
Sins of Society, The *09–19*, 397
Sins of the Night *94–99*, 150
Sir Anthony *99–09*, 526
Sir Harry Lauder *29–30*, 527
Sire *09–19*, 437
Siren, The *09–19*, 448
Sister Against Sister *46–47*, 497
Sister Beatrice *99–09*, 560; *09–19*, 415, 446
Sister Mary *99–09*, 353
Sisters *27–28*, 474
Sisters of Susanne *09–19*, 579
Sisters of the Chorus *30–31*, 436
Sisters' Tragedy, The *29–30*, 533
Sita *30–31*, 478
Site, The *63–64*, 368
Sitting Pretty *23–24*, 418
Six *70–71*
Six Characters in Search of an Author *22–23*, 482; *23–24*, 396; *30–31*, 516; *46–47*, 485; *55–56*, 366; *62–63*, 328
6 From La Mama *65–66*, 432
Six Months' Option *09–19*, 616
Six Persons *94–99*, 160
Six Who Pass While the Lentils Boil *09–19*, 588
Six-Cylinder Love *21–22*, 402
Six-Fifty, The *21–22*, 448
Sixth Finger in a Five Finger Glove *56–57*, 321
Skating Vanities of 1942 *41–42*, 459

Skeletons *48–49*, 426
Sketch Book (1; see *Earl Carroll's Sketch Book*)
Sketch Book (2) *47–48*, 341
Sketches of Frontier Life *99–09*, 443
Skidding *27–28*, 556
Ski-Hi *99–09*, 563
Skin Deep *27–28*, 431
Skin Game, The *20–21*, 398
Skin of Our Teeth, The *42–43*, 443; *55–56*, 337; *60–61*, 48
Skin Tight *67–68*, 412
Skipper & Co., Wall Street *99–09*, 433
Skipper Next to God *47–48*, 394, 395
Skirt, The *21–22*, 455
Skits-oh-Frantics! *66–67*, 417
Skull, The *27–28*, 544
Sky Farm *99–09*, 407
Sky High (1) *24–25*, 551
Sky High (2) *50–51*, 375
Skydrift *45–46*, 406
Skye *70–71*
Skylark *39–40*, 401
Skylark, A *09–19*, 416
Skylark, The *21–22*, 388
Skyrocket *28–29*, 454
Sky's the Limit, The *34–35*, 423
Skyscraper *65–66*, 384s
Skywriting *67–68*, 406
Slag *70–71*
Slapstick Tragedy *65–66*, 399
Slave, The *64–65*, 350
Slave Ship *69–70*, 354, 372
Slavery records, letters, statements, etc. (untitled sources) *63–64*, 350
Slaves All *26–27*, 437
Slaves of Gold *94–99*, 87
Slayer of Dreams *38–39*, 492
Sleep, My Pretty One *44–45*, 395
Sleep No More *44–45*, 372
Sleep of Prisoners, A *51–52*, 286
Sleeping Beauty and the Beast, The *99–09*, 398
Sleeping City, The *94–99*, 244
Sleeping Clergyman, A *34–35*, 389
Sleeping Partners *09–19*, 640

Sleeping Prince, The *56–57*, 330; *63–64*, 315
Sleepless Night, A *09–19*, 652
Sleepy Hollow *48–49*, 375s
Sleuth *70–71*
Slice It Thin *44–45*, 395
Slice of Life, A *09–19*, 464
Slight Ache, A *62–63*, 322; *64–65*, 349
Slight Case of Murder, A *35–36*, 403
Slightly Delinquent *54–55*, 53
Slightly Delirious *34–35*, 435
Slightly Imperfect *45–46*, 405
Slightly Married *43–44*, 420
Slightly Scandalous *43–44*, 482
Slim Princess, The *09–19*, 435
Slow Dance on the Killing Ground *64–65*, 318; *69–70*, 368
Slow Memories *70–71*
Slumbering Gods *38–39*, 484
Small Hours, The *50–51*, 351
Small Miracle *34–35*, 378
Small Timers, The *24–25*, 531
Small War on Murray Hill *56–57*, 348
Small Wonder *48–49*, 380s
Smaller Than Life *70–71*
Smell of Burning, A *62–63*, 338
Smile at Me *35–36*, 401
Smile of the World, The *48–49*, 406
Smiles *30–31*, 455
Smilin' Through *19–20*, 408; *31–32*, 471; *44–45*, 436
Smiling Faces *32–33*, 382
Smiling the Boy Fell Dead *60–61*, 360s
Smith *09–19*, 423
Smokeweaver's Daughter, The *58–59*, 51
Smoldering Flame, The *09–19*, 508
Smooth as Silk *20–21*, 429
Snafu *44–45*, 391
Snakes *60–61*, 294
Snapshots of 1921 *20–21*, 452
Snark Was a Boojum, The *43–44*, 408
Snatch of Sliphorn Jazz *60–61*, 294

Snickering Horses *35–36*, 475
Sniper, The *59–60*, 49
Snobs *09–19*, 449
Snookie *40–41*, 426
Snow Maiden, The *59–60*, 40
Snow White and the Seven Dwarfs (1) *09–19*, 483
Snow White and the Seven Dwarfs (2) *38–39*, 490
Snow White and the Seven Dwarfs (mn) *36–37*, 498; *37–38*, 466
Snowangel *63–64*, 343
Snows of Spring *70–71*
So Am I *27–28*, 499
So It's All Rashomon *63–64*, 367
So Long, Letty *09–19*, 584
So Many Paths *34–35*, 421
So Much for So Much *09–19*, 540
So Proudly We Hail (1) *36–37*, 409
So Proudly We Hail (2) *37–38*, 469
So Red the Rose *62–63*, 326
So This Is London *22–23*, 445
So This Is Politics *24–25*, 426
So Was Napoleon *29–30*, 475
So Who's Afraid of Edward Albee? *62–63*, 327
Soap (1) *39–40*, 473
Soap (2) *70–71*
Soap Opera *67–68*, 412
Social Highwayman, A *94–99*, 145, 235
Social Register, The *31–32*, 426
Social Whirl, The *99–09*, 512
Society and the Bulldog *99–09*, 555
Society Circus, A *99–09*, 503
Society Girl *31–32*, 456
Society Shadows *94–99*, 190
Sociological Type Jokes *60–61*, 295
Soeur, La *99–09*, 548
Softly, and Consider the Nearness *63–64*, 365
Sohn der Wildniss, Der *99–09*, 461
Soil *38–39*, 486
Sojourner Truth *47–48*, 428
Sol Hyam's Brocanteur *23–24*, 333
Sold and Paid For *99–09*, 381
Soldier of France, A (see *Joan*)
Soldiers *67–68*, 376

Soldiers and Women *29–30*, 385
Soldiers of Fortune *99–09*, 407
Soldier's Wife *44–45*, 387
Solid Gold Cadillac, The *53–54*, 316
Solid Ivory *25–26*, 497
Solid South *30–31*, 430
Soliloquy *38–39*, 432
Solitaire *41–42*, 436
Solo *61–62*, 330
Sombra, La *31–32*, 501
Some Baby! *09–19*, 555
Some Comments on the Harmful Effects of Tobacco (see *On the Harmfulness of Tobacco*)
Some Like 'Em Cold *29–20*, 236
Some Night *09–19*, 638
Some One in the House *09–19*, 636
Some Party *21–22*, 534
Somebody's Luggage *09–19*, 578; *22–23*, 522
Somebody's Sweetheart *09–19*, 647
Someone From Assisi *61–62*, 318
Someone Waiting *55–56*, 374
Someone's Comin' Hungry *68–69*, 449
Something About a Soldier *61–62*, 279
Something Different *67–68*, 353
Something for Nothing *37–38*, 401
Something for the Boys *42–43*, 458; *64–65*, 357
Something Gay *34–35*, 474
Something More! *64–65*, 311s
Something More Important *35–36*, 397
Something to Brag About *25–26*, 426
Something Unspoken *57–58*, 53
Sometime *09–19*, 639
Sometime Jam Today *66–67*, 412
Somewhere Else *09–19*, 492
Son, Come Home, A *67–68*, 391
Son of the People, A *09–19*, 415
Son Who Hunted Tigers in Jakarta, The *69–70*, 349
Son-Daughter, The *19–20*, 387
Sondra *66–67*, 420

Song and Dance Man, The *23–24,*
    380; *30–31,* 398
Song for a Certain Midnight *59–60,*
    40
Song of Bernadette, The *45–46,* 434
Song of Norway *44–45,* 369
Song of Songs (1) *58–59,* 50
Song of Songs (2) *66–67,* 36
Song of Songs, The *09–19,* 541
Song of Sorrows *41–42,* 458
Song of the Dnieper, The *46–47,*
    497
Song of the Flame *25–26,* 526
Song of the Grasshopper *67–68,* 342
Song of the Lusitanian Bogey *67–68,*
    396; *68–69,* 421
Song of the Sword, The *99–09,* 352
Song Writer, The *28–29,* 358
Songs by Carmines *68–69,* 425
Songs From Milk Wood *69–70,* 311
Songs on the Death of Children
    46–47, 491
Sonnets From the Portuguese *68–69,*
    407
Sonnette d'Alarme, La *23–24,* 373
Sonny *21–22,* 396
Sons and Soldiers *42–43,* 474
Sons o' Fun *41–42,* 417
Sons o' Guns *29–30,* 451
Sonya *21–22,* 395
Soon *70–71*s
Sophie (1) *19–20,* 434
Sophie (2) *44–45,* 405
Sophie (3) *62–63,* 305s
Sophie Halenczik, American *44–45,*
    405
Sophisticrats, The *32–33,* 461
Sorcerer, The *09–19,* 551; *31–32,*
    380; *43–44,* 488; *45–46,* 458;
    46–57, 494; *51–52,* 334
Sorceress, The *(La Sorciere)* *99–09,*
    468; *09–19,* 432
Sorrows of Satan, The *94–99,* 247
So's Your Old Antique *29–30,* 535
Sotoba Komachi *60–61,* 44
Soul Kiss, The *99–09,* 556
Soul of My People, The *47–48,* 432

Sound of a Different Drum, The
    69–70, 373
Sound of Hunting, A *45–46,* 408;
    46–47, 485
Sound of Music, The *59–60,* 303s;
    66–67, 386
Sound of Silence, A *64–65,* 355
Sour Grapes *26–27,* 373
Sourball *69–70,* 339
South Pacific (1) *43–44,* 445
South Pacific (2) *48–49,* 418s;
    54–55, 412; *56–57,* 369; *60–61,*
    337; *65–66,* 366; *67–68,* 339s
Southern Exposure *50–51,* 315
Southern Romance, A *94–99,* 206
Southerners, The *99–09,* 461
Southwest Corner, The *54–55,* 397
Sowing the Wind *94–99,* 120
Span of Life *94–99,* 102
Spanish Armada, The *61–62,* 327
Spanish dances (untitled dance
    programs) *47–48,* 415, 416
Spanish Dancers, The (mn) *36–37,*
    498
Spanish Love *20–21,* 366
Spanish musical themes (untitled
    sources) *56–57,* 353
Spanish poems (untitled) *38–39,* 483
Sparkin' *42–43,* 490
Spartacus *94–99,* 226
Speak Easy *27–28,* 414
Speak for Yourself *46–47,* 498
Speak for Yourself, Joan *35–36,* 511
Speak of the Devil *39–40,* 468
Speaking of Murder *56–57,* 346
Special Delivery *94–99,* 112
Speckled Band, The *09–19,* 430
Speculator, The *94–99,* 172
Speed *09–19,* 450
Spell, The *99–09,* 545
Spellbinder, The *99–09,* 464
Spellbound (1) *26–27,* 481
Spellbound (2) *27–28,* 450
Spenders, The *99–09,* 439
Spendthrift, The *09–19,* 417
Sphinx, The *94–99,* 138
Spice of 1922 *22–23,* 433

Spider, The *26–27*, 496; *27–28*, 517
Spider and the Fly, The *94–99*, 128
Spiritisme *94–99*, 195
Spiritualist, The *09–19*, 498
Spiro Who? *68–69*, 453
Spite Corner *22–23*, 462
Spitfire, The *09–19*, 418
Spitting Image *68–69*, 446
Spofford *67–68*, 357
Spoilers, The *99–09*, 535
Sponge Room, The *63–64*, 359
Sponono *63–64*, 330
Spook House *29–30*, 547
Spook Scandals *44–45*, 368
Spook Sonata, The *23–24*, 382
Spooks *24–25*, 599
Spoon River Anthology *63–64*, 304
Sport McAllister, One of the 400
    94–99, 113
Sport of Kings *25–26*, 596
Sporting Days *99–09*, 567
Sporting Duchess, The *94–99*, 139
Sporting Life *94–99*, 240
Sporting Thing to Do, The *22–23*,
    532
Spots of the Leopard, The *63–64*,
    345
Spread Eagle *26–27*, 503
Spreading the News *09–19*, 459,
    494
Sprightly Romance of Marsac, The
    99–09, 380
Spring *34–35*, 411
Spring, The *21–22*, 425
Spring Again *41–42*, 411
Spring and Port Wine *67–68*, 341
Spring Chicken, A *94–99*, 244
Spring Chicken, The *99–09*, 522
Spring Cleaning *23–24*, 349
Spring Dance *36–37*, 404
Spring Fever *25–26*, 422
Spring Fever (mn) *38–39*, 483
Spring Freshet *34–35*, 385
Spring in Autumn *33–34*, 447
Spring Is Here *28–29*, 478
Spring Maid, The *09–19*, 434
Spring Meeting *38–39*, 436

Spring Production *43–44*, 488
Spring Returneth, The *38–39*, 486
Spring Sonata *46–47*, 491
Spring Song (1) *27–28*, 472
Spring Song (2) *34–35*, 381
Spring Thaw *37–38*, 433
Spring 3100 *27–28*, 510
Spring Varieties *34–35*, 483
Springboard, The *27–28*, 430
Springtime *09–19*, 402
Springtime Folly *50–51*, 354
Springtime for Henry *31–32*, 446;
    32–33, 489; *45–46*, 450; *50–51*,
    357
Springtime of Youth *22–23*, 479
Spy, The *09–19*, 492
Spy of Spain, A *94–99*, 230
Spy of the Government, The *99–09*,
    547
Squab Farm, The *09–19*, 625
Squall, The *26–27*, 425
Square, The *60–61*, 44
Square Crooks *25–26*, 560
Square in the Eye *64–65*, 360
Square Peg, A *22–23*, 525
Square Root of Wonderful, The
    57–58, 297; *62–63*, 339
Squaring the Circle *35–36*, 414;
    44–45, 436
Squat Betty *63–64*, 359
Squaw Man, The *99–09*, 207, 498;
    09–19, 436; *21–22*, 484; *27–28*,
    480
Squealer, The *28–29*, 415
Squire Kate *94–99*, 182
Squire of Dames, The *94–99*, 163
Squirrel *61–62*, 332
St. Columba and the River *54–55*,
    376
St. Helena *36–37*, 414
St. Joan of the Stockyards (see *Saint
    Joan of the Stockyards*)
St. Louis Woman *45–46*, 436
St. Luke (Gospel of; Parable of the
    Prodigal Son) *09–19*, 593; *62–63*,
    321
St. Mark (Gospel of) *38–39*, 318

St. Matthew (Gospel of) *62–63,* 321; *70–71*

St. Simeon Stylites *25–26,* 593

Stag Movie *70–71*s

Stag Party, A, or A Hero in Spite of Himself *94–99,* 158

Stage Affair, A (see also *A Story for a Sunday Evening*) *61–62,* 320

Stage Door *36–37,* 421

Staircase *67–68,* 358

Stairs, The *27–28,* 447

Stalag 17 *50–51,* 368, 374

Star and Garter (1) *99–09,* 380

Star and Garter (2) *42–43,* 420

Star Gazer, The (1) *94–99,* 197

Star Gazer, The (2) *09–19,* 615

Star Spangled *35–36,* 493

Star Spangled Family *44–45,* 428

Star Time *44–45,* 384

Starbucks, The *99–09,* 431

Starcross Story, The *53–54,* 336

Starlight *24–25,* 553

Stars and Stripes *67–68,* 406

Stars in Your Eyes *38–39,* 458

Stars of Tomorrow *44–45,* 441

Stars on Ice *42–43,* 421

Stars on Strings (mn) *35–36,* 479, 513

Star-Spangled Girl, The *66–67,* 379

Star-Wagon, The *37–38,* 373

State of the Union *45–46,* 407

Stay Away, Joe *58–59,* 314

Steadfast *23–24,* 343

Steal the Old Man's Bundle *69–70,* 368

Steam Roller, The *24–25,* 484

Steambath *70–71*

Steel (1) *31–32,* 435; *36–37,* 497

Steel (2) *39–40,* 422

Step on a Crack *62–63,* 280

Step Right Up *45–46,* 459

Step This Way *09–19,* 575

Stepdaughters of War *30–31,* 425

Stephen D *67–68,* 386

Stephen Hero *67–68,* 386

Stepping Out *28–29,* 505

Stepping Sisters *29–30,* 530

Stepping Stones *23–24,* 348; *24–25,* 443

Steps Leading Up *40–41,* 432

Step-Sister, The *99–09,* 547

Steve *09–19,* 478

Stevedore *33–34,* 516; *34–35,* 383

Stewed Prunes *60–61,* 354

Stick-in-the-Mud *35–36,* 441

Still Alarm, The *94–99,* 98

Still Life *36–37,* 437; *45–46,* 450; *48–49,* 426; *66–67,* 393

Still Waters *25–26,* 560

Stingy *09–19,* 649

Stitch in Time, A *09–19,* 640

Stockholm Marionette Theater of Fantasy, The (mn) *66–67,* 366

Stolen Fruit *25–26,* 465

Stolen Orders *09–19,* 558

Stolen Story, The *99–09,* 521

Stomp *69–70,* 345

Stone and Star *(Shadow of Heroes; The Murderers)* *61–62,* 150

Stop! Look! Listen! *09–19,* 567

Stop Press *38–39,* 466, 486

Stop the World—I Want to Get Off *62–63,* 278s

Stop Thief *09–19,* 490

Stop, You're Killing Me *68–69,* 448

Stop-Over *37–38,* 415

Stork, The *24–25,* 528

Stork Is Dead, The *32–33,* 390

Stork Mad *36–37,* 412

Stork Who Married a Dumb Wife, The *62–63,* 310

Storm, The (1) *99–09,* 363; *61–62,* 325; *63–64,* 364

Storm, The (2) *19–20,* 361

Storm Center *27–28,* 461

Storm Operation *43–44,* 447

Storm Over Patsy *36–37,* 470

Story for a Sunday Evening, A (see also *A Stage Affair*) *50–51,* 326

Story for Strangers, A *48–49,* 382

Story of Ferdinand, The (mn) *38–39,* 483

Story of Mary Surratt, The *46–47,* 459; *61–62,* 332

Story of Rodion the Student, The
  94–99, 92
Story of the Nativity, The (dance
  program) 47–48, 415
Story of the Rosary, The 09–19, 530
Story of Waterloo, A 94–99, 151
Story Theater (see Paul Sills' Story
  Theater)
Stowaway, The 94–99, 109
Strada, La 69–70, 308s
Straight From the Heart 94–99, 192
Straight Road, The 99–09, 531
Straight Thru the Door 28–29, 389
Strange Adventures of Miss Brown,
  The 94–99, 157
Strange Bedfellows (1; see So This Is
  Politics)
Strange Bedfellows (2) 47–48, 376
Strange Child 34–35, 453
Strange Fruit 45–46, 410
Strange Gods 32–33, 484
Strange Interlude 27–28, 500; 62–63,
  300
Strange Orchestra 33–34, 464;
  45–46, 457
Strange Play, A 43–44, 481
Strange Rider 63–64, 352
Strange Woman, The 09–19, 515
Stranger, The (1) 09–19, 461
Stranger, The (2) 44–45, 417
Stranger in a Strange Land 99–09,
  350
Stranger in New York, A 94–99,
  208
Stranger Than Fiction 09–19, 596
Strangers at Home 34–35, 372
Strangler Fig, The 39–40, 460
Strangulation 70–71
Stratonice 46–47, 498
Straw, The 21–22, 459
Straw Hat 37–38, 408
Straw Hat, The 26–27, 403
Straw Hat Revue, The 39–40, 400
Strawberry Blonde, The 26–27, 478
Stray Leaves 33–34, 422
Street Scene (p) 28–29, 453; 48–49,
  425; 65–66, 371

Street Scene (m) 46–47, 454; 58–59,
  54; 65–66, 371
Street Singer (1) 29–30, 396
Street Singer (2) 47–48, 431
Street Sounds 70–71
Street Wolf, The 28–29, 448
Streetcar Named Desire, A 47–48,
  366; 49–50, 380; 54–55, 53; 55–56,
  375
Streets Are Guarded, The 44–45,
  398
Streets of New York, The (or
  Poverty is No Crime; p) 94–99,
  245; 31–32, 404; 47–48, 429;
  50–51, 375; 61–62, 320
Streets of New York, The (m)
  63–64, 349s
Streets of Paris, The 39–40, 394
Strength of the Weak, The 99–09,
  513
Strictly Dishonorable 29–30, 397;
  33–34, 495
Strife 09–19, 404
Strike Me Pink 32–33, 472s
Strike Me Red 34–35, 485
Strike up the Band 29–30, 479
String 68–69, 440
Strings, My Lord, Are False, The
  41–42, 451
Strip for Action 42–43, 432
Strip Girl 35–36, 421
Stripped 29–30, 424
Strollers, The 99–09, 392
Strolling Players 99–09, 485
Strong, The 23–24, 404
Strong Are Lonely, The 53–54, 307
Strong Breed, The 67–68, 393
Strong Man's House, A 29–30, 393
Stronger, The 09–19, 497; 26–27,
  524; 55–56, 376; 65–66, 425
Stronger Sex, The 99–09, 573
Stronger Than Love (1) 25–26, 524
Stronger Than Love (2) 47–48, 431
Strongheart 99–09, 483
Struck Oil 94–99, 94
Struggle Everlasting, The 99–09, 545
Struggle of Life, The 94–99, 148

Strugglers, The *09–19,* 457
Strut Miss Lizzie *22–23,* 432
Stubborn Cinderella, A *99–09,* 576
Stubbornness of Geraldine, The
    99–09, 421
Student Gypsy, The, or The Prince
    of Liederkranz *63–64,* 304s
Student King, The *99–09,* 529
Student Prince, The *24–25,* 500;
    30–31, 485; *42–43,* 475; *61–62,*
    304, 332
Styles in Acting *31–32,* 501
Subject of Scandal and Concern, A
    65–66, 437
Subject Was Roses, The *63–64,* 339
Subscriber, The *68–69,* 432
Substitute for Murder *35–36,* 422
Subtleties of Jealousy *94–99,* 224
Suburban Tragedy *65–66,* 431
Subway, The *28–29,* 462
Subway Express *29–30,* 403
Subways Are for Sleeping *61–62,*
    276s
Success *09–19,* 621
Success Story *32–33,* 391; *46–47,*
    485
Successful Calamity, A *09–19,* 593;
    33–34, 495; *49–50,* 385
Such a Little Queen *09–19,* 398, 511
Such Is Life (1) *09–19,* 588
Such Is Life (2) *27–28,* 395
Sudden and Accidental Re-education
    of Horse Johnson, The *68–69,* 399
Sudden End of Anne Cinquefoil, The
    60–61, 39
Suddenly Last Summer *57–58,* 53;
    64–65, 362
Suds in Your Eye *43–44,* 447
Sue *94–99,* 177
Sue, Dear *22–23,* 434
Sue Hastings Marionettes *32–33,*
    439; *33–34,* 534; *34–35,* 484;
    35–36, 512; *36–37,* 498; *37–38,*
    466, 467; *38–39,* 489; *39–40,* 472
Sugar Hill *31–32,* 451
Sugar House, The *09–19,* 579
Suicide Club, The *28–29,* 490

Sultan of Sulu, The *99–09,* 425
Sumidagawa (see *The River Sumida*)
Summer and Smoke *48–49,* 386;
    51–52, 334; *59–60,* 43
Summer Ghost, A *61–62,* 329
Summer Night *39–40,* 408
Summer of Daisy Miller, The *62–63,*
    337
Summer of the 17th Doll *57–58,*
    310; *59–60,* 42; *67–68,* 396
Summer on Parade *34–35,* 483
Summer Pygmies *60–61,* 39
Summer Widowers, The *09–19,* 420
Summer Wives *35–36,* 500
Summertime *69–70,* 378
Summertree *67–68,*394;*69–70,*350
Sumurun *09–19,* 463
Sun and I, The *36–37,* 496
Sun Dodgers, The *09–19,* 487
Sun Field, The *42–43,* 450
Sun Kissed *36–37,* 471
Sun Showers *22–23,* 529
Sun Up *22–23,* 579; *28–29,* 403;
    29–30, 537
Sunday *99–09,* 473
Sunday Breakfast *51–52,* 328
Sunday Dinner *70–71*
Sunday in New York *61–62,* 272
Sunday Man, The *63–64,* 336
Sunday Night Events *37–38,* 462
Sunday Night Varieties *38–39,* 486
Sunday Nights at Nine (1934)
    34–35, 483
Sunday Nights at Nine (1935)
    35–36, 512
Sunday Nights at Nine (1936)
    36–37, 497
Sunday Promenade, The *68–69,* 458
Sundown Beach *48–49,* 378
Sunken Bell, The *99–09,* 365, 470
Sunkist *20–21,* 451
Sunny *25–26,* 452
Sunny Days *27–28,* 505; *28–29,* 386
Sunny Morning, A *35–36,* 447
Sunny River *41–42,* 418
Sunrise at Campobello *57–58,* 313
Sunset *65–66,* 435

Sunset Sonata *(The Time of Your Life)* *39–40*, 205
Sunshine *26–27*, 366
Sunshine Girl, The *09–19*, 494
Sunshine of Paradise Alley, The *94–99*, 173
Sunstroke *69–70*, 349
Sun-up (see *Sun Up*)
Sunup to Sundown *37–38*, 420
Superba *94–99*, 118
Superfluous Husband, A *94–99*, 191
Superman *65–66*, 405
Superstition of Sue, The *99–09*, 458
Supper Club, The *99–09*, 401
Supper for the Dead *54–55*, 56
Suppressed Desires *09–19*, 612
Sur la Dalle *23–24*, 333
Sur le Banc (see *On the Bench*)
Sure Cure, A *94–99*, 240
Sure Fire *26–27*, 408
Surena Varada, La *37–38*, 470
Surgeon, The *32–33*, 410
Surprise Package *52–53*, 307
Surprises du Divorce, Les *94–99*, 134
Surprises of Love, The *99–09*, 361
Survival of St. Joan, The *70–71*
Survival of the Fittest, The *20–21*, 435
Survivors, The *47–48*, 378
Susan and God *37–38*, 379; *43–44*, 435
Susan in Search of a Husband *99–09*, 526
Susan Slept Here *61–62*, 304
Susanna and the Elders *47–48*, 397
Susanna, Don't You Cry *38–39*, 475
Susie Is a *Good* Girl *68–69*, 433
Suspect *39–40*, 454
Suspected Slipper, The *29–30*, 497
Suspense *30–31*, 401
Suzanne *09–19*, 434
Suzanna and the Elders *40–41*, 390
Suzari Marionettes *39–40*, 472; *47–48*, 431
Suzette *21–22*, 467
Suzi *09–19*, 538

Swan, The *23–24*, 341; *37–38*, 467
Swan Song *45–46*, 446
Swan Song, The (A) *40–41*, 432; *42–43*, 489; *43–44*, 490
Swedish dances (untitled dance programs) *47–48*, 415
Sweeney Agonistes *51–52*, 333
Sweeney in the Trees *46–47*, 498
Sweeney Todd *24–25*, 431
Sweet Adeline *29–30*, 386
Sweet Aloes *35–36*, 491
Sweet and Low *30–31*, 454
Sweet and Twenty *99–09*, 402
Sweet Anne Page *99–09*, 380
Sweet Bird of Youth *58–59*, 328
Sweet Chariot *30–31*, 440
Sweet Charity (1) *42–43*, 455
Sweet Charity (2) *65–66*, 395s
Sweet Enemy, The *64–65*, 355
Sweet Eros *68–69*, 436
Sweet Genevieve *44–45*, 442
Sweet Iniscarra *94–99*, 192
Sweet Kitty Bellairs *99–09*, 448; *09–19*, 613
Sweet Land *36–37*, 496
Sweet Land of Liberty *29–30*, 401
Sweet Lavender *99–09*, 480
Sweet Little Devil *23–24*, 390
Sweet Marie *99–09*, 397
Sweet Miani *62–63*, 314s
Sweet Mystery of Life *35–36*, 417
Sweet Nell of Old Drury *99–09*, 383; *22–23*, 576
Sweet of You to Say So *61–62*, 332
Sweet River *36–37*, 423
Sweet Seventeen *23–24*, 409
Sweet Stranger *30–31*, 437
Sweet Thursday *55–56*, 364
Sweetheart Shop, The *20–21*, 375
Sweetheart Time *25–26*, 531
Sweethearts *09–19*, 506; *29–30*, 400; *46–47*, 457
Sweetshoppe Myriam, The *70–71*
Swell Mrs. Fitzwell, The *94–99*, 215
Swifty *22–23*, 475
Swim Low Little Goldfish *65–66*, 421

Swing It *37–38*, 447

Swing Mikado, The *38–39*, 472, 480

Swing Your Lady *36–37*, 419

Swingers, The *70–71*

Swingin' the Dream *39–40*, 417

Swiss dances (untitled dance programs) *47–48*, 415

Switchboard, The *09–19*, 497

Sword by His Side *47–48*, 432

Sword of the King, The *99–09*, 418

Swords *21–22*, 409

Sybil *09–19*, 568

Sydney Thompson *34–35*, 484

Sylvia *22–23*, 562

Sylvia Runs Away *09–19*, 528

Symphony *34–35*, 473

Symphony in Two Flats *30–31*, 412

Synthetic Sin *27–28*, 426

System du Docteur Goudron et du Professeur Plume, Le *23–24*, 333

System of Dr. Tarr (and Professor Feather), The *99–09*, 485

TV *66–67*, 405

Ta Bouche *23–24*, 363; *28–29*, 476

Table by the Window *56–57*, 327

Table Number Seven *56–57*, 327

Tablecloths *60–61*, 294

Taboo *21–22*, 531

Tailor Becomes a Store Keeper, The *37–38*, 460

Tailor Made Man, A *09–19*, 604; *29–30*, 426

Tainted Philanthropy *09–19*, 487

Take a Bow *43–44*, 484

Take a Chance *32–33*, 430s

Take a Giant Step *53–54*, 306; *56–57*, 55

Take Care of Business *69–70*, 371

Take Her, She's Mine *61–62*, 274

Take It as It Comes *43–44*, 454

Take It From Me *09–19*, 654

Take It From the Top *67–68*, 395

Take Me Along *59–60*, 299s

Take Me to Bed *69–70*, 334

Take My Advice (1) *09–19*, 459

Take My Advice (2) *27–28*, 444

Take My Tip *31–32*, 504

Take the Air *27–28*, 457

Taking Chances *09–19*, 548

Taking the Count *37–38*, 463

Tale of Corsica, A *94–99*, 102

Tale of Kasane, The *68–69*, 406

Tale of the Morning Glory, The (mn) *65–66*, 403

Tale of the Wolf, A *25–26*, 465

Tale of Two Cities, A *99–09*, 349; *52–53*, 301

Tale Retold, A *27–28*, 550

Tales of Hoffmann (opera rep) *09–19*, 638; *43–44*, 471; *64–65*, 297

Tales of Rigo *26–27*, 531

Tales of the South Pacific *48–49*, 419; *54–55*, 412; *56–57*, 369; *60–61*, 337; *65–66*, 366

Tales to Be Told *70–71*

Talk About Girls *26–27*, 534

Talk of New York, The *99–09*, 552

Talker, The *09–19*, 462

Talking Parrot, The *23–24*, 366

Talking to You *42–43*, 425; *61–62*, 310

Tall Prussian, The *94–99*, 221

Tall Story *58–59*, 318

Talley Method, The *40–41*, 417

Tamaris (dance programs) *34–35*, 460

Tambor y Cascabel *31–32*, 500

Tambourines to Glory *63–64*, 312s

Tamburlaine the Great *55–56*, 370

Taming of Helen, The *99–09*, 431

Taming of the Shrew, The *94–99*, 113; *99–09*, 452, 469, 536; *09–19*, 413, 447, 478, 508, 523, 627; *19–20*, 363; *21–22*, 446; *23–24*, 328; *24–25*, 483; *27–28*, 438; *29–30*, 516; *32–33*, 424; *35–36*, 413; *39–40*, 435; *42–43*, 489; *43–44*, 490; *48–49*, 406, 426; *50–51*, 365; *56–57*, 356; *60–61*, 46; *62–63*, 327; *65–66*, 97

Taming of the Shrew, The (mn) *37–38*, 466

Tangerine *21–22*, 391
Tangletoes *24–25*, 544
Tango *68–69*, 444
Tantalizing Tommy *09–19*, 479
Tante *09–19*, 512
Tantrum, The *24–25*, 447
Tanyard Street *40–41*, 413
Tapestry in Gray *35–36*, 454
Taps *99–09*, 466; *24–25*, 576
Tarnish *23–24*, 324
Tarot *70–71*
Tarrytown Widow, A *94–99*, 229
Tartuffe, Le *(The Impostor)* *60–61*,
   325; *63–64*, 327; *64–65*, 309;
   67–68, 405; *68–69*, 374; *69–70*,
   313
Tarzan of the Apes *21–22*, 410
Taste of Honey, A *60–61*, 297
Tatterman Marionettes *35–36*, 512;
   37–38, 466
Tattle Tales *32–33*, 499
Tattooed Countess, The *60–61*, 41
Tattooed Man, The *99–09*, 534
Tavern, The *20–21*, 385, 451; *29–30*,
   544; *39–40*, 462; *61–62*, 326;
   63–64, 359
Tchin-Tchin *62–63*, 283
Tea and Sympathy *53–54*, 308
Tea for One *62–63*, 310
Tea for Three *09–19*, 638
Tea Party *68–69*, 429
Teach Me How to Cry *54–55*, 56
Teahouse of the August Moon, The
   53–54, 310; *56–57*, 332; *70–71*
Teaser, The *21–22*, 389
Teaspoon Every Four Hours, A
   69–70, 294
Teatro dei Piccoli Marionettes
   32–33, 439; *33–34*, 534; *39–40*,
   472
Technique *30–31*, 525
Ted Montague (see *Eva Lorraine &
   Ted Montague*)
Ted Shawn Dancers (dance
   programs; see also *Ruth St. Denis
   & Ted Shawn; Jacobs Pillow Dance
   Festival Troupe*) *34–35*, 460, 484

Teeftallow *27–28*, 515
Telemachus Clay *63–64*, 351
Telephone, The (or L'Amour a
   Trois) *46–47*, 477; *48–49*, 399;
   50–51, 311
Telephone Girl, The *94–99*, 219
Telephone Pole *65–66*, 437
Tell Her the Truth *32–33*, 411s
Tell Me More *24–25*, 574
Tell Me Pretty Maiden *37–38*, 403
Tell My Story *38–39*, 464
Temper the Wind *46–47*, 452
Temperamental Journey, The *09–19*,
   506
Temperance Town, A *94–99*, 89
Tempest, The *94–99*, 200; *09–19*,
   410, 573; *32–33*, 424; *44–45*, 412;
   45–46, 392; *58–59*, 316; *59–60*, 43;
   62–63, 305, 354
Tempest Tossed *94–99*, 244
Temporary Husband, A *32–33*, 447
Temporary Island, A *47–48*, 395
Temptation (1; dance program)
   09–19, 444
Temptation (2) *47–48*, 421
Ten Little Indians *44–45*, 365
Ten Million Ghosts *36–37*, 422
Ten Million Others *35–36*, 510
Ten Minute Alibi *33–34*, 443
Ten Nights in a Barroom *31–32*,
   467; *53–54*, 358
Ten Per Cent *27–28*, 405
1066—And All That *38–39*, 491
Tenacity (see *The S.S. Tenacity*)
Tender Trap, The *54–55*, 368;
   61–62, 304
Tenderfoot, The *99–09*, 454
Tenderloin *60–61*, 301s
Tendresse, La *22–23*, 461
Tenement Tragedy, A *99–09*, 526
Tennessee's Pardner *94–99*, 89
Tennis Anyone? *67–68*, 414
Tenor, The *09–19*, 560
Tentation, La *94–99*, 209
Tenth Avenue *27–28*, 390
Tenth Man, The *59–60*, 302; *67–68*,
   346

Tenth of an Inch Makes the
  Difference, A *62–63*, 318
Tenting Tonight *46–47*, 474
Tents of the Arabs, The *09–19*, 650
Terence *99–09*, 451
Termagant, The *94–99*, 249
Terminal *69–70*, 369; 376; *70–71*
Terra Baja *36–37*, 499
Terrible Jim Fitch *68–69*, 448
Terrible Meek, The *09–19*, 469
Terrible Swift Sword, The *55–56*,
  362
Terzo Marito, Il *09–19*, 656
Tess of the D'Urbervilles *94–99*,
  169, 195; *99–09*, 409
Testament de Caesar Giradot, Le
  94–99, 132
Tethered Sheep *09–19*, 548
Texas, Li'l Darlin' *49–50*, 361s
Texas Nightingale, The *22–23*, 492
Texas Steer, A *94–99*, 199
Texas Town *40–41*, 431
Thais (1) *09–19*, 441
Thais (2) *31–32*, 375
Thalia Mara (see *Arthur Mahoney &*
  Thalia Mara)
Thank You *21–22*, 430
Thank You, Miss Victoria *65–66*,
  432
Thank You, Svoboda *43–44*, 460
Thanks for Tomorrow *37–38*, 464;
  38–39, 485
Thark *49–50*, 385
That Awful Mrs. Eaton *24–25*, 460
That Day *22–23*, 469
That Ferguson Family *28–29*, 437
That 5 A.M. Jazz *64–65*, 344s
That French Lady *26–27*, 494
That Girl at the Bijou *56–57*, 333
That Hat! *64–65*, 342
That Imprudent Young Couple
  94–99, 145
That Lady *49–50*, 361
That Man *94–99*, 251
That Man and I *99–09*, 453
That Old Devil *43–44*, 481
That Overcoat *94–99*, 221

That Rib of Adam *37–38*, 463
That Sort *09–19*, 538
That Summer—That Fall *66–67*,
  385
That Thing at the Cherry Lane
  64–65, 359
That Worthless Fellow Platonov
  39–40, 446
That's All *69–70*, 345
That's Gratitude *30–31*, 410; *31–32*,
  522
That's the Woman *30–31*, 407
That's Your Trouble *69–70*, 345
Theater *41–42*, 413; *45–46*, 450
Theater of Peretz, The *63–64*, 351
Theater of the Absurd *61–62*, 322
Theater of the Balustrade *70–71*
Theater of the Piccoli (see *Teatro*
  dei Piccoli)
Theater of the Soul *41–42*, 459
The-Merry-Go-Round *99–09*, 562
Them's the Reporters *34–35*, 482
Then . . . *62–63*, 339
Theodora, The Quean *33–34*, 490
Theodore Tiller Marionettes *38–39*,
  489
There and Back *99–09*, 432
There and Return (opera rep)
  42–43, 487
There Is a Play Tonight *60–61*, 44
There, Is No End *49–50*, 384
There Shall Be No Night *39–40*,
  457; *40–41*, 376
There Was a Little Girl *59–60*, 324
There You Are *31–32*, 513
There's a Girl in My Soup *67–68*,
  345
There's Always a Breeze *37–38*,
  429
There's Always a Murder *53–54*,
  358
There's Always Juliet *31–32*, 478;
  32–33, 412; *46–47*, 485
There's Many a Slip *99–09*, 416
There's Wisdom in Women *35–36*,
  427
Therese *45–46*, 397

Therese Raquin *94–99*, 124; *45–46*, 397

These Charming People *25–26*, 464

These Days *28–29*, 415

These Few Ashes *28–29*, 408

These Modern Women *27–28*, 508

These People *37–38*, 466

These Tender Mercies *47–48*, 412

These Two *33–34*, 526

Thespis *52–53*, 308

They All Come to Moscow *32–33*, 494

They All Want Something *26–27*, 402

They All Want to Get Married *44–45*, 443

They All Want to Play Hamlet *60–61*, 295

They Came *70–71*

They Don't Mean Any Harm *31–32*, 484

They Fought for What *38–39*, 485

They Got Jack *65–66*, 437

They Had to See Paris *30–31*, 453

They Knew What They Wanted *24–25*, 492; *39–40*, 401; *48–49*, 413; *55–56*, 387; *65–66*, 407

They Never Grow Up *29–30*, 520

They Refuse to Be Resurrected *38–39*, 492

They Refuse to Be Resurrected (mn) *37–38*, 466

They Shall Not Die *33–34*, 499; *49–50*, 383

They Should Have Stood in Bed *41–42*, 440

They Walk Alone *40–41*, 419

Thief, The *99–09*, 544; *09–19*, 453; *26–27*, 512

Thieves' Carnival (*Le Bal des Voleurs*) *38–39*, 492; *54–55*, 52, 56; *63–64*, 369

Thin Ice *22–23*, 465

Things That Almost Happen *70–71*

Things That Are Caesar's *32–33*, 403

Things That Count, The *09–19*, 516

Things We Do *32–33*, 377

Third Best Sport *58–59*, 316

Third Degree, The *99–09*, 577; *48–49*, 425

Third Ear, The *63–64*, 366

Third Floor Back, The (see also *The Passing of the Third Floor Back*) *47–48*, 427

Third Little Show, The *30–31*, 530

Third Party, The *09–19*, 528

Thirst *28–29*, 502

Thirsty Soil *36–37*, 458

13 Daughters *60–61*, 327s

Thirteenth Chair, The *09–19*, 587

30 Days Hath September *38–39*, 409

39 East *09–19*, 654

This Bird of Dawning Singeth All Night Long *68–69*, 430

This Earth Is Ours *39–40*, 446

This Fine-Pretty World *23–24*, 336, 377

This Flower *29–30*, 272

This Happy Breed *51–52*, 334

This Here Nice Place *66–67*, 405

This Is New York *30–31*, 462

This Is Our Play *47–48*, 430

This Is the Army *42–43*, 421

This Is the End *63–64*, 368

This Is the Rill Speaking *65–66*, 432

This Man's Town *29–30*, 507

This Music Crept by Me Upon the Waters *59–60*, 49

This One Man *30–31*, 438

This Our House *35–36*, 449

This Picture and That *94–99*, 169

This Property Condemned *45–46*, 450

This Proud Pilgrimage *39–40*, 470

This Rock *42–43*, 464

This Side of Paradise *61–62*, 324

This Thing Called Love *28–29*, 374; *45–46*, 457; *47–48*, 425

This Time Tomorrow *47–48*, 363

This, Too, Shall Pass *45–46*, 439

This Was a Man *26–27*, 431

This Was Burlesque (1) *61–62*, 325

This Was Burlesque (2) *64–65*, 329s; *69–70*, 358s

This Way Out *09–19*, 605

This Way to the Tomb *61–62*, 314

This Woman and This Man *99–09*, 578

This Woman Business *26–27*, 438

This Year of Grace *28–29*, 410

Thistle in My Bed *63–64*, 352

Thomas and Sally *37–38*, 412

Thomas Jefferson *42–43*, 29

Thora *37–38*, 407; *62–63*, 325

Thoroughbred (1) *94–99*, 172

Thoroughbred (2) *33–34*, 455

Thoroughbreds *24–25*, 449

Those Endearing Young Charms *43–44*, 400; *44–45*, 436; *45–46*, 450

Those That Play the Clowns *66–67*, 373

Those We Love *29–30*, 498

Those Who Walk in Darkness *19–20*, 345

Thoughts on the Instant of Greeting a Friend on the Street *67–68*, 406

Thousand Clowns, A *61–62*, 296

Thousand Generations and One, A *22–23*, 571

Thousand Summers, A *31–32*, 515

Thousand Years Ago, A *09–19*, 518

Thracian Horses, The *61–62*, 307

Three and One *33–34*, 449

Three at the Cherry Lane *63–64*, 362

3 Bags Full *65–66*, 401

Three Bears, The *09–19*, 614

Three Bears, The (mn) *35–36*, 512

Three Blind Mice *39–40*, 466

Three by Ferlinghetti *70–71*

3 by Ghelderode *63–64*, 352

3 x 3 *61–62*, 325

Three Cheers *28–29*, 395

Three Cities *38–39*, 493

Three Daughters *39–40*, 474

Three Daughters of Monsieur Dupont, The *09–19*, 417

Three Doors *24–25*, 580

Three Dragoons, The *94–99*, 251

Three Faces East *09–19*, 632

Three for Diana *09–19*, 656

3 for Tonight *54–55*, 403s

Three Fountains, The *62–63*, 326

Three Gifts *45–46*, 460; *46–47*, 496

Three Grotesques *70–71*

Three Guardsmen, The *94–99*, 133, 195, 234; *35–36*, 511

Three Hand Reel *66–67*, 407

Three in One *52–53*, 309

Three Kingdoms, The *29–30*, 497

Three Lights, The *09–19*, 456

Three Little Girls *29–30*, 523

Three Little Lambs *99–09*, 358

Three Little Maids *99–09*, 435

Three Live Ghosts *20–21*, 388

Three Men and a Girl *38–39*, 493

Three Men and a Woman *31–32*, 463

Three Men on a Horse *34–35*, 446; *37–38*, 462; *41–42*, 423; *42–43*, 435; *61–62*, 260; *69–70*, 300

3 Modern Japanese Plays *60–61*, 44

Three Musketeers, The (source) *94–99*, 133, 195, 234, 254, 255; *20–21*, 450; *27–28*, 526; *68–69*, 374

Three Musketeers, The (p) *68–69*, 374

Three Musketeers, The (m 1) *20–21*, 450

Three Musketeers, The (m 2) *27–28*, 526

Three of Hearts *09–19*, 553

Three of Us, The *99–09*, 523

Three One-Act Plays *61–62*, 311

Three One-Act Plays With Songs *70–71*

Three Pills in a Bottle *22–23*, 574

Three Plays by Ed Bullins *67–68*, 36

Three Romeos, The *09–19*, 457

Three Showers *19–20*, 444

Three Sisters *22–23*, 517; *26–27*, 414; *37–38*, 465; *39–40*, 402; *42–43*, 452; *46–47*, 485; *54–55*, 56; *59–60*, 42; *64–65*, 295, 323; *69–70*, 297

Three Thousand Red Ants *70–71*

Three Times the Hour *31–32*, 382

Three to Make Ready *45–46*, 431

Three Twins *99–09*, 563

Three Waltzes *37–38*, 405

Three Wise Fools *09–19*, 642;
    35–36, 489

Three Wishes for Jamie *51–52*, 315s

Three . . . With Women in Mind
    70–71

Three Wonder Tales *09–19*, 410

Three-Cornered Moon *32–33*, 477

Threepenny (3-Penny) Opera, The
    32–33, 483; *53–54*, 358; *63–64*,
    342; *67–68*, 401

Threepenny Opera, The (mn) *66–67*,
    366

Three's a Crowd (1) *19–20*, 395

Three's a Crowd (2) *30–31*, 432

Three's a Family *42–43*, 475; *43–44*,
    489

Thrilby *94–99*, 137

Thrills *24–25*, 579

Through the Looking Glass (source)
    09–19, 548; *32–33*, 434; *46–47*,
    439

Through the Night *30–31*, 402

Through the Years *31–32*, 471s

Thumbs Down *23–24*, 296

Thumbs Up *34–35*, 432

Thunder *19–20*, 354

Thunder in the Air *29–30*, 438

Thunder on the Left *33–34*, 453;
    44–45, 441; *53–54*, 358

Thunder Rock *39–40*, 411; *45–46*,
    450

Thunderbolt, The *09–19*, 430, 458

Thurber Carnival, A *59–60*, 322;
    60–61, 289; *65–66*, 436

Thurber Country *59–60*, 226

Thursday Evening *22–23*, 572

Thus *61–62*, 329

Thy Name Is Woman *20–21*, 404

Thy Neighbor's Wife *09–19*, 450

Tia Juana *27–28*, 453

Tiao Ch'an (see *The Beautiful Bait*)

Ticket of Leave Man, The *94–99*,
    99, 235; *34–35*, 483; *61–62*, 316

Tickets, Please (1) *43–44*, 490

Tickets, Please! (2) *49–50*, 379s

Tickle Me *20–21*, 367

Tick-Tack-Toe *19–20*, 431

Ti-Coq *50–51*, 348

Tidbits of '46 *45–46*, 458; *46–47*,
    415

Tidbits of 1946 *46–47*, 415

Tide of Life, A *94–99*, 94

Tide Rises *34–35*, 483

Tide Rising *36–37*, 456

Tidings Brought to Mary, The
    (*L'Annonce Fait a Marie*) *22–23*,
    510; *64–65*, 357

Tied to a Stick (*Boshibari*) *70–71*

Tiger, The *62–63*, 325

Tiger at the Gates *55–56*, 349;
    59–60, 43; *67–68*, 348

Tiger Cats *24–25*, 475

Tiger Rag, The *60–61*, 41

Tiger Rose *09–19*, 609

Tiger! Tiger! *09–19*, 644

Tiger, Tiger Burning Bright *62–63*,
    291

Tight Britches *34–35*, 370

Tightwad, The *26–27*, 508

Till I Come Back to You *43–44*,
    433

Till the Day I Die *34–35*, 464

Tiller Marionettes (see *Theodore
    Tiller Marionettes*)

Tillie *09–19*, 649

Tillie's Nightmare *09–19*, 419

Timber House *36–37*, 407

Time *23–24*, 361

Time and the Conways *37–38*, 410

Time for Bed—Take Me to Bed
    69–70, 334

Time for Elizabeth *48–49*, 384

Time for Singing, A *65–66*, 410s

Time for the Gentle People, A
    66–67, 421

Time, Gentlemen Please *61–62*, 312s

Time Is a Dream *23–24*, 336

Time Limit! *55–56*, 371; *59–60*, 43

Time of Storm, The *53–54*, 359

Time of the Cuckoo, The *52–53*,
    260; *58–59*, 52; *64–65*, 330

Time of the Key, A *63–64*, 345

Time of Vengeance *59–60,* 46

Time of Your Life, The *39–40,* 406; *40–41,* 380; *46–47,* 495; *54–55,* 392; *69–70,* 303

Time Out for Ginger *52–53,* 272

Time Remembered *57–58,* 301

Time, the Place and the Girl, The *99–09,* 541; *42–43,* 438

Time to Burn *40–41,* 431

Time to Go *59–60,* 49

Times (London) *64–65,* 303

Times Have Changed *34–35,* 457

Tin Drum, The *65–66,* 434

Tin Pan Alley *28–29,* 409

Tin Top Valley *46–47,* 495

Tinker's Dam *42–43,* 486

Tinker's Wedding, The *56–57,* 55; *67–68,* 409

Tinted Venus, The *43–44,* 417

Tiny Alice *64–65,* 322; *69–70,* 297

Tip Top *20–21,* 393

Tipping the Winner *09–19,* 532

Tip-Toes *25–26,* 525

Tired *23–24,* 433

Tired Business Man *28–29,* 510

'Tis of Thee *40–41,* 389

'Tis Pity She's a Whore *58–59,* 52; *70–71*

Tit for Tat *99–09,* 460

Title, The *21–22,* 460

Title Mart, The *99–09,* 509

Titus Andronicus *67–68,* 94

To Be Continued *51–52,* 320

To Be or Not to Be—What Kind of a Question Is That? *70–71*s

To Be Young, Gifted and Black (or The World of Lorraine Hansberry in Her Own Words) *68–69,* 442

To Broadway With Love *63–64,* 372s

To Bury a Cousin *66–67,* 420

To Clothe the Naked *66–67,* 418

To Damascus *60–61,* 45

To Dorothy, a Son *51–52,* 293

To Have and to Hold *99–09,* 389

To His Coy Mistress *62–63,* 322

To Love *22–23,* 476

To Make My Bread *35–36,* 431

To My Husband *35–36,* 508

To Nemesis, or Love and Hate *94–99,* 109

To Quito and Back *37–38,* 378

To See a World *62–63,* 322

To See Ourselves *34–35,* 475

To Tell You the Truth *47–48,* 426

To the Chicago Abyss *65–66,* 421

To the Ladies *21–22,* 512

To the Water Tower *62–63,* 330

Toast of the Town, The *99–09,* 502

Tobacco Road *33–34,* 467; *36–37,* 488; *42–43,* 427; *43–44,* 409; *49–50,* 375; *59–60,* 43

Tobias and the Angel *36–37,* 493; *49–50,* 385

Toby's Bow *09–19,* 652

Today *09–19,* 510

Today We Saw a Turtle *69–70,* 378

Toddles *99–09,* 560

Todo un Hombre *36–37,* 499

Toilet, The *64–65,* 350

'Toinette *61–62,* 313s

Told in the Hills *99–09,* 533

Tom Jones *99–09,* 550

Tom Moore *99–09,* 393

Tom Paine *66–67,* 36; *67–68,* 404

Tom Pinch *99–09,* 384, 385

(The Adventures of) Tom Sawyer (source) *94–99,* 231; *31–32,* 449; *56–57,* 371

Tom Sawyer (p) *31–32,* 449; *34–35,* 484; *37–38,* 467; *47–48,* 430

Tom Sawyer (mn) *36–37,* 498

Tom Sawyer—Ballad of Mississippi *47–48,* 430

Tom Thumb revue *37–38,* 467

Tombeau Sous l'Arc de Triomphe, Le *28–29,* 404; *31–32,* 416

Tommy *26–27,* 457; *33–34,* 425

Tommy Rot *99–09,* 420

To-morrow *28–29,* 446

Tomorrow and Tomorrow *30–31,* 479; *46–47,* 485

Tomorrow the World *42–43,* 472

Tomorrow's a Holiday *35–36,* 456

Tomorrow's Harvest *34–35*, 420
Tomorrow's Yesterday *44–45*, 441
Tone Pictures *26–27*, 504
Tongues of Men, The *09–19*, 514
Tonight at Eight-Thirty (8:30)
   36–37, 435; *45–46*, 450; *47–48*,
   384, 385; *66–67*, 392
"To-night at 12" *28–29*, 416
Tonight in Living Color *69–70*, 334
Tonight in Samarkand *54–55*, 398
Tonight or Never *30–31*, 456;
   40–41, 410
Tonight's the Night *09–19*, 542
Tony Sarg Marionettes *32–33*, 439;
   33–34, 534; *34–35*, 484; *35–36*,
   512; *36–37*, 498; *37–38*, 467;
   38–39, 489
Too Close to Comfort *59–60*, 49
Too Hot for Maneuvers *44–45*, 430
Too Late the Phalarope *56–57*, 322
Too Many Boats *34–35*, 369
Too Many Cooks *09–19*, 522;
   22–23, 484
Too Many Girls *39–40*, 404
Too Many Heroes *37–38*, 389
Too Many Husbands *19–20*, 368
Too Much Johnson *94–99*, 107;
   09–19, 432; *63–64*, 356
Too Much Party *33–34*, 503
Too True to Be Good *31–32*, 502;
   62–63, 300
Toot Sweet *09–19*, 656
Toothbrush, The *70–71*
Toot-Toot! *09–19*, 624
Top Banana *51–52*, 290s
Top o' th' World, The *99–09*, 548
Top o' the Hill *29–30*, 450
Top Speed *29–30*, 467
Topaze *29–30*, 493; *30–31*, 403, 491;
   47–48, 371
Topics of 1923 *23–24*, 358
Toplitzky of Notre Dame *46–47*,
   450
Top-Hole *24–25*, 440
Top-Notchers *41–42*, 454
Topsy and Eva *24–25*, 511
Topsy-Turvy *38–39*, 494

Torch Bearers (Torchbearers), The
   22–23, 444; *60–61*, 48
Torch Song 30–31, 404
Torches *22–23*, 574
Torches, The *09–19*, 611
Toreador *70–71*
Toreador, The *99–09*, 403
Tornado *37–38*, 464
Tornado, The *94–99*, 168
Torquato Tasso *49–50*, 383
Tortilla Flat *37–38*, 416
Tortue, La *94–99*, 237
Tosca, La (p) *94–99*, 163, 222;
   99–09, 380; *09–19*, 432
Tosca, La (opera rep) *43–44*,
   438, 474; *44–45*, 378; *45–46*, 387,
   441; *46–47*, 409, 480; *47–48*, 347,
   399
Toto *20–21*, 438
Toto, the Clown *34–35*, 484
Touch *70–71*s
Touch and Go *49–50*, 357s
Touch of Brimstone, A *35–36*, 407
Touch of the Poet, A *58–59*, 293;
   66–67, 392
Touchstone *52–53*, 283
Tour *67–68*, 407
Tour de Four *63–64*, 343s
Tourists, The *99–09*, 517
Tovarich (p) *36–37*, 418; *38–39*,
   492; *51–52*, 324; *62–63*, 302
Tovarich (m) *62–63*, 302s
Tower Beyond Tragedy, The *50–51*,
   331
Town Boy *29–30*, 411
Town House *48–49*, 383
Town Topics (see *Ned Wayburn's
   Town Topics*)
Town's Woman, The *28–29*, 478
Toy for the Clowns, A *62–63*, 313
Toymaker of Nuremberg, The
   99–09, 552
Toys in the Attic *59–60*, 322
Traffic, The *09–19*, 539
Tragedian in Spite of Himself, A
   47–48, 346
Tragedy of Homer Stills, The *70–71*

Tragedy of Nan, The *19–20*, 427;
  44–45, 436
Tragedy of the Future, A *09–19*,
  497
Tragedy Rehearsed, A *94–99*, 122
Tragic 18 *26–27*, 398
Tragic Jest *45–46*, 460
Tragical History of Doctor Faustus,
  The (see *Doctor Faustus*)
Trail of the Lonesome Pine, The
  09–19, 464
Train of Death, The *35–36*, 511
Trainer, Dean, Liepolt and Company
  68–69, 430
Traitor, The (1) *29–30*, 532
Traitor, The (2) *48–49*, 417
Tramp Abroad, A *65–66*, 404
Transfers *69–70*, 356
Transgressor, The *94–99*, 148
Transgressor Rides Again, The
  68–69, 453
Transit *37–38*, 465
Transit of Leo, The *94–99*, 157
Transplanting Jean *20–21*, 419
Trap, The *09–19*, 546
Trapp Family Singers, The *59–60*,
  303; *66–67*, 386
Trapped *28–29*, 372
Trapps *59–60*, 118; *65–66*, 430
Traveling Lady, The *54–55*, 371
Traveling Salesman, The *99–09*, 564
Traveller Without Luggage *64–65*,
  301
Travelling Man, The *09–19*, 591
Traviata, La (opera rep) *43–44*, 442,
  473; *44–45*, 378; *45–46*, 388, 440;
  46–47, 409, 479; *47–48*, 343, 347,
  399
Tread the Green Grass *49–50*, 385
Treasure, The *20–21*, 391
Treasure Girl *28–29*, 411
Treasure Hunters, The *48–49*, 430
Treasure Island *09–19*, 566; *31–32*,
  449; *37–38*, 460
Treasure Island (mn) *38–39*, 490
Treasury of Loyal Retainers, The
  (Chushingura) *69–70*, 296
Treat 'Em Rough *26–27*, 393

Treatment, The *67–68*, 412
Tree, The *31–32*, 505
Tree Grows in Brooklyn, A *50–51*,
  363s; *65–66*, 437
Tree of Knowledge, The *94–99*, 223
Trelawny of the "Wells" *94–99*,
  246; *09–19*, 435; *24–25*, 598;
  26–27, 471; *61–62*, 332; *69–70*,
  377; *70–71*
Trench Fantasy, A *09–19*, 616
Trevor *69–70*, 348
Trial *39–40*, 469
Trial, The *(Le Proces)* *52–53*, 269;
  64–65, 363
Trial by Fire *47–48*, 427
Trial by Jury *09–19*, 551; *31–32*,
  379; *32–33*, 485; *33–34*, 516;
  34–35, 365; *35–36*, 399, 400, 498;
  36–37, 399; *38–39*, 446; *39–40*,
  469; *40–41*, 382, 430; *41–42*, 432,
  458; *43–44*, 455; *45–46*, 458;
  47–48, 372, 375; *49–50*, 356;
  50–51, 347, 375; *52–53*, 263;
  55–56, 346; *62–63*, 286; *64–65*,
  313; *66–67*, 399
Trial by Jury (mn) *45–46*, 458
Trial Honeymoon *47–48*, 363
Trial Marriage *26–27*, 473; *27–28*,
  520
Trial Marriage, The *09–19*, 482
Trial of Dr. Beck, The *37–38*, 447
Trial of Joan of Arc, The *(Le Proces
  de Jeanne d'Arc)* *09–19*, 432, 589
  (and 605); *20–21*, 440
Trial of Lee Harvey Oswald, The
  67–68, 351
Trial of Mary Dugan, The *27–28*,
  407
Trial of Pontius Pilate, The *63–64*,
  371
Trial of the Catonsville Nine, The
  70–71
Trials of Brother Jero, The *67–68*,
  393
Triangle, The *99–09*, 510
Trick for Trick *31–32*, 481
Trifler, The *99–09*, 486
Trifles *09–19*, 579; *27–28*, 550

Trigger *27–28*, 468
Trigon, The *65–66*, 421
Trilby *94–99*, 121, 132, 235; *99–09*, 491; *09–19*, 549; *21–22*, 481
Trimmed in Scarlet *19–20*, 423
Trimplet, The *09–19*, 588
Trio *44–45*, 407
Triomphe de l'Amour, Le *58–59*, 295
Trip Around the World, A (mn) *35–36*, 513
Trip to Bountiful, The (A) *53–54*, 315; *58–59*, 53
Trip to Chinatown, A *94–99*, 96; *09–19*, 470; *50–51*, 374; *60–61*, 48
Trip to Coontown, A *94–99*, 227
Trip to Japan, A *09–19*, 398
Trip to Scarborough, A *28–29*, 482
Triple Crossed *26–27*, 525
Triple Play (1) *58–59*, 333
Triple Play (2) *68–69*, 432
Triple-A Plowed Under *35–36*, 472
Triplets *32–33*, 389
Tristan *40–41*, 422
Tristan and Isolde (opera rep) *43–44*, 440
Triumph *35–36*, 420
Triumph of an Empress, The *09–19*, 441
Triumph of Love, The *99–09*, 454
Triumph of Robert Emmett, The *68–69*, 452
Triumph of X, The *21–22*, 401
Triumphant Bachelor, The *27–28*, 405
Troilus and Cressida *31–32*, 520; *56–57*, 324; *63–64*, 353; *65–66*, 95
Trois Filles de Monsieur Dupont, Les *09–19*, 417
Trois Jeunes Filles Nues *28–29*, 475
Trois Maries, Les *32–33*, 458
Trois Masques, Les *23–24*, 333
Trois Rois, Les *32–33*, 458
Trojan Incident (dance program) *37–38*, 458
Trojan War Will Not Take Place, The *67–68*, 350

Trojan Women, The *37–38*, 463; *40–41*, 431; *46–47*, 485; *63–64*, 345, 354; *65–66*, 420
Trolly Party, The *94–99*, 172
Tropical Revue *44–45*, 440
Troubadour, A *99–09*, 367
Trouble in Tahiti *54–55*, 406; *64–65*, 363; *65–66*, 418
Trouble in the Works *69–70*, 345
Troubled Island, The (opera rep) *48–49*, 428
Troubled Waters *65–66*, 416
Troupe du Roi, La *69–70*, 313
Trouper, The *25–26*, 563
Trovatore, Il (opera rep) *43–44*, 474; *45–46*, 440; *46–47*, 480; *47–48*, 399
Troyka *29–30*, 519
Truckline Cafe *45–46*, 429
Trudi Schoop (dance programs) *46–47*, 487
True American, A *94–99*, 87
True Blue, or The Press Gang *37–38*, 412
True Irish Hearts *94–99*, 255
True to Life *94–99*, 189
Truly Valiant *35–36*, 458
Trumpet Shall Sound, The *26–27*, 439
Trumpets and Drums *69–70*, 377
Trumpets of the Lord *63–64*, 354s; *68–69*, 413s
Truth *(Ododo)* *70–71*
Truth, The *99–09*, 531; *09–19*, 526; *69–70*, 371
Truth About Blayds, The *21–22*, 527; *31–32*, 504
Truth Game, The *30–31*, 472
Truth Wagon, The *09–19*, 466
Try and Get It *43–44*, 403
Try It With Alice *24–25*, 429
Trysting Place, The *22–23*, 571
Tsar Fyodor Ivanovitch *22–23*, 517; *23–24*, 356
Tseril Mirel From Galicia *47–48*, 431
Tug of War *70–71*
Tumble In *09–19*, 654

Tumbler, The *59–60,* 321
Tunnel of Love, The *56–57,* 354
Turandot (see *Princess Turandot*)
Turista, La *66–67,* 421
Turn of the Screw, The (source)
  47–48, 423; *49–50,* 371; *58–59,* 52
Turn of the Screw, The *47–48,* 423
Turn of the Tide *94–99,* 184
Turn to the Right! *09–19,* 578
Turning Point, The *09–19,* 415
Turpentine *36–37,* 496
Turtle, The *94–99,* 237
Tweedles *23–24,* 298
Twelfth Disciple, The *29–30,* 540
Twelfth Night *94–99,* 107, 167;
  99–09, 363, 454, 469, 470, 480,
  534; *09–19,* 412, 413, 447, 478,
  508, 523, 539; *19–20,* 363; *21–22,*
  445; *23–24,* 328; *26–27,* 444;
  29–30, 516; *30–31,* 431; *32–33,*
  424; *40–41,* 394; *41–42,* 418;
  44–45, 436; *49–50,* 355; *54–55,* 56;
  56–57, 55; *58–59,* 52, 310; *60–61,*
  48; *63–64,* 347, 360; *67–68,* 397,
  398; *69–70,* 337; *70–71*
Twelve Dancing Princesses, The
  38–39, 490
Twelve Miles Out *25–26,* 497
Twelve Months Later *99–09,* 365
Twelve Pound Look, The *09–19,*
  439
Twelve Temptations *94–99,* 143
12,000 *27–28,* 525
Twentieth (20th) Century *32–33,*
  444; *50–51,* 337
Twentieth Century Girl, The *94–99,*
  119
Twentieth Century Guy, A *61–62,*
  317
Twenty Days in the Shade *99–09,*
  555
Twenty-five Cent White Cap, The
  61–62, 325
$25 an Hour *32–33,* 494
Twenty-four Inventions *64–65,* 297
2905 or Tomorrow Land *99–09,*
  519

27 Wagons Full of Cotton *54–55,*
  406, 407
23 Pat O'Brien Movies *65–66,* 436
Twiddle-Twaddle *99–09,* 506
Twilight Walk *51–52,* 283
Twin Beds *09–19,* 528
Twin Sister, The *99–09,* 407
Twinkle, Twinkle *26–27,* 429
Twirly Whirly *99–09,* 416
Two Angry Women of Abingdon
  36–37, 497
Two at Les Deux *61–62,* 317
Two Blind Beggars and One Less
  Blind *09–19,* 547
Two Blind Mice *48–49,* 414
Two Blocks Away *21–22,* 406
Two Bouquets, The *37–38,* 446
Two by Ibsen *70–71*
Two by Saroyan *61–62,* 310
Two by Two (1) *24–25,* 548
Two by Two (2) *70–71s*
2 × 2 = 5 *27–28,* 459
Two Camps by Koutoukas *67–68,*
  403
Two Colonels, The *94–99,* 128
Two Escutcheons, The *94–99,* 162
Two Executioners, The *63–64,* 362
Two Fellows and a Girl *23–24,* 295
Two for Fun *60–61,* 48
Two for the Seesaw *57–58,* 309
Two for the Show *39–40,* 436
Two for Tonight *39–40,* 468
Two From Lost and Found *70–71*
Two From Ulysses *70–71*
Two Gentlemen of Verona *94–99,*
  125; *57–58,* 324
Two Girls Wanted *26–27,* 377
200,000 *36–37,* 497; *37–38,* 470
200 Were Chosen *36–37,* 433
Two Is Company *09–19,* 558
Two Little Brides *09–19,* 471
Two Little Girls in Blue *20–21,* 446
Two Little Sailor Boys *99–09,* 460
Two Little Vagrants *94–99,* 184
Two Married Men *24–25,* 523
Two Mr. Wetherbys, The *99–09,*
  516

Two Mrs. Carrolls, The *43–44*, 405; *44–45*, 369

Two New American Plays *67–68*, 408

Two Old Cronies *94–99*, 159

Two on an Island *39–40*, 431

Two on the Aisle *51–52*, 278s

Two Orphans, The *94–99*, 107, 235; *99–09*, 456; *25–26*, 579; *36–37*, 500

Two Roses, The *99–09*, 474

Two Schools, The *99–09*, 418

Two Seconds *31–32*, 407

Two Serious Ladies *53–54*, 84

Two Sisters *94–99*, 102

Two Slatterns and a King *36–37*, 499

Two Strange Women *32–33*, 449

Two Strangers Breakfast *60–61*, 294

Two Strangers From Nowhere *23–24*, 417

Two Times One *69–70*, 341

Two Virtues, The *09–19*, 561

Two Wanderers, The *94–99*, 247

Two Women *09–19*, 431

Two Women and That Man *09–19*, 402

Two's Company *52–53*, 275s

Tyger, The (Tyger, Tyger) *62–63*, 322; *68–69*, 407

Tyger! Tyger! and Other Burnings *68–69*, 407

Typhoon, The *09–19*, 467

Typists, The *62–63*, 325

Tyranny of Love, The *20–21*, 434

Tyranny of Tears, The *99–09*, 347; *09–19*, 509

Tyrant, The *30–31*, 451

Tzigane, The *94–99*, 135

Tzipke Fire *47–48*, 431

U.S.A. *59–60*, 350

U.S. vs. Julius and Ethel Rosenberg, The *69–70*, 328

UTBU *65–66*, 394

Ubu *69–70*, 375

Ubu Cocu *68–69*, 457

Ubu, the King *(Ubu Roi)* *52–53*, 308; *68–69*, 425

Uday Shan-Kar Hindu Dancers (dance programs) *33–34*, 520

Ugly Daughter, The *37–38*, 470

Ulysses (source) *58–59*, 55; *63–64*, 368

Ulysses *99–09*, 437

Ulysses in Nighttown *58–59*, 55; *63–64*, 368

Umbrella, The *64–65*, 361

Unborn, The *09–19*, 565

Unchastened Woman, The *09–19*, 239, 561; *25–26*, 555

Uncle Don's Easter Circus *37–38*, 467

Uncle Harry *41–42*, 452; *46–47*, 485

Uncle Remus (mn) *33–34*, 534

Uncle Sam *09–19*, 456

Uncle Sam's Money *09–19*, 526

Uncle Tom's Cabin (source) *94–99*, 134; *99–09*, 389; *24–25*, 511; *32–33*, 498; *36–37*, 423

Uncle Tom's Cabin (1) *94–99*, 134; *99–09*, 389

Uncle Tom's Cabin (2) *32–33*, 498

Uncle Vanya *23–24*, 356; *28–29*, 507; *29–30*, 524; *30–31*, 417; *45–46*, 443; *55–56*, 55; *70–71*

Uncle Willie *56–57*, 346

Uncommon Denominator, The *62–63*, 335

Unconquered, The *39–40*, 436

Under Conviction *22–23*, 571

Under Cover (1) *99–09*, 437

Under Cover (2) *09–19*, 529

Under Fire *09–19*, 555

Under Glass *33–34*, 452

Under Many Flags *09–19*, 474

Under Milk Wood *57–58*, 291; *60–61*, 359; *62–63*, 320; *69–70*, 311

Under Orders *09–19*, 633

Under Pressure *09–19*, 623

Under Sentence *09–19*, 584

Under Southern Skies *99–09*, 399

Under the Counter *47–48*, 356s

Under the Dome *94–99*, 247

Under the Gaslight *28–29*, 488;
67–68, 410

Under the Greenwood Tree *99–09*,
553

Under the Lash *94–99*, 108

Under the Lilacs *34–35*, 484

Under the Polar Star *94–99*, 174

Under the Red Globe *94–99*, 179

Under the Red Robe *94–99*, 190

Under the Sycamore Tree *59–60*,
355

Under the Weather *66–67*, 366

Under the Yum-Yum Tree *60–61*,
307; *63–64*, 366

Under This Roof *41–42*, 441

Under Two Flags *99–09*, 387

Undercover Man *66–67*, 399

Undercurrent, The *24–25*, 535

Underground *70–71*

Underpants, The *68–69*, 458

Undesirable Lady, An *33–34*,
439

Undine *09–19*, 458

Unexpected Husband *30–31*, 532

Unexpurgated Memoirs of Bernard
Mergendeiler, The *67–68*, 407

Unfair to Goliath *69–70*, 356s

Unforseen, The *99–09*, 426

Unicorn in the Garden, The *47–48*,
416, 417; *59–60*, 323; *60–61*, 289;
62–63, 310

Unicorn From the Stars, The *69–70*,
372

Uniform of Flesh *48–49*, 427; *50–51*,
101

Uninvited Guest, The *27–28*, 417

Union Pacific (dance program)
33–34, 519

Union Soldier, A *94–99*, 230

Universal Nigger, The *69–70*, 372

Unknown *94–99*, 226

Unknown Purple, The *09–19*, 637

Unknown Soldier, The *39–40*, 473

Unknown Soldier and His Wife, The
67–68, 340

Unknown War, The *60–61*, 295

Unknown Warrior, The *28–29*, 404;
31–32, 416

Unknown Woman, The *19–20*, 382

Unleavened Bread *99–09*, 386

Unmarried Father, The *28–29*, 252

Unnamable, The *70–71*

Unofficial Patriot, An *94–99*, 251–2

Unseen Hand, The *69–70*, 362, 375

Unsinkable Molly Brown, The
60–61, 304s

Unsophisticates, The *29–30*, 471

Until the Monkey Comes . . .
66–67, 400

Untitled Play (work in progress)
67–68, 411

Unto Such Glory ·*35–36*, 510; *36–37*,
496; *37–38*, 459

Unto the Third *32–33*, 486

Unusual Concert, An (mn) *63–64*,
305

Unwelcome Mrs. Hatch, The *99–09*,
400

Unwritten Chapter, The *20–21*, 394

Unwritten Law, The *09–19*, 495

Up and Down Broadway *09–19*, 421

Up East and Way Down West
70–71

Up and Up, The *30–31*, 408

Up Eden *68–69*, 436

Up From Nowhere *19–20*, 346

Up in Central Park *44–45*, 413;
46–47, 413

Up in Mabel's Room *09–19*, 649

Up Pops the Devil *30–31*, 406;
31–32, 409

Up She Goes *22–23*, 484

Up the Ladder *21–22*, 522

Up the Line *26–27*, 431

Up the Rebels *41–42*, 458

Up to Thursday *64–65*, 354

Up York State *99–09*, 395

Ups and Downs of Life *94–99*, 123

Ups-a Daisy *28–29*, 392

Upstart, The *09–19*, 423

Upstairs and Down *09–19*, 582

Uptown West *22–23*, 553; *32–33*,
377

Uriel Acosta *39–40,* 474
Usurper, The *99–09,* 475
Utopia, Limited *61–62,* 332

V for Victory *41–42,* 439
V.I.P (Very Important Phallus), The
  70–71
Vagabond King, The *25–26,* 451;
  43–44, 402; *61–62,* 332
Vagabondia *94–99,* 248
Vagrant, The *61–62,* 323
Vale of Avoca, The *94–99,* 132
Valerie Bettis (dance programs)
  46–47, 486; *47–48,* 415; *48–49,*
  429
Valiant, The *25–26,* 591; *27–28,*
  549; *41–42,* 459
Valley Forge *34–35,* 422
Valley of Content, The *24–25,* 525
Valmouth *60–61,* 349s
Values *26–27,* 523
Vamp, The *55–56,* 360s
Vampire, The *99–09,* 576
Van Dycke, The *99–09,* 547
Vanderbilt Cup, The *99–09,* 507
Vanderbilt Revue, The *30–31,* 447
Vanities (see *Earl Carroll's Vanities;*
  Murder at the Vanities)
Vanity Fair (source) *99–09,* 348;
  09–19, 436; *28–29,* 509
Vanity Fair *09–19,* 436
Vanity of Nothing *62–63,* 326
Van Volkenburg Marionettes (see
  Ellen Van Volkenburg Marionettes)
Variations *64–65,* 297
Varying Shore, The *21–22,* 472
Vaudeville (untitled material &
  programs) *45–46,* 459; *66–67,*
  386; *67–68,* 362; *69–70,* 298;
  70–71
Vegetable, The *28–29,* 492; *63–64,*
  367
Veille d'Armes, La *20–21,* 423
Veils *27–28,* 530
Veldt, The *65–66,* 421
Velvet Glove, The *49–50,* 365
Velvet Lady, The *09–19,* 650

Vendetta, The (1) *94–99,* 138
Vendetta, The (2) *94–99,* 231
Veneer *29–30,* 441
Venetian, The *31–32,* 419
Venetian Glass Nephew, The *30–31,*
  496
Venetian Romance, A *99–09,* 460
Venetian Twins, The *(I Due Gemelli*
  Veneziani) *67–68,* 379
Venturi, The *69–70,* 378
Venus *27–28,* 476
Venus and Adonis *63–64,* 360
Venus at Large *61–62,* 296
Venus Observed *51–52,* 310
Venus-Shot *66–67,* 400
Vera Violetta *09–19,* 458
Verbena de la Paloma, La *68–69,*
  415
Verge, The *21–22,* 461
Verlorene Paradies, Das *94–99,* 201
Verlorene Sohn, Der *09–19,* 593
Vermont *28–29,* 450
Veronica *65–66,* 426
Veronique *99–09,* 499
Versunkene Glocke, Die *36–37,*
  500
Very Good, Eddie *09–19,* 567
Very Good Young Man, A *09–19,*
  633
Very Idea, The *09–19,* 602
Very Little Faust and Much
  Marguerite *94–99,* 205
Very Minute, The *09–19,* 598
Very Naked Boy, The *09–19,* 588,
  650
Very Rich Woman, A *65–66,* 372
Very Special Baby, A *56–57,* 334
Very Warm for May *39–40,* 412
Very Wise Virgin, A *26–27,* 532
Via Crucis *23–24,* 343
Via Wireless *99–09,* 572
Viceroy, The *99–09,* 367
Viceroy Sarah *41–42,* 402
Vickie *42–43,* 430
Victim, The *51–52,* 332
Victims, The *67–68,* 402
Victims of Amnesia, The *70–71*

Victims of Duty *59–60,* 49; *63–64,*
　366; *67–68,* 402
Victor Borge's One-Man Show
　53–54, 308
Victor, or The Children Take Over
　68–69, 425
Victoria Cross, The *94–99,* 85
Victoria Regina *35–36,* 453; *36–37,*
　402; *38–39,* 410
Victors, The (1) *37–38,* 468
Victors, The (2) *37–38,* 468
Victory Belles *43–44,* 421
Vida es Sueno, La (see *Life Is a*
　Dream)
Vie de Boheme *94–99,* 167
Vie Parisienne, La *42–43,* 487;
　44–45, 380; *63–64,* 326
Vienna at Night *44–45,* 444
Vienna Life *(Wiener Blut)* *99–09,*
　386; *64–65,* 299s
Vient de Paraitre *32–33,* 490
Vierge Folle, La *23–24,* 410
Viet Rock *66–67,* 407
View From the Bridge, A *55–56,*
　347; *64–65,* 353
View From Under the Bridge, A
　64–65, 341
Viewing, The *66–67,* 422
Vigil, The *47–48,* 405
Vik *09–19,* 526
Vikings, The *29–30,* 543
Villa of Madame Video, The *59–60,*
　46
Villa Primrose *09–19,* 479
Village Green *41–42,* 393
Village Lawyer, The *99–09,* 560
Village Postmaster, The *94–99,* 172;
　99–09, 382
Village Wooing *42–43,* 489
Vimazoluleka *68–69,* 456
Vincent *59–60,* 40
Vinegar Buyer, The *99–09,* 433
Vinegar Tree, The *30–31,* 457
Vintage, The *49–50,* 384
Vintage '60 *60–61,* 292s
Vinyl *67–68,* 409
Violet *44–45,* 390

Violet, The *30–31,* 423
Violin Maker of Cremona, The
　94–99, 93
Virgin, The *25–26,* 558
Virgin Man, The *26–27,* 462
Virgin of Bethulia, The *24–25,* 547
Virgin of the Lake, The *47–48,* 420
Virginia *37–38,* 367
Virginia Courtship, A *94–99,* 223
Virginia Reel *46–47,* 463
Virginia Runs Away *23–24,* 327
Virginia Sale *45–46,* 458
Virginian, The *99–09,* 451
Virginius *94–99,* 105; *99–09,* 545
Virtue (?) *22–23,* 491
Virtue's Bed *29–30,* 524
Vision of Vasavadatta, The *63–64,*
　368
Visit, The *57–58,* 332; *59–60,* 326;
　67–68, 410
Visit to a Small Planet *56–57,* 354
Visitor, The *44–45,* 389
Visitor From Forest Hills *67–68,*
　363
Visitor From Hollywood *67–68,*
　363
Visitor From Mamaroneck *67–68,*
　363
Vitrail, Le *09–19,* 589 (and 605)
Viva Madison Avenue! *59–60,* 330
Viva O'Brien *41–42,* 403
Vivian's Papas *99–09,* 434
Vogues of 1924 *23–24,* 413
Voice From the Minaret, The *21–22,*
　500
Voice in the Dark, A *19–20,* 341
Voice of Israel *48–49,* 429
Voice of McConnell, The *09–19,*
　648
Voice of the Turtle, The *43–44,* 434;
　61–62, 304
Voice to Call Your Own, A *70–71*
Voices *09–19,* 588
Volpone *27–28,* 535; *29–30,* 509;
　46–47, 467; *47–48,* 345; *56–57,* 55,
　353; *63–64,* 325; *67–68,* 94
Voltaire *21–22,* 528

Voodoo dramas & songs (untitled programs) *44–45*, 438; *44–45*, 440

Vortex, The *25–26*, 445; *45–46*, 450

Votes for Women *99–09*, 579

Voyage de Monsieur Perrichon, Le *37–38*, 469

WPA Federal Theater Project (see *Federal Theater Project*)

Wages for Wives *23–24*, 321

Wages of Sin, The *94–99*, 135

Waifs of New York, The *94–99*, 108

Wait a Minim! *65–66*, 401s

Wait 'Til We're Married *21–22*, 426

Wait Until Dark *65–66*, 396

Waitin' *26–27*, 524

Waiting for Godot *55–56*, 385; *56–57*, 350; *58–59*, 53; *67–68*, 405; *70–71*

Waiting for Lefty *34–35*, 465; *35–36*, 402; *38–39*, 484; *45–46*, 450; *67–68*, 413

Wake up and Dream *29–30*, 473; *64–65*, 357

Wake up, Darling *55–56*, 386

Wake up, Jonathan! *20–21*, 420

Walk a Little Faster *32–33*, 433s

Walk Down Mah Street! *68–69*, 424s

Walk Hard *45–46*, 435

Walk Hard—Talk Loud *45–46*, 435

Walk in Dark Places, A *65–66*, 429

Walk in Darkness *63–64*, 349

Walk Into My Parlor *41–42*, 415

Walk Together Children *68–69*, 433

Walk Together Chillun *35–36*, 466

Walk With Me *63–64*, 371

Walk With Music *39–40*, 466

Walking Delegate, The *94–99*, 229

Walking Gentleman, The *41–42*, 450

Walking Happy *66–67*, 374s

Walking to Waldheim *67–68*, 394

Walk-Offs, The *09–19*, 638

Walk-Up *60–61*, 39

Wall, The *60–61*, 300

Wall Street *26–27*, 515

Wall Street Girl, The *09–19*, 470

Wall Street Scene *37–38*, 381

Wallace Puppeteers *38–39*, 489

Wallflower *43–44*, 451

Walls *70–71*

Walls of Jericho, The *99–09*, 496

Walls of the Ghetto *70–71*

Walrus and the Carpenter, The *41–42*, 410

Waltz Dream, A *99–09*, 556

Waltz in Goose Step *38–39*, 423

Waltz of the Dogs, The *27–28*, 545

Waltz of the Toreadors, The *56–57*, 349; *57–58*, 322; *58–59*, 53; *59–60*, 43

Wanderer, The *09–19*, 593

Wandering *67–68*, 406

Wandering Jew, The *21–22*, 449; *26–27*, 474

Wandering Stars *46–47*, 497

Wang *94–99*, 170; *99–09*, 459

Wanhope Building, The *46–47*, 460

Wanted *28–29*, 354

War *63–64*, 370; *65–66*, 432

War and Peace *41–42*, 458; *64–65*, 348; *66–67*, 371

War Bubbles *94–99*, 230

War Games *68–69*, 450

War of Wealth, The *94–99*, 165

War President *43–44*, 471

War Scare *38–39*, 487

War Song, The *28–29*, 379

War Wife *42–43*, 488

Ward of France, A *94–99*, 218

Ware Case, The *09–19*, 566

Warm Body, A *66–67*, 391

Warm Peninsula, The *59–60*, 298

Warning—A Theme for Linda, The *69–70*, 338

Warrens of Virginia, The *99–09*, 552

Warrior's Husband, The *23–24*, 430; *31–32*, 493; *41–42*, 455; *66–67*, 410

Wars of the Roses, The *70–71*

Wars of the World *09–19*, 530

Wasantha Wanasingh (dance programs) *47–48*, 415

Washington, All Change *39–40,* 472

Washington Heights *31–32,* 399

Washington Jitters *37–38,* 442

Washington Square *47–48,* 353

Washington's First Defeat *99–09,* 547

Wasp, The *22–23,* 549

Wasp's Nest, The *27–28,* 439

Watch on the Rhine *40–41,* 422

Watch Your Neighbor *09–19,* 635

Watch Your Step *09–19,* 541

Watched Pot, The *47–48,* 425

Watcher, The *09–19,* 412

Water Carrier, The *36–37,* 500

Waterbury Tales, The *41–42,* 461

Watercolor (& Criss-Crossing) *69–70,* 312

Watering Place, The *68–69,* 409

Waterloo *99–09,* 353, 442

Waterloo Bridge *29–30,* 474; *47–48,* 429

Waters of Babylon, The *65–66,* 437

Watt *70–71*

Waves, The *60–61,* 48; *67–68,* 410

Wax Museum, The *68–69,* 455

Way, The *40–41,* 430

Way Down East *94–99,* 223; *99–09,* 399, 448, 449

Way of a Woman, The *40–41,* 432

Way of Life, A *68–69,* 418

Way of the World, The (1) *99–09,* 399

Way of the World, The (2) *24–25,* 489; *30–31,* 530; *31–32,* 501; *54–55,* 56; *60–61,* 45

Way Out, The *32–33,* 436

Way Things Happen, The *23–24,* 392

Way to Win a Woman, A *94–99,* 96, 131

Ways and Means *36–37,* 437; *47–48,* 385; *66–67,* 393

Wayward Saint, The *54–55,* 399

Wayward Stork, The *65–66,* 394

We All Do *26–27,* 489

We Americans *26–27,* 401

We Are No Longer Children *31–32,* 499

We Are Seven *09–19,* 517

We Bombed in New Haven *68–69,* 385

We Can't Be as Bad as All That *09–19,* 434

We Comrades Three *66–67,* 371

We Girls *21–22,* 458

We Have Always Lived in the Castle *66–67,* 365

We Live and Laugh *35–36,* 479

We Moderns *23–24,* 407

We Never Learn *27–28,* 496

We the Living *39–40,* 436

We, the People *32–33,* 453

We Uns of Tennessee *94–99,* 260

We Were Dancing *36–37,* 436

We Will Dream Again *46–47,* 493

We Will Live *44–45,* 444

Weak Link, The *39–40,* 441

Weak Sisters *25–26,* 472

Weak Woman, A *25–26,* 538

Weary Blues, The *66–67,* 423

Weasel, The *25–26,* 591

Weather Clear—Track Fast *27–28,* 435

Weather Hen, The *99–09,* 367

Weather Permitting *34–35,* 479

Weavers, The *09–19,* 566

Web, The *32–33,* 377

Wedding, The *47–48,* 346; *60–61,* 45

Wedding Bells *19–20,* 383

Wedding Breakfast *54–55,* 376

Wedding Day, The (1) *94–99,* 200

Wedding Day, The (2) *09–19,* 406

Wedding Feast, The *(Die Kleinburgerhochzeit) 70–71*

Wedding Gown, The *47–48,* 432

Wedding in Town, A *47–48,* 431

Wedding Night *46–47,* 497

Wedding Presents *27–28,* 549

Wedding Trip, The *09–19,* 461

Wednesday's Child *33–34,* 481

Week From Today, A *65–66,* 436

Weed-End (1) *29–30,* 427

Weekend (2) *67–68,* 367

Weep for the Virgins *35–36,* 444

Welcome Stranger *20–21,* 381

Welcome to Our City *09–19,* 423

Welded *23–24,* 409

Well of Romance, The *30–31,* 448

Well of the Saints, The *09–19,* 458;
   31–32, 468; *34–35,* 410; *37–38,*
   463

Wen, The *66–67,* 366

Wep-Ton-No-Mah, the Indian Mail
   Carrier *94–99,* 225

We're Civilized? *62–63,* 318s

Werewolf, The *24–25,* 437

Werther (opera rep) *47–48,* 343

West of the Moon *61–62,* 304

West Point Cadet, The *99–09,* 468

West Side Story *57–58,* 286s; *59–60,*
   336; *63–64,* 333; *65–66,* 418;
   68–69, 373

Western Folkways *34–35,* 484

Western Waters *37–38,* 407

Westerner, The *94–99,* 228

Wet Blanket, A *94–99,* 135

Wet Paint *64–65,* 358s

We've Got to Have Money *23–24,*
   305

What a Guy! *48–49,* 429

What a Killing *60–61,* 42

What a Life *37–38,* 438

What Ails You? *09–19,* 485

What Ann Brought Home *26–27,*
   484

What Big Ears *41–42,* 447

What D' You Call It *39–40,* 444

What Did We Do Wrong? *67–68,*
   347

What Do We Know? *27–28,* 473

What Every Woman Knows *99–09,*
   575; *25–26,* 583; *46–47,* 436;
   52–53, 289; *54–55,* 384

What Happened *63–64,* 346

What Happened at 22 *09–19,* 529

What Happened to Jones (?) *94–99,*
   205; *09–19,* 605; *36–37,* 499

What Happened to Mary *09–19,*
   498

What Is Love? 09–19, 532

What It Means to a Woman *09–19,*
   539

What Makes Sammy Run? *63–64,*
   327s

What Money Can't Buy *09–19,* 561

What Never Dies *26–27,* 449

What Price Glory? *24–25,* 448;
   48–49, 426

What Shall We Tell Caroline?
   61–62, 314

What the Butler Saw (1) *99–09,* 513

What the Butler Saw (2) *69–70,* 367

What the Doctor Ordered (1) *09–19,*
   451

What the Doctor Ordered (2) *27–28,*
   392

What the Public Wants *21–22,* 541

What Use Are Flowers *68–69,* 442

What Would You Do? *09–19,* 522

Whatever Goes Up *35–36,* 439

Whatever Possessed Her *33–34,*
   485

What's in a Name? *19–20,* 439

What's the Big Idea *25–26,* 576

What's the Matter With Susan?
   99–09, 446

What's the Use *26–27,* 375

What's Up *43–44,* 426

What's Your Husband Doing?
   09–19, 614

What's Your Wife Doing? *23–24,*
   326; *24–25,* 575

Wheel, The *21–22,* 403

Wheel of Fortune, The *94–99,* 245

Wheels Within Wheels *99–09,* 358

When a Man's Married *94–99,* 192

When Claudia Smiles *09–19,* 521

When Crummles Played *28–29,* 384

When Did You Last See My
   Mother? *66–67,* 410

When Differences Disappear *40–41,*
   431

When Dreams Come True *09–19,*
   504

When George IV Was King *94–99,*
   160

When Greek Meets Greek *94–99*, 240

When Hearts Are Young *47–48*, 432

When I Was a Child *60–61*, 48

When I'm Old *68–69*, 435

When in Rome *33–34*, 503

When Johnny Comes Marching Home *99–09*, 424; *09–19*, 601

When Knighthood Was in Flower *99–09*, 386, 464

When Knights Were Bold *99–09*, 542

When Ladies Meet *32–33*, 396; *39–40*, 397

When London Sleeps *94–99*, 175

When Sweet Sixteen *09–19*, 450

"When the Bough Breaks" (1) *31–32*, 479

When the Bough Breaks (2) *49–50*, 384

When the Cat's Away *94–99*, 188

When the Owl Screams *63–64*, 345s

When the Roll Is Called Up Yonder *29–30*, 536

When the Whirlwind Blows *23–24*, 431

When the Young Vine Blooms *09–19*, 564

When We Are Married *39–40*, 424

When We Are Young *20–21*, 407

When We Dead Awake(n) *99–09*, 487; *44–45*, 436; *65–66*, 433

When We Were Forty-One *99–09*, 491

When We Were Twenty-one *99–09*, 362, 521

When You Smile *25–26*, 463

Where Do We Go From Here? *38–39*, 427

Where E'er We Go *42–43*, 477; *43–44*, 404

Where Ignorance Is Bliss (see also *The Guardsman*) *09–19*, 506; *24–25*, 3

Where People Gather *67–68*, 389

Where Poppies Bloom *09–19*, 634

Where Stars Walk *47–48*, 382

Where the Cross Is Made *27–28*, 550

Where There's a Will *09–19*, 413; *38–39*, 450

Where's Charley? *48–49*, 388s; *50–51*, 346; *65–66*, 407

Where's Daddy? *65–66*, 400

Where's Your Husband? *26–27*, 461

Where's Your Wife? *19–20*, 362

Which Way Is Home? *52–53*, 308

Which Way the Wind *59–60*, 40

While Parents Sleep *33–34*, 531

While the Iron's Hot *63–64*, 371

While the Sun Shines *44–45*, 384

Whims *09–19*, 560

Whims of '37 *37–38*, 461

Whip, The *09–19*, 486

Whipping Boy, The *60–61*, 357

Whirl of New York, The *20–21*, 453

Whirl of Society *09–19*, 467

Whirl of the Town, The *94–99*, 202

Whirl of the World, The *09–19*, 519

Whirl-i-gig *99–09*, 350

Whirlpool *29–30*, 456

Whirlwind, The (1) *09–19*, 416, 456

Whirlwind, The (2) *19–20*, 405

Whisper in God's Ear, A *62–63*, 316

Whisper Into My Good Ear *62–63*, 315

Whisper to Me *60–61*, 39

Whispering Friends *27–28*, 513

Whispering Gallery, The *28–29*, 467

Whispering Wires *22–23*, 435

Whispers on the Wind *70–71*

Whistle in the Dark, A *69–70*, 341

Whistler's Grandmother *52–53*, 275

Whistling in the Dark *31–32*, 466; *32–33*, 415

Whistling Wizard and the Sultan of Tuffet, The (mn) *69–70*, 351; *70–71*

White Cargo *23–24*, 347; *25–26*, 582; *60–61*, 46

White Cat, The *99–09*, 499

White Collars *24–25*, 546

White Desert *23–24*, 339

White Devil, The *46–47*, 485;
   54–55, 52; *65–66*, 427
White Dress, The *32–33*, 436
White Eagle *27–28*, 480
White Feather, The *09–19*, 546
White Flame *29–30*, 433
White Flower, The *94–99*, 188
White Gold *25–26*, 489
White Guard, The *34–35*, 453
White Headed Boy, The (see *The
   White-Headed Boy*)
White Heather, The *94–99*, 216
White Hen, The *99–09*, 534
White Horse Inn *36–37*, 413
White House, the *63–64*, 338
White House Murder Case, The
   69–70, 358
White Lie, A *94–99*, 114, 115
White Lies *66–67*, 381
White Lights *27–28*, 428
White Lilacs *28–29*, 370
White Magic *09–19*, 464
White Man *36–37*, 419
White Peacock, The (1) *21–22*, 483
White Peacock, The (2) *26–27*, 504
White Peacock, The (3) *27–28*, 551
White Rat, The *94–99*, 144
White Rose and the Red, The
   63–64, 361
White Sister, The (p) *09–19*, 400;
   26–27, 529
White Sister, The (m) *26–27*, 529
White Slave, The *94–99*, 165
White Snake, The *(Peh Shuh
   Tchuwan)* *62–63*, 285
White Squadron, The *94–99*, 103
White Steed, The *38–39*, 448; *41–42*,
   459; *44–45*, 436; *47–48*, 430
White Villa, The *20–21*, 427
White Way, The (mn) *36–37*, 498
White Whore and the Bit Player,
   The *68–69*, 455
White Wings *26–27*, 404; *53–54*,
   358
White-Headed Boy, The *21–22*, 419;
   32–33, 407; *37–38*, 463; *38–39*,
   484

Whiteoaks *37–38*, 434
Whiteoaks of Jalna *37–38*, 434
Whitewashed *23–24*, 424
Whitewashing of Julia, The *99–09*,
   447
Whitman Portrait, A *66–67*, 402
Whitsuntide *70–71*
Who Cares *30–31*, 400
Who Did It? *09–19*, 658
Who Goes There? *99–09*, 484
Who Is Ophelia? *62–63*, 335
Who Is There to Ask? *63–64*, 368
Who Is Who (1) *94–99*, 224
Who Is Who (2) *38–39*, 493
Who Ride on White Horses *39–40*,
   473
Who Was That Lady I Saw You
   With? *57–58*, 322
Whole Town's Talking, The *23–24*,
   311
Whole World Over, The *46–47*, 473
Who'll Save the Plowboy? *61–62*,
   318
Whoop-Dee-Doo *99–09*, 437
Whoopee *28–29*, 431
Whoop-Up *58–59*, 314s
Whores, Wars & Tin Pan Alley
   69–70, 335s
Who's Afraid of Virginia Woolf?
   62–63, 279; *67–68*, 401; *68–69*,
   425
Who's Brown *99–09*, 484
Who's Got His Own *66–67*, 403;
   68–69, 457
Who's Hungry *70–71*
Who's Happy Now? *69–70*, 347
Who's Who? (1) *09–19*, 507
Who's Who (2) *37–38*, 429
Who's Who (3) *67–68*, 400
Who's Who, Baby? *67–68*, 400s
Why Did the Children Put Beans in
   Their Ears? *60–61*, 294
Why Do I Deserve This? *(Womit
   Haben wir das Verdient?)* *65–66*,
   429
Why Marry? *09–19*, 315, 618
Why Men Leave Home *22–23*, 452

Why Not? *22–23*, 511
Why Smith Left Home *99–09*, 347
Why Wait for Science *62–63*, 322
Why Was Lincoln Murdered?
 42–43, 422
Why Worry? *09–19*, 634
Wicked Age, The *27–28*, 446
Wicked Cooks, The *66–67*, 411
Wicklow Postman, The *94–99*, 133
Wide Awake Lil *34–35*, 483
Wide Open Cage, The *62–63*, 321
Widow by Proxy *09–19*, 495
Widow Goldstein *94–99*, 202
Widow in Green, A *31–32*, 438
Widow Jones, The *94–99*, 144;
 99–09, 401
Widowers' Houses *99–09*, 535;
 38–39, 484; *52–53*, 307
Widow's Might, The *09–19*, 399
Wiener Blut (see *Vienna Life*)
Wife Decides, The *09–19*, 457
Wife Hunters, The *09–19*, 456
Wife Insurance *33–34*, 515
Wife of Scarli, The *94–99*, 156
Wife of Willoughby, The *94–99*, 188
Wife With the Smile, The *21–22*,
 468
Wife Without a Smile, A *99–09*, 477
Wild Birds *24–25*, 568
Wild Duck, The *09–19*, 625; *24–25*,
 549; *28–29*, 420; *37–38*, 439;
 44–45, 436; *51–52*, 301; *66–67*,
 371
Wild Man, The *35–36*, 511
Wild Man of Borneo, The *27–28*,
 404
Wild Oats Lane *22–23*, 451
Wild Rose, The (1) *99–09*, 409
Wild Rose, The (2) *26–27*, 408
Wild Waves *31–32*, 481
Wild Westcotts, The *23–24*, 372
Wildcat *60–61*, 313s
Wildcat, The *21–22*, 467
Wilde Evening With Shaw, A
 62–63, 327
Wilderness, The *99–09*, 401
Wildfire *99–09*, 568
Wildflower *22–23*, 529

Will, The *09–19*, 509; *29–30*, 533
Will Geer's Americana *65–66*, 436
Will o' the Wisp, The *22–23*, 574
Will Shakespeare *22–23*, 515
Will Success Spoil Rock Hunter?
 55–56, 353
Will the Mail Train Run Tonight?
 63–64, 355s
Willie *70–71*
Willie Doesn't Live Here Anymore
 66–67, 422
Willie the Germ *67–68*, 413
Willie the Weeper *47–48*, 398
Willow and I, The *42–43*, 451
Willow Tree, The *09–19*, 596;
 26–27, 499
Wilson in the Promise Land *69–70*,
 330
Wind and the Rain, The *33–34*, 491
Wind in the Sassafras Trees, The
 68–69, 390
Wind Is Ninety, The *45–46*, 379
Window Panes *26–27*, 482
Window Shopping *38–39*, 437
Windows *23–24*, 329
Wine of Anubis, The *31–32*, 462
Wine of Choice *37–38*, 426
Wine of Life *27–28*, 549
Wine, Women and Song (1) *94–99*,
 239
Wine, Women and Song (2) *42–43*,
 431
Winesburg, Ohio *57–58*, 316
Winged Victory *43–44*, 429
Wingless Victory, The *36–37*, 445
Wings of the Dove, The (source)
 56–57, 334; *61–62*, 309
Wings of the Dove, The *61–62*,
 309s
Wings Over Europe *28–29*, 432;
 47–48, 427; *48–49*, 427
Winkelberg *57–58*, 56
Winner, The *53–54*, 341
Winner Take Paul *44–45*, 394
Winners *68–69*, 375
Winners and Losers *46–47*, 495
Winnie the Pooh (mn 1) *34–35*, 484;
 37–38, 467; *38–39*, 489

Winnie the Pooh (mn 2) *67–68*, 395; *68–69*, 437; *69–70*, 351; *70–71*

Winning Girl, The (see *The Social Whirl*)

Winslow Boy, The *47–48*, 362

Winsome Widow, A *09–19*, 470

Winsome Winnie *99–09*, 446

Winter Bound *29–30*, 440

Winter Garden *09–19*, 442

Winter Journey *67–68*, 403

Winter Soldiers *42–43*, 448

Winterfeast, The *99–09*, 574

Winter's Tale, The *99–09*, 350, 480; *09–19*, 416; *45–46*, 421; *58–59*, 316; *62–63*, 305; *63–64*, 360, 387

Winterset *35–36*, 410; *44–45*, 436; *52–53*, 309; *65–66*, 429

Wisdom Tooth, The *25–26*, 551

Wise Fool, A *38–39*, 493

Wise Have Not Spoken, The *53–54*, 359

Wise Tomorrow *37–38*, 380

Wisecrackers, The *25–26*, 518

Wiser They Are, The *30–31*, 511

Wish Me Luck *45–46*, 460

Wish You Were Here *52–53*, 253s

Wishing Fairy and the Discontented Donkey, The (mn) *34–35*, 484

Wisteria Trees, The *49–50*, 376; *54–55*, 396

Witch, The (1) *94–99*, 157

Witch, The (2) *09–19*, 414; *26–27*, 429

Witch, The (3) *61–62*, 323

Witch Woman, The *33–34*, 533

Witches' Sabbath *61–62*, 329

Witching Hour, The *99–09*, 271, 550

With a Silk Thread *49–50*, 377

With Privileges *30–31*, 411

Within Four Walls *22–23*, 559

Within the Gates *34–35*, 395; *52–53*, 309

Within the Law *09–19*, 475; *27–28*, 521

Without Love *42–43*, 442

Without the Law *09–19*, 486

Without Warning *36–37*, 482

Witness *68–69*, 436

Witness for the Defense, The *09–19*, 460

Witness for the Prosecution *54–55*, 383; *65–66*, 436

Wives, The *64–65*, 359

Wives of Henry VIII, The *31–32*, 432; *32–33*, 429; *34–35*, 467; *36–37*, 498

Wizard of Oz, The *99–09*, 427

Wizard of Oz, The (mn) *68–69*, 436

Wizard of the Nile, The *94–99*, 152

Wolf, The *99–09*, 561

Wolf at the Door, The *59–60*, 322; *60–61*, 289

Wolf Who Went Places, The *62–63*, 310

Wolves *31–32*, 459

Woman *65–66*, 423

Woman, The (1) *09–19*, 451

Woman, The (2) *64–65*, 322

Woman and Wine *99–09*, 366

Woman Bites Dog *45–46*, 437

Woman Brown, The *39–40*, 421

Woman Denied, A *30–31*, 497

Woman Disputed, The *26–27*, 389

Woman Hater, The *94–99*, 236

Woman Haters, The *09–19*, 480

Woman in Black, The *94–99*, 193

Woman in Room 13, The *09–19*, 649

Woman in the Case, The *99–09*, 483

Woman Is My Idea *68–69*, 378

Woman Killed With Kindness, A *09–19*, 524

Woman of Bronze, The *20–21*, 378; *26–27*, 535

Woman of Destiny, A *35–36*, 469

Woman of Impulse, A *99–09*, 579

Woman of It, The *09–19*, 492

Woman of No Importance, A *09–19*, 574

Woman of the Soil, A *34–35*, 464

Woman on the Index, The *09–19*, 634

Woman on the Jury, The *23–24*, 300

Woman Who Laughed, The *22–23,*
438
Woman's a Fool—To Be Clever, A
38–39, 419
Woman's Honor, A *09–19,* 628
Woman's Pity, A *99–09,* 485
Woman's Reason, A *94–99,* 164
Woman's Silence, A *94–99,* 104
Woman's Way, A *99–09,* 578;
39–40, 470; *42–43,* 489
Women, The *36–37,* 446; *59–60,* 43
Women at the Tomb, The *60–61,* 44
Women Go on Forever *27–28,* 400
Women Have Their Way, The
29–30, 483; *35–36,* 448
Women of Trachis, (The) *60–61,*
347
Women of Twilight *51–52,* 311
Women Through the Ages *60–61,*
295
Women Without Men *41–42,* 459
Womit Haben wir das Verdient? (see
Why Do I Deserve This?)
Wonder: a Woman Keeps a Secret,
The *94–99,* 198
Wonder Bar, The *30–31,* 507
Wonder Book, The *09–19,* 410
Wonder Boy *31–32,* 415
Wonder Hat, The *36–37,* 498
Wonderful Journey *46–47,* 449
Wonderful Night, A *29–30,* 431
Wonderful Thing, The *19–20,* 428
Wonderful Town *52–53,* 290s;
57–58, 323; *62–63,* 297; *65–66,*
418; *66–67,* 386s
Wonderful Visit, The *23–24,* 399
Wonderful World of Burlesque, The
64–65, 358
Wonderland *99–09,* 499
Wood Demon, The *66–67,* 422
Wooden Dish, The *55–56,* 351;
65–66, 426
Wooden Idol, The *29–30,* 539
Wooden Kimono *26–27,* 448
Wooden Slipper, The *33–34,* 475
Wooden Soldier, The *31–32,* 375
Woodland *99–09,* 474

Woodrow Wilson *41–42,* 34
Woof, Woof *29–30,* 467
Wooing of Eve, The *09–19,* 613
Wookey, The *41–42,* 394
Worcester Account, The *58–59,* 309
Words and Music (1) *09–19,* 617
Words and Music (2) *70–71*
Work and Wages *94–99,* 110
Work Is for Horses *37–38,* 393
Workers Laboratory Marionettes
34–35, 484
Workhouse Ward, The *09–19,* 458,
494; *36–37,* 497
World Against Her, The *94–99,*
118
World and His Wife, The *99–09,*
572
World Full of Men, A *52–53,* 308
World of Carl Sandburg, The *60–61,*
294; *67–68,* 410
World of Charles Aznavour, The
65–66, 377s; *69–70,* 314
World of Gunter Grass, The *65–66,*
434
World of Henry Orient, The *67–68,*
347
World of Kurt Weill in Song, The
63–64, 342s
World of Mrs. Solomon, The *69–70,*
333
World of Pleasure, A *09–19,* 562
World of Ray Bradbury, The *65–66,*
421
World of Sholom Aleichem, The
53–54, 359
World of Suzie Wong, The *58–59,*
296
World Trembles, The *38–39,* 493
World Waits, The *33–34,* 448
World War 2½ *68–69,* 449
World We Live In, The (see *The
Insect Comedy)*
World We Make, The *39–40,* 413;
45–46, 451; *52–53,* 309
World's a Stage, The *68–69,* 415
World's Full of Girls, The *43–44,*
433

Worlds of Oscar Brown Jr. *64–65,* 355

Worlds of Shakespeare, The *63–64,* 353

Worm in Horseradish, A *60–61,* 39

Worse Things Happen at Sea *37–38,* 465

Worth a Million *94–99,* 246

Worth of a Man, The *09–19,* 526

Worth of a Woman, The *99–09,* 558

Would-Be Gentleman, The (see *The Bourgeois Gentleman*)

Woyzeck *65–66,* 406; *67–68,* 412; *70–71*

Wrecker, The *27–28,* 517

Wrecking Ball, The *63–64,* 363

Wren, The *21–22,* 437

Wretched the Lionhearted *62–63,* 313

Wrists on the Door, The *23–24,* 429

Write Me a Murder *61–62,* 267

Writing on the Wall, The *99–09,* 582

Wrong Box, The *09–19,* 595

Wrong Mr. Right, The *94–99,* 199

Wrong Number *33–34,* 506

Wrong Way Light Bulb, The *68–69,* 408

Wuthering Heights *38–39,* 472

Wuziz *70–71*

X Has No Value *69–70,* 377

Xingu *43–44,* 490

Xmas in Las Vegas *65–66,* 383

Yale Puppeteers *32–33,* 439; *34–35,* 484; *35–36,* 512; *36–37,* 498; *38–39,* 489

Yankee Circus on Mars, A *99–09,* 489

Yankee Consul, The *99–09,* 455

Yankee Girl, The *09–19,* 414

Yankee Point *42–43,* 445

Yankee Prince, The *99–09,* 562

Yankee Princess, The *22–23,* 467

Yankee Tourist, A *99–09,* 541

Yankee-Doodle-Dandy *94–99,* 232

Yankele *47–48,* 431

Y'Avait un Prisonnier *37–38,* 469

Yeah Man *31–32,* 517

Year Boston Won the Pennant, The *68–69,* 437

Year of Pilar, The *51–52,* 333

Year One, The *94–99,* 152

Year the Yankees Lost the Pennant, The *54–55,* 413

Yearling, The *65–66,* 390s

Years Ago *46–47,* 445

Years Between, The *41–42,* 459

Years of Discretion *09–19,* 490

Years of the Locusts, The *36–37,* 497; *39–40,* 470

Yegor Bulitchev *34–35,* 472

Yellow *26–27,* 385

Yellow Jack *33–34,* 504; *38–39,* 468; *46–47,* 438; *64–65,* 362

Yellow Jacket, The *09–19,* 483, 587; *28–29,* 411

Yellow Kid, The *94–99,* 154, 181

Yellow Roses *94–99,* 236

Yellow Sands *27–28,* 400

Yellow Ticket, The *09–19,* 520

Yellow, Triangle, The *24–25,* 585; *28–29,* 502

Yenuine Yentleman *94–99,* 135

Yeomen of the Guard, The (or The Merryman and His Maid) *09–19,* 551; *32–33,* 485; *33–34,* 426; *34–35,* 366; *35–36,* 398, 400; *36–37,* 400; *38–39,* 448; *41–42,* 458; *43–44,* 458, 488; *45–46,* 458; *46–47,* 494; *47–48,* 374, 375; *55–56,* 345; *63–64,* 328; *65–66,* 419; *67–68,* 373

Yerma *66–67,* 36, 361; *70–71*

Yes Is for a Very Young Man *49–50,* 383; *62–63,* 327

Yes, M'Lord *49–50,* 356

Yes, My Darling Daughter *36–37,* 462; *67–68,* 410

Yes or No *09–19,* 617

Yes Yes, No No *68–69,* 442

Yes, Yes, Yvette *27–28,* 421

Yeshiva Bucher, The *47–48,* 431

Yesterday's Magic *41–42*, 447
Yesterday's Orchids *34–35*, 386
Yiddish folklore, songs, etc.
  (unidentified sources) *66–67*, 367;
  70–71
Yiddish plays (untitled programs)
  34–35, 483; *65–66*, 438
Yip Yip Yaphank *09–19*, 633
Yokel Boy *39–40*, 395
Yom Bonditten, Die *51–52*, 334
Yon Yonson *94–99*, 96
York State Folks *99–09*, 492
Yosemite *09–19*, 539
Yoshe Kalb *33–34*, 472; *46–47*, 497
You and I *22–23*, 535
You Can't Change Human Nature
  35–36, 510
You Can't Do That to Svoboda
  43–44, 460
You Can't Take It With You *36–37*,
  440; *44–45*, 381; *50–51*, 375;
  65–66, 387; *66–67*, 371
You Can't Win (1) *25–26*, 554
You Can't Win (2) *32–33*, 429
You Know I Can't Hear You When
  the Water's Running *66–67*, 384
You Never Can Tell *99–09*, 481,
  495; *09–19*, 550; *47–48*, 389;
  52–53, 308; *66–67*, 422
You Never Know *38–39*, 406;
  64–65, 357; *69–70*, 377
You Reach for Your Hat *63–64*,
  346
You Said It *30–31*, 480
You Touched Me! *45–46*, 385
You Twisted My Arm *50–51*, 375
You With Me *46–47*, 499
You'll See Stars *42–43*, 456
Young Abe Lincoln *60–61*, 42
Young Alexander *28–29*, 480
Young America *09–19*, 556
Young American, A *45–46*, 400
Young and Beautiful, The *55–56*,
  348
Young and Fair, The *48–49*, 396,
  397
Young Blood *25–26*, 501

Young Couple Wanted *39–40*, 433
Young Go First, The *34–35*, 479
Young Idea, The *31–32*, 494
Young Love *28–29*, 405
Young Madame Conti *36–37*, 475
Young Man's Fancy, A (1) *19–20*,
  375
Young Man's Fancy, A (2) *46–47*,
  477
Young Marrieds Play Monopoly
  65–66, 431
Young Master Dante, The *68–69*,
  430
Young Mr. Disraeli *37–38*, 387
Young Mrs. Winthrop *94–99*, 234
Young Sinners *29–30*, 454; *30–31*,
  518; *32–33*, 473
Young Turk, The *09–19*, 412
Young Visitors, The *20–21*, 409
Young Wife, A *99–09*, 347
Young Wife, The *94–99*, 234
Young Wisdom *09–19*, 518
Young Woodley *25–26*, 484
Younger Generation, The *09–19*,
  508
Younger Mrs. Parling, The *99–09*,
  453
Youngest, The *24–25*, 507
Your Humble Servant *09–19*, 408
Your Loving Son *40–41*, 423
Your Own Thing *67–68*, 398s
Your Uncle Dudley *29–30*, 442
Your Woman and Mine *21–22*, 518
You're a Good Man Charlie Brown
  66–67, 415s
You're in Love *09–19*, 594
Yours, A. Lincoln *42–43*, 422
Yours Is My Heart *46–47*, 418
Yours Till Yesterday *51–52*, 332
Yours Truly *26–27*, 467; *27–28*, 525
Youth (1) *94–99*, 113
Youth (2) *09–19*, 446; *20–21*, 399
Youth (3) *09–19*, 612
You've Got Something There *37–38*,
  468
Yr. Obedient Husband *37–38*, 414
Yum Chapab *09–19*, 612

Yvette (1) *99–09*, 460
Yvette (2) *09–19*, 577

Zander the Great *22–23*, 556
Zapfenstreich *99–09*, 466
Zarzuela *68–69*, 415
Zaza *94–99*, 250; *99–09*, 373, 472,
    481
Zebra, The *09–19*, 438
Zelda *68–69*, 409
Zeno *23–24*, 308
Zeppelin *28–29*, 456
Ziegfeld Follies of 1907 *99–09*, 540
Ziegfeld Follies of 1908 *99–09*, 563
Ziegfeld Follies of 1909 *99–09*, 584
Ziegfeld Follies of 1910 *09–19*, 420
Ziegfeld Follies of 1911 *09–19*, 446
Ziegfeld Follies of 1912 *09–19*, 481
Ziegfeld Follies of 1913 *09–19*, 502
Ziegfeld Follies of 1914 *09–19*, 527
Ziegfeld Follies of 1915 *09–19*, 553
Ziegfeld Follies of 1916 *09–19*, 576
Ziegfeld Follies (1917) *09–19*, 601
Ziegfeld Follies of 1918 *09–19*, 631
Ziegfeld Follies (1920) *20–21*, 355
Ziegfeld Follies of 1921 *21–22*, 388
Ziegfeld Follies, 1922 *21–22*, 555
Ziegfeld Follies (1923) *23–24*, 340

Ziegfeld Follies (1924) *24–25*, 429
Ziegfeld Follies (1927) *27–28*, 391
Ziegfeld Follies, 1931 *31–32*, 377
Ziegfeld Follies (1934) *33–34*, 476
Ziegfeld Follies (1936) *35–36*, 465
Ziegfeld Follies of 1936–1937 *36–37*,
    405
Ziegfeld Follies (1943) *42–43*, 471
Ziegfeld Follies (1957) *56–57*, 357s
Ziegfeld Girls of 1920 *19–20*, 436
Ziegfeld Midnight Frolic (1919)
    19–20, 361
Ziegfeld Midnight Frolic (1921)
    21–22, 464
Ziegfeld 9 O'Clock Frolic *20–21*,
    425
Ziegfeld's Revue *26–27*, 359
Zira *99–09*, 496
Zizi *64–65*, 315s
Zombie *31–32*, 476
Zoo Story, The *59–60*, 352; *61–62*,
    305, 323; *62–63*, 313, 337; *65–66*,
    416; *68–69*, 379
Zorba *68–69*, 393s
Zorba the Greek *68–69*, 393
Zulu and the Zayda, The *65–66*,
    383s
Zwei Wappen *94–99*, 162